THE UNITY
MOVEMENT

THOUGHT, 48-page
Magazine, $1.00 per year.

UNITY, Monthly Paper,
50 cents per year.

Metaphysical Series,
15 cents per copy.

METAPHYSICAL
BOOK DEALERS
AND PUBLISHERS,
820 Walnut Street,
KANSAS CITY, MO.

Dedication and Covenant.

We, Charles Fillmore and Myrtle Fillmore, husband and wife, hereby dedicate ourselves, our time, our money, all we have and all we expect to have, to the Spirit of Truth, and through it, to the Society of Silent Unity.

It being understood and agreed that the said Spirit of Truth shall render unto us an equivalent for this dedication, in peace of mind, health of body, wisdom, understanding, love and an abundant supply of all things necessary to meet every want without our making any of these things the object of our existence.

In the presence of the Conscious Mind of Christ Jesus, this 7th day of December A.D. 1892

Charles Fillmore.
Myrtle Fillmore

THE UNITY
MOVEMENT

Its Evolution and Spiritual Teachings

NEAL VAHLE

Templeton Foundation Press

Philadelphia & London

Templeton Foundation Press
Five Radnor Corporate Center, Suite 120
100 Matsonford Road
Radnor, Pennsylvania 19087

Designed and typeset by Kachergis Book Design

Printed by Versa Press, Inc.

Cover photo: Window at 917 Tracy, Kansas City, Missouri.
Used by permission of Unity School of Christianity

Photos courtesy of Unity School of Christianity,
Unity Village, Missouri

LIBRARY OF CONGRESS CATALOGING-IN-PUBLICATION DATA
Vahle, Neal.
  The Unity movement : its evolution and spiritual teachings /
Neal Vahle.
    p. cm.
  Includes bibliographical references and index.
  ISBN 1-890151-92-0 (alk. paper) — ISBN 1-890151-96-3 (pbk. : alk.
paper)
  1. Unity School of Christianity. I. Title.
BX9890.U535 V34 2002
289.9'7—dc21
                                                    2002004780

Printed in the United States of America

02 03 04 05 06 07   10 9 8 7 6 5 4 3 2 1

CONTENTS

FOREWORD

The story of the beginning of the Unity movement has been told and retold within Unity for years, so that many details have formed a kind of myth about the lives and the teachings of the founders. Countless times someone has approached me to say: If your great-grandfather were alive today, I know he would *(think, say, do) (this,* or *that)*. For some time I have thought what a gift it would be to the Unity movement if someone would go directly to the source material and distill the facts about Unity's early days. I am glad to say that Neal Vahle, Ph.D., has done just that.

Both Dr. Vahle's credentials and his process lent themselves to this task. Trained as a historian and well acquainted with the New Thought movement, Dr. Vahle spent hours in our archives studying the actual words written and spoken by the important figures of Unity's early days. I believe the result is an objective, comprehensive study that will be of interest to virtually everyone within the Unity movement and to many outside of it. Dr. Vahle has made it possible for Unity students to read and consider Unity's teachings in the actual words of its founders and early leaders. This well-researched study can also serve as a valuable resource to scholars and students in the field of American religious history, because the book presents an intimate picture of the people, beliefs, and societal influences that shaped this uniquely American religious movement.

Personally, I feel gratified to see the publication of this book, for I believe it will make it possible for people who currently know nothing or little about Unity to sense the influence that Unity teachings have had on American culture through the years. My great-grandparents were firm believers in both faith and education, and I believe they would be pleased to know that their story continues to make a contribution to society long after their personal lives have ended. I trust that you will find this book not only interesting but also helpful in your own life in some way, because this is the purpose to which the work of the Unity movement is dedicated.

Unity Village, Missouri   CONNIE FILLMORE BAZZY
November 21, 2001

ACKNOWLEDGMENTS

Four people deserve special acknowledgment for their contribution to the preparation of this book. They are Vern Barnet, Connie Fillmore Bazzy, Joseph P. Schultz, and Philip White. Connie Fillmore Bazzy, president of Unity School of Christianity, originally proposed the topic to me in 1996. She wanted a study that described the origins and development of the Unity teaching and the evolution of the Unity movement, and she wanted it prepared by someone outside Unity with appropriate credentials. As a researcher in the literature of the New Thought movement, I had written biographies of both Ernest Holmes, founder of the Church of Religious Science, and Myrtle Fillmore, co-founder of Unity. As a result, I was familiar with the archival materials needed to produce this book and had the expertise to access them.

In an effort to facilitate scholarly independence and objectivity, a review committee was formed comprised of experts in the field of American religion from both inside and outside of Unity. Those chosen from outside Unity included Vern Barnet, D.Mn., director of the Center for Religious Experience and Study, Overland Park, Kansas, and religion columnist for the *Kansas City Star,* and Joseph P. Schultz, Oppenstein Brothers distinguished professor emeritus and director of the Center for Religious Studies at the University of Missouri-Kansas City. In addition to Connie Fillmore Bazzy, Philip White, an ordained Unity minister who had served as the director of the school's Continuing Education Program and as dean of education for Unity School for Religious Studies, represented Unity School. During the four years this book was being written, the committee met several times to review sections of the manuscript. The depth of knowledge and insight the review committee provided significantly enhanced the quality of the work. The review committee's role, however, was advisory, and final decisions about the contents of the book were left up to me.

For insight into the lives and work of the three founding teachers— Charles, Myrtle, and Lowell Fillmore, I was able to draw upon the first-hand knowledge and experience of three people who have been associated with Unity for many years. James Dillet Freeman came to Unity as a teenager in 1931, presented the teachings for many years in his own writings, and served as director of Silent Unity. Charles R. Fillmore, whose service in Unity began in 1946, became the school's chief executive officer in 1962 and chairman of its board of trustees in 1982. Rosemary Fillmore Rhea, who like her brother Charles R. is a third generation Fillmore, served for many years as director of Unity's radio and television programs and was active in Unity churches as a minister and speaker. Another granddaughter of the founders, Frances Fillmore Lakin, who is no longer associated with Unity, provided information on the family.

For information on the operation of Unity School I was able to draw upon the knowledge of the school's chief executive officers, including, in addition to Connie Fillmore Bazzy, its two executive vice presidents, Chris Jackson and Jim Rosemergy. Members of the staff of the Unity School for Religious Studies were particularly helpful, providing information on the Unity teaching as well as recollections on the development of the Unity movement. These included: John Anderson, Robert Barth, Laura Barrett Bennett, Robert Brumet, Claudel County, Christine Dustin, Jim Gaither, Don Jennings, Gary Jones, Jimmie Scott, and Tom Thorpe. Past and present members of the Unity School staff provided much useful information. Those who granted interviews included: Gary Baebenroth, Lynne Brown, Bob Bryan, Debbie Bryan, Eric Butterworth, Johnnie Colemon, Bill Dale, Stan Hampson, Charles Lelly, Allen Liles, Michael Maday, Allen Noel, Dorothy Pierson, David Williamson, and Colleen Zuck.

A useful perspective on the development of Unity churches was provided by Glenn R. Mosley, president and CEO of the Association of Unity Churches.

The Unity archives and library were an important source of much of the information contained in this book. Priscilla Richards, Unity School's librarian, took a deep interest in this work and, in addition to giving counsel and advice, lent her full support to the project. I also owe a large debt of gratitude to Caroline Stewart, the Unity archivist, who through diligent effort uncovered important information that only a person well versed in the contents of this large archive could provide. She was aided during the course of my work by three able assistants: David Jackson, Walter Le-Conte, and Eric Page. For assistance in locating materials throughout the library, I also wish to thank Freda Butner, Judy Cournyea, Judy Elizabeth, and Janet Staten of the library staff.

Several people from outside the Unity movement provide important input in the preparation of the manuscript. Included among these are Alexander Everett, Milton Friedman, Arthur Vergara, and Curt Wells. I have benefited from the copyediting and proofreading skills of several people: Sherry Brennan, Allen Burdick, Christine Finnegan, Lisa A. Smith, and the copy services department of Unity School, which included Beth Anderson, Marlene Barry, Tom Lewin, and Kay Thomure. All of them suggested important improvements in the copy and footnotes.

Finally, I owe a personal debt of gratitude to my wife Nancy, who listened with the ear of someone who understands spiritual principles and practices as I sorted through problems in the writing. She offered much-needed advice, support, and care.

INTRODUCTION

The Unity Movement

Many spiritual teachers have created a body of doctrine and presented it, orally or in writing, to sizable numbers of people. Few, however, have been successful in developing organizations for promulgating the teaching over time. The Fillmores, Charles and Myrtle, and their sons, Lowell, Rickert, and Royal, are among the few gifted spiritual innovators who created, over the course of the twentieth century, a successful worldwide spiritual movement—the Unity movement. The organizations that carry forth their work are the Unity School of Christianity and the Association of Unity Churches. Unity School is located at Unity Village, Missouri, on a sixteen hundred-acre tract twenty miles southeast of Kansas City, Missouri. Its origin can be traced to prayer meetings held in 1889 in the Kansas City living room of Charles and Myrtle Fillmore. Included in the school's current activities are:

• A twenty-four-hour prayer ministry responding to over two million prayer requests each year, including approximately 1.1 million phone calls and one million letters. The prayer ministry operates 365 days a year.

• One of the largest religious publishing houses in the Midwest. One publication alone, the *Daily Word,* has a circulation of over 1.1 million, is printed in nine languages, and is distributed in 175 countries.

• A twenty-four-month ministerial education program.

• Nine sessions of adult curriculum provided annually through a continuing education program as well as twelve retreats for adults.

Unity School handles approximately thirty-four million pieces of outgoing mail each year, employs a staff of six hundred at its headquarters, and operates on a yearly income of about $35 million. The grounds and buildings are debt-free, and the school holds liquid assets of approximately $22 million.

The Association of Unity Churches provides services to over one thousand ministries worldwide. Just over two hundred are outside the United

States, Canada, and Puerto Rico. The number of congregants now totals 170,000. The association's services now include: guidance for church administration, consultation for development and fund-raising, ministerial assistance, mentoring and spiritual renewal programs, training for key leaders, communication through a variety of publications, placement of ministers, conflict management, and assistance in the starting of new study groups and churches. Unity's programs, both through the school and through the churches, continue to expand with each passing year.

Religion, Science, and Medicine in America

The Unity movement developed at the turn of the twentieth century during a period when the healing practices of those who claimed to be medical professionals were highly ineffective and when traditional Christianity was being challenged by advances in science and by new spiritual philosophies whose doctrines were considered heretical. Calvinist Christianity, which formed the theological basis for several Protestant denominations, had been a powerful force in American religion from colonial times. In the nineteenth century, it was subjected to a severe challenge from Unitarians, Universalists, Transcendentalists, Spiritualists, mesmerists, and Theosophists, as well as those engaged in mental healing or New Thought.

The Unitarians and Universalists were among the first to revolt against the stern doctrines of predestination and eternal punishment. The Transcendentalists rejected traditional Christian teaching regarding the Trinity and the nature of the divine. The Spiritualists, who were anticlerical and antidenominational, believed humanity could be perfected. They expressed an aversion to ideas of human depravity, vicarious atonement, and final judgment. At the height of its popularity in the United States, a reported two million out of a total population of twenty-five million practiced Spiritualism.[1] The Theosophists drew more from Eastern religions than from Christianity, and viewed the divine as permeating all life, rejecting traditional Christian ideas on the nature of God. The mental healing and New Thought movements criticized traditional Christianity for abandoning healing, which they considered to be the principal work of Jesus.

Advances in science in the nineteenth century posed a serious threat to the teachings of traditional Christianity. New knowledge in several physical sciences, including astronomy, anatomy, geology, and paleontology, fostered confidence in human reason and a belief in human progress. As the educated classes put their trust in science, they discarded traditional Christian teachings regarding sinfulness, miracles, the need for grace, and the focus on heaven and hell. The application of the scientific method to biblical studies indicated to many that the Bible was a combination of folklore, discourse, history, and poetry rather than divinely inspired writings. The publication of Charles Darwin's *The Origin of Species* convinced many that human life evolved over vast ages. It challenged traditional Christian teachings regarding creation.[2]

While advances in medical knowledge were taking place in the nineteenth century, particularly in Europe, the French were formulating modern clinical methods and combining clinical observation with pathological anatomy. For the most part, this new learning was not put into practice in the United States.[3] Ineffective, even harmful therapeutic practices, such as bloodletting and the use of medicines that included heavy doses of mercury, were still in use.[4]

The training of physicians was sadly lacking. With no state controls and no accreditation procedures, medical schools proliferated, offering easy terms, quick degrees, and little in the way of substantive training. State licensing requirements were either weak or nonexistent; anyone could practice medicine. In agrarian America, lay practitioners using herbs and folk remedies flourished in the countryside where most people lived.[5]

The situation in Missouri, where Unity was founded, exemplified the problem. The state passed a licensing law in 1874 that required a physician to register a degree from a legally chartered medical school. The statute had little effect, since the incorporation laws permitted anyone to start a school by applying for a charter. Medical colleges proliferated. Almost all were diploma mills. As a result, many people claimed to be medical doctors, but few were qualified.[6]

The impoverished state of American medicine was acknowledged in the 1850s by Jacob Bigelow of Harvard University when he stated, "The unbiased opinion of most medical men of sound judgment and long experience is that the amount of death and disaster in the world would be less if all disease were left to itself."[7] He called on physicians to recognize nature as "the great agent of cure" and to use art only as an auxiliary. There was little demand for the services of general hospitals in America. Even the well to do did not use them. Hospitals were regarded with dread, and for good reason. They were dangerous places. People were better off if treated at home.[8]

Considering the inadequacies of allopathic medicine, it is not surprising that therapies emphasizing the use of the mind, such as "mind cure" and Christian Science, flourished. Even as eminent an authority as William James, a member of the faculty of the Harvard Medical School, tried an assortment of methods to heal a heart condition, including Christian Science, hypnotism, and mind cure. James opposed medical licensing before the Massachusetts legislature in 1898 because he felt it would interfere with freedom of research in medicine. At the time he was pursuing his own research on psychic healers. He defended the right of "mind cures" to test out new modes of therapy.[9] Major improvements in American medical practice did not occur until well into the twentieth century.

Original Formulators of the Unity Teaching

When the Fillmores began their public spiritual work in April 1889 with the publication of *Modern Thought* magazine, they had no intention of presenting a new and original spiritual teaching. Their purpose was to provide larger public exposure to those nineteenth-century metaphysical teachings and healing practices that had been useful in their own spiritual development. Over the course of several decades, with the help of their eldest son Lowell and H. Emilie Cady, they pieced together a body of spiritual teachings called "Practical Christianity." They presented these teachings in books, articles, and letters.

It is evident from the literature cited in their writings that they drew upon the works of four nineteenth-century American spiritual thinkers: Ralph Waldo Emerson, Warren Felt Evans, Mary Baker Eddy, and Emma Curtis Hopkins. They also consulted the works of Madame Helena Blavatsky and the Theosophists. The writings of Emanuel Swedenborg, Franz Anton Mesmer and his followers, and Phineas P. Quimby had an important, although indirect, impact on their work.

Myrtle Fillmore spelled out the teaching in depth in hundreds of letters written in response to correspondence from Unity students. Excerpts of these letters are contained in *Myrtle Fillmore's Healing Letters*, edited by Frances Foulks, and *How to Let God Help You*, edited by Warren Meyer. Both books are available from Unity School of Christianity. Quotations from many of her letters are presented in my book, *Torch-Bearer to Light the Way: The Life of Myrtle Fillmore*.

Charles Fillmore presented the teachings in thirteen books and hundreds of articles published in *Unity* magazine between 1889 and 1948. His writings, while difficult to read, contain a comprehensive presentation of Unity teaching. Three of his works still find an audience among Unity students: *The Twelve Powers* (1930), *Prosperity* (1936), and *Keep a True Lent* (1953). All of his books remain in print.

H. Emilie Cady, a New York City homeopathic physician and author, began writing for Unity periodicals in the early 1890s at the invitation of the Fillmores. In 1901, Unity published Cady's *Lessons in Truth*, a book that presented with clarity the basic elements of the Unity teaching. Myrtle Fillmore described Cady's work as a "foundation stone" of Unity work. *Lessons in Truth* immediately became a Unity bestseller. By 1937, over 500,000 copies had been sold. By 2001, sales had exceeded 1.6 million. It remains among the top five of Unity's best-selling books. *Lessons in Truth* is used for classes at Unity School and in the churches.

Lowell Fillmore, general manager and president of Unity School for over five decades, presented the teaching in *Weekly Unity* magazine, the most widely read of the early Unity publications. From 1912 to 1972, he served as editor and wrote over three thousand columns entitled "Things to Be Remembered." Accessible because of their down-to-earth quality, for many years Lowell's writings were highly popular throughout Unity. Two books containing materials from his columns in *Weekly Unity* are still available from Unity School.

PART I

THE UNITY TEACHINGS

Yesterday and Today

Introduction

It would be reasonable to assume that, because the Unity movement and the Unity School of Christianity were co-founded by Charles and Myrtle Fillmore, the metaphysical teaching identified with Unity called "truth principles" would be based solely on their teachings and writings. Such is not the case. There are two versions of the Unity teachings presented today by the Unity School of Christianity and in Unity churches worldwide. In addition to that of the Fillmores, there is another version that is the product of the writings of H. Emilie Cady (1848–1941), a New York City homeopathic physician, and Lowell Fillmore (1882–1975), the eldest son of Charles and Myrtle. Both versions can be characterized as "Practical Christianity," because they apply Christian principles to improving the quality of everyday living.

Charles and Myrtle organized their metaphysical teaching under the rubric "the twelve powers of man." The teaching was developed by the Fillmores in their classes, letters, and articles, and published by Charles in his book, *The Twelve Powers of Man.* The spiritual ideas expressed in their various writings on the twelve powers can be summarized as follows:

GOD IS LIMITLESS and without bounds, transcendent as well as immanent, and actively present within every man and woman as the indwelling Presence. God, as Principle, operates impersonally in the universe through Divine Law. While God is not a person, God relates to humankind in personal ways, and works both as a partner with men and women in the work of the world and through the activities of the Holy Spirit.

DIVINE NATURE AND HUMAN NATURE have the same characteristics, for humankind is made in the image and likeness of God. While men and women are endowed with God's nature, the divine attributes are latent, existing in potential only. Men and women possess free will. They have used this attribute, however, in destructive ways, and as a result, fail to manifest the indwelling Presence. Negativity, fear, malice, sensual pleasure, ignorance, selfishness, and willfulness are manifestations of humankind's self-destructive tendencies.

MEN AND WOMEN can overcome their faults and shortcomings, and manifest the indwelling Presence by complying with Divine Law and the Will of God. This can be accomplished by activating twelve faculties of the mind or centers of consciousness—the Twelve Powers of Man. The powers are spiritual understanding, judgment, faith, divine love, imagination, will, zeal, power, strength, elimination, order and life. The powers are activated through spiritual practice. The practices include "right thinking," which involves disciplining the mind, affirmations and denials, prayer and meditation or sitting in the silence.

TRADITIONAL CHRISTIANITY, both Catholic and Protestant, has misinterpreted the life and teachings of Jesus. He was born human, not the incarnation of God. Jesus realized the indwelling Presence, activated the Twelve Powers, and manifested the Christ Consciousness through spiritual work over the course of several lifetimes. Jesus did not die on the cross to save humankind from its sins. At the time of his presumed death on the cross, he realized the highest possible state of consciousness and made himself "God-incarnate." By so doing he regenerated his body, overcame physical death and entered the "spiritual ethers of this world," or the "fourth realm of consciousness." Jesus exists in that state today and is available to aid men and women in developing and activating the Twelve Powers. Jesus is not waiting in heaven at the right hand of the Father to greet those who have led virtuous lives. There is no heaven for the saved nor is there a hell where the damned will suffer for all eternity.

JESUS BY HIS WORDS and deeds serves as a source of inspiration to men and women, an exemplar for humankind. The primary goal of human life is to reach the consciousness level of Jesus: the Christ within or the indwelling Presence. Those who make progress in activating the Twelve Powers and become more fully conscious of the reality of their divine heritage will become healthier, happier, and more prosperous. They will also have the ability to heal others physically, psychologically and spiritually.

WHEN, THROUGH LONG and ardent spiritual practice, the "Life" faculty located in the genitals is activated, the cells of the body become youthful and vigorous despite advancing years. The regenerative process moves forward until the body becomes so sublime that it is no longer visible to the human eye. Those who regenerate their bodies no longer suffer from declining health or experience the death of the human body.[1]

One of Charles's clearest presentations of his beliefs on bodily regeneration is contained in the following commentary:

Every organ of the body is capable of being constantly renewed through the inflow of an unseen force called mind or Spirit. . . . Your body will be so transformed within and without that it will never go through the change called death. It will be a resurrected body, become more and more refined as you catch sight of the free truths of Being, until it will literally disappear from the sight of those who see with the eye of sense. This is the way in which the last enemy, "death," is to be overcome.[2]

The Fillmores recognized that progress on the spiritual path may not occur in one lifetime. Reincarnation would be the lot of humankind until the spiritual work was complete. They believed that the soul entered an afterlife of peace and tranquility, where it prepared itself for the next incarnation.

Another version of the principles of truth, also identified as Unity teaching, was formulated by H. Emilie Cady and Lowell Fillmore. Cady's book *Lessons in Truth,* published by Unity in 1901, was an immediate Unity bestseller and continues to be so in 2001. For five decades in the twentieth century, Lowell Fillmore edited and wrote for *Weekly Unity,* Unity School's most widely read magazine. The major difference between the Cady/Lowell version of the teaching and that of Charles and Myrtle Fillmore concerns the twelve powers. Cady's writing makes no mention of them and Lowell refers to the powers only briefly, and then only in passing. Cady leaves out reincarnation in her teaching and saw no merit in extending the life of the physical body and no purpose in overcoming physical death. "The possibility of living here in these bodies indefinitely," she declared, "seems altogether foolish and short-sighted."[3]

Cady viewed physical death as a positive life event. It freed the "real self," the "spiritual body" as she called it, from the limitations of the physical body. "Death," she asserted, "is simply being born out of this hampered sphere into a grander, fuller, freer life."[4] Cady believed divine law required that the soul live in an afterlife that was an improvement upon human conditions. She used the biblical metaphor "In my Father's house are many mansions" to characterize conditions in the afterlife. The mansion to which you were assigned depended upon your level of spiritual attainment. Everyone was at peace. No one suffered or was in pain, and no one went to hell for all eternity. Her formal writing contains no mention of reincarnation. Given her ideas on the nature of the afterlife, reincarnation would be unnecessary.

There are major areas of agreement in both versions of the teaching. All four writers agree on the attributes of divine nature and human nature. They acknowledge the existence of free will and the harmful consequences to humankind from the abuse of free will. They also agree that the way men and women overcome their shortcomings is to come into alignment with the indwelling Presence and manifest the Christ Consciousness. The two versions diverge over the means to achieve the higher states. Unlike Charles and Myrtle, Cady and Lowell place no emphasis on developing the twelve powers. They stressed the importance of spiritual education to gain knowledge of truth principles and spiritual practice to prepare the body/mind/spirit for its role in divine selfhood. The practices include the discipline of the mind through "right thinking," the use of affirmations and denials, prayer, meditation (or going into the silence), the exercise of faith and divine love, acts of forgiveness, and focusing the attention on the present moment.

Both versions of the teaching are presented in classes for Unity students at Unity School and in Unity churches. The aspect of the twelve powers teaching of Charles and Myrtle involving bodily degeneration, however, has been de-emphasized. During Unity's century-long history and at the present time, the Cady/Lowell version of the teaching, presented in *Lessons in Truth* and *Weekly Unity*, has enjoyed greater popularity among Unity students than the twelve powers version. Two factors are responsible. The twelve powers teaching itself is difficult to understand. Only Unity students who have studied it carefully have adopted it. Secondly, Charles, who presented the teaching for the general public in his books, wrote in a style that is incomprehensible to many readers, particularly beginning Unity students.

CHAPTER I

Myrtle Fillmore: Spiritual Visionary

Spreading This "Saving Gospel"

Myrtle was a forty-year-old wife and mother when she began her work as a spiritual teacher and practitioner of mental healing. Her early years give no indication that she someday would catalyze and co-lead a spiritual movement that would attract thousands. Born two decades before the Civil War, she was the daughter of an Ohio businessman-farmer and the seventh of eight children. To be sure, she was bright. From an early age she was a curious child who loved learning. "I remember my school days and my eagerness to read and learn what others knew," she recalled. "I always wanted to read the books that were supposed to be for big boys and the grown-ups, but little girls were not encouraged to do such reading, so I had to take my brother's books quietly and go secretly to a little corner to enjoy them."[1] As she grew older, her reading tastes expanded. "I liked the old myths, fairy tales, histories and scientific works," she recalled. "I have found that those stories, and the visions of scientists of those days and of hundreds of years ago, all have to do with our present-day life."[2] Her parents were strict Methodists, adhering to a puritanical moral code and a belief in a punishing God. From an early age, Myrtle was repulsed by these teachings. She noted:

I found my dear ones did not have an understanding of God, who ruled in their lives, which satisfied me . . . My mother was a very spiritual woman. She always kept the principles of right and wrong before us by her own example. But she accepted the church creed. And had such a devotional spirit that she felt that if her God saw fit to punish, or do any of the many things that were attributed to God, He must have reason for it and it was all right. I marveled that my wonderful mother, who loved so devotedly, could have a God who might punish, or take the lives of His children.[3]

Unlike many of her Protestant contemporaries, Myrtle was repelled by puritanical teachings on sin and the nature of evil. "There was something in me," she recalled, "that protested against the declaration that I was by nature evil and sinful."[4] Disease lay like a dark cloud over much of her youth. She was afflicted at a young age by tuberculosis. Family members on her father's side had been stricken with it, and Myrtle was assumed to have contracted it because the disease ran in the family. She was well enough, however, to finish high school and hold down a job as a writer for a newspaper in Columbus, Ohio. At age twenty-one she enrolled in "The Literary Course for Ladies" at Oberlin College. The studies lasted for only one year because women were not eligible for the regular four-year college programs. Upon graduating in 1867, she received her teaching license and the following year accepted a job teaching in the public schools in Clinton, Missouri, a small town about sixty miles southeast of Kansas City. Except for a year in Denison, Texas, (1877–1878), recovering from tuberculosis, she spent the next thirteen years teaching in the Clinton school system.

She met Charles Fillmore during her stay in Denison and married him three years later on March 29, 1881. Nine years his senior, she was thirty-five years old at the time of her marriage. The couple initially lived in Gunnison, Colorado, where Charles was engaged in the mining and real estate business. They moved to Pueblo shortly thereafter, where their first child, Lowell, was born on January 4, 1882. A second son, Rickert, was born two years later on June 1, 1884. The family moved to Omaha, Nebraska, and then on to Kansas City, Missouri, in 1885, where they settled permanently and where their third son, Royal, was born.

Myrtle often suffered from poor health during the early years of her marriage. "I was fearfully sick," she recalled. "I had all the ills of mind and body that I could bear. Medicine and doctors ceased to give me relief and I was in despair.[5] . . . I was supposed to be dying or very close to it.[6] . . . Along with tuberculosis trouble in my lungs, I had disorders through the abdominal walls. At times hemorrhoids made life miserable for me."[7] In the spring of 1886, a Christian Science practitioner from Chicago, Eugene B. Weeks, came to Kansas City to present a course of lectures on Christian Science. The Fillmores attended, and Myrtle left with insights that changed her life. She explained how she and Charles came to attend the course, and its impact:

It was at the solicitation of friends, already interested, that my husband and I attended the first class taught in this city. I must have been fully ready for the initial lesson, for it filled and satisfied all empty, hungry longings of my soul and heart. There is nothing in human language able to express the vastness of my possibilities, as they unrolled before me . . . The physical claims that had been considered such a serious nature faded away before the dawning of this new consciousness, and I found that my body temple had been literally transformed through the renewing of my mind.[8]

In letters to friends, she gave a fuller explanation of the illumination that took place as a result of attending Weeks's course. To one, she wrote: "I remember with great joy the time when it dawned upon me that God was my Father and that I need not be bound by human limitations. I had been laboring under the belief in inherited ill health, and the Truth of my divine parentage freed and healed me."[9] She told another, "It was such a wonderful time for me when I awakened to the Truth that God is my Father and that I inherit from him only that which is Good. It seemed to loosen all the binding thoughts of the race belief in inherited weakness and I breathed so freely and joyously."[10]

Myrtle, with her newfound spiritual understanding, healed herself of tuberculosis. She chose to apply the healing principles herself rather than engage another practitioner. "I did most of the healing myself," she revealed, "because I wanted the understanding for future use."[11] She gave a detailed account of how she discovered affirmations and was persistent in the use of them until she fully recovered from tuberculosis:

It flashed upon me that I might talk to the life in every part of my body and have it do just what I wanted. I began to teach my body and got marvelous results. I told the life in my liver that it was not torpid or inert, but full of vigor and energy. I told the life in my stomach that it was not weak or inefficient, but energetic, strong and intelligent. I told the life in my abdomen that it was no longer infested with ignorant ideas of disease, put there by myself and by doctors, but that it was all athrill with the sweet, pure, wholesome energy of God. I told my limbs that they were active and strong. I told my eyes that they did not see of themselves but that they expressed the sight of Spirit, and that they were drawing on an unlimited source. I told them that they were young eyes, clear, bright eyes, because the light of God shone right through them. I told my heart that the pure love of Jesus Christ flowed in and out through its beatings and that all the world felt its joyous pulsation. I went to all the life centers in my body and spoke words of Truth to them—words of strength and power. I asked their forgiveness for the foolish, ignorant course that I had pursued in the past, when I condemned them and called them weak, inefficient and diseased. I did not become discouraged at their being slow to wake up, but kept right on, both silently and aloud, declaring the words of Truth, until the organs responded.[12]

Myrtle pored herself into the study of Christian Science. "I know and feel that my work must be the spreading of this saving gospel," she testified. "I want before I go out to preach it, to be so *one* with my doctrine that nothing will move or upset me, that I shall not by my inconsistencies bring reproach upon the cause."[13] When she was confident that she fully understood the principles and the practice, she sought to help others. She believed she had been given a mission, commenting:

From the moment I perceived the healing law I could not let my neighbors alone. If there was anything the matter with them it had to be put aright; they had to know that there is a better way. I did not do this meddlesomely. No one objected if the pain left him and he became perfectly well; in fact, our neighbors got so interested in healing that they would not let me alone and our parlors were filled nearly every morning.[14]

It was in this way that her career as a practitioner of spiritual healing was launched.

Myrtle's forty years of professional life were busy ones. As a practitioner of spiritual healing, she carried a full, daily client load. She served as co-central secretary of the Society of Silent Help (renamed the Society of Silent Unity in 1891), and provided editorial material for a department of the magazine devoted to the society. In April 1893, she became the editor of a new monthly magazine for children called *Wee Wisdom,* which told about the healing power of God. She published a book for children in 1896 entitled *Wee Wisdom's Way,* based on her own healing experiences. She co-taught with Charles, beginning in 1897, a two-week course in Practical Christianity which was given three to four times annually. She co-led a Sunday service with Charles for the Kansas City Society of Practical Christianity, the first church organization in the newly emerging Unity movement. In addition, she carried on an active correspondence with Unity students.

As years passed, Myrtle saw her life's purpose as being "a torch-bearer to light the way for all sincere true followers of the Master Metaphysician Christ Jesus."[15] She explained: "My work is a work of love and encouragement and blessing, a work with the individual, with a view to lifting him into a greater light and consciousness of freedom and power and plenty, that he may the better *do* his part in unity with others."[16]

In 1910 Myrtle was sixty-five years old and in excellent health. Retirement was something she never considered. She had no intention of growing old, either in body or in spirit, and was convinced that humans were ageless beings capable of living far beyond the normal life span. She told a woman correspondent, "We consider seventy years a mere childhood! The soul is just getting a well-rounded knowledge of the world in which it lives, and preparing to really live, after being here for seventy summers."[17] She firmly believed that children were given the wrong message about the nature of life and death. She wrote:

It is a common mistake for children to be taught that they are born, full of life, and strength and mental enthusiasm; that the years bring heavy responsibilities, unavoidable disappointments and sickness; and that the approach of the three-score-and-ten milestone on life's journey marks a decline in the life flow and the active interest and the ability to cope with problems, and that the end is weakness and death. Children do not like to accept such an erroneous concept of life, and they vigorously resist it.[18]

Myrtle lived and worked for another twenty-one years, going to the office every day and often working far into the night. She never retired, dying at age eighty-six on October 6, 1931. Active until the end, her last letter, in which she responded to a request for healing, was written the day before she died. While she had some minor ups and downs in health during her last years, she never encountered serious illness. Her family reported that she died peacefully in her home at Unity Farm, a few miles outside Kansas City.

Divine Nature and Human Nature

Myrtle filled her letters with her ideas on the nature of the divine. While she adopted a Christian perspective, she was often at odds with the teachings of Protestantism and Catholicism. Her alienation from traditional Christianity was evident in a comparison she made between Christian ideas on the nature of God and those of the American Indian. She observed: "I often think that the Indians' concept of a Great Spirit brought them, consciously, nearer to the Creator than the Christians' concept of a personal God could ever bring civilized man to his God. We are to form no 'graven images' that will materialize into a one-man source of Being."[19]

Myrtle believed in a multifaceted God, one that had qualities of transcendence as well as immanence, a God that was omnipotent, omniscient, and omnipresent. While statements about the indwelling Spirit filled the pages of her correspondence, Myrtle did not ignore the transcendent aspects of God. It is clear that Myrtle recognized God as an all-powerful being. Yet she made relatively few references to God as omnipotent, omnipresent, and omniscient, and when she did, her characterizations were typically short. "God is all powerful—All Power," she noted. "And there is no lack."[20]

Myrtle repeatedly told Unity students that God was an inseparable, intimate part of their lives. She sought to impress upon them the central "truth of man's being," that God existed in each cell of their bodies, lived in their thoughts and feelings, and occupied a place that was at the center of the inner self. The language she used to describe God's indwelling presence was always fresh and inventive. She rarely repeated herself or gave patented answers. "Each one of us is inseparably one with God," she noted, "the source and Substance of life and wisdom and every good."[21]

Myrtle also viewed God as operating impersonally in the universe through laws of cause and effect. She described this impersonal manifestation of God as "Principle." Many passages in her letters referred to God as principle operating through divine law. She declared, "God is Law and Principle, as well as Life and Love. God is all in all, and the Source of our every good."[22]

Myrtle also viewed God as having a personal, one-on-one relationship with men and women. She rejected, however, common Christian teaching regarding the personal relationship of God and humankind, particularly those regarding sin and salvation. She made her views explicit in the following statement:

I was thinking of the difference between our present understanding of God, and the old idea we, some of us, held about God—as though He were a great ruler on a throne, away off somewhere, far above the earth. Personally, I am not interested in a God who is chiefly concerned about the moral shortcomings of His subjects! The God I know is a Father who knows that all His children are like Him—loving, and happy, and kind, and considerate, and eager to show forth the glorious things contained in the realm of Mind.[23]

Myrtle was convinced that, even though God made personal connection with men and women, God did not have a personality, nor was God a person. "God is not a person," she declared, "God is Spirit."[24] Myrtle often characterized the personal relationship she saw existing between God and humankind as a partnership. She counseled Unity students to allow God to take the lead. "Did you go to the Father and acknowledge Him as the senior partner," she asked a Unity student, "and seek divine guidance in your undertakings?"[25] She indicated that a further manifestation of the personal connection between God and humankind could be seen in the work of the Holy Spirit. Myrtle viewed the Holy Spirit, which she described as "the action of God ideas in the individual mind and heart," as working in the lives of men and women to facilitate their spiritual development.[26] Myrtle believed that humankind and God shared similar divine natures. She believed that the faculties and powers attributed to God were also present in humankind. Consequently, children were born into the world with a divine heritage, possessing in potential all the attributes of God. Nowhere in her writing does Myrtle acknowledge the Christian idea that men and women are tainted with original sin at birth, or that human beings are fundamentally flawed and in need of God's redemptive grace to merit salvation.

Myrtle described the common nature of God and humankind as resulting from God's creating humans in his "image and likeness," therefore, "perfect." She indicated that "God and man are one and the same—it is God in us who gives us mind, and life and love, and substance."[27]

While men and women were created in the "image and likeness" of God, Myrtle was under no illusion that humans were born into the world with fully developed divine faculties. Men and women were "God-like" in potential only. The purpose of human life, she insisted, was to realize the divine possibilities inherent in human nature, to actualize fully human potential; in short, to manifest divinity. Myrtle believed that if individuals turned their attention "to the energies of the spiritual world,"[28] they would be "awakened spiritually," and realize their God-like nature. She and Charles called this state of advanced spiritual awakening the "Christ Consciousness"—the same state of consciousness Jesus attained in his lifetime. Reaching the Christ Consciousness was seen as the primary goal of human life on earth. She declared, "That is the purpose of life, to find the Christ and live the Christ life."[29]

Recognizing that manifesting the Christ Consciousness took place in stages, Myrtle advised patience, for time was required to bring this spiritual work to fruition. She counseled, "The transformation into the Christ type of man is a matter of growth; and none of us can say just when, or how long [it will take for] the full awakening."[30]

Myrtle acknowledged that men and women were free to choose whether or not to develop their God-like qualities. "Man had inherited free will," she noted, "and the privilege of developing as he chooses."[31] Many people failed to grasp the importance of devoting themselves to developing their spiritual potential. "Even God," Myrtle acknowledged, "cannot force man's highest good upon him."[32] Men and women were prone to making "mistakes," and by so doing bringing about "undesirable results."[33] Humankind had a propensity to make errors or to "sin." Sin, as Myrtle defined it, was "an unwise use of the powers and faculties and qualities of Being."[34] Myrtle warned a Unity student of the temptation: "If you are like most of us, and I believe you are, you almost hourly think, or do something or are moved by some impulse which admits your unbelief, lack of faith, lack of assurance that God is all in all, and ever shall be the fullness of good of every kind."[35]

Myrtle acknowledged her own weakness and inability at times "to interpret and express God's perfect plan."[36] She confessed: "Sometimes I feel that I'd like to just slip away from all this that is going on about us. But when I feel this way it is because of some negation, or bubbling to the surface of some old subconscious ugliness, or some remnant of belief in the reality of suffering and inharmony."[37]

The source of human difficulty lay in an aspect of consciousness that she called "the carnal mind." Myrtle reported:

The carnal mind is the only devil there really is, and of course, it doesn't intend to give up its reign in the individual; so when the Spirit of Truth sends its "angels" of light into human consciousness, the "old devil" of carnal mind does all in its might to destroy the messengers of Truth. Unless the soul is strong and positive, and can maintain its hold upon Christ, the Truth, it is apt to suffer adverse experiences.[38]

Negative thought, an aspect of carnal mind, was a major perpetrator of evil in the world and responsible for the greed, avarice, intolerance, and bigotry that characterized much of humankind's behavior. Myrtle noted: "Man, through error thought, has fallen from his high estate as the Son of God. He has lost sight of his unity with God, all good."[39] Negative feelings or emotions also raised havoc with human consciousness. Myrtle indicated, "when some of our thought energy is expended in negative beliefs and feelings . . . we get those old negative results."[40]

It was clear to Myrtle that negativity was deeply ingrained in the human consciousness, instilled in everyone from childhood. She noted: "We have been trained in looking for and seeing and being disturbed by the appearances of inharmony and discord and selfishness and lack since we were born."[41]

Myrtle indicated that her own religious upbringing was responsible for the negative attitudes she held for many years regarding her own health. She said that she demonstrated good health when she changed her belief system and began trusting the indwelling Spirit.

Manifesting Our God-like Nature

"The purpose of human relations," Myrtle once observed, "is the glorification of the divine. The purpose of life is to manifest God."[42] Myrtle believed it highly important for men and women to claim their "inseparable oneness with God."[43] She urged her correspondents "to abide in the realization that God and the Good are omnipresent."[44] She believed that men and women who develop themselves spiritually and experience the indwelling presence, live in accord with God's will and abide by the principles of divine law. Those who succeed in becoming God-realized, according to Myrtle, are rewarded in this lifetime.

Myrtle stressed the need for men and women to follow "God's will and plan."[45] She equated God's will with "the Father's direction,"[46] or what "His Spirit has prompted you to do," or "what God has given you to do."[47]

Myrtle believed that definite benefits accrued to those who conformed their lives to God's will. She told a Unity student that when he was doing "what God in the midst of him would have him do," he would "keep well and happy and be prosperous."[48] She elaborated: "When we let God have His way in us and in all our affairs, He brings to pass blessings beyond our greatest expectations. He does things for us in a large, splendid, glorious, divine way."[49]

Myrtle referred to divine law as "God's laws,"[50] as "universal law,"[51] and as "the Law of Good."[52] She urged Unity students to align themselves with divine law, declaring that those who live their lives in conformity with divine law will enjoy health, happiness and prosperity. "The Law is that we reap according to what we have sown," she indicated. "When we are diligent in sowing [thinking] thoughts of eternal life, health, peace, perfection . . . we shall transcend the carnal law of sin and death."[53]

To Myrtle, those who fail to observe divine law pay a steep price. She reported: "There is a divine law of life, which establishes rules which make for . . . sickness, unhappiness and lack, if we fail to understand them and live by them."[54]

THE TWELVE POWERS

Men and women, according to Myrtle, live according to the principles of divine law and aligned themselves with the will of God by activating twelve faculties of the mind called the twelve powers. Myrtle believed that the "divine inheritance of faculties and powers" consisted of twelve specifically defined attributes implanted in each human being at birth. She observed: "We have found that there are twelve centers or basic centers of consciousness, which are the result of the soul's use of the God qualities of Life, and Love, and Wisdom and Power and Substance."[55]

Myrtle believed that the centers of consciousness, though a part of humankind's mental faculties, existed in twelve different places in the body. She noted: "These centers of consciousness are mental, but they have built the physical organism through which they express. So, we have twelve locations in the body, where the soul expresses definite qualities."[56] She urged her correspondents to focus their attention on the development of the Twelve Powers. "We must come to know ourselves, and our God-given faculties and powers," she declared. Myrtle listed the powers individually as "faith, and love, and power, and life, and wisdom, and zeal, and order, and judgment, and will, and renunciation, and imagination and strength."[57]

Myrtle recognized the importance of each of the twelve God-like faculties, and believed that all must be developed uniformly to attain the Christ Consciousness. She indicated: "The Christ man needs all his faculties—power and strength, wisdom and love, order, praise, zeal, imagination, faith, judgment, understanding, elimination—organized and unified in constructive activity.[58]

While Myrtle stressed the importance of developing all the faculties, in letters to Unity students she devoted her attention to discussing only eight of the twelve—spiritual understanding, faith, divine love, power, imagination, zeal, will, and life. Her writings give no explanation as to why she neglected to discuss strength, order, judgment, and renunciation.

SPIRITUAL UNDERSTANDING

Myrtle was convinced that understanding the truth of man's being was an essential first step for all who sought to experience God in their lives. Myrtle was under no illusion that truth principles, as taught by Unity, could be grasped without diligent study. She warned students that it was impossible to benefit from association with Unity without becoming thoroughly familiar with the teaching. She told a student: "You can't really be sure you are living anything you do not understand . . . If you fail to understand the Law, and your thinking is not in harmony with the Truth, you get undesirable results."[59]

Myrtle stressed the fact that spiritual awakening depended upon gaining knowledge of the nature of God and an understanding of human nature and the purpose of life on earth. She restated the point again and again in communications with students, declaring: "There is nothing to compare with understanding of Truth . . . Truth principles are laws which, when they are understood and followed, will result in peace of mind, health of body and prosperity in affairs."[60]

FAITH

Myrtle believed that an individual's spiritual development was dependent on the depth of his or her faith in the power of the indwelling Spirit. Myrtle described how faith worked in human affairs when the faculty was fully developed. She explained: "Faith is the very substance of 'things hoped for.' Faith is the faculty for seeing and realizing the good that is eternally established in Omnipresence. Through faith we see our good as something real, tangible, substantial, already ours."[61]

Myrtle made specific reference to faith as one of the God-like powers when she observed:

When you keep your eye single to that which is good, that which is perfect, you are seeing that which is real and permanent. So when you keep your eye of faith single to life, joy, health you are beholding attributes of God that are innate in you and in all people. Whatever you think about and see with your eye of faith, will come into manifestation.[62]

DIVINE LOVE

Myrtle continually stressed the need for Unity students to develop their capacity to love. To Myrtle, divine love went beyond the personal love that men and women have for each other. Deeper and more all encompassing than the love between humans, divine love facilitated the common good of all. Those who gave love in its pure, divine form nurtured all with whom they came in contact. She asserted, "Love must radiate from you—happy, positive love, to those who will be blessed by it. Then, there will be more and more room for love to come back to you."[63]

Myrtle warned that the faculty of love alone, without the support of the other faculties, would not bring spiritual enlightenment. She noted, "Love, without the cooperation of wisdom and good judgment and will and substance, would not give you the well-rounded expression that you desire."[64] She believed that the faculties of faith and love, when present in a highly developed state in a person, produced "many blessings."

Myrtle indicated that love of another person could come from a selfish motive. We need to be aware of the limitations of the love between human beings. She explained: "When we permit ourselves to take God's love and pour it out upon persons or things, to the degree that we bind them to ourselves, the very virtue of loving becomes a fault."[65] While Myrtle wanted her students to be careful of love gone awry, she nevertheless considered love in its purest form to be of the highest value. She observed:

"Love is the greatest thing in the world, for 'God is love.' It is the 'spiritual currency' that makes those who give and those who receive it, rich beyond any material standard of comparison."[66]

POWER

Myrtle was convinced that the words we speak have the power to create the conditions we experience in our lives. The "power faculty," which she observed lay in the throat, could be activated with words that were positive and uplifting. She explained: "Power manifests in the body in a little brain center in the throat. By concentrating there your words which declare your unity with All-power, you quicken the brain center into activity."[67]

Myrtle believed that those who had an understanding of truth principles used words more effectively. She commented: "As you study and seek to prove the Truth you read, you will find that you have the power to speak words of Truth, and that these words of Truth do just what you say. They become alive and active in you and for you."[68]

Myrtle felt that there was "unlimited power in the Word spoken in faith,"[69] and indicated that powerful words of truth had a greater spiritual impact than several other religious practices. She commented: "Not in church-going and praying and observance of moral laws, but in vital, loving, powerful words and acts of helpfulness to others do we live divinely."[70]

Myrtle wanted it understood that words alone could not create desired conditions. If the power faculty functioned alone—without aid from the other eleven—she believed that one could not expect good results. She warned, "The repetition of words, however true they are, cannot make conditions right, if they are not right at the foundation." Words by themselves would have no impact "without the inner confirmation of Spirit, and without the purposeful cooperation of all the faculties."[71]

IMAGINATION

Myrtle viewed the imagination as a faculty that facilitated direct contact with God. Active and intelligent use of the imagination could enable one to create health and well-being in daily living and to attain the good things in life. One could become spiritually alive and inspired through the effective use of the imagination. She told a Unity student, "You have a vivid imagination. Use it for building purposes. Imagine the good, the true, the lovely, the perfect, the purposeful."[72]

Myrtle related a personal experience in which she used her imagination to overcome negativity in her own life. She reported: "I had tried and tried so hard to overcome a negative condition. It occurred to me to image just how I'd feel if I were free from it. I entered fully into the imagination of freedom and wholeness, and Lo! I discovered *I was, in actual manifestation,* all that my imaging faculty declared me to be."[73]

ZEAL

Myrtle told Unity students that spiritual development required concerted effort. Lazy persons and those who preferred a life of ease to one in which they applied their talents and abilities diligently would not reap the benefits. Contact with God required alertness, awareness, and action. She acknowledged, "we don't usually accomplish many things worthwhile, without steadfastness and persistent effort, as well as prayerful contemplation of all factors involved."[74]

Given her rural upbringing, it is not surprising that Myrtle often used agricultural metaphors to make her point, as she did in the following characterization of the importance of zeal. She observed, "all of us are 'farmers,' given the fields of mind action to cultivate, and the harvest we shall reap depends upon how diligent and industrious we are in our 'farming.'"[75]

WILL

Myrtle believed that one of our major human attributes is the will, that the will enables us to make choices and decisions. Her letters contained little about the operation of the will, only enough to make it clear that she understood its importance and was aware it needed nurturing. She stated: "Even God cannot force man's highest good upon him ... the way of experience may be rough and stony, but it is up to man to choose whether or not he will take the short cut, or go the road of experience."[76]

LIFE

When the life faculty was fully activated, Myrtle believed, men and women would be completely renewed in body and spirit, might live on indefinitely, and would never again suffer bodily deterioration and physical death. She indicated, "the body which is inhabited by the soul that is in tune with God's love and peace and life, is not going to wear out, and none of its organs are going to suffer."[77]

Myrtle believed that those who sought to activate the life faculty needed to refrain from sexual intercourse. She observed:

Sex passion is a taint; it is lust that sets the cells of the body on fire, which causes death ... When the sex force is purified, uplifted and consecrated to the Lord, it maintains the body in health, youth, strength; it quickens the mental and spiritual faculties and makes the mind alert, keen, and capable of discerning the deep things of Spirit. It makes the soul radiant and the body alive.[78]

In none of her writings does Myrtle indicate that sexual activity of husband and wife should be curtailed at the expense of producing children. Myrtle placed high value on childrearing. *Wee Wisdom* magazine, which she edited for several decades, and the "Family" and "Motherhood" columns in *Unity* magazine, which she edited for many years, were directed towards those involved in raising children. She told *Unity* readers:

I believe in the bringing forth of perfect children and in the establishment of the ideal home. And I am doing what I can in the Home Department to enthuse all homemakers with like ideals ... We like to call to ourselves that which expressed the beauty and symmetry that are developing in our souls, so we want children that we may bestow upon them the loving care and protection which we feel welling up within us as our capacity to do and enjoy broadens and deepens.[79]

Only after the family's last child was conceived was it appropriate to pursue bodily regeneration, and this most likely would occur during a later phase of life. She commented:

There comes, farther on, another phase of growth, when all the energies and powers of mind and soul are demanding that we bring forth a new and imperishable habitation of the Divine Self . . . This process is called "regeneration" and means, for those who attain it, conquest over all the limitations of mankind, and the restoration of dominion which was given in the beginning to God's Man.[80]

When questioned in March 1921 as to whether Unity teachings on parenthood and regeneration were in contradiction, Myrtle, as editor of the Motherhood Department in *Unity,* commented:

The work carried on in the Motherhood Department is in no way contradictory in the teaching of regeneration as presented in our literature. Regeneration is for those who have decided that the idea is the upbuilding and spiritualization of their own bodies. For those in whom the urge for parenthood prompts the bringing forth of children, the motherhood ministry offers its teachings. Regeneration and parenthood do not antagonize each other. They are different views and aims of life.[81]

One of Myrtle's loftiest spiritual aspirations was to regenerate her own body. In 1928 she told a correspondent, "We are working diligently every day to save the body from the ravages of unwise living, and to quicken it and keep it expressing more and more of the life of God, to the end that it may be transformed, even as Jesus transformed his body."[82]

ACTIVATING THE TWELVE POWERS

Myrtle devoted a great deal of time, energy, and attention in her correspondence advising Unity students how their shortcomings could be overcome by activating one or more of the twelve powers. Her advice often depended upon how she viewed the spiritual development of her correspondent and her sense of which of the faculties needed the most nurturing. A new student who knew little about truth teaching, who needed to work on "spiritual understanding," would be given some introductory instruction and materials to read. For the student who was lost in analytical thinking and had little sense of a divine inner spark, she would recommend going into the silence and listening for the still, small voice. For people who focused constantly on the negative, she would suggest ways to discipline the mind and to think positively. For those who were full of doubts, she would recommend prayer. For the sad, lonely, and unloving, she would suggest ways of becoming more joyful. For those who made little use of the imagination, she suggested visualizations or the use of creative ideas. For those whose attention was focused on the mistakes of the past, she recommended living in the "now." For all students, she recommended affirmations and denials as a way of developing faith, love, power, zeal, and life.

STUDY AND LEARNING

Myrtle indicated that the faculty of spiritual understanding was pivotal, since it served as a catalyst for the development of all the other faculties. She urged students, both new and old, to become thoroughly acquainted with truth principles. "You must learn to know what Truth is," she told a Unity student, "and to let the Principle of Truth prompt your every thought."[83] She told another, "There is much to learn, if we would be in command of all our wonderful faculties and powers, and do with them what we came into the world to do."[84] Pamphlets and articles that addressed a particular aspect of truth accompanied many of her letters to students. She was convinced that Unity School needed to do its best to help students gain a knowledge of truth. She acknowledged: "Our spiritual ministry of prayer is only half done unless we give those to whom we minister an explanation of the Christ principles that will enable them to demonstrate spiritual laws for themselves."[85]

Myrtle often recommended enrollment in the Unity correspondence course, telling students, "you will receive inspiration and instruction that would organize and clarify your ideas and open the door to a new unfoldment of Truth."[86] Myrtle was full of ideas on how to activate the faculty of spiritual understanding: "Put aside doubting, questioning thoughts for the time being at least, and open your mentality to Truth principles. Study the literature through and through, thoroughly and often, asking your indwelling Lord (Light) to give you spiritual discernment, spiritual faith, and spiritual understanding."[87]

Myrtle's letters often contained passages that students might reflect upon, and by so doing, add to their spiritual understanding. The following passage, which Myrtle advised a student to study "until you understand it and realize its power,"[88] is an example of the kind of instruction she gave for the purpose of helping students activate that faculty:

The Father-Mother elements of divine mind are blended in you, and you are now expressing your sonship in Christ. You are the illumined child of God, filled with the spirit of divine love and wisdom, by which you are guided in all ways, and led into that which is for your highest good. Because of your divine relation to others, you readily understand what is your spiritual attitude toward them, and how you are to express what the Father would have you do, in dealing with them. You are free from delusions of sense and mortal beliefs; free to receive your good and use it wisely. Those who are near and dear are inspired by the Christ in you, and great peace and joy are established in your home.[89]

DISCIPLINING THE MIND OR "RIGHT THINKING"

Myrtle believed that the human mind was very powerful. She was convinced that the circumstances of our lives were the product of our thoughts. She underscored this point when she declared: "The conditions of your life are the result of your own thinking. Each condition that appears in your body and affairs corresponds to the kind of thought that produced it. You can readily see, then, that in order to change your conditions you must first change your thoughts."[90]

Those who wish to activate the twelve powers need to discipline their minds by filling them with healthy, life-enhancing, positive thoughts. Myrtle advised a Unity student to: "Send only thought currents of a good, constructive, harmonizing, upbuilding, healing character over your nervous system so that there will be no obstruction to the free-flowing energies of the Holy Spirit."[91]

Myrtle had strong views on what qualified as "right thinking." She shared her ideas with her students, pointing out: "Our affairs are just an extension of our consciousness, and as a man thinketh in his heart, so is he in mind, body, and affairs."[92]

Myrtle had equally strong opinions on the impact of the correct use of the mind on the development of the faculties. She counseled: "Keep your mind filled with thoughts of life, strength, health, joy, Truth and you will express these blessings. You will radiate life, joy, health, because, 'as he thinketh within himself, so is he.'"[93]

Myrtle recommended that students focus their attention as much as possible throughout the day on the presence of the indwelling Spirit or the "Christ mind." She told students, "The same mind of Christ Jesus is in all of us. 'We have the mind of Christ.' 'Christ in you the hope of glory.'"[94] She urged her correspondents to turn their thoughts inward, stating: "The more you think about your indwelling Christ mind the greater will be its expression in you. Your consciousness will be illumined by the Christ light. Gradually your whole consciousness will be spiritualized."[95]

Myrtle believed that because the mind had such great power for both good and ill, it had to be disciplined; every effort needed to be made to keep the mind focused in positive ways. "You must discipline your mind day after day, and control your thoughts," she advised, "so that you will not be full of faith one moment, and doubting, wavering, and unstable the next."[96]

Myrtle pointed out that powerful ideas had an important impact on consciousness. She presented a variety of arguments for the importance of keeping divine ideas constantly in mind. She indicated: "Every divine idea you meditate upon and incorporate into your consciousness does a mighty regenerating, transforming spiritualizing work in your mind, soul, body, and even in your outer world of affairs. Each time you grasp an idea of Truth you lift your consciousness a little higher, and the word of transformation goes on, 'until Christ be formed in you.'"[97]

USING INTUITION

Myrtle indicated that one of the ways to develop deeper spiritual understanding was through intuition. She urged a Unity student "to awaken and unfold the knowing faculty of mind-intuition."[98] She continued: "Then you will not have to stop and reason out seeming conflicts and inconsistencies that appear. Intellect reasons, but intuition knows."[99]

She saw intuition as particularly valuable in separating truth from error and right from wrong, pointing out: "Your own intuition will show you whatever degree of truth there may be in all the doctrines that come to your attention. When the Mind of Truth within you shows you that a thing is true, accept it; but do not accept a proposition as true merely because somebody says it is truth."[100]

Myrtle had great faith in the power of the "inner knowing" faculty. She encouraged students to recognize its value and to develop and use it: "Your intuition is your faculty for knowing beyond a shadow of a doubt the Truth about God and your oneness with Him. Do not try to reason out things intellectually—that is, spiritual things, but trust the Spirit of Truth to make them clear and plain to you. Have faith in the guiding light of your indwelling Spirit."[101]

FOCUSING THE MIND ON THE PRESENT MOMENT

Myrtle believed that one of the best ways to develop the faculties leading to Christ Consciousness was to keep the mind continually focused on the present. She advised Unity students over and over again to "live in the now." She emphasized the point in a letter to a Unity student, observing that we "must get hold of the idea that it is what we are, here, NOW, that really counts."[102] Myrtle indicated: "Right now we have fresh mind substance, fresh in this new moment of existence, and the God-given power to use it to absolutely renew, regenerate, and spiritualize mind and body . . . We must live in the now and let our new thoughts be nourished by this spiritual bread, this manna from heaven."[103]

She saw no point in worrying about past mistakes or obsessing about the future, and felt that if we live fully in the present moment, the future will take care of itself. She commented: "We are glad to leave the past behind . . . We see, in the present moment, the fulfillment of our highest ideals, and the supply for our present needs."[104]

USING SILENT MEDITATION OR "GOING INTO SILENCE"

Myrtle felt it essential for Unity students to spend time each day sitting in silence. It was in this quiet space that she believed the voice of the indwelling Spirit could be heard. Most important, it was in this peaceful, centered state that the faculties were awakened. She observed, "When you get quiet and come in touch with this higher Self it is the most natural thing for your . . . powers and faculties to begin to express."[105]

Since contact with the divine inner Spirit was a primary objective of Unity spiritual practice, it is not surprising that Myrtle placed strong emphasis on the inner work that took place in the silence. She did not suggest a fixed type of sitting, as designated, for example, in Eastern meditation practices. "Unity does not teach that any special physical posture is necessary," she commented. "Sitting comfortably helps to bring about a more restful attitude." One's state of mind, however, was most important. She pointed out, "It is the attitude of the mind and heart, your interest and earnestness, that helps you most to the 'Still Place' within."[106] She wanted it understood that going into the silence could be done in a variety of ways, and that one's own creativity could be enlisted in finding useful approaches. She wrote: "The silence is not a habit of sitting for hours. Perhaps the nearest you come to the silence is during some quiet, receptive, faithful attitude of mind and heart. That should give you something definite to work on immediately after the period of quiet communion."[107]

Myrtle felt strongly about the value of going into the silence and believed that the quiet space was essential for those who wanted to develop their faculties. She observed: "The daily quiet time, for study and meditation, and identification with our Source, helps us to grow—to come into understanding of our sonship and our full, free use of our God-given faculties and powers."[108]

USING AFFIRMATIONS

One of the principal ways of awakening the power faculty was through affirmations. Myrtle defined affirmations as "just the right arrangement of words to train the Thoughts in harmonious ways."[109] She considered affirmations to be "vital, powerful, living words of Truth," which to be most effective should be spoken "confidently and regularly and with conviction." She believed that clarity of thought and purpose were also important in speaking "words of Truth." Myrtle urged Unity students to "declare them in a way to convince every thought, every brain center, every nerve, every member of your soul and body."[110] She emphasized the need for persistence in working with affirmations and specific advice on how to use them. She told a Unity student:

Go down into the body—instead of soaring off into the mental realms—to tell the various organs and functions the Truth. Learn to know what mental faculty is back of a given organ or center of nerves; study into your use of this faculty, to see whether or not you are measuring up to God's idea of that phase of life. After a while you will be acquainted with an entirely new man, and will know how to link up all these faculties and powers, and to use them under the direction of the Christ Mind.[111]

Myrtle felt that affirmations that took the form of praise and blessings were also useful. She told a Unity student, "There is unlimited power in praise and blessings to bring good into [your] life."[112] For a woman who wanted to know how to advise a friend on the use of praise and blessing, Myrtle suggested: "Tell her to praise and bless her eyes, her hands, her feet—her whole body temple, and if they seem to make mistakes and fall short in any way, to pour out upon them words of love, courage, blessings, Truth. When she trains herself to do this, all her faculties . . . will readily respond and become more alert, strong, vital, perfect."[113]

Myrtle believed that affirmations were particularly powerful when spoken while sitting in the silence. She advised: "Go into the silence and declare the Word; then rest in the faith that the power of the Word is working to bring forth the wisdom, health, strength and supply you need."[114]

Myrtle explained that the most powerful affirmations were contained in "I AM statements of Truth." She told a Unity student: "Instead of letting your thoughts run along old lines of materiality, when you are busy with your daily duties as well as when you pray, use the 'I AM truths.' Make them an established part of your consciousness. The more you think about 'I AM' your Christ Self, the greater will be the realization of your inner righteousness and purity."[115]

Myrtle considered the I AM statements attributed to Jesus to be particularly effective. She recommended the following: "I am the resurrection and the life. I am the light of the world. I am the health of my people. I am and there is naught beside me."[116] She suggested that each day might begin with the following I AM affirmation: "I am stepping out to face blessings, to face prosperity, to face the glory of life."[117]

USING DENIALS

Myrtle considered denials to be an important tool in counteracting negative states of consciousness. Words of denial were necessary "to dissolve negative conditions and weak tendencies" before affirmations could do their creative work.[118] She urged Unity students not to neglect denials, offering the following advice: "Deny out of both your conscious and your subconscious, all thought of fear, in all its phases, along every line . . . You need to deny those fears that are trying to hide in your consciousness, and your subconscious mind."[119]

PRAYER

Prayer and affirmations, for Myrtle, had many similarities. "Prayer," she wrote, "is simply an exercise to change our thought habits, and our living habits."[120] Prayer could take the form of affirmations, Myrtle indicated, if while praying, "we read and declare words of Truth."[121] She pointed out that prayer could also be done silently, with the mind focused on connecting with the divine within. Myrtle described this type of prayer as "the quiet, attentive, receptive coming to the divine Father-Mother for example and counsel and light and assurance."[122]

Silent prayer was particularly significant because it brought the person in contact with the divine presence. Myrtle suggested: "Be faithful to periods of silent prayer for it is the only way we can know God, and knowing Him you have the conviction of oneness with Him."[123]

Myrtle indicated that prayer, when done silently, "really relaxes one and relieves tension, and turns thoughts into new channels."[124] When praying, she advised, "enter into your closet and shut the door. We are taught to center our thoughts within, and then to shut the door, that is, to close our minds to all other thinking and think about God and His goodness and wonderful love."[125]

BEING JOYFUL

Myrtle recognized that joyfulness had a powerful spiritual impact, and she urged her students to recognize its importance. She indicated, "Joy is one of our powerful spiritual assets. Joy relieves all strain and stress and opens the way for the outpouring of divine goodness."[126]

Myrtle revealed in a comment to a friend how she herself discovered the impact of positive thought in creating the experience of joy. She asserted: "I want to tell you a wonderful truth. I have made a discovery that when one's thoughts are busy with good, and happy, and loving things, one's heart is full of a joy that lights up the consciousness, and brings to the individual every blessing and delight that can be imagined."[127]

Myrtle suggested the following exercise for creating "a joyful consciousness":

Start with the top of your head and go to the very bottom of your feet, into every organ, every function, every nerve, every cell in your body temple, giving each the word of joy. Do not simply speak the word joy to them, but make this work ringing, sparkling, living, and vibrant. [Do this] every day and many times a day both silent and aloud until your whole being is actively, vibrantly awake and alive with the joy of living.[128]

DEVELOPING ALL THE FACULTIES

Myrtle was convinced that if some of the faculties remained undeveloped, the others would languish. She argued for a "well-rounded development" of all the faculties, warning that difficulties would arise if some failed to receive proper attention. "If we neglect some parts of our consciousness," she observed, "we must sooner or later suffer weakness and lack."[129] She believed that "right use" of the faculties would assure the greatest progress. She elaborated on what she meant by "right use," stating:

Right use of wisdom will prompt you in doing that which will result in good success. Right use of power will give you mastery and poise and the ability to work well with your fellows. Right use of life will keep your whole system built up, and a good healthy satisfied feeling in every part. Right use of love will make you kind and considerate and diligent in doing that which is best for all your dear ones; and also keep your mental faculties and your members and the various functions of your body doing what is best for each other, so that harmony will prevail, and there will be no craving for unnatural stimulants. Right use of substance will build you up, and provide well for your family and give you something to keep you really interested in your progress.[130]

BODILY REGENERATION

Myrtle believed that when men and women fully manifested the Christ Consciousness and lived their lives according to truth, their bodies would be "quickened and renewed."[131] These dedicated souls would ultimately defeat "the last enemy" and overcome physical death. While Jesus was the only human known to have accomplished this extraordinary feat, it was possible for others to achieve it, Myrtle believed, if they fully developed their God-like attributes. Myrtle wrote extensively on how demonstrations of bodily regeneration might occur:

Those who are following Christ Jesus in the regeneration are going through a transformation; they are letting go of the material mind, the mind of the flesh and are unfolding the Truth consciousness; they are letting the Christ Mind express in and through them ... We believe that those who are steadfast in practicing the principles that He demonstrated will overcome the death of the body, just as He did. One of the essentials in the attaining of eternal life, and in the redemption of the body, is to keep the attention undivided and fixed upon the Life of God Within Us.[132]

REINCARNATION

Myrtle recognized that, for most people, the spiritual development required to achieve bodily regeneration could take several lifetimes. "Everyone is going to have to reincarnate," she explained, "until we make the union of Spirit, soul and body, and spiritualize these bodies of ours."[133] While she did not promise heaven for all eternity with Jesus to those who fulfilled the law and became spiritual beings, she predicted a state of lasting happiness for them. She declared: "While those who do not learn to completely transform the body and raise it up as Jesus did, will no doubt return in new bodies to finish their work, those who are illumined and who have fulfilled the law of life and love in so many ways will have a wonderful opportunity, and a more glorious experience than that from which they were translated."[134]

Myrtle viewed death not as an ending or a beginning, but as a time of transiting from one lifetime to another. It was a time in which the soul "left us to dwell for a while in the Great Invisible."[135] She explained: "You will learn that those who go through the change called death are really passing through a transition—the soul giving up the body temple which for some reason or other it can no longer express through or bring health."[136]

Myrtle harbored no doubts about humankind's immortality. "Life cannot be defeated," she declared, "Life is Eternal and unchangeable."[137] She believed that consciousness existed beyond physical death, explaining: "There is no reason to suppose that a soul out of the physical body is not aware of what is going on about it. At least, since the soul is consciousness, it is most reasonable to assume that it is aware of all that really interests it and all that it desires to identify itself with."[138]

Myrtle viewed the time between incarnations as a time of rest, with the soul living in a state that resembled sleep. She commented: "The soul continues to exist just as it is, except that it no longer has the vehicle of expression. The thing called death is more like sleep than living. It is a sort of rest—like our night's sleep and rest."[139]

She believed that life between incarnations was without stress or strain. She saw the soul existing in a place where "every need is supplied . . . a haven of rest, just out of sight, but not away from those it loved."[140] Many people wrote to Myrtle after the loss of a loved one, seeking solace, counsel, and advice. Myrtle reassured them that all was well, that their loved one was, as she told one correspondent, "just as happy in her present state as she was when in a body of flesh."[141] She comforted another, saying, "The Angel of His Presence is always at hand to make easy, beautiful and joyous the way, when we go from one place of manifestation to another."[142]

Myrtle saw no pain, deprivation, or suffering in the afterlife. She did not subscribe to the traditional Christian view that sinners were condemned to hell for all eternity and criticized religious leaders who warned of the awful fate in the afterlife awaiting those who lived a life of sin. She explained: "Our preachers have sought to frighten their people into being good, by describing this state of torment and burning as a condition which they would face after death . . . Those who have learned this version of 'hell' are sometimes less spiritually minded than they might be."[143]

Myrtle did not subscribe to the Spiritualist view that those who had died were available to give spiritual advice to the living through the intercession of a medium. While she acknowledged that those "who go through the transition which takes them from our sight have not gone anywhere," she wanted it understood that she did not favor efforts to communicate with them. She believed that the Spiritualist conception of life after death was erroneous, and she saw no value in "the efforts of those in the flesh to see and talk with those who have withdrawn from the physical for the time being."[144]

Myrtle viewed reincarnation as an opportunity rather than as an unfortunate fact of life or a burden. She told a Unity student who had lost a loved one: "When the time comes the way will open so that she can through reincarnation again take up a vehicle of flesh, and come into the world to do the will of I AM, her own indwelling Lord."[145]

She had similar words for another. "In the event that its shortcomings did wear out the body, or sever the connection, with it," she told a correspondent, "the soul would bide its time, and await the right opportunity for re-embodiment."[146] Writing about the passing of a Unity center leader who had been one of the first local healers and Silent Unity workers at Unity headquarters, Myrtle gave words of hope, noting, "All that was good in her soul will continue to live on, and sometime she will manifest only the Christ in all her ways."[147]

Unlike her husband Charles, who sought information on his past incarnations, Myrtle had little interest in past lives, her own or others. She told a friend, "I have never been able to work up any enthusiasm over past incarnations, or even to feel that I knew anything about my past."[148]

ASSESSMENT OF THE ROLE OF JESUS

Myrtle rejected much of the traditional Christian teaching on the role and mission of Jesus. She did not view Jesus as sent by God to save humankind from sin by dying on the cross, nor did she believe that Jesus' mission was to show men and women how to live in a state of sanctifying grace so as to merit heaven for all eternity after death. She did not hold to the Christian view that Jesus was now "away at some distant place called heaven."[149] She had no tolerance for negative "subconscious religious impressions" that indicated Jesus was "[u]p in the heavens somewhere and that He comes and gathers up those who are ready to accept him, and takes them up in the clouds with Him to abide in perfect bliss for all eternity."[150]

She considered this a "childish concept," a view that had been, "ground into the soul by religious leaders and the writings of those who had but glimpses of the true spiritual character of life."[151]

Myrtle did not view Jesus as a moralist who chastised people for wrongdoing. Her impressions of Jesus were expressed in a question she raised with a Unity student who, she felt, held an erroneous view of the teachings of Jesus. She asked: "I wonder if you have a habit of thinking of Jesus as a sanctimonious old church-goer, one who is ever looking about to find fault with folks, or to give them a lecture on morals or on loving their neighbors?"[152]

She believed that the false information about Jesus had discouraged many from understanding Jesus' true mission. She declared: "Some of our ambitious old sin-hunters have almost spoiled our best story of life as it should be lived, and so, many of us haven't cared much about reading the reports of Jesus' doings, or getting our faculties to work to enable us to really know him and to make us want to do what he told us to do."[153]

Myrtle felt that traditional Christian churches bore most of the responsibility for the lack of appreciation for the teachings of Jesus, noting: "The churches have failed to live up to His doctrine and life, and the result is confusion and restlessness, which is not according to Christ's promise, 'In me ye shall find peace.'"[154]

Christian teaching, in Myrtle's opinion, placed far too much emphasis on the transcendent nature of God, failing to focus sufficiently on the reality of God's immanence, the inward presence in humankind. Myrtle told a Unity student: "Stop looking to a God way off somewhere in the outer, but stand steadfastly in the realization that in God 'we live, and move, and have our being,' and center your attention upon God in the midst of you."[155]

Myrtle did not accept traditional Christian teaching on the Triune nature of God. Consequently, she did not consider Jesus to be the second person of the Blessed Trinity, possessing omniscience, omnipresence, and omnipotence at birth—in short, all the attributes of God. Rather, she viewed Jesus as born human, like every other man and woman, developing his God-like qualities over several lifetimes. Myrtle indicated that Jesus "lived many lifetimes until He became the perfect man," and that he was "the incarnation of David."[156]

Myrtle concluded that Jesus realized his God-like nature by fully developing the twelve powers. She observed:

Jesus exercised all the God qualities we have yet been able to discern in a masterly way. God-love was expressed by him; but it was complemented and balanced by God-wisdom, and power, and judgment, and will, and zeal, and life, and renunciation, and strength, and order, and imagination, and faith. Love drew him to people, but good judgment held him to a course of action which resulted in a success which was more far-reaching than any of us have yet realized.[157]

Jesus became, in Myrtle's view, completely unified with his divine inner nature. By so doing, he reached a high level of consciousness, a level that she characterized as the "Christ Consciousness." She reported: "Jesus is the individual who made the complete union of mind, soul and body in Spirit. He brought forth into expression the Christ, the God Mind within and consciously identified Himself with the Father."[158]

When Jesus preached "the Gospel of Truth," Myrtle testified, "his very flesh radiated the Light and Power and Love of Spirit."[159] She considered Jesus to be "the greatest of all men," because, to her knowledge, he was the only human being who developed his divinity every step of the way.[160]

According to Myrtle, Jesus' greatest achievement was overcoming the physical death of his body—the "last enemy," as she referred to it. Myrtle rejected the idea that Jesus raised himself from the dead on the third day after his crucifixion and ascended bodily into heaven forty days after the resurrection, as traditional Christianity taught. Jesus, Myrtle indicated, "disappeared [and] lifted his physical body into the invisible."[161] Myrtle considered "the invisible" to be "the spiritual world"[162] or "the fourth realm of consciousness." Though she referred to this realm often, she never fully identified or described it.[163] According to Myrtle, Jesus never went through the process of dying but kept his body constantly alive. Myrtle asserted: "Jesus did not die and let His body remain in the tomb. He raised it up to the fourth dimensional realm and lives in it right now—right here with us."[164]

Myrtle believed not only that the spirit of Jesus continued to live, but also that he was available to help humanity. She postulated that Jesus "lives in His glorified body right now in the fourth dimensional realm of Spirit. He is in the world right now helping those dear souls that are earnestly looking to Him for aid."[165] While Jesus was available to help humankind with their problems, one of his greatest gifts to humanity, according to Myrtle, was his service as a "Way shower."[166] He both taught and demonstrated truth and provided an example for humankind by manifesting his God-like powers. Myrtle indicated: "Jesus helped humanity, not by giving them temporal wealth, material things, but by showing them how to find their own innate Divinity, and demonstrate the Law of Good for themselves, so that they would have permanent, lasting health, happiness and prosperity."[167]

Myrtle's interpretation of the life, work, and teachings of Jesus provides a key to understanding the spiritual teaching of Unity School. Her ideas on the nature of God and humankind and her emphasis on the activation of the twelve powers and the development of the Christ Consciousness are all modeled after the example of Jesus, as she perceived it.

CHAPTER 2

Charles Fillmore: Spiritual Teacher and Leader

"In this babel I will go to headquarters."

During the first thirty-five years of his life, Charles Fillmore gave no indication that he would co-found and co-lead a spiritual healing movement
that would spread around the globe and involve thousands of people. Religion or spirituality played practically no part in his upbringing or in his
early adulthood. The profession he prepared himself for was business, not
that of a metaphysical, spiritual teacher and healer.

CHILDHOOD ON THE FRONTIER

Charles was born in 1854 to pioneer parents on a Chippewa Indian
reservation in northern Minnesota near present-day St. Cloud. His early
years were spent dealing with the rigors of life on the frontier. Northern
Minnesota at the time was disputed Indian territory. The Sioux and the
Chippewa were struggling with each other and with white settlers over
land. His father, a young man of twenty-six when Charles was born, was
an Indian agent and farmer whose family was from Buffalo, New York.[1]
His mother, Mary Georgiana Stone, a dressmaker, grew up in Brunswick,
Nova Scotia, of Welsh and English parents.[2]

When Charles was six months old, he was alone with his mother at a
trading post operated by his parents when a roving band of Plains/Sioux
rode up and took him away. Evidently his captors had second thoughts
about keeping him, because they returned him unharmed a few hours later.[3] Experiences like this evidently were common during his boyhood.
"Such incidents made my early years," he reported, "romantic, but crude
and unprofitable."[4] A broken hip from an ice-skating accident at age ten

became a major life-shaping event. The break and the ensuing infections disabled him physically.[5] He reported:

When I was ten my life was crossed by what the doctors pronounced a fatal illness. It began with what was at first diagnosed as rheumatism in the right leg, which gradually developed into tuberculosis of the hip. . . . I was bled, leeched, cupped, lanced, seatoned, blistered and roweled. Six running sores were artificially produced on my leg to draw out the diseased condition which was presumed to be within. Physicians of different schools were employed and the last one always wondered how I ever pulled through alive under the treatment of the "quack" that preceded him; and as I look back at it now it's a miracle to me how I ever got away from them all the little bundle of bones and sinews which I found in my possession after they finished their experiments.[6]

The doctors told Charles that the abscesses on his leg would kill him before he was forty. Charles was, for several years, so incapacitated that he could not lead a normal life.[7] He explained: "I managed after years to get on my feet, although my right leg was several inches shorter than the left, and I was to all appearances destined to chronic invalidism. I managed to get about on crutches and cane and attend school in a desultory way until I was eighteen."[8]

EARLY ADULTHOOD IN TEXAS
AND COLORADO

By the time Charles reached maturity, one leg was three-and-one-half inches shorter than the other, and he required a leg brace to walk.[9] As the years passed his health improved, and by the time he was twenty he felt confident enough to leave Minnesota for Texas. Evidently, the move was in part the result of the breakup of his parents' marriage. He and his younger brother Norton, his only sibling, were left, he stated, "without a permanent home."[10] Charles moved first to Caddo, where he had a cousin, and then to Denison, where he lived for five years working as a clerk in the freight office of the Missouri, Kansas and Texas Railway. His mother joined him in Denison and lived with him for most of the remaining fifty years of her life.

In 1877, in Denison, he met Myrtle Page. The two struck up only a brief acquaintance before he left for Colorado. Residing in Leadville, he took a course in metallurgy and then became a metals assayer. Little information is available about his contact with Myrtle between his leaving Texas in 1879 and his returning to marry her in Clinton, Missouri, in the early spring of 1881. They most likely corresponded, though no copies of their letters remain. The couple left for Colorado after their marriage and settled in Gunnison. When the mining boom broke later in the year, they moved to Pueblo, where Charles engaged in real estate. It was there that Lowell and Rickert, their first two sons, were born. Charles was not ready to settle permanently there and moved the family to Omaha in 1884 and to Kansas City in 1885. Charles attributed the constant moving to his search for his true calling. He explained:

I never seemed satisfied with my surroundings nor at peace with my work, and the urge to go elsewhere was always with me. So I began looking for a location, without knowing exactly where to look. We broke our home in Pueblo in 1884, and we spent one winter in Omaha, Nebraska. However, there was a constant urge to go to Kansas City, and in the spring of that year we moved.[11]

Charles spent the first five years in Kansas City engaged in what he called "real estate plunging," acknowledging that he was "quite successful."[12] When he moved with his family to Kansas City in 1885, he had no interest in religion. He reported, "I did not believe in Jesus Christ and I did not want anything in the way of religion."[13] His lack of involvement dated back to childhood. He was not given a religious upbringing. Though his father, Henry G. Fillmore, came from a religious family—he had two uncles who were Methodist ministers in upstate New York—he did not raise his son as a Methodist. His mother appears to have been equally disinterested. "My religious education," Charles testified, "was quite limited."[14] As a young adult, Charles was not a churchgoer. During his pre-Kansas City years, God, he said, was "an unknown factor in my conscious mind."[15]

SPIRITUAL AWAKENING

A series of lectures he and Myrtle attended in Kansas City in 1886 on spiritual healing, presented by a Christian Science practitioner from Chicago, Eugene B. Weeks, proved to be a turning point for Charles, although not an immediate one. "The doctrine," he admitted, "did not at first appeal to me."[16] Charles's shift from doubt to faith was based in part on Myrtle's experience. He was impressed with the results of her efforts in curing herself of tuberculosis. He testified: "I was in sympathy with Mrs. Fillmore's continued demonstrations. In fact my interest became so pronounced that I neglected my real estate for the furtherance of what my commercial friends pronounced a fanatical delusion."[17]

The Fillmore's oldest son, Lowell, testified that his father joined the work after he saw the results of Myrtle's own healing and the success she had in helping others. Lowell observed: "My father, who was gifted with a keen power of perception and good judgment, as well as love of Truth, was quick to see the possibilities for helpfulness in Mother's new inspiration. . . . He began at once to spend time in study and prayer and soon became a great strength to many who called upon him to help them find healing of mind, body and affairs."[18]

Although Myrtle was a catalyst, Charles's developing religious convictions were based on his own inner work. Through study, prayer, meditation, and dream analysis, sometime in the late 1880s Charles developed a strong belief in the reality of the indwelling presence, the divine within. He explained:

I was much interested and took lessons in all the different schools. For a time I was mentally disturbed by the many conflicting statements of Truth, who had it, etc., made by the various teachers. The muddle was so deep that for a time I was inclined to ridicule, yet I could not get away from the evidence of a greater power back of the flood of contradictory statements. Neither could I understand why there should be so many divisions and schools, and such assortment of opinions about an exact science.[19]

He addressed this situation by seeking to make contact with the divine within by sitting regularly in quiet meditation. He observed:

I noticed, however, that all the teachers and writers talked a great deal about the omnipresent, omniscient God who is Spirit and accessible to everyone. I said to myself, "In this babel I will go to headquarters. If I am spirit and this God they talk so much about is Spirit we can somehow communicate, or the whole thing is a fraud. I then commenced sitting in the silence every night at a certain hour and tried to get in touch with God. There was no enthusiasm about it; no soul desire, but cold, calculating business method. I was there on time every night and tried all conceivable ways to realize that my mind was in touch with the Supreme Mind. In this cold, intellectual attitude one can easily understand why I did not seem to get any conscious result, but I kept at it month after month, mentally affirming words that others told me would open the way.[20]

Charles soon began having "exceedingly realistic dreams," which finally convinced him that Spirit was giving him guidance. He testified: "For months I paid no attention to them, my business at that time being of the earth—buying and selling real estate. The first connection I remember to have observed between my dreams and my affairs was that after closing the purchase of a piece of property I remembered having dreamed the whole transaction months before."[21]

While this particular dream sequence seemed to have no relationship to his spiritual development, the experience nonetheless convinced him of the need to explore more carefully. He reported: "After that I watched my dreams closely and found that there was a wider intelligence manifesting in my sleep than I seemed to possess in the waking state, and it flashed over me one day that this was the mode of communication that had been established in response to my desire for information from headquarters."[22]

Thereafter Charles paid closer attention to his dream life and received important spiritual information:

This has been kept up ever since with growing interest on my part, and I could fill a large book with my experiences. Everything which it is necessary for me to know is shown to me and I have time without number been saved from false steps by this monitor. Again and again I have had mapped out the future along certain lines for months and years ahead, and the prophecies have so far never failed, although I have sometimes misinterpreted the symbols which are used.[23]

As he worked with his dreams, Charles came to believe that Spirit was speaking to him in the same way the prophets of the Old Testament had been spoken to. He observed: "I can distinguish no difference between my symbolic dreams and those of Jacob, Joseph and other Bible characters. This is one of the many ways by which the Lord, or higher consciousness, communicates with the lower, and is just as operative today as it was centuries ago."[24]

Sitting in the silence became a part of the daily regimen for Charles for the rest of his life. Soon after, he developed a regular practice and acknowledged its importance. He observed: "All manifestations of life originate in the silence. The thoughts that rise up in you and come to the surface in deed and act, are they not from the silence? Do you take a step or lift a hand that has not its motive from the depths of that mighty sea of throbbing life within your own being? Then why look to the eternal for that which comes only from the silence within?"[25]

Later in life, Charles summarized his early experiences with meditation and dreams and their impact on his spiritual growth. He recalled: "The most important phase of my experience, however, was the opening of my spiritual nature. I gradually acquired the ability to go into the silence, and from that source I received unexpected revelations and physical sensations."[26]

Charles interpreted the information he obtained meditating in the silence as objective fact rather than subjective experience. In his writings, he presented information obtained while meditating as spiritual truth. He noted: "I developed a dream code through which I could get information and answers of marvelous accuracy to my questions. I do not remember that I asked who the author of my guidance was; I took for granted it was the Spirit."[27]

Given the value Charles attached to sitting in the silence, it is not surprising that he developed a deep interest in meditative practice. In his writing, he gave advice on posture, breathing, controlling thought, and focusing the mind.[28] After exploring differing styles of meditation, he concluded that the meditative techniques of Eastern practitioners, particularly Hindu meditators, were more effective than practices taught in the West. He observed:

The concentration usually taught by western metaphysicians is the antithesis of the higher spiritual concentration . . . The acme of concentration is the discovery in oneself of the real I. This is accomplished through meditation and inner attention. Hindu adepts levitate and do other seemingly marvelous feats by concentrating upon I, and intoning their name for the Deity. They use virtually the same name that Jehovah gave to Moses, I AM. They have over sixty intonations of the sacred name, some silent and some audible. The key to the power they exhibit is the silent affirmation of and audible expressions of AUM or OM. The higher the realization of the spiritual character of I, the greater power in the manifestation.[29]

Charles's experiences in meditation convinced him of the importance of an inner knowing, which he called "the light within."[30] If you want "eternal Truths," he declared, "you must seek it [sic] in your own heart."[31] "Intuition" was the term he often used to describe this capacity for inner knowing of spiritual truth. He indicated: "Truth is not the formulated doctrine of any church, nor the creed of any sect . . . That Truth is written in the inner sanctuary of every soul, and all know it without external formulas. It is the intuitive perception of what is right in the sight of God and men."[32]

Sometimes Charles referred to this inner knowing or intuition as "the Spirit of Truth," indicating the confidence he had in the information he received from this source. He stated: "The Spirit of Truth is our teacher and we look to that source alone for our authority. . . . We have closely followed the guidance of the Spirit of Truth, and on all points have boldly proclaimed the instruction given us."[33] Many times in his writing he would preface his remarks with "it was revealed to us that . . ." or, "I have been shown by the Spirit."[34]

It seems surprising that Charles also relied heavily on logic in ascertaining spiritual truth, given the fact that he downgraded the value of information received from the evidence of the senses or from rational analysis of factual information. His belief in the value of logic was stated forthrightly in the following passage:

Logic is the fundamental constituent of man's being, and all minds acquiesce to statements of logical sequence. We all see the relation and unity of cause and effect, mentally stated, but because the realm of forms does not carry out our premise, we fall away from the true standards and try to convince ourselves that our logic is somehow defective. The one important thing the student of spiritual science must learn is to trust the logic of the mind. If appearances are out of harmony with your mental premise, do not let them unseat your logic.[35]

Spiritual propositions, for Charles, either were right or wrong, true or false. There was no in-between or gray area; truth was not relative. Charles's basic philosophical approach was revealed in a response to a reader's question about the nature of truth. He explained:

Truth is absolute. Its laws are as exact as those of mathematics, and its standard of demonstration is as fixed. Some people think that the way will be easier if they do not at once make the highest claims of Truth for themselves and all men. They are like one who says, it is not expedient that I admit that three and two equal five, so I will let myself down easy by saying three and two equal four.[36]

Divine Nature and Human Nature

Charles devoted a great deal of time and energy to describing the nature of the divine and the activities of God in the universe. He returned to the subject again and again, addressing some aspect of God in all of his writings. Charles's belief that God was limitless and without bounds led him to postulate the existence of a God with immense power. He declared, "God is Spirit, the Universal Mind in whom we 'live, move and have our being.' This Mind is Omnipotent, Omniscient and Omnipresent."[37] The most appropriate designation for a transcendent God, Charles indicated, were the words I AM THAT I AM. Citing the Hebrew Scriptures on Yahweh (Charles used "Jehovah," the characterization of God in the King James version of the Bible), he noted:

When the great Jehovah sent Moses to bring the children of Israel out of Egypt he gave the name by which he was to be known, "I AM THAT I AM." This non-committal way of designating the Unnamable One stamps this scripture with a peculiar metaphysical authority. It reveals, in this particular instance, that it came forth from one who knew the truth, that God could not be named as man names, by describing. To describe God is to give Him limitation, hence He could not be given a fairer designation than "I AM THAT I AM." This is without confines or bounds and it allows unlimited expansion in every direction.[38]

While Charles acknowledged the transcendence of God, he also believed that God was actively present within every man and woman. Rather than looking outward for a supreme being existing separate and apart from humankind, as traditional Christianity looked for God, he felt the search should focus on the inner self of every human being. "Theology," he wrote, referring to mainstream Christianity, "has wandered away from the very present sentient and vitally active spirit permeating all things, man not excepted."[39] Much of Charles's writing on the nature of God was focused on the reality of the indwelling presence. Charles's belief that God existed within humankind was made explicit when he stated: "God is not an exclusive being, nor does He dwell in an inaccessible place apart from His creations. He is around you, about you, within you, without you. You are God yourself, in a sense. Ignorance has blinded you to your real self."[40]

Charles also viewed God as "Principle," operating impersonally in the universe through divine law. "To clearly understand that God or Good is Principle and not person," he testified, "is to have the key that will unlock all the mysteries of creation."[41] "The true concept of God," Charles asserted, "is that He is the Intelligent Principle of the universe, and, like all principles, totally impartial in His expressions."[42]

Despite the foregoing, Charles saw God relating to humankind in personal ways. "God is personal to every one of us," he observed, "and we must know Him intimately before we can be truly religious."[43] The following prayer of affirmation, used by Charles, indicates how he related personally to God. He affirmed:

Father Almighty! We bow before Thy goodness, and invoke in prayer and supplication Thy silent presence as Love. May its steady currents of power draw us into Thy mighty arms where we shall rest secure from all the buffets of the world. We come as little children into the sacred precincts of Thy Love, knowing full well that no hand of force ever finds welcome here.[44]

While Charles seemed to find no disparity in viewing God as both personal and impersonal, many students of religion have found it difficult to reconcile what appears to be a contradiction between the conception of God as principle and God as personal. This tension can be found in many religious traditions. In Christian thought, the tension is between the transcendence of God and the immanence of God. In Hinduism, it is between Nirguna Brachman and Saguna Brachman. In the Jewish tradition, it is between God as Elohim (the transcendent God) and God as Adonai (the personal God).

While Charles saw God as relating personally to humankind, he did not believe that God is "a person." He was critical of traditional Christianity and Judaism's efforts to make a person out of God. He commented:

People have been taught that God is a personal being who rules the universe much after the manner of an arbitrary monarch. This erroneous and contracted teaching has led to a belittlement of God in the concepts of men ... Let us dismiss the thought that God is a man ... So long as the concept of man-God exists in consciousness, there will be lack of room for the true concept, which is First Cause, composed of principles from which all manifestations flow.[45]

God operated in the earthly realm, according to Charles, through the activities of humankind. Men and women enjoy a cooperative relationship with God; they occupy a "place in the universe as cocreator and coworker with God." Charles thought that health, prosperity, and well-being were the result of this cooperative endeavor.[46] He indicated: "Some metaphysicians teach that man makes himself, others that God makes him, and others that the creative process is a cooperation of God and man. The latter is proven true by those who have had the deepest spiritual experience."[47]

Charles viewed God as relating personally to humankind through the workings of the Holy Spirit. Using as synonyms "the Comforter," "the Holy Ghost," and "the Spirit of Truth," Charles indicated that the Holy Spirit's primary function is to facilitate the connection between humankind and God: "It is the mission of the Holy Ghost to bring all men and all women into His open communication ... It is the mission of the Holy Spirit to so guide man that he shall not mistake the way into that light, nor wander off into the darkness of the many delusive paths of mortal sense."[48]

Charles felt that the work of the Holy Spirit was not properly acknowledged by traditional Christianity. He noted: "The failure by the orthodox Christian church of today to recognize this Holy Spirit as the one and only Guide and Inspirer, is the fatal departure from the teachings of Jesus Christ which has made all the worldly methods and spiritual atrophy so painfully manifest in the so-called followers of the true church."[49]

Charles was convinced that the Holy Spirit was at work in the lives of many creative, spiritually alive people, even though they themselves did not recognize it. The Holy Spirit, he believed, infused them with the power to connect with the divine. He observed:

The poets, the writers of Truth, both profane and sacred, are inspired of the Most High. Quiet citizens in every walk of life are the recipients of the divine Word. Every man and woman who has earnestly desired to do right in the sight of God and man, has been the guest of the Holy Spirit. They may not have recognized the strong conviction which has suddenly come over them to say or do certain things—they may not have discerned the source of the passage of Scripture or line of poetry, or some other form of a great truth . . . Yet these are all methods of the Holy Spirit for reaching consciousness.[50]

Charles viewed humankind as born divine and free from sin. He did not accept the traditional Christian doctrine of original sin that viewed men and women as flawed at birth, predisposed to destructive behavior, and by nature inferior to a transcendent deity. He wrote: "Man is not 'conceived in sin' nor 'born in iniquity.' Man is conceived in purity and born in holiness. This man is spiritual, the I Am, born of God. He makes a form of the dust of the ground and breathes into it the breath of life and it becomes living soul. This 'form' or man, an Adam consciousness, is also pure and holy at its birth."[51]

Charles saw no distinction between the nature of man and the nature of God. Their natures were one and the same. "Man is the idea of God," he asserted, "and must in essence be like God." As was his predisposition, Charles used logic to support this view:

"It is strictly logical and scientific to assume that man comes forth from this One, who is named variously, but whom all agree is the origin of everything. If man is the offspring of the Almighty, he must have the fundamental character of his parent."[52]

According to Charles, if the Bible was accepted as the ultimate authority, there could be no other explanation for the nature of man. "Man is created in the 'image and likeness' of God," Charles declared. "God looks in the mirror of the universe, and sees himself as man; he gives himself to man, and man in his highest is God manifest."[53]

While he felt that men and women are endowed with God's nature, he pointed out that the divine attributes are latent, existing in potential only. "None of us has attained that supreme place in consciousness where he wholly gives up the material man and lives in the spirit."[54] Charles observed that "Man, as we find him today, is at best but a partial product of the perfect image in which Divine Mind holds him. He has not fulfilled the orderly steps involved in bringing forth the Image."[55]

Charles believed that Jesus of Nazareth was the only human being who had fully activated the divine powers. Humankind's primary goal in this life was to follow the example of Jesus and to realize its true divine nature. Following Paul's admonition, Charles advised, "Let this mind be in you which was also in Christ Jesus."[56] Charles called this realization of the divine presence a "second birth," or being "born anew," in which we "put on Christ."[57] In other passages, Charles described this universal or higher consciousness as "the Christ Principle,"[58] or "the Christ state of mind,"[59] or "what we term the Christ Consciousness."[60] He elaborated:

The fact that Jesus of Nazareth lived and manifested the Power of the Christos, or spiritual man, is of vital importance to every soul. Not only is it important as an example, showing the possibilities latent within each of us, but in a deeper sense the testimony of the Gospels, and all who have come onto His spiritual plane, is that He bridged the way or formed a connecting link, between humanity and God.[61]

Charles was convinced that it was possible for all men and women to attain the same level of consciousness attained by Jesus. Those who followed his methods could also attain it. He emphasized that the purpose of life was not about creating wealth or attaining material goods, but about living the Christ life. He observed:

We sometimes think that we must succeed in some business or occupation before we can become rich or famous. This is a missing of the mark of the "high calling of God in Christ Jesus," which is to demonstrate the divine idea of a perfect man. The real object of life is not making money or becoming famous but the building of character, the bringing forth of the potentialities that exist in every one of us.[62]

To Charles, those who attain the Christ Consciousness will live healthy, happy, fulfilled lives.

Charles considered free will one of humankind's major attributes. Without it, he felt, men and women would be unable to develop the inner divine presence. "The absolute freedom of the individual," he asserted, "must be maintained at all hazards."[63] He rejoiced in the fact that men and women were free to determine the course of their lives. "Man is free," he declared. "We are never forced to be good nor truthful nor holy. We can live on the animal plane or the spiritual plane as we choose."[64]

Charles reasoned that men and women enjoy free will because it is an attribute of God. If God possesses it, so must humankind: "Man is the idea of God and must in essence be like God. God being the All of Being— without apposition—absolutely free, must necessarily have perfect free will. Then man, being in His 'image and likeness,' must also partake of that free-will, which he exercises according to his wisdom."[65]

While to Charles free will was an essential part of a person's makeup, it also enabled men and women to choose evil over good. In Charles's view, evil in the world took many forms. It came forth in human behavior as envy, malice, jealousy, lust, anger, covetousness, deceit, wickedness, and pride. He also saw it manifesting as negative thought, fear, sensual pleasure, ignorance, selfishness, and willfulness.

In his opinion, negative thought was particularly paralyzing. He indicated: "If you continually think and say, 'I can't,' 'I'm sick,' 'I'm poor,' you deny away power, health and prosperity. If you hold thoughts of envy, malice, jealousy, lust, anger, pride, hypocrisy, hate or fear, your body will show forth disease and you will be subject to accidents and all destructive agencies which such thoughts call about you."[66]

Charles indicated that fear had a debilitating effect on the mind and considered it an extremely harmful emotion. "Fear is the prime factor in every case of sickness," he observed. "On the thought plane, it is a disintegrating element which shadows forth in the human body in disease, and frequently results in death."[67]

Pleasure derived from the senses was a major cause of humankind's spiritual demise, according to Charles. While taste, touch, sight, hearing, and smell were not harmful in themselves, he observed that men and women constantly abused the senses.

He felt that sexual pleasure was a particular example of sensation gone awry. Charles continually advised against indulging the sexual appetite: "Sex-sensation has made a broken cistern of man's consciousness; for generations the life stream has been turned into this receptacle, and the lust for more has robbed the bodies of the whole race, making them mere shells. The failed eye, the deaf ear, the festering or withering flesh, all bear testimony to this perversion of God's life."[68]

Charles saw ignorance as a severe stumbling block to spiritual development. Charles elaborated on how, through it, we misuse our powers: "Every undesirable condition that we behold in the world is the result of ignorance. If men knew the truth about themselves, their relation to the Supreme Mind, and how to get into touch with it, and acted upon that knowledge, unhappiness would pass away and the millennium be rapidly ushered in."[69]

Lack of concern for the well-being of others was another inhibitor of spiritual development. Charles observed: "selfishness and greed make men grovel in the mire of materiality when they might soar in the heavens of spirituality."[70] He felt that willfulness also stood in the way of spiritual growth, observing: "stubborn, willful, resistant states of mind congest the life flow . . . The determination to have one's own will, regardless of the rights of others, stops the free action of the heart."[71]

Charles's study of the developing field of modern psychology convinced him of the existence within the human psyche of a "subconscious mind." He believed it was extremely powerful. It "transcends the conscious mind," he declared, "in knowledge and ability."[72] Charles indicated that the subconscious mind contained possibilities for good as well as evil. The subconscious mind, he said, included within it "the wise man and the foolish man, the kind man and the cruel man, the loving man and the hateful man, the stingy man and the generous man."[73]

Despite the fact that Charles was painfully aware of the manifestations of evil in the world, he steadfastly held, as a matter of philosophical principle, that evil was illusion, and had no existence. He defended his position with the following argument:

The statement of the unreality of evil is one that makes Truth a stumbling block to many, yet it must in essence be correct. If there is *real evil* it must have a basis in Principle, and as God is the One and Only Principle, it must be in God, hence God is evil. But the mind instantly rebels against this conclusion. There is an intuitive recognition that God is Good. Then what place shall we give the sin, sorrow, misery and discord which we see in the world? We can only give it a secondary place, brought about by misuse of the powers of Pure Being by man, God's free agent. Then evil does not inhere in Principle. It can be erased from man's life, hence it cannot be real because all reality is enduring. But it seems real to those who have been so taught, and its seeming reality can be erased from the tables of the mind only through understanding the truth of God's Being, and then willing that the truth alone shall be built up in thought and character.[74]

Unity readers on occasion wrote to Charles asking for clarification. To one who commented "I don't understand how you can deny that there is sin and evil when you see it all about you day and night," Charles responded:

You mistake our teaching if you think we deny that there is seeming evil. What we do deny is that evil has Principle back of it. It does not come from God—man creates it, hence it is not permanent and has no power except what we give it. We give it this power in two ways, first by doing evil, and second, by fearing evil. Many refrain from doing evil, but they talk about it as a reality. They believe it is sustained by a personality called the Devil, or that it is a Principle potential in Being.[75]

Manifesting the Christ Presence, Our God-like Nature

Charles's primary interest as a person and as a spiritual teacher was in manifesting the indwelling presence, the Christ Consciousness, and helping others do the same. Charles believed that men and women counteracted negative human behavior and realized the divine indwelling presence by living in accord with the will of God and by complying with divine law.

Knowing the will of God and aligning oneself with it was of the utmost importance. Charles declared:

Oh, my friends, there is a Supreme Will over us that when accepted shall lead us into all harmony and peace, if we will but acknowledge its presence every moment of our lives and follow to the letter the high ideals which it flashes before us. We cannot plead ignorance of this Supreme Spirit of Wisdom for we have all at some time come into conscious relation with it.[76]

Charles believed it was necessary for men and women to be willing to relinquish their own personal agendas to follow the will of God. He commented: "There can be but one course for the obedient devotee. If you have surrendered all to the omnipresent wisdom, you must take as final what it tells you. You will find its guidance is the right course for you, and, in the end, that it was the only course that you could possibly have taken."[77]

Charles referred to the divine law as the "Law of Being," the "Law of Divine Nature," and the "Law of God."[78] Charles believed that men and women who complied with divine law were in alignment with the will of God. Charles declared, "The greatest work that one can do is to strive to know God and to keep His law. God pays liberally for this service and the reward is sure."[79]

He thought that the difficulties human beings experience in the course of their lives are the result of failure to observe divine law. Charles reported: "The sin, sickness, suffering, and death that men experience are not punishment willed by God; they are the results of broken law. . . . All the woes of humanity have their root in disregard of law."[80]

According to Charles, knowing, understanding, and interpreting divine law required a high level of spiritual consciousness. He asked, "Who can tell what the law is?" Answering his own question he declared, "Only those who study man as a spiritual and mental being."[81] Charles viewed divine law as unchangeable, established for all eternity from the beginning of time. "The law is already fixed," he explained. "There is nothing in it to be changed because God is the lawgiver and does not change."[82] Therefore, there are no miracles. Charles admonished his students not to look for miracles to be performed for them. Rather, he advised, "look for the law with which you have identified yourself to work out the problem."[83] He continued: "God never performs miracles, if by this is meant a departure from universal law. Whatever the prophets did was from the operation of laws inherent in Being and open to the discovery of every man."[84]

In addition, he indicated, nothing happens by chance. The universe operates by cause and effect. He declared, "There are no accidents in the laws of Being. 'As a man sows so shall he also reap' is another way of saying that for every cause there is an adequate effect."[85]

THE TWELVE POWERS

As men and women align themselves with the will of God, comply with divine law, and thereby find union with the indwelling Spirit, they realize the divine within by activating twelve faculties or centers of consciousness. Charles referred to these faculties as "the twelve powers," declaring them "essential in the development of the perfect man."[86] Included were spiritual understanding, judgment, will, divine love, faith, imagination, zeal, strength, power, elimination, order, and regenerative life.

Charles believed that each of the twelve faculties could be located somewhere in the human body. He noted that each "has a focal point in the body through which it manifests."[87] Some were located in the head and neck, and others in the torso. Self-observation had led him to conclude that thought manifested itself from each of these body centers, not just from the brain itself. Man, he indicated, "has established twelve states of consciousness which have centers in his body."[88] Each of these "twelve great centers of action," he explained, "works through an aggregation of cells that physiology calls a 'ganglionic center.'"[89] According to Charles, if men and women want to activate these centers and make them functional, they need to direct thought into each of the body centers.

Charles indicated that each of the twelve powers was represented by the life of one of the twelve apostles of Jesus. He listed them as follows:

Peter—Faith
Andrew—Strength
James, son of Zebedee—Discrimination or Judgment
John—Love
Philip—Power
Bartholomew—Imagination
Thomas—Understanding
Matthew—Will
James—Order
Simon—Zeal
Thaddaeus—Renunciation or Elimination
Judas—Life Conserver[90]

Charles urged all practitioners of truth principles to undertake the development of the twelve faculties of mind. He believed that for generations, men and women had suffered from negative thought and lack of spiritual development, leaving the faculties in weakened condition. It was humankind's job "to get control of these centers"[91] and develop them in appropriate ways. Charles explained, "What we are all aiming at is restitution—a perfect balancing of all our faculties which have fallen into inharmonious action through ages of wrong thinking."[92]

SPIRITUAL UNDERSTANDING

Charles indicated that spiritual understanding was the starting point for anyone who wanted to develop the twelve powers. It was necessary for everyone to become "deep and strong in spiritual understanding."[93] He commented: "How important it is that we strive to quicken the spirit and live its life. We can afford to make any sacrifice to bring about the development of the pearl of great price—spiritual understanding."[94]

Charles often equated spiritual understanding with intuition, indicating, "this wisdom of Spirit is man's through the all-knowing and all-discerning power of Spirit within him, and he need never fear going wrong if he listens to his divine intuition."[95]

WISDOM

Charles's description of the faculty of wisdom indicated that he viewed it as related to spiritual understanding. He explained: "Wisdom is the power that lighteth every man that cometh into the world, and without it man is not man but a tempest-tossed barque that continually seeks but never reaches port. The quality of Wisdom is necessary to the adjustment of many conflicting questions of existence."[96]

One needs to look inside oneself for wisdom, Charles observed. "Look not abroad for power or wisdom. Seek at home. There, in the silent recesses of your own soul, you will find the pearl of great price. The well of living water must spring up in you."[97]

FAITH

In Charles's view, faith was the key element enabling men and women to accept the reality of the indwelling presence. Throughout his written works, Charles focused on the nature of faith and the importance of developing it. He observed: "The development of the faith faculty in the mind is as necessary to the work in spiritual principles as is the development of the mathematical faculty in the worker in mathematics. Neither of these faculties comes at a bound fully formed into consciousness, but both grow by cultivation."[98]

Charles stressed the fact that in exercising faith, men and women needed to use discretion. It was not wise to seek things that were outside the realm of possibility. He advised: "You must have reasonable faith in the possibility of your asking being answered. That is, do not ask for things wholly outside of your sphere and which you do not have in mind as eventually to be accomplished."[99]

DIVINE LOVE

Charles often wrote about divine love. He returned to the subject time and again. "The Spectrum of Love," he observed, "has nine ingredients." Included were:

Patience—"love suffereth long."
Kindness—"and is kind."

Generosity—"Love envieth not."

Humility—"Love vaunteth not itself, is not puffed up."

Courtesy—"seeketh not her own."

Good Temper—"Is not easily provoked."

Guilelessness—"Thinketh no evil."

Sincerity—"Rejoiceth not in iniquity, but rejoiceth in truth."[100]

Charles attached utmost importance to divine love because he felt that, to manifest God, this pure form of love must be in the consciousness of every seeker after truth. He asserted: "Love is the power that moves the world, and the sooner mankind finds out and takes advantage of its resistless currents, the sooner will prosperity, happiness and harmony come to all."[101]

Human love, Charles believed, was very different from divine love. He declared: "Divine Love and human love should not be confounded, because one is as broad as the universe and is always governed by undeviating laws, while the other is fickle, selfish and lawless. It was out of this personal aspect of the love-center in man that Jesus referred when He said, 'Out of the heart proceed evil thoughts.'"[102]

Human love, particularly romantic love, needs to be supported by the other faculties, specifically wisdom and understanding. He observed:

The most mysterious part of man's nature is the heart. As the seat of affections it is the center of forces that are difficult to harmonize. Love is of itself blind. It is a force, an energy, a wild, untamed cyclone of energies, swaying us this way and that way, until we are dazed and weary of the struggle. We learn by experience that *love must be directed* by wisdom. If we give up blindly to the impulses suggested by our loves we shall suffer many downfalls.[103]

Charles was aware that love of God needed to flow forth from a deep place inside, a place that was free from self-hate or self-disgust. In short, he recognized that love of self was a prerequisite for divine love. "Self condemnation," he asserted, "is also a great error and leads to dire results. You must love yourself because you are the child of God."[104]

IMAGINATION

Charles viewed the imaginative faculty as being extremely powerful: it created the outer reality in which people lived their lives. "That there is a limit to the ability of the mind is unthinkable," Charles declared. "What a man imagines he can do, he can do."[105] Charles elaborated, "You may attain to everything you can imagine. If you imagine it possible to God, it is also possible to you. Whatever possibility your mind conceives, that is for you to attain."[106]

WILL

Charles considered volition, the power to choose, as "the focal point around which all action centers."[107] Through our "innate power of choice," Charles stated, we have the freedom "to be what we wish to be."[108] He elaborated: "Man is free to give up his mind to the rule of the Holy Spirit or retain it in whole or in part. We are never forced to be good nor truthful nor holy. We can live on the animal plane or the spiritual as we choose."[109]

ZEAL

Charles defined zeal as "the affirmative impulse of existence; its command is 'Go Forward.'"[110] He observed that many beginners in the study and practice of truth expected immediate gratification. "Many fail," Charles observed, "because they are not patient. They want results at once."[111] Charles often stressed the fact that success required time and effort. He cautioned, "A man cannot expect his ideas to be transformed at once by the Spirit of God. He must be patient and receptive to the Word, and await the result."[112]

Charles felt that humankind's weakened condition, caused by generations of men and women who thought negatively and lacked spiritual understanding, made it unrealistic to expect immediate results in developing the twelve powers. Success would come, however, to those who were zealous enough to keep practicing in spite of apparent failure.

POWER

To Charles, words were the product of the power center, a faculty that lay in the throat. "The throat controls all the vibratory energies of the organism," he observed. "Every word that goes forth receives its specific character from the power faculty."[113] Charles cited the Bible as the authority for the power of words. He indicated: "If the word of God created all that was created, it follows that everything must be subject to transformation through the power of the word on its plane of formation."[114]

Men and women who fully employed the power of words took an important step in raising their spiritual consciousness. The power faculty,

Charles declared, "swings open all the doors of soul and body. . . . One can feel the power of unity with the higher self, [through] the vibrator center in the throat quicker than in any other way."[115] Charles believed that words were more powerful if spoken aloud than contemplated in silence. "Silent words do their work," he noted, "but audible words, rightly said, bring quicker results."[116]

STRENGTH

Located in the small of the back, the faculty of strength, Charles stated, "represents the all-around stability that lies at the foundation of every true character."[117] The strength that Charles refers to here was, as he stated, "not physical strength alone, but mental and spiritual strength."[118] Men and women, Charles indicated, should focus on becoming "steadfast, strong and steady in thought," so as to develop "mastery of the spiritual over the material."[119]

Charles indicated that men and women who develop this faculty demonstrate the "strength-giving attitudes" of joy and gladness. Charles also indicated that, with the faculty of strength, men and women can more easily overcome thoughts of "timidity and fear" as well as mental weakness.[120]

ELIMINATION OR RENUNCIATION

The faculty of elimination or renunciation is located, according to Charles, in the lower part of the back near the base of the spinal column and is primarily concerned with eliminating offensive thoughts. Charles indicated, "A healthy state of mind is attained and continued where the thinker willingly lets go of the old thoughts and takes on the new."[121]

ORDER

Charles provided little information on the faculty of order. In addition, his only writing on the subject lacked clarity. His most extensive treatment of this subject, "Spiritual Law and Order," published in *The Twelve Powers of Man* and in the February 1930 issue of *Unity,* rambled from one unrelated subject to another without providing a coherent treatment of the topic. To Charles, order does not seem to possess mental attributes inherent in humankind or in the other eleven faculties. As a result, an observer might easily conclude that order does not qualify as a "faculty of the mind."

LIFE

Charles believed that men and women were endowed with a faculty that was capable of permanently regenerating the cells of the human body. Located in the generative organs or "loins," this transforming faculty Charles called the "focal life center," or simply, "life."[122] Charles viewed the regenerative process as beginning in the mind and then ultimately manifesting in the body; as the life faculty was activated, the physical bodies of men and women would be transformed from the material to the spiritual plane of existence. He explained: "First, the Spirit, the Mind is regenerated, then sets in actual physical regeneration, in which every atom of the soul and body organism goes through a transformation. This is the corruptible putting on the incorruptible."[123]

He believed that as the regeneration process advanced through rising spiritual consciousness, men and women would reach a point in their lives when they would be able to dematerialize. Physical death would then no longer be a part of the human experience. Charles explained:

Your body will be so transformed within and without that it will never go through the change called death. It will be a resurrected body, become more and more refined as you catch sight of the free truths of Being, until it will literally disappear from the sight of those who see with the eye of sense. This is the way in which the last enemy, "death," is to be overcome.[124]

Activating the Twelve Powers

Charles indicated that a variety of spiritual practices might be used to activate the twelve powers. He believed that gaining control of the mind through right thinking was a necessary first step. Then, affirmations as well as denials produced positive states of consciousness, so essential in the development of each of the powers. Prayer—when it took the form of praise, thanksgiving, and blessing—also helped. Sitting in the silence calmed the mind and provided the setting for experiencing the divine inner presence.

RIGHT THINKING

Charles believed in the vast power of human thought. "The greatest discovery of all the centuries," he asserted, "is the power of thought."[125] He often commented on the wide-ranging impact of thought. He declared:

"Everything that appears in your life and affairs, physically, mentally or otherwise has at some time been sent forth from your thinking faculty. It is only through the power vested in it that you can come into consciousness of anything. It makes your heaven and it makes your hell."[126]

Charles had no doubt that men and women had the ability to control thought and direct it in positive directions. He asked, "What can a man do with the thought in his mind?" His answer indicated his confidence in humankind's mental powers. He asserted: "He can do everything with them. They are under his absolute control. He can direct them. He can coerce them. He can hush them or crush them. He can dissolve them and put others in their place. There is no other spot in the universe where man has mastery."[127]

Charles believed that "thinking right thoughts"[128] was humankind's biggest challenge and the key to activating the twelve powers. He indicated: "If [man] recognizes the Universal Principle of good and 'thinks the thoughts of God after Him' . . . he swings out into space, carried onward and upward by a boundless power—conscious of no opposing force, no friction, ever-floating in the ethereal arms of love."[129]

Charles indicated that men and women need to discipline their minds to think right thoughts: "You cannot do what the Father has set before you without an orderly discipline of your powers. Your thinking faculty is the first to be considered. It is the inlet and outlet of all your ideas. It is always active, zealous, impulsive, but not always wise. Its nature is to think and think it will."[130]

AFFIRMATIONS

Charles believed that affirmations provided men and women with the clarity of thought needed to develop the latent potential in each of the twelve faculties. He recommended that men and women spend an hour each day "in silent or audible affirmation."[131] Specific affirmations were to be used, worded to have the greatest effect in developing "the centers," as he called the individual faculties. "Keep this up," he urged, "until you have all the centers *alive* and under your mental direction." He acknowledged it was not an easy task. "This requires persistence and patience," he noted, "but it is the only way to get control of the body and renew it."[132]

Charles indicated that activating the life faculty required more work than activating the other eleven faculties. He declared: "We must concentrate, we must bend every energy along the line of life, acknowledging life, speaking life, thinking life. If anything comes up that opposes it, we must dismiss it, deny it; the thought of the absence of life does not belong where life is."[133]

Charles was convinced that the most powerful affirmations were cloaked in I AM statements of truth. "Metaphysicians," Charles observed, "have learned by experience the power of words and thoughts sent forth in the name of the Supreme I AM."[134] Charles viewed the I AM" as the central identity of every human being. The I AM he observed, "is the metaphysical name of the spiritual self."[135] The use of the I AM had its basis in Scripture. Charles indicated that I AM THAT I AM was the preferred designation of Jehovah, the God of the Old Testament.[136]

Charles urged Unity students to use the I AM in their affirmations: "Every time you send out a thought of whole-hearted dependence upon the I Am of yourself for all your needs, you set in motion a chain of causes that are bound to bring to you that which you need."[137]

Charles's own favorite affirmations were I AM statements of truth. He stated that his own "seven supreme affirmations" were: "I am Life Omnipresent. I am Love Omnipresent. I am Power Omnipresent. I am Substance Omnipresent. I am Order and Harmony Omnipresent. I am Strength Omnipresent. I am Intelligence Omnipresent."[138]

DENIALS

Denials, according to Charles, were the mental constructs needed to offset the impact of negative thought on consciousness. He believed that denials were as essential as affirmations in creating positive states of mind, and should be used in conjunction with them. He provided a detailed rationale for their use:

If we merely affirm the good ideas, and create the thought forms which they represent, we are but half doing our work, because we have a lot of old stock on hand. The old furniture of the mind must be put out before the new is moved in. One cannot keep a room thoroughly sweet and clean by merely letting in plenty of air and sunshine; the dust must be swept out.[139]

Charles wanted to make it clear that affirmations and denials in themselves did not do the spiritual work; rather, it was the state of consciousness that was established through their use. He indicated: "We do not claim that 'denials and affirmations' do the healing, but that through this dual thought process a state of consciousness is formed that is open to Divine Harmony, which ultimates in health."[140]

PRAYER

To Charles, prayer was also a means of activating the twelve powers. Prayer, he suggested, often takes the form of affirmations. "True prayer," he observed, "the prayer that gives thanks as if we had 'already received,' is the highest affirmation, and it is used by Christian metaphysicians universally."[141] Praise, blessings, and thanksgiving are effective forms of prayer, Charles observed: "The knowledge that you can, by blessing, increase everything, is of more value to you than all the riches of the world, because through it you can make yourself happy, healthy and prosperous."[142]

Prayers of supplication or petition have little chance of activating the twelve powers, according to Charles, because these prayers fail to create the required mental state. He made a clear distinction between prayers of petition and affirmative prayer, asking: "Are you begging some distant God to give you light, or are you *praising* the light in your very presence? One is praying for something we have not; the other is praying as if we had 'already received.' Thus we see that praising and thanksgiving is the only key that will open the door for Spirit to reveal itself in our consciousness."[143]

Charles was firm in his belief that asking God for favors did no good:

The strained use of the prayer of petition for special material favors is standing evidence of the selfish materialism of humanity. If God be Infinite Love and Wisdom and knows better what we need than we can know, how can we presume to counsel or enlighten Him. Can we ask even for needed spiritual blessing, expecting a change on His part in response? We misapprehend the nature of prayer. His Spirit is already Omnipresent, awaiting our recognition.[144]

SITTING IN THE SILENCE

Activating the twelve powers required the truth student, according to Charles, to spend significant amounts of time sitting in the silence and meditating. Only in the silence, he explained, does one make conscious contact with the indwelling presence. He indicated:

All manifestations of life originate in the silence . . . The thoughts that rise in you and come to the surface in deed and act, are they not from the silence? Do you take a step or lift a hand that has not its motive from the depths of the mighty sea of throbbing life within your own being? Then why look to the external for that which comes only from the silence within?[145]

ACTIVATING THE "FOCAL LIFE CENTER"

In order to activate the "focal life center" and regenerate the physical body, Charles believed it necessary to conserve the seminal fluid that was normally discharged during sexual intercourse. This fluid, in his view, contains powerful life-giving properties and must remain in the body to facilitate the regenerative process. He stated:

When the seminal substance in the organism is conserved and retained the nerves are charged with a force that physiologists have named *Vitamine*. This is another name for spiritual energy, which runs like lightning through an organism well-charged with the virgin substance of the soul. . . . In the conservation of this pure substance of life is held the secret of body rejuvenation, physical resurrection and the final perpetuation of the whole organism in its transmuted purity.[146]

It followed that men and women must refrain from sexual relations to conserve the "seminal substance" and make it available to revitalize the body. He asserted, "Those who desire to come into closest unity with the Spirit of Truth and construct here on earth the true temple of God—a regenerated body—must abstain from the sex relation."[147]

In his readings in Hinduism, Charles may have come across the Tantric practices connected with the raising of the kundalini energy in which the loss of semen is considered a weakness of the body. He also may have been influenced by the Augustinian tradition in Christianity, with its restrictive attitudes concerning sexual relationships.

BODILY REGENERATION

Charles dedicated his life to the performance of practices required to activate the twelve powers to regenerate his body and overcome physical death. Charles's experiences in meditative states convinced him that through dedicated spiritual practice, the cells of the human body could be renewed, body parts regenerated, youth restored, and illness overcome. In addition, it would no longer be necessary for humans to pass through physical death. He expressed these views in print for the first time in April 1889, when he was only thirty-five years old. Referring to the work of the Society of Silent Help, a prayer and healing group that he and Myrtle had recently founded, he predicted:

"This Society will produce individual members who, through soul concentration, will have so spiritualized the atoms of their bodies as to be able to make themselves visible or invisible at will, and will have the power to live upon this earth plane any length of time they may desire."[148]

Charles continued to suffer in his mid-thirties from the effects of his childhood leg injury. He testified that he was "a bodily wreck"[149] and still a "chronic invalid and seldom free from pain."[150] Believing now that bodily regeneration was possible, the first body part he sought to regenerate was his shortened leg. He explained, "When I began to study what Jesus taught in the Bible about God as the source of life and health, I had faith that I could be healed."[151]

He began the inner work, and within a short time he began to see progress. He reported: "I began to apply the healing principle to my own case with gratifying results. My chronic pains ceased and my hip healed and grew stronger and my leg lengthened until in a few years I could dispense with the steel extension that I had worn since I was a child."[152]

In an interview in 1902 with Charles Brodie Patterson, editor of the well-respected metaphysical magazine *Mind*, Charles, now age forty-eight, reported major improvement. He commented:

The gradual healing of this diseased limb, and its growth to nearly normal size during the last ten years, has been to me, at least, one of the strongest proofs of the power of metaphysical treatment, especially in view of the fact that the physicians who attended me as a boy prophesied that when I reached the age of forty I would undoubtedly be a helpless cripple in a wheel-chair."[153]

Charles explained to Patterson the mental practice he employed to regenerate not only his diseased limb, but also his entire body. He declared:

I am transforming, through mental dynamics, the cells of my whole body, the ultimate of which will be immortality in the flesh. I have discovered that all the ganglion centres in the organism are in reality brains, who think thoughts in a measure independent of the central thinker, whose seat of action is usually confined to the head. In order to control these various brains I have found it necessary to project into them my conscious thought and fill them so full of true ideas that there is no room for the false. This task has not been a light one, and I have spent years in silent willing, denying and affirming, actually rebuilding every cell in my organism from centre to circumference. I would say that in this work I have been guided by an invisible intelligence, which I call the Holy Spirit. I have also found that the whole process is symbolically outlined in the life of Jesus Christ, and is what is technically called *regeneration*.[154]

A year later, Charles described the actions he had taken to turn back the aging process. He reported:

About three years ago the belief in old age began to take hold of me. I was nearing the half century mark. I began to get wrinkled and gray, my knees tottered, and a great weakness came over me. I did not discern the cause at once but I found in my dreams I was associating with old people, and it gradually dawned on me that I was coming into this phase of race belief. Then I went to work with a vim. I repudiated the whole world of old age and decrepitude. I denied them any place in my mentality. I spent hours and hours silently affirming my unity with the Infinite Energy of the One True God. I absolutely refused to sympathize with old people in any way. I associated with the young, I danced with the boys, sang "coon" songs with them and for a time took on the thoughtless kid. In this way I "switched" the old age current of thought. Then I went deep down within my body and talked to the inner life centres. I told them with firmness and decision that I should never submit to the old age devil—that I was determined never to give in and that they might just as well give up first as last. Gradually I felt a new life current coming up from the Life Center. It was a faint little stream at first, and months went by before I got it to the surface. Now it is growing strong by leaps and bounds. My cheeks have filled out, the wrinkles and "crow feet" are gone, and I actually feel like the boy that *I am*. "God is not the God of the dead, but of the living."[155]

Four years later, in 1907, Charles, now past fifty, reported continuing progress in regenerating his leg. He commented: "Through spiritual realization the leg has gradually lengthened, until now it is less than two inches short, and its shrunken muscles and flesh have been restored. I know this spiritual power will make it perfectly whole, although as men count time, I am over a half century in this body."[156]

In 1913 Charles again described the spiritual practice he engaged in to regenerate his body and the results that he observed. He noted:

In my own case I can testify to a gradual physical renewal. I can feel the new life coursing through my nerves in living streams of energy. The energy I have learned to direct to the various organs of the body, and through daily practice of thought concentration I am renewing both mind and body. My skin is getting pink, as in youth, and my gray hair is changing at its roots to its natural color. I am satisfied that I shall overcome the disintegration of my organs and finally conquer death. As men count years I am nearly sixty, but I have for the past twenty years lived so constantly in the thought of perpetual life that I have no consciousness of loss of force or body energy.[157]

His concern for overcoming the death of his body was again expressed in 1924. He indicated that his faith in the teachings of Jesus was an important element in his spiritual work. He reported:

My body is not disintegrating. Why not? Because I am believing in God's life in me; I am affirming that life. I know that if I follow Jesus Christ in this respect I shall overcome death. I know that it is incumbent upon me to enter into the realization of the eternal life of the body and to teach the world that it is possible to overcome the great and last enemy, death.[158]

In a letter to a friend in 1928, Myrtle told how, through spiritual practice, Charles had overcome deafness in one ear. She wrote:

Mr. Fillmore was once deaf in his right ear. And as soon as he saw that the life and intelligence in him was very active, and responsive to the direction of his mind, he began to work with his ears. He would give his undivided attention to God, and open his mind and hold it receptive to the ideas which he felt God had for him. He would declare that he was hearing mentally, through his ears. He would think of the abundant life which was flowing up from his life center and heart, through the glands of his neck, and into his ears. He would mentally see this life stream stimulating the nerves and cells there, and setting them into action. And one day, there was a great throbbing, and a rush of wax thrown out of his ear. And his hearing has been perfect ever since.[159]

One year later Myrtle, in another letter to a longtime correspondent, indicated that Charles had still more work to do to heal his injured leg. In response to her friend's request that the Fillmores make a visit to California, Myrtle explained: "I have tried, ever so many times, to get him to join me in a lovely trip somewhere. But the dear man just doesn't like to get out among crowds; and really feels that he'd better wait until he has completed his demonstration of healing his leg before going out, either for lecture work or pleasure."[160]

That same year, 1929, Charles, at age seventy-five, was asked by Unity students: "Does Charles Fillmore expect to live forever?" His response indicated that he was still fully committed to regenerating his body and continuing to do the inner work:

Because I have emphasized the eternal-life-in-the-body teaching of Jesus, the question is often asked by Unity readers. Some of them seem to think that I am either a fanatic or a joker if I take myself seriously in the hope that I shall with Jesus attain eternal life in the body. But the fact is that I am very serious about the matter and am striving earnestly to follow Jesus in the regeneration, which I am satisfied will result in a transformation of my body. I am renewing my mind and, at the same time, working out body transformation. As I study and apply the words of Jesus I cannot see any way to fulfill the law of God for man except through overcoming death. That death is the most dreaded enemy of the human race goes without argument. The Bible from Genesis to Revelation so teaches. . . . It seems to me that someone should have initiative enough to make at least an attempt to raise his body to the Jesus Christ consciousness. Because none of the followers of Jesus has attained the victory over this terror of humanity does not prove it cannot be done. Every great forward movement of the race has been preceded by repeated failures. Every pioneer in untried fields has been called either a fool or a dreamer. So instead of ridiculing those who are striving to follow Jesus in the overcoming of death, we should encourage them to go forward, knowing as we must that they will finally attain the mastery—if not in this incarnation, then in the next, or the next. So do not throw cold water on me when I say that I am doing my best to follow Jesus in overcoming death of my body. I need your help, and the helpful thoughts of all loyal members of the brotherhood of Jesus Christ, in my battle against the most grievous enemy of mankind.[161]

Ten years later, in his mid-eighties, Charles again reflected on his long-time journey to transform his body and the status of that effort. He reported:

I gradually acquired the ability to go into the silence, and from that source I received unexpected revelations and physical sensations. . . . I was informed by the Presence that I was beginning the body regeneration as taught by Jesus Christ. Neither physiology nor psychology offers a nomenclature describing it. The first sensation was in my forehead, a "crawly" feeling when I was affirming life. Then I found that I could produce this same feeling at the bottom of my feet and other nerve extremities by concentrating my attention at the place and silently affirming life. I spent several hours every day in this process and I found that I was releasing electronic forces sealed up in the nerves. This I have done for nearly fifty years until now I have what may be termed an electric body that is gradually replacing the physical.[162]

In 1938 when he was eighty-four, Charles was interviewed by Ralph Teener, a doctoral candidate at the University of Chicago who was preparing a Ph.D. dissertation on the Unity movement. Teener, who was not a Unity student, was well aware of Charles's commitment to bodily regeneration. Teener's observations indicate that Charles still had much work to do to regenerate his hip. He commented:

Today, Mr. Fillmore is a quite interesting, humorous, white-haired man, some 84 years young. His right leg is much shorter than his left. He wears a higher heel on his right shoe and walks with a decided hitch. When in discussion, his mind is likely to wander from the point at issue. To a superficial observer, his teeth show dental work, certainly not of the "spiritual substance" kind. . . . He is almost retired from the business of Unity School, coming in from his country home to the headquarters only one or two afternoons each week.[163]

Charles was interviewed in 1942 at age eighty-eight by the religious historian Marcus Bach. A University of Iowa faculty member, Bach, who traveled to Kansas City for the meeting, found Charles to be an extremely lively, vital, and energetic man. He reported:

I first met Charles Fillmore in 1942 at Unity headquarters, 917 Tracy Avenue, in Kansas City. It was a rainy autumn morning, but the smallish, energetic man had utter disregard for the weather. He was bareheaded, exhilarated, it seemed to me, by the touch of the rain in his wisps of thin, white hair, and thrilled at the fact that his hands were opening the copper-grilled door to what might have been some celestial hideaway. His face was strong but gentle. Deep-set blue eyes and the confident hint of a smile had a way of saying that all was well with the world because all was well with him. His manner was that of a young man who had run through the rain catching the drops in his mouth, flushed with a sense of nature's friendly response. His ears were large, a fact I recalled particularly because of my impression that he did not really need them at all. As he sat at his rolltop desk and I on a cushioned kitchen chair in his modest office, his art of listening, as far as I was concerned, was psychic, as if interpreting the spirit of my questions rather than the spoken word. Had you been with me as we entered his office you might not have noticed that he limped slightly, and it would have stretched your credulity to believe that for twenty years and more he walked with the aid of a brace.[164]

In 1946, just two years before his death, Charles acknowledged that his leg was not yet fully healed, but it was still improving. He indicated: "I do not claim that I have yet attained perfection, but I am on my way. My leg is still out of joint but it is improving as I continue to work under the direction and guidance of Spirit."[165]

Shortly before he died in 1948, he again gave an overview of the progress he had made in his work with his leg. He commented:

I can testify to my own healing of tuberculosis of the hip. . . . When I began to apply the spiritual treatment there was for a long time slight response in the leg, but I felt better, and I found that I began to hear with the right ear. Then gradually I noticed that I had more feeling in the leg. Then as years went by the ossified joint began to get limber, and the shrunken flesh filled out until the right leg was almost equal to the other. Then I discarded the core-and-steel extension and wore an ordinary shoe with a double heel about an inch in height. Now the leg is almost as large as the other, the muscles restored, and although the hip bone is not yet in the socket, I am certain that it soon will be and that I shall be made perfectly whole. I am giving minute details of my healing because it would be considered a medical impossibility and a miracle from a religious standpoint. However, I have watched the restoration year after year as I applied the power of thought, and I know it is under divine law. So I am satisfied that here is proof of a law that the mind builds the body and can restore it.[166]

In the summer of 1948, as he approached his ninety-fourth birthday, he was suffering from the effects of kidney failure. He recognized that the sixty-year effort to regenerate his body and overcome physical death was not going to succeed. He told a friend: "As for myself I would like to keep this body, but it seems that the lord of my being has decided otherwise, and I am ready to do what has to be done."[167]

As he neared the end he said: "It looks like I'll have to go, but don't worry, I'll be back. . . . I am going to have a new body, anyway, and this time it's going to be a perfect body."[168]

Among his last words were "Christ in you, the hope of Glory."[169]

Charles's ideas on bodily regeneration probably were derived from his interpretation of Hindu literature, the New Testament, and the writings of Eastern and Western mysticism. He was deeply interested in the capability of Hindu spiritual adepts who, through yogic practices, were reportedly able to demonstrate feats of teleportation (moving from one place to another) and bilocation (being in two places at the same time). These adepts were also credited with being able to dematerialize their bodies. Charles's reading of the New Testament, particularly those passages dealing with the transfiguration of Jesus, indicated that Jesus passed from a physical to a spiritual body. The conception of the fourth dimension of consciousness came from an old mystical tradition found in both Eastern and Western religion that was taken up by the Theosophists and became part of New Thought beliefs.

Afterlife

While physical death represented failure to realize God, Charles did not view it as terminating life. He believed the soul continues to live on. Charles indicated that the soul did not go to a far-off heaven or hell but continued to exist in close relation to family, friends, and loved ones in a mental environment similar to the earthly one. He explained: "When the body falls asleep, the soul, or mental part, passes into the mental plane of consciousness, which is right here in our midst. Consequently, they do not go anywhere. They come in close relation with us mentally."[170]

Charles described the process of continued life as "perpetual incarnation."[171] The soul, in his view, never died. He stated:

Man cannot die nor can he go anywhere when he "shuffles off this mortal coil." Those who have changed their consciousness to that of a people whose thought vibrations are at a rate higher or lower than those of earth are said to have passed on. . . . They may believe that they are off in some heaven or some spiritual sphere, but the fact is that they are right here in our midst, because mind is always "right here," and there is nothing in existence but Mind.[172]

Since they really hadn't gone anywhere, those who left their bodies through physical death did not need to be mourned. "Don't mourn about anybody's being dead," Charles declared, "Death is not even a change, but to consciousness."[173]

It was Charles's belief that after a period of inactivity the soul would incarnate and take on another body. "After a period of recreation and rest," Charles indicated, "they will again take up active overcoming of the flesh body through reincarnation."[174]

Charles viewed the need to reincarnate as a kind of penalty for having failed to activate the twelve powers. He stated:

Repeated human births are the persistent efforts of the One Great Mind to restore that unity in creation which man disturbed—and continues to disturb—through his ignorant use of its powers and elements. . . . So you see, we do not believe in reincarnation but in perpetual incarnation, without a break in the continuous life chain of expression of soul and body.[175]

Reincarnation was a subject of major interest to Charles. Those who failed to manifest the Christ Consciousness and regenerate their physical bodies would return in new bodies for more spiritual work. On occasion Charles reflected on his own past incarnations, believing he got accurate information on them while meditating. He indicated that he was once incarnated as the Apostle Paul. In a statement made in *Unity* magazine in October 1896, he commented, "We happen to know Paul in his present incarnation and have his word for this." While he didn't specifically identify himself, he gave more detail when a *Unity* reader wrote to him asking for clarification. "Are we to understand that Paul reincarnated is now upon the earth, and an acquaintance of yours?"[176] the writer asked. Charles, who had informed Charles S. Braden, a highly respected historian of religion,[177] that in an earlier incarnation he was the Apostle Paul, was probably referring to himself when he responded to the *Unity* correspondent:

He who once manifested as Paul the Apostle is now expressing himself through another form right here in America. . . . Paul lived over thirty-eight years in his

present form, a plain American citizen, before he knew that he was the same ego
that had once expressed itself in the flesh as Saul the Jewish zealot; afterwards,
Paul the Christian pioneer. . . . He who once manifested as Paul is only now getting a practical understanding of the scientific laws underlying the so-called miracles of the religious world, and his aim is to so develop his own powers that he can
demonstrate to materialistic science that there exists a connecting link between
their world and the supernatural world of the church, which they have not understood for lack of that link. To do this successfully requires an extraordinary
amount of silent work with physical, psychical, and spiritual powers.[178]

Contrary to what one might expect, Charles did not hold the Apostle
Paul in high esteem. Charles considered Paul to have been deeply flawed,
one whose work did more harm than good. Paul, according to Charles,
failed to follow the instructions of the Holy Spirit and led Christianity
away from the true teachings of Jesus. Charles declared:

Paul, the chief Apostle, was a persecutor of women and children and a man-slayer,
having been the ring leader and abettor of those who stoned Stephen to death.
Paul was by nature a fighter. He belonged to that class of irrepressibles that when
fired by an idea cannot be hushed up. He just would talk about the subject that
possessed his mind. He talked incessantly, argued and expostulated—an intellectual debater. In this day he would be called a wordy crank.[179]

Paul was willful, according to his own admissions, and went contrary to the guidance of the Holy Spirit. For example, the Spirit warned him not to go up to
Jerusalem the second time. But his combativeness was up, and he was so determined to have a bout with those old Jews that he went anyway. The result was his
imprisonment, appeal to Caesar, and long incarceration at Rome. Had Paul been
more obedient and less ambitious to defend his religion, the history of Christianity
would have been vastly different. To be successful in a spiritual work, we must not
only be obedient to the leading of the Spirit part of the time, but *all the time*.[180]

Charles did not cite biographies or outside authorities as sources of information on his life as Paul. The information was revealed to him personally, presumably while he was in a meditative state. Charles considered
Paul to be sincere, but with grave defects. He testified:

In the history of his life, as revealed to me in the thought realms, I read that he
died of consumption in a mountain town near Rome. The popular idea that the
so-called saints were good and powerful enough to sit with Jesus in His power,
will not bear close analysis. It is, in fact, a mere assumption. Paul in his own writings left a hundred admissions of his disobedience, weakness, ambition and dou-
ble-mindedness. . . . Paul was a good man, and sincere, but he had his faults. He

was possessed of a towering ambition. Ambition is a subtle mental force. . . . Paul, like Caesar, was ambitious, and that ambition was not converted when he turned his zeal from the Jews to the Christians; it was simply transferred. . . . During his lifetime his work did not come to fruitage, and he died in disappointment.[181]

Before incarnating as Charles Fillmore, the spirit that was in Paul the Apostle, according to Charles, incarnated as Napoleon Bonaparte. Again, Charles indicated he received this information while in a meditative state. In a sermon given in December 1902, which was published in *Unity* magazine, Charles explained: "You may be surprised, and some of you may doubtless be shocked, if I tell you that Paul the Apostle and Napoleon Bonaparte were one and the same individual. Yet I know this to be a fact. I have gone deep into the subject of man and his subjective life, and I tell you that I have found his character, not as theory but as fact."[182]

Charles's identification of Napoleon as the reincarnation of Paul created a stir in the *Unity* readership; Charles received several letters of inquiry and protestation. A Protestant minister declared he was "shocked and disappointed" by Charles's statement that "Paul the Apostle and Napoleon Bonaparte were one and the same individual." The minister commented:

It is the very essence of Christianity to teach that when men in whom the Christ-nature is distinctly formed, as it was in St. Paul, pass out of the limitations of the earthly life, they enter upon that life of glorified manhood into which Jesus was raised. . . . Such a supposition, as you make it, in the case of Paul is not only contrary to Scripture, and to all that Science teaches concerning the evolution of humanity; it is a backward and humiliating step in the Divine plan of human life.[183]

Charles responded by reasserting his belief in reincarnation and defending the means he used in uncovering the information. He again indicated his conviction that information that came to him in the silence was reliable, objective data rather than subjective personal experience. Charles observed:

Our good brother wishes me to reconsider my teaching in this matter of so-called reincarnation, as if it were a question that rested upon belief. I know that man does not die—that he lives right on, sometimes in a natural body, sometimes in an astral body, and sometimes in no body at all. I do not get this as a special revelation, but I have developed faculties that have enabled me to, in a measure, see behind the veil of sense. It is not a supposition on my part—I know the facts as I know about the events that have taken place and are taking place in the lives of myself and those with whom I come in contact.[184]

All who dedicated themselves to inner work, he believed, could develop the intuitive powers Charles was claiming for himself. He explained: "This ability to see deeper than the sense consciousness may be developed by anyone who is willing to let go of the outer world, and patiently seek the inner."[185]

In responding to the minister, Charles again reasserted his position that Paul had reincarnated as Napoleon. Charles reported, "His [Paul's] ambition did not die." Charles further indicated that through the workings of Divine Law, the spirit of Paul was bound to reincarnate. "As a mental energy," he stated, "it was generating its force in the intellect, and under the law of mind action it must have a vent. That vent was found in the Napoleon incarnation."[186]

Assessing the Role of Jesus

Charles criticized traditional Christianity, both Catholic and Protestant, for its inaccurate interpretation of the life and teachings of Jesus. Christianity erred by worshipping Jesus as God rather than by treating him as a man. "Orthodox Christianity has deified Jesus of Nazareth," Charles asserted, "and pronounced Him not man, but God."[187] He elaborated: "The secular world has been taught that Jesus was so superior to the moral man that He can be thought of only as a god. This removes Him from us all as a man whose character we may emulate and as an example of what we may become, and places His attainments far beyond human possibilities."[188]

Charles considered Jesus to be human at birth rather than divine as taught by traditional Christianity. Jesus transformed himself and realized the indwelling presence, Charles believed, by developing and implementing in his life all twelve of the faculties of mind. Charles stated: "He was not in the beginning the perfectly rounded genius that He became. He knew the law of obedience, however, and was a willing pupil. He resolutely went to work to weed out His weaknesses and build them up with the fullness of the Omnipotent Father."[189]

By making Jesus divine, Charles thought that Christianity created a false idea of Jesus' mission. He stated:

Through believing that Jesus was more divine than other men the church has assumed that He had certain privileges that are not extended by the Father to all men, and that through the exercise of these privileges He made good all our shortcomings, and saved us . . . by suffering for our acts, by simply believing in Him and in a perfunctory way accepting Him as our savior.[190]

Charles faulted the teachings of the Apostle Paul for this misconception: "Paul is responsible for a good share of this throwing the whole burden upon the blood of Jesus—doubtless the result of an old mental tendency carried over from his Hebrew idea of the blood sacrifices of the priesthood."[191]

Charles did not believe Jesus taught that men and women would be sent to hell after death as punishment for sin, and took issue with traditional Christian teaching on punishment for sin in the afterlife. He commented: "It is not a saving of the soul from a mythical place called hell that Jesus talked of, but the purification of the soul while yet in the body to the end that this same body may be raised up out of its tomb of matter and spiritualized until it is a fit home for that illumined soul."[192]

Charles believed that Christianity was also wrong in indicating that the reward for leading a good life was heaven with Jesus after death. He stressed the need to be concerned with the here and now, not with the hereafter, declaring, "God is, and we are. Let us live in His world, not in a world-to-be tomorrow, next month, next year, or next century, but here and now."[193] He noted: "When we finally understand the facts of life and rid our minds of the delusion that we shall find immortal life after we die, then we shall seek more diligently to awaken the spiritual man within us."[194]

Charles could find no support in Scripture for the notion that there was a place called "heaven" where souls went after death. He observed: "No one should be deluded with the vague assumption that there is a place in the skies, or on some far away planet, called heaven. There is not the shadow of foundation in either the old or new Testaments for such doctrine."[195]

Christianity had failed to interpret Scripture accurately, Charles believed, because its leaders were not sufficiently evolved spiritually. Charles concluded that it took a high level of spiritual perception to interpret correctly the teachings of Jesus. He stated: "The Bible and the prophets can be understood only by those who arrive at that place in consciousness where the writers were when they gave forth their messages. It requires the same inspiration to read the Scriptures with understanding that it required originally to receive and write them."[196]

Christianity also erred by teaching that Jesus was sent by God the Father to save humankind from sin by dying on the cross. "The popular thought, based on Theology, that Jesus died upon the cross for our sins," Charles noted, "is not reasonable nor true."[197] Charles elaborated:

It is quite evident that theology hasn't understood the true character of Jesus' death. Instead of dying upon the cross like the two thieves that were crucified with Him, He simply passed through the human consciousness of death and came out fully alive on the other side. The bodies of the robbers were turned to clay, while that of Jesus became alive again, and was glorified.[198]

Although Jesus was nailed to the cross on Calvary, Charles believed he remained alive, that he never died. Charles explained:

Jesus did not die upon the cross to save men from their sins, but He *lived*. This is an important distinction, and clears up points that have always been stumbling blocks to those who wanted a reasonable theology . . . Jesus still lives in the spiritual ethers of this world and is in constant contact with those who raise their thoughts to Him in prayer.[199]

Jesus was important, in Charles's view, because during his lifetime he fully developed the twelve faculties, unified his spirit with God, and realized his inner divine nature. By so doing, he reached the highest possible state of consciousness, a state that Charles called "the Christ Consciousness" or the "Christ mind." In describing the Christ Consciousness as Jesus manifested it, Charles stated:

The fact that Jesus of Nazareth lived and manifested the Power of the Christos, or spiritual man, is of vital importance to every soul. Not only is it important as an example, showing the possibilities latent within each of us, but in a deeper sense the testimony of the Gospels and all who have come onto His spiritual plane, is that He bridged the way or formed a connecting link, between humanity and God.[200]

To Charles, Jesus developed the twelve faculties and attained the Christ Consciousness through diligent spiritual practice that included thinking correctly, using powerful affirmations and denials, praying, and sitting in the silence.

He believed that Jesus, by fully manifesting his inner divine nature, regenerated his body and overcame physical death. Charles observed: "Jesus' body did not go down to corruption, but He, by the intensity of His spiritual devotion, restored every cell to its innate state of atomic light and power. . . . Jesus lives today in that body of glorified electricity in a kingdom that interpenetrates the earth and its environments. He called it the kingdom of the heavens."[201]

Charles was convinced that it was possible for all men and women to attain the Christ Consciousness. Jesus showed the way and demonstrated to humankind that it could be done. Those who followed his methods could also attain it. Charles indicated: "Whosoever dedicates his whole life to the Supreme Good, through devotion, right thinking, right doing, right acting, pure living and pure speaking fulfills the law and may have all the power of Jesus."[202]

Charles felt that Christianity was mistaken by failing to recognize that men and women reincarnate repeatedly on their spiritual quest. He was convinced that Jesus had incarnated many times and developed the twelve faculties of mind over a series of lifetimes. He commented:

Jesus did not reach unity with the Father in the space of a single lifetime. He had been sent back to His task many times. He did part of the work under the names of Moses, Elisha, David, et al. These lives were His day at school, and He arrived at a state of consciousness while manifesting as Jesus of Nazareth where He remembered His past lives.[203]

Charles Fillmore enjoyed a long and productive career as a metaphysical editor, publisher, and author; as a practitioner of spiritual healing; and as a spiritual teacher both in the classroom and in the pulpit. His achievements are remarkable considering his lack of formal education, his initial disinterest in organized religion, and his early commitment to a career in business. Charles's organizational and leadership skills, financial acumen, dynamic energy, and huge capacity for work were essential for the growth and development of the Unity movement. Charles's career in Unity spanned six decades. His work during the last fifteen years of his life—he died at age ninety-four in 1948—was facilitated by his second wife, Cora. She provided a support system that enabled him to teach, write, travel, and lecture until well into his nineties.

CHAPTER 3

H. Emilie Cady: Articulator of the Unity Teaching

Unity's Best-Selling Author

H. Emilie Cady, a New York City homeopathic physician and contemporary of Charles and Myrtle Fillmore, merits the distinction of having written the most widely read book on the Unity teachings since the beginning of the Unity movement. During its century-long history, *Lessons in Truth,* which appeared in book form in 1901, has sold over 1.6 million copies, outselling all other Unity books.

Cady was one of the first metaphysical authors to be featured in Unity periodicals. *Finding the Christ in Ourselves,* a twenty-two page pamphlet sent unsolicited to the Fillmores by Cady, appeared in the October 1891 issue of *Thought.* It contained what was to become the core of the Unity teaching. Its popularity, and the wide acceptance of other articles submitted by Cady in the early 1890s, convinced the Fillmores to invite Cady, in August 1894, to publish a course of twelve lessons on the truth principles in *Unity* magazine. Seven years later, because of continuing demand, the lessons were published in book form.

Lessons in Truth became further established as a key element in the Unity teaching in 1909 with the establishment of the Unity Correspondence School. Materials from the book were included in the first two sections of the Unity correspondence course, a course that was to be widely used by Unity students outside Kansas City for the next fifty years. *Lessons in Truth* quickly became Unity's best-selling book. In February 1917, *Weekly Unity* commented on its popularity. *"Lessons in Truth,"* it reported, "leads all other Unity books and booklets in sales, and has every year since it was first published." Three reasons were given for the wide appeal of the book:

1. It is fundamental. The principles that it sets forth are the foundation for all metaphysical study, no matter how scientific or thorough that study is to be.

2. It is practical. Its truths are the basis for more than mere theory and study. They are the basis for healthy, happy, prosperous living.

3. It is easily understood; simply and clearly written in a sympathetic vein that gives the reader the comfortable feeling that it was written in direct answer to his own needs.[1]

By 1920 the regard for the book had grown to the extent that it was being published in several languages. *Unity* magazine commented on why the book had generated such worldwide interest. It reported: "It grounds the student in the fundamentals of higher thought teachings, kindles faith, quickens spiritual understanding, and leads him to the 'Secret Place of the Most High,' where the fetters of false beliefs in sin, sorrow, sickness and death drop away, leaving the spirit radiantly joyous in its new-found freedom."[2]

Myrtle Fillmore's high regard for Cady's writing was undoubtedly expressed many times during the course of their long association. The following letter, sent on January 7, 1929, shows clearly her appreciation of Cady's work:

I think you must surely know as we do what your own blessed contributions to Truth literature are doing. The words you have spoken out to the world through our publications are Spirit and Life, and they are bringing forth their kind all over this great round earth, and they are ringing their messages of Truth and good will to man wherever he has found a foothold.[3]

A letter written on September 11, 1929, indicated that Myrtle considered *Lessons in Truth* a "foundation stone" of the Unity teaching.

In 1933 Unity School set aside one week in September for the study of *Lessons in Truth*. Called "Lessons in Truth" Week, its purpose was to encourage Unity centers worldwide to conduct an in-depth study of the contents of Cady's teachings. *Unity* magazine commented: "This is a time of united study when thousands of persons, either in groups at Unity centers or alone in the quiet of their own home, find a new sense of freedom in Truth by reading and studying H. Emilie Cady's book *Lessons in Truth*."[4]

Lowell wrote Cady personally to explain Unity's intention and to give her some idea of how valuable an in-depth review of the book could be:

Did you know that we have just completed a worldwide "Lessons in Truth" Week? Thousands of Unity readers all over the world made a special study of your little book during that time, and we at Unity did, too. Each time we review it we find new ideas revealed to us, and thank you again and again for giving us such a wonderful guide for our spiritual unfoldment.[5]

Lessons in Truth's continuing popularity was indicated by the fact that by 1937 its sales reached the half-million mark. It retained its rank as Unity's best-selling book. Given that Charles Fillmore was co-founder of the Unity movement and president of Unity School, one might assume that his book *Christian Healing,* published in 1909, which presented many of the same teachings, would have supplanted Cady in the Unity literature. Such was not the case. In 1937 *Weekly Unity* explained that Charles's work was more applicable for advanced students, while Cady's was more useful for beginners. *Weekly Unity* pointed out:

If you have never made a study of the Unity teachings, you should begin with [*Lessons in Truth*]. In twelve lessons it explains the basic Truth ideas, and shows how you can use them to make yourself happier, richer, and vibrantly healthy. *Christian Healing* by Charles Fillmore takes up where *Lessons in Truth* leaves off, helping the advanced student with the power of faith and imagination as well as with thoughts and words.[6]

Martha Smock, who for thirty years served as editor of Unity School's *Daily Word* magazine, noted in 1959 how the book had stood the test of time. After reading *Lessons in Truth* as a young adult, she let several years pass before returning to it. She reported her delight in rediscovering it: "In rereading *Lessons in Truth* during 'Lessons in Truth' Week, I discovered in it the source of my fundamental beliefs about Truth. I thought to myself, 'It is all here, the Truth that has grown and enlarged and expanded in my consciousness.'"[7] Smock then commented on the timeless nature of the message for her life, stating:

In rereading it we stand once more at the beginning, as it were, of our search for Truth. We read it in almost two states of mind. We see it as it first made an impact on our mind and life. We see it from the perspective of time and experience. We see how changeless Truth is, how timeless the quality of its principles are. We see how sure the ground is that we now stand on. We see how sure it was even when in the past we first began to seek out the Truth . . . The ideas found in *Lessons in Truth* are like a lamp that throws light on our paths, that calls to our remembrance things that we have always known, that reminds us that we have within us the Spirit of Truth that Jesus promised.[8]

Despite the fact that "Lessons in Truth" Week was discontinued in 1968 and the correspondence school was closed in 1974, *Lessons in Truth* continued to be popular with Unity students. The *Foundations of Unity Series,* a three-volume set "written around the chapters from *Lessons in Truth,*" was developed by Unity School to replace the correspondence course. The editors explained the value of the series for Unity students, stating:

This specially designed *Foundations of Unity* course will help you feel the presence of God within you. It will help you . . . to discover and apply your own power of faith . . . In these books you will find a positive, constructive approach to life and living that has helped thousands of people over the years. Here is your opportunity to apply the principles that will enable you to live a healthy, prosperous, and happy life.[9]

In the 1980s and 1990s, excerpts from Cady's writings continued to be featured in *Unity* magazine. These consisted primarily of reprints of chapters from *Lessons in Truth*. In 1998 her writings began appearing in *Unity* as a part of the "Unity Classics" series. After a century of availability, *Lessons in Truth* is still considered by Unity School to be its "foundation text"; the book continues to be studied in classes in Unity churches, in Unity's Continuing Education Program (CEP), and in the ministerial training program at Unity School.[10]

Who was H. Emilie Cady and how did she prepare herself to write the book that was to occupy such a central place in the Unity teaching? Born in 1848 on a farm near Dryden, New York, a small town south of Syracuse, Cady grew up there and as a young woman taught near Dryden in a one-room schoolhouse.[11] In her early twenties, she went to New York City and studied at the Homeopathic College of New York City, graduating at age twenty-three in 1871. While practicing homeopathic medicine in Manhattan, she became interested in spiritual healing. When asked by a friend, Ella Pomeroy, how she became interested in truth and New Thought, Cady responded that the impetus was provided by the work of a "faith healer" by the name of Simpson, who practiced in the 1870s in New York City.[12] Cady told Pomeroy, "I could recall reports of his work in the daily papers of the hundreds of persons he had helped and of his marvelous powers." Pomeroy reported:

She heard the man Simpson many times. He was the revivalist type and spoke in a large tent set up in a field. Her admiration for his accomplishments was unbounded, but her good sense told her that there must be a way of solidifying and retaining such healings as he gave his followers, and to her came the revelation of the way—simple discipline and thanksgiving to God. She went on to say that it seemed to her that there must be a bridge between his "faith" and the practice of medicine.[13]

While Simpson may have provided a catalyst for Cady to become interested in spiritual healing, her writings in *Lessons in Truth* and her other works stress the teachings of Jesus as she interpreted them. Her commentaries on the teachings of Jesus demonstrate a familiarity with the New Testament. Jesus, in her view, manifested the God-self more than any other human being who ever lived.

Cady's works are also filled with quotes from Ralph Waldo Emerson, the American transcendentalist and forefather of the New Thought movement. Cady viewed Emerson as "grandly simple . . . a man large in individuality (Divine Self or God Self)." She continued: "He was of a shrinking, retiring nature (or personality). But just in proportion as the human side of him was willing to retire and be thought little of, did the immortal, the God in him, shine forth in greater degree."[14]

Cady was also influenced by the works of Warren Felt Evans, a spiritual healer and a major late-nineteenth-century metaphysical writer. The titles of the books by Evans that she "especially remembered" were *Esoteric Christianity or Mental Therapeutics, Mental Medicine,* and *Divine Law of Cure.*[15] It was Cady's opinion that Evans "transcended the writers of his day," indicating that his books "were too fine for large popular sale." Cady observed: "He most frequently used material analogies to make plain to people the deep spiritual truths which up to that time had been thought to be almost completely of another world and not to be at all applicable to the every day problems of life here."[16]

In her conversations with Pomeroy, Cady acknowledged the influence of Evans in the development of her spiritual ideas. Pomeroy reported: "His [Evans] books fell into Dr. Cady's hands, and, in the older copies of her noted book *Lessons in Truth,* his name is used by her. Evans's style of writing was lucid and simple, his ideas sound and he evidently helped her to lay hands on that mental bridge between the outer facts of life and the nature and presence of Spirit which she sought."[17]

Cady was one of the many writers and teachers who studied under the founder of New Thought, Emma Curtis Hopkins. Beginning in the late 1880s, Hopkins, who taught and ordained the Fillmores, gave classes in New York City. Cady, in her letters to Myrtle, indicated the respect and appreciation she had for Hopkins's work. By private correspondence during her lifetime, Cady maintained a close personal as well as professional relationship with both Myrtle and Lowell Fillmore. Both acknowledged Cady for making a vitally essential contribution to the development of the Unity movement.

Human Nature and Divine Nature

Cady viewed God as a divine being with unlimited capacity. While Cady seldom dwelled on God as all-powerful, her writing contained passages that indicated that she had no doubts about God's transcendent qualities. She wrote:

God is power. In other words, all the power there is to do anything is God. God, the source of our existence every moment, is not simply omnipotent (all-powerful), He is omnipotence (all power). He is not only omniscient (all-knowing); He is omniscience (all knowledge); He is not only omnipresent, but more omnipresence . . . Everything that you can think of that is good, when in its absolute perfection, goes to make up that invisible Being we call God.[18]

Cady viewed God as an indwelling presence in humankind. She sought to convince her readers that if they wanted to find God, they needed to look within themselves. She declared: "This Divine Substance—call it God, Creative Energy, or whatever you will—is ever abiding within us, and stands ready today to manifest itself in whatever form you and I need or wish."[19]

Cady believed God existed not only in humankind but in all things, in every atom that composed the universe. She explained: "Each rock, tree, animal, every visible thing, is a manifestation of the one Spirit—God, differing only in degree of manifestation, and each of the numberless modes of manifestation or individualities, however insignificant, contains the whole."[20]

Cady wanted to assure her readers that hers was not a "pantheistic view" of the universe, which, she indicated, postulated "the visible universe taken as a whole is God."[21] She explained: "God is the living, warm, throbbing life that pervades our being. He is the quickening intelligence that keeps our mind balanced and steady throughout all the vicissitudes of life. He never is and never can be for a moment separated from His creation."[22]

When Cady wrote about the nature of God she usually described God as principle rather than as personal. She indicated: "God is the name we give to that unchangeable, inexorable principle at the source of all existence . . . God as Life, Wisdom, Love, Substance fills every place and space of the Universe, or else He is not omnipresent."[23]

Because God functioned as principle, God did not grant favors to men and women, or respond to pleas for help. Cady asserted: "The light that we want is not something that God has to give; it is God himself. God does not give us life or light as a thing. God is life and light and love."[24] Rather than responding to personal requests, God operated in human affairs through divine law. She indicated: "You cannot change God's attitude toward you one iota by either importuning or affirming. You only change your attitude toward Him. But thus affirming, you put yourselves in harmony with Divine Law, which is always working toward your good and never toward your harm or punishment."[25]

Cady was perfectly comfortable with the idea that God operated both personally and impersonally. Her views on the motherhood of God best expressed her point of view. She asserted:

Every metaphysician either has reached or must reach the place where God as cold principle alone will not suffice any more than in the past God as personality alone could wholly satisfy . . . We must have, and we do have, the motherhood of God, which is not cold Principle any more than your love for your child is cold . . . God (Father-Mother) is a present help in time of need.[26]

While Cady acknowledged the reality of God as "Father-Mother," she at the same time held that God was not a person. She stated:

Many have thought of God as a personal being. The statement that God is Principle chills them, and in terror they cry out, "They have taken my Lord, and I know not where they have laid him." Broader and more learned minds are always cramped by the thought of God as a person, for personality limits to time and place . . . To the individual consciousness God takes on personality, but as the creative underlying cause of all things He is Principle, impersonal, as expressed in each individual.[27]

Cady especially rejected the ideas about God as a person that are held by traditional Christians. She declared:

God is not a being or person having life, intelligence, love [or] power ... God is not, as many of us have been taught to believe, a big personage or man residing somewhere in a beautiful region of the sky called "heaven," where good people go when they die, and see Him clothed in ineffable glory, nor is He a stern, angry judge only awaiting opportunity somewhere to punish bad people who have failed to live a perfect life here.[28]

Despite the fact that the Bible indicated men and women were created in "the image and likeness of God," Cady rejected the notion that this passage should be interpreted to mean that God took human form. She commented: "No intelligent person can make the mistake of supposing that God has parts like unto a human body, or that the external man is in any way in the image and likeness of God."[29]

Cady was convinced that many human problems could be traced to erroneous ideas about the nature of God. She commented:

We have believed wrong about God and about ourselves. We have believed that God was angry with us and that we were sinners who ought to be afraid of Him. We have believed that sickness and poverty and other troubles are evils put here by this same God to torture us in some way into serving Him and loving Him. We have believed that we have pleased God best when we became so absolutely subdued by our troubles as to be patiently submissive to them all, not even thinking to rise out of them or to overcome them. All this is false, entirely false. The first step toward freeing ourselves from our troubles is to get rid of our erroneous beliefs about God and about ourselves.[30]

Cady believed that men and women perform an extremely important function for God. They serve as vehicles for God to become manifest in the world. Without humankind, God would be unable to express His true nature. She told her readers:

If you are inclined to wilt before strong personalities, always remember that God has need of you through whom, in some special manner, to manifest Himself— some manner for which He cannot use any other organ. . . . However humble your place in life, however, unknown to the world you may be, however small your capacities may seem at present to you, you are just as much a necessity to God in His efforts to get Himself into visibility as the most brilliant intellect, the most cultured person in the world.[31]

A vitally important way God manifested himself in humankind was through the activity of the Holy Spirit. Cady believed that the Holy Spirit was the aspect of God that lived within men and women, serving as a valuable guide. She indicated, "The Holy Spirit lives within you. He cares

for you, is working in you that which He would have you do, and is manifesting Himself through you."[32]

Cady believed that men and women possess divine attributes and that
the presence of God occupies a central part of each person. She observed:
"Man is made in the image of God . . . The divine spark at the center of
his being, the ever-renewed breath of God, which is life, the intelligence of
this man, be it full or limited, is God's image, is part of God Himself."[33]

Cady saw in human nature an "animal or sense part,"[34] an "eating,
drinking and sensual creature"[35] that was not at all God-like or divine.
She labeled this weak, limited, erring part of humankind as the "personality." The personality, she declared, "is the outward appearance, not the
real self."[36] It represents the animal part of us. "Always remember," she
warned, "that the personality is of the human." She described the various
ways the personality manifested itself in human affairs, identifying it with
the "carnal mind." She explained:

Besides the real innermost self of each of us—the self that is the divine self because
it is an expression or pressing out of God into visibility . . . there is the human self,
a carnal mind, which reports lies from the external world and is not to be relied
upon fully. . . . This intellectual man, carnal mind, or whatever you choose to call
him, is envious and jealous and fretful and sick because he is "self." The human
self sees its own gratification at the expense, if need be, of someone else.[37]

Cady's ideas on the personality are not original with her. They have
their origins in the teachings of Saint Paul and in the writings of the Gnostics. The terminology was used by Christian Science as well as by Emma
Curtis Hopkins in New Thought.

The goal of human life, according to Cady, was to realize fully the divine nature within. Only Jesus, Cady asserted, had accomplished this objective. Cady characterized Jesus as "our noblest type of the perfect life
. . . the fullest, most complete manifestation of the One Mind that has ever
lived."[38] She believed that Jesus realized, during His lifetime, "the divine
self,"[39] the highest level of human consciousness. Jesus achieved this goal,
the Christ Consciousness, through spiritual work. She explained, "Jesus
lived almost wholly in the Christ part Himself, so consciously in the center
of His being, where the very essence of the Father was bubbling up in
ceaseless activity."[40]

Cady believed that every man and woman, deep down inside, wants
an inner connection with the divine, seeking "to realize oneness with the
Father at all times." She explained:

Every person in his heart desires, though he may not yet quite know it, this new birth into a higher life, into spiritual consciousness. Everyone wants more power, more good, more joy . . . Many today are conscious that the inner hunger cannot be satisfied with worldly goods, and are with all earnesty [*sic*] seeking spiritual understanding, or consciousness of an immanent God.[41]

What kept men and women from fully realizing their divine potential, particularly since, in Cady's view, each had been created in the image and likeness of God? Cady acknowledged the dilemma, telling her readers: "It is difficult for you to understand why, if God lives in us all the time, He does not keep our thoughts right instead of permitting us through ignorance to drift into wrong thoughts, and so bring trouble on ourselves."[42]

God allowed humankind to err, Cady believed, because men and women, like God, possess free will: "We are not automatons."[43] She explained: "We are made in the image and likeness of God, and like Him we have the power of choice, the power of deciding each for himself . . . There is but one force, but we each have the power of opening ourselves to this force or closing ourselves against it, which ever we choose."[44]

To Cady, free will made it possible for men and women to take actions that were ultimately hurtful; they could choose the negative as well as the positive. She explained: "The power that is in man is divine. It is all from God, who is omnipotent, but man is given the choice of using or directing this power for either good or evil."[45]

Cady recognized that humankind, except for Jesus, had failed to manifest the divine spirit within. The "personality," or the human, had dominated the consciousness of men and women. She observed: "Heretofore we have lived more in the human region. We have believed all that the carnal mind has told us, and the consequence is that we have been overwhelmed by all kinds of privation and suffering."[46]

Acknowledging the human dilemma, Cady asked the question: "Now, if God in Christ is the life of all life, if He is the light of all light, the force of all forces, how is it that some are suffering from lack of life, some are sitting in darkness, some are handicapped by weakness of character and body?"[47]

Cady outlined several factors she believed were responsible for humankind's failure to reach its divine potential. These included negative thought, ignorance, willfulness, fear, false belief, and selfishness. To Cady, humankind's inability to use the mind effectively was a primary cause for its failure to manifest the indwelling Spirit; specifically, the propensity of the mind to harbor negative thoughts. "Bad results follow false thinking," she reported. Improper thoughts have a significant impact. "Strong negative thoughts," she declared, "may render the blood acid, causing rheumatism."[48] Cady asked: "Have you been living in negation for years, denying your ability to succeed, denying your health, denying your Godhood, denying your power to accomplish anything, by feeling yourself a child of the Devil or of weakness?"[49]

Cady indicated that "wrong thinking" was one of the particularly harmful forms of negative thought.[50] She noted, "we have thought wrong because we are misinformed by the senses, and our troubles and sorrow are the result of our wrong thinking."[51] She thought that negative words were equally inhibiting: "If you speak the 'I Am' falsely, you will get the result of false speaking. If you say, 'I am sick,' you will get sickness; 'I am poor,' you will get poverty; for the law is, 'Whatsoever a man soweth, that shall he also reap.'"[52]

Cady believed the two major factors inhibiting the development of the Christ-self were ignorance and willfulness. The two were juxtaposed probably because she was aware of their juxtaposition in the book of Psalms (see, for example, Psalm 14:1 and Psalm 92:7). Willfulness was considered the more serious offense. She stated: "The inner light comes to 'every man of God coming into the world' but we may close ourselves to this light either through ignorance or willfulness—the result is the same—and live in darkness."[53] These ideas came out of the Christian mystical tradition. They can also be found in the writings of Jonathan Edwards and in the Hebrew Bible.

Cady believed that fear was probably the greatest deterrent to achieving oneness with the Divine. She reported: "Oh, the awful paralyzing effect of fear. It makes us helpless babes. It makes us pygmies, whereas we might be giants were we only free from it. It is the root of all of our failures, of nearly all sickness, poverty and distress."[54]

Erroneous beliefs, Cady noted, were also destructive. Men and women, by holding false beliefs, sacrifice their ability to demonstrate the divine presence. She felt that false beliefs about the nature of God were particularly harmful, observing: "Believing that God regards us as 'miserable sinners,' that He is continually watching us and our failures with disapproval, brings utter discouragement and a sort of half-paralyzed condition of the mind and body, which means failure in all our undertakings."[55]

Cady listed selfishness as another major inhibitor of spiritual development. She noted: "We cultivate personality in which lives pride, fear of criticism, and all manner of selfishness, by listening to the voices outside ourselves and by being governed by selfish motives, instead of the highest within us."[56]

Despite the fact that Cady recognized the evil nature of negative thought, ignorance, willfulness, selfishness, and fear, she steadfastly maintained that evil did not exist. She defended the seeming contradiction in her teaching by stating:

There is no evil, sickness is not real, sin is not real . . . I repeat, nothing is real which is not eternal; and all conditions of apparent evil, sickness, poverty, fear, etc., are not things, not entities in themselves, but they are simply an absence of Good, just as darkness is the absence of light. In the deepest reality there is never an absence of Good anywhere for that would mean the absence of God there.[57]

While Cady recognized that jealousy, avarice, hate, ill will, condemnation—negativity of any kind—prevent men and women from experiencing the divine inner self, she passionately believed that evil should not be acknowledged. She urged truth students to deny its reality. She asserted:

Let us go back to our straight, white line of Absolute Truth. *There is only God.* All that is not God is no thing, that is, has no existence—is simply a nightmare. If we walk on this white line where we refuse to see or acknowledge anything but God, then all else disappears. In dealing with everyday problems of life we will succeed in becoming free just in proportion as we cease absolutely to parley with apparent evils as though they were entities. We cannot afford to spend a moment's time agreeing with their claim, for if we do, we ourselves will become the overcome instead of the overcomers.[58]

Cady appears to be suggesting that when humankind manifests the indwelling Spirit, evil cannot and does not exist. Evil arises as selfishness, fear, negative thought, malice, and hate, only when the consciousness of a man or woman is centered in the human self or personality. Cady believed that holding to the idea of the unreality of evil had major benefits. She indicated: "The very circumstances in your life that seem heartbreaking evils will turn to joy before your very eyes if you will steadfastly refuse to see anything but God in them."[59]

The views expressed by Cady on the unreality of evil were contained in William James's major work, *The Varieties of Religious Experience.* While Cady did not specifically acknowledge James, it is likely that she was aware of his work. Her ideas were in the philosophical tradition of Neo-platonism. A fundamental question of all religion is the nature of ultimate reality. In Cady's view, ultimate reality was good, not evil, a view she shared with many who adopt a metaphysical worldview.

"The Highest Manifestation of God Is in Man."

How do men and women achieve "a clear, vivid consciousness of the Indwelling Presence?"[60] How can humankind attain "this new birth into a higher life, into spiritual consciousness?"[61] How do we let go of the human self or personality and live as Jesus did, "in the Christ part" of ourselves?[62] Cady believed these things are accomplished through observing the principles of divine law and by doing the will of God. As men and women manifest the indwelling presence, she maintained, they enjoy greater success, prosperity, more happiness, better health, and an enhanced sense of personal well-being.

Cady asserted that men and women achieve oneness with God by knowing and understanding divine law and by living in accordance with it. "Knowing Divine Law and obeying it," Cady assured her readers, "we can forever rest from all anxiety."[63] Cady's writing was filled with references to the importance of divine law and the necessity of aligning with it. She declared:

The mental and spiritual worlds or realms are governed by laws that are just as real and unfailing as the laws that govern the natural world. Certain conditions of mind are so connected with certain results that the two are inseparable. If we have the one, we must have the other, as surely as the night follows the day . . . The whole matter is based on laws that can neither fail nor be broken.[64]

Knowing the will of God and following it was equally important to Cady; if men and women wanted "to come into consciousness of the indwelling God," it was necessary that they discover the will of God for themselves and take steps to live in accordance with it. Cady advised people to: "Cease to desire anything less than the fulfillment of God's will in you. His thoughts are higher than yours as the heavens are higher than the earth. Let nothing short of the perfect fulfillment of His thought in and through you satisfy you."[65]

Cady recognized that it took courage to seek and follow the will of God: "Oh, for more men who have the courage to abandon themselves utterly to infinite will—men who dare let go of every human being for guid-

ance and seek the Christ within themselves. Let the manifestation be what
He wills!"[66]

Cady predicted good things for those who submit themselves to God's
will rather than following human desires: She declared: "When we thus
burst the bounds of personal desire and rise to a willingness that the Father's will be done through us every moment, how sure we are of the fa-
therly care which shall clothe us with the beauty of the lilies and feed us as
the birds of the air."[67]

Cady outlined a variety of spiritual practices that would enable humankind to comply with the will of God and observe the principles of divine law, thereby realizing the existence of the divine within. The list includes disciplining the mind, going into the silence, using affirmations and
denials, exhibiting faith in God, expressing divine love, and living in the
present. This approach differed from that of Charles and Myrtle Fillmore,
who stressed the need to activate twelve faculties of the mind to realize the
inner presence.

DISCIPLINING THE MIND

Cady believed that the human mind is very powerful. It can work either for us or against us, depending on how we use it. "Our way of thinking," she declared, "makes for our happiness or unhappiness, our success
or nonsuccess."[68] One of the ways to maximize the use of the mind, according to Cady, was through "right thinking." "Every right thought that
we think," she explained, "every unselfish word or action, is bound by immutable laws to be fraught with good results."[69]

Cady was certain that through proper mental discipline, men and
women could learn to hold positive rather than negative thoughts. "We
can," she asserted, "by effort, change our thinking."[70] She believed results
could be obtained through practice and by perseverance. "I ask you," she
implored her readers, "to try thinking true, right thoughts awhile, and see
what the results will be."[71] She assured her readers: "We can all learn how
to turn the conscious mind toward universal Mind, or spirit, within us.
We can by practice learn how to make this everyday, topsy-turvy 'mind of
the flesh' be still and let the mind that is God (all wisdom, all love) think
in us and out through us."[72]

To Cady, right thinking was but one of the attributes of the disciplined
mind. Intuition, she indicated, was a much more valuable tool, one that
needed to be developed and continually used. She commented: "Intuition,

or the Spirit of truth, [is] ever living at the center of our being. Its action is infinitely higher than that of intellectual conclusions. . . . Intuition is the open end, within one's own being, of the invisible channel ever connecting each individual with God."[73]

Cady argued that the intellect needed to be informed by the intuition. Those who discounted intuition and relied solely on analytical reasoning would be unable to develop spiritual understanding or manifest their divine nature. She declared:

Intuition and intellect are meant to travel together, intuition always holding the reins to guide intellect . . . If you have been thus far cultivating and enlarging only the mental side of Truth . . . you need, in order to come into the full understanding, to let the mental, the reasoning side, rest awhile. "Become as little children," and learn how to be still, listen to that which the Father will say to you through the intuitional part of your being.[74]

Cady seemed to equate intuition with listening to the "still small voice." One needed to shut out all distractions, all outside noise, and simply listen. She advised: "Still the intellect for the time being and let universal mind speak to you; and when it speaks, though it be but a 'still small voice,' you will know that what it says is Truth."[75]

Based on her own experience, Cady was certain that when the indwelling Spirit spoke, its message was unmistakable. "How will you know?" There could be no doubts. Your intuition would tell you. She observed: "You will know just as you know that you are alive. All the argument in the world to convince you against Truth that comes to you through direct revelation will fall flat and harmless at your side . . . Spirit takes the deep things of God and reveals Truth to man. Spirit does not give opinions about Truth. It is Truth, and it reveals itself."[76]

SPIRITUAL UNDERSTANDING

According to Cady, by listening to the "still small voice"—or using intuition—it was possible to gain spiritual understanding. Cady placed high value on its attainment. Through spiritual understanding, she felt, a person became conscious of "the immanent God,"[77] the "flash of the most high within your consciousness."[78] Cady's spiritual understanding took the form of "a spiritual birth, a revelation of God within the heart of man."[79] She had a clear idea of what was needed to gain it and the benefits it provided. She asserted: "Until, down in the depths of your being, you are conscious of your oneness with the Father, until you know within yourself that the spring of all wisdom and health and joy is within your own being, ready at any moment to leap forth at the call of your need, you will not have spiritual understanding."[80]

Cady was sure that spiritual understanding did not come from book learning. She advised: "If you want to make rapid progress in growth toward spiritual understanding, stop reading books. They only give someone's opinion about Truth, or a sort of history of the author's experience in seeking Truth. What you want is a revelation of Truth in your own soul, and that will never come through the reading of many books."[81]

She thought that spiritual understanding was not the product of the use of logic or analytical reasoning, pointing out:

If you are one who seeks and expects to get any real knowledge of spiritual things through argument or reasoning, no matter how scholarly your attainments or how great you are in worldly wisdom, you are a failure in spiritual understanding. You are attempting an utter impossibility—that of crowding the Infinite into the quart measure of your own intellectual capacity.[82]

Intuition provided the path inward. She declared: "A person must be willing to 'become as little children,' and just be taught how to take the first step toward pure understanding (or knowledge of Truth as God sees it), and then receive the light by direct revelation from the All-Good."[83]

The path inward to spiritual understanding, she believed, was an individual trek. Each person must proceed unaccompanied, without church, teacher, or spiritual confidante. "Books and lectures are good teachers,"[84] she indicated. The final leg of the journey, however, had to be taken alone. She explained: "Each man must come to a time when he no longer seeks external help, when he knows that the inner revelation of 'my Lord and my God' to his consciousness can come to him only through an indwelling power that has been there all the time, waiting in infinite longing and patience to reveal the father to the child."[85]

Cady believed that a teacher might give a prescription or an instruction, but the student must be receptive to it and do the inner work. She counseled: "I cannot reveal God to you. You cannot reveal God to another. If I have learned, I may tell you, and you may tell another, how to seek and find God, each within himself. But the new birth into the consciousness of our spiritual faculties and possibilities is indeed like the wind that 'bloweth where it will.'"[86]

These ideas are in contrast to those of Henry Nelson Wieman (1884–

1978), a liberal theologian at the University of Chicago, whose principal works include *The Source of Human Good* and *Man's Ultimate Commitment*, and the German philosopher Martin Buber (1878–1965), author of *I and Thou*, who concluded that the divine was revealed in the creative interchange between human beings.

IN THE SILENCE

Cady believed that the best place to gain spiritual understanding was in a quiet meditative state, "in the silence." By spending sufficient time alone with God, she thought, we deepen our spiritual knowledge and power and emerge ready to face the demands of life. She reported: "We go apart into the stillness of divine presence that we may come forth into the world of everyday life with new inspiration and increased courage and power for activity and overcoming."[87]

Cady felt that for new students unfamiliar with meditation, it was important to find a quiet space alone where there were no distractions. "Seek light from the Spirit of Truth within you," she suggested. "Go alone. Think alone. Seek light alone."[88] Cady suggested that while in a meditative state, men and women concentrate their thoughts on God rather than on their own problems. She advised:

When you withdraw from the world for meditation, let it not be to think of yourself or your failures, but invariably to get all your thoughts centered on God and your relation to the Creator and Upholder of the universe. Let all the little annoying cares and anxieties go for a while and by effort, if need be, turn your thoughts away from them to some of the simple words of the Nazarene, or of the Psalmists. Think of some Truth statement, be it ever so simple.[89]

Cady stressed the need for quiet time each day to commune personally with God. She suggested: "Every man must take time daily for quiet and meditation. In daily meditation lies the secret of power. No one can grow in either spiritual knowledge or power without it. Practice the presence of God just as you would practice music. . . . Daily meditation alone with God focuses the divine presence within us and brings it to our consciousness."[90]

Cady indicated that people need to be patient, waiting as long as it takes for Spirit to speak. She declared: "Do not be discouraged if you do not at once get conscious results in the silent sitting. Every moment that you wait, Spirit is working to make you a new creature in Christ—a creature possessing consciously His very own qualities and powers. There may be a working for days before you see any change; but it will surely come."[91]

While it was important to wait, Cady wanted it understood that it was an attitude of waiting which was important, not the amount of time spent sitting in the silence. She advised: "Of course I do not mean that you are to give all the time to sitting alone in meditation and silence, but that your mind shall be continually in an attitude of waiting upon God, not an attitude of clamoring for things, but of listening for the Father's voice and expecting a manifestation of the Father to your consciousness."[92]

PRAYER

Cady believed that the best way to begin the silence was with prayer. She suggested: "Begin your silence by lifting up your heart in prayer to the Father of your being. Do not be afraid that, if you begin to pray, you will be too orthodox . . . Spending the first few moments of your silence in speaking directly to the Father centers your mind on the Eternal."[93]

Cady reminded her readers that prayer was not about asking for things. She indicated: "You know better than to plead with or to beseech God, with an unbelieving prayer. . . . You are not going to supplicate God, who has already given you things whatsoever you desire."[94]

She told her readers that prayer was not for the purpose of influencing God in any way. "Prayer," she surmised, "does not change God's attitude toward us."[95] The real purpose of prayer, Cady believed, was for giving thanks. "True prayer," she indicated, "is just a continual recognition and thanksgiving that All is good."[96]

AFFIRMATIONS

One of the principal ways to discipline the mind so that it functions effectively, according to Cady, is through affirmations. She explained: "The saying over and over of any denial or affirmation is necessary training of the mind that has lived so long in error and false belief that it needs this constant repetition of Truth to unclothe it and to clothe it anew."[97]

Cady saw a direct connection between thoughts held in the mind and words of affirmation on the lips. Both were necessary if results were to be attained. She reported:

"All things which we desire, already are now in being in the spiritual or Invisible. But, as someone has said, 'Thought and the spoken word stand between the Invisible and visible.' By the action of these two—thought and the Spoken word—is the Invisible made visible."[98]

Cady was convinced that affirmations, if used correctly, had the power to change the circumstances of life for good or ill, depending on what was stated. If used rightly, she noted, affirmations "build up, and give strength and courage and power."[99]

Cady was convinced that affirmations worked well when made in direct contradiction to existing life circumstances. If you were sick, you affirmed that you were healthy; if financially strapped, you affirmed you had plenty. She declared: "To affirm anything is to assert positively that it is so, even in the face of all contrary evidence. We may not be able to see how, by our simply affirming a thing to be true, a thing that to all human reason or sight does not seem to be true at all, we can bring this thing to pass, but we can go to work to prove the rule, each one in his own life."[100]

Cady believed that the words themselves were critical and should be chosen carefully. The best results came from the use of the most powerful words. She reported:

"As God created by the spoken word, 'without which was nothing made that was made,' so man can create by his spoken word. In fact, there is no other way under heaven to bring into existence the visible conditions and things which we want."[101]

Cady believed that affirmations could be used at all times and in all places. One did not need to be in a meditative state for them to be effective. She urged people: "Practice these denials and affirmations silently in the street, in the car, when you are wakeful or during the night, anywhere, everywhere, and they will give you a new, and to you a strange, mastery over external things and over yourself."[102]

Cady believed the I AM statements of truth that Jesus used were particularly powerful. She suggested a simple exercise to demonstrate the benefits of the I AM. She suggested a person do the following: "Go alone, close your eyes, and in the depth of your own soul say over and over the words 'I Am.' Soon you will find your whole being filled with a sense of power which you never had before—power to overcome, power to accomplish, power to do all things."[103]

Cady recommended using "I am the way, and the truth, and the life."[104] She wanted to be sure her readers used the I AM as a statement of being in the present, here and now. She indicated, "Notice that it is 'I am,' not 'I will be,' present tense, not future."[105] Cady viewed I AM statements as focusing the mind in a positive direction, no matter what the context.

Cady testified how the persistent use of an affirmation in her own life helped her heal a relationship in which she had felt powerless and victimized. She reported:

Some years ago I found myself under a sense of bondage to a strong, aggressive personality, with whom, externally, I had been quite intimately associated for several months. I seemed to see things through another's eyes and while I was more than half conscious of this, yet I could not seem to throw it off. This personality was able, with a very few words, to make me feel as if all that I said or did was a mistake, and that I was a most miserable failure. I was always utterly discouraged after being in this person's presence, and felt I had not the ability to accomplish anything.

After vainly trying for weeks to free myself, one day I was walking along the street, with a most intense desire and determination to be free. Many times before, I had affirmed that this personality could not affect or overcome me, but with no effect. This day I struck out further and declared (silently of course), *There is no such personality in the universe as this one,* affirming it again and again many times. After a few moments I began to feel wondrously lifted, as if chains were dropping off. Then the voice within me urged me on a step further to say, *There is no personality in the universe: There is nothing but God.* After a short time spent in vigorously using these words, I seemed to break every fetter. From that day to this, without further effort, I have been as free from any influence of that personality as though it had never existed.[106]

DENIALS

Denials were as important as affirmations, in Cady's view. "All systems for spiritualizing the mind," she reported, "include denial."[107] The purpose of denial, Cady asserted, was "to eradicate apparent evil and bring the good into manifestation."[108] To deny, she stated, "is to declare to be not true, to repudiate as utterly false."[109] That which was declared not true, according to Cady, was "a thing that seems to be true."[110]

Denials were important, she believed, because they rid the mind of negative thoughts and ideas. Denial, she explained, "is the first practical step toward wiping out of our minds the mistaken beliefs of a lifetime."[111] Cady continually emphasized the positive impact of denials on the mind, stating, "Everything undesirable passes away if we refuse absolutely to give it recognition by word, deed or thought as a reality."[112]

Cady observed that some people responded better to denials than to affirmations. It depended on their mental makeup. She explained: "Denials have an erasive or dissolving tendency ... Persons who remember vividly, and are inclined to dwell in their thoughts on the pains, sorrows and troubles of the past or present, need to deny a great deal, for denials cleanse the mind and blot out the memory of all seeming evil and unhappiness."[113]

FAITH

Cady recognized that her spiritual teaching was based on faith in the power and presence of the divine indwelling Spirit. She was certain that without faith it was impossible to connect with the divine inner light. Men and women, in her view, demonstrated success, prosperity, and health based on their ability to access the Christ mind, the divine inner self. Faith was the key that opened the door. Cady declared: "God is forever in process of movement within us, that He may manifest Himself (all-good) more fully through us. Our affirming, backed by faith, is the link that connects our conscious human need with His power and supply."[114]

The real test of faith, according to Cady, was the ability to trust, in the face of contrary evidence, life circumstances that provided no grounds for belief. "Faith has nothing to do with visible circumstances," she observed. "The moment one considers circumstances, that moment one lets go of faith."[115]

Cady distinguished between hope and faith, suggesting that Christians often incorrectly considered them to be one and the same. She noted:

Many Christians mistake hope for faith. Hope expects answers sometime in the future; faith takes it as having already been given. Hope looks forward; faith declares that she has received even before there is the slightest visible evidence. Man's way is to declare something done after it has become obvious to the senses; God's way is to declare it done before there is anything whatever in sight ... This declaring, "It is finished," when there is still no visible evidence, has power to bring the desired object into visibility.[116]

DIVINE LOVE

Cady believed that one of the best ways to connect with the divine inner self, the indwelling Christ mind, was through love. Men and women experience greater consciousness of the indwelling Spirit, thought Cady, as they become more loving and more giving. "The higher we rise in recognition and consequent manifestation of the Divine," she asserted, "the more surely we think always of giving, not of what we shall receive."[117] She asked, "Is our heart cold, and is our love dead?"[118] If so, we need to realize that "God is love and love is God."[119]

Cady equated divine love with giving to others; men and women comply with divine law and express divine love to the extent that they give unconditionally. She observed: "God is forever giving, giving, giving, with no thought of return. Love always thinks of giving, never of receiving. God's giving is the spontaneous outflow of perfect love."[120]

LIVE IN THE NOW

Cady believed that those who fully experienced the indwelling presence had learned to live fully in the present. As a result, all of Cady's teaching was focused on present time: the future would take care of itself if we lived in the now. Quoting Jesus, she wrote, "Now is the accepted time; behold; now is the day of salvation."[121] She was explicit in her declarations about the importance of staying focused on what was happening in the present moment. She declared: "Let go of the notion of being or doing anything in the future . . . God's work is finished in us now. All the fullness abides in this indwelling Christ now. And whatever we persistently declare is done now, is manifested now."[122]

ASSESSMENT OF THE ROLE OF JESUS

Cady's writings are filled with references to the life and teachings of Jesus. The Nazarene, as she referred to Jesus, was important to her because she believed that he alone had overcome the limitations of the human self or personality and manifested the one mind, the divine self.

Cady did not view Jesus as born God-like or divine. She did not believe he was God incarnate, the second person of the Blessed Trinity, sent by God the Father to save humankind from its sins. Jesus possessed the same human qualities as other men and women. At birth he was no different from anyone else, possessing attributes of the human and of the divine. "He went through all the years of His early manhood—just as you and I are doing today—overcoming the mortal."[123] Cady commented: "There was in Jesus' being two distinct regions. There was the fleshly, mortal part, which was Jesus, the son of man; then there was the central, living, real part, which was the Spirit, the Son of God. That was the Christ, the Anointed."[124]

Cady believed humankind possessed the same innate attributes as Jesus, that men and women had the innate capacity to rise to the same level of consciousness as Jesus had. "The very mind of Christ that was in Jesus is in you,"[125] she assured her readers. She continued: "The same Christ lives within us as it lived in Jesus. It is the part of Himself which God has put within us, and which ever lives there with an inexpressible love and desire to spring to the circumference of our being, or to our consciousness, as our sufficiency in all things."[126]

Cady rejected the traditional Christian idea that Jesus died on the cross to atone for the sins of humankind. She stated: "Simply believing that Jesus died on the cross to appease God's wrath never did, nor can, save anyone from present sin, sickness or want, and was not what Jesus taught."[127]

Cady viewed the death and resurrection of Jesus as important because it demonstrated human immortality: men and women now know that there is an afterlife. Cady explained: "Because He went down and came up again a glorified man, He brought life and immortality to light. Immortal life existed before, but it remained for Jesus to bring it to light, to our human understanding, and thus prove to us that all life is One."[128]

Cady was convinced that the impact of Jesus' life and teachings would have been greatly lessened if he had extended his life through bodily regeneration. She asked: "Is He not rather infinitely more to all the world today than He could possibly have been had He simply prolonged, for endless years, life in the physical body?"[129]

AFTERLIFE

Given her belief that men and women are created in the image and likeness of God, it is not surprising that Cady believed the spirit, or the "real man," survives the death of the body. "Life is one and continuous," she declared, "even though there comes a seeming break which we call death."[130] She was convinced that through the physical act of dying, men and women remain conscious of themselves.[131]

Cady rejected the traditional Christian idea that many people suffer after passing through the curtain called death. People view oncoming death with dread, she declared, "due to certain religious teachings of punishment and hell."[132] Cady reassured her readers that there was nothing to worry about. "The future," she commented, "is not a system of rewards and punishments."[133] Death, in her opinion, was a positive rather than a negative experience, "an unspeakably good fortune."[134] Death, she believed, "is simply being born out of this hampered sphere into a grander, fuller, freer life."[135] Cady's articles and books do not focus on the prospects for reincarnation.

BODILY REGENERATION

Writing in 1908, Cady saw no merit in the idea espoused by the Fillmores (Charles, Myrtle, and Lowell) that, as men and women grow in spiritual understanding and manifest the Christ Consciousness, the cells of their bodies regenerate, growing more youthful and vigorous with age. Nowhere did she indicate her belief that the human body through this process would ultimately overcome physical death. She declared: "There is much said in these latter days about the desirability and the possibility of living here in these bodies indefinitely. This seems altogether foolish and shortsighted. Why continue, even if it were possible, clinging to this old body after it has served its purposes?"[136]

CHAPTER 4

Lowell Fillmore: Clarifier and Popularizer

"Things to Be Remembered"

The eldest son of Charles and Myrtle Fillmore, Lowell Fillmore probably did more to popularize the Unity teaching in the twentieth century than either of his parents. The audience he attracted during his sixty years as editor of *Weekly Unity* magazine and as author of the column "Things to Be Remembered" was much wider than the audience his father attracted through books and articles or his mother attracted through articles and letters. Lowell's popularity was due in large part to the clarity with which he presented the Unity spiritual teaching. Lowell had the ability to make the teachings understandable to people who were being exposed to it for the first time.

Lowell Fillmore, along with his parents and H. Emilie Cady, deserves credit as a founding author of the Unity teaching. This view is not based on the fact that he attracted a wide audience. He, together with H. Emilie Cady, provided a formulation of the Unity teaching that differed in significant ways from that of Charles and Myrtle Fillmore. Unlike his father and mother, Lowell did not use the theory of the twelve powers as the context for presenting the teachings. Lowell referred to the twelve powers only sporadically in his writing. In the sixty-plus years he wrote for *Weekly Unity*, he mentioned them fewer than two dozen times. He never presented a comprehensive treatment and mentioned them only in passing.

Lowell was primarily interested in describing the practices that enable men and women to live in conformity with the will of God and the precepts of divine law, practices that enable humankind to manifest the Christ Consciousness. In addition, he sought to inspire people to use those practices. Lowell's interpretation of the Unity teaching has been widely used throughout Unity's century-long history and continues to be used today in the teachings of Unity School and in many Unity churches.

Lowell also played a key role in the development of the Unity movement. He originated the Prosperity Bank plan, which was responsible for Unity's vast growth during the first three decades of the twentieth century. Unity's worldwide impact is in large part due to the contribution of Lowell Fillmore.

"One of God's spiritual millionaires"

Born in Pueblo, Colorado, on January 4, 1882, Lowell Fillmore was involved with working for Unity at an early age. "I must have been about ten years old when I first went to work in Unity," he recalled. "On Saturdays when there was no school I would go down to the office, or as we called them, the 'Unity Rooms,' and there I would wrap for mailing the magazines that my father and mother were publishing."[1] His mother, who began editing *Wee Wisdom* magazine in 1893, involved her eleven-year-old son in important ways. She often asked his opinion on articles she was publishing for her reading audience of elementary-school-age children. Lowell Fillmore's home life during his boyhood was apparently a happy one. In later years he remarked, "I believe it can be truly said that my boyhood home was a household of faith."[2]

Lowell graduated from high school in Kansas City at age seventeen in 1899. Unlike his two younger brothers, he did not seek higher education. Instead, he went to work for the Unity Tract Society immediately upon graduation, embarking on a career that was to last sixty-four years. At the outset he learned to type and take shorthand and he performed a variety of menial chores around the office. In 1907 business manager Charles Prather resigned, and Lowell's parents asked him to take over the duties. Just twenty-five at the time, Lowell doubted whether he had sufficient knowledge and experience. "I was fearful lest I could not do the job, but my father insisted: 'You can do it,' he said, 'and if something comes up I will help you.'"[3]

Lowell was also active in the local Unity Society of Practical Christianity, the church organization that held services on Sundays as well as meetings during the middle of the week. In addition to attending services on Sunday, Lowell taught Sunday school, beginning as a teenager when the boys in his classes were almost his age.[4] When the first Unity youth group, the "Joyful Circle," was organized in the early 1900s, Lowell was one of its first members. He participated for many years.[5] In May 1909 Lowell became the editor of a small weekly paper that the local Unity Society established to help its members keep in close touch with all phases of the work. Called *Weekly Unity,* its initial purpose was to publish news items along with a schedule of meetings and reports on the society's business. Intended for local distribution only, its original mission did not include an outreach to Unity readers outside Kansas City.

With the incorporation of the Unity School of Christianity in 1914, Lowell, then thirty-two, became the school's general manager. It was Lowell's job to run the school and its expanding publications program. He took over as head of Unity School in 1933 when his father, then seventy-nine, withdrew from day-to-day involvement in running the school. With his father's passing in 1948, he became president of Unity School, a position he held until 1964 when he became president emeritus. He remained active until his passing in 1975.[6]

Reports from his coworkers indicate that Lowell was industrious, disciplined, and energetic. One coworker noted that he was a man "of great physical vigor. I have rarely seen him walk up the stairs. He runs up two at a time."[7] He was at work early in the morning, usually at 7:30 A.M., and left long after the normal workday ended. Throughout most of his long career, he spent little time away from Kansas City. His administrative assistant, Retta Chilcott, remembered that he was hardly ever ill. "I never remember Lowell staying home, not even half a day."[8] He rarely took a vacation. "I don't need a vacation," he once said. "I have a vocation. Everything I do is a vacation."[9]

Lowell's parents, Charles and Myrtle, had great confidence in him and an appreciation of his abilities. In a letter to a friend in 1928, Myrtle commented:

Lowell has always been ready to make the best of conditions. He spends some of his time in quiet, getting his ideas, and deciding just what he would do; then he works out his plans with all the confidence in the world—knowing that God the Father is back of him, and that there are those who will be willing to encourage and aid, where that is necessary, and that he can handle whatever is his to do.[10]

Charles, on the occasion of Lowell's forty-ninth birthday on January 4, 1931, wrote the following note of acknowledgment:

I want you to realize what a joy and blessing you have been to us all these years you have spent with us in our close relationship of son. You came to us in the guise of a wee babe—a gift from the hand of the Infinite Father. We welcomed you gladly, for we felt dimly what we now realize. You are a great soul in the making, given into our charge for a season for care and guidance in your unfoldment on this experimental plane we call living. You have been through it all with us, and we have never had reason to regret.[11]

Lowell was well liked and respected by his coworkers. On May 1, 1928, *Unity News,* the newsletter put together for the in-house Unity School staff by the Unity workers, published a picture of Lowell at age three. He was dressed up in a suit and hat and looked like a little businessman. Under the picture was the following caption: "The future manager and treasurer of Unity School, a child who, with each succeeding year, has grown in wisdom and understanding until now he stands among his corps of workers, a shining light, kind, just, and much beloved."[12]

In the January 18, 1933 issue of *Unity News,* a particularly warm testimonial to Lowell was written by one of the women workers. She stated:

It is always a red letter day around the office when Lowell Fillmore drops casually round to each worker with a friendly smile and a cheery word. This is a custom with him from time to time, and do we like it! On the occasion of his last visit he came burdened with flowers, and whenever he departed a pink rosebud remained behind. Is it any wonder we girls are all "that way" about him?[13]

Retta Chilcott, who for forty years worked closely with him as his administrative assistant and personnel manager, recalled that Lowell focused on the positive, was sympathetic to the needs of employees, and supported them the best way he knew how:

One of his outstanding traits is that he never agrees with negation. Many times through the years, when some disturbing incident has occurred in the office, when someone has fallen sick or some inharmony has arisen, I have turned to Lowell. I have always found him understanding of people and their needs, but he keeps his thought positive. When people in the office have fallen sick he has always told me to do what I had to do to help them, while he himself has remained quietly and calmly in prayer, and held in his mind the Truth about them.[14]

Lowell was genuinely concerned about the welfare of Unity workers. One employee reported: "He is constantly trying to think of ways of helping people. When changes are suggested in the work, one of his first questions is always, 'can this be done without hurting anyone?'"[15] A niece,

Frances Fillmore Lakin, who from the age of five was raised by Lowell and his wife Alice, recalled how he cared for others. "He loved people, he just loved people. Even when he was in his nineties he wouldn't miss a coffee with Unity retreatants for anything."[16] Part of Lowell's success was due to the quality of his relationships with the Unity staff. From all reports, Lowell was a warm, outgoing man who treated his coworkers with care and respect. He made it a point to periodically go through every department of the school and shake the hand of every person who worked there. "These are the hands that do the work," he once explained. "I love to shake them."[17]

Lowell made it a practice to eat lunch with other workers at Unity Inn. Taking his place in the cafeteria line like any other worker, he would eat lunch with anyone beside whom there was an empty seat. "It is not unusual," one observer commented, "for the newest worker at Unity to hear someone say, 'Do you mind if I eat with you?' And when he looked up that someone was the president of Unity School." When lunch was over, Lowell carried his dishes away like any other worker. Before Lowell returned to his office, this observer continued, "He usually goes from table to table. Usually he has a new joke. He especially likes to stop behind a table where there has been laughter."[18] Retta Chilcott also testified to Lowell's capacity for genuine caring, indicating that he would be the one she would go to in time of need. "If I have a physical need," she stated, "I would rather get in touch with Lowell Fillmore than anyone I have ever known—and you can't imagine how much faith I had in Charles Fillmore."[19]

Prayer and meditation were part of Lowell Fillmore's spiritual practice, and he put them to use in running the everyday affairs of Unity School. One observer recalled how Lowell would go into the silence before making a major decision:

When Lowell is called upon to help someone, he becomes very still, his face becomes a study in tranquil concentration. He folds his hands in front of him, one upon the other motionless. No one seeing him can help knowing that here is a man who through a long life has practiced the art of meditation and whose first thought is always of going to God.[20]

A coworker who interviewed several people on the Unity staff while writing an article on Lowell sought information on Lowell as a person. The writer discovered that his coworkers all commented on how they had been changed by their interaction with him:

I talked with many people who had been associated with him in the Unity work. I was seeking, above all, stories about Lowell as a person, but after a time I discovered an interesting thing. Instead of telling me stories about Lowell, these people were soon telling me stories about the effect Lowell Fillmore had had in their lives, about how Lowell's devotion to principle, Lowell's simplicity, Lowell's modesty, Lowell's goodness had influenced them to be the kind of person they were and to do the things that they had done in running the affairs of their department of Unity School. When people think of Lowell Fillmore they do not think of fine anecdotes, and glittering personal exploits, they think only of the influence he has cast quietly and impersonally on their lives. . . . Unassuming, thoughtful of others, ready to exchange the latest funny story, or to discuss some profound metaphysical theme that the occasion demands, Lowell Fillmore is "just folks."[21]

Lowell was not the kind of person who needed adulation or the applause of coworkers or of Unity students. He was uncomfortable with people who came to Unity headquarters for classes with inflated notions about the spirituality of the people who worked there. He once commented: "People out in the field have the idea that when they come to Unity headquarters they will find people wearing wings, but we are just folks learning, as they are, to apply the principles of Truth in every day life."[22]

Barney Rickets, who worked directly for Lowell for thirty-five years as treasurer of Unity School and as head of its accounting department, gave Lowell high marks: "He comes nearer to living up to what he sees to be the Truth than anyone I know."[23] Rickets provided an important insight on how Lowell handled the financial affairs of the school. He reported: "If you want to get Lowell to do something, you don't tell him how much it will cost or how much money it will bring, you tell him how much good it is going to do. In all the years I have worked with him, I have never seen Lowell make a decision on any other basis than that of service. How many people will it bless? This is the question he asks."[24]

Lowell's niece Rosemary Fillmore Rhea remembers her uncle with great affection. She echoed what others had to say about him:

Lowell got along with everybody. He was the sweetest, dearest man that you could ever meet in your life. He was just too good to be true. He was one of these people who saw no evil, spoke no evil, thought no evil. He was in every ounce of him innocent. His whole life was Unity. He believed, he lived it. He was like his mother. He was totally dedicated to Unity work.[25]

Lowell's nephew Charles R. Fillmore, who succeeded him as head of Unity School in 1964, held him in high esteem. "The older I get," Charles

R. reported, "the more appreciation I have for my Uncle Lowell . . . In many ways he lived exactly what he believed."[26]

Marcus Bach, a professor of religion at Iowa State University and author of several books on the religions of the world, interviewed Lowell in the 1940s when Lowell was in his sixties. Bach characterized him with these well-chosen words:

Handsome, healthy, white-haired, this manager of the Unity School of Christianity is an interesting combination of a realistic business executive and the totally unrealistic naiveté of an ancient saint . . . There was a certain snap and substance about him not usually found in saints, ancient or modern. He wasn't showing off, or was he? No, he was too guileless, too genteel and too extraordinarily secure. His vitality had something to do with a physical healthfulness as well as a state of mind.[27]

Bach's observations on Lowell's daily habits indicate that he knew how to relax and enjoy life. Bach reported, "Lowell is an indoor type, a quiet-nature-walk kind of person, quite contented to settle for a vanilla soda, leisurely sipped and thoughtfully enjoyed."[28]

Lowell chose never to work in an office far removed from other workers. Charles R., who observed his work habits over the course of almost fifty years, recalled that Lowell "never wanted an office with walls around him . . . He wanted to be right out in the center of things."[29] Marcus Bach, who observed Lowell's office environment, commented: "His easily accessible office was pointed out to me just off the main lobby in the 917 Tracy building. If this office was easily accessible, so was Lowell. I wondered then, and I wonder now, whether this genial first son of the founders of Unity had ever heard about the image maker's admonition to keep a psychological distance between one's professional self and the public."[30]

Lowell maintained this same accessibility when Unity headquarters was moved from Kansas City to Unity Village. A Unity worker noted the lack of separation between Lowell and the staff, reporting:

Although he is responsible for the decisions of an organization with more than 800 workers, this man does not even have a private office. He sits at a desk in a corner of a large room on the ground floor of the Unity building, just to the right of the main entrance. Behind him are banks of books. Along side of him are many filing cabinets. On top of one of these he has a collection of dolls and animal figures that people have sent him from all parts of the globe. Any visitor who cares to can walk freely up to Lowell's desk and introduce himself, and to all of them he is simply "Lowell."[31]

Lowell reminded Marcus Bach of the Buddhist monks he had met at the Soji temple in Japan. Bach asked how the monks maintained their poise in the midst of the rush and turmoil of life in the workaday world. One of them told Bach that if there was any secret, it was that they never left their place of meditation. "He meant," stated Bach, "that although he was physically occupied elsewhere, his mind and consciousness were always in his center of spiritual orientation. He never left it, and it never left him." Bach felt that Lowell maintained this same level of consciousness. "There was something of this bilocation in [him]. Wherever he was, he was never far from his place of oneness with God." Bach saw Lowell as a rich man, but not in a material sense. "He was one of God's spiritual millionaires."[32]

Lowell was the editor of *Weekly Unity* magazine from its inaugural issue in 1909 until the magazine was discontinued in 1972, a remarkable span of sixty-three years. The magazine, which began as a newsletter for the local Unity Society of Practical Christianity, was transformed in 1911 into an instructional and inspirational magazine for the expanding national and international Unity audience. The Prosperity Bank plan was used to attract new subscribers, and the magazine grew quickly once the banks were put into the hands of subscribers. *Weekly Unity* grew from 35 subscribers in 1910 to 8,500 in 1912. Subscriptions doubled by 1915 and by 1920 there were 38,704 on the list, reaching 100,000 in 1923. By 1927, with a list of 160,900, it surpassed *Unity* magazine in numbers of subscribers. Throughout the remainder of Lowell's editorial career, *Weekly Unity* remained more popular with Unity readers than *Unity* magazine. By 1948, the year of Charles Fillmore's passing, *Weekly Unity,* with 220,000 subscriptions, had more than double the number of *Unity* subscribers. Considering that *Weekly Unity* appeared fifty-two times each year to *Unity's* dozen, *Weekly Unity* made four times as many reader contacts in 1948 as did *Unity* magazine.

Lowell Fillmore's column, "Things to Be Remembered," appeared in almost every issue of *Weekly Unity* during Lowell's sixty-three-year tenure as editor—an astonishing achievement. The essays in the early years were short, about five-hundred words, and less comprehensive than his later work. By the late 1920s, the columns increased significantly in size, doubling and tripling in length, and in quality. Only in his final years (he died in 1975 at ninety-three), with his mental faculties failing him, did the content decline. In almost every piece, he wrote about the immanence of God and how it was manifested in men and women. He regularly discussed the power of thought, both positive and negative, with specific applications to everyday situations in life. Invariably Lowell suggested affirmations that might be used to deal with specific problems. He continually stressed the need for increased understanding of the principles of truth.

Divine Nature and Human Nature

Lowell considered God's divine nature to be multifaceted, transcendent as well as immanent, personal as well as impersonal. Lowell acknowledged the all-powerfulness of God but did not dwell on this aspect of God's nature. Rarely did he reflect upon God as all-powerful, though when he did he was definite in his statements. "God is all there is," he observed, "and is all-powerful."[33] Much of Lowell's writing focused on the reality of the indwelling presence of God in humankind. He wanted to encourage those who had a strong desire to discover God to look inside themselves, to delve into their own hearts and minds. He strongly believed God dwelled there and could be found there. He declared: "God is within you, because your intelligence and your life and your power are within you. They are not outside you. You recognize God within yourself, and the better you understand Him the better you will understand the fullness of life."[34]

Lowell asserted that God dwelled in our inner consciousness or mind and manifested himself in our thoughts. He wrote: "God is everywhere present, but we must contact Him within us, because that is where our thoughts are. We can know only that which we are able to contact with our thoughts, and God, our Great Supplier, our very life, is close to us."[35]

Lowell equated the indwelling presence with the kingdom of heaven. He did not believe that heaven existed outside oneself, as most traditional Christians place it. He observed:

The first thing to realize is that heaven is not a place far distant but that it is a harmonious state of mind that each must endeavor to establish in himself. The kingdom of heaven is man's true estate . . . When you realize your unity with God and that you, the real you, are a son of God, you will begin to see that the kingdom of heaven is truly at hand.[36]

Lowell also considered God present not just within humankind, but present in all the universe, in all existence. He asked: "Where is God? He is here in His universe. You will find Him within you. He cannot be separated from His creation because He is one with all His good works. This is true unity."[37]

Lowell believed that God manifested himself primarily as principle operating through divine law. Divine law, which he equated with the law of God, operated impersonally in the universe and formed the basis for all other laws—physical, human, or spiritual. Lowell indicated: "God's divine laws or principles transcend the physical laws that men understand and try to obey in the physical world. His divine principles are at the service of all persons who will study them and become obedient to them."[38]

Lowell assigned a variety of impersonal attributes to God as principle—"God-qualities," as he characterized them. He observed: "The great Truth of the universe is that God is good and that God-qualities are everlasting. The God-qualities include love, peace, harmony, life, wisdom, power, abundance, forgiveness, purity, joy and beauty. These God-qualities are Truth. They are enduring."[39]

Lowell also equated God with the principles of truth, asserting, "God is Spirit, God is Truth."[40] "Truth," for Lowell, had nothing to do with the development of theoretical interpretations of reality based on empirical data. "Truth" had to do with spiritual reality. Lowell explained:

Truth is eternal and unchanging. We say that Truth is certain, pure and real; these are but man-made descriptions of Truth. Truth itself is a living thing and can be known only to those who contact it in Spirit. Truth is something that has existed from the beginning and is revealed to us as we grow in understanding. When I speak Truth I am talking about my real spiritual self, and that self must be perfect.[41]

In almost every piece he wrote, Lowell reflected upon the workings of the principle of divine love. "God is love," he stated over and over again.[42] Lowell was convinced that love was *the* fundamental part of God's nature, asserting: "If God seems to anyone to be cold when considered as Principle, it is because he has not made friends with the principle of love . . . To know God as the Principle of love, you must love, you must become a channel for its expression."[43]

Lowell saw no contradiction in his belief that God operates impersonally through divine law as well as personally in the universe. He directed his comments to those who had difficulty accepting this point of view, stating: "There should be no controversy between those who hold that God is Principle and those who believe that God is personal. We all agree that God is infinite, all-powerful, and everywhere present. Surely then He must be capable of manifesting Himself both as Principle and in a personal sort of way."[44]

In almost every "Remember" column, Lowell had something to say about the way God related personally to men and women. He wrote, for example: "When God-love is expressed by an individual it becomes personal. 'God is love,' and God's love, when it touches an individual capable of consciously receiving it, becomes as personal as any father's love for his children."[45]

A further manifestation of the personal relationship between God and humankind could be seen in their partnership in the work of the world. Lowell often suggested to his readers that God needed them, observing, "man is one of God's means of expressing himself."[46] To Lowell, God needs the cooperation of men and women so he can carry out his divine plan for the universe. He indicated: "God in His love made man in His own image and likeness to become a companion and helper to Him . . . God's intention, it seems to me, was to create a physical being who would be able to help Him bring His spiritual world into manifestation on the physical plane."[47]

While Lowell acknowledged that God relates to men and women on a personal basis, he believed that God himself is not a person, that while human characteristics are expressed in the personalities of men and women, it is inaccurate to think of God as having a personality. Lowell explained: "If God were only a person He would be greatly limited in His scope of expression . . . Because man is masquerading as a personality is no reason for him to try to limit God to so small a field of activity."[48]

Lowell was particularly concerned that men and women view God as judgmental, vengeful, and expressing anger. In disagreeing with those who attributed emotional characteristics to God, Lowell reasserted his belief that God is principle. He observed: "Many people have developed strange ideas concerning the nature of God, and His power. They have felt that God is moved by emotions similar to human emotions, and that at times He cracks down with His vengeance on those who oppose Him. This is contrary to the nature of God, for God is love."[49]

God as Holy Spirit was in Lowell's view a further manifestation of the personal connection between God and humankind. Lowell believed that the Spirit of truth inspires men and women and aids them in developing spiritual understanding. He observed: "God speaks in universal language through his spiritual minister, the Spirit of Truth . . . The Spirit of Truth brings us the truth direct from God in a language that we can understand. Every person in the wide world who sincerely believes in God can be taught by the Spirit of Truth."[50]

Lowell viewed humankind as created in the image and likeness of God, with God-like powers in potential at birth. These divine attributes need to be developed, however, and in his opinion, the purpose of human life is to bring them into manifestation.

CREATED IN THE "IMAGE" AND "LIKENESS"

Lowell believed that, as stated in Scripture, men and women are created in the image and likeness of God. It seemed logical to Lowell that since God himself was perfect, human beings must by nature possess the same God-like perfection. Lowell declared: "Spiritual man, created in the image and likeness of God is perfect, good, and wise also . . . We must remember that God made man perfect in the beginning and that perfection is still the reality back of him."[51]

Lowell was under no illusion that humankind's God-like powers were fully developed. He recognized that divine attributes were in potential only. Men and women have much spiritual work to do before they can manifest their true God-like nature. Lowell noted: "We are working toward our salvation as a race slowly and cautiously. We are unfolding slowly toward the goal of the perfect man who was made in the image and likeness of God."[52]

Lowell believed that men and women were "threefold beings" consisting of spirit, soul, and body. He observed: "When Unity speaks of the Spirit in man, we mean the Christ, the true Son of God, and when the soul is mentioned, we refer to the mental and emotional part of us, including memory as well as the conscious and the subconscious mind. Unity thinks of the body as the physical part of us, the vehicle through which the Spirit and soul find expression."[53]

Lowell believed that each of the three parts needs to be perfected for humankind to experience its God-like nature. He commented: "In order to be perfect as God expects him to be, man must become conscious of these three necessary members of one harmonious whole. . . . Soul, spirit and body must be unified and harmonized with no lack of understanding and cooperation between them if man is to express his Son of God perfection."[54]

Humankind's principle resource or instrument for attaining God-like perfection, according to Lowell, is the conscious mind, an aspect of the soul. The mind, he believed, is extremely powerful and, if used properly, can unify spirit, soul, and body. Lowell believed that Jesus, through spiritual work during his lifetime, perfected the conscious mind and "became unified with Christ."[55] He was convinced that humankind would ultimately unify soul, spirit, and body and reach the same level of consciousness attained by Jesus. By following the example of Jesus and developing the Christ Consciousness, men and women, according to Lowell, become "new creatures." Their minds and hearts are "brought back to their original vitality and purity by the new life of Christ."[56] As men and women fully incorporate the mind of Christ, they express the attributes of God, which Lowell characterized as "love, wisdom, life, harmony, peace, joy, strength and power."[57] By doing so, they demonstrate "prosperity and health" in their lives.[58] The purpose of human life, according to Lowell, is to realize our Christ-like nature and, by doing so, to realize the existence of the indwelling presence. "The goal of every man is to become the son of God in manifestation," Lowell proclaimed. "Christ in you and me is our hope of glory."[59]

Lowell believed that humankind as a whole is still deeply flawed and had much ground to cover to reach the Christ perfection. He indicated: "The human race is still in its infancy. Judging by the newspaper headlines, we have not ceased to be barbarians. We continue to love war and strife more than peace and harmony . . . Much of the human race is still in the savage state as far as spiritual progress is concerned."[60]

One might ask why, if human beings are created in the image and likeness of God, was Jesus—as Lowell describes him—the only "typical expression of this perfect man that God created."[61] What's more, we might ask why, more than two thousand years after the birth of Jesus, do men and women remain in the "kindergarten state of mind"?[62]

Lowell attributed the snail's pace of human development primarily to the power of negative thought. These thoughts included fear, doubt, worry, greed, inharmony, anger, sorrow, hate, willfulness, selfishness, ambition, envy, and jealousy. Lowell believed that negative thought has a powerful effect on the human condition. He declared: "It is the negative thought habits of the human race that are keeping the affairs of the world in turmoil . . . Thoughts of hate, fear, greed, revenge, and other human emotions are breaking up the world today in whirlwinds of destruction."[63]

Among negative thoughts, Lowell believed that fear was probably the most damaging. Lowell observed, "Fear is about the worst troublemaker in the world today, and more of our troubles than we realize are caused by it."[64]

He felt that negative attitudes are equally inhibiting and are often based on social conditioning that has gone on for generations. Lowell commented: "The race mind contains many ideas that are not in harmony with Truth, but they have been passed along and taken for granted because they have been in the minds of our ancestors for many thousands of years."[65] Had Lowell been writing today, he might have used Jung's term, "the collective unconscious," instead of "the race mind."

To Lowell, the Devil symbolized the negative conditioning that had so inhibited spiritual development. He explained: "The Devil is the state of mind that is averse to the perfect creation. The Devil is really the embodiment of your wrong attitude toward life, and he can be overcome only when you eliminate your adverse state of mind and put in its place a Christlike state of mind."[66]

Lowell believed that unhealthy states of mind, wrong attitudes, and negative thoughts and feelings are all possible because humankind possesses free will. "Man is a free agent," Lowell pointed out. Man is created "in the image and likeness" of God.[67] Therefore, men and women can use that freedom "for good or evil."[68] Lowell reported:

"Because he is free every person may choose whether he will accept God's good creation and enjoy it, or refuse it and accept instead fear, misunderstanding, worry, doubt, greed, hatred, and other thoughts that create discord, poverty, sadness, strife and sickness in his life."[69]

Lowell acknowledged that free will is essential if humankind is to qualify as "created in the image and likeness of God." He believed that God provides men and women with free will for a purpose. Freedom of choice is a necessary condition for spiritual development. God gave humankind free will, Lowell observed, "to develop their inner powers, to give each one full opportunity to become conscious of his unity with God, and to realize the full meaning and joy of unity."[70]

Putting on the Mind of Christ

According to Lowell, people overcome negative conditions, develop themselves spiritually, put on the mind of Christ, and realize their God-like potential by leading lives in accordance with the will of God and by observing the precepts of divine law. For Lowell, the will of God and divine law were one and the same. "God's will works through his laws," Lowell observed. The principles of divine law, he noted, "are in essence the will of God for us."[71] Lowell believed it was equally necessary for men and women to devote themselves to knowing and understanding both the will of God and the principles of divine law.[72]

Lowell believed that people comply with the will of God and with divine law by engaging in a variety of spiritual practices. These include: disciplining the mind, using affirmations and denials, engaging in prayer, going into the silence, having faith in the power of God, giving divine love, practicing forgiveness, being joyful, living in the now, and educating themselves in spiritual matters. Lowell never stressed the need to develop twelve faculties of mind or "twelve powers" to comply with divine law and manifest the Christ Consciousness. In this regard, his presentation of the Unity teaching differed markedly from that of his parents.

Lowell believed that compliance with the will of God and divine law results in a rich, full life characterized by prosperity and good health. He urged Unity students to "Encourage faith, fearlessness, love, goodwill and joy. Open wide the gate to them; let them come in day or night. They will bring you health and prosperity."[73]

It should be noted that Lowell defined prosperity broadly. "Prosperity" meant much more to him than the mere acquisition of material goods and the making of money. He advised Unity students to "Believe in prosperity and think prosperity, not of mere money-getting, which destroys true prosperity, but of the larger blessings which include all things necessary to your happiness and well-being, both spiritual and material."[74]

Lowell believed that the will of God is always directed toward human well-being. God's will, Lowell indicated, "is that man shall be well, happy and prosperous."[75]

He felt it essential that men and women live in harmony with God's will. He indicated: "When a man is willing to let God's will be done in his life, he permits divine order to become established. When he cooperates with God's will, he opens the way for God's abundance of good things to flow into his life."[76]

Lowell believed that men and women who follow the dictates of their own selfish human will rather than God's will cause themselves nothing but trouble, that they deprive themselves of any chance of realizing their

God-like potential. Lowell noted: "When a man follows the dictates of his own personal will, he often brings confusion into his affairs, especially when his will is selfish and lacking in consideration of others."[77]

Much of Lowell's writing was devoted to encouraging Unity students to comply with the will of God and with divine law. He outlined a variety of spiritual practices that would help students in this endeavor.

RIGHT THINKING

Lowell believed that the mind, if used correctly, is a powerful transforming instrument. "We are given the power to think," he declared, "in order to better ourselves and rise above difficulties."[78] Lowell believed that the mind needs to be trained and disciplined. "Happy is the man," he indicated, "who by right thinking is daily strengthening the good in his life, and creating new and brighter things for himself."[79] He felt that men and women benefit greatly when they eliminate negative thoughts, attaining "health, happiness, and prosperity."[80] He told Unity students that success in life, in both the spiritual and material worlds, was dependent upon gaining control of thought, stating:

Your thoughts are like a great nation of people dwelling within you. These thought people must have supervision and guidance. If they are not directed and trained they will run helterskelter into confusion and discord, wasting your energy and substance. But when they are trained and kept in order they are capable of quickly overcoming the difficulties that confront you in the world. If you would have a happy, healthy, harmonious life, you must rein in your thoughts.[81]

Lowell explained that the process of controlling thought begins with the belief that it is possible to do so. Awareness of thoughts is an essential next step:

The first step in controlling our thoughts is to believe that it is possible to control them, and the next step is to desire to control them, and to watch them continually. As you begin to put constructive thoughts and words in place of negative and destructive ones, you will notice an improvement in your general outlook upon life. Conditions will grow more prosperous, you will feel happier, and you will grow more healthy.[82]

Lowell identified the negative thoughts that needed to be observed and replaced. "Doubt, fear, worry, jealousy, hatred, and the like are all troublemakers. Do not let them in," he advised. "As the gatekeeper you must learn how to keep them out." Putting on the mind of Christ was an important help. "You must be firm," he declared. "You must be fired with an intense desire to let the Christ manifest in you."[83]

Lowell described the procedure by which the mind was renewed:

You will conform your thinking to the Christ standard when you replace thoughts of hate with thoughts of love; thoughts of pride with thoughts of humility; thoughts of impurity with thoughts of purity; thoughts of ignorance with thoughts of wisdom; thoughts of unforgiveness with thoughts of forgiveness; thoughts of discord with thoughts of harmony; thoughts of sorrow with thoughts of joy and thanksgiving; thoughts of doubt with thoughts of faith; and thoughts of death with thoughts of life.[84]

Lowell believed that this approach held great promise. "By this procedure," he noted, "a man gradually redeems his thoughts and rebuilds his mind and body until he becomes a 'new creature.'"[85]

Lowell recognized that disciplining the mind requires effort and commitment. "Making these changes in your method of thinking," he acknowledged, "will take practice." Important benefits accrue to those who succeed in engaging in "right thinking." "You will understand," Lowell promised Unity students, "that you are truly a spiritual being and have dominion over all things."[86]

AFFIRMATIONS

In the work of disciplining the mind, Lowell considered affirmations, essential. Lowell had definite ideas on the nature and purpose of affirmations. He believed that by using them correctly we can change our thoughts and attitudes and, by doing so, improve our circumstances. He explained: "An affirmation of Truth is an exercise for the purpose of remodeling our thinking processes. It is not a magic statement that in some mysterious way takes hold of material objects and tosses them about. The affirmation changes our thought habits, and these change our outer conditions."[87]

Lowell cited a particularly powerful affirmation, one he apparently used himself, which he believed helped overcome adversity. He testified:

No matter what conditions may be in my life, no matter what problems I may have to meet, I can overcome them by taking such thought as this: "There is but One Presence and One Power in my life, God Omnipotent." If I desire this attitude to be a ruling trend of thought, it will be so. . . . If I expect this affirmation of One Presence to produce results for me I must be persistent in holding it and in letting it become a real part of my life . . . My success in overcoming adverse conditions will depend on my ability to become unified with this thought.[88]

Lowell pointed out that even though an affirmation "contradicted material conditions as they appeared to be," the affirmative statement itself was not false. A person might, for example, affirm that *I am in perfect health* when in fact the person is riddled with cancer. The affirmation, according to Lowell, "would be a true statement of conditions as they are in God's plan."[89]

Lowell wanted it understood that affirmations could do nothing to change the mind of God. Affirmations are not for petitioning God for help; their sole function is to "help the devotee to ascend into a new state of mind."[90] Lowell reported: "Affirmations are not for the purpose of changing God but for bringing our mind into a perfect understanding of our true nature, and thus lining up our thinking so that it will be constructive and produce good results in our life."[91]

Lowell indicated that an affirmation becomes more effective through repetition. He pointed out: "It accumulates power by being said over and over. . . . An affirmation of Truth organizes the scattered powers of the mind and directs them into one channel. Helter-skelter thoughts about this, that, and the other will not accomplish much constructive good, but when they are lined up by the continued repetition of a truth, they do wonders."[92]

It was important that an affirmation reflect more than a mere wish. Strong conviction was required for an affirmation to be effective. Lowell explained:

If an affirmation is spoken without conviction it is like a wish instead of a prayer and lacks vitality. . . . If I repeat the affirmation "God is my health," while at the same time I am thinking how wonderful it would be if God would really become my health, I am making a very weak affirmation. I am expressing a wish instead of sending forth a dynamic prayer.[93]

Lowell considered I AM statements of truth to be particularly useful affirmations. He indicated that, according to the prophet Moses, I AM is the name of God. Lowell described the power of the I AM as he viewed it: "'I Am' statements of Truth are those that proclaim the truth about God . . . When we speak words in connection with 'I Am,' we set something in motion, down deep within ourselves, that produces results in harmony with the words spoken."[94]

Lowell cited some particularly helpful I AM statements. These included "I am life. I am love. I am wisdom. I am power. I am strength. I am good. I am that I am, and there is no one besides me."[95]

Lowell recognized that one could easily become discouraged using affirmations. He assured Unity students that affirmations produce results if used faithfully and correctly. He stated: "It may seem to you that it is like lifting yourself by your bootstraps to change your life by affirmations, but you can prove that it works. Use affirmations faithfully, with a relaxed mind and you will find yourself gradually lifting your whole thought process out of ignorance and discord and into wisdom and harmony."[96]

DENIALS

Lowell believed that denials are useful in counteracting negative states, cleansing the mind of unhelpful thoughts, and preparing the way for affirmations. Denials, he suggested, are to be used to indicate that negative thought has no power over the mind and no capacity for creating negative circumstances. Denials are inextricably tied to affirmations. "Denials should be followed by affirmations," Lowell counseled.[97] He explained: "The dish should be cleansed before we put food into it. After we have cleared an erroneous idea from our mind a true idea should be put into the vacant place. This is done by making a definite, good affirmation."[98]

While he thought that denials were to be used less frequently than affirmations, Lowell viewed them as equally important in elevating consciousness. He declared: "Denials and affirmations are the two mighty tools of the mind, and if they are rightly used they bring health, happiness, and prosperity."[99]

PRAYER

In Lowell's view, prayer and affirmations in some ways have similar goals. He believed that, like affirmations, prayer is "calculated to change ourselves by first changing our attitudes."[100] Lowell saw prayer, however, as having a broader purpose: prayer is directed toward "finding our unity with God and His creation."[101] It was, therefore, "the greatest power in the world."[102]

Lowell believed that prayer is primarily about giving thanks. "We should always be giving thanks on general principles,"[103] he declared. Lowell placed great value on constantly giving thanks. He commented: "Giving thanks is a very effective way of aiming high because it lifts one's thoughts above selfish desires to an appreciation of spiritual worth. When we are thankful we open the way for more good to come to us. It is praiseworthy to direct our thanks to men, but we can look still higher and offer our thanks to God."[104]

Lowell indicated his belief that we should give thanks even though that which we seek has not yet been received. He explained:

When we give thanks we should do so realizing that we have already received. We should not withhold our thanks because appearances indicate that we have nothing to be thankful for. As we cultivate the spirit of thankfulness, we at the same time develop our potential good. Our good has been ready for us all the time, waiting for us to accept it. The first step in accepting it is to give thanks for it.[105]

Lowell distinguished between a large prayer and a smaller one. He noted: "When your prayer is backed only by a personal desire it is little ... The little prayer asks for something personal and usually outlines the way in which the answer is to come. We limit the power of God's wisdom by working out the details in the prayers for him. When we leave the method of answering entirely in God's hands we pray the larger prayer."[106]

Lowell believed that repetitive prayer was very helpful, mainly because of its impact on the soul of the one doing the praying. He commented: "By repeating our prayer many times we do not please God but we discipline and educate our own soul to appreciate and understand better the richness of the ever-present kingdom of God."[107]

Lowell's expanded notion of what constitutes prayer was outlined in the following statement: "Thanksgiving is praying. Basking in the sunshine of God's goodness is prayer. Loving God is praying. Doing your daily tasks for the glory of God is praying. Having faith that God is taking care of your life, your substance, and your family is praying."[108]

Success in life is in part the result of how well we pray, according to Lowell. He noted, "Success grows out of praise, thanksgiving, and constructive thoughts, words and work."[109]

GOING INTO THE SILENCE

One of the most effective ways of discovering the will of God in Lowell's view is to "go into the silence." The silence is a place where one can, according to Lowell, "listen more attentively and more obediently to the still, small voice of God."[110] He urged his readers to go into the silence because close contact with God was possible there. "God speaks to you in the silence," he told Unity students. "When confused personal emotions are quieted it is possible for clear, sane thoughts to come to you from a higher source than the world of appearance."[111] Lowell was convinced that sitting in the silence speeds up progress along the spiritual path. He indicated: "All our earthly problems can be solved in the silence if we go direct to headquarters and speak the truth about them in the presence of God."[112]

Lowell described what it was like for him to sit quietly and listen. He reported:

There is a stillness that is more eloquent than oratory, sweeter than a love song, and more satisfying than a feast. It is the stillness that a person finds when he quiets his personal desires, worries, ambitions and grievances and listens to God. A person enters the stillness when he stops for a time the flow of his thoughts about his affairs and takes his attention from the outer sounds and mundane interests to listen to the still, small voice of God within him.[113]

Lowell provided a detailed description of how he focused his mind as he sat quietly communing with the infinite. He reported:

I first try to relax my mind. I choose a time to practice when I am not likely to be disturbed, and I sit or lie quietly in a restful place, thinking at first as little about my physical body as possible. All good comes from God, therefore my first step is to go to headquarters by concentrating my attention upon the sublime truth that God is omnipresent goodness. I spend a little time in thinking about how wonderful it is that God's love is present in me and through me and all about me. I let the vision of his loving presence unfold before my inner sight. I feel His love like a great ocean in which I am immersed. I feel happy and contented in the assurance that the presence of His love is protecting and harmonizing me. I place all my earthly affairs lovingly in the Father's hand, and I trust Him to look after all these things for me while I take time out to make a business of relaxing.[114]

Lowell believed that the way to perceive truth principles was intuitively, while in a quiet, meditative state of mind, rather than through any one of the five senses. He commented: "Truth is really more than a doctrine of a church or a creed, for it is something that underlies and is more important than any creed, doctrine or dogma. We cannot know the eternal verities of Truth with our physical senses, but we can, in the quietness and confidence, know it in our intuitive perception of what is right in the sight of God."[115]

Lowell urged Unity students to spend time alone each day in the silence. He advised: "Spend some time each day, if it is no more than five minutes in the morning and five minutes in the evening getting acquainted with God. Become absolutely quiet as you listen, for the words of God are in your heart."[116]

FAITH

Lowell described faith as "the inner eye of the mind." Through faith, he indicated, "we see beyond the things that are revealed to us by the five senses." Most important of all, he asserted, "It is through faith that we find God . . . and through faith we understand that life is eternal."[117] Lowell believed that strong faith is required to live one's life according to the will of God and in keeping with divine law. He stated: "Faith is a most important part of our spiritual make-up . . . It is only through faith that we can know God; it is through faith that we contact His wonderful blessings at their source, and it is as a result of faith that His blessing finally becomes actually manifest to our physical senses."[118]

DIVINE LOVE

To Lowell, one of the most effective ways men and women can follow the will of God, obey divine law, and realize their God-like potential is by manifesting divine love. Lowell wrote extensively about love, which he described as "the most powerful force in the world . . . the greatest expression of God's power in the Universe."[119] Lowell viewed divine love as an aspect of divine law. He explained: "When we love God with all our heart, soul, and mind we are cooperating with the Creator in the most perfect way possible, and our affairs will then come under the perfect law of love. In loving, we comply with all good laws."[120]

Lowell believed that many benefits accrue to those who fulfill the law of divine love. He indicated:

There is a law of love that, when invoked, will free a person from the dire consequences of his past mistakes. It may be stated in these familiar words, "Forgive, and ye shall be forgiven." The law of love will help us get even with our enemies by giving them good for evil, thus terminating the bad results that come from bad causes. The only way we can absolutely destroy an enemy is to turn him into a friend.[121]

Lowell distinguished between divine love and the love that exists between persons, declaring that divine love was by far the most important. He explained: "We often speak of 'divine' love, 'personal' love, and 'human' love as though there were many kinds of love. While there may be no harm in speaking of different manifestations of love as kinds of love, we should remember that there is in Truth but one kind of love: divine love."[122]

Lowell felt that "personal, sentimental love" not only fails to manifest the qualities of divine love but can, under certain circumstances, cause more harm than good. He indicated: "The love of man is changeable because it is controlled by his personal will and it therefore falls short of the divine idea or principle of love. Personal love is often mixed with egotism, jealousy, unforgiveness and various selfish motives."[123]

Lowell had definite ideas on how one might become more loving; he gave the following advice to those who wanted to express more divine love:

If you feel the need of more of God's love in your life, the first thing to do is to begin to practice love by feeling more friendly toward everyone and everything, putting this good feeling in place of envy, hate, jealousy and peevishness. When you have practiced expressing divine love, you will find that you are able to recognize love everywhere and that all people and all things are filled with love and goodwill toward you. You will wonder what has happened to the world to make it so loving.[124]

Lowell believed that the best way to express divine love is through service to others. He indicated: "We find that service is the true expression of Godlove in every walk of life—in the business world, in the professions, and in the home . . . Service is the most important thing in life. Through service we express or use the good that God has given us."[125]

FORGIVENESS

Lowell believed that we take a major step in realizing our God-like potential when we forgive others for any wrongdoing. "Forgiveness releases the power of God in you," Lowell declared. He believed that forgiveness is another aspect of divine law. In describing "the law of forgiveness," Lowell commented: "When we forgive others we set our own hearts right. When we forgive others we open the way for divine justice to work in our lives. Our forgiveness will set us free from the law of condemnation and will help other evil-doers to be free eventually."[126]

Lowell believed that forgiveness produces many benefits, not just for the person or persons who were being forgiven, but in particular for the one doing the forgiving. "The act of forgiving," he declared, "benefits the forgiver more than the one he forgives."[127]

BEING JOYFUL

Lowell viewed joy as a powerful "spiritual asset." Joy is present in our lives, according to Lowell, to the extent that we are in touch with the divine within. "When a person continually contacts the Spirit of Truth," Lowell observed, "he is filled with joy all the time."[128] Joy helps us realize our God-like potential because, according to Lowell, "joy really helps us to find the Christ."[129]

LIVING IN THE NOW

Lowell stressed the importance of living in the now, believing that as we develop our divine potential, our minds will be focused on the present rather than on the past or the future. God lives in the now, and so must we. Lowell surmised: "In Truth there is only the now. The Spirit of God does not change, but is the same yesterday, today and forever. God lives in the eternal now, unaffected by time, place or events. Should we not continually rejoice in the consciousness of God's loving presence which gives us an everlasting foundation of stability and firmness?"[130]

SPIRITUAL EDUCATION

Lowell believed that men and women need to educate themselves in spiritual matters if they are to learn how to use their minds productively, express divine love, and find the divine within when going into the silence. Lowell stressed this point on several occasions, stating: "Spiritual education is a process of awakening and drawing forth our inner spiritual powers, which God has placed within us to find and use . . . The most important part of our education comes when we enter into our inner chamber, and shut the door against worldly, negative thoughts so that we can find the Truth that is within us."[131]

Lowell believed that the study of truth principles is necessary for all who want to manifest their God-like potential. He wrote: "A definite course of study in Truth is very beneficial. This course of study should be trained into our everyday life through coordination with our thoughts, words and deeds. We must learn to relax and let Truth work through us. This requires faithful practice."[132]

Lowell indicated that one of Unity School's primary responsibilities was to provide students with an opportunity for education in spiritual matters. He reported:

"Unity feels that no greater work can be done than lifting up the individual's point of view to a realization that peace, righteousness, love and good will . . . will bring more happiness into his life than any of the negative ways of thinking."[133]

IMPACT OF THE LIFE OF JESUS

Almost all of Lowell's weekly columns, "Things to Be Remembered," contained references to the life, teachings, or spiritual development of Jesus of Nazareth. Jesus was highly significant for Lowell because Jesus, in Lowell's view, was the only person in the history of mankind to realize his divine powers. "Jesus influenced the history of the world," Lowell stated, "more than any other man."[134] Lowell asserted that Jesus' mission on earth "was to show all men how to find and express their Christ-self just as He did."[135] Lowell continually commented on Jesus' achievement in becoming Christ Conscious, noting, "Jesus unified the perfect spiritual man with the manifest man, causing the manifest man to have eternal life."[136]

Jesus was able to achieve this dramatic result, according to Lowell, because he followed the precepts of divine law, and allowed the will of God to work in him. Lowell observed: "Jesus demonstrated to all men the right use of God's eternal laws. He taught that it is possible for any man to follow Him into the kingdom of God. He promised that His followers will be able to do even greater things than He did if they will follow him in using the laws aright."[137]

REGENERATION AND REINCARNATION

Like his father and his mother, Lowell was convinced, based on his interpretation of the life of Jesus, that it was possible for men and women to follow the example of Jesus and overcome physical death. He did not shy away from this belief, even in the face of his mother and father's deaths. He never wavered from it in his sixty-plus years of writing spiritual essays for *Weekly Unity*. "If the body is lifted up, its cells spiritualized, and it and the soul unified with the Spirit," Lowell declared, "it will not die."[138]

Lowell was firm in his conviction that to be fully human, men and women must commit themselves to this goal. He declared:

We must follow Jesus Christ in the regeneration and unify our body and soul with the Christ within us, thus bringing our whole being—spirit, soul, and body—into perfect manifestation of a child of God . . . The life of the Son of God must enter into our body and soul through the Christ Spirit so that we can prove that we are indeed sons of God.[139]

Men and women could regenerate their bodies and overcome physical death if, like Jesus, they conformed their lives to the principles of divine law. Lowell indicated:

When one aligns his life with Spirit he no longer comes under the law of destruction. . . . In divine law there is no death; man's spirit never dies. When man realizes and proves to himself that he is in reality a spiritual being, composed of spirit, soul, and body, he will break himself of the habit of losing his body, and it will become an expression of undying Spirit.[140]

The key to bodily regeneration, Lowell indicated, is steadfast belief. It is absolutely essential that those who seek to regenerate their bodies display deep faith. He declared: "The resurrecting power of God is within everyone ready to cooperate with him who believes in it. We must believe in God's life as a reality; we must believe in God's life as undying; we must believe in Godlife as having power over death."[141]

Lowell believed that those who fail to regenerate their bodies in this lifetime will be given another chance. "Those who fail to overcome death in the present body," Lowell explained, "will be given an opportunity to try again and again in new physical bodies."[142] Lowell indicated that reincarnation takes place to fulfill the principles of divine law. He observed: "Because people insist on letting their bodies die, the law of life has to bring millions of new bodies into the world to take their place. This is because God's life is eternal and if man refused to go along with it the life must find a new body to express itself in."[143]

In several passages, Lowell expressed his conviction that men and women will reincarnate until they achieve the Christ Consciousness, become unified with God, and overcome physical death. He observed: "Spirit and soul live on, and since they have not gained control of the powers of the body and attained perfection, they must seek a new body to go through a new life experience on earth in order to grow toward the perfection that God conceived for man in the beginning."[144]

Unlike his mother and father, who stressed the importance of sexual abstinence as a necessary precondition for bodily regeneration, Lowell does not mention sex in his writing. Nothing in Lowell's writing indicated that he believed that refraining from sexual activity was a necessary first step in the regeneration of the body.

CHAPTER 5

Unity's Spiritual and Intellectual Antecedents

The teaching of the Unity founding authors appears to have been fed by two streams of spiritual information and ideas. One began with Emanuel Swedenborg and Franz Anton Mesmer and flowed through the works of Ralph Waldo Emerson, Phineas P. Quimby, Warren Felt Evans, and the Theosophists. The other originated with Mary Baker Eddy and was filtered through the lenses of Christian Science dissidents Eugene B. Weeks, Joseph Adams, and Emma Curtis Hopkins.

Charles Fillmore acknowledged that the Unity teaching was derived from widely divergent sources when he noted: "We have been readers among all the schools of thought and we find good in all of them . . . We do not claim to have discovered any new truths, nor have had any special revelation of truth. There is truth in every religion. It is my privilege to take Truth from any source, put it into my religion, and make it a fundamental rule of action in my life."[1]

It appears that the Fillmores, in developing their doctrine, were spiritual eclectics, using intuition to pull together the mix of teachings that they called "Unity," which, for them, represented spiritual truth.

Emanuel Swedenborg: Seer and Mystic

In describing the origins of the Unity spiritual teachings, it is impossible to ignore the work of the Swedish spiritual philosopher Emanuel Swedenborg (1688–1772), even though only a few references are made to his works in Unity publications. J. Gordon Melton, author of *The Encyclopedia of American Religions* (Detroit: Gale, 1988) includes Swedenborg as one of five authors who influenced the leaders of New Thought.[1] Others were Ralph Waldo Emerson, Warren Felt Evans, Phineas P. Quimby, and Emma Curtis Hopkins. In his *Religious History of the American People* (New Haven: Yale University Press, 1972), Sydney E. Ahlstrom recognized the impact Swedenborg's work had on religion and spirituality in nineteenth-century America, noting: "His influence was everywhere: In Transcendentalism and at Brook Farm, in Spiritualism and the free-love movement, in the craze for communitarian experiments, in faith healing, mesmerism, and a half-dozen medical cults, among great intellectuals, crude charlatans, and innumerable frontier quacks."[2]

Stephen Larsen, a Ph.D. psychologist on the faculty of Ulster County Community College and author of *The Shaman's Doorway* (New York: Harper & Row, 1976), credited Swedenborg with being an important catalyst for the nineteenth-century mental healing movement of which Unity School of Christianity was a part. Larsen commented: "Swedenborg's visionary worldview became seminal in a number of healing systems, from Christian Science to homeopathy, all of which emphasize the dependence of physical health on the inner or causal level of spiritual well-being."[3]

In his book *Representative Men,* Ralph Waldo Emerson commented on the "genius of Swedenborg" and credited him with being, "the largest of all modern souls."[4] Emerson observed:

Swedenborg styles himself in the title pages of his books, "Servant of the Lord Jesus Christ," and by force of intellect, and in effect, he is the last Father of the Church, and is not likely to have a successor. The moral insight of Swedenborg, the correction of popular errors, the announcement of ethical laws, take him out of a comparison with any other major writer and entitle him to a place among the lawgivers of mankind.[5]

Charles Fillmore read the works of Swedenborg and found them "consistent with modern metaphysical teaching."[6] The works of Swedenborg's were listed among recommended books in the first issue of *Modern Thought* magazine in April 1889. Swedenborg's literary output during the twenty years of his life that he devoted to writing spiritual works was prodigious. His writings, coupled with biographies and commentaries, today occupy a full library shelf.

Although the Fillmores referred only briefly to the works of the Swedish seer and mystic, his teachings had an impact on their work. The spiritual ideas of Swedenborg that ultimately filtered through to the Fillmores can be summarized as follows:

GOD IS A TRANSCENDENT, all-powerful being. God is also immanent in humankind as men and women are the receptacles of divine energy. Their very life principle is the indwelling presence of God. Men and women possess free will because they have been created in the image and likeness of God. Everything that manifests in the physical world has an inward spiritual cause (the doctrine of correspondences). The health of the human body corresponds to what is going on spiritually in the person. Intuition rather than reason is the proper guide in ascertaining spiritual truth. Souls enter a spiritual world after death in which there is continued opportunity for spiritual attainment. Heaven in the Christian sense, as a place where there is constant praising and celebrating the Lord, does not exist. Nor is there a place of eternal damnation called hell where there is unending suffering.

Franz Anton Mesmer: The Healing Power of the Mind

Born on May 23, 1734, at Iznang on Lake Constance, Franz Anton Mesmer (1734–1815) was the son of an Episcopal gatekeeper. He studied divinity and became a doctor of philosophy before moving to Vienna, where he studied medicine. At age thirty-three he was granted the degree of doctor of medicine from the University of Vienna and went into private practice in Vienna. By nature interested in research and experimentation, Mesmer was inspired by the work of the Swiss physician Paracelsus (1493–1541) and his disciples, who believed that magnets could be used to facilitate health by redistributing the body's magnetic fluids.[1] Using iron magnets in treating his patients, Mesmer, at the outset of his work, applied them to the throat, the heart, or whichever portion of the body needed relief. He assumed that health was restored as the body's fluids were brought into balance.[2]

As many of his clients reported amazing recoveries, news of his successes spread. He was soon overrun with clients. People came from all over Austria to be touched by the miraculous magnet. Within a short time, hundreds of patients testified to the efficacy of his method in restoring health. Mesmer was so pleased with his initial success that he called magnetism the "invisible fire" of Hippocrates.[3] Further experimentation, however, led Mesmer to realize that the cure was not due to the lifeless mineral he held in his hand, but to human touch itself. It was he himself, the magnetizer, he concluded, that restored health.[4] Like Van Helmut (1577–1644)[5] before him, Mesmer discovered that he could relieve symptoms by making passes over the afflicted parts of the patient's body with his hands alone.[6]

The mental healing movement that blossomed in the United States in the mid-nineteenth century grew, in part, out of the research and experimentation of this Enlightenment-era Viennese medical doctor. While this tradition was well established in Western and Eastern mysticism, Mesmer and his followers are credited with developing the first modern scientific method of mental healing.[7] Approaching their work from outside a religious or mystical context, they demonstrated the impact that one mind could have upon another for the purpose of restoring health.

Leaders of the mental healing movement in the United States (including Warren Felt Evans, Phineas P. Quimby, Mary Baker Eddy, Emma Curtis Hopkins, and the Fillmores, as well as the Theosophists and the Spiritualists) were indebted, in one way or another, to Franz Anton Mesmer. Modern twentieth-century psychotherapy is, in part, derived from his discoveries.[8] Charles Fillmore credited Mesmer with providing one of the proofs "that the mind can produce conditions in the mental world that ultimate in the material world."[9] Mesmer's theory of "animal magnetism" or "mesmerism"—as it was popularly labeled until the word "hypnotism" was substituted for it by medical science in the 1840s—can be defined as the healing power that suggestion, words, persuasion, and commands can exert for curative purposes, particularly for those illnesses which affect the mind-body interface.

Ralph Waldo Emerson:
The Transcendentalist Connection

Transcendentalism was a nineteenth-century literary, philosophical, and spiritual movement that the essays of New England sage Ralph Waldo Emerson (1803–1882) did much to popularize. In their magazines from *Modern Thought* to *Unity*, the Fillmores recommended Emerson's essays. Quotations from Emerson's works appeared in issue after issue. Unity students were urged to become familiar with his writings. The Fillmores declared:

All students of metaphysics should read Emerson. His writings contain the essence of all the higher thoughts that are now being lavishly given to the world through

Christian Science, Metaphysics, Theosophy and the various systems of soul culture
... Emerson anticipates the modern school of metaphysics and gives voice in his
essays to all the truths which have been formulated in Divine Science. His writings
are growing more and more popular daily and no metaphysical student should be
without his works.[1]

Emerson was born in 1803 in Boston into a family with deep roots in
Massachusetts.[2] His mother was the daughter of a prosperous Boston dis-
tiller. His father was a liberal Boston minister from a family that had produced clergymen in eight previous generations. Only eight when his father
died, Emerson had the good fortune to be raised by and around women,
including his mother, of notable intellectual and spiritual accomplishments. Emerson considered his aunt (his father's sister, Mary Moody
Emerson, who deeply influenced him as he was growing up) one of the
most brilliant women in New England.

Emerson attended the eminent Boston Latin School and, following in
the family tradition, studied for the ministry and graduated from Harvard.
He was ordained in 1826 at age twenty-three and was appointed the junior minister at the Unitarian Second Church in Boston. He quickly established himself as an eloquent, inspirational speaker. He was less successful,
however, in fulfilling duties related to pastoral care, probably because of
lack of interest. He resigned after six years, in 1832, because of disagreements with his parishioners over the administration of the sacrament of
the Lord's Supper.

After leaving the ministry and traveling abroad for a year, he took up
residence in Concord, Massachusetts. Emerson read widely in philosophical, literary, and religious literature. He also kept a daily journal and in
the early 1830s began writing the essays that were to make him famous.
"Nature," published in 1836 when he was thirty-three, was the first that
gained him notice. In a Harvard Divinity School address in 1838, he outlined the tenets of Transcendentalism, the philosophical system that owes
its beginnings to his work. In the speech he disavowed many of the teachings of traditional Unitarianism, bringing him wide notoriety in New England.

The attention he got set a pattern for the rest of his career. There were
strong objections and attacks from one side and personal, witness-bearing
praise, almost adulation, from another. His fame grew rapidly in the early
1840s with the publication of two volumes of essays, works that included
the two that made his reputation, "Self-Reliance" and "The Over-Soul."

During the course of his lifetime his literary output, including journals, letters, lectures, and essays, was prodigious.

Along with writing, he began working as a platform lecturer. He made a good living at it; by the time he was in his fifties, he was giving over sixty lectures a year, a total of approximately fifteen hundred during his forty-year career. In 1847 he traveled to England where he gave sixty-seven lectures to audiences averaging 750 people. By the late 1850s, he was fast becoming an institution—his growing reputation preceding him wherever he went. By the 1870s he had become a fixture in American life. Moncure Conway, a religious commentator who met him in 1850, considered him a titanic iconoclast. "Emerson," Conway wrote, "has the distinction of being the first repudiator of sacraments, supernaturalism, biblical authority, and Christianity itself in every form, who suffered no kind of martyrdom."[3]

The spiritual ideas contained in Emerson's teaching that the Fillmores and H. Emilie Cady adopted can be summarized as follows:

GOD IS AN ALL-POWERFUL PRESENCE, transcendent and immanent, everywhere present in the universe. There is a oneness in all things as the spirit of God permeates humankind as the indwelling supreme presence. Those who seek to find God need to look inside themselves.

WHILE THE DIVINE IS IN THE HUMAN, the inner presence is in potential only. Spiritual work is required to experience the reality of the God-life within. Self-understanding is a key attribute that needs to be developed. Humankind has the power of choice (free will), because human behavior is not determined. Human freedom opens up the possibility for all forms of negative conditions and allows for the expression of the dark side of human nature.

THERE ARE LAWS OF SOUL, which, if observed, enable men and women to express their true nature. The human mind has great creative power, and that power is expressed through thought and the use of intuition. Men and women, as they learn to trust and rely on intuition, become more self-reliant and self-responsible.

PRAYER AND MEDITATION ARE ESSENTIAL spiritual practices. The most beneficial form of prayer celebrates the connection with the divine inner spirit. Meditation enables the seeker to connect with the indwelling presence. The divine is expressed in the human as the mind is kept focused on the present moment.

THE LIFE OF JESUS IS IMPORTANT for humankind because Jesus

was a supreme example of how divinity manifests itself. Jesus is an instructor to men and women because he taught how to become more God-like. Traditional Christianity misinterprets the teachings of Jesus and misconstrues the meaning and purpose of his life. It is a mistake to separate Jesus from the human and treat him as God. Jesus was not God incarnate and he did not redeem humankind from sin by his death on the cross.

Warren Felt Evans: The Recording Angel of Metaphysics

Warren Felt Evans (1817–1889) was the first American writer to give literary form to the ideas and methods of spiritual healing. His book *Mental Cure*, published in 1869, is considered to be the first of the New Thought books.[1] It was read widely in this country and in Europe, went through several editions, and was published in several languages. Horatio Dresser, the early historian of New Thought (writing in 1919, fifty years after the book was published), considered it to be "still superior . . . to most of the New Thought literature of today."[2] Charles Braden, a widely respected authority on metaphysical movements in America, commented that Evans "was the only important figure, aside from Mrs. Eddy, who attempted to work out a consistent and philosophically supported system of metaphysical healing and mental healing after Quimby."[3]

H. Emilie Cady highly praised Evans's work, indicating that he "transcended the writers of his day." She considered his work particularly valuable because he made use of "material analogies to make plain to people the deep spiritual truths which up to that time had been thought to be of another world."[4] The works of Evans that she considered important were *Esoteric Christianity, Mental Medicine,* and *The Divine Law of Cure.*

Charles Fillmore read all of Evans's books and was generous in his praise. In 1908 he commented:

W. F. Evans is called "The Recording Angel of Metaphysics." He has hunted out all the vital issues in ancient and modern spiritual writing, and sifted them thoroughly. I have read the seven volumes which he has written and think them the most complete of all metaphysical compilations. He is not an original thinker, but knows the Truth when he sees it.[5]

A farmer's son, Evans was born to Eli and Sarah Edison Evans at Rockingham, Vermont, on December 23, 1817, the sixth of seven children. Unlike Quimby, Evans was the recipient, by nineteenth-century standards, of an excellent education. Private schooling at Chester Academy

was followed by one year at Middlebury College and a year and a half at
Dartmouth. He left in the middle of his junior year to study for the
Methodist ministry, then served in a variety of Methodist churches for
over two decades.

In 1840 he married M. Charlotte Tinker, a union that was to last until
his death in 1889. Two important events occurred in 1863: Evans left the
Methodist church and joined the Swedenborgian Church of the New
Jerusalem, and went to Portland, Maine, to be treated by Phineas P.
Quimby. Evans apparently had contracted a serious illness, "a nervous af-
fliction complicated by a chronic disorder."[6] The high regard in which he
held Quimby thereafter indicates that he benefited from the treatment.[7]

During the remaining quarter century of his life, he worked with his
wife, primarily in Boston, as a practitioner of mental healing. During this
period he saw patients, taught students the principles of mental healing,
and wrote seven books on its theory and practice. They are: *The New Age
and Its Messengers* (1864), *Mental Cure* (1869), *Mental Medicine* (1872),
Soul and Body (1876),) *The Divine Law of Cure* (1881), *Primitive Mind
Cure* (1884), and *Esoteric Christianity* (1886). His books presented many
of the spiritual ideas and healing principles that later became a part of the
teaching of Unity School of Christianity.

The spiritual teachings of Warren Felt Evans that appear in the works
of the Fillmores and H. Emilie Cady can be summarized as follows:

THE POWER OF GOD is all-encompassing. God is the first and the
last, the alpha and the omega. Men and women are manifestations of God
because humankind is made in the image and likeness of God; consequently, the divine exists in the human. The divine inner presence, however, is a latent attribute, a possibility that could be made real through spiritual practice. Humankind's ultimate challenge is to act in and from God.
Men and women possess the power of free will but have used it in harmful
ways. Ignorance, fear, negative thought, sense consciousness, and selfishness are manifestations of humankind's abuse of its freedom. The innate
universal divine humanity can be realized through observing divine law
and following the will of God. This can be accomplished through spiritual
practice. Men and women need to harness the transformative power of
thought, develop and use intuition, connect with the indwelling presence
through prayer in the silence, and have confidence in these higher truths
through acts of faith.

JESUS EVOLVED during his lifetime from the human to the divine; he exhibited to the world a perfect humanity, a complete humanized expression of the Christ. Because Jesus had become an incarnation of the Christ, he had an extraordinary ability to heal others both physically and spiritually. What Jesus accomplished others could do also if they followed his example, because men and women possess the same potential. Those who develop themselves spiritually can work successfully as practitioners of spiritual healing. By manifesting their divine attributes men and women can also regenerate the human body, realize the Christ within, and overcome physical death. Those who fail to achieve the Christ Consciousness before physical death enter an afterlife of peace and tranquility. Traditional Christianity has erred in its teachings on hell for the damned and heaven for the saved. Both Catholicism and Protestantism have been unwilling to follow the example of Jesus. Christianity has prepared men and women to die rather than to transform the physical body and live eternal life on earth.

Evans made a unique contribution to New Thought and to the work of the Fillmores. He was the first to combine the work of Mesmer, which proved the beneficent impact of the mind on the body for purposes of health, with the spiritual teaching of Ralph Waldo Emerson, which addressed the value of becoming one with the divine indwelling presence. Evans deepened the mental healing movement by demonstrating its spiritual basis. The method developed by Evans, which emphasized the action of the divine inner spirit, was used by the Fillmores in their practitioner work.

The areas of divergence in the teachings of Evans and the Fillmores are relatively small. Evans believed that with a certain few patients, hypnosis was helpful. The Fillmores did not employ hypnosis. Evans also saw some benefit in hands-on healing, although he used it rarely. Hands-on healing was not a part of the Unity teaching. Evans was receptive to Western medical practices while the Fillmores were leery of them.

Phineas P. Quimby: Mental Healer

Phineas P. Quimby (1802–1866), a native of Belfast, Maine, was a clockmaker, an inventor, and a man fully engaged in the scientific spirit of his time. He was one of many mid-nineteenth-century amateurs who became interested in the newly developed techniques of hypnotism and somnambulism, commonly known as mesmerism. In 1838, at age thirty-six, Quimby learned the techniques from a traveling mesmerist and used them for purposes of mental healing. His work, although apparently highly effective with many clients, would probably have gone unnoticed but for the notoriety of his most famous client—Mary Baker Eddy.

Quimby recorded his experiences with clients; they were published in 1921, many years after his death, as *The Quimby Manuscripts*. It was on the strength of these writings and because of his presumed influence over the development of Christian Science that he was credited by J. Stillson Judah, author of *The History and Philosophy of the Movements in America*, as "the forefather of the mental science healing groups";[1] and by Charles Braden, author of *Spirits in Rebellion: The Rise and Development of New Thought*, as "the original source of the New Thought movement."[2]

Quimby's practice of mental healing appears to have been markedly different from that of either Warren Felt Evans or Mary Baker Eddy. His method, after discontinuing his work as a somnambulist, consisted of identifying through clairvoyance a patient's presumed physical malady or psychological difficulty. Then, through argument, persuasion, or suggestion, he attempted to change the client's beliefs regarding the ailment. Healing took place when the client accepted Quimby's suggestions.

When working with clients, Quimby began by attempting to ascertain the nature of the presumed disease and the patient's emotional response. He used his own psychic or intuitive abilities to make this determination. His success in making an accurate assessment, he believed, established his credibility with the client. He reported: "I give no medicine and make no outward applications, but simply sit with the patient and tell him what he thinks is his disease . . . As it is necessary that he should feel that I know more than he does, I tell his feelings."[3]

Quimby believed his ability to cure was dependent upon his success in changing a client's attitude or point of view. "If I change your mind," he told a patient, "the change is the cure."[4] Unlike Christian Science and New Thought teachers who came after him, Quimby did not attempt to reframe a client's thought processes through affirmations and denials, nor did he recommend prayer. Quimby explained the process by which he helped patients adopt more healthy attitudes: "My way of curing convinces him that he has been deceived, and, if I succeed, the patient is cured.[5] . . . As the truth changes his mind, light takes the place of darkness, till he sees through the error of disease. The light of wisdom dissipates the matter, or disease, and the patient once more finds himself freed of opinions and happiness is restored."[6]

The Fillmores never adopted Quimby's healing practices. The Fillmores, as mental healers, worked with clients in a very different way than Quimby. What's more, the Fillmores had little firsthand knowledge of his spiritual teaching or practices. Their acquaintance with Quimby came several years after they began their own work. While they no doubt were aware of charges by Annetta and Julius Dresser that Mary Baker Eddy plagiarized Quimby's work, the first published information about his spiritual ideas, sketchy though it was, came with the publication in 1892 of Annetta Dresser's biography. This book provided an indication of how Quimby worked as a mental healer but did not provide an explication of his spiritual ideas.[7]

Quimby's manuscripts remained unpublished long after the Fillmores had established their own work. Consequently, the impact of Quimby on the teaching and healing practices of the Fillmores was at best secondhand. While Quimby may have had an important impact on the practices of those who worked directly with him, such as Mary Baker Eddy and the Dressers, it would be incorrect to assert that Quimby had a direct effect on the Fillmores. Nevertheless, it must be acknowledged that it is unlikely that the Fillmores would have become spiritual teachers and healers had it not been for Quimby. It was through Quimby that Mary Baker Eddy became acquainted with spiritual healing. Her contact with Quimby was an essential first step in creating Christian Science. It was from those who learned spiritual healing as a result of their association with Christian Science (Joseph Charles and his student, E. B. Weeks) that Myrtle Fillmore healed herself of tuberculosis and began the practice of spiritual healing.[8]

Mary Baker Eddy and Christian Science

Of the nineteenth-century spiritual healers, Mary Baker Eddy (1821–1910) was without doubt the most successful, if success is measured in terms of impact on the widest number of people. In 1866, at age forty-five, she reported she was divinely healed from a serious injury through an experience of being fully conscious of the divine presence. She dedicated her life thereafter to divine healing as a practitioner, teacher, and church leader. Calling her work "Christian Science," she was remarkably able to teach others her healing technique and to inspire middle-aged women in particular to become practitioners of Christian Science and return to their communities to teach, heal, and establish institutes and churches. Her book *Science and Health,* which publicized her work, ultimately became a bestseller.[1]

Though poorly educated and unlearned, Eddy was shrewd, highly intelligent, and a gifted organizer. Her religious roots were in Puritan Congregationalism and she was a lifelong student of the Bible. Through personal charisma and organizational savvy, she established Christian Science as a new religion that she believed would "reinstate primitive Christianity and its lost element of healing."[2] She saw her work as a continuation of the Congregational tradition, not a departure.

She attracted a fiercely loyal and dedicated following. As Christian Science developed a following that numbered in the hundreds of thousands, Eddy came under strong attack from a variety of sources, including the Protestant establishment, which considered her a heretic and a fraud; the American press, which saw her as a money-hungry kook; the medical establishment, which considered her a quack; followers of her former teacher Phineas P. Quimby, who charged her with plagiarism; and dissident former students who considered her an autocrat.

A tough-minded and resilient woman, she was unfazed by criticism and refused to be sidetracked from what she believed was her God-given mission to make Christian Science available to the world. By the time of her death in 1910 at age eighty-nine, she had developed a corps of practitioners who carried the movement forward. She had established a church in Boston (the First Church of Christ, Scientist) with a reported membership of thirty thousand, and she had supported the founding of Christian Science churches and institutes in most major American cities, claiming a following of eight hundred thousand Christian Scientists worldwide.

The influence of Mary Baker Eddy on the Fillmores lay primarily in the practice of divine healing. The Fillmores accepted Eddy's position that successful practitioner work depended upon the ability of the practitioner to achieve conscious union with God. Charles Fillmore's adoption of this method of practice is indicated in the following statement: "He who realizes most thoroughly that God is the Supreme Perfection, and that in Him can be no imperfection, and speaks forth that realization with conviction, will cause all things to arrange themselves in divine order."[3]

While the Fillmores' practitioner work was similar in part to Eddy's, they rejected key points in her spiritual teaching. Eddy was a conventional Trinitarian; they adopted a metaphysical interpretation of the doctrine of the Trinity. Eddy viewed Jesus as Calvinist Christianity saw him, as God incarnate, the Savior and Messiah. The Fillmores viewed Jesus as born human and as manifesting his divine inheritance over several lifetimes through spiritual practice. Eddy was constantly addressing the manifestations of sin in human behavior and seeking the means to eradicate it. Sin and salvation, as traditional Christianity viewed them, were not of primary concern to the Fillmores. Eddy's religious background was Congregationalist, with Puritan and Calvinist underpinnings. The Fillmores spiritual path was more eclectic, drawing from Swedenborgianism, Transcendentalism, Theosophy, New Thought, and Eastern religions. Having learned Christian Science from Eddy dissidents, and been persuaded by Annetta Dresser's 1892 biography of Quimby that Eddy was a plagiarist, the Fillmores did not have a high regard either for Eddy or for Christian Science.

Emma Curtis Hopkins: Teacher of Teachers

Charles and Myrtle Fillmore began studying Christian Science with Emma Curtis Hopkins (1849–1925) in January 1890, when Hopkins came to Kansas City to deliver a series of lessons. The Fillmores were enthusiastic about her personal qualities, her ability to heal, and her teaching, as the following testimonial published in *Modern Thought* magazine indicated:

Those who went to the class as the most vehement scoffers came out enthusiastic champions of truth, and members without exception declared themselves wakened to new life. To detail their individual experiences in the healing of bodily and mental ills, would fill several such papers as this . . . A new universe has opened to them . . . It is safe to say that this course of lectures has given an impetus to the work in this city which will ultimate in the freedom of every mind from the thralldom of sin, sickness and death, and open the way for the new heaven and earth.[1]

Hopkins returned to Kansas City for another series of lectures in March 1890. Again the Fillmores attended, and again they were touched by her presence and the content of her message. They reported:

The prominent characteristic of Mrs. Hopkins is her charity. She has such a broad generous grasp on Truth, her reading is so extensive and her knowledge so thorough that she charms and disarms the most prejudiced. Yet she is inflexible in her persistent adherence to the one principle of Good and he who wanders from the straight Science cannot say that she has not clearly pointed the way.[2]

The Fillmores completed Hopkins's metaphysical curriculum and were ordained by her as Christian Science ministers in December 1890. Four years later, in September 1894, the Fillmores wrote a beautiful testimonial to the work of Hopkins, stating:

In our experience among teachers we never met anyone who could bring out the latent faculties of the mind so swiftly as Mrs. Hopkins. She knows just what words you need to hold to develop your brightest talents, and the little army of metaphysicians in the western country who have come forth from her instruction, brilliant writers, speakers, and healers, are living testimonials to her genius.[3]

J. Gordon Melton, a leading academic authority on New Thought, considered Hopkins instrumental in the development of the movement. He commented: "Though many are the names of people who influenced the development of New Thought—Franz Anton Mesmer, Emanuel Swedenborg, Ralph Waldo Emerson, Phineas Parkhurst Quimby, and Warren Felt Evans, Hopkins stands above all of them as the founder of the movement."[4]

Little is known about the life of Emma Curtis Hopkins before she met Mary Baker Eddy in 1883 at age thirty-four and became involved in Christian Science.[5] Born in 1849 in the farming community of Killingly, Connecticut, she was the eldest of nine children. Her father, Rufus Curtis, was a farmer and part-time realtor; her mother, Lydia Phillips Curtis, was a farmer's wife. Emma was raised in the Congregational church and received a secondary school education at the Killingly high school. Afterward she taught in local schools. She married George Irving Hopkins, a high school English teacher, in July 1874; she was twenty-four. A son, John Carver, was born in the summer of the following year. At the time of the 1880 census, the family was living in Nantucket, Massachusetts, and Emma was identified as a housewife. In the early 1880s the family moved to Manchester, New Hampshire, where George Hopkins continued to work as a teacher.[6]

In October 1883, Hopkins met Mary Baker Eddy at the home of a mutual friend, Mary F. Berry of Manchester. Berry, a graduate of Eddy's Massachusetts Metaphysical College, had invited Eddy to give a talk on Christian Science healing. Hopkins was immediately attracted to the work and wrote to Eddy in December, telling her that the "beautiful theory" she had advanced had taken "a firm hold on my heart." Hopkins expressed an interest in coming to Boston to study with Eddy. Hopkins told Eddy that she was happily married and had "a sweet little son," but could not "command a single dollar" because of her husband's continued indebtedness for his college education. She asked if she could pay Eddy for the primary course, which was to begin on December 27, after graduating and working as a practitioner.[7]

Eddy evidently agreed, since Hopkins came to Boston, completed the twelve lessons in the course, and qualified as a Christian Science practitioner. In a letter to Eddy from Manchester in January, Hopkins testified to healing her husband of a throat infection and expressed her dedication to the work, stating, "I give myself and all my time to the Master's work wherever it lies, here, there and yonder."[8]

In April 1884 she contributed an article entitled "God's Omnipresence" to Eddy's *Christian Science Journal,* and in August Eddy offered her the editorship of the publication, a job that did not pay a salary. Assuming she would make enough money to support herself from practitioner work, Hopkins left home in September, placed her son with surrogates, and took the job of editor. One month later, she expressed her loyalty to Eddy in a letter, stating, "I am at your service," and signed it, "lovingly, your disciple."[9]

Hopkins remained on the job until she was dismissed eleven months later in October 1885. The reasons for her firing are unclear; most likely it was due to disagreements over editorial policy. Shortly thereafter, Hopkins, again leaving husband and son behind, joined with Mary Plunkett, another Christian Science student who also had fallen out of favor with Eddy, and moved to Chicago. There they set up a Christian Science metaphysical college and teachers' association modeled after Eddy's organizations in Boston. Plunkett was the administrative president and Hopkins, the teacher. The first class, which was directed toward practitioner training, graduated in June 1886. Shortly thereafter Hopkins, though not an ordained minister herself, broadened the scope of the Chicago work and opened a seminary for the training and ordination of ministers.[10] Eddy, who was continually plagued by students who abandoned her, castigated Hopkins as one of "the unprincipled claimants" guilty of "dishonesty" and "fraud."

Unfazed by Eddy's criticisms, Hopkins continued to teach classes in Chicago and in other cities in the Midwest and Far West, including Kansas City. When Mary Plunkett dissolved their partnership in 1888 and set up a rival Christian Science work on the East Coast, Hopkins found it necessary to both teach and administer. She continued her work until 1895, when she closed her seminary and moved to New York City. Although Hopkins enjoyed teaching and ordained 111 ministers during her stay in the Midwest, she did not enjoy administrative work. By 1895 she was apparently burned out.[11]

From 1895 until her death in 1925, Hopkins taught students individually from her New York apartment, worked as a practitioner of mental healing, and spoke occasionally to metaphysical groups. In letters written to friends during her New York years, she told of a busy schedule. Apparently it was difficult to get an appointment with her. She evidently made a comfortable living from her work.[12]

Hopkins earned the title "teacher of teachers" because during her long career she taught, in addition to the Fillmores, the following leaders of New Thought: Ida Nichols, co-founder of Divine Science in Denver; Annie Rix and Paul Militiz, who established the Homes of Truth in Los Angeles; H. Emilie Cady, who wrote the bestseller *Lessons in Truth;* and Ernest Holmes, founder of the United Church of Religious Science in Los Angeles.

Hopkins, though a gifted teacher and practitioner of spiritual healing, was not an able writer. She wrote occasional articles for New Thought periodicals and one book, *High Mysticism,* in 1907. A book entitled *Scientific Christian Mental Practice,* which pulled together information from her classes, was published posthumously. Her writing is disjointed and difficult to follow, moving precipitously from topic to topic with little or no follow-through. Only the most dedicated reader would pursue her written work.

The following is a summary of Hopkins's teaching, most of which can be found in the work of the Fillmores and H. Emile Cady:

GOD IS ALL-POWERFUL, omnipotent, omnipresent and omniscient. God is not a great being on a throne in the air, but the principle of holiness, goodness, and truth. Mind, Life, Soul, Spirit are the names of God. God interpenetrates all things, the natural world as well as the human. While humankind shares the same nature as God, the God-like qualities are in potential only. Men and women have strong powers of the mind. They are free, however, to use these powers as they see fit, and they often choose to use them in negative ways. Humankind often chooses to be selfish, envious, jealous, angry, greedy, and fearful. Realizing the divine in the human can be accomplished through study and spiritual practice. The mind needs to be disciplined, because thoughts about God or "Absolute Truth" have powerful impact. Affirmations are also important, but they must be preceded by denials. Life's most difficult problems can be alleviated through the correct use of denials. Words themselves have hidden power, and must be chosen carefully. Like affirmations, prayer plays a vital role in shifting consciousness from the negative to the positive. Those who fully raise their level of consciousness and manifest the indwelling presence overcome poverty, disease, aging, and death. Jesus, by fully manifesting the Christ within and overcoming death, showed that he is a forerunner of a new race of human beings. The task of humankind is to put on the mind of Christ, the mind that was in Jesus.

The impact of Hopkins on the Fillmores appears to have been the result of her personal presence and skills as a teacher. Her written works fall far short of conveying the message she was able to communicate in person. Her talent seems to have been as an effective articulator and synthesizer of the works of others, particularly Emerson, Evans, Swedenborg, and Eddy. Although the content of Hopkins's teaching more closely matches that of the Fillmores than that of any other teacher, it would be wrong to assume that the teaching was original with her or that she was transmitting large amounts of new information or ideas. By the time the Fillmores met Hopkins, they had already read the writings upon which the content of her teaching was based.

Madame Helena Petrovna Blavatsky and the Theosophists

The teachings of Madame Helena Petrovna Blavatsky (1831–1891) and the early Theosophists became publicly available in the two decades before the Fillmores began their own work. The Fillmores' high regard for theosophical teachings was indicated in 1889 in reviews of literature in the first issue of *Modern Thought* magazine. No less than thirteen books on Theosophy were recommended. Included was the landmark work by Madame Blavatsky, *Isis Unveiled*. In addition, a book entitled *Christian Theosophy* by John Hamlin Dewey was recommended as "one of the very best books on the subject." It was given a lengthy review and highly praised. The periodical entitled *The Wilkins Letter on Theosophy* was suggested for all who wanted to learn theosophical doctrines.[1] Charles Fillmore acknowledged his own intellectual debt to Theosophy when he commented: "I myself was a very earnest student of Theosophy and quite familiar with its literature, and found much truth therein. . . . I have studied [it] carefully, both from the exoteric and esoteric standpoints."[2]

The growth and development of the theosophical movement in the

United States, Europe, and India in the late nineteenth century can be attributed in large part to the work of two disparate and unlikely middle-aged collaborators: Madame Helena Petrovna Blavatsky, a brilliant, captivating, and eccentric Russian émigré to the United States, and Henry Steel Olcott, a diligent, pragmatic, New York lawyer with family ties back to the Pilgrims. Blavatsky articulated the teaching in several books on the occult. Olcott's work as an administrator and organizer was essential to the development of the theosophical movement.

From an early age, Blavatsky felt a sense of mission, telling a friend at age nineteen: "I will bless mankind by freeing them from their mental bondage . . . I know I was intended to do a great work."[3] Nevertheless, Blavatsky's personal history prior to her creating the written works that articulated the teaching gave little indication she had the background and ability to develop a complex and appealing system of spiritual beliefs and to co-found a worldwide movement. Born in 1831 into an upper-class Russian family, she was married at age seventeen to the forty-year-old Nikifor Blavatsky, the vice-governor of the province of Yerevan in Armenia. After a brief time, she abandoned her husband and, until her mid-forties, traveled in Europe, America, and the Middle East. She never remarried, although she had long liaisons with a Russian opera singer as well as with several others.[4] She had a business relationship with Olcott that was apparently platonic.

In the 1860s she became involved with Spiritualism, conducted séances, worked as a medium, and spelled out messages from invisible entities.[5] She claimed at the time she left Europe in 1873, sailed for the United States, and settled in New York City, that she had been a Spiritualist for over a decade. In October 1874, she met Olcott, who was also deeply involved in Spiritualism, at the Eddy brothers' farmhouse in Chittenden, Vermont, where both had gone to observe Spiritualist manifestations. They immediately became friends.[6]

In the spring and summer of 1875, Blavatsky conducted séances and hosted Spiritualist lecturers at gatherings in her New York apartment. Olcott attended, along with persons interested in Kabbalism, Rosicrucianism, and Spiritualism. Olcott considered Blavatsky to be the most unusual medium he had ever met, observing: "[I]nstead of being controlled by Spirits to do their will, it is she who seems to control them to do her bidding."[7] At a meeting in Blavatsky's apartment on September 7, 1875, Olcott proposed that those in attendance form a society to pursue occult research. The seventeen present agreed, and on the following evening the group met and passed a resolution that formally established the Theosophical Society. In October, bylaws were approved and officers elected, with Olcott chosen as president.[8]

In his inaugural address, Olcott defined the purpose of the society as helping free "the public mind of theological superstition and a tame subservience to the arrogance of science."[9] One of the chief goals of the society was to transcend the cleavage between science and religion and to return to concerns of an ancient-wisdom tradition. Olcott distinguished Theosophy from Spiritualism, indicating that Spiritualism was plagued by "imposture, tricky mediums, lying spirits, and revolting social theories."[10] He indicated that the primary task of the society was investigation. Its twice-monthly meetings would be devoted to "researches and experiments of our members and of eminent correspondents in this and other countries . . . [and to] tests, experiments, and practical demonstrations."[11]

Madame Blavatsky indicated that there were three major objects of the society: to form the nucleus of a universal brotherhood of humanity without distinction of race, color, or creed; to promote the study of Scripture, particularly those of the East; and to investigate the mysteries of psychic and spiritual powers.[12] Like Olcott, she had become disenchanted with Spiritualism, particularly its teachings about the afterlife.

The word "theosophy" was chosen to represent the society's philosophy because it expressed the esoteric truths the group sought to uncover.[13] Etymologically, the term means "wisdom about God."[14] It was not the first time the term was used in a spiritual context. The word appears in works of several Church Fathers, both Greek and Latin, as a synonym for theology.[15] "Theosophy" was also used from ancient to modern times to refer to a particular form of mysticism.[16]

The morning after the second meeting of the society, Madame Blavatsky traveled to Ithaca, New York, to visit friends and to begin work on her first book, *Isis Unveiled*. Written when she was forty-five and published in 1877, it was a massive and comprehensive treatise of an ancient wisdom religion. It was divided into two volumes, the first entitled "Science," the second, "Theology." Included were chapters on modern science, psychic phenomena, Spiritualism, mesmerism, the Kabbalah, the Devil, and esoteric interpretations of Christianity.[17] The book has become a modern occult classic.

Blavatsky wrote prolifically during the remaining decade of her life.

Her collected writings consist of a dozen volumes. Her two-volume masterwork, *The Secret Doctrine,* was published in 1888. It is a recasting of *Isis Unveiled,* making the development of the inner man the reason for human evolution.[18] It combined ideas from Asian religions within a cosmic framework that gave meaning to human destiny and is considered by some authorities to be the major work of occultism in the nineteenth century.[19] Blavatsky's last book, *The Voice of Silence,* is a theosophical devotional classic that continues to be popular in the present day and had a significant effect on shaping the outlook of Theosophy. Theosophists consider it to be the most widely read and beloved of all her writings.[20]

Madame Blavatsky claimed that the theosophical doctrines she presented were not her own, but were obtained through a kind of thought transference from so-called "Masters" or adepts. She claimed that these personages, also called "Mahatmas," were highly evolved living beings who possessed the hidden truths of the universe and whose chief residence was Tibet.[21] Mahatmas were believed to live to a great age and were called "great-souled-ones" because of their moral development and intellectual attainment. Blavatsky claimed that entire passages were "entirely dictated by them and verbatim."[22] In other parts of her writing, the Mahatmas inspired the ideas. "They are our teachers," she declared, "because from them we have derived all the Theosophical truths."[23]

Bruce F. Campbell, who has written a balanced and thorough study of the work of the early Theosophists *(Ancient Wisdom Revived: A History of the Theosophical Movement),* indicated that the existence of the Masters is among the weakest of the Theosophists' claims. He cites reputable sources that indicate Blavatsky derived most of her information from Hindu and Buddhist spiritual literature as well as from nineteenth-century works on occultism.[24] Whatever their source, Blavatsky was among the first to present Eastern philosophy in a popular way that was accessible to Western readers.[25]

Most Theosophists accepted Blavatsky's assertions that the Mahatmas were the real source of theosophical doctrine and the true founders of the Theosophical Society.[26] Many believed they could communicate with these teachers in the same way Blavatsky did. The large number of theosophical works created in the late nineteenth century, many of which were read by the Fillmores, are probably attributable to these beliefs.

Olcott and Blavatsky had better success at developing the theosophical movement in India than in the United States. In 1878, three years after the founding of the Theosophical Society, they left America for India, eventually setting up headquarters in Adyar. A hundred branches of the society were chartered in India during their first five years there.[27] In 1884 the founders returned to the West, stopping first in England to facilitate the work of the London lodge.[28] By 1888 there were about twenty-five lodges in the United States with an aggregate membership of fewer than five hundred. By 1896 there were 103 American branches, comprising about 25 percent of those worldwide, and a membership of about six thousand.[29]

During the twentieth century there have been three separate theosophical organizations, two with headquarters in the United States and one in India. Membership peaked at fifty thousand in the 1920s; most members were in India. Worldwide membership as of 1980 was approximately forty thousand. The activities of branches and centers include courses and lectures in Theosophy; a publications program; and sponsorship of bookstores, libraries, and summer camps.[30] After the deaths of Blavatsky and Olcott, three twentieth-century spiritual teachers, Annie Besant, C. W. Leadbeater, and J. Krishnamurti, gained renown for their theosophical works.

The following is a summary of the spiritual teaching of the Theosophists. The teaching of the Fillmores included many of these ideas, including those regarding reincarnation:

GOD IS AN EVER unknowable principle beyond the range of human understanding. God is not a personal father, ruler, and governor of the universe. God is everywhere in every atom of the universe and immanent in humankind. Men and women have within themselves, in potential only, goodness, perfection, and divine attributes. Humanity possesses free choice and the disharmony and evil in human behavior are the result of faulty choices. Selfishness, malice, and hatred are major human defects. Contact with the spiritual realm is made through prayer and meditation. Prayer consists of ardently bending the soul toward the divine. Prayer is not asking for things. The law of cause and effect (karma) operates in human affairs, rewarding and punishing with equal impartiality. Karmic law presupposes reincarnation because sins of the current life are not redressed until a future incarnation. Vicarious atonement, or the self-sacrifice of Jesus for the salvation of humankind, is an erroneous Christian doctrine. Spiritual development is a slow process and is experienced during the course of many incarnations. The afterlife is one of peace and rest while the soul readies itself for its next incarnation.

Theosophy has its roots in Eastern religion, Swedenborgianism, mesmerism, Transcendentalism, and Spiritualism. Its teachings on karma and reincarnation can be found in Buddhism and Hinduism; its ideas on the afterlife come from Swedenborg; its beliefs in the positive impact of one mind upon another are no doubt derived from the work of Franz Anton Mesmer and his followers; its views on the immanence of God are Transcendentalist ideas; and its effort to bridge the gap between science and religion and to acknowledge human evolution are also evident in Spiritualism.

Fillmore family *Top (L to R):* Lowell, Rickert, Royal Fillmore; *Bottom (L to R):* Myrtle, Charles, Georgianna (Grandma) Fillmore (ca. 1910–1915)

Myrtle Fillmore (1928)

Charles S. Fillmore (1940s)

H. Emilie Cady, M.D.

Emma Curtis Hopkins

Lowell Fillmore (1934)

W. Rickert Fillmore (1932)

Charles R. Fillmore

Connie Fillmore Bazzy

Roy Howard

Charles Edgar Prather (1904)

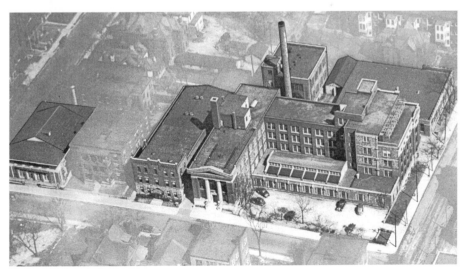

Unity School of Christianity at 9th and Tracy (1940s)

Unity Ministerial Students (August 22, 1934). Charles and Cora Fillmore are on the right.

Silent Unity Workers Attending a Prayer Meeting Led by Charles Fillmore. May Rowland in front row on far left (1943)

Silent Unity Letter Writers, 9th and Tracy, Kansas City (1923)

Silent Unity Telephone Associates and Letter Writers, Kansas City (1940s)

Rosemary Fillmore Rhea

Cora Dedrick Fillmore (1946)

May Rowland (1939)

Frank B. Whitney (1934)

Martha Smock (1970)

Imelda Octavia Shanklin

Celia Ayers (1936)

Elizabeth Sands Turner (1946)

James Dillet Freeman

Emmet Fox

Alexander Everett (1962)

Warren Kreml

Norman Vincent Peale with Rosemary Fillmore Rhea during a TV Interview

David Williamson

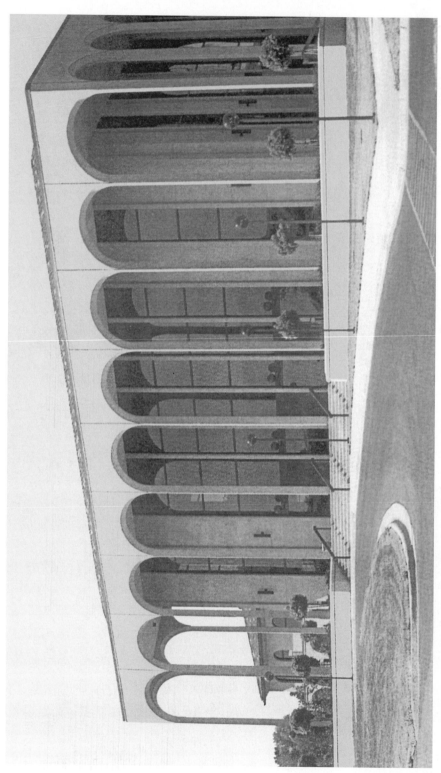

Village Chapel and Activity Center, Unity Village

Unity Village

Ministerial Students at Unity Village. Faculty members are in the last row (late 1970s)

PART II

THE GROWTH AND DEVELOPMENT OF THE UNITY MOVEMENT

Introduction

Unity came onto the American religious scene in the nineteenth century at a time when advances in science posed a significant threat to traditional Christianity. It was also a time when Unitarianism, Christian Science, Spiritualism, Theosophy, and New Thought were challenging the doctrines of Catholicism and Protestantism. Metaphysical healing was gaining in popularity as allopathic medicine was still in its infancy.

Beginning in the late 1880s, Unity evolved over the course of the twentieth century from prayer meetings in the living room of Charles and Myrtle Fillmore to a worldwide spiritual movement. Unity published magazines and books to spread the teaching, prayed and healed through the Silent Unity prayer ministry, trained students and ministers, built Unity School of Christianity at Unity Village, Missouri, and developed centers and churches in the United States and abroad.

Described in the following chapters are the key factors that led to the growth and development of the Unity movement.

Organizing and Financing Unity School of Christianity

Organizing a Spiritual Movement (1889–1914)

Very few spiritual teachers succeed in creating an organization that can carry on their work after their deaths. The Unity movement, which grew and developed in the twentieth century, established itself in large part because of the organizing ability of its co-founder, Charles Fillmore. Unlike many nineteenth-century metaphysical spiritual teachers—who were either uninterested or unable to organize around their work—Charles was a gifted organizer who worked best in an organizational setting.[1] Before its activities were incorporated in 1914 as the Unity School of Christianity, the spiritual work of the Unity movement was carried on under several organizational designations, and Charles headed each of them. The first was the Society of Silent Help, founded in 1889, which in 1891 became the Society of Silent Unity. The Silent Unity Healing Department, which began employing prayer workers in the late 1890s, benefited greatly from Charles's guiding hand. *Modern Thought, Christian Science Thought,* and *Thought* magazines, which Charles edited, were published by Thought Publishing Company, which he owned and operated. The Unity Book Company, established in 1892, and the Unity Tract Society, founded in 1897, were successor organizations. They were unincorporated private businesses, most likely single proprietorships. The Unity Tract Society published all Unity books, tracts, and magazines, including *Unity* magazine, until 1914.

In addition, in 1903 Charles facilitated the incorporation of the Kansas City Unity Society of Practical Christianity, the nonprofit church organization he led until his retirement in 1933. In the 1890s he was actively involved, as leader, in each of its predecessor groups. In 1909 he developed a course in Practical Christianity for Unity students that could be taken by correspondence. He then founded the Unity Correspondence School to manage the workload associated with the course.

In 1909, *Unity* magazine began referring to the "Unity Society" as the organizational vehicle for all the Fillmores' teaching and healing work and for their publication activities. No attempt was made to incorporate the Unity Society, although the organizational purposes of the group suggested that nonprofit status would be appropriate for its work. In answer to the question, "What is the object of the Unity Society?" in 1909 *Unity* magazine explained:

The object of the Unity Society is to harmonize and unify the Christian religion with modern metaphysics. It sees in the pure doctrine of Jesus and the apostles the same truths that modern independent investigators claim as original discoveries. It teaches that all the modern discoveries of the constitution of man are set forth in the doctrine of Jesus and his apostles . . . The literature published by the Unity Society explains in detail the Divine Law and however man can take advantage of it and be restored to health, prosperity and happiness.[2]

The Unity Society was featured in a large headline on the front page of *Weekly Unity* on July 3, 1909, in which the following announcement appeared: "The Unity Society is not the offshoot of any organization, but is an original and independent movement in religious study."[3]

The origins of the society were traced back to the beginning of the Fillmores' activities as spiritual teachers. "The Society has been in existence about twenty years," a *Weekly Unity* article stated, "having been started by Mr. and Mrs. Fillmore."[4] The article further pointed out that there were twelve departments in the Unity Society, "but all work as one."

In March 1910, *Unity Magazine* reported on the good work being done by the Unity Society, observing: "Our friends write that they are with us in the work of the Unity Society and are glad to see reports of progress every month . . . People from all over the land are telling us that a very great work for humanity is being done by the Unity Society and that it should be generously supported."[5]

Though it had no official legal status, by 1910 the Unity Society had become the preferred organizational designation for the Unity movement. In a Sunday morning address on November 24, 1910, entitled "What Has the Unity Society to Be Thankful For?" Charles emphasized the steady growth in all aspects of the work and the impact of the teaching: "Other societies had outstripped us from the worldly point of view, but we are satisfied to know that there has been here planted a great Truth that shall never pass away, but shall grow and be given to the whole earth. We have established here a school which is founded on Principle."[6]

In April 1913, *Weekly Unity* referred to the Unity Society as a "school" rather than a religious organization, indicating that a new designation for Unity work was in the offing. The magazine observed:

The Unity Society is not a church, but a school for the training and discipline of all who would develop spiritually. It aims especially to prepare teachers for the work of spreading the Truth. In keeping, therefore, with our mission, every session should bear out the school idea and each member of the various classes should enter heartily into his privileges as a student.[7]

In June 1913, in a letter addressed to "Members and Friends of the Unity Society," Charles recalled the Unity Society's long history, tracing it back to the earliest days of his and Myrtle's teaching. He wrote: "The Unity Society has for twenty-five years taught this Truth 'without money and without price,' and has paid its bills from the sale of books and the free-will offerings that have been sent to our healing and teaching departments. This work has achieved a good measure of success."[8]

A logical step for the Fillmores would have been to incorporate the Unity Society as a nonprofit organization. Incorporation was long overdue by the time it was decided upon in 1914. By then, however, the name "Unity Society" did not accurately reflect the nature of the Unity work. Since Unity had become an institution with a major interest in spiritual education in a Christian context, the name "Unity School of Christianity" seemed to fit the work the organization was undertaking. The September 1914 issue of *Unity* described the purposes of the new organization:

To establish and maintain a school, institute or college for the instruction and promotion of mental, moral, spiritual and physical principles and qualifications deemed best for the promotion of the harmony, health and happiness of mankind, and to apply such principles and qualifications to such purposes as healing diseases and ailments anywhere.[9]

The school, which was incorporated under the General and Business Corporation Act of Missouri on April 14, 1914, included within its organizational structure the Unity Tract Society, the Society of Silent Unity, the Unity Correspondence School, the Silent-70, and the Unity Pure Food Company.[10] Fifty shares of stock were issued at that time, all controlled by members of the Fillmore family. The school was established as a commer-cial business rather than as a nonprofit educational organization, because the Fillmores were led to believe that a business charter was necessary if the school was to engage in the publication of books and magazines. This information was brought to light in 1926 in a "Finding of Fact" by the U.S. Board of Tax Appeals. The board ascertained:

Long before the incorporation, the Fillmores and their two sons were occupied en-tirely with the Unity movement and had devoted their property to it. They organ-ized the corporation because they believed that by doing so the work would be carried on more conveniently and more impersonally. They then transferred their property, including real estate, to the corporation in exchange for its entire 50 shares of stock of $5,000 par value, which was divided equally among the four. The Corporation was organized under the business corporation law instead of that for religious and charitable corporations because they [The Fillmores] were ad-vised that their desire to print literature made this necessary.[11]

In an address on January 1, 1915, at the dedication of a new Unity building in Kansas City, Charles described the objectives of the School and the ideas upon which it was based. He told the audience:

Every great work must have as its foundation a great idea. If the idea is not present the work will fail in attaining the object for which it stands. The great idea upon which the Unity work is founded is the right concept of God. Our God is not an enlarged man but the one Great Principle of Being. God is Spirit—the direct oppo-site of matter. God is Supreme Mind—the storehouse of all perfect ideas. God is the One Spirit-Mind in whom all ideas of life, love, substance, intelligence, power, originate. Spirit-Mind is the indwelling idea at the center of everything that has real existence.[12]

Fillmore ended his address by claiming a broad scope for the school's work and making an optimistic prediction of its future.

The object of this school is the redemption of the human race. It is a link in the great educational movement inaugurated by Jesus Christ, which not only taught the Truth, but demonstrated it also. . . . This is but the beginning of a work that will in due season encircle the earth. This vision of the future which the Lord has shown us is of a magnitude beyond present description. The New Jerusalem is not to be in Palestine, but in the heart of the American continent.[13]

Status as a Nonprofit Organization

While the Fillmores sought to establish the educational and religious nature of the school's activities in the minds of those attracted to its teachings and to develop closer ties with Christian churches, the Federal Commissioner of Revenue was not convinced that Unity's purpose was religious and sought to tax the Unity School of Christianity as a commercial enterprise. In 1926 Unity School appealed a Federal Commissioner of Revenue ruling that the corporation owed $32,466 in back taxes from 1917 to 1920. The government contended that Unity should pay federal tax because the Unity Inn and the Unity publications were conducted in competition with other purely commercial ventures, and because the organization was formed under the business law rather than the law for religious, scientific, and educational organizations.

The Fillmores felt that because Unity School carried out an educational and religious function, it should be exempt from taxes even though the corporation was organized under the General and Business Corporation Act of Missouri. As a way of establishing its charitable purposes, the stockholders of Unity School had declared themselves ineligible for the benefits normally accorded stockholders of commercial enterprises. In 1921 they stipulated, by amendment to the bylaws, "no dividends shall ever be declared or paid out, but all profits and property of this organization shall be used to carry out the purposes of the organization or some part thereof." In another amendment to the bylaws in 1923, they disclaimed any right to private property in the organization. In a 1918 amendment, the Fillmores reserved to themselves, however, and to their successors "the right to manage and control the business and its properties."[14] This amendment enabled members of the Fillmore family to serve as managers of the school throughout the twentieth century.

In defending the school's right to nonprofit status, Charles spoke before the court, emphasizing the spiritual nature of the teaching and the prayer work of Silent Unity. He testified:

We have what is called the silent prayer method, and we follow out the command of Jesus that we should get together in His name. We recognize that Jesus is the head of the work: that Jesus Christ is right in our midst today carrying on His work. We are one department of that work. We reach such a state of consciousness that we function through a spiritual ether very much like the radio. People who follow our teachings lay down the personal and rise into the spiritual, and get the consciousness we have. It is not only a psychological consciousness, but it is a teaching. We teach the people directly what we think they should do, especially as to the law of love and justice and righteousness, trying to iron out all the differences in life, as we recognize the difference in the life of any man is the result of discord in states of mind.[15]

The U.S. Board of Tax Appeals, with Judge Sternhagen rendering the opinion on April 23, 1926, ruled in Unity's favor. Judge Sternhagen, speaking for the three-member panel, declared:

In considering whether a corporation is religious, charitable or educational, we must always be guided by the character of the organization and its activities. We are of the opinion that the purpose of the petitioner is within the statute, that its financial activities are only incidental to this purpose and do not change it, and that its earnings are all devoted to this purpose. The petitioner is therefore exempt from tax and there is no deficiency.[16]

With this ruling Unity School of Christianity was allowed the same tax privileges as nonprofit educational, scientific, or religious organizations, even though it was not organized under the laws that typically apply to these groups.

At Unity's Fourth Annual Convention held October 3–7, 1926, the Fillmores felt it necessary to make sure Unity students knew how Unity School was owned and operated. The question "Who owns Unity property?" was answered quite specifically:

Unity School of Christianity is a corporation that was created on April 14, 1914, under the Business Corporation Law of Missouri. The Unity School of Christianity was incorporated as a business corporation because of the fact that it prints books and does other things that are considered business. However, it is organized for religious and educational purposes and not for profit. There is a paragraph in the Articles of Incorporation which reads as follows: "Provided that no dividend shall ever be declared or paid but all profits and property of this organization shall be used to carry out the purpose of the organization or some part thereof." The sole purpose of the school is to set forth in a practical way the teachings of Jesus Christ and to establish the kingdom of heaven here on earth.[17]

As is necessary with business corporations, stock was issued, but this stock is held in trust by four members of the Fillmore family who are acting directors. A Declaration of Trust was made on August 3, 1918, and another on June 22, 1923, in which the Fillmore family transferred to Unity School all their right, title, and interest in all properties of the corporation. The Fillmores give their entire time to the work of the School and receive, therefore, regular salaries, just as other employees of the School receive salaries. No one owns anything at the farm except furniture and personal property. The Fillmores as well as others living at the farm pay a rental for the use of their dwellings and they also pay for their meals at Unity Inn, just as others do.[18]

The nonprofit status of the Unity School remained unchanged throughout the remainder of the twentieth century. The U.S. Internal Review Service continued to allow the school tax-exempt status based on the educational and spiritual nature of its work. The only amendment to the Articles of Incorporation was made on August 26, 1951, when the sixth article was changed to reflect the decision of the Board of Trustees to extend "the corporation duration to perpetual."[19]

Management by the Fillmore Family

Throughout the twentieth century, operational management of Unity School of Christianity was controlled by the Fillmore family. Presidents of the school and those holding chairmanships of the board of trustees have all been the sons, grandchildren, and great-grandchildren of Charles and Myrtle. The school has thrived under their leadership, growing to become a worldwide spiritual organization and operating on a budget of approximately $35 million annually. Management control has been maintained through ownership of the corporation's fifty shares of stock. When the corporation was formed in 1914, the stock was divided equally between four persons: Charles, Myrtle, Lowell, and Royal Fillmore. With the death of Royal in 1923, his shares were transferred to his brother, Waldo Rickert Fillmore. This was accomplished by a provision in the bylaws stipulating that when a trustee and stockholder either resigns or dies, the remaining trustees determine the disposition of the outstanding shares. Each trustee votes according to the number of shares he or she holds.[20]

With the death of Myrtle in 1931 and Charles in 1948, a portion of their shares was allocated to their sons, Lowell and Waldo Rickert Fillmore—enough shares to allow them to maintain control of the corporation. Approximately one-third of the total shares, however, were assigned to May Rowland, who was not a member of the Fillmore family. Rowland, who since 1916 had been director of Silent Unity, was awarded stock in recognition of her valuable service to the school and out of gratitude for her family's contribution to Unity. Her father, Daniel Hoagland, had provided funding for Unity in the early 1900s at a time of financial crisis.[21]

Shares of stock in the corporation were passed on to a third generation of Fillmores with the appointment to the board of trustees of Charles R. Fillmore, the son of Waldo Rickert Fillmore, after his return to Unity School from service in the Navy in World War II. In 1964 Charles R., after a twenty-year career in Unity, was appointed executive vice president and chief operating officer. He became majority stockholder with the retirement of Lowell in 1964, the death of his father Waldo Rickert in 1965, and the retirement of May Rowland in 1972. Charles R. served as president until 1987 and as majority stockholder and chairman of the board of trustees until 2001. His daughter Connie Fillmore Bazzy, who began her career in Unity in 1971, served as president from 1987 to 2001. She had been awarded sufficient shares so that if her father had died or resigned and returned his shares to the corporation, she would have had authority to manage the school.

Operational Management in the Twenty-first Century

On March 13, 2001, Connie Fillmore Bazzy announced that the school planned to make a transition from the operating system that placed management control in the hands of the Fillmore family to a "more traditional non-profit management and Board structure."[22] A new board of trustees would be selected to replace the internal board, which had been comprised of Unity School employees. Connie announced that she would be "the last Fillmore" to occupy the post of president and chief executive officer, that she would be resigning from that post and selecting a successor. She indicated that she would assume the post of chairman of the new board of trustees and that her father would become chairman emeritus. The new president and CEO would be a qualified Unity person who understood and embraced the core values of the Unity movement, who had proven experience in operating a nonprofit organization, and who possessed strong management and leadership skills. As chairman of the board of trustees, Bazzy planned work closely with the new CEO for the next few years to ensure a smooth transition.[23]

Connie indicated that members of the board of trustees would be "chosen by virtue of their understanding of and commitment to the values and work of the Unity School." New board members would represent various areas of expertise needed to move the school successfully into the future. Their responsibilities would include setting policy as well as engaging in fiscal and fund-raising activities.[24]

Financing Unity School of Christianity

Throughout its history, the programs and facilities of Unity School have been supported financially primarily by donations from those who received prayer work from Silent Unity and by two promotional programs: Prosperity Banks and Premium Booklets. Income produced by the Prosperity Bank plan funded Unity's growth from 1910 to the 1950s. The Premium Booklet promotion program generated the income that kept Unity School afloat from the 1960s through the year 2000. The educational programs of Unity School (which include adult education classes and workshops, ministerial training programs, and retreats) have seldom produced enough income to pay for their operating costs or to contribute to Unity School overhead.

Prosperity Banks: Key Factor in Unity's Growth

Why did Unity School grow so rapidly after 1910? The answer is simple: Prosperity Banks. In 1910, Lowell Fillmore, the eldest son of Charles and Myrtle Fillmore and editor of *Weekly Unity* magazine, devised a plan for generating new subscriptions. Called the Prosperity Bank plan, it proved highly successful and was soon used to promote all of Unity's publications. The plan was ultimately responsible for the sizable growth of the Unity movement between the years 1910 and 1960.

Prosperity Banks were first used in 1910 to help members of the Kansas City Unity Society of Practical Christianity pay for annual subscriptions to *Weekly Unity* magazine. At the time, *Weekly Unity* was a new and untried publication addressed specifically to the members of the Society. Using a four-page, newsletter-type format, *Weekly Unity* was first published in April 1909. Its pages contained news of interest to members; a column by Lowell Fillmore entitled "Things to Be Remembered," which focused on Unity principles and practices; excerpts from Charles Fillmore's Sunday talks to the Society of Practical Christianity; and a series of Bible lessons. The Kansas City group itself was not large: its average weekly attendance at Sunday services in 1910 was a little over one hundred persons.[25]

When Prosperity Banks were first introduced, only thirty-five members of the society subscribed to *Weekly Unity*.[26] A small news item in the May 5, 1910, issue of *Weekly Unity* described the banks. It noted: "Every friend is invited to become a subscriber to the *Weekly Unity* and receive one of the new Prosperity Banks. Each bank has a strong prosperity statement printed on it. This statement is to be repeated each time a dime is deposited in the bank."[27]

Society members were asked to come by the office of the editor or librarian at Unity headquarters in Kansas City to pick up their little cardboard banks. In addition to the prosperity affirmation printed on one side, there was a slot for depositing dimes. A key feature was the method of payment. The subscription price of $1 for fifty-two issues was to be paid over the course of ten weeks, with members depositing a dime each week. Subscriptions began at the time members signed up for the bank. Each member was also told, upon requesting a Prosperity Bank, that his or her name would be taken to the Silent Unity room and "its owner given special prosperity treatments for a month."[28]

Within a week, it was apparent that many members were willing to try the bank proposal. *Weekly Unity* reported, "Many are taking advantage of the offer which we made in last week's paper."[29] The offer was restated, "*Weekly Unity* one year, a Prosperity Bank and a month of prosperity treatments for the asking." The steps a member needed to take to participate were again described:

One wishing to take this combination signs a little card prepared for the purpose and receives from the Librarian a Prosperity Bank. His name is both entered on the mailing list for *Weekly Unity* for one year and sent to the Silent Unity room for a month's prosperity treatment. He takes the bank and deposits a dime in it each week, holding the Special Prosperity Statement which is printed on the side of the bank. At the end he brings the dollar thus saved to the Librarian.[30]

As the year 1910 progressed, reports appearing in *Weekly Unity* indicated that the banks were generating a good deal of interest. In April 1911, the Fillmores decided to use Prosperity Banks to promote *Weekly Unity* to the thirteen thousand subscribers to *Unity* magazine.[31] *Unity* readers were told of the advantages of receiving *Weekly Unity:*

We believe that if more people knew about our little paper, called *Weekly Unity,* the list of subscribers would be much larger, so we desire to say a few words for it. It is a four-pager at present, and is in its second volume. It was published at first in the interest of the local Unity Society, but we feel now that the time has come for it to do a larger work in connection with the one it originally took up. Each issue of the *Weekly Unity* contains extracts from Charles Fillmore's talk of the Sunday morning just preceding publication. It also gives a Bible reading which is used in the Unity service, but which can be used by any society or individual. Part of a column is given to "Things to Be Remembered," and many items of interest to the members of the local Society and outsiders are printed. All announcements and reports of the Society are made through this paper. The subscription price of $1 per year brings you fifty visits from the newsy and helpful little caller.[32]

Unity readers were then advised that a Prosperity Bank could be used to pay for the subscription. The offer and steps needed to participate were spelled out:

If you wish the paper for one year, send us your name and address and state that you want to become a subscriber and take the Prosperity Bank. Upon receipt of your request we will enter your name on the mailing list of the *Weekly Unity* for one year and send you a bank, in which you are to save a dime a week, and at the end of ten weeks return the $1 thus saved in the bank to pay for your subscription. As soon as we receive the application we will enter your name on the Prosperity list for one month's prosperity treatment.[33]

The Fillmores stressed the need for users of the Prosperity Bank to participate fully in a drill that required the use of affirmations at specific times. They explained: "You will also hold in meditation the statement printed on the side of the bank, in co-operation with the members of the Society. This has been tried with much success by those who have taken the banks."[34]

In May 1911, one month after the introduction of Prosperity Banks to *Unity* readers, positive results were reported. "A large number of our friends," it was indicated, "have responded to the offer."[35] The appeal for new participants was made again in June. In July, more success was reported. In August, it was announced that Prosperity Banks had enabled people to get over the idea of lack. *Unity* stated, "The Prosperity Bank is teaching many people how to apply the law of prosperity in a practical way."[36] Testimonials soon began appearing in *Unity* in the form of letters of "thanksgiving and commendation" from Prosperity Bank users who experienced an increase in finances.[37] A satisfied bank user commented:

I am sending the one dollar paper money in exchange for ten dimes from Unity Prosperity Bank. The empty thoughts of my mind are being filled with His inexhaustible substance, and many desires of my heart are being satisfied. I have had more money come in payment for work than in a long time. I feel success is mine in the near future. I enjoy *Weekly Unity* so much.[38]

The success of Prosperity Banks in increasing the number of sub-scribers to *Weekly Unity* convinced the Fillmores in December 1911 to use the banks in promoting holiday books and subscriptions. *Unity* magazine announced: "Our friends have found the Prosperity Banks so helpful in connection with saving the *Weekly Unity* subscription money that we have decided to give everyone a chance to make the prosperity demonstra-tion in a more extended way."[39]

Unity prepared what they called a "Christmas Prosperity Bank Book" that would be sent to anyone who applied for one. Those who ordered the bank book could select from a list of books, pamphlets, and subscriptions. No money was to be sent in, as two months would be allowed for bank users to save the full amount of the order. As participants deposited ten cents, they were to silently affirm the prosperity statement appearing on the bank. The user's name was to be sent to the Silent Unity room for "one month's general prosperity treatment."[40]

Prosperity Banks attracted sufficient new business during Christmas of 1911 to convince the Fillmores in 1912 to expand their coverage and use them to promote subscriptions to subscribers of *Unity Magazine*. In Janu-ary the editors of *Unity* informed their readers: "The Prosperity Banks have met with so much success, and in a majority of cases have been so markedly beneficial to those making deposits in them, that we feel justified in keeping them before *Unity* readers, so that all may have an opportunity of proving their worth and receiving their benefits."[41] *Unity* subscribers could use Prosperity Banks to pay for their own subscription renewals or to pay for subscriptions of three friends who might be interested in receiv-ing the magazine. The editors of *Unity* presented the following proposal to their subscribers:

Here is our offer. Upon receipt of your request we will enter three subscriptions to *Unity* for one year each, and at the same time send you a Prosperity Bank in which you will save the subscription price. While you are saving the money by dropping a dime at a time in the bank, our Silent Unity Department will give you one month's general prosperity treatment. A prosperity statement will be sent you with the bank, which you are to repeat silently each time you deposit a coin. At the end of two months you are to send us the two dollars saved in the bank, to pay for three subscriptions to Unity, thus taking advantage of our offer of three subscrip-tions for two dollars.[42]

Unity magazine editors pointed out that by becoming a Prosperity Bank participant, it was possible to increase one's own prosperity while at the same time serving others, indicating: "This is an excellent opportunity for you to prove the Law and at the same time introduce *Unity* to three of your friends. Send in your request at once, and begin the cultivation of a daily prosperity thought."[43] *Unity* guaranteed that as soon as a subscriber requested a Prosperity Bank, his or her name would be sent "to the Silent Unity room for a month's general prosperity treatment." A response to a letter inquiry about what the banks looked like explained: "It is a cardboard container that can be folded flat to fit in an envelope. When it arrives you unfold it and stand it up in a convenient place. One of the tiny stars around the border should be crossed out each time you drop a coin into the Bank."[44]

Prosperity Banks proved highly popular with *Unity* subscribers. In December 1912 the magazine reported that during the preceding twelve months, "several thousand" had taken advantage of the special offer of three subscriptions for $2 and sent them to three friends as presents. Throughout 1912, bank users wrote to Unity telling of the benefits of participation. Many indicated that in addition to increased financial well-being, they felt connected spiritually at a deeper level. Prosperity Banks had been so successful that by the end of 1912, there were thirty thousand subscribers on the magazine's lists, up from thirteen thousand in 1911.[45] Never before in Unity's twenty-three year history had subscriptions risen so dramatically.

In 1913, Prosperity Banks were promoted in each issue of *Unity* magazine. In their messages to subscribers, the editors presented ideas on the nature of true prosperity, indicating that it encompassed far more than financial gain. "Many persons spend their entire lives seeking prosperity," they wrote, "but few realize it is really a state of mind. The material comforts of life are controlled by mind."[46] The editors said that the thoughts and ideas people dwell upon are crucial, and that people who keep their minds focused on God are the most successful. The magazine advised: "Make your mind prosperous through cultivating large ideas of God's abundance, and learn to bless and praise everything that you possess, even though it be small in appearance. You will then be on the royal road to Prosperity."[47]

As the months passed in 1913, more and more *Unity* subscribers became participants. *Unity* magazine reported in August that thousands of banks had been used during the preceding year. The editors expressed the wish that everyone would try the plan. They stated, "We invite every reader to become 'a prosperity banker.'"[48]

It comes as no surprise that in 1914 *Unity* continued to push Prosperity Banks. Almost every issue of the magazine carried a two-page advertisement promoting their use. In April, the editors again commented on the banks' widespread popularity. They indicated: "Thousands of persons have learned the truth concerning the wonderful laws of prosperity through the instructions given with the Unity Prosperity Bank, and through it they have also learned to apply the laws in their daily lives and realize unlimited prosperity."[49]

In 1915, the editors continued to broaden the definition of prosperity. "Prosperity," they indicated in the May issue, "is the manifestation of the fullness of good. It is a universal force, and its source of supply is inexhaustible."[50] In July the editors observed that those who were more successful in using the banks were those who believed most fully in their efficacy: "Faith is absolutely necessary in demonstrating prosperity and success through spiritual laws. It is undoubtedly true that many earnest students fail to realize greater abundance because they overlook this essential factor. Lack of faith prevents the drawing into manifestation of the creative elements of Being."[51]

By 1915 Prosperity Bank patrons received, in addition to the affirmations printed on the side of the bank, prosperity lessons and a drill in concentration. "With each bank," it was noted, "is sent a folder which gives instructions pertaining to the bank and treatments."[52] The lessons and drill were "to impress clearly upon the minds of students the true idea of the creative force of Mind." It was important that bank users follow the instructions. The editors indicated: "the law never fails when we work with it understandingly. If you should send for a Prosperity Bank, we ask you to study the instructions carefully."[53]

The popularity of Prosperity Banks continued to rise, and the editors of *Unity* commented on the increasing demand, noting:

Our mails are heavy with letters of thanks from those who have found the Unity Bank plan helpful in demonstrating prosperity and finances. There is no doubt in the minds of the thousands who have been successful demonstrators of this plan, but that permanent prosperity can be realized if the instructions given with the special treatment from Silent Unity are applied.[54]

Subscription figures for 1916 bore out the fact that Prosperity Banks continued to be responsible for sizeable growth in the *Unity* subscription list. Fifty thousand subscribers were listed on the rolls, five times the number of subscribers in 1909.[55]

Unity continued to publish, on a regular basis, testimonials from those who had benefited from the use of Prosperity Banks. The following extracts from letters of Prosperity Banks users are representative of the commentaries of those who believed they benefited from using the bank.

Port Neches, Texas—The ten weeks since receipt of Prosperity Bank were accomplished yesterday, and I have really had increased material prosperity, and prospects of larger earnings are in view. My greatest blessing has been grasping and realizing the true idea of prosperity, that the true riches are the riches of the kingdom of God, and that in proportion as we acquire these they will show forth in material form in obedience to the law of manifestation.[56]

Hynes, California—Since sending for the Prosperity Bank our financial cloud seemed to lift. Money came from an unexpected source, and we do not feel depressed. We feel very grateful to Unity and the true source of all Good.[57]

In 1916, the editors of *Unity* continued to expand upon the reasons for using Prosperity Banks. When asked why the banks were necessary, they commented:

Men and women everywhere are searching for, and will be satisfied with only that which is practical. When the hidden principles of life are discerned by them, they will not accept those principles wholly until their practical values have been discovered. It seems quite necessary to find a working basis for the science of life before mankind will endeavor to apply its laws. In this respect the Unity Prosperity Bank Plan supplies the demand by giving the word a practical lesson in demonstrating the truth and the reality of the principle of Prosperity.[58]

The "object of the Plan," they continued, "is to furnish a simple Prosperity lesson that teaches the unfailing Law of Supply." The editors assured readers that the bank plan patrons had found it very helpful. "From the time that the Plan was first used," they stated, "it has been an extraordinary success." A large number of readers had requested banks, they reported, "because they realize that the Plan would help them establish their prosperity on a more permanent foundation, and at the same time give an opportunity to send *Unity* magazine to three persons who need the ministry of this helpful periodical."[59]

From 1917 to 1920, the editors of *Unity* continued to publish in almost every monthly issue a two-page advertisement for Prosperity Banks that addressed three topics—"Why Necessary?," "The Object of the Bank," and "The Use of the Bank." In July 1920, the editors attempted to answer a question that they must have been asked on many occasions:

"Does it really free a person from poverty?" Their affirmative response declared:

Well, just give the Bank a chance! In using it with the accompanying drill, you break up old thought conditions of lack, thus allowing the spirit of plenty to express through you. Opulent abundance obtains in the universal Mind, and ever seeks to flow out through multitudinous channels. If you have harbored poor thoughts, the free riches of Spirit could not work out into manifestation through you, because you haven't given them the chance . . . Rich and poor alike find the plan effective. Those who already have an abundance learn to establish their prosperity on the granite foundation of spiritual understanding; and those who have experienced lack learn to appropriate what is already their own.[60]

Testimonials to the effectiveness of the plan were continually featured in *Unity*, lending credibility to the editors' claims for its effectiveness. The following are extracts from testimonials published in 1920:

I am well pleased with the investment. Harmony has been established out of financial chaos. I realize as never before that God is the source of all good. The Bank certainly brings rich returns.[61]

Enclosed find three dollars from my Prosperity Bank. The Lord has surely blessed us wonderfully since I sent for the Bank. Not only financially, but even more have we become prosperous in the consciousness of our oneness with the Father. Life is now a joy to us, and in ministering to others we ourselves receive a blessing many times greater.[62]

In August 1920, the editors felt it necessary to disabuse users of the notion that the bank plan could be implemented without using the drill. Several were apparently sending in money for subscriptions without following the set of instructions that accompanied the banks. The editors saw no benefit in this approach. They indicated:

Some of our free-hearted friends feel that they wish to send in money for publications at once, rather than to let it accumulate in the Prosperity Bank, and send it later. Now let us make this bank proposition a little clearer. You get benefits in prosperity in proportion to the mental attitude you take. The object to be attained in the use of the Prosperity Bank is educative in two respects. First, when the depositor affirms in words as the deposit is made, it establishes a continuous thought current of prosperity; and second, one learns not to waste God's Substance, for the fund grows easily from the small change which might otherwise be spent for trifles. Hence, it is better to follow the Bank Plan, in preference to paying at once for subscriptions.[63]

In January 1921, the editors of *Unity*, in promoting Prosperity Banks, asked the question: "Dare I depend entirely on God?" It is the question, they acknowledged, "which we all put to ourselves at a certain stage of unfoldment."[64] Answering the question in the affirmative, they explained:

When intuition and reason have just about convinced us that we can rest safe in the "everlasting arm," the adversary begins putting in his word about the bank account, the rainy day, life insurance, and all the rest of the false beliefs which never get us anywhere. This is the reason for the Prosperity Bank. The old fear thoughts of lack must be cast out and the mind must be trained to a perfect dependence on God.[65]

In June 1921, *Unity* announced that there were then ninety thousand subscribers on the rolls, almost double the number enrolled in 1916.[66]

In 1922, the editors of *Unity* continued to expand upon the benefits of the bank plan. One of its principal values, they stated, was that it helped create in the minds of bank users a "prosperity consciousness." Repeated use of the bank drill made it possible for people to create financial well-being without keeping "the nose to the grindstone for a mere existence."[67] The editors explained:

That it is not necessary to be in any form of financial bondage, has been proved by the thousands of Unity Prosperity Bank patrons. By the use of the Prosperity Bank Drill, they have learned to "let go" of money cares and worries; they have linked up with the Universal Substance which is only waiting for a chance to rush in; they have through repeated successes built up a strong prosperity consciousness.[68]

The bank drill, the editors believed, had a salutary effect on the user's reasoning power and subconscious mind, creating more positive mental states regarding financial matters as well as more serenity. They explained: "Prosperity Banks bring to the faithful users that peace and poise which result from an entire dependence on God. Only those who have had the experience can realize the care-free, light, happy feeling attendant upon this perfect trust in the infinite Good."[69]

The editors presented the testimony of a bank plan user to support this assertion. The user declared: "A wonderful change has taken place in my affairs since I began using the Prosperity Bank. I find myself strangely calm when faced by obstacles, where once I would have been overwhelmed by fear of failure. My faith in God is more substantial and I seem to be literally shown how to manage every difficulty."[70]

With each succeeding year, the editors of *Unity* devised new and fresh language to characterize the benefits of Prosperity Banks. The year 1923 was no exception. The editors listed nine benefits to be derived from using the plan and urged Unity students to become bank plan patrons. They were encouraged to become involved for these reasons:

• Because it gives a working knowledge of mind and soul action in contacting the dynamic things of Spirit.

• Because it trains you to look back of appearances for all that you can possibly need or want.

• Because it teaches you how to create what you need from the formless substance of the invisible realm of God.

• Because it relieves your mind of all care, uncertainty, and fear regarding money matters.

• Because its use makes you strictly honest, just, free, generous and forgiving in all monetary dealings.

• Because it helps to take your attention from petty, sordid considerations of making ends meet, of rainy days, of hoarding and scrimping.

• Because it leaves you free to put the best of yourself into your work, knowing that God brings the increase.

• Because it puts you in touch with Silent Unity, which holds you in prayerful meditation for success.

• Because—and this is the most important "because"—it makes you know yourself as an heir of God, and as a coworker with him in bringing forth into visible expression his perfect universe. This is your prerogative. Now exercise it.[71]

On the strength of these arguments, it is understandable why *Unity* readers familiar with Unity teaching were inclined to give the bank plan a try.

The year 1922 marked an important milestone in the growth of *Unity* magazine. The circulation for the first time went over the one hundred thousand mark. *Unity* was reported to be servicing 112,203 subscribers.[72] The rapid growth in the subscription list was no doubt attributable to the use of Prosperity Banks by *Unity* subscribers. A total of 48,482 cardboard banks were sent out by Unity School in 1921.[73]

In 1923 another eight thousand banks were being sent out each month to subscribers who wanted to participate in the bank plan.[74] Sources within Unity School acknowledged the contribution of the bank plan and credited it with the dramatic increase in the number of subscribers. On August

4, 1923, *Unity News,* the in-house organ of the workers at Unity School, indicated: "Thousands of testimonials tell of finances established soundly and kept in order by the use of the Prosperity Bank. It is apparent that the Unity publications owe to the Bank much of their increase in circulation."[75]

The newspaper went on to explain the reasons why the bank plan worked so well: "The Bank Plan has established its merit in various ways. Persons who have discovered its efficacy have told their friends of its value. Then, too, the bank is an easy medium of contact with Unity; thousands of subscribers have learned about Unity only after the Prosperity Bank plan had made it possible for them to obtain our periodicals."[76]

The growth in numbers of subscribers is even more remarkable considering that in the 1920s Unity School had a policy of promoting only to those already inside Unity channels of communication. *Unity* magazine reported: "Unity School does not advertise its service and its publications except in Unity publications and through the mediums afforded by the Unity organization. It is dependent for its growth on the present subscribers and the efforts they make to spread to all the world its aims and ideals, and its publications."[77]

In 1924, Unity mailed 94,083 Prosperity Banks. It was the principal in-house vehicle for promoting Unity publications and no doubt the primary source of new readership.[78] *Unity* magazine reached new heights in 1924, reaching 165,000 subscribers, triple the number on the rolls in 1916 and sixteen times as many as in 1909.[79]

In August 1924, the editors of *Unity,* in describing the efficacy of the banks, let the trappings of success overcome their good sense. In characterizing the effectiveness of the banks, the editors made promises that seemed unwarranted and beyond what could be justifiably claimed. They called the bank plan "a master key which unlocks the doors to success" and further stated that the bank drill "cures stinginess . . . cures dishonesty . . . cures soul cramp . . . and cures one of a sense of injustice."[80] In this instance, the editors promised more than one might reasonably assume could be delivered.

Evidently, Unity School was criticized by some for materialistic motives because of its constant promotion of Prosperity Banks. In 1927, in response to a question about why Unity emphasized the prosperity idea, the editors of *Weekly Unity* met the issue head-on, indicating:

The prosperity Unity talks about is not merely an accumulation of gold. Webster says that prosperity is advance or gain in anything good or desirable and Unity uses it in this larger sense—an abundance of health, or of happiness, or of friends, or of money . . . There is nothing sinful or mercenary about the accumulation of goods. We are told that plenty is our birthright. If we are thinking right, we cannot escape prosperity in all its phases.[81]

A key to the success of the Prosperity Bank plan was the patron's selection of three friends who would receive a year's subscription to *Unity* magazine. If the "friends" were not open to Unity teaching, the Unity literature would probably end up in the garbage can. In July 1927, the editors of *Unity* advised prospective bank patrons on how to identify those persons who might be receptive to Unity teaching. They commented:

You have dozens of friends who are seeking the very things that *Unity* magazine has to offer them . . . Your first work is to select among your friends those whom you feel are really sincerely seeking something of what Unity has to offer them. May we help you in choosing "Who?"

First—the wide awake, well-read person who rather prides himself on keeping informed on any current line of thought that is attracting attention. *Unity* magazine offers interesting ideas and discussions that pertain to metaphysics, a subject much discussed everywhere.

Second—the tired mother and housewife whose family is getting beyond her and who is blindly seeking help, sympathy, understanding and advice about her problems. The Home Department offers all of these.

Third—the friend battling with some problem of finances or of health, of business or home, meeting seeming failure with a determination to win.

Fourth—The Sunday school teacher or the earnest Bible student who has felt the need of a more practical interpretation of the Bible lessons—an interpretation that may be applied to the daily affairs of life. The International Sunday School lessons and their metaphysical interpretation are a regular feature of *Unity Magazine*.[82]

This advice to subscribers, given as an aid in choosing people for gift subscriptions, provides a glimpse of the kind of men and women Unity believed were most interested in the teaching.

In December 1929, no doubt as a result of their excitement over the success of Prosperity Banks, the editors of *Unity* again went overboard in promoting them, promising more than could be delivered. A brief ad in *Unity* read as follows:

> A MATHEMATICAL CERTAINTY
>
> A desire to prosper
> + The help of the Prosperity Bank Plan
> + The application of the Bank Drill
> = Prosperity[83]

It was quite appropriate to cite testimonials of bank plan participants as to the value of the banks or to indicate what might reasonably be expected from their use. *Unity* editors went too far when they promised prosperity to the bank plan user as "a mathematical certainty."

During the two decades before the Great Depression (1912–1929), Unity School used Prosperity Banks to promote *Weekly Unity* in the same way it had used them to promote *Unity* magazine. In-house advertisements similar to those used in *Unity* were placed in *Weekly Unity*. The first announcement encouraging *Weekly Unity* subscribers to become bank participants and to give the magazine as a gift to three friends was made in December 1912. It noted:

Weekly Unity is proving to be so helpful to its readers that we are persuaded that it would also make an excellent gift. We are, therefore, offering three yearly subscriptions to *Weekly Unity* for $2. Here is a gift that brings to three persons and their families a message of good cheer, uplift, health, happiness and prosperity. Send your list of three names, with addresses and $2 to the Unity Tract Society.[84]

In most issues of *Weekly Unity* thereafter, the editors encouraged subscribers to become bank plan patrons. Their efforts were highly successful. Subscriptions increased from 8,500 in 1912 to 185,000 in 1928, as the chart below shows:

Year	Number of Subscribers[85]	Year	Number of Subscribers[85]
1912	8,500	1921	90,000
1915	18,190	1924	115,000
1916	22,000	1925	117,523
1919	24,995	1927	156,500
1920	38,704	1928	185,680

In 1928, with a total of over 185,000 subscribers, for the first time *Weekly Unity* outdistanced Unity School's flagship publication, *Unity*. *Weekly Unity* surpassed its older sibling probably because Unity School recommended it for beginning students, while *Unity* was being directed toward the more advanced, indicating:

Weekly Unity offers a terse discussion of metaphysical subjects, as relating to current matters, vegetarian diet, gleanings from the press; and practical, homely problems are handled from a Truth standpoint. *Unity* magazine, published monthly, gives a more comprehensive treatment, a more advanced study of things spiritual, a growth in understanding of things like advanced metaphysics, and the practical application of the Christ teachings.[86]

Wee Wisdom made its first appearance in 1893. Edited by Myrtle Fillmore, it taught "Truth" to children in pictures, poems, and stories. *Wee Wisdom*, taking the persona of an older sister or kindly aunt, sought to show children "the beauties of love and Truth." It was a magazine that the editor hoped children would be delighted to have because it was "beautiful, sweet, helpful, encouraging and entertaining." In 1901 *Unity* magazine urged parents to subscribe to *Wee Wisdom* for their children. The magazine was viewed as unique, "the only metaphysical magazine for children" in the United States. The editors of *Unity* saw it filling an important need and believed it "should receive the hearty support of everyone who wants this Truth taught to rising generations."[87]

Subscribers did not stay on the list for long, for children grow up quickly. As a result, in the early years *Wee Wisdom* had difficulty paying its way. It was suspended for three years between 1896 and 1899; by 1913, twenty years after it was launched, it had only 3,700 subscribers.[88] In an effort to broaden its appeal, it was decided to expand the scope of the magazine to include teenagers and parents. This intention was announced in *Weekly Unity*:

Wee Wisdom has decided to grow up a little bit herself, so that she can entertain and help the larger children as well as do general good about the house by aiding mamma and papa in solving the little problems that come up in home life. Beginning with the August number, *Wee Wisdom* will be enlarged so as to contain not only stories and good things for our Wee readers, but also a department devoted to youths and one for the mothers of Truth children.[89]

The enlarged scope seemed to have little impact on numbers of subscribers—by 1919, there were still only 4,200 on the list. Shortly thereafter, *Wee Wisdom* returned to the audience for which it was originally intended, "the little folks." Its objective was to save children from "years of wrong thinking and consequent suffering." It did so by stories and poems "that entertainingly teach Truth, more by suggestion than actual words."[90] The magazine's new mission was stated as follows: "For the Children. Beautiful pictures, lovely poems, charming stories, telling lessons, combine to make this monthly magazine a delight to the eye as well as to the mind. The main purposes of the magazine are character formation and soul culture. Subsidiary purposes are instruction, entertainment and diversion."[91]

For some unexplained reason, it appears that Unity School did not use the Prosperity Bank plan until 1919 to promote *Wee Wisdom*. When it did so, it appealed to children's interest in nice things, and their desire to help their friends. The following promotional copy reflects how the bank plan was presented to children and their parents:

Most grown people have forgotten that God has provided the best of everything for us, and enough of it; so they have looked outside of themselves for the good things of life; in doing so, they have lost the good that is for them.

The Unity grown folks are now training their minds back to the knowledge that God has everything good ready for their use, if they will only see it that way. They are using a little helper for this purpose, called the Prosperity Bank.

When mother has a cape, little daughter has to have a cape, too. And isn't it every boy's ambition to have a watch like father's? Now, you should have a little Prosperity Bank, in which you can save your pennies for subscriptions to *Wee Wisdom,* just as grown-ups are saving for *Unity* and *Weekly Unity* subscriptions.

You can learn, day by day, that God will give you every good thing; and, at the same time, you can save your pennies, nickels, and dimes to send Wee Wisdom to a little friend.

Below is a blank, which you can either fill out yourself, or have some older person fill out for you.[92]

The following subscription totals reflect the impact on the growth of *Wee Wisdom* when the bank plan was introduced.[93]

Year	Subscriptions to Wee Wisdom
1913	3,700
1916	4,800
1919	4,200
1920	15,000
1922	35,500
1928	52,680

For a few years beginning in 1896, *Unity* magazine published a special feature entitled "A Daily Word." It was, according to Charles Fillmore, "for the benefit of those who want a healing thought for each day of the week."[94] The column recommended that subscribers: "Take up the word for the day upon rising, and repeat it aloud a number of times. Repeat again at twelve and six. During the intervening hours repeat it mentally."[95]

"A Daily Word" took the form of phrases like those below, which *Unity* recommended be used during the week of September 20, 1902.

Monday: The good that is for me is my God. My God is Life, Truth, Love, Substance, Intelligence, Omnipresence, Omnipotence, Omniscience. I do not accuse the world or myself of having lustful passions or sensual appetites. God is all.

Saturday: I understand the secret of instantaneous spiritual demonstration. I am omniscience, I am understanding, I am strength.

Sunday: While knowing all things and doing all things, I am identified with nothing. I am absolutely free.[96]

This feature was eliminated from the magazine shortly after the turn of the century and it never reappeared. In early 1924, Unity School decided to publish an expanded version of the 1890s column in a monthly magazine format with the title *Unity Daily Word.* In announcing the new publication *Unity* magazine observed:

It has long been the desire of Unity to meet the demand for instructions which can be put to daily use by Truth students. To be sure, the Unity periodicals, books and booklets all contain material for daily Christian practice. But people who live in the rush of things want something definite and explicit they can lay hold of at the instant—a booklet that can be carried around in the pocket or handbag, that can be used on the train or the street car, on the desk, or the work bench or at the kitchen table, or on the dresser.[97]

The magazine later announced that a longtime Unity worker and current dean of the correspondence school, Frank B. Whitney, would serve as editor. Charles Fillmore would also be involved, because each issue would have his "sanction and supervision." The magazine would have strong leadership. "These able and consecrated workers," it was pointed out, "will see that Unity students are provided each day with a powerful lesson that will insure them peace, health, and prosperity."[98]

The magazine was promoted as giving "a devotional program for the morning, noon or evening period of meditation," including "a brief affirmation to be held in the silence, and a Bible reference in support of the affirmation"; as providing "daily lessons in demonstrating Truth"; and as helping persons "begin the day in the right state of mind." It was suggested that, in addition, the magazine "draws the reader close to the Source of his being, and prepares him to receive the blessing that the Father has in store for him. . . . Often the lesson fits the very problem that confronts the reader that day."[99]

Unity Daily Word was successful, probably beyond all expectations. At the outset it was promoted directly to Unity School magazine subscribers, who by 1925 totaled over 350,000.[100] In November 1926, Unity announced that during the twenty-eight months *Unity Daily Word* was published, "half of the Unity readers have become friends and subscribers."[101] In February 1928, a little over three years after beginning publication, the magazine reached the one hundred thousand mark. The good news was announced in *Unity:*

Three years ago last July, *Unity Daily Word* made its first appearance. Tuesday of this week, when making the official monthly count, the Addressograph department discovered that the magazine had passed the 100,000 mark during the last month. At that time the record showed 102,499. This is a gain of over 70% over the list of a year ago. 128,000 copies of the January number have been printed. The sales department reports that 17,869 copies of the magazine were sold to individuals by Unity centers last month.[102]

Unity Daily Word obviously hit an extremely responsive chord with readers of Unity School magazines. While it cannot be claimed that Prosperity Banks were directly responsible for the rapid four-year growth of *Unity Daily Word,* the pool of Unity School magazine subscribers from which readers of *Unity Daily Word* were drawn was developed largely through the efforts of bank plan patrons.

With *Wee Wisdom* focusing again solely on the needs of children, Unity School decided it was necessary to provide for the teaching of teenagers, who were no longer served by its publications. In November 1926 Unity School announced that, beginning in January 1927, it would commence publication of *Youth* magazine. The editors viewed its mission as being: "a genuine companion to boys and girls of high school age, to face their problems with them, to inspire them to high ideals and fine action, to show them the true values in life, and to lead them to recognize Truth."[103] Its aim was to entertain, instruct, and inspire. Fiction was one of its principle features, but fiction of a special kind. "It will be a fiction with Truth in it . . . stories that show Truth at work in the lives of young people." Biblical stories would also be presented. "Each month there is a youthful interpretation of some story from the Bible, showing that the Bible is a book of practical instruction, conforming to the findings of modern science and psychology."[104]

Like *Unity Daily Word*, this magazine was promoted to those already on Unity School subscriber lists. In its first year of publication, *Youth* attracted a total of 19,518 subscribers. The magazine grew much more slowly after its inaugural issues, attracting only 27,623 subscribers in its second year. *Youth* magazine did not enjoy the immediate response or the wide appeal of *Unity Daily Word*. The magazine could be purchased through the Prosperity Bank plan, but it failed to attract a large following among existing Unity School magazine subscribers.[105]

Charles Fillmore had a long-standing interest in the application of Christian ethics to modern business practices. A real estate businessman himself before becoming involved in Unity work, he understood the difficulties that businessmen face in living up to Christian ideals. As editor of *Unity* magazine, he often published articles that focused on the implications of Christian principles in the conduct of business enterprise. Given his lifelong interest and involvement in business affairs, it is not surprising, with both *Unity* and *Weekly Unity* enjoying phenomenal success in the early 1920s, that Unity School decided in June 1922 to publish a magazine "devoted to the application of Christianity to business in a practical way." The purposes were spelled out in *Unity:*

It seems that the time is now ripe for men to follow the teachings of the Master all the way, in business as well as in other walks of life. In this magazine for business people, we shall show that business health, business success, and business harmony can be attained and maintained when businessmen become partners with God—coworkers with Him.[106]

Like *Youth* magazine, *The Christian Business Man* never caught on with Unity School magazine subscribers. It attracted approximately 20,000 subscribers in its first year but never grew much beyond that. There were only 23,784 names on its subscription list in 1928.[107] While subscriptions could be obtained through the Prosperity Bank plan, Unity magazine subscribers did not show the same interest in it as in *Unity Daily Word*.[108]

Prosperity Banks: The Brainchild of Lowell Fillmore

Until the 1930s, nothing was said in Unity publications about the origins of the bank plan, who was responsible for developing it, or how it came about. In 1934 Inez Russell, a Unity School editor, wrote a profile of Lowell Fillmore for *Progress* magazine. Lowell was the eldest son of Charles and Myrtle and had been manager of Unity School since 1916. [Although his title was "manager," his role was more like that of an executive vice president.] The profile shed light on how the bank plan was conceived. Russell reported:

Almost a quarter of a century ago Lowell Fillmore sat at his desk in deep meditation—seeking inspiration from God. Then, as now, his attention was primarily focused on the dissemination of Truth throughout the world. As he sat at his desk he was pondering the question: How can Unity best serve its subscribers? His first thought had been of the children who subscribed to *Wee Wisdom,* how they might save their pennies to pay for their subscriptions.

As everyone knows who has studied Truth, he who turns to the Father in faith, believing, will get a solution to any problem. Lowell Fillmore was no exception, and suddenly an inspiration flashed into his consciousness. It was the birth of the Prosperity Bank Plan, a plan that has been in operation constantly since its inception, and it came to Lowell Fillmore full fledged ... At first it was used only in connection with subscribers to *Weekly Unity.* But for many years now thousands of persons all over the world have been saving in their banks for subscriptions to every Unity periodical and other Unity literature also.[109]

In 1931 Lowell, in correspondence with a potential bank plan participant, described how the idea came to him. He wrote:

A number of years ago it came to our attention that many persons who would like to subscribe to Unity literature felt that they could not spare the amount of a full year's subscription price at one time. So the idea occurred to us to issue little banks in which these folks might save their coins until they had enough to pay for the subscriptions desired.

Then we decided that merely providing banks was not going far enough. We wanted these persons to learn that their supply is unlimited, and that God, the source of all good, is their unfailing supply. Now, the only way to learn this and to manifest it is to think it and believe it; to change old habits of thinking about lack and "hard times"; to build into consciousness the truth that God is the source of all supply, and that there is no lack of any good thing.

With this thought in mind we planned the Prosperity Bank drill. With the bank we send a little Truth statement, which should be repeated and held in silent meditation whenever a coin is dropped into the bank, also whenever a thought of lack tries to creep into the mind. The secret of success with the bank plan lies in putting to flight all thoughts of fear, sickness, and lack, and substituting thoughts of joy, health, and plenty, for the Bible tells us, "As he thinketh within himself, so is he." He who looks to God for his supply, and thinks only thoughts of right kind, will attract to himself the good that he desires.

The little bank is for one's convenience in saving for Unity literature or for offerings to our work, if one is interested in helping the cause along. Seven weeks constitute the period of the prayer drill.[110]

Financing Unity School During the Great Depression and World War II

In the decade of the 1930s, the industrial world experienced a severe economic decline. Throughout the United States, every aspect of the nation's economy was hard hit. The downturn in the economy became known as the "Great Depression," probably because every economic indicator reflected a collapse. New investments declined from $10 billion in 1929 to $1 billion in 1932; national income fell from over $80 billion in 1929 to $50 billion in just three years. Over five thousand banks closed their doors during this same period. Industrial production declined dramatically. Automobile output fell from 4.5 million units in 1929 to 1.1 million in 1932. Unemployment skyrocketed, rising from 4 percent in 1929 to over 25 percent in 1933, with 15 to 20 percent of the workforce unable to find jobs each year until 1940. By 1932, one-third of the entire population of Pennsylvania was on relief, and in every major city, homeless families gathered in ramshackle communities called "Hoovervilles."[111]

Unity School magazines were little affected by the cataclysmic decline in national income. While not achieving the tremendous gains in numbers of subscribers experienced in the 1920s, Unity magazines countered the prevailing national economic trend and emerged in the late 1930s with more subscriptions on the lists than before the Depression began. In February 1929 Unity School reported 594,000 total subscribers.[112] In 1938, subscriptions to Unity magazines totaled 659,623. Two years later, in 1940, the total had risen to 700,000.[113]

The staying power of Unity School's three principal teaching and healing magazines (*Unity Magazine, Weekly Unity,* and *Unity Daily Word*) during the Great Depression can be seen from a comparison of subscription totals from 1924, when *Unity Daily Word* was first introduced, and subscription totals in 1938, nine years after the onset of the Depression. As seen in the chart below, there were almost 162,000 more subscribers to the three publications in 1938 than in 1924.[114]

Year	Unity	Weekly Unity	Unity Daily Word	Total	Difference
1924	165,000	116,000	5,300	286,300	
1938	96,000	170,000	182,000	448,000	+ 162,000

Although *Unity* magazine lost subscribers during the fourteen years between 1924 and 1938, the loss was probably attributable to causes other than the Depression. In November 1926, Unity School decided to direct *Unity* magazine to those interested in "a more advanced study of things spiritual."[115] *Weekly Unity,* on the other hand, was recommended for a broader group of students, those interested in "relating to current matters." *Weekly Unity,* therefore, would have been more attractive than *Unity* magazine to those being introduced to Unity teaching through the Prosperity Bank plan. Second, before the introduction of *Unity Daily Word,* those interested in Unity's basic teaching and healing work had two publications to choose from: *Unity* and *Weekly Unity.* Apparently many people subscribed to both. After 1924 these Unity students had three choices. Those who picked *Unity Daily Word* probably decided to satisfy themselves with either *Unity* or *Weekly Unity,* rather than both.

Throughout the 1930s, Unity School continued to urge Unity students to become Prosperity Bank users, stressing the fact that the banks aid people in shifting consciousness from poverty to abundance. Promotional material for Prosperity Banks in the 1930s often addressed issues of declining personal income. On March 10, 1934, *Weekly Unity* observed: "Many a person puts obstacles in the way of approaching good fortune by talking hard times and by indulging in fear and worry. Prosperity does not materialize in such an atmosphere."[116] The Unity School *Catalogue, 1934* also addressed the issue of poverty indirectly, stressing how the bank plan helped create the positive mindset so essential for success. It indicated: "The Unity Prosperity Bank Plan is based on the power of the mind to bring about certain desired results. It has been proved that the mind, through definitely directed thought, has the power to draw to itself an abundance of all good things from the universal source."[117] Creating the right state of consciousness was essential, and the bank plan facilitated this process: "The Bank Plan is designed to enrich the consciousness of the one who uses it, to help him overcome all thoughts of lack and failure and cultivate instead a sense of well-being and plenty. The Bank Drill furnishes a working method by which to make practical application of the law of prosperity, and bring one's good into manifestation."[118]

Testimonials in Unity periodicals focused on the effect of the bank drill in creating employment opportunities, as the testimonials below indicate:

My salary had been cut but the week following the receipt of my Prosperity Bank it was restored to its former basis, and things in general have improved very much.[119]

I sent for a Prosperity Bank when I was out of a position. A few weeks later I found a notice in my mail telling me to come to work at one of our large stores and I am still there. Everything points to a steady position.[120]

Unity editors commented that one's state of mind held the key: "Before any person can actually demonstrate prosperity he must feel rich within. His mind must be filled with rich thoughts—of love, peace, forgiveness, joy, health and plenty."[121]

The editors of Weekly Unity had specific advice for a wife whose husband wanted a better job. She had an important role to play, because her thoughts could easily affect the outcome of his job search. The woman was told: "You play an important part in your husband's finding the job he wants. You can help him by thinking prosperity instead of lack, success instead of failure. This creates a calm and encouraging atmosphere in your home and enables you both to rely on God's willing arms to lift the burden of your cares."[122]

Unity editors advised that the bank drill could have a major positive impact only if performed on a regular basis. A woman correspondent was told: "When you accept a Bank you agree daily, as you drop a coin into your Bank, to meditate upon the prosperity thought and to keep your mind centered on prosperity all day long."[123]

Prosperity Banks continued to enjoy popularity with Unity subscribers in the 1930s. In 1931 Unity School reported, "in a period of world-wide adjustment, we sent out more Prosperity Banks than in any previous year."[124] In 1932, an average of 620 Prosperity Banks were mailed out daily from Unity headquarters. In all, there were over 193, 473 Prosperity Banks issued by Unity School in 1932, the largest number ever.[125] Subscriptions, other than to Unity, never really tailed off. The continuing responsiveness of subscribers to Unity School magazines was indicated by Lowell Fillmore in a letter to H. Emilie Cady on August 6, 1935. Lowell reported:

Our subscription lists have increased tremendously . . . renewals and new subscriptions have poured in, and there have been twice as many gift subscriptions ordered this season than there were last. *Wee Wisdom* and *Weekly Unity* are bounding ahead. Over 4,000 school teachers have subscribed to *Wee Wisdom* since school began last September.[126]

Prosperity Banks continued to be sent out from Unity headquarters in large numbers throughout the 1930s. In 1938 Retta Chilcott, a longtime employee of Unity School, compared Prosperity Bank work at Unity headquarters with that which took place in 1914. She reported: "In those days our Prosperity Bank files consisted of four small trays of cards with one worker in charge. Now several large tables bearing row after row of cards comprise the prosperity bank department, and about thirty workers are required to handle this work; all of which testifies to the fact that the Prosperity Bank Plan does work."[127]

In 1938 Unity School magazine subscriptions totaled 659,623, an overall increase of 11 percent from the 594,000 reported in 1929.[128] A comparison of subscription levels between 1928 and 1938 is shown below:

Magazine	Subscribers/1928	Subscribers/1938
Unity	148,642	96,000
Weekly Unity	185,680	170,000
Wee Wisdom	52,805	134,000
Daily Word	144,366	182,000
The Christian Business Man	23,784	27,623
Youth (renamed *Progress*)	34,000	50,000
TOTAL	589,277	659,623

Unity continued to rely on Prosperity Banks during World War II and into the postwar era as the principal vehicle for attracting new subscribers to its publications. The rationale for involvement with the banks was similar to that put forward in the past. That Unity School was satisfied with the results is indicated by the following statement made in *Weekly Unity* in 1943: "The Prosperity Bank plan has long enjoyed a unique position. It originated here at headquarters, but Unity friends everywhere have stepped out on their faith in the Bank idea and proved that it is based upon a scientific principle."[129] The article further indicated that improvements were being made in the bank drill, with the goal of making it "the last word in scientific prayer."[130]

Magazine subscriptions grew during the 1940s, though not at the rate experienced in the 1920s. *Daily Word* and *Weekly Unity* and *Wee Wisdom* led the way. The chart below provides a comparison between 1938 and 1948.[131]

Magazine	Subscriptions/ 1938	Subscriptions/ 1948	Difference[132]
Unity	96,000	97,627	+ 1,627
Weekly Unity	170,000	220,020	+ 50,020
Wee Wisdom	134,000	300,000	+ 166,000
Daily Word	182,000	397,313	+ 215,313
The Christian Business Man	27,623	34,197	+ 6,574
Progress	50,000	41,731	− 8,269
TOTAL	659,623	1,070,888	

Unity School magazines emerged from World War II in a very healthy position. Prosperity Banks, which for almost four decades were the principal vehicle for reaching out to new subscribers, continued to make an important contribution to the Unity publication program. While no longer producing the outstanding results of the 1920s, the bank plan still helped Unity School increase circulation continually throughout the 1940s, enabling the school to reach the million mark in subscribers by 1948.

Prosperity Banks continued to be an effective vehicle for increasing subscriptions to Unity publications into the 1950s. In the 1960s, however, the bank plan lost its appeal to subscribers of Unity periodicals. Economic and social conditions changed, and the idea of saving money for subscriptions by depositing coins in a cardboard bank no longer attracted people. As subscription prices rose, the banks didn't work.[133] In short, Prosperity Banks became outdated.

Premium Booklets: The Unity Fund-Raising Program (1966–2000)

Unity School faced a financial crisis in the 1960s when the bank plan no longer generated the funds needed to finance Unity's educational activities. No replacement promotional program had been developed that produced income sufficient to support the activities of the school. Contributions to Silent Unity brought in the largest percentage of the school's total income, but it was not enough to cover the deficit. Expenses were exceeding income and the school was drawing down its reserves. Money was not available for educational initiatives or for maintenance, and many of the school's lovely buildings began falling into disrepair. It was imperative that the school find a new way to raise money.[134]

In the summer of 1966, the school hired Charles Lelly as director of its advertising and promotion department. Lelly had come to Unity School in 1964 as a ministerial student. Forty-three years old at the time, he had served in World War II, graduated from pharmacy school, and, before coming to Unity, owned and operated a drugstore in Delray Beach, Florida. His abilities as a communicator were identified while he was in ministerial school, and he was hired before graduating as editor of *New,* Unity's magazine dedicated to "a positive way of life."[135] Shortly after his appointment he was asked to write a letter introducing the magazine to new subscribers. The letter, which was mailed to all six hundred thousand people on the Unity School active mailing list, generated great interest and produced many new subscriptions.

Lelly's ability to write effective promotional copy gained the attention of one of Unity's top executives, William Underwood. At the time Underwood was seeking to fill the job of director of advertising and promotion. The job was open because the previous director had failed to raise money for the school and had resigned. Underwood offered the position to Lelly. Lelly was urged to develop a promotional plan as quickly as possible, one that would generate the funds needed to cover the school's growing budget deficit. Lelly, whose experience in the field was limited, proceeded to train himself in marketing techniques. He was tutored by a nationally known Kansas City direct-mail consultant and completed an in-house course in direct mail marketing from the Direct Marketing Association in New York City. Lelly recognized that in devising a promotion plan, he had to work within one of Unity s financial ground rules: "Don't ask for money." Lelly saw himself in the ambivalent position of being a fundraiser who couldn't make an appeal for funds.

One of the basic tenets of the Unity spiritual teaching is that in order to receive, one must first give. Something of value must be given unconditionally. Only then will something be received in return. Lelly developed a promotional plan based on this tenet and conceived the idea of producing attractive booklets on basic Unity themes: prayer, healing, meditation, prosperity, Practical Christianity, and so on. The booklets would be made available free to Unity supporters who requested them. The availability of a booklet on a particular theme would be announced in a personalized letter to those on the Unity-supporter list. The mailing envelope would contain a return card that could be used to order the booklet. At the top of the return card was a place for a prayer request. At the bottom left corner was a dollar sign and the words FREE WILL OFFERING. The person requesting the booklet would be given the opportunity to make a donation, although no direct request for funds would be made. A donation would not be required for a person to qualify to receive a booklet. Large Unity donors, those who contributed $100 or more annually, would be treated somewhat differently than others on the mailing list.[136] Large donors would not need to request a booklet; complimentary copies would be sent to them each time a new booklet was published. Promotional letters to them would indicate that a booklet on a specific subject would be arriving. A return card, which gave them an opportunity to donate, would be included in the promotional package.

Lelly did not believe it necessary to test this direct-mail program. He wanted to mail the offer of a free booklet to all six hundred thousand names on the Unity mailing list, even though a significant cash outlay was required to produce the mailing piece and booklet and to pay postage. Before Unity School would release funds for Lelly's proposed program, the school's advertising and promotion committee needed to give its approval. This committee consisted of the school's top executives, including the chief operating officer, Charles R. Fillmore. Opposition from within the committee came from financial officers who believed the proposal was too risky and too expensive. Charles R. saw possibilities in the Lelly plan and, despite opposition within the committee, gave the go-ahead. The mailing of six hundred thousand letters went forward in the fall of 1966.

The response was far beyond the expectations of everyone involved, including Lelly. Income from freewill offerings far exceeded the expense of the promotional effort. Lelly immediately got the green light to proceed with additional premium booklet promotions. Over the course of the next twelve months, another seven promotional mailings were sent out. Each one was successful, and millions of dollars rolled in, enabling the school to again meet its costs of operation. During the six years (1966–1972) that Lelly was director of advertising and promotion—he left Unity School in 1972 to pursue a ministerial career—eight promotional mailings went out each year. Only one failed.

Lelly indicated that it would have been impossible to implement the promotional program if the Unity mailing list of six hundred thousand names had not been computerized. When the premium booklet promotional program began, the conversion from addressograph plates to computer had just been completed. This complex job had been accomplished through the efforts of Roy Howard, Unity's director of operations. Lelly indicated that the promotional program was dependent upon the efficiencies in list production made possible by the use of a computer as well as by the speed with which the computer processed orders. Lelly considered the work of Howard, who planned and executed each of the promotions, as instrumental to the promotional program's success.

Lelly also indicated that the quality of the material published in the premium booklets was a major factor in motivating recipients to make financial contributions to the school. Lelly convinced the advertising and promotion committee to upgrade the quality of the booklets by increasing their size. Though objections were raised within the committee on grounds of cost, premium booklets were enlarged from eight pages to sixteen, to thirty-two, to forty-eight, and finally to sixty-four pages. Lelly credited Elvira Hicken, who was hired as editor of the booklets, with selecting interesting articles that effectively presented important aspects of the Unity teaching. Hicken had prepared herself for the work through wide reading of Unity literature and through acting as a prayer worker and teacher in Silent Unity. Lelly believes the initial success of the program was in part due to her work.

Lelly applauded Charles R. Fillmore for having the courage to proceed with a plan that many Unity staff members considered too risky. Fillmore, according to Lelly, had the wisdom to see the potential in the program and to disregard the advice of his principal financial advisers. The premium booklet promotional program that Lelly created in 1966 continues to be used by Unity School. In the three-plus decades of its existence, millions of dollars have been received annually by Unity. Charles Lelly himself, who is currently retired and living in Louisville, Kentucky, deserves credit for his creativity in designing and implementing a program that has been of immense benefit to the school.

Surprisingly, over the years. only a few minor changes have been made in the production and delivery of the Lelly-designed promotional package.[137] Instead of eight promotions per year, the number is now twelve. The themes are basically the same: prayer, peace of mind, prosperity, healing, meditation. A "World Day of Prayer" and an "Advent Blessing" promotion have been added. In 1990 the practice of sending booklets to large donors without a request was discontinued. The message at the bottom left of the return card that offered the Unity supporter the opportunity to donate has also been changed. It now reads: "We welcome your support for our continuing ministry. My gift is_____."[138] The response to Unity from those receiving the mailings continues to be high by industry standards. For every twenty-seven cents spent on promotional costs, one dollar in returns is received by the school.[139]

Lelly believes that premium booklets, like the Prosperity Bank plan, will ultimately become outdated. He is surprised that the premium book promotional plan has worked so well for such a long time. He feels that the school will soon need to find a new way to generate income to support its activities.

CHAPTER 7

W. Rickert Fillmore and the Development of Unity Village

As the Unity movement grew steadily from a staff of twenty-five in 1910 to over five hundred in 1930, the Fillmores faced the question of how to house a publishing program, a healing group, a church, and a school. In 1906, through the auspices of the Kansas City Unity Society of Practical Christianity, a small two-story building was constructed at Ninth Street and Tracy, a residential district near downtown Kansas City. As space requirements grew, the organization purchased adjacent property and constructed additional buildings. By 1929 Unity School occupied an entire square city block.

The Fillmores recognized that the long-term needs of Unity would not be served by these structures. In 1920 they bought farmland outside Kansas City with the intention of building a school on the property. They assigned the task of developing the property to their second son, Waldo Rickert, an artist and designer then in his thirties. Rick, as he was called, devoted his life to the project. The success of Unity School is due in part to the facility that was built on what is now a 1,400-acre tract of land near Lee's Summit, Missouri. Unity Village, as it was later named, has become a center for spiritual healing as well as a spiritual home for generations of Unity students.

Two years younger than his brother Lowell, Waldo Rickert Fillmore was born in Pueblo, Colorado, on June 1, 1884. He was the second Fill-more son to be named after a famed American Transcendentalist. Lowell was the namesake of James Russell Lowell and Rickert was named after Ralph Waldo Emerson.

Family life throughout Rickert's youth was centered around Unity work. Free time from school was often spent running errands at the offices of the Unity Tract Society. His talents as an artist surfaced early, and his mother involved him as a teenager in drawing illustrations for *Wee Wisdom* magazine. Growing up, he was particularly close to his mother. In a huge elm in the family's backyard, Rick had built a series of platforms and ladders that enabled one to climb high up into the tree. Often he and his mother would climb up together. He would play the guitar while she sat and meditated.[1]

While in high school he wrote a piece for *Wee Wisdom* magazine entitled "The Evolution of Santa Claus." It was a clearly written and carefully constructed piece that contained some unusual insights for a young man of seventeen. It seemed to reveal Rick as a promising young writer. It was not until the next issue of the magazine appeared that the editor, his mother, notified readers that she had rewritten the manuscript before publication, and that her son was deeply offended by changes. He wanted it known "that he wasn't going to own the story at all, and wasn't going to write for anybody that meddled with his stories."[2]

Rickert's response was the first public display of a strong, independent, audacious, self-believing, self-assertive personality—a persona he exhibited throughout his lifetime. Not drawn to writing and teaching like his father and mother, he pursued the world of art after finishing high school in 1901. He enrolled in the Chicago Art Institute, spending four years studying there. Returning to Kansas City, he worked as an illustrator and graphic designer for several years before leaving in 1910 for a six-month tour of Europe, studying art for a time in Rome. His education and travel abroad provided him with a more cosmopolitan outlook than his older brother Lowell, who rarely left Kansas City, never went to college, and devoted his life to Unity from the age of seventeen.

Returning from Europe in 1911, Rickert, with a friend, opened an interior design studio, doing business under the name "Fillmore & Rindskopf, Interior Designers."[3] The two engaged in commercial artwork, decorating such things as the walls of the main rooms of the new Hill Crest Country Club with individually designed murals. He also designed the patio of the University Playhouse (no longer in existence) at the University of Missouri, Kansas City. His design business, according to a memo in the Unity Archives files, "was prosperous." He also continued drawing illustrations for *Wee Wisdom* magazine and maintained an office at Unity headquarters.

Highly inventive, his mind often turned to mechanical things. In 1913 his mother observed a talent he was to use many times during the building of Unity Village. In a letter to her sister, she wrote:

Rick is turning out inventions that are very practical and promising. He is working on a folding bed now. It seems like a fairy tale that a bed can hide itself and furnish a room, and I could not get it straightened out in my mind till I saw it demonstrated. People who are building flats and apartments are wild over it. It should bring a royal income. His brain seems to be teeming with all kinds of new ideas, and he has about him those who are able to carry them right into practice.[4]

Like many other young men of his era, Rick was called into military service during World War I. He served as a corporal in the U.S. Tank Corps. Returning from the war in 1918, he began to involve himself more fully in Unity work and married Harriet Collins, whom he met through Unity. The couple had two children, Charles Rickert, born in 1921, and Rosemary, born in 1925.

In 1919, when Unity School was in a rapid phase of expansion, Charles Fillmore and his sons began looking for a new site for Unity headquarters. Space for expansion at 917 Tracy Avenue in Kansas City was limited. It also seemed that the inner-city environment would not serve the long-term needs of the movement. They began looking in rural areas outside Kansas City for more suitable property. Land was selected seventeen miles southeast of Kansas City near the little village of Lee's Summit in 1919, then purchased in early 1920. Rickert, though he had no architectural or engineering training, was authorized by his father to begin planning and designing the first buildings. When he was a student in Rome he had learned to love buildings in the Italian Renaissance style. He decided to copy that style along with the English Cotswold design in the construction of buildings on the new property.[5] He immediately began landscaping and designing the Unity Tower and the Silent Unity building, which were completed in 1929, collaborating with architects Elmer Boillot and Jesse Lauck. He also constructed recreational facilities for Unity workers (tennis courts, a golf course, and swimming pool), and operated a farm.

During the early 1920s, Rickert worked out of offices at Unity headquarters in Kansas City and occasionally took a good-natured razzing from *Unity News,* the house organ for the Unity School staff. On December 30, 1921, *Unity News* characterized him as follows:

W. Rickert Fillmore is in truth "the man higher up." Having himself the entire five-and-one-half floor (or the mezzanine to the editorial room), his studio allows him views in every direction except through the floor. When he works, our artist has practically the whole Unity School behind him, and enjoys knowing that nearly 300 employees are under him. He has it soft too—with upholstered chairs and subdued skylight. Also, in discovering that the fireplace draws so well, he finds he has not so much to do. The room is equipped with every feature of which the modern studio might boast. A library, alcove seats with portfolio chests beneath, a clothes closet, and a lavatory grace the ivory den of Unity's Michelangelo.[6]

When it came to office humor, Rickert Fillmore could give as well as take. In 1925 he boasted that he would be the first in the area to get an airmail letter. Of course, no one believed him. The next day at Unity Farm, a letter came floating down from a small airplane. It was addressed to Rick, "much to the amazement of everyone." The workers soon realized "the joke that Rick had played upon them."[7]

It was his humor that drew Unity minister and training school official Dorothy Pierson to him. She commented:

His sense of humor was terrific. We sat together at all the banquets for the students of the training school and laughed the entire time. He was funny. Once when I was master of ceremonies I told the students that I had Mr. Rick and Mr. Lowell here. If they had any question for them, they would be glad to answer. One woman got up and said she would like to know more about vegetarianism. I said that would be Mr. Lowell. Lowell got up and said, among other things, "I haven't eaten meat for fifty years," and Rick, who was sitting next to me, said in a loud stage whisper, "and I haven't had any since breakfast."[8]

Rev. Pierson, who knew many of the Fillmore family members when she served at Unity School in the 1940s and 1950s, felt that Rick was more colorful than Lowell. He had "pizzazz. . . . He was a darling man."[9]

While Rickert was involved in planning, building, and operating Unity Farm during the 1920s, he was also extremely active in community affairs. He joined the Rotary in 1924 and was active in it all his life. He served as president of the Kansas City club in 1927 and 1928 and was district governor in 1929 and 1930. He was a strong supporter of the Rotary Boys' Camp project and gave much time and attention to the general welfare of the property, year in and year out. In his community activities, he was not someone who could be pushed around. The Rotary Club recognized him as "a plain-talking individual whose beliefs were staunchly followed and defended."[10] The *Kansas City Times* quoted him as asking his fellow Rotarians when he was president, "Are we standing for anything in this community or are we just talking?" He threatened to resign "if members did not support a bond drive he headed."[11] His interest in art led him to the Kansas City Art Institute where he served as president of the board of directors and later as a trustee. The organization ultimately conferred upon him an honorary doctor of fine arts degree.[12]

He was interested in righting wrongs he saw in the community. When he was chairman of the finance committee of the Citizens Fusion Party campaign in 1934, he told a group of Kansas City businessmen: "I find a lot of people don't believe the facts of election frauds as we know them."[13] He bluntly described the ballot abuses of that year and what might be done about them. When in 1932 he headed the Allied Charities campaign (forerunner to the United Way), he was blunt in telling members what the group was about. "We are out to feed people," he declared.[14]

He belonged to and served on the boards of an impressive list of civic organizations. They included, in addition those listed above, the following: The Playgoer's League, The Kansas City Art Commission, the Kansas City Museum Association, the Business District League, United Charities of Kansas City, and the Kansas City Chamber of Commerce. As "host" to the Republican National Convention, held in Kansas City in the summer of 1928, Rickert worked out a plan that, according to a Washington, D.C., press release, "would ensure the extension of hospitality for which Kansas City is noted to every convention visitor, from the most obscure alternate to the greatest of the great bankers, statesmen and political chieftains who were to be Kansas City's guests." Rickert, "who would talk politics at the drop of a hat," his son Charles noted, served not only on the national, but also on the local level. He was elected as the first mayor of Unity Village after it was incorporated in 1953.[15]

While he was active in the Kansas City community, his major interest in life was building Unity Village and making it available as a spiritual center. What he wanted more than anything else, recalled Dorothy Pierson, "was to bring people to the village, whether for education or the sharing of a wonderful atmosphere. . . . He had a real feeling for that ground, believing his family was spiritually directed to it. He saw it as a hallowed place."[16]

George Leroy Dale, an official in the Unity Training School, located on the property, also testified to Rickert's dedication. "Rick loved beauty—the trees, natural scenery, growing things," Dale recalled. "He was interested in making Unity a place for people to study, to pray, and to relax. He had grand ideas about the future."[17]

Rickert apparently never worried about money. "He would build first," reported Dale, "knowing that the money to pay for the work would be forthcoming."[18] Dorothy Pierson recalled how sure he was that resources to build would be available. "Lack of money never entered his mind." she marveled. Whenever he was questioned about the money that paid for the remarkable growth of the village, he responded, "The Lord helps us."[19]

Rickert was given leeway to build Unity Village by his father. Dorothy observed: "His father had total confidence in him, respecting his audacity and his vision. Every Saturday evening for several years after Myrtle's death in 1931 Charles went to his son's home for dinner, and they talked about the work. Charles Fillmore put a lot of trust in Rick and supported him to the fullest."[20]

One of his major projects at the farm was the Unity Training School. Efforts had been made on several occasions, over a period of three decades, to set up training facilities in downtown Kansas City for out-of-town Unity students. It never worked. Finally, in 1931 Rickert was given the authority to establish a school at the farm. He was made chancellor and operated the training school from a beautiful building originally constructed for Silent Unity in the 1920s. Even though the Great Depression was in full swing, for the first time Unity School was able to attract enough students on a regular basis year-round to create a financially viable training program for students from outside Kansas City.

A ministerial training program, under Rickert's overall direction, was established in 1933 at Unity Farm. It turned out to be a major success, graduating an increasing number of students as the years progressed. Dorothy Pierson saw him as the chief promoter and the person with primary responsibility for all the educational programs of the training school. In the early 1930s, when the training school was getting off the ground, other officials at Unity headquarters in Kansas City were uninterested. Dorothy reported: "The people downtown didn't want to claim the training school."[21]

A board of Unity staff people ultimately worked with Rickert in operating the school. According to Dorothy, who at the time was co-director of the training school, Rickert was the key figure on the board. She recalled that at the time he was more concerned with building a suitable campus for the work than in the contents of the curriculum, and his behavior at board meetings reflected that interest. Dorothy described a typical board meeting: "Nothing really happened until Rick got there, and he was usually late. He always led out, usually didn't address the curriculum or the business of the training school so much as telling us about his vision and the big things he was about to do, which he went ahead and did. We were always entranced by his vision and his spirit. It never stopped."[22]

While Rickert was a pusher, he was also respectful of the talents of the people on the training school committee and allowed them to apply their expertise in developing the contents of the study program. Dorothy Pierson further reported:

Rick appreciated what we were trying to do. We were more interested in the sequential study plan than he was. He went along with it. We didn't sit down and talk to him about the educational process, because his mind was really on the development of the place as a whole. He saw that our need was for a campus. The property at 917 Tracy in Kansas City was in a residential district that would not meet the school's long-term needs. Unity Farm gave us a campus, and he saw his job as developing it. His main interest was in drawing people to Unity Village as a spiritual center.[23]

Rickert's daughter, Rosemary Fillmore Rhea, concurred with this assessment. She observed: "My Dad was interested in Unity Village. He was interested in building a spiritual community. The original idea was they would live off the land, have their own water, and produce their own food. They wouldn't be dependent on the outside world. It would be a self-sustaining spiritual community."[24]

Rickert, according to Rosemary, put a lot of effort into Unity Farm. He developed the orchards of apples and peaches, planted the berry bushes, grew fresh vegetables, raised chickens, operated a dairy and a large greenhouse, and sold farm produce from a stand on the road alongside the property. "People from all over Kansas City came," recalled Rosemary, "because we had the best apples."[25]

Starting in 1924, one of the major events at the farm each year was the Unity annual conference. Held in the fall of the year, it drew Unity students from around the world. Rickert was in his element during the conference. "The biggest thing in the world for Rick," recalled Dorothy, "was the annual meeting of Unity students when people came to the village." One of his greatest pleasures was showing people the property. "He was so cute," she recalled. "He would be all dressed up on top with a good-looking blazer or sport jacket with tie and shirt, and have on the baggiest old pants you ever saw, and big old work shoes, which were appropriate for taking people out in the orchards and around the farm, something he loved to do."[26]

Part of his idea of a spiritual community was to have lots of activities for workers, Unity students, and members of the community. He built an amphitheater big enough for stage shows and musical comedy. Gilbert and Sullivan productions such as *The Mikado* were performed. According to Rosemary, "All of Kansas City came out for the performances."

Saturday nights featured farm dances in the club house; farmers from all around came, Rosemary recalled. There were May Day celebrations and a May Day queen was crowned. Everyone danced around the May-pole. Employees would get the day off and have a picnic. Each year there was a big Halloween party, with hayrides for workers and their families. In the winter there was ice-skating, and in the summer there was tennis on the Unity courts and golf on the beautiful Unity golf course.

Rickert's contribution to the development of Unity Village was also ac-knowledged by May Rowland, longtime director of Silent Unity and mem-ber of the Unity School board of directors. She reported: "Rick had great vision and was a genius for developing original ideas. With his expansive consciousness, his artistic ability, and his drive to get things done, our beautiful and utilitarian buildings here at Unity headquarters were brought forth."[27]

Rickert's daughter Rosemary believes that without her father's vision and driving force, Unity Village would never have been built. She felt that Lowell "wasn't that much interested," and at times resisted going to the Farm. He was happy working downtown and preferred to focus energy on spreading the teaching through publications and the correspondence course. She feels that her grandfather Charles would not have taken the initiative. He was persuaded by Rickert to channel Unity funds into build-ings and land. She remembers her father as forceful and assertive. His atti-tude was "This is the way it is going to be, and we're going to do it."[28]

Perhaps Rick's biggest weakness, observed Dorothy Pierson, was that he was "opinionated, very biased, and judgmental of people." He had strong likes and dislikes. She recalled, "He was very open about who he liked and who he disliked." She was one of the people he liked: "In 1940 he wanted me and my husband to take the church on the farm. He was not pleased with the woman who was leading it. He got her out and us in. He liked us, and supported us to the hilt. Whatever we wanted, we got."[29]

When he disliked someone, "he showed it." Dorothy observed his behavior at the conference. "If he didn't like someone who was talking," Dorothy recalled, "he would let everyone around him know how he felt. He would sit with his head in his hands, or he would shake his head in disapproval."[30]

Dorothy recalled that Rickert, like his father Charles, had "a thing" about being religious, about being pious. If he got the impression that people were seeing him as pious, he would tell a joke, sometimes off-color, to dispel the notion. She observed that Rickert "never put on any religiosity at all." Called upon spontaneously to say grace at a dinner party, he responded, "Good bread, good meat; good Lord, let's eat."[31]

Religious historian Marcus Bach saw Rickert's spirituality expressing itself in the building of Unity Village: "What is the Christ within but the discovery and conviction that I am a Child of God. I had heard it as a cardinal Unity precept ever since I met Rick, who, as far as I was concerned, manifested the truth of the indwelling Christ by manifesting creative thought into structured things."[32]

"I think he was as spiritual as any of them," his daughter Rosemary indicated, "but it was more in the sphere of art and architecture, because he felt he was guided about every building on the property."[33] Rickert himself expressed his views on the relationship of architecture and spirit in 1947 when showing guests around the growing complex of buildings. He explained, "Everything you see is but a physical counterpart of the spiritual process of the teaching . . . When man works in harmony with God, the right things come at the right time."[34]

CHAPTER 8

The Fillmore Family and the Operation of Unity School

In addition to Charles and Myrtle Fillmore, three sons, a grandson, a granddaughter, and a great-granddaughter were actively involved in the operation of Unity School throughout the twentieth century. Lowell Fillmore served as general manager of the school from 1916 until the death of his father in 1948. He then assumed the presidency, a post he held until his own death in 1975. (See Chapter 4 for a description of his work.) Charles R. Fillmore, son of Rickert Fillmore and grandson of Charles and Myrtle, assumed management control of the school in 1964 as executive vice president. He became president in 1971. Charles R.'s daughter, Connie Fillmore Bazzy, replaced her father as president and CEO in 1987. Three other Fillmores played significant roles in the operation of the school. W. Rickert's contribution has been described in the preceding chapter. Charles and Myrtle's son Royal Fillmore was actively involved in the management of the school until his premature death in 1923 at the age of thirty-four. Rickert's daughter, Rosemary Fillmore Rhea, assumed a variety of responsibilities on the Unity staff for several decades.

Charles R. Fillmore: Astute Businessman and Faithful Steward

The son of Rickert and Harriet Fillmore and only the grandson of Charles and Myrtle Fillmore, Charles R. was born in 1921 and grew up at Unity Farm. His early interest in animals, the out-of-doors, and golf was revealed in an item in *Unity News* in 1925 when he was four. *Unity News* reported:

Harriet Fillmore's brother sent Charles Rickert a hound pup from California. It was evidently a case of love at first sight for Charles Rickert spends most of his time with the pup, to the exclusion of everything else. And this reminds us that the above named young man appeared Wednesday afternoon in a nifty golf outfit, and as they say nowadays, "strutted his stuff" over the links. Keep your eye on Charles Rickert: he may be one of our future golf champions.[1]

Though from a family deeply immersed in Unity teaching, he was not instructed by his parents. "Listen to what Papa Charley says," his father told him, when the subject of religion came up. This was not an easy task, since the boy didn't understand much of what his grandfather had to say. It was in Sunday school that he learned the Unity teaching.[2]

Charles R. grew up in a rural community, attended elementary and high school in the small town of Lee's Summit, graduated with a degree in journalism from the University of Missouri in 1943, married his high school sweetheart Anne Jones, received a commission in the U.S. Navy, and served as an executive officer aboard a minesweeper in World War II. He returned home at war's end and in 1946 began working for Unity School. His father, two uncles, and grandparents had devoted their lives to Unity—as the only grandson of Charles and Myrtle Fillmore, he was undoubtedly expected to follow in the family's footsteps. His first assignment was a comedown from the responsibilities he had held in the Navy. He was put to work cleaning the printing presses and sacking mail. During his first decade as a Unity employee, he worked in every department in the school.[3]

He credits May Rowland, director of Silent Unity and member of the Unity board of trustees, with pushing him ahead and enabling him to prepare for his future role as president of Unity School. It seems that in the 1950s neither his father nor his uncle, both in their seventies, were concerned about moving him up and giving him the necessary experience to serve as the school's president.[4] He was in line for the presidency because of the legal structure of Unity School. The school, though granted nonprofit status by the IRS in 1926, has a unique corporate charter. Organized under the Corporation Law of Missouri in 1914, a majority of the school's fifty shares of stock have always been held by members of the Fillmore family. While ownership of the stock did not entitle them to receive dividends, majority ownership did authorize the family to operate the business tax-free. Charles R., the only male in the third generation of Fillmores, was the logical choice to become majority stockholder and take over management of the school at the retirement of his uncle and his father.

May Rowland, whom Charles R. viewed as a guiding spirit of the Unity work and a power behind the scenes, prodded both his father and uncle to take steps to prepare him for his future role. She told them: "Charles needs to be directed in the work," and urged that he be enrolled in the Unity Training School's ministerial education program.[5] They complied and Charles R. matriculated and graduated. Although he had no desire to be ordained or serve in a ministerial capacity, the program, he reported, "opened new vistas" for him.[6]

In 1955 he was appointed public relations director of Unity School and in 1963 became executive vice president and chief operating officer. In 1971, shortly before the death of Lowell Fillmore, he became president and chairman of the board of trustees. He served as president until 1987. He retained his position as board chairman, a position he continues to hold. His longtime associate, William B. Dale, reports that for the past thirteen years, Charles R. has "continued to keep his finger on the pulse of the organization."[7] While not active in the day-to-day management of Unity School, Dale reported, Charles still keeps an eye on the financial bottom line.[8]

Charles R. has never considered himself a spiritual teacher or leader and has not been the kind of person who calls attention to himself. In an interview published in *The Kansas City Star* in 1979, he explained: "I'm not the spiritual leader of Unity. I'm much more a custodian, a steward."[9] In a more recent interview, he conveyed the same message. He viewed himself as a "caretaker," as one who saw his role as "carrying out the philosophy, goals, and wishes of the founders and in preserving the Unity teaching as presented by them."[10] With these words, Charles R. validates the insight of Max Weber, the great sociologist of religions. Weber noted that all religious movements begin with charismatic founders, often prophetic figures, who energize the movement with their charisma and give it direction. But after their death, if the movement is to survive, charisma must be routinized by competent and honest stewards who administer the movement's institutions. This preservative function is crucial for the continued existence of organized religion. Charles and Myrtle were two charismatic founders of Unity. Lowell, Rickert, and May Rowland, while possessing a degree of charisma, began the process of routinization.

Charles R. and Connie Fillmore Bazzy, daughter of Charles R., completed the routinization process.[11]

Charles R. has spoken at Unity churches in the United States and abroad but has been more comfortable in the out-of-doors than on the lecture platform. He considers himself a "throwback," as someone who, in spirit, is much more like his pioneer great-grandfather, Henry G. Fillmore, than like his father or grandfather. Henry G. Fillmore migrated from the East Coast to northern Minnesota in the mid-nineteenth century, when it was Indian country. He was an outdoorsman who lived off the land, farmed, and traded with local Indian tribes.[12]

As president of Unity School, Charles R. did not exercise spiritual leadership through writing, teaching, and speaking, as his grandfather and uncle before him. He nevertheless has firm ideas about the value of the Unity teaching and the spiritual tradition that has grown up around it.[13] He sees Unity as a religious philosophy with an "open end," seeking to "find God's truth in all of life, wherever it may be." He also views Unity as "an adventure," because, as he indicated, it arouses our interest in our spiritual nature, teaches us to pray affirmatively, enables us to go into the silence and be receptive to "a still small voice," brings God down into the here and now, and makes God available as a partner in our daily living.[14] He summarized his views on the contribution made by the Unity teaching when he declared: "It is scientifically sound, psychologically healthy, intellectually challenging, and spiritually satisfying."[15] He believes that the teaching is able to "satisfy the spiritual needs of all peoples" in a time of "stress, strain, and misunderstanding."[16]

Charles R.'s major contribution to Unity has been through strong administrative and financial management. James Dillet Freeman, who worked closely with Charles R. for several decades, characterized him as "a damn good businessman, intelligent and totally committed to Unity."[17] William B. Dale, who served Unity School in a variety of capacities and currently serves as a member of the board of trustees, has found him to be "bright, shrewd, interested, committed to the work, and a good delegator of authority."[18] Unity School prospered during the years of Charles R.'s presidency—he has kept the organization operating in the black throughout his tenure in office. Some specific accomplishments that took place under his leadership include:

• A promotion program that resulted in a significant increase in Unity income.

• The introduction of a computer-based system in Silent Unity that resulted in better service at a lower cost and a significant reduction in staff.

• An educational expansion program that led to the creation of Unity School for Religious Studies. The school is responsible for the education of beginning and advanced Unity students, including teachers and ministers.

• A retirement program for Unity workers.

• Development of the Unity retreat program.

• Building in 1975 of a $5 million activity center. That building now houses Unity Chapel, serves as a meeting place for retreatants, and is a place where public events from band concerts to lectures and workshops take place.[19]

In 1965 Charles R. took steps to transfer the management of Unity centers and churches from Unity School to an organization funded and operated by Unity ministers. It was a decision that, at the time, was not favored by a significant number of Unity ministers. The move required the ministers themselves to take responsibility for fulfilling their own organizational needs and for developing a support system for their churches. Today the organization they created, the Association of Unity Churches, is strong, independent, self-supporting, and successful, and is making a major contribution to the Unity movement. Unity ministers have no interest in returning control of the administration of churches to Unity School.

Part of Unity School's success can be attributed to the acceptance it has enjoyed in the local community. Given the school's unorthodox spiritual teachings and the criticism that has been leveled at Unity from traditional Christianity, the school could have easily been a target for unfavorable comment in the local press. Respect for the school, as evidenced by favorable press reports over the years, is due in part to the work of both Charles R. and his father Rickert in the Kansas City metropolitan community. Charles R. has served as chapter chairman of the Greater Kansas City American Red Cross; chairman of the Citizen's Committee for Conservation in the Lee's Summit area; member of the Citizen's Advisory Committee for the Missouri Conservation Commission, chairman of the William R. McKee for Congress committee, board member of the Little Blue Valley Sewer District, mayor of Unity Village, and a member of the board of directors of the Midland Bank in Lee's Summit, Missouri. In addition, he has been an active Rotarian for forty years.[20]

His avocations have been golf and the experience of nature. "I have spent a great deal of my life in the out-of-doors," he reported, "and have loved hunting and fishing."[21] He continues to hunt wild turkeys in locales both inside and outside of Missouri, a passion that he has engaged in for over thirty years. He is also an accomplished golfer, having spent a considerable amount of time on the Unity Village golf course, and has competed in local tournaments. In 1968 he was the winner of the championship trophy of the Unity Golf Association. Charles R. continues to live with Anne, his wife of over fifty years, at Unity Village.[22] He has two grown daughters, Connie, who succeeded him in 1987 as president of Unity School, and Harriet. Harriet graduated from Duke University, married a Kansas businessman, and lives with her husband in New Hampshire. She has two grown daughters, Sarah and Leslie. Neither Harriet nor her daughters are involved in Unity.[23]

Connie Fillmore Bazzy: Continuing the Fillmore Tradition of Responsible Management

Connie Fillmore Bazzy is the fourth generation of Unity's founding family to serve as president of Unity School. The daughter of Charles R. Fillmore and the great-granddaughter of Charles and Myrtle Fillmore, Connie is the first woman to become the school's chief executive. Like her father, Connie grew up at Unity Village and attended Lee's Summit High School, graduating in 1966 as class valedictorian. She completed her undergraduate work at Pomona College in Claremont, California, receiving a degree in psychology and graduating in 1970 with honors.[24]

She traveled in Europe after completing her undergraduate work and then returned to Unity School in 1971 to work in the editorial department as a copy editor. In her early twenties at the time, she was still in the process of figuring out what she wanted to do with her life. She wasn't sure that a career in Unity was right for her. "At first," she indicated, "I didn't think I was interested in Unity."[25] While working in the editorial department, she made her first in-depth investigation of the Unity teachings. In the process, she prepared two premium booklets for the promotion department, one on healing and the other on prosperity. Viewing it as a learning experience, she went through the Unity literature on these topics and pulled out "the nuggets."[26] The booklets she produced proved very popular; they were expanded and published as small books titled *The Unity Guide to Healing* and *Unity Guide to Prosperous Living*. Both works are well regarded by Unity professionals and continue to be used in the movement.

In 1974, at the suggestion of James Dillet Freeman, Connie enrolled in the Unity ministerial training program. Unlike most others in the program, she did not intend to become a Unity minister in a center or church. She accepted Freeman's argument that, since she was a Fillmore and involved with Unity School, she should avail herself of ministerial education.[27] She completed the program in 1976 and then left Unity School with John Strickland, a fellow ministerial student whom she married, to accompany him on a church assignment in Santa Rosa, California. The couple went to Jacksonville, Florida, in mid-1977 before returning to Unity School in 1979. While in the field, she supported her husband in his work but never served as a field minister, since she was not drawn to the work. "As a result," she acknowledges, "I don't take credit for field service."[28]

Upon returning to Unity School, Connie made a commitment to work with her father and to accept a position as assistant to the president. She also went through a divorce. Over the course of the next four years, she prepared herself for the responsibilities of the school's chief executive. Part of that preparation included a thorough study of all aspects of the school's activities, as well as graduate studies in business at Rockhurst College in Kansas City. In addition, Connie wrote Sunday school material for the Association of Unity Churches and was instrumental in developing the Unity Help Line, a telephone counseling and referral service.[29] In December 1983 she was appointed executive vice president and chief operating officer. Like her father and grandfather, Connie assumed civic responsibilities in metropolitan Kansas City. She served on the board of directors of the American Red Cross, Greater Kansas City Chapter, and on the board of directors of the Commerce Bank of Lee's Summit. In January 1987, she became Unity School's fourth president. She is responsible for long-term planning and coordination of Unity School operations, including the administration of school policy, decision making, and overseeing of the worldwide ministries of the school.[30]

Early in her managerial career, she indicated a strong interest and attraction to administrative work. "I like administration," she reported. "Some people wouldn't touch it with a ten-foot pole, but I like it a lot."[31]

As time has passed and she completes her second decade as Unity's chief operating officer, she has come to acknowledge the difficulties inherent in the work. "What I find after twenty years is that one meets the same kinds of problems over and over." She now views the management of Unity School "as challenging and also difficult. I see how important it is, and I am a little more worn out now than what I was twenty years ago."[32] She is well aware of the importance of effective administration to the success of the school. She noted: "Good administration is necessary to enable Unity to continue to present its teaching in an organized, accessible, efficient, and fiscally responsible way."[33] Over the past two decades, she has committed herself to providing this kind of service to the school.

Like her father, Connie does not see herself as a spiritual teacher, leader, or guru. She recognizes that spiritual leadership in Unity has been exercised not only by the founders, but also by Lowell Fillmore and May Rowland. She believes that those who head Unity School, now and in the future, no longer need to play the role of spiritual leader. "My father broke that mold," she noted. She knows that some people in Unity expect spiritual leadership from her, and she believes it's an expectation she need not fulfill. "I didn't assume that role," she commented, "because I don't have it in me. My father and I have tried to keep Unity 'a work,' and not something about the Fillmores." While spiritual teaching and leadership are not her calling, she nevertheless feels a strong bond with the school and with its teachings. "I feel so connected to the work," she commented, "even though I am not the spiritual leader of the work."[34]

Connie sees Silent Unity as now playing a key role in the spiritual leadership of the movement. Silent Unity, she indicated, "carries the lamp and represents the heart of the Unity work." She sees the group effort of Silent Unity entirely in keeping with the vision of Charles and Myrtle Fillmore. They believed that the Unity work "should not be about a person or individual. They were not interested in setting up something around themselves."[35]

Connie sees her role as president of Unity School as "keeping Unity on track in the world, honoring the unique ideas we have and making them accessible to people."[36] She sees Unity as having a spiritual purpose in the world that was originally articulated by her great-grandparents and her role as facilitating the advancement of that original vision. She is often asked to comment on the future of Unity. She sees no need to make predictions, because she believes that Unity "has a life of its own. It has its own spiritual energy that moves it forward. It has a way to serve in the world, a way to meet the spiritual needs of people."[37]

Connie sees herself as committed to the basic Unity teachings. She indicates that Unity teaching can be condensed into a series of five core ideas that can be used on a daily basis by everyone in the world, no matter where they live. They are:

• God is absolute good, everywhere present.

• Human beings have a spark of divinity within them, the Christ spirit within. Their very essence is of God, and therefore they are also inherently good.

• Human beings create their experiences by the activity of their thinking. Everything in the manifest realm has its beginning in thought.

• Prayer is the creative thinking that heightens the connection with God-mind and therefore brings forth wisdom, healing, prosperity, and everything good.

• Knowing and understanding the laws of life, also called Truth, are not enough. A person must also live the Truth that he or she knows.[38]

Connie considers prayer to lie at the heart of the Unity work. "Our history is filled," she noted, "with stories of answered prayer, prosperity demonstrations, miracles of healing and peace."[39] Her belief in the primacy of prayer and her conviction that a principal goal of Unity is to foster prayer among peoples of all religions and beliefs were made evident in the following statement: "Our primary purpose is to pray with people and help them, no matter what the denomination. The people we serve come from all denominations. We also serve many unchurched people. We try to serve the spiritual hunger of everyone."[40]

In 1994 Connie married L. Allan Bazzy, a minister and businessman from Bradenton, Florida. Though it meant leaving Unity Village, she moved to Florida to keep her marriage together. When asked how living in Florida and performing the job of president of a Missouri-based school has worked out, she responded, "It works surprisingly well." She noted that being away from Unity Village has helped her keep her focus and stay out of operational issues that are best handled by others. She feels that working at a distance helps her "keep an eye on the big picture and continue to make sure that we are being true to the purposes of the founders."[41] She commented:

I thought it would benefit the School if I had a little distance from it. People on the staff tend to defer too much to me because I'm a Fillmore. When I'm in Florida, others take up the day-to-day matters. They make decisions they should make. I stay in touch by computer, telephone, and fax, and I'm involved in the decisions that need to be made by me. Living in Florida has worked very well for me. It has allowed me to have a very important relationship. I think it has not created undue hardship for the organization.[42]

William Dale, director of publishing and a longtime member of the Unity board of trustees, concurs with Connie's assessment, observing that the managerial system has functioned effectively with Connie in Florida. He reported:

We are continually in touch by e-mail, fax, and telephone. Contact works better with her in Florida on a day-to-day basis because it is easier to get her attention by e-mail than to schedule a personal meeting. Being in Florida gets her away from the attention-getting day-to-day details, prevents micro-management, and enables her to focus on the bigger issues, thereby making it easier for her to lead. What needs to be handled face-to-face is done in periodic board meetings, which she comes to Unity Village to attend.[43]

Other Unity employees, further down the chain of command, feel that in order to fulfill all the responsibilities associated with the job, the school's president and chief operating officer must be present full-time on the campus.

When asked what she considers her most significant accomplishments, Connie mentioned the 1987 formation of the Unity Movement Advisory Council, the 1989 construction of a new building for Silent Unity, and the creation of the school's development department. She also noted administrative accomplishments such as computerizing Unity's internal office operation and putting in place a salary structure for the organization. She will probably add to this list the current $7 million fundraising program for the building of a new retreat center at Unity Village, which has a planned completion date of 2002.[44]

Connie was instrumental in establishing the Unity Movement Advisory Council (UMAC), which is made up of executives of Unity School and the Association of Unity Churches. She believes its formation has been highly important because it provides an ongoing structure of meetings, three times each year, that demands that officials of the association and school communicate. "Before we always communicated," she reported, "but it was hit and miss. Now we know we are going to sit down face-to-face and talk things over."[45] The conflict that developed between the school and the association over the proposal for the creation of Unity International made her particularly aware of the need for a formal method of communicating. "I didn't want the environment out of which that dispute grew to happen again."[46]

Connie recognizes that the school and the association, although growing out of the same philosophy, have different missions and serve different people. She observed that UMAC has provided a forum for resolving issues where there are overlapping responsibilities, particularly regarding ministerial education and international outreach. Through meetings and discussions, she noted, "we clarify the work that each of us is doing and gain a better awareness and understanding of each other's perspectives and goals."[47]

Connie was integrally involved in the organization, planning, and implementing of the Silent Unity building project, which resulted in the school's raising $14 million in funds. The building, which houses several departments related to the prayer ministry, was dedicated during Unity's centennial celebration in 1989. The organization of the school's development department came out of the experience of the Silent Unity fund-raising campaign. During the building project, an outside consultant helped identify people, Connie noted, "who really loved us and wanted to support the work." Unity has a broad base of small donors, "and a few who support us strongly. The development department has helped identify our most loyal supporters and build personal relationships with them." Connie pointed out, "we don't pressure people. I am proud that we are doing it the Unity way." Millions of dollars flow into the school annually through the work of the development department.[48]

On March 13, 2001, Connie announced her intention to oversee a transition from the organizational system that gave management responsibility for Unity School to a member of the Fillmore family to a nonprofit structure similar to that of other organizations engaged in spiritual education. During the process she will create a new board of trustees comprised of qualified people from outside Unity School, assume the role of chairman of that board, and relinquish her duties and responsibilities as president and CEO. Her replacement will be selected from among those who understand and embrace the core values of the Unity movement, have proven experience in operating a nonprofit organization, and possess strong management and leadership skills.[49] On July 18, 2001, in a memo to Unity School employees, Connie expressed her hope that the new leadership team would be in place by the end of 2001.[50]

Royal Fillmore: An Unrealized Potential

Royal Fillmore was the third and youngest son of Charles and Myrtle Fillmore. Like his two brothers, Lowell and Rickert, he was deeply involved in the Unity movement during his short lifetime. He died prematurely at age thirty-four. Charles R. Fillmore, his nephew, believes that of the three sons of Charles and Myrtle, Royal was "the dominant son," the one with the strongest personality, the one with the greatest potential for leading the Unity movement. Charles R. believes that had Royal lived, he would have succeeded his father as president of Unity School.[51] Thomas Witherspoon, author of *Myrtle Fillmore: Mother of Unity*, reported that Royal, by the testimony of his contemporaries, was the most lovable and loving of the three sons and the most charismatic.[52] Unity field lecturer E. V. Ingraham observed that Royal had one outstanding interest that overshadowed everything else, "and that was making practical in everyday life the teachings of Jesus Christ."[53]

Born July 16, 1889, Royal was a child in the 1890s when his mother began publishing *Wee Wisdom*, a magazine that at the time was devoted to teaching children "the way to attain the real Truth underlying Christianity."[54] She involved him in the work of the magazine, publishing his first piece of writing when he was only ten years old.[55] *Wee Wisdom* was to become a big part of his life. As a teenager, he was secretary of the *Wee Wisdom* booster club and carried on correspondence with young subscribers around the world.[56] He also wrote a column of positive, loving thoughts that children might consider.[57] His mother turned over the editorship of the magazine to him in 1912 when he was twenty-three. He was involved with the magazine in various capacities for the remainder of his life. He continued as secretary of the booster club. The object of the club, he said, "was to radiate sunshine even in the darkest corners of the world." Its activities were parties, picnics, and get-togethers.[58]

Royal attended the University of Missouri in Columbia for three years from 1907–1910. He was associate editor of the yearbook and a member of the varsity football team. Royal was very large, and from his pictures appeared to have carried much excess weight. At age seven, he weighed one hundred pounds and was called "Baby Elephant" by his classmates.

His weight had risen to close to three hundred pounds when he was in college, and the football team had to order special gear for him. The day of the three hundred-pound football player had not yet arrived.[59]

He returned to Kansas City in 1910 and immediately went to work for Unity. He contributed articles for both *Unity* and *Weekly Unity* magazines, and for many years edited a column on vegetarianism for *Weekly Unity*.[60] He also gave Sunday evening lectures on Unity principles to the Kansas City Unity Society of Practical Christianity.[61] After one lecture, the *Kansas City Daily Sun* reported, "he was surrounded and congratulated by his friends."[62] The newspaper expressed the wish that he would lecture on a regular basis. In 1914 a New York City Unity center leader, a British woman by the name of Sophia Van Marter, took the summer off to visit friends and relatives in England. Royal traveled east to take her place.[63]

Royal was close to his mother. He was the only one of her sons with whom she worked professionally. They also made several trips to the East Coast together, sightseeing and visiting friends who had come into Unity.[64] In a birthday note to her on August 6, 1921, he wrote:

> To my beloved Mother—who bore me;
> nurtured me through my forming days;
> befriended me in my growing days;
> prayed for me in my stress and storm;
> guided me wisely in mating season;
> and rejoices with me in my approaching parenthood;
> God bless my wonderful Mother.[65]

Myrtle had high praise for Royal's work habits at Unity. She commented: "He was so wonderfully responsive. There didn't seem to be a thing in any department that he could not lend a hand to help out on. His clear-sightedness and sympathy were great factors in the work."[66]

Royal also participated administratively in the management of Unity School. He was secretary of the corporation and handled the school's purchasing. He made trips to the East Coast to promote Unity magazines, to negotiate printing contracts, and to speak at Unity centers.[67] He also played a role in convincing his parents to buy the farmland southeast of Kansas City that ultimately became the site for the future location of Unity School. Despite Royal's size, he was accepted into the U.S. Army during World War I and commissioned as a second lieutenant. He did not serve overseas. When he returned to Unity in 1919, he picked up where he left off, working on *Wee Wisdom* magazine, handling administrative chores at Unity School, and involving himself as a columnist for *Wee Wisdom*.

Like his brother Rickert, Royal was active in the community life of Kansas City, undoubtedly making it easier for Unity School to be looked upon favorably by the city's power structure. He was gregarious and popular with his contemporaries. Upon returning to Kansas City after his marriage, he was captured by his friends when he stepped off the train, placed in a makeshift lion's cage, and hauled through the business district of Kansas City by a parade of automobiles with horns blaring.[68] Royal was both a Mason and a Rotarian. After his death, Albert Hutchings, former president of the Kansas City Rotary, reported that Royal was "what we term a true Rotarian." This included being "a Christian" as well. Hutchings indicated that Royal regarded Rotary as a way of performing public service.[69]

On one of his business trips to the East, he met Frances Sleater of Merchantville, New Jersey. On November 27, 1920, after a short courtship, they married and settled in Kansas City. Frances soon became pregnant and bore a baby girl on October 1, 1921. Six weeks later Frances died of complications resulting from the birth. After her death, Royal's health declined; he suffered from both diabetes and high blood pressure.[70] On September 2, 1923, Royal, then thirty-four, in an effort to find a way to improve his health, went to Battle Creek, Michigan, to spend time recovering in a well-known sanitarium. When he arrived, the medical staff took his blood pressure. It was high—216/180. Royal refused medication, believing that prayer and rest would enable him to regain his health. He died a week later on October 9 of heart and liver disease. The death certificate described the primary cause as "chronic interstitial nephritis" and "myocarditis." A contributory cause was "hypertension" and "arteriosclerosis."[71]

There was a large turnout for his funeral in Kansas City. His mother reported: "Everybody loved him. The city must have given up all its flowers. I never saw so many at any one time. Loving friends crowded the chapel, and hundreds drove away that could not even find room inside. The Rotary and the Masons, though not invited to take part, sent and brought flowers and loving sympathy."[72]

It is impossible to predict whether, had Royal Fillmore lived, he would have become president of Unity School and led the movement. It seems clear, however, that his depth of involvement in the work, his commitment

to the teaching, and his many stellar personal qualities could have qualified him for that role.

Rosemary Fillmore Rhea: Radio and TV Ministry

The granddaughter of Myrtle Fillmore, Rosemary Fillmore Rhea is the
second Fillmore woman to become deeply involved in the Unity Movement. Born in 1925, four years after her brother Charles R., she is the
daughter of W. Rickert Fillmore and Harriet Collins Fillmore. Rosemary
grew up in the peaceful atmosphere of Unity Village, which at the time
was known as Unity Farm, a spiritual oasis located in an undeveloped rural area southeast of Kansas City, near the town of Lee's Summit, Missouri. As a child, she was very close to her grandfather, Charles Fillmore.
Some of her fondest memories growing up were of times spent with him.
She recalls in particular times when she was ill. He would come and sit beside her bed, and she would begin to feel better.

After high school, she went to Christian College in Columbia, Missouri, graduating in 1944 from its two-year program. She then studied radio broadcasting at Pasadena Playhouse for one year in metropolitan Los
Angeles. During the summers she worked at Unity School in various departments. In 1946 she began working full-time at the school as assistant
to the editor of *Daily Word* magazine.[73]

In 1947 she married Stanley Grace, a local resident, and became a wife
and mother. The couple had two children, Stanley Rickert Grace and Ros-
alind Fillmore Grace. In 1956, when her children were school age, she
went to work for WHB, a Kansas City radio station, hosting a show called
Young Ideas. It featured interviews with young persons concerning current
events. The following year the president of WHB became president of
KMBC, Channel 9 in Kansas City, and asked her to adapt Unity's *Daily
Word* magazine for television. The result was a five-minute program consisting of the word for the day, a passage from the Bible, a short meditation, and an inspirational thought. Presented as a nondenominational film
featuring Rosemary as host, the program enjoyed a twelve-year run. At its
height, it appeared on seventy-five television stations nationwide.[74] In
1968 when the program closed, she reported: "It is the most gratifying
work I ever have done . . .We get several hundred letters a week from all
over the country, and it is most comforting to realize the messages are
helpful in the daily lives of people."[75]

In 1966, after almost twenty years of marriage, Rosemary divorced Stanley Grace. Two years later she married Ralph Rhea, a minister who had enjoyed a long and successful career in Unity. She found Rhea to be an amazing person and her marriage to him, she reported, "was everything that my first marriage wasn't."[76] In 1969, shortly after their marriage, they began working together on a program entitled *The Word*. Like her previous program *The Daily Word*, it was meant to be inspirational. In an effort to make *The Word* more attractive to stations during public service time, the program was condensed from five minutes to sixty seconds and taped for distribution to area radio stations. Ralph Rhea wrote the script and Rosemary narrated.[77] A single word used in everyday language was selected; the word was then built upon to give it new meaning. Rosemary reported:

We attempt to make "The Word" a capsule of positive thinking—it is good news that comes as a pleasant surprise in contrast to the somewhat depressing news of the day . . . The programs ask for nothing and are nonreligious and use a single word as a basis for every segment. The words are selected because of their applicability to everyday living—something helpful which people can use in their day-to-day activities.[78]

The program's ultimate success in television was due in large part to the Rheas' ability to attract celebrities from the entertainment and sports fields to handle the broadcasts. The Rheas went to Hollywood, not knowing anyone. A chance encounter with the mother of Robert Wagner, who was a Unity student, opened the door. "One star introduced us to another," Rosemary recalled.[79] A long list of well-known people handled the broadcasts, including Steve Allen, Phyllis Diller, Anne Francis, Ernest Borgnine, Phil Silvers, Jane Russell, and football star Mike Garrett.[80] In 1980, in recognition of her long work with Unity, Rosemary was granted special ordination in the Unity ministry.

In 1980 Rosemary initiated legal action against Unity School and her brother Charles R., an action she was later to regret.[81] It grew out of sibling rivalry, she indicated, which dated back to childhood. Rosemary had grown angry because she was not a member of the Unity board of directors and possessed none of the fifty shares of stock that had been traditionally held by Fillmore family members. She was aware that stock formerly held by her father and her uncle, as well as that held by former Silent Unity director May Rowland—all of whom were now deceased—had been placed in the hands of her brother, Charles R. She wanted to know why she was excluded.[82] Although the stock had no monetary value to her, since the corporation operated on a nonprofit basis, it had importance because stockholders controlled the management of Unity School. On January 7, 1980, along with her husband Ralph Rhea, she filed a petition in the Circuit Court of Jackson County, Missouri, to give her access to all the documents (board minutes, etc.) and transactions that resulted in the transfer of shares.[83]

After filing the suit, she left Unity School for Miami, Florida, where she and her husband took over an active Unity ministry. In Florida, she had second thoughts about the wisdom of her actions and, as a result, began to experience great personal pain. She concluded that she had made a mistake. The suit had caused a rift in the Fillmore family—not only between herself and her brother, but between their children as well. She withdrew the suit before the court acted upon it.[84] In retrospect, she wishes that she had never filed it. For herself, she decided it was best to forgive and forget.[85] Her relationship with her brother improved and she returned to Kansas City in 1983 to found, with her husband, the Myrtle Fillmore Center, a Unity ministry in Kansas City.

In 1989, after the death of Ralph Rhea, she came back to Unity School to serve on the staff of the Unity School for Religious Studies. She became an "ambassador of goodwill" for Unity, accepting speaking engagements in Unity churches and centers around the country. She had the special ability to connect her listeners to the Unity message as she had received it from her parents and grandparents. She continued at Unity School until she retired in 1998. Rosemary now lives in Jamaica, where she is involved in supporting Unity ministries on the island. She reported that her relationship with her brother is warm and cordial, the best that it has ever been.[86]

CHAPTER 9

Silent Unity and the Practice of
Spiritual Healing

Healing others—physically, psychologically, and spiritually—has been central to Unity work from its earliest beginnings. In the spring of 1889, Charles and Myrtle Fillmore began working with people, both individually and at a distance, as practitioners of what they ultimately called "spiritual healing." In the early years, both Fillmores devoted most of their energies to practitioner work, seeing clients personally in their Kansas City healing rooms. As time passed and people from outside Kansas City wrote to them for help, they shifted their focus to "absent healing." Charles gave up practitioner work entirely in 1909, although Myrtle continued to see clients throughout her lifetime. The organization they developed to help them with absent healing became known as Silent Unity. At Unity School of Christianity, over three hundred people are employed in this ministry. The evolution of Silent Unity—from a prayer group in the living room of a Kansas City couple to the organization it is today—is described below.

Practitioner Work in Kansas City

During the first two decades of their careers as spiritual healers, the Fillmores appear to have supported themselves financially through practitioner work with individual clients in Kansas City. They called this work "local healing." By local, they meant that the healing was carried on locally in their Kansas City healing parlors, face-to-face with clients. A significant part of their workday during the first two decades of their spiritual healing work seems to have been spent working personally with clients.

They were both certified as practitioners of Christian Science in July 1887 by Joseph Adams (a graduate of the Massachusetts Metaphysical College of Boston that was founded by Mary Baker Eddy). During the 1890s, a sign reading MENTAL HEALING, CHARLES AND MYRTLE FILLMORE, TEACHERS AND HEALERS hung outside their headquarters in Room 320, Hall Building, Kansas City. Their office hours were "10–4."[1]

Apparently, the Fillmores were busy people with plenty of clients. In 1909, shortly after Charles retired from "local healing,"[2] he gave an idea of how much time and effort he had given to the work. He stated, "I have treated an average of probably twenty cases a day for the last twenty years, and the results have been uniformly good."[3] Myrtle treated at least as many, probably more.[4] Their eldest son Lowell, who was still a boy when his parents began their healing work, personally observed the busy office. "I remember," he recalled, "how the reception room would be lined with people."[5] Unity magazine reported in 1896, "a continuous stream of people come and go."[6]

Myrtle continued working personally with local clients long after Charles stopped. She also wrote much more about her experiences as a practitioner than did her husband.[7] Unity magazine never featured the work of the "local healers" with the same depth of coverage given to the Silent Unity Healing Department. Evidence of their existence was provided only occasionally, and then in obscure places in Unity magazine. In February 1908, under the headline MR. FILLMORE WITHDRAWS FROM LOCAL HEALING, Unity magazine reported that the work would continue despite his leaving. It indicated: "Local healers will be in attendance at our Headquarters who will look after patients who desire the personality of the practitioner to appear before them, and they will continue to be served with careful attention."[8]

In November 1909, Weekly Unity published a news item entitled OUR HEALING DEPARTMENT. In additional news about the work of Silent Unity, there was a brief announcement about the work of Myrtle Fillmore and the local healers. It reported: "On the second floor of the Unity Building, 913 Tracy Avenue, are our local healing rooms, where city patients are treated. Mrs. Myrtle Fillmore, Mrs. A. H. Ray, Mrs. Sophia Van Marter, and Mrs. Rudesill have charge of this ministry, and will be in attendance daily at certain hours. Call Home Phone, Main 5653."[9]

In September 1911 Weekly Unity published the Fillmores' response to requests from visitors to Unity headquarters who wanted to be treated by

a Silent Unity healer. Personal contact with Silent Unity workers, it was indicated, would interrupt the department's absent healing work. It was suggested that a local healer might be consulted. *Weekly Unity* stated: "If we
tried to meet personally all the friends who come, the absent work would
be seriously interfered with; so we leave all that, as well as the giving of
personal treatments, to the Local Healing Department."[10]

Although Charles practiced local healing for twenty years, Myrtle was
obviously more interested than he, as she continued with the work until
the time of her death in 1931. She commented on the qualities a practitioner needed to work successfully as a local healer. Myrtle wrote:

There are many points on which one must qualify before taking up local work.
For in the local work there is very little supervision—here at least. Those who
meet the public are supposed to be poised, and well-rounded in their spiritual development, and so filled with love and joy and health and consciousness of supply
that they fairly radiate it to all who come near—not starved for kindness and understanding and love and encouragement. Those who need help themselves, don't
belong in the work where they are continually faced with the problems of others.[11]

Myrtle commented on the effectiveness of a Unity practitioner in the
case of a man suffering from cancer who stopped by Kansas City on his
way to the Mayo Clinic in Rochester, Minnesota. After working with local
healers, there was no need for the man to continue on to Minnesota. Writing in March 1931, she observed:

I remember an instance of healing more than five years ago, when a man stopped
here at Unity on his way to Mayo's to undergo treatment for cancer of the stomach. I talked to him, and referred this friend to one of our Unity Society local healers. He took dinner at our Unity Inn, and seemed to enjoy his meal. He stayed a
while longer, and continued to improve. His wife returned home, but he stayed a
short time with us, attending our Unity classes and receiving spiritual instruction,
and the prayers of our healers. It turned out that he did not go on to Mayo's but
returned home healed. The last we heard from him, he was getting along fine.[12]

The confidence Myrtle had in gifted practitioners was expressed in a
letter to a friend. She explained that a woman by the name of Marguerite
had been persuaded to come to Unity headquarters "and take treatments
from our Mrs. Hatfield, who is especially quick to sense one's needs and
who is one of our best healers." Commenting on the healing that was
about to take place, she wrote, "We are sure that Marguerite will very
soon manifest health and a good wholesome appetite, now that she has

decided to depend upon the Great Physician to make her every whit whole."[13]

Myrtle indicated that, like the Silent Unity healers, the local healers did not charge for their services but worked on a freewill offering basis. She reported: "The local healers and spiritual advisors do their work on the love-offering plan, giving gladly and freely of their time and understanding, and receiving whatever their students and patients feel prompted to give."[14]

It seems that the Kansas City practitioners were willing to make house calls if a potential client was physically unable to come to Unity headquarters. In a letter to a Kansas City woman who was apparently incapacitated, Myrtle indicated, "Our healers would be glad to give you their help, in treatments, and no doubt they would call on you if you were unable to come to the Unity rooms."[15]

During Unity's Third Annual Convention, held June 15–28, 1924, Myrtle conducted a healing meeting in which she was "assisted by the healers of the local Unity Society." Their objective was to do healing work with participants who were interested in experiencing it. Myrtle told the participants:

In this healing meeting we intend to show you our faith by showing you our works. We want you to be so one with us in Spirit that you will know the mighty healing power of God as we know it. We want to have an illuminating revelation within our souls and a mighty outpouring of the Holy Spirit. We have come together for a purpose, not aimlessly, not to be amused or entertained; we have gathered here to lay hold of the healing power of Jesus Christ.[16]

Myrtle participated personally in the work of the local healing department until the last month of her life. In a letter written just one year before her death, she told a friend about her continuing connection with the local healers. She stated, "Always I am at Headquarters on Wednesday, to help 'mother' the work of the Local Unity Society, so that it is quite a busy day. We have a meeting at 2:30 and another at 8 o'clock in the evening."[17] On Wednesday, March 19, 1930, she wrote a friend, "This is my busy day in the local work and I get to my desk for short periods to give Elizabeth her work."[18] Myrtle's temporary secretary, Ila White, confirmed the fact that Myrtle spent important time with the local healing group as a part of her busy schedule. White reported:

Mrs. Fillmore divides her time between the town office and the office at Unity Farm. Friday evening she goes to the city and stays until Sunday afternoon. Then she is at the Farm Mondays and Tuesdays. Every Tuesday afternoon she again goes to the city and stays until Thursday afternoon. The work of the local Unity society needs Mrs. Fillmore's wonderful mother-Love and care and she devotes Wednesdays to it.[19]

In August 1930, Myrtle and other practitioners traveled to Unity Village from downtown Kansas City to work with students attending the 1930 summer school and help them gain a better understanding of local work. She reported, "Wednesday our Local Healers will be represented, and will tell how the Law of Holiness has worked in their experience as teachers and healers."[20]

After the death of Myrtle Fillmore in October 1931, the work of the Unity local healing department was dropped from the pages of Unity publications. The group apparently went out of existence sometime in the 1930s. If Charles had been a stronger proponent of practitioner work, this most likely would never have happened. Charles's preference was for absent healing. He indicated he could "reach patients as effectually through absent treatments as present, and with the same effort heal many more."[21] Given these views, it is not surprising that Unity School concentrated on the work of the Silent Unity healing department rather than on practitioner work after Myrtle's death.

The Society of Silent Unity: A Community for Mental Healing

The work of the Society of Silent Unity was begun by the Fillmores in April 1890 with the establishment of the Society of Silent Help. The organization's name was changed in June 1891 with the founding of *Unity* magazine. The Society's purpose was to foster the expansion of the Fillmores' teaching and healing work beyond Kansas City.[1] *Unity* magazine was founded to provide spiritual advice and counsel to people who enrolled as members of the society.[2] The masthead of the inaugural issue of the magazine reflected the connection between the society and the magazine, stating that *Unity* is "published by the Society of Silent Unity."[3] Leadership of the society was in the hands of the Fillmores, since Charles and Myrtle were listed as its "central secretaries."

The Society's mission was spiritual rather than religious. "The object and aim," the Fillmores stated, was "to lead men and women to the God within them."[4] They provided a clearer indication of what they meant by this when they stated: "The only object and aim of this society is to get people to listen to that 'still small voice' and to know that God will lead them into all wisdom, health and happiness if they will but spend a few moments each day in His company."[5]

Myrtle indicated that it was the responsibility of the central secretaries to reach out to those who "cannot for any reason have the benefit of personal healing and teaching"[6] and to help them "come into harmony with the Divine Spirit" and thereby "overcome their sins, ills, and troubles."[7] Members of the society were encouraged to develop themselves spiritually by studying truth principles, by practicing meditation, and by doing healing work.

Unity magazine was to play a major role in this effort. Its mission was to "have its columns devoted to the Society of Silent Unity and such points of Truth as are suitable for beginners."[8] In the 1890s the Fillmores continually emphasized the connection between the society and the magazine, stating, "We want all subscribers and members of Silent Unity to feel that they are equally interested with us in this good work."[9]

The Fillmores were convinced that the society would play a vitally essential role in the future development of humankind. Writing in June 1891, they prophesied:

It is promised that the Society of Silent Unity shall be an important factor in the reorganization of society which is now imminent, and that those of its members who have in view only the good, without a thought of self, shall be given charge over some of the silent forces that move the thoughts of men . . . This society will eventually prove the most potent controlling power on this planet in this establishment of the new order of things which is now being inaugurated.[10]

THE USE OF AFFIRMATIONS

"Whoever will may join the Society," the Fillmores promised. Membership was open to "every soul in the Universe."[11] The only requirements were to sit in the silence at 9:00 P.M. each evening and to hold in mind an affirmation entitled the "class thought" that was published in each issue of *Unity* magazine. The class thought was a central feature of the spiritual work assigned to members. Many of the class thoughts were for the purpose of connecting the member with the spirit of God within, as the following examples indicate:

"I am now manifesting the perfect harmony of Omnipotent Mind."[12]

"I am now conscious of thy indwelling Presence."[13]

"God wills through me to will and do that which ought to be done by me."[14]

The Fillmores continually stressed the need to hold the class thought in mind daily at the regularly stated time. They described in detail the benefits of doing so. They explained:

This "Class Thought" given each issue of *Unity* is the mental center about which we all revolve, and any one who wishes may take up that thought, and by silently holding it in mind, connect himself with us, and also with that Universal mind to which the "Class Thought" is an open sesame[15] . . . To hold the Class Thought means to silently repeat it over in mind until you realize the Presence of the Spirit all about us.[16]

In addition to the class thought, the Fillmores recommended that members repeat "a healing thought for each day." Published in *Unity* under the byline "A Daily Word," this affirmation was to be taken up, as they stated, "upon rising in the morning and repeated aloud many times." They suggested that it be repeated aloud specifically at noon and 6:00 P.M., and during the intervening hours be repeated mentally. The following are examples of "A Daily Word."

"The Father and I are one, therefore, the Truth is my personal belief."
"That they may be one even as we are one."[17]

MEDITATION

The Fillmores periodically emphasized the importance of silent meditation and the need to make it a regular part of the day's activities. Meditation was a spiritual practice they strongly encouraged, because they were convinced that the divine in the universe could be discovered by looking inward. They used a variety of arguments to convince members, undoubtedly unaccustomed to meditative techniques, to take time out from a busy day for at least fifteen minutes to sit alone in silence. They indicated:

All manifestations of life originate in the silence. Run over in your mind the main visible evidences of power and intelligence in the world of effects, from the delicate poise of the daisy to the mighty arms of silence that swing the planet out in space, and you will find that without exception they depend for existence upon that realm we call invisible. The thoughts that rise in you and come to the surface in deed and act, are they not from the silence? Do you take a step or lift a hand that has not its motive from the depths of that mighty sea of throbbing life within your own being? Then why look to the external for that which comes only from the silent within?[18]

The Fillmores were concerned that members did not have sufficient knowledge to go into the silence and to handle their minds when spending time in quiet. They recognized that most members were neophytes at the practice, so instructions on how to meditate were occasionally provided. They informed members that:

The "inner chamber" is the inner consciousness, and the closed "door" is the shutting out of external thoughts, sights and sound. Beginners find it helpful to close the eyes, and sit in a place where no external sound can reach the ears. This aids that inner concentration of mind so important in realizing the Divine Presence. Whether you get this consciousness of the Presence at first or not, you should sit in the silence regularly until you do get it.[19]

TESTIMONIALS FROM MEMBERS

The Fillmores continually received testimonials from members describing the benefits of the 9:00 P.M. time of silence. Myrtle summarized the experience of several members when she reported:

Splendid reports are coming to us from many who are taking advantage of our Silent Help sittings. It is proving a boon to those who are so situated that they have no opportunity of mingling with the spiritually minded . . . They soon find their mental atmosphere refreshed and invigorated . . . Hence, when a number of people sit down and go in mind to the higher realms, they come into rapport with not only the one primal mind, but with each other; there is thus established an intercommunion that is far reaching in its benefits.[20]

On occasion, Myrtle shared communications from members of the society with the *Unity* readership, as she did with the report of a woman who felt more peaceful as a result of the evening silences. The woman commented: "I do feel I must tell you of the help I have received from our 9 o'clock sittings. I have been helped so much mentally. When waves of seeming trouble threatened me I used the words, 'nothing but good can come to me,' and all was peace, peace and joy unspeakable, and the seeming troubles vanished away."[21]

As time went on, members reported benefits that were not only physical and psychological, but financial as well. In November 1894 the Fillmores reported: "The success of Silent Unity in helping people financially is greater than in any other direction. Last week in one day we got a dozen letters from different members acknowledging financial help in their affairs from unexpected sources."[22]

The Fillmores gave society members periodic pep talks, encouraging them to persist, have patience, and put in the time and effort required to get results. Most important of all, they needed to believe. The Fillmores advised: "No one is picked up by the Spirit and carried to success on beds of roses. Only those who are faithful to the cooperative thought, and who trust in the spirit, and watch for the good, are helped. Let your asking be definite, and then be persistent in looking for fulfillment."[23]

LOCAL CHAPTERS

One of the best ways to take advantage of the spiritual work of the society, the Fillmores believed, was through the formation of chapters of the society in local communities. In June 1891 they began urging members to take the initiative and establish groups in their communities. They gave specific instructions as to how this might be done. The guidelines below were repeated in *Unity* magazine several times each year. Members were told:

Start a society at once, if you have but two persons to begin with. Do not seek numbers, but harmony in those who meet with you. Meet regularly every Tuesday night and the Spirit will eventually draw you to those desired. Begin with music and sing frequently during the entire time of the meeting. Immediately after each song hold in the Silence for a moment of some thought of Truth. You cannot overdo this feature of the meeting. It is always uplifting and harmonizing to hold in unison some high spiritual thought . . . The early part of the evening may be passed in a general discussion of matters spiritual.[24]

Key features of the evening were the 9:00 o'clock silence and the affirmations that followed. The Fillmores recommended:

When the clock strikes nine go into the silence and hold in consciousness for a few moments, *"Be Still and Know that I am God."* Then after music hold the class thought for the month, in unison for a few moments. It is sometimes advisable to repeat it audibly, then silently, until the mental vibrations become harmonious. In holding these universal thoughts let your consciousness go out and take in all the minds of men. Feel that you are talking to every soul in the universe and that all are listening to your call. The mental drill will center your thoughts, and those of you who are spiritually alive will sense the vibrations of the Unity Spirit.[25]

The evening culminated with the healing work that could be accomplished by taking the following steps:

Take up those who you desire to help and hold them in thought by name separately, always saying to each: "In the name of Divine Unity—or Jesus Christ," as you prefer. Always remember that the thoughts you send out are pregnant with power and will sooner or later produce effects . . . See only the good—the pure, the perfect, the just, the true—then will the Divine Principle of Life, Love and Truth manifest in all you do.[26]

MEMBERSHIP

In July 1892 the Fillmores began encouraging those who had heretofore informally considered themselves members because they participated in the 9:00 o'clock silences to apply for formal induction. Those who sent in a personal written application to the Fillmores would receive a certificate acknowledging their official membership in the Society of Silent Unity. Along with the application, the Fillmores asked members to describe any "troubles" they might be having. The Fillmores told members that their heavy workload precluded them from making individual replies, but assured them they would "respond as Spirit directs" and take up requests for help during the 9:00 o'clock silences.[27]

In October 1896 the Fillmores began publishing the numbers of people who had received certificates of membership. As of October 1, 1896, there were 6,124 people with certificates. The number grew to 7,500 in August 1900 and to 15,000 by January 1907. In 1909, shortly before the Fillmores began de-emphasizing the Society's membership activities, the number of certified members totaled 16,000.[28]

SPIRITUAL COUNSELING

In addition to articles in *Unity* that spelled out truth principles, one of the chief ways the Fillmores clarified points in their teaching was through publishing in the magazine their written responses to members' questions. In answer to one member who asked, "Do I have to understand the Truth before I can be healed?" Charles responded: "No. You can be healed instantly through faith. Jesus of Nazareth did His healing by exercising the faith of the patient. If you will cultivate your faith in the healing power of Christ, by silent invocation, prayer, praising or singing, you can be healed, because the same Omnipresent Spirit is with you that was with Jesus."[29]

Another member wanted to know whether it was necessary to demonstrate truth before teaching it. The Fillmores did not view this as a precondition, indicating that knowing the truth was the first and most important step. They advised:

Go forth and teach, preach and do the works just as soon as you mentally perceive the Truth. Do not wait for demonstration; that will come in the process of the work. The perception of a truth is just as legitimate as its demonstration . . . When Truth comes to you with great conviction it is your duty to tell it to others regardless of your physical limitation in health or finances . . . But we should not lose sight of the fact that demonstration is the fulfillment of perception, and that it must come to you as a result of your faith in it.[30]

Another asked, "Will you kindly inform me whether it is necessary for a member of Silent Unity to sit in the silence every evening?" The Fillmores recommended flexibility in the practice:

Members observe the silent hour just as regularly as they can without stress and burden to themselves. The more faithful we are the greater our reward; you should not be so wedded to rules of action as to interfere with the freedom of ourselves or others. If you observe the hour whenever you can do so without inconvenience to anyone you will be doing quite right. Many of our members make it a rule to mentally run over the class thought or any uplifting thought at nine every night for a month.[31]

Still another member asked whether membership in the society precluded attendance at Christian churches. In their response, the Fillmores clarified the organizational rules of the society. They stated: "Members of Silent Unity are at perfect liberty to belong to any and all churches or any organization. We do not dictate as to what any member shall do, what they shall believe, or what they read . . . Our only rules relate to the silent hour. Outside of that our organization lays down no rules for anyone."[32]

The Fillmores wanted to make it clear that the society was not a church or a sect. They felt that there were already too many religions and when asked, continually denied that the society was just another religious denomination. They explained: "Silent Unity is not a sect, and lays down no points of doctrine or rules of life to be rigidly carried out. We say, join us in the daily recognition of an All Wise, All Powerful and All Present father, and you will find a new factor entering into all your affairs of mind and body."[33]

Some of their correspondents seemed to believe that membership in the society alone would solve all of their problems. The Fillmores wanted them to understand that hard work and study were required to grasp truth principles. Members needed to know that permanent healing was the result of diligent effort. They indicated:

Members should not look upon the Society as something that will overcome their errors without an effort on their part. There is an idea abroad among people who do not clearly understand the principle of Being that their cases can be taken up and permanently healed by another without their making any effort to understand what caused the disease or why it disappeared . . . As a Society of Silence we invoke this teaching spirit and assure all who mentally reach out to it, that it will come to them; yet this is but a sign of the more thorough work which must be done.[34]

Some members seemed to believe that spiritual healing could be done without mastering the teaching. The Fillmores wanted to make sure members understood that awakening to the truth of being was the principal goal of the teaching and came first. The ability to do healing work followed upon the deepening of spiritual understanding. They emphasized this point on several occasions in communicating with members, indicating:

Pain and suffering are not accidental, but they are the visible manifestation of wrong thinking and acting. Hence if I heal one without instructing him as to the cause, I have deferred the lessons which the law was teaching him, and to that extent put him aback in his understanding . . . so we should be teaching always, and thus be in a position to tell the patient what line of thinking brought about the ill, so that he may avoid it in the future. If all bodily ills of all the people in the world were healed instantly, they would soon be sick again, unless they were taught the Truth. It is the experience of old practitioners that the disease which they heal, in time reappears, unless the mind of the patient has been renewed through spiritual understanding. Healing is right and people can never give it too much attention. We are not *healers* but ministers of the gospel of Jesus Christ and our one idea should be to proclaim its Truth, letting the perfect results follow in harmony and wholeness of body and affairs.[35]

ROLE OF THE SOCIETY OF SILENT UNITY
IN THE UNITY MOVEMENT

In 1905, in a communication entitled "Items for Silent Unity Members," the Fillmores reflected upon the fruitful, mutually beneficial connection they enjoyed with the society's growing membership. They stated:

The power of the Spiritual Words spoken by this Society grows more pronounced in its work as the membership increases . . . Our ultimate aim is to educate all our members in the true way of thinking and living, but we do not wish to make it too hard. The fact is, it is the easiest way of all ways. Those who get into this way never desire another . . . Members who are in the habit of sitting in the 9 o'clock Silence can reach us when in special need by simply sitting quietly and *thinking* about us and our Spiritual power. We get many such messages every day. Our members appear before us in our mind's eye, and sometimes we see them in form, and we speak the Word, and the servant is healed.[36]

In 1907, seventeen years after the society was established, Myrtle Fillmore acknowledged the important role it had played in the development of the Unity movement. Her remarks were made as a part of a celebration of "The first Annual Jubilee" of their occupation of new headquarters at 913 Tracy Avenue, Kansas City. Myrtle explained:

The Society of Silent Unity is a branch of the Unity work whose importance and extent is very little understood or appreciated by those at the local center who have recourse to healers and teachers, but which in reality is "The Power Behind the Throne" of all Unity's prosperity and success. The Society was instituted in 1890 to help those who were seeking light through the ministry of our publication, *Thought,* and its object was to prove the power of silent cooperation in holding in thought some vital truth at 9 o'clock every night. These thoughts were given monthly in the magazine *Thought,* and this silent cooperation was found to be of great value to those who practiced it.[37]

Myrtle described what she considered the phenomenal growth of the society in terms of size of membership. She also referred to the fact that relating to the needs of its membership required the work of several people at headquarters:

From a nucleus of about a half a dozen to start with, the Society has grown to number almost 16,000. And from so small a correspondence that Mr. Fillmore and I could easily handle it, it has come to require the services of a half a dozen secretaries, besides ourselves, and the force of local healers. Its membership belts the globe . . . and if all members are faithful to the given thought at their local time there is not an hour in the day that someone is not sending forth this truth.[38]

THE RED LEAF CONTROVERSY

In October 1905 the Fillmores invited members of the Society of Silent Unity to participate in a test of the healing power of thought. For the next several months, one page was devoted to society activities in *Unity* magazine. The page containing the class thought was to be used for the test. This page was to be printed entirely in red ink and "treated and saturated with the direct thought emanations of eight members of the Silent Unity Healing Department, 913 Tracy Avenue, Kansas City, Missouri."[39] Those members of the society outside Unity headquarters in Kansas City who were willing to participate in the test were to remove the page, or the red leaf as this special page was called, from the magazine. Members were then requested to hold the red leaf between clasped hands and repeat the class thought for between five and fifteen minutes. The class thought for December 1905, for example, was this: "The promise of Jesus Christ: 'Ye shall receive power when the Holy Ghost is upon you' is now fulfilled." The Fillmores also published a "prosperity thought" on the red leaf. The prosperity thought for January 1906, for example, was: "I am enriched by the abounding sufficiency of God, now making me a magnet for plenty."[40] After working with the red leaf for thirty days, society members were asked to report on their results.

Letters from members soon began pouring in. Some of the testimonials indicated that the affirmations printed on the red leaf were the key factor in improving the member's life circumstances. Others, however, seemed to give the red leaf itself—the piece of paper, a material object—the credit. Writers of the testimonials listed below appear to have attributed their success to the red sheet of paper rather than to the affirmations printed on it. They wrote:

While holding the Red Leaf between my hands it caused vibrations through my whole system, and rheumatic pains that I was troubled with disappeared as if by magic. MJR.[41]

Our hired man had a pain around his eye, and was somewhat frightened by it. I told him about the Red Leaf; he placed it over the painful spot and it soon began to get better. Mrs. LAH.[42]

I cannot say too much in praise of the Red Sheet. I spent a silent hour alone with it in my hands, and felt a thrill all through me, a white light was pictured before me, and with it the head of a lion. It came to me as a symbol of strength; indeed, I have gained strength every day. The demonstration in my case was wonderful. Mrs. AET.[43]

While many reported substantial benefits in working with the red leaf, others objected on grounds that the red leaf test could mislead people into believing that a physical object, a page out of a magazine, did the healing. The Fillmores acknowledged that "widespread protest" came from their "most devoted friends," who criticized them for "departing from their true doctrine" and for "supplying a material aid."[44] Believing the criticism unjustified, in January 1906 the Fillmores published an "Explanatory" that provided further justification for the use of the red leaf. They wrote:

"This Red Leaf bears testimony of that invisible Omnipresence, the Spirit of Truth, promised by Jesus Christ. We have blessed it, and spoken the Word into it, and given through it a message of health and prosperity to all who *believe.*"[45]

The Fillmores wanted it clearly understood that the affirmations contained on the red leaf did the work. They asserted: "The Healing Leaf that goes with this issue carries the healing thought in larger measure than ever. Every one of them has been given the Word of Divine Life and Love. Believe in the power of the Omnipresent life, which the words on this leaf will call to your mind, and you will be healed."[46]

By February it was apparent that society members needed further instruction in the use of the red leaf. The Fillmores recognized they needed to address criticism by members who felt that they were "lowering their standards of thought by using these helps," and that the red leaf test "would lead credulous ones away from the Spirit."[47] In an article entitled "How to Use the Red Leaf," Charles provided a detailed justification for the red leaf, indicating his strong belief that the spiritual faculties of Kansas City members of the society added to the red leaf's effectiveness as a healing agent. He wrote: "We would not be truthful if we did not plainly tell you that the Red Leaf is charged with a spiritual, mental and physical potency not common to the outer world, and does put those who use it into a certain unity with higher realms of consciousness, according to their faith."[48]

The red leaf possessed its unusual potency, Charles asserted, because it had been spiritually treated by the Unity Society members in Kansas City. "It is charged with healing-thought power, and will connect all who use it with the Jesus Christ Consciousness."[49] In response to a question by a society member who wanted to know why they got a stronger realization of spiritual power when holding the class thought in their hands, Charles stated that it was in part due to the spiritual potency of the Kansas City healers. He wrote:

We have, through nearly twenty years of effort, established a spiritual thought-centre, and we have the power to connect all people, who have faith in things spiritual with the Christ Consciousness. Do not understand that we claim an exclusive power, but we have attained a very positive degree of this consciousness, and our decrees are established and carried out by the Higher Law. When we declare that even a sheet of paper shall carry our Word, and do a certain work in the name of our Lord Jesus Christ, it is accomplished.[50]

Charles then described how society members might correctly use the red leaf. He advised: "Hold it in your hands and slowly read the words over, then close your eyes and repeat them mentally. Do this until your mind is *saturated* with the thought. Then meditate upon its meaning, and let it sink deep into your consciousness. This is the *right* use of the Red Leaf."[51]

Charles wanted members to be sure they recognized that the red leaf was not to be used as "a mustard plaster or a magnetic belt."[52] He also wanted to be certain that members understood that the piece of paper itself did not do the healing. He reported: "People do not look upon that little piece of red paper as having in itself any virtue. They know that it is representative only and merely as an aid to the wandering thought that has lost its connection with the One Great Mind."[53]

Charles then described the red leaf's many benefits. He wrote: "As an aid to concentration, the Red Leaf is without peer. In the throes of pain it is hard to gather one's thoughts, and here the Red Leaf takes the place of a good healer. It is charged with the Power of the Spirit-Word, and helps to concentrate the discordant thoughts."[54]

Charles believed that, if working with the red leaf was unsuccessful, the user's negative thoughts were to blame. He declared: "All failures are due to the thought that it is a piece of material paper, or that it is superstition and materialism to believe it has power. 'As a man thinketh in his heart, so is he.'"[55]

By May 1906 criticism was still mounting and Charles recognized that he needed to deal with it. "The Red Leaf is still a question of high and low degree by our readers," he acknowledged.

Some of them consider it a species of necromancy (sorcery) . . . The Red Leaf is helping many, yet others are afraid of it. Because the thought is printed on a piece of material paper, and they are told to hold that paper in sight while meditating upon that thought, they jump to the conclusion that it is like taking medicine, or believing in the healing power of some sacred relic.[56]

He then restated the case for its use and described the impact of the prayer work of the society members in Kansas City.

We might tell you how frequently our whole Healing Board prays and invokes the Omnipotence, Omniscience and Omnipresence of the Infinite Good upon those sheets before they are put into *Unity* and we might describe the Holy Ghost power that is frequently poured out upon us at such times . . . The Red Leaf is a thought gatherer. The printing press has put upon it the "Class Thought" of the Silent Unity Society, and it has again been imprinted by the direct imaging of the power of our Board of Healers. Thus it carries a twofold power as a thought gatherer, and many are finding that they can concentrate more successfully when using it as such an aid.[57]

In September 1906 Charles further clouded the issue by choosing to reprint in *Unity* a letter to the editor of *The New York Times* that used the red leaf episode to satirize Unity, Mary Baker Eddy, and Christian Science. Written by a New York man unfamiliar to the Fillmores by the name of Edward Branch Lyman, it was entitled CHRISTIAN SCIENCE OUTDONE: NEW CULT IN KANSAS CITY BEFORE WHICH MRS. EDDY'S DOINGS PALE. The letter began with the following biting piece of sarcasm:

I wonder if you have given the Red Leaf cure a trial? I note that Christian Science is too gaseous and idealistic for you. But here you have practically the same thing in tangible, applicable and much more concentrated form. The Red Leaf cure may be said to be Christian Science in plaster shale . . . Have you a toothache, a cancerous growth—anything that can be classed as an ill of the flesh? Merely apply the Red Leaf into or near the affected part or organ, and presto you are healed.[58]

The letter went on to cast scorn on the red leaf's capacity to improve personal circumstances. Lyman wrote:

Perhaps your health is good, but your financial status is not just what it ought to be, from your unselfish point of view (by you I mean, Mr. Editor, anybody, whoever he may be). Simply apply the little Red Leaf to pocketbook or business letterhead, or sleep with it under your pillow, and you will experience a turn in the tide of your affairs and you will get a prompt harvest of "long greens." Or perhaps you are wealthy and well but are not content with your psychological makeup. Apply the Red Leaf as direction and get confidence, trust, courage, etc., a-plenty. Oh, it's beautiful! Lovely Red Leaf![59]

The writer then presented several enthusiastic testimonials of the healing power of the red leaf extracted from letters written to the Fillmores and printed in *Unity* magazine. Again, tongue-in-cheek, Lyman asked: "What it has done for them, may it not do for you?" The writer then made the following snide comment: "There are dozens of other quite wonderful cures. Even were this side of the work of the Red Leaf all there was to its activities, it would surely be worth a dollar a year. But it cures drunkenness, stops fires, gives prosperity, etc., as note the following few more extracts from the letters of the helped."[60]

In his last paragraph Lyman concluded by ridiculing both Unity and

Christian Science: "*Unity* contains a photograph of the nearly completed new Unity Building in Kansas City. It is built upon the "love offerings" of beneficiaries of the little Red Leaf. Doesn't that beat Christian Science 'all holier' in inexpensiveness and expeditiousness—this little Red Leaf?"[61]

Charles's response to the letter indicates that he did not see or chose to overlook Lyman's apparent purpose—which was to lump Unity with Christian Science and cast both in an unfavorable light. Charles observed:

The foregoing appeared in the *New York Times* July 15th. It was evidently written in a spirit of semi-ridicule, but quite mild; in fact, we are finding that the author is a friend in disguise . . . We could have not summed up more completely the virtues of the Red Leaf, and we are truly grateful to this unknown friend for his comprehensive estimate of its varied powers.[62]

It appears Charles did not recognize that Lyman presented through biting satire the same criticism of the red leaf that society members had made; in other words, that the healing was done by a material object—a page printed in red ink cut from a magazine. By misreading both Lyman's objective in writing the letter and *The New York Times'* interest in printing it, Charles left himself open to further criticism.

The red leaf controversy simply would not go away, and the Fillmores struggled to cope with it. In the two months following *The New York Times* piece (October and November 1906), they removed the red leaf from the magazine. It was returned, however, in December, due (they announced) to popular demand. The opponents of the red leaf had apparently been outvoted. Charles reported:

With this issue we return the Red Leaf to the pages of *Unity*. The demand for it has been so universal, and its absence so keenly felt by so many, as expressed in their letters, that we are satisfied that it is meeting a need that cannot well be ignored. The charge that its tendency is to lead the minds of people away from Spirit, is not sustained, if these letters may be taken as indicative of the general trend of thought of those who are using it. They indicate as a rule a great devoutness and dependence upon God as the source of all good. The Red Leaf helps them to more firmly fix their attention upon the words that bring the One Great Mind into expression.[63]

The Fillmores were still unable to put this matter to rest and the criticism continued. Two months later in February 1907, Charles extracted from a letter from one of the critics, who commented: "Since you have added the Red Leaf, a number of people to whom I introduced *Unity* say, they do not care for it since it became superstitious. The testimonials on the back seem like patent medicine recommendations. Why publish them?"[64]

Charles responded by continuing to justify his position on the red leaf with these comments:

That the Red Leaf has more than fulfilled our most earnest expectations, is attested by the hundreds of testimonials of healing, through its use, coming from all parts of the world; and when we omitted it, our mail was, for a time filled with requests to have it restored. Some may call it "superstition," but who will undertake to draw a line between superstition and faith? . . . That which one may call superstition today, may be living reality tomorrow, in the light of increased knowledge.[65]

Objections to the use of the red leaf continued, and the Fillmores recognized that something needed to be done to put an end to the controversy. They finally came to recognize that the red leaf, as a symbol, misrepresented their real intentions in attempting to test the power of thought. A name change was long overdue, and they finally decided to make one. They also made it clear that the real purpose of the "concentration leaf" was to help people shift consciousness. In an editorial in the January 1908 issue of *Unity* entitled THE RED LEAF—THE CONCENTRATION LEAF, Charles formulated their new position:

We have always called it the Red Leaf. A better name would be the Concentration Leaf. That is what it is—an aid to concentration of thought on several planes of consciousness . . . That this is a fact we are having proven to us in everyday experiences. Nearly all people apply these concentration leaves in bodily healing, but few at once realize the Spirit power that does the work. But that power is there because we put it into the Leaf by charging it with a message of Truth. We are in a constant spiritual radiation in our healing room at Headquarters, and this we put into the leaves through prayer.[66]

Unity continued for several years to feature a concentration leaf containing two affirmations, one a class thought and the other a prosperity thought. These short statements were usually printed in large type on one full page in the Silent Unity section. This page was not, however, printed in red ink. This visually appealing page usually appeared in two colors: yellow, green, or blue, in addition to black. This new approach apparently met with the approval of the membership of the Society of Silent Unity and the subscribers to the magazine, because no further criticisms appeared in the magazine. The following commentary, contained in the May 1915 issue of *Unity,* is indicative of the revised policy. It stated:

The Concentration Leaf which appears each month in the magazine *Unity* has a baptism of the Word before it is sent out. For one whole month before mailing, the leaves are kept on the table in the Silent Unity healing room, and this alone would make them vibrant with the living Word; but the power of the Word is also given them directly and definitely in a special meeting of the Silent Unity workers. One day each month the ten o'clock Silence is devoted to blessing these leaves preparatory to their going forth in *Unity* . . . The statement on the leaf that is being sent out gives the keynote for the meeting, and the texts and affirmations and songs are usually in line with the printed word. All who take part in this service of blessing feel themselves spiritually uplifted and strengthened through the power of the spoken Word. Some who have felt the power of the leaves that we send out in *Unity* and in letters have tried to use them as mustard plasters, but the leaves themselves have no power. It is the Word which they carry that makes them different from the ordinary printed page. There is nothing occult nor material about them.[67]

The red leaf controversy could have been avoided had the Fillmores more clearly understood that their legitimate desire to test the power of thought could be misinterpreted by focusing attention on a material object, a page printed in red in a magazine. Had they called it a concentration leaf test and printed the page without color, not focusing attention on the printed page itself, they most likely would have avoided the controversy that swirled for two years around their teaching and healing practices.

PHASING OUT THE WORK OF THE SOCIETY

Not long after the end of the red leaf controversy, the Fillmores, for no explicit reason, began to phase out the work of the Society of Silent Unity. No longer were articles or commentaries in *Unity* specifically addressed to the membership. Articles and columns were aimed primarily at the subscribership-at-large. Spiritual counseling that took the form of open letters to members ceased. No longer did the Fillmores publish letters from members requesting help. No longer were members asked to particpate in tests like the red leaf. Reprints of letters of advice from the Fillmores or from the Silent Unity staff addressed members who were now absent from *Unity's* pages. No longer were members encouraged to establish local chapters of the society, and no longer did *Unity* magazine publish guidelines on how to go about setting up local chapters. The only indication of membership activity was an occasional listing, possibly two to three times each year, of the total membership. For no apparent reason the numbers kept increasing, as there was no visible effort in the magazines to enlist new members. In the late 1920s the total was over one hundred thousand.

Silent Unity

ABSENT HEALING

The Fillmores discontinued the major outreach work of the Society of Silent Unity because they were able to reach Unity students outside Kansas City more effectively through the healing work of an offshoot of the Society called the Silent Unity Healing Department. In February 1910, in an article entitled "The Society of Silent Unity," *Weekly Unity* described the absorption of the Society by the Kansas City-based Silent Unity Healing Department. The editors indicated: "The third floor of the Unity building is occupied by the Society of Silent Unity which is the department of Unity work devoted to absent healing. A dozen workers here unite in sending forth the Word of life and healing to people in all parts of the world in response to the request of those who desire help."[1]

In January 1912 the Fillmores acknowledged the demise of the membership activities of the society when they published an announcement in *Unity* that totally ignored the fact that the organization had members outside Kansas City. In describing the nature of the society, they made the following brief, to-the-point statement: "The Society of Silent Unity *is* (emphasis added) the absent healing department of the Unity work."[2]

Absent-healing work was first performed by Myrtle and Charles in the 1890s. In their communications in *Unity* magazine with the members of the Society of Silent Unity, the Fillmores made it known they were available should members choose to write requesting help. The approach was low-key, and they did not actively solicit the work. They warned members that because of their busy schedules they "could not undertake to answer such letters personally." They did assure members, however, that they would "respond in the silence as Spirit directs."[3]

As the decade of the 1890s progressed, more and more members of the society wrote for healing. As the workload increased, the Fillmores engaged other Kansas City practitioners to handle some of the letter requests. A woman who identified herself as "Secretary McMahon" apparently was the first healer to be employed by the Fillmores in the Silent Unity Healing Department. She wrote an article for *Unity* in 1893 in which she commented on the cases being treated by the department and described her work as a letter writer. She cited the cases of several people whose physical ills had been alleviated through the absent healing.[4]

The Fillmores had absolute faith in the power of absent healing to bring about positive results. "No individual," they indicated, "can ever have the power of several united in absent work."[5] Testimony of those who had been treated successfully in absentia convinced them of its efficacy. "The wonderful success of absent healing," the Fillmores wrote in 1891, "demonstrated that bodily presence is not necessary to those in spiritual harmony."[6] Based on their own experience, they concluded that absent healing was more effective than practitioner work. They noted:

Some folks think they will get better results if they are treated by an individual healer, but our experience is that the healing averages higher where cases are handled from an impersonal standpoint. There is a good reason for this—the work is not done by the healer, but by the Spirit of Truth, and where both patient and helper forget self and centre all power in the Great Supreme, the consciousness is raised to a higher plane and the result Divine.[7]

The spoken word was a key element in absent healing. The Silent Unity Healing Department employed it exclusively. In fact, the Fillmores reported that the group "does all its work through the Word spoken in the name of Jesus Christ." The Fillmores had great confidence in the power of the spoken word. They declared: "The Word having in it all the potentialities of Being has quickening, vitalizing, strength-giving, harmonizing, health-creating, prospering power, and all who have the faith that makes one receptive to the Word get the benefit of it in new thoughts, new states of mind, new conditions in body and affairs."[8]

The Fillmores insisted on doing healing work on a freewill offering basis only.[9] They considered it improper to charge for spiritual work. "Our work is not to be bought with a price," they indicated. "We make no bargain or ask any pay."[10] Freewill offerings, the Fillmores had observed, were a well-established practice in religious circles in America. "The religious institutes of this whole country depend upon freewill offerings of the people for their support," they wrote. It followed that since Unity was engaged in the same ministry as the churches, Unity should use the same methods to obtain financial support.[11]

While they did not charge for their healing work, the Fillmores strongly disapproved of charity, and did not consider the Silent Unity Healing Department to be a charitable organization. They explained:

We do not advocate charity in healing. Many people pride themselves on giving their services, expecting nothing in return. This is error. It attracts a pauper mentality that is always looking for something to be given it without having to reciprocate. One of the [common] mortal errors of humanity is that something can be gotten for nothing. This one-sided idea has become a disease, and a large portion of the people spend their time in cultivating it.[12]

In fact, the Fillmores' distaste for charity was so strong that they felt that those who dispensed charity did a disservice to the recipients. They noted: "People who pose before the world as benefactors and dispensers of charity should rightly be counted as enemies of mankind ... Thousands are held in bondage to the belief that they must be helped, when the blessings would be to make them see that their salvation lies in helping themselves."[13]

While they did not charge for their services, the Fillmores believed they should be adequately compensated for their work. They were convinced of the value of their efforts and those of the Silent Unity healers associated with them in the Kansas City headquarters and were forthright in pointing out the benefits of their work. Writing in 1907, when the Unity movement was almost two decades old, they explained: "We are not giving out drugs, or anything that can be measured or seen, yet there is a constant outpouring of Spiritual Life Energy from this center, and all who put themselves *en rapport* with us get its effect. It has taken twenty years' constant work to get this current established, and we know that it is the greatest healing agent in the universe."[14]

The Fillmores believed there should be a fair exchange between client and healer. "Spiritual reciprocity" was the name they gave this relationship, and they defined it as "the spontaneous reciprocal exchange of values between healer and patient." It was a concept they often referred to and wrote about. They commented: "The healer gives his time and the word of the Spirit just as fully as he knows how; this is his value. The patient is expected to give in return that which he counts valuable, be it money, jewels, books, goods or whatever."[15]

In determining how much money to give for healing work, the Fillmores asked recipients to be fair. If society members were truly seeking justice, they would compensate Unity healers adequately for their services.

On several occasions in *Unity* magazine, the Fillmores appealed to members' sense of equity:

We appeal to your sense of justice—be fair with us. Remember that we have through years of mental experience developed the power of handling Universal Life Substance, and we pour it into your consciousness, and through it you are healed. And we have by years of study come into understanding of Divine Wisdom, which we impart to you freely. If you have made sacrifices to pay doctors, should you do anything less to pay those who place you in touch with the very elixir of life?[16]

In January 1901, the Fillmores summarized the work of the first twelve years of the Silent Unity Healing Department and commented on the status of the work. Describing both the activities at Unity headquarters in Kansas City as "The Silent Unity Center" and the progress made since the movement began, they stated:

This Center of the Silent Unity Society begins the new year and new century with a consciousness of great spiritual power. For over twelve years we have without interruption centered our hearts, our souls, our minds, upon the one omnipresent God working in and through us, and in and through all people, until there has been established in our minds a consciousness of Spiritual Power having substance and mental tangibility. That God is Life and Substance is no longer a theory, but His presence has become to us a mental visibility, and we know and feel the power of the Divine Word as plainly as one having hold of the wires of a great battery.[17]

In addition to the Fillmores, three others (Mr. and Mrs. Cassius Shafer and Jennie Croft) were engaged in absent healing at Unity headquarters. The Fillmores informed society members that the healers at Unity headquarters welcomed their requests for spiritual work, and assured them that valuable help would be provided. They stated:

We are ready to help you all to come into the Christ Presence and Power. The power is mighty in us, and we are assured that we can help others to realize it . . . As a Spiritual Center we send forth the Christ Word for all members and for the friends of members. There is no limit to the power of the Divine Logos where there is a faith center in working order. If you have faith that God can reach your friends in their trials, mental or physical, send forth your spiritual word and God will prove it for you. If you have faith in Silent Unity, write or wire us, and our power will be joined with yours.[18]

In early 1905 the Fillmores began on a regular basis to actively encourage subscribers to write to them for healing work. It was the first time that they used a full page of *Unity* magazine to print an application form. They declared: "We can help you in matters pertaining to health, finances, spiritual understanding, and, in fact, everything that is desirable, and for your highest good . . . We put no limit on the power of the Holy Spirit, through which the work is done. Write us freely just what you most desire."[19]

Direct invitations produced more requests for prayer work than the more passive approach previously taken. While no statistics are available prior to 1907 on the number of letters and telegrams received or sent, the number of healers working at Unity headquarters rose from three to eleven from 1900 to 1906.[20] In an effort to make it easier for those who wanted "healing and spiritual assistance," the Fillmores stipulated: "Write short letters. A little silent prayer before you write concerning the question of what and how much is necessary to be told, will help you to tell us your needs clearly and concisely."[21]

More detail was also provided to members regarding how prayer was used by the staff at Unity headquarters:

Many write us that they feel the vibrations of love and life and strength carried by the letters received from us, and one who mentions it asks, "Do you treat the letters before you send them?" Yes. As soon as letters are received, the Word of help is sent forth, and the reply is written with prayer. The Word is spoken again and sent with them as they are sent out. Prayer characterizes all the Silent Unity work.[22]

It was also revealed that the Silent Unity healing work was done in privacy, on a floor of the building where only Silent Unity staff was allowed. The report indicated:

The Silent Unity Healing Department is on the top floor of the Unity Building where no one is allowed except the healers and the correspondents. Eight healers and seven correspondents now constitute the staff. This "upper room" is a great healing pool, from which flows a perpetual stream of health—giving life and substance to all who ask, in faith believing.[23]

In January 1907 the first report of Silent Unity Healing Department's workload was made. *Unity* magazine stated that about one hundred letters were being written daily.[24] In addition, the magazine published extracts from letters "written by Silent Unity healers to patients." These extracts provided "excellent lessons," therefore were "worthy of repeating to all our readers."[25] The Fillmores viewed these letters as presenting the teaching in a direct and accessible form.

The following question written by a *Unity* subscriber, and the answer provided by a Unity correspondent, are examples of the kind of questions and answers that began appearing in *Unity* in 1907 and continued for many years.

Question: I understand New Thought, and have practiced it for five years, declaring myself lucky, and praying in the name of the Spirit, yet I have been unlucky. Now I am thoroughly discouraged. This is the third month you have treated me.

Answer: We are doing all we can for you, and you are under daily treatment by the Society. No, we have not forgotten to speak the Word for you, but you may have over looked the fact that, before the Word can be made manifest unto you, there is something for you to do in making conditions for it. Your letter does not indicate that you have any desire for the realization of the kingdom of heaven within, your desires seeming to go out for material things alone . . . There is no such thing as "luck." All things come through the operation of an immutable law, and if that law is put into operation, it will bring results as sure as the day follows the night. That thing sometimes called "luck" is nothing but a golden calf, which men too often bow down to worship. Remember this, in the realm of good there is nothing left to chance. We suggest you take this thought into the silence. "I have faith in the One God, the Father which dwelleth within me, whose power is now working for the manifestation of my highest good. All that is mine shall come to me, and there is no power that can come between me and a full realization of that which is for my highest good."[26]

Periodically, further details about the workings of the Silent Unity Healing Department were presented in *Unity*. The following report made in August 1908 reflected its growing importance:

The absent healing and correspondence department of our work is seldom mentioned in these columns but it is none the less important. A dozen people give their entire efforts to this part of the work, and have set apart a large room in the Unity Building where no one enters but those who are dedicated to the ministry. Here the power of the Omnipresent One is realized until its presence fills the room and goes forth with every word that is there—thought, written, or spoken. The correspondence of this Silent Unity Department is strictly private, but many letters testify to the healing, spiritualizing and comforting effects of the ministry.[27]

Two years later, in February 1910, the details of the daily 5:00 P.M. staff healing meeting were revealed. *Weekly Unity* reported: "Every afternoon at 5 o'clock the special meeting for the realization of God's Presence and power is held, and at this time all cases presented for treatment are taken up. At the close of the meeting, extracts from the many good letters received are read."[28]

The article further indicated that in 1910 about a dozen workers comprised the staff and about one hundred letters were received daily, suggesting that little growth had taken place since the size of the staff and the workload was first reported on three years earlier in January, 1907.[29] One of the more detailed accounts of the work of the Silent Unity Healing Department (which by now was beginning to be called simply "Silent Unity") was written in October 1911 by Edna L. Carter, who had worked at Unity headquarters for almost a decade. In an article entitled POINTS FROM SILENT UNITY, Carter reported that the workday began early and was punctuated by periods in which all the workers gathered for silent meditation. Carter stated:

Every morning at ten o'clock the sixteen local workers of the Society of Silent Unity drop the letterwriting, gather in the Silence room, and join in this word: "Christ is the head of the Movement." In the afternoon at three o'clock they again have a Silence, and then spend a half hour in discussing various points that come up in the letter-writing . . . At five o'clock in the afternoon the regular healing silence is held.[30]

Maintaining the inner peace established during periods of silent mediation was essential in establishing a proper context for the work in Silent Unity. "Everything possible is done to establish and maintain a strong healing power and atmosphere of Truth," Carter reported, "and outside thoughts are excluded as much as possible."[31] Carter then discussed the manner in which letter requests for healing were handled.

In studying a letter preparatory to answering it, we find that we can often get the keynote to the writer's mind; that is, the letter the patient has written reveals the cause of his inharmony. When the keynote is found it is easy to give help . . . As a part of our study of the art of writing healing letters, some of the letters containing special problems are brought up in this three-o'clock meeting, and a general expression as to the needs of the writers comes from the workers. In this way we get broader views and find that we help one another as well as the patients.[32]

Carter also revealed that letter writers had been instructed not to go too deeply into the factors that may have produced ill health in the patient. She indicated: "In answering letters we often find it necessary to explain that we do not think it wise to search too much for causes of ailments. All real healing follows overcoming of errors, but the error should not be emphasized in any way. Instead, it should be allowed to pass out of consciousness."[33]

Describing the workers in the department as "the Silent Unity 'bees,'"

Carter went on to provide insights into how the actual work was carried on, particularly when the workload grew heavy. She reported:

Sometimes, especially when the workers are taking vacations, our baskets of letters to be answered get so full that extra time is needed for them, and that there may be as little delay as possible in answering the letters, we stay now and then of an evening and have a "bee" from seven until nine, with supper at six. A long table is made of desks and spread with a generous outlay of the good, wholesome foods that vegetarians eat. The cut glass and china and silverware are somewhat on the picnic order; but it is a merry crowd that gathers around the table, and we don't care whether the dishes match or not. Sometimes we go over to the Inn for the supper; but wherever it is eaten there is always a merry time at the meal, a short recreation after it, followed by two hours of good work.[34]

Between 1910 and 1915, the Silent Unity healing work grew rapidly. Several hundred letters were now being received daily and the staff grew from twelve to thirty-five. Larger quarters were required, and space was designed in a new building specifically to meet Silent Unity's needs. Healers were available on a twenty-four-hour basis, including weekends, with someone available throughout the night to respond to telegrams. Details of the work were reported in the March 1915 issue of *Unity*. The workday began at 8:00 A.M. with a silent prayer that lasted fifteen minutes. "During the Silence," it was reported, "workers sit at their desks ready to begin on their letters as soon as they have prayed for Divine Guidance and help."[35] Letter writing was interrupted for prayer and meditation at 10:00 A.M. At 3:00 P.M. each day the workers met in the healing room "to take up some special feature of the work." In modern parlance these meetings might be called "staff training." The sessions lasted for about an hour and covered a variety of topics:

On Monday afternoon the time is given to the reading of extracts from letters, bearing witness that the Word which we speak is fulfilling its mission in awakening, quickening, healing and prospering those who are under our ministry.

On Tuesday afternoon an hour is spent on the study of Truth. The Complete Correspondence Course has been covered in this way, and Part One has been studied twice. At present we are studying the leaflets so that the workers may be thoroughly familiar with the teaching in them.

On Wednesday afternoon is "Joy Day." The meeting begins with this thought, or one similar: "The joy of the Lord is my strength." The heartier we can laugh on this day, the more successful we think the meeting has been, so everybody comes with an offering of the best in the way of humor he has been able to find through the week.

On Thursday afternoon, points for the good of the work are considered. Better methods and greater efficiency along all lines are desired, and suggestions to this end are in order at this meeting.

Friday is prosperity day. We hold the prosperity thought and discuss points that have to do with the demonstration of prosperity. The idea is to build up our own consciousness of God as the one Resource, that we may demonstrate supply for the needs of the work, and also be better able to help others in their demonstrations.[36]

Classes given by Charles for the Silent Unity staff were conducted in an unusual way. Two weeks before a scheduled hour-long session, Charles presented four workers with a question that they were to be prepared to answer in depth when the class met. While answers could be presented orally, most workers preferred to write them out and present them as a "paper." Each took from three to fifteen minutes to present. After each presentation, Charles would ask for comments from the staff. Harry L. Reed, a Silent Unity worker who participated in many of the classes, reported on the lively discussions. "There was no telling," he noted, how the presenter "might be questioned, praised or torn apart."[37] Reed praised Charles for the way he handled these sessions, indicating:

In all the classes and meetings, Mr. Fillmore retained his poise, his kindly good humor, his humanity, his great understanding and patience, and he imparted to each student something of his light and love and appreciation of life, if the student was at all receptive. And no student remained long in the group without becoming receptive and without being drawn into the friendly but serious and helpful discussions.[38]

At the end of each training session, Charles closed it with a short period of meditation and thanksgiving. The staff returned to their tasks renewed and ready again to take up the work. Reed reported that as the meeting ended, "The workers, refreshed, instructed and inspired, would file out sometimes to the accompaniment of a joyful hymn, and go back to various duties in the files, in the letter writing rooms, in the telephone room, in the supply department, and in the prayer room, the 'Healing Room.'"[39]

Silent Unity continued the rapid growth that began in 1910; by 1920, 186,000 letters were sent out, requiring a staff of forty to process them. By 1925 the number of outgoing letters had risen to 500,000 and the staff totaled approximately sixty workers. By 1930 the workload in healing letters mailed was over 600,000, and a total of ninety healers were employed. In a piece appearing in *Weekly Unity* entitled FACTS ABOUT SILENT UNITY, the department's procedures, which provided careful, loving attention to all letters, was described. The report stated:

Each letter that is received by Silent Unity is opened and blessed. The letter is then taken to the file room where a worker looks over the records to see whether the writer has had previous correspondence with Silent Unity . . . When a record of the letter has been made in the file room, the letter is then prayerfully considered and answered by a Silent Unity worker who gives special attention to the case. Prayers are later offered for the writer in the Silent Unity healing meeting. Unless otherwise instructed, Silent Unity prays for its correspondents every day for thirty days.[40]

After a letter was answered, it was placed in the Silent Unity prayer room for thirty days. At least one Silent Unity worker was on duty there all day, praying. Unity believed that this practice amplified the prayer work originally done when the letter was first received. *Weekly Unity* reported in 1919 that of the forty Silent Unity healers, "one is in prayer a half hour, when another comes and takes that one's place for his or her half hour, and so it goes throughout the day . . . So there is someone to do healing constantly."[41]

SILENT UNITY AND THE WORK OF MYRTLE FILLMORE

Myrtle was very close to the work of the Silent Unity Healing Department, participating daily in healing meetings and answering letters to people, both friends and total strangers, who wrote to her for prayer and spiritual guidance. She nurtured Silent Unity's growth from the time it was a small group of letter writers and prayer workers in the 1890s until it was a healing group ninety strong, responding to the needs of thousands of people around the world at the time of her death in 1931. Throughout her forty-two-year involvement with the Unity movement, Myrtle maintained daily contact with the work of Silent Unity, describing it in 1930 as "a radiant, dynamic center of spiritual life, joy, health and power."[42] Myrtle often described to her correspondents the advantages of regular contact with Silent Unity and urged them to write whenever they were in need of help. She told an acquaintance: "As you 'tune in' with Silent Unity spiritually, you are bound to be quickened, illumined, and blessed according to the needs. This mighty power station of Spirit is always in operation, and when you become receptive spiritually, you are in all ways blessed."[43]

As more and more people sought Silent Unity's help, Myrtle commented on the difficulty Unity experienced in finding people who had the combination of personal qualities required to do the work. She described the
kind of person Silent Unity needed:

The combination of executive ability, level headedness, harmoniousness and first
of all spirituality, seems very difficult to find. Many who have a marvelous consciousness have not developed and trained themselves in all that goes to make for
accuracy and efficiency in the executive end of our Unity work . . . At the present
time we have a very high quality in Silent Unity.[44]

Myrtle appreciated the fact that in her last years she was often asked
by Silent Unity workers to lead the late afternoon healing service. In 1931
she wrote to a friend: "All the Silent Unity work has my heart's blessing
and whenever I'm out there in my office (Silent Unity was headquartered
at Unity Farm at the time), they ask me to lead the healing service."[45]
Myrtle Fillmore was active in the work of Silent Unity until the time of her
death at age eighty-six on October 6, 1931.

THE DIRECTORSHIP OF MAY ROWLAND
(1916–1971)

As the Unity work grew larger, it was impossible for Charles and Myrtle, both over sixty by 1915, to direct the work of Silent Unity without
help. In 1916 they appointed a young woman by the name of May
Hoagland (she was later known by her married name, May Rowland) to
direct Silent Unity. Rowland grew up in Unity. Her father was a board
member of the Unity Society of Practical Christianity in Kansas City, and
she attended services from the age of five. By the time Rowland assumed
the leadership of Silent Unity, she had been studying the teachings for over
a decade.[46] May Rowland turned out to be highly suited for the work and
remained director of Silent Unity until her retirement in 1971, providing
inspired leadership to scores of workers for over a half century. Only one
year out of high school when appointed, she immediately gained the trust
of both Charles and Myrtle. Assuming leadership of the rapidly growing
Silent Unity Healing Department was a major challenge for the young
woman. Shortly after taking the job, she recalled asking Charles how to
handle some of the more difficult letters. She reported: "He would read
them carefully and tell me what to say. Finally, about the fourth time I
went in and he said, very positively, 'The Christ mind is in you, use it.' So

that was his answer. I know he didn't want me to be asking any more questions, and I didn't."[47]

Rowland periodically wrote articles for magazines published by Unity describing the work of Silent Unity. In each piece she wrote, she emphasized the fact that prayer was central to the department's function and that this was in keeping with the fact the Unity movement itself had its roots in prayer. She stated: "Prayer has been continuous in the Unity work ever since it was started. Ours is one of the few groups in the world that are organized for continuous prayer . . . The constant prayer work going on in Silent Unity released a feeling of peace and security, a sense of well-being and spiritual uplift."[48]

Rowland described the benefits of prayer as she saw them, indicating: "As you pray, you generate the spiritual energy that renews and heals you in mind, soul, and body. One of the best things about prayer is that it awakens and arouses within you the self that is capable of standing regardless of what comes."[49]

Prayers of supplication or petition, Rowland believed, were useless. Like the Fillmores, Rowland believed the most effective form of prayer took the form of affirmations.[50]

Affirmative prayers containing "I Am statements of Truth" were particularly powerful. Rowland particularly liked "I am the ever-renewing, ever-unfolding expression of infinite life, love and wisdom," and "I am alive, alert, awake, joyous and enthusiastic about my work."[51]

In Rowland's view, prayer produced positive results. The increasing number of people contacting Silent Unity for prayer work, and the constant flood of testimonials of people who said they were healed as a result of Silent Unity's help, gave concrete evidence of the power of prayer. She declared: "We believe that Silent Unity is successful because we are organized for constant prayer."[52]

Rowland pointed out that people in all walks of life and from widely diverse sections of society called upon Unity for prayer work—young and old, rich and poor, women and men, Catholic and Protestant. She described the diversity of people seeking prayer work, commenting:

If you were to read the letters on the desks of the workers at this time you might find: A farmer asking to pray that his crops bring a good yield; a little boy asking prayers for his pet that has been lost or stolen. A mother asking prayers for herself and her family, that they may have a happy, harmonious home, and a united family. A minister asking for our viewpoint about a Bible passage. A well-known movie actress asking that she give a good performance, that she have the strength and endurance and health to do a good job. A government official asking us to pray that he may use wisdom in connection with his office. A doctor asking prayers for his patient. You may be surprised to know that the world is full of praying people. We are very happy to be a part of this great praying group. "God is your Help in Every Need."[53]

In an address in 1922 to students attending classes at Unity School, Rowland addressed some misconceptions people had regarding Silent Unity. A common though erroneous opinion held by many in Unity was that the best workers in Silent Unity were those whose primary interest was in their own spiritual development. Rowland believed that this alone would not suffice. She explained:

We have grouped together about fifty workers in this department, most of them very efficient, capable people, filled with the desire to serve God's children everywhere. It is this desire for spiritual service that has drawn us together. Added to this desire for service, is a great ability to do what some people might call work. Most of our members are splendid typists. As those of you who have corresponded with us know, nearly all of our replies to letters are typewritten . . . We are finding more and more that the people who expect to do God's work, should be efficient, wide awake, capable people. We used to feel that if an individual had spiritual aspirations, that was about all that was necessary to entitle him to a place in the Silent Unity Department. But we have been shown the fallacy of that idea. We have found that spiritual desire must be stronger than merely aspiration. Truth must be practical and demonstrable, so that it can be put into use in our work, every moment of the day. People are sometimes surprised to learn that we work in Silent Unity.[54]

Another common though mistaken belief was that Silent Unity healers cloistered themselves like medieval monks and spent the day in prayer, meditation, and fasting. Rowland disabused readers of that belief also. She explained:

We are sometimes asked if it is not lovely just to pray all day long, because meditation and prayer give one such a wonderful chance for spiritual development. It is a wonderful opportunity, and we do "pray without ceasing." If you heard the typewriters humming, when you visited the Silent Unity Department, you probably thought: "I don't call that praying without ceasing." But it is! Do you know what the humming of those machines means? Each one is giving form to and emphasizing a living message of Truth. The worker is saying over and over all day long, "God is your life, God is your Strength, God is your Prosperity, God is your All-sufficiency," or words to that effect, which mean life and light to the soul longing for help. Would you not call this an effective form of prayer?[55]

Rowland wanted it understood that Silent Unity healers did not work miracles. She carefully dissected the steps in the process by which the client was healed, focusing on the roles played by both the Silent Unity healer and the client. She stressed the fact that it was God, not the Unity worker, that did the healing. The Unity healer merely facilitated the process. She observed:

The soul does not need to wait until he gets our written reply, telling him in so many words that we are praying for him, in order to get a response to his letter. Our letter merely emphasizes the fact that the spiritual work is already done. Before the letter has been received by the letter writing department, where it is answered, it has had our attention in silent prayer. And even before we have received the letter here at Unity, God has heard and answered the prayer, for the promise is: "Before they call, I will answer; and while they are yet speaking, I will hear." That you have not recognized the response, does not mean that your prayer is not yet answered. God's part is finished. Your part is to thank the Father that He has heard and answered. This attitude of praise and thanksgiving will open the door into your consciousness, and you will receive more easily.[56]

Rowland emphasized that faith in God on the part of the Silent Unity healer paved the way for the healing work. It was essential that the Silent Unity prayer worker have deep faith in the healing power of the indwelling Spirit. She wrote:

Silent Unity claims for itself no miraculous power, except that by faithfulness in prayer, and obedience to the Spirit of Truth, it has become a channel through which God's love is continually poured out upon all who ask . . . Our faith makes a bridge for us across the inharmonious appearances or limitations of the natural man, to the place in consciousness where we see man as he is—the child of God, free, whole, perfect. When one has placed his faith in God, he need never fear the outcome.[57]

Rowland described how the workday was organized, how it was important that breaks from letter writing (which included meditation and instruction) were provided for the purpose of nurturing and enriching the Silent Unity healers themselves, making them better able to serve clients. Rowland provided a detailed description of how the workday was organized in Silent Unity in 1922. She reported:

We work in eight hour periods, commencing at eight o'clock in the morning. All our work is conducted in an orderly, harmonious way, and we feel the strength of a deep spiritual unity. Even though we are many members, we are one Spirit.

We start our morning's work with a silence; each worker is at his desk, and takes part in the meditation. "Where two or three are gathered together in my name, there am I in the midst of them." Each day in Silent Unity, we gather together several times, and claim the fulfillment of the promises made to those who ask in Christ's name.

At ten o'clock, we meet in our healing room. We sing a song, then for meditation take up the class word, as given in *Unity* magazine. We not only use these prayers for ourselves, at this time, but we also pray for all those who are asking our cooperation.

At eleven o'clock, we have another silence, and send forth a word of truth to all the world. We adopted this hour during the war, as a special time to declare a word for peace, but have continued to observe it ever since. This period of silence is observed by all the Unity workers, in every part of the building.

When we come back from our lunch, we have another silence period, each worker at his desk.

At two-thirty each afternoon, we have a meeting in the healing room, taking up a different subject each day. One afternoon each week, we have a Bible class; one afternoon, a prosperity class; another afternoon is devoted to taking up points for the improvement of our work. We are always alert to find new and better ways of handling our work. We must be progressive in order to carry on our large correspondence. Each worker feels free to express himself, just as he feels led.

Our healing meeting comes in the afternoon, at four-thirty or five o'clock. Then there is also, always, the nine o'clock healing meeting. People join us all over the world at this hour, in speaking our prayers for health and prosperity, as given each month in *Unity Magazine*.[58]

If Rowland herself needed assistance with a personal problem, she turned to the department for help, submitting her prayer request just like any other Unity student might. Other members of Silent Unity apparently followed the same practice. Rowland testified:

"When a worker in Silent Unity has a need for prayer, he turns his name into our prayer room. When I have a need, I turn my name into the prayer room, the Room of Light. Every worker has great faith in the spiritual work that is being done."[59]

The prayer life of Silent Unity workers also focused on getting support for the work they were doing for others. "We pray daily for keener spiritual discernment," stated Rowland, "so that we may better know how to minister unto those needing instruction and healing."[60] Rowland aptly summed up the mission of Silent Unity when she observed: "Our work is to help the individual find God through Christ, and to get the right understanding of him and his laws. This is the only road to permanent healing, prosperity, and happiness."[61]

Silent Unity's rapid growth was slowed by the national economic catastrophe known as the Great Depression. While the nation's economy suffered a major downturn, with unemployment as high as 20 percent in the 1930s, prayer requests to Silent Unity apparently did not decrease, and the department was able to maintain its pre-Depression level of ninety employees throughout the 1930s. Cutbacks in employment in other departments at Unity School, the result of declining income, did not have a major effect on Silent Unity. During the 1930s, Unity School did not provide regular updates on the numbers of letters and telegrams received and letters written by Silent Unity as it had done in the 1920s, when the workload was constantly on the rise. A report prepared in January 1940 indicated that between 1,800 and 3,000 letters were received daily, which was approximately the same level as a decade earlier, in 1929. In February 1939 one hundred workers were listed on staff, an increase of ten over 1929.[62]

Silent Unity was entering its fifth decade at the outset of the Great Depression. Its operating principles and procedures had been established and had met the test of time. Because many of its new clients came from descriptions of Silent Unity's work published in Unity School magazines, the department periodically published news about its work and restated its objectives. One of the more in-depth descriptions of Silent Unity's mission was contained in a 1938 piece in *Weekly Unity* entitled THE WORK OF SILENT UNITY. The following characterization of the work could have been written two decades earlier and still have been accurate:

For the benefit of readers who are not wholly familiar with the Silent Unity Department of Unity School, we may say that it is a group of consecrated workers who minister to those seeking spiritual help through prayer.

Besides the healing services held during the day, there is a healing service each evening at nine o'clock conducted in their little chapel by the Silent Unity workers on night duty. They are joined in thought by all Truth students everywhere who declare the healing thought for the current month.

For forty years workers in Silent Unity have been on duty day and night to minister at any hour to those who seek help. During that time millions of persons have found help and comfort in their hour of need. Through prayer with Silent

Unity their faith has been bolstered and they have found healing of body and adjustment of affairs.[63]

In May 1940 *Weekly Unity* published a piece for those seeking basic information about the work of Silent Unity entitled THE SOCIETY OF SILENT UNITY: THE HEALING DEPARTMENT OF UNITY SCHOOL. The unnamed author, most likely a Silent Unity worker, answered several of the most often asked questions. To the query "What is Silent Unity?" it was reported: "Silent Unity is a group of consecrated workers who give spiritual ministry through prayer to persons everywhere without seeing them personally."[64] As to who might write for help: "Any person who has faith in God and who feels the need of spiritual aid through prayer." As to the "underlying principle" behind the work: "Faith in God as the one great healing, harmonizing and prospering power."[65] As to how Silent Unity was supported financially: "Through love offerings that are sent by grateful friends." As to whether it was necessary to send offerings when requesting help: "Love offerings are always gratefully received, but our service is given gladly and lovingly to all alike, whether an offering is enclosed or not." As to what problems Silent Unity might give aid with: "No matter what your problem may be—physical, social or financial—it can be solved through prayer. God is the one great healer of all disease, the harmonizer of every untoward condition, and the supply of all those in need. Let Silent Unity help you to make contact with God through prayer." The explanation of the work and the description of the life problems that prayer might help were simple, straightforward, and direct, and in keeping with long-established practices and traditions.

In a revealing piece published in *Unity* in October 1940, AN OPEN LETTER FROM SILENT UNITY, the author, again unnamed though obviously a Silent Unity worker, answered many questions that Unity students had been asking for years. The article touched on the workers themselves, what they were like, how they lived, and what motivated them. Many clients who sought help from Silent Unity attempted to establish personal contact with healers but were rebuffed. From the beginning, the Fillmores refused to allow Silent Unity workers to identify themselves personally when answering letters or to handle those individual cases that stretched out for long periods of time. A cogent defense for this policy was provided, as was a strong case for continuing it. In response to a client who wrote, "So often when I sit down, as now, to write to you, I find myself wondering just what you who read this letter are like," the Silent Unity worker explained:

Were we not convinced that an impersonal role makes a more efficient vehicle for the help we give, we should no doubt let the personal element play a greater part in our relations with you . . . When our names and our personalities are kept in the background you are not tempted to impute to us any of the human traits that so often arouse likes, dislikes, preferences . . . Our being impersonal does not imply lack of human interest in your letters and your problems . . . In spite of the fact that it would please us as individuals to follow many of your cases through to completion by having your letters directed to particular desks, we follow the wiser plan of allowing them to go to various workers. We feel that each one of us has been drawn into the Silent Unity work because of some special gift, and we like our correspondents to have the benefit of our different gifts or talents. For this reason we do not assign your case to an individual worker for his sole attention, but we use the strength of the united group to pray for the fulfillment of your needs.[66]

Clients often speculated as to whether the Silent Unity workers had grown wealthy while doing the work. The writer's reply showed how workers' involvement with Silent Unity had enriched their lives. The Silent Unity worker reported:

Sometimes we are asked if the Unity workers are all rich. Some of our friends would like to believe that we are, for then, they feel, we should be justifying the claims that we make about God's willingness to supply us abundantly. Others feel that it would hardly be in keeping with the Jesus Christ ministry for His servants to live in luxury. We believe that our financial status would be pleasing to both. We are rich—there is no doubt about it—so rich in mind and spirit that there is no abnormal desire in us for the excess of outer things that discontented minds desire. We all dress well, eat as well, live as well as any well-employed group of people. Some of us drive cars, but others do not and are happy without them.[67]

The writer also provided insights into the personal and professional experiences of people before becoming Silent Unity workers. Ages of the workers varied widely, with some in their twenties and others in their eighties. Charles Fillmore, who still took an active interest in the work of the department and participated in its daily healing meetings, was eighty-six years old when this article was written. The writer made a comment containing an important insight about the relationship between age and spirituality, stating: "We have found that age is not always the decisive factor in determining spiritual depth and understanding. Some of the youngest that we have are young with the wisdom of old soul and of things learned from God by journeying with Him since 'before Abraham was.'"[68]

The variety of professional backgrounds indicated that most people came to Unity after already having had significant life experiences. The writer noted: "many walks of life have been and are represented." The report continued: "From teaching, law, ministerial, nursing and medical professions, we have drawn several members. Others have come from the home and the office, the college and high school. Many states are represented, and some have come from foreign countries. For a time we had a young man from Czechoslovakia."[69]

The writer then described the impact the Unity teachings had on many of the Silent Unity workers and how they had been changed by it:

We are all of us people who have walked and continue to walk in the stream of life, and we know whereof we speak when we say that the Truth we teach is applicable to all life's problems. Some of us literally owe our life to the Truth that we send you in our prayers and our letters ... There is not one of us who has not proved that justice and freedom and joy and supply bless him who opens his heart to receive.[70]

Almost as an aside, the writer provided a detailed description of the Silent Unity healing room—the place where much of the prayer work had been done for several decades. The author reported:

Our healing room is an attractive and quiet place. It is filled with a beauty that cannot be wholly accounted for by color scheme and furnishings, not even by the pictures representing Jesus in Gethsemane and in the Temple at the age of twelve, Christ of the loving heart, the Presence, and other pictures that hang on our walls. There is a beauty there that is felt rather than seen, a beauty that is the result of many prayers of love, of trust, of praise and joy. No room could serve for many years as a house of prayer, a sanctuary of holy thoughts, without becoming a hallowed place, beautiful to those who enter it daily.[71]

The writer took solace in the fact that someone is always in the healing room praying, day and night, twenty-four hours a day, seven days a week. "There is always someone in the healing room, keeping trust with you and God, praying for you and affirming the health, harmony and rich abundance that we are so sincerely convinced that God wants you to have."[72]

Because prayer was an essential feature of the work of Silent Unity, May Rowland, in Unity periodicals, offered her views on the nature and power of prayer. In a *Daily Word* article written in 1953, she indicated that Unity's great contribution was in the field of "affirmative prayer." She contrasted affirmative prayer with the petitionary prayer of traditional Christianity in which the person praying asked, "Oh God, give me this, if it be thy will." Implied in prayers of petition, Rowland believed, is the idea that "perhaps God's will is negative."[73] Rowland considered this to be an impossibility.

Rowland was convinced that Silent Unity enjoyed continued success because affirmative prayer produced tangible results in people's lives. She observed: "The thousands of letters received weekly in Silent Unity testify to this. Prayer moves the mind, body, and affairs, and heals, adjusts, and prospers."[74]

By the 1950s, the healing work of Silent Unity had become so widely known outside the Unity movement that it was, on occasion, written about in the popular press. In an article in *True Confessions,* Wainwright Evans, a journalist, compared the Silent Unity healing work to that of the Roman Catholic shrine at Lourdes and to the work of some of the Protestant churches and Christian Science. Evans reported:

One of the greatest of all centers for spiritual healing through prayer is conducted by the Unity School of Christianity whose headquarters is at Lee's Summit, Missouri, near Kansas City. Silent Unity, as this particular Unity prayer function is called, is really a gigantic prayer group. Membership includes Protestants, Roman Catholics, Jews, Muhammadans [sic] and Buddhists. It is not only interdenominational, but interfaith. Ten thousand requests come every week, some by mail, some by long-distance telephone, across the continent or from half a world away, from desperate people in need of healing of the body and the mind—people who are reaching out for God.[75]

In 1960 *Daily Word* published an article by an unnamed Silent Unity worker that reviewed the current prayer work of Silent Unity, describing the typical requests for prayer, and the people who made them, including a farmer, a mother and a son, a government official, and even a medical doctor. The writer explained why he believed that many people called on Silent Unity for help, noting that Unity prayer workers provided an open channel for people who had no outlet to express their trials and tribulations. The writer noted: "Many people are unable to reveal their hearts to their families or their friends, but they feel a need to unburden themselves. When they are led to come to Silent Unity for help, they can know that their thoughts and feelings will be understood and that we will pray with them without any feelings of curiosity, condemnation or doubt."[76]

The writer concluded by indicating that the prayers of Silent Unity released "a feeling of peace and security, and a sense of well-being and spiritual uplift into every part of the Unity work."[77] The writer closed by commenting on the contribution of Silent Unity, not only to the Unity movement but also to the world at large, declaring: "Silent Unity is the great loving heart of Unity. Its animating spirit is felt throughout the Unity movement and throughout the world. Silent Unity's power for good lies in its love for humanity and its understanding of human nature, as well as in its deep appreciation of the divinity that is found in every man."[78]

In the mid-1960s, the methods by which prayer work was handled in Silent Unity were changed. At the instigation of Charles R. Fillmore, the grandson of Charles and Myrtle who in 1963 took over direction of Unity School of Christianity as executive vice president, the method of manually typing each letter was abandoned in favor of a computer-based system. The computer was viewed as a huge filing cabinet and a large typewriter. Although computerization speeded up the process by which letters were handled, it did not change the responsibility of the Silent Unity letter writer. Each letter continued to be answered individually.

When May Rowland retired in 1971 after fifty-five years of service, Silent Unity was responding to 750,000 letters compared to approximately 100,000 when she became director in 1916.[79] In addition, in 1971 approximately 200,000 phone calls were handled. In 1916 the telephone had yet to become a major part of Unity work. In 1971 approximately 140 prayer workers were employed by Silent Unity compared with 35 in 1916.[80] It is not surprising that May Rowland, who had served so long and faithfully, was universally admired throughout the Unity movement. Phil White, a Unity minister and for several decades a member of the professional staff of Unity School, said that she was regarded as "the second Mother of Unity" because of the way she symbolized in her way of conducting herself and in her demeanor the basic Unity teachings—prayer, meditation, affirmations, and denials. White knew of no one "more devoted to the Fillmore principles."[81] Rosemary Fillmore Rhea, granddaughter of Charles and Myrtle Fillmore, a Unity minister whose radio and television ministry reached thousands during her career, viewed May Rowland as someone who lived Unity in every part of her life. "She was a presence, had a great exuberance about her, and was loved by everyone who knew her." Rhea viewed May Rowland as "the reigning Queen of Silent Unity, the spiritual leader."[82] James Freeman, a leading contemporary articulator of the Unity teachings who in 1971 replaced Rowland as head of Silent Unity, saw her as "a wonderful person . . . the leader." Freeman noted that Rowland was not the type of leader "who threw her weight around."[83]

THE LEADERSHIP OF SILENT UNITY (1971–2000)

During the remaining twenty-nine years of the twentieth century, after the retirement of May Rowland, five different Unity ministers led Silent Unity, including: James Dillet Freeman (1971–1983), John Strickland (1983–1990), Mary-Alice and Richard Jafolla (1991–1997). The current director is Lynne Brown, who replaced the Jafollas in 1997.

James Dillet Freeman brought a wealth of Unity experience to the work. He had been a letter writer and telephone prayer worker for Silent Unity in the 1930s. In addition, in 1948 he wrote *The Story of Unity*, the first book describing the growth and development of the Unity movement. He also headed the Unity ministerial training program from 1950 to 1966. Drawing on his longtime connection with Unity, he described in 1972 how he viewed the impact of Silent Unity on those who called for help. Reflecting on his own work answering Silent Unity telephones, he recalled: "One night I got a call from a man in Chicago. He told me, 'I'm an old man . . . It's snowing . . . I'm in my office and I'm afraid to go out into the night and go home.' We prayed together. As we prayed you could feel the fear edging out of the man's voice. Finally, he said, 'I think I can go home now.'"[84]

Freeman considered this call typical of the kind that came to Silent Unity. "That's what we're here for," he noted. "We're here to help you go home in the dark."[85] Freeman felt that it was important to note that Silent Unity was not in the business of counseling. Prayer work and the kind of advice that comes with counseling were very different. "We're not a counseling organization," Freeman declared "We're a praying organization."[86] He observed: "When we pray with a person, we do not dwell on the problem or condition, and we never give advice. We offer positive reassurance that the creative, intelligent life force, the Father within, can overcome the situation. We encourage the person to become open to the flow of his own innate power, that spark of divinity within each of us."[87] Several years later he said: "We try not to advise people. We don't think we're that wise. God is. That's what we tell them . . . When we are in tune with God and with the universe, then we overcome our problems."[88]

Freeman indicated that one of Silent Unity's more valuable services was to reassure people of their connection with the divine. "Perhaps," he noted, "the most important thing Silent Unity does for the caller or writer is help him renew his faith and tell him that he is not alone."[89] Freeman did not assume that he knew precisely how the Silent Unity form of prayer worked. Asked by Scripps Howard religion writer George G. Plagenz about the effectiveness of Silent Unity prayers, Freeman replied:

In my 48 years at Unity I've thought quite a bit about the question of how prayer works. I don't really know. We're dealing with a mystery. I think prayer for other people may work because we are all closely linked together in ways we don't understand. Certainly love is a link between people because healing thoughts are loving thoughts.[90]

Freeman indicated that when men and women prayed, they changed themselves. Their prayers did not influence or change the mind of God. He observed: "The purpose of prayer is not to change things but to change ourselves, our attitudes and perspectives. When we begin to look at things differently, we have hope; we begin to think and act differently and things start to happen."[91]

Like his predecessor May Rowland, Freeman saw no value in prayers of petition. He indicated that the meditative prayer used by Unity got better results. He observed:

Most prayers are the petition kind. A petition prayer is one in which someone says, "Lord, help me to do this or that." Our prayers are more of a meditation. They are not petitions. We meditate on God. To meditate is to dwell on a topic. You don't have to ask God for help. His love is freely given already. You don't have to change God. You have to change yourself and realize you are one with Him. When we meditate we take a subject like "God is my help in every need." We tell people to relax and let it flow through their minds. As the thought flows through the person's mind he realizes that God's love surrounds him; he is more able to cope with or overcome his problems.[92]

When James Dillet Freeman retired as director of Silent Unity in 1983 after fifty years of service to Unity School, he was replaced by John Strickland, a 1976 graduate of the Unity ministerial school. Strickland, who had served in Unity churches in Santa Rosa, California, and Jacksonville, Florida, viewed Silent Unity as "an anchor, a rock, a shelter in a storm."[93] The work of Silent Unity grew dramatically during his eight-year directorship. Telephone prayer requests, which totaled 350,000 in 1975, doubled by 1991.[94] In addition, during Strickland's tenure, a new 78,000-square-foot, three-story building costing $10 million was constructed at Unity Village to house the two hundred-person Silent Unity staff. Completed in 1988, it included a 334-seat chapel, a facility for processing mail, a twenty-four-hour telephone prayer room that occupied one floor of the building, and a prayer vigil chapel. Strickland was particularly sensitive to the use of an impersonal technology based on computers in an area of high personal endeavor such as prayer. He acknowledged the "tension between technology and the personal touch,"[95] and recognized that "a fervent response to a healing request" required the skills of a good letter writer who brought a deep sense of caring to the work.[96]

During the early 1990s Silent Unity was directed by the husband-and-wife ministerial team of Mary-Alice and Richard Jafolla. Both were trained in counseling psychology and had served as ministers in Vero Beach, Florida. They were also authors of *The Quest: A Journal of Spiritual Rediscovery*, a book that has been widely used in classes for teaching Unity principles. The Jafollas took over Silent Unity at a time when the organization was challenged by an overload of work in the telephone room. In the summer of 1992, about 40 percent of the toll free calls and 20 percent of the regular calls were blocked because of limited capacity.[97] Many callers had to call again and again to get through. It was reported that while Silent Unity responded to 840,000 telephone requests in 1992, another 350,000 went unanswered because the phone lines were overloaded.[98] Unity School took steps to solve the problem by investing $2.5 million in equipment and personnel.[99] In 1994 the Silent Unity prayer service went over the million mark, handling 1,065,000 calls.

In 1997 the Jafollas decided to devote all their time and talents to writing and resigned as co-directors of Silent Unity. Lynne Brown, a Unity minister who had served in a number of positions in Silent Unity including director of correspondence services, assumed the position of senior director. Brown explained that Silent Unity functions today much the same as it has in the past, except that the volume of work continues to grow and approximately three hundred staff members are employed. People contact Silent Unity by mail, telephone, fax, and e-mail. Over two million prayer requests are received annually, with 1.2 million by telephone. There are approximately 150 Silent Unity staff members involved in prayer room-related work. These people respond to calls twenty-four hours a day, and most, but not all, are handled immediately. When the volume is particularly high, a caller may have to wait a few minutes before Silent Unity responds.[100]

Anyone who calls Silent Unity will note that the prayer room associate engages the caller in a warm and supportive way. He or she will lend a compassionate ear as the caller talks. No advice or counsel is given. The approach is nonjudgmental and callers are treated with respect. After identifying the caller's particular need, the prayer room associate chooses the affirmative prayer statement that addresses the need. (The prayer associate is aided by a listing developed by Silent Unity of twenty-eight categories of basic human need including physical healing, inner peace, love, justice, prosperity, success, employment, etc.) At this point in the interchange, the prayer associate begins praying with the caller. The prayer associate then shifts the focus and invites the caller to move from his or her need to an awareness of the presence of God, to the spirit of God within.[101]

If the caller requests it, a letter of prayer support and a leaflet that addresses the caller's need are sent by the letter-writing department. In addition, for thirty days the names of the caller and those for whom prayer was asked are placed in the prayer vigil chapel. Prayer room associates, taking half-hour shifts day and night, pray continually in that room. No charge is made for the prayer work of Silent Unity, although freewill offerings are accepted. The prayer work of Silent Unity is supported by these offerings. Brown assures that Silent Unity maintains confidentiality with all its callers.[102]

Given that the work of Silent Unity is spiritual and accomplished through prayer, it is not surprising that the staff itself gathers periodically during the day for prayer. A morning prayer meeting is conducted daily using the message contained in Silent Unity's magazine, *Daily Word*. At 11:00 A.M. the staff joins employees of Unity School in the Silent Unity chapel for a prayer service. There is consecrated prayer for the staff alone at noon, 2:30 P.M., and 10:30 P.M. every day.[103]

One might suppose that Unity church members would be the primary source of contact with Silent Unity. Such is not the case. Brown indicates that a high percentage of the callers (90–95 percent) are not associated with the Unity movement. Many are from various Christian denominations. Women rather than men represent the vast majority of the callers.[104]

Daily Word

In 1924 Unity School began publishing a devotional magazine that was to become, by the year 2000, one of the longest continuously published magazines of its kind. It was also one of the largest in terms of numbers of subscribers. *Daily Word* made its debut in July of that year and became immediately popular with readers of Unity literature. Promoted initially to subscribers of *Unity* and *Weekly Unity,* whose combined subscriber lists in the mid-1920s contained over 300,000 names, *Daily Word* had 100,000 subscribers in its fourth year of publication. Today, with 1.2 million subscribers, it remains Unity School's most popular publication. It is published in eight languages and in Braille.

In March 1924, four months prior to *Daily Word's* appearance, *Unity* magazine described the contents of the new publication. That description, with minor updating, might be used today in presenting the magazine to potential readers:

It has long been the desire of Unity to meet the demand for instructions that can be put to daily use by Truth students. To be sure, Unity periodicals, books, and booklets all contain material for daily Christian practice. But people who live in the rush of things want something definite and explicit they can lay hold on at the instant—a booklet that can be carried around in the pocket or handbag, that can be used on the train or the street car, on the desk, or the workbench, at the kitchen table, on the dresser.[1]

The cover of the first issue of *Daily Word* contained a statement that was to characterize the magazine's continuing purpose. It declared, MAN FINDS THE LOST WORD WHEN HE FINDS WITHIN HIMSELF HIS GOD-GIVEN POWER TO CREATE THROUGH HIS WORD. The magazine was the brainchild of Frank B. Whitney, who for several years had been employed by Unity School in a variety of professional capacities. It was his work in Silent Unity as a letter writer that gave him the idea for *Daily Word*. While answering letters to people who wrote for prayer, the thought came to him, "if only these people had something before them every day to remind them of Truth."[2] For the remaining fourteen years of his life, Whitney single-handedly produced most of the copy for the magazine including the affirmations that appeared for each day of the week. Charles Fillmore, who took a strong interest in the magazine, had a high regard for Whitney, characterizing him as "a meteor flashing against the dark blue of the night, a shaft of silver floating in the sunlight for a moment, a brilliant soul shedding his rays in our midst."[3]

Martha Smock, whose thirty-three-year tenure as editor of *Daily Word* was marked by a dramatic increase in readership, described the editorial formula that contributed to the magazine's continuing success. She observed: "Each day of the week has a lesson which is meant to be a personal meditation for the reader. It is taken from a Bible text and is brief, positive and backed by prayer . . . The writing is meant to fulfill a need and the topics range from health and emotions to freedom and justice."[4]

Each day's lesson or meditation, which takes about a minute to read, is written around a central word or phrase that can be read aloud or silently. The "Daily Word" for April 18, 2000, is typical of those that have been published over the course of the magazine's seventy-six-year lifetime. It addressed a specific spiritual topic, "inner peace." Included were a Scriptural reference, an affirmative prayer, and a meditation. It reads as follows:

THE PEACE OF GOD IS MY ANCHOR. I AM SECURE AND TRANQUIL.

The eye of the storm is a center of calm in the midst of outer chaos. The peace of God centers me in a place of absolute peace and tranquility. The spirit of God within me is peace—peace that soothes and comforts me when I need it most. So if events in my life seem out of control or if others are trying to pull me into a whirlpool of activities that may not be what I want or need to do, I let God's peace shine on me and on each situation. Then I know what to do and how to respond to both opportunities and challenges. I am poised and calm as I stay focused on the spirit of God within, the spirit of peace and love and harmony that will always bless me. Sheltered in God's presence, I have peace in mind and heart.

It is to peace that God has called you. . . . Let each of you lead the life that the Lord has assigned, to which God called you.—1 Corinthians 7:15, 17

Smock characterized the inclusive nature of the *Daily Word* readership when she observed: "We have readers from all walks of life, and all ages. Some of our subscribers are Ph.Ds and some can barely write their names. We have regular readers as young as nine, and on up to people in their hundreds."[5]

Smock described the magazine's broad appeal when she noted that it was "non-denominational and nonsectarian." She continued: "We have readers from every denomination and with no religious affiliation from nuns to Protestant ministers. We are not trying to convert people, but to remind them of things most of us already know."[6]

Colleen Zuck, who has been the editor of *Daily Word* since 1986, indicated that readership continues to be broad-based, explaining: "*Daily Word* is written for a diverse audience and, because of that, reaches out to each reader." Zuck further indicated, "*Daily Word* continues to be useful because people are inspired by its concise, positive, and powerful message."[7]

Smock viewed the magazine as providing "a day by day reminder that nothing is hopeless or impossible, that the power to overcome is within each individual."[8] Readers receive "a reminder of who and what they are." They were reminded, she continued, "[t]hat they are spiritual beings and . . . that they can meet matters happily, effectively and constructively, and with faith in God and good . . . Daily Word reminds people of something they have known without being aware of it—the spiritual side of them."[9]

Smock, who worked in Silent Unity before becoming editor, believed that the magazine's close association with the work of Silent Unity is important to its success. Smock reported, "Daily Word is edited under the inspiration of Silent Unity. The messages in Daily Word are part of Silent Unity's work and word."[10] During Smock's long tenure as editor, Daily Word was written by staff members of Silent Unity, freelance writers, and Unity ministers and students. Smock continued: "Because of our close association with Silent Unity, we are aware of the needs of people and in touch with them. Through the daily lessons we try to meet some of these basic needs that they tell us about when they write and call asking for prayer help."[11] The practice of involving Silent Unity in the work continues to the present day.

The comments of long-term readers of the magazine indicate the inspiration it has provided. The following testimonials are typical of those sent over the years to the magazine:

"The answer in that little booklet helps you in whatever you're going through. Reading Daily Word sets the tone for the day—it fortifies you. You start the day from strength." WA, Kansas City, Missouri.[12]

"Ninety percent of the time it's as though the message for the day was written just for me. My life has been richly blessed by Daily Word and I am grateful for it." PT, Mesa, Arizona.[13]

"Daily Word keeps me in touch with myself, my feelings and my life." Bernie Siegel, author of Love, Medicine and Miracles.[14]

"It points me in the direction I need to go. It always says the right things every day. Those words are something I eat like food. I take them deep down inside where my feeling nature is. They give me answers to choices I need to make, when I need to make them." RS, Dallas, Texas.[15]

"*Daily Word* is a substantial spiritual meal. If I feel something in my life isn't quite right, if something is amiss, I go to my *Daily Word.*" ML, *Kansas City, Missouri.*[16]

"It makes me feel centered and reminded of what I believe and I feel that I've done something good for myself. I think that the benefits that I receive from it are reflected in my day, and in my interactions with other people. If I get cut off in traffic, I can look at it from a bigger perspective." KD, *Ahwautukee, Arizona.*[17]

Daily Word and Silent Unity have an important connection. The contents of the magazine are inspired by the work of the healing ministry. At the same time, many of the requests for prayer come from readers of *Daily Word.* The magazine and the prayer ministry are dependent upon each other in significant ways for their continued success.

CHAPTER 10

Training Unity Students

Introduction

The Fillmores gave high priority to instructing Unity students in metaphysical principles. In the early years their teaching was directed at adults who were being introduced for the first time to Christian metaphysics. As years passed and men and women became more deeply immersed in the teaching and involved in Unity healing work, the Fillmores began training teachers and leaders for service in Unity centers around the country. In the 1930s ministerial training was begun in earnest. While advanced work became a key element in the Unity training program, instruction has continued for all levels of students. Retreats have been an important part of the Unity program since 1951. Currently Unity School for Religious Studies provides three areas of service: continuing education for Unity students, ministerial education, and retreats.

Continuing Education Programs for Adults

Throughout its century-long existence, Unity has sought to interest students in its metaphysical teaching through class work at Unity School and in Unity centers and churches. Beginning in the 1890s in Kansas City, the Fillmores themselves taught the first classes in Practical Christianity and spiritual healing. Following their example, Unity has presented continuing education programs for students at all levels, from beginners to those who seek leadership positions as licensed Unity teachers. Described in this chapter are the types of educational programs Unity has offered in the past and those it currently offers, including a description of course contents, the goals and purposes of the work, and the intended audience.

FILLMORE CLASSES IN UNITY PRINCIPLES
(1896–1909)

In their early classes, the Fillmores presented the elements of the teaching that they deemed most important. Spiritual healing was the central focus of the first class offered by Charles for Unity students in Kansas City, which began on July 26, 1896.[1] The next class, Practical Christianity, again offered solely by Charles, began March 15, 1897, and consisted of twelve evening sessions over a two-week period. Charles indicated that he had developed the class based on his own inner development, specifically the mind/body connections, which he felt were essential for bringing about bodily regeneration. He explained: "These lessons are in a large measure the outgrowth of my own experience in the regeneration through which I have been passing for several years, and are therefore very practical."[2]

In June 1897 Myrtle joined Charles in teaching a class entitled "Practical Christianity and Christian Healing." In response to a question about course content, the Fillmores stated it "covered all the ground of the higher courses in Metaphysics."[3] Again, they pointed out that teaching and healing went hand in hand, indicating: "The whole aim of our method is to quicken the Spirit until it grasps for itself the Truth in all its phases. Healing is done also in connection with the instruction, and excellent results nearly always follow."[4]

In May 1899 the Fillmores listed for the first time the topics covered in these classes. In addition to discussing the nature of God and man and the role of Jesus, they provided information on "the twelve faculties of mind." Several of those faculties were treated in depth, including faith, imagination, love, power, will, and spiritual understanding. In addition, advice was given on how to activate the powers through affirmations, denials and the "generative power of thought."[5]

In December 1902, in addition to the course on Practical Christianity and Christian healing, which they now called the primary course, the Fillmores initiated a second, more in-depth class, which they called the "Advanced Course in Concentration."[6] The Fillmores acknowledged that for several years they had given lessons in interior concentration to a few advanced students, but had never presented it in a formal classroom setting.

To meet the needs of several students who had completed the primary course and desired more advanced work, they created the new course. They indicated:

We find that there is a larger number of metaphysicians each year who are seeking to know more about the body and the details of the law by which it is controlled by the mind. We have therefore decided to open our Concentration classes to all those who have reached a certain point in the understanding and application of the law, which fits them for the drills which are included in these lessons.[7]

The Fillmores further stated that students would focus on seven principal centers of consciousness in the body and would be instructed "on how to awaken, purify, educate, and control these centers of consciousness." This course was to be offered over a period of seven weeks, with one lesson per week.[8] Brief notices that "concentration classes" were being held on an ongoing basis appeared from time to time in the magazine.[9]

With the development of the advanced course, the Fillmores settled into a pattern of teaching that was to continue until 1909. In addition to the advanced course, a primary course was offered three or four times yearly on "Christian living and healing," with twelve evening sessions over a two-week period. The course was open to the general public and the focus was on both teaching and healing, with the latter being emphasized. The Fillmores promised that "a practical demonstration of the way to heal is given at the close of each lecture by audibly treating someone in the audience who asked for help."[10] Charles believed that the primary class was of particular value for beginners on the path of spiritual development. He explained:

The muscles of the soul are as flabby in most people as those of the infant. They have lost control of them through ignorance and neglect. Jesus said, "What doth it profit a man if he gain the whole world and lose his own soul?" Another translation of His words is, "What gain is there in getting material possessions if you thereby lose control of your soul?" At no other place on this globe is this system of soul culture taught and demonstrated. It was given to us direct from the Spirit and we give it forth freely to those who are ready for it. We know that it is of such importance in its practical effects that were a mercenary thought back of it we should be charging hundreds of dollars for these lessons. The Spirit has revealed to us that in a few years this system of soul development will be accepted as scientific by all enlightened metaphysicians.[11]

THE CORRESPONDENCE SCHOOL (1909–1973)

Charles and Myrtle Fillmore continually sought ways to reach people outside Kansas City with Unity teaching and healing work. Classes taught in Kansas City were attended primarily by Kansas City residents, with an occasional outsider traveling to Missouri for the fourteen-day course. In an effort to reach students outside Missouri, in 1909 the Fillmores created a course in Unity teaching that could be taken by correspondence.[12] In April 1909 they announced: "in response to widespread demand we have arranged to give lessons in Christian Healing and the true science of Christianity by correspondence."[13]

The content of the course was similar in most respects to the primary course described previously and taught by the Fillmores in Kansas City for over a decade. The course was presented, as were all the Fillmores' courses, in twelve lessons. Students received one lesson at a time. Printed copies of the lesson, usually eight to ten typewritten pages, were sent to the student. Students were instructed to copy the lesson verbatim, go over it until they felt certain they fully understood the material, and then request the questions on the lesson from the school. Upon completing the questions—which the Fillmores estimated might take about one month—students were instructed to return their answers to Unity headquarters for grading. The Fillmores explained: "If answers are not satisfactory we will point out the errors and require further study. This system will be continued until all the points in the twelve lessons are understood and can be set forth by the student in his own language."[14] The Fillmores foresaw important benefits for those taking the course. They observed: "These lessons will give every student a training in the demonstration of prosperity, as well as health, and with each lesson he will manifest the teaching in health, harmony and understanding."[15]

The correspondence course was immediately popular with Unity students. By June 1909, 268 students were enrolled.[16] By November the total had risen to 700,[17] and by the end of the first year (March 1910), over 900 were taking the course.[18] Many students wrote to headquarters expressing their belief in the value of the course. Several testimonials, of which the following two are representative, were published in *Unity*.

The lessons grow more beautiful all the time. If I had never believed in inspiration before, I should now at the close of Lesson five. Surely the mind of mortal man could not conceive such statements. While sublime and powerful, they are so simple as to be perfect in expression. They fill me with wonder and pride in your achievement. MM.[19]

I am now returning lesson six which I have copied, and am now ready for the questions on same. I am more interested all the time in the lessons, and I think I am getting along fine. It is certainly the most wonderful and interesting study I have ever known anything about. IR.[20]

By December 1910 the enrollment had risen to 1,600 and, in addition to students throughout the United States, there were enrollments from Cuba, Brazil, England, Scotland, France, Germany, Russia, India, Japan, Australia, New Zealand, and South Africa. The Fillmores announced: "the course is especially recommended for all who wish to become teachers and healers."[21] In 1911, with enrollment rising to 2,000, potential students were advised that they should have read Unity literature for at least one year before enrolling.[22] A preparatory course of six lessons with auxiliary reading, called part one, was introduced in 1912—evidently because beginning students were having difficulty with the basic course.[23]

The twelve original lessons that comprised the primary course were now called part two. *Unity* magazine indicated that part two contained most of the material published in 1909 by Charles Fillmore in his book *Christian Healing*. Students, however, were assured that the course differed from the book. "While these lessons cover the same ground as those given by Mr. Fillmore," it was explained, "they are differing, having been prepared especially for the Correspondence School work."[24] In March 1913, the Fillmores indicated their confidence in the results of the correspondence course by noting: "Every student of our Correspondence School who has completed the course is competent to do thorough healing and should not hesitate to begin at once giving the Word of Truth, knowing that the Spirit will fulfill the law."[25]

Within a short time the correspondence course became the basic text for the teachings of the Unity School, or as the Fillmores described it, "the written instruction of the Unity School of Practical Christianity."[26] By 1913 the Fillmores were so convinced of the value of the correspondence course that they dubbed it "the basis of the teaching," or as it was later called, "the recognized Unity course of study."[27] Announcements for classes in Kansas City beginning in 1912 stated that teachings would be based on the "lessons of the Unity Society Correspondence School."[28] All involved with Unity work were expected to complete the course and receive a passing grade. *Unity* magazine reported:

One of the first questions asked one who wishes to enter our healing work at headquarters or who wishes to conduct study classes in his community is, "Have you taken the Unity Correspondence Course?" ... Our field lecturers, magazine contributors, and healers, in many cases owe their success to these lessons and are most enthusiastic in pointing the way to their students and friends.[29]

As with all Unity class work, the correspondence course was offered on a freewill offering basis. The Fillmores asked students in 1912 to consult with the Spirit within to determine proper compensation. They advised: "Our Correspondence School is sustained by free-will offerings, and every student is expected to settle the amount of his offerings by referring the question directly to the Spirit of Justice as expressed within himself."[30]

In March 1913 the Fillmores provided further suggestions to students on how to gauge the appropriate compensation for the course: "This school is not funded in any way on commercial methods. There is a Divine Law of giving and receiving, and we keep this law, giving fully and freely, and expecting to receive in the same manner. All our compensation there comes as free-will offerings."[31] Comments made by the Fillmores the next year might be construed as indicating that students were not providing sufficient resources to pay for the costs of the course. The Fillmores indicated: "The work of setting up these lessons, the grading of the matter submitted by students, and the enormous correspondence and postage connected therewith is one of the heaviest taxes upon our Society, and we pray earnestly that every student will appreciate this and make a just financial return for each lessons."[32]

By 1918 the correspondence course had been further refined, the introductory course being called the primary course. The lessons had the following titles: How to Pray, Healing, Prosperity, The True Church and Its Sacraments, Restoration of Man and Restitution of the Earth, Man's Inherent Power to Overcome, and The Demonstration of Eternal Life.

Part two, which previously had been called the primary course, was now called the advanced course. Students were now required to rewrite the lessons in their own language. It was indicated: "In sending in their work, students generally use paper of the size of that on which the original lesson is given. The average lesson can be written on from three to five sheets, using one side of the paper. Answers should be from a positive and impersonal standpoint. 'Personal doubts' should not be included."[33]

In an effort to provide an intellectual underpinning for the value of courses taken by correspondence, the Fillmores quoted from the writings of Dr. William R. Harper, former president of the University of Chicago (1890–1906). Harper commented: "The work done by correspondence is even better than that done in the classroom. The correspondence student does all the work himself. He does twenty times as much reciting as he would in a class where there were twenty people. He works out the difficulties himself and the results stay with him."[34]

Periodically the Fillmores cited the benefits derived from taking the correspondence course, indicating that it was helpful both for those who wanted to do healing work as well as for those who wanted an introduction to Unity teaching. In October 1923 they provided a particularly clear statement of the rationale for enrollment. They observed:

We have established a system of instructing Unity students in their homes so they may have the same advantage as if they were in personal attendance at the Unity meetings in Kansas City. It is our desire to have students develop into Unity teachers and healers so they may minister to their own families and to those in their communities. It is not necessary, however, for one to signify his intention of becoming a public healer or teacher in order to have our personal instruction. If you do not understand Truth well enough to demonstrate it, you will find those Lessons very helpful. Many religious and metaphysical questions which puzzle and confuse are clearly explained.[35]

The benefits to be gained from taking the correspondence course were restated in *Unity* in March 1933, in a piece entitled "The Joy of Living." The editors noted:

The plan of the Unity correspondence course is to teach you the fundamental truths of Being so that you may experience now the real joy of living. There is no need to spend years in the search for health and happiness. They lie within you, and you have the power to bring them forth. A great many of those whose testimonials appear in these pages have been enabled to rise out of conditions of disease and lack through the application of the Christian principles taught by the correspondence school. Some readers imagine that our course of study is for those who wish to become teachers and healers in a public way, but it is also particularly valuable to those who wish to unfold spiritually, to discover their own divine nature, to have the mysteries of life made plain, to live in a frictionless environment.[36]

In November 1933 in an article titled "An Ideal Time for Study," the life-enhancing benefits of the course were again emphasized, along with the practical help given by staff members of the school at Unity headquarters. *Unity* magazine reported:

The Unity Correspondence School offers you a course in Practical Christianity, which will help you to know the heavenly Father better, and to discover your true relationship to Him. No other subject offers you such great returns in peace, health, happiness, and success, as the subject of Truth earnestly studied and applied. You have the individual attention of a teacher at Unity headquarters, and the rate of your progress depends upon your own interest and efforts.[37]

From the 1930s until 1973, when it was discontinued, Unity School indicated that the correspondence course was designed primarily for those who could not come to Unity headquarters for class work. The program was designed to provide students with an opportunity to gain a thorough understanding of truth principles and to unfold spiritually.[38] The course continued to consist of the principal works of H. Emilie Cady and Charles Fillmore. In the 1940s, a series of twenty-four Bible lessons was added, and by the 1960s the course consisted of a total of forty-one lessons.[39] The course was available in French, German, and Spanish.

The correspondence school was disbanded in 1973 because more and more Unity students were coming to Unity School for personal instruction. Extension courses in local Unity centers had also become an attractive alternative to study by correspondence. In addition, by 1972 most people who began the course never finished it. As a result, the correspondence school, with its large staff, became a drain on Unity finances. When the program was discontinued, only five papers were graded daily, and freewill offerings of just $5 per paper were being received.[40] In the 1970s, Unity School replaced the correspondence course with a nongraded home-study course entitled "Foundations of Unity." Made up of a compilation of lessons from the original correspondence school, the Foundations program included readings from Unity authors, a home-study guide, and "test-yourself" questions.[41]

INTENSIVE TRAINING SCHOOL (1919–1922)

With the development of the correspondence course in 1909, the Fillmores no longer offered primary and advanced courses in Practical Christianity at Unity headquarters in Kansas City. For almost a decade, the Fillmores abandoned class work in Kansas City.

Classes at headquarters in Kansas City were no longer viewed as an effective way to reach a wide audience of students, particularly non-Kansas City residents. Then, in the summer of 1919, the Fillmores, as they had from 1896 to 1909, again sought to encourage adults from outside Kansas

City to come to Unity School for metaphysical instruction. An announcement appearing in the May 1919 issue of *Unity* noted: "Plans are now being made for a short-term Unity Summer School in Kansas City. Beginning Sunday, July 20, there will be a two-week intensive course of lessons in the Science of Being and Practical Christianity."[42]

Classes were offered by teachers on the Unity School staff and covered topics the Fillmores had treated in the past in the primary and advanced courses. These included: meditation, basic Unity principles, mind training, prosperity, and healing. One hundred twenty-five students attended the 1919 summer school, sufficient for Unity to deem the program "a big success." Unity School immediately announced plans for another two-week "intensive course"—to be called the "Thanksgiving School"—which was to begin November 16.[43]

Attendance at the Thanksgiving School exceeded that of the summer school, with an enrollment of 150 students. The success of both intensive training courses encouraged school officials to schedule yet another two-week intensive course for spring. Called the "Easter School," it opened March 21 and closed on Easter Sunday, April 4, 1920. The curriculum was similar to the previous two courses with the addition of classes on meditation called "The Silence." After Easter School ended, plans were announced for a summer session. Based on the enrollment experience of the previous year, Unity School predicted an even bigger turnout for the 1920 summer school than for the one in 1919. *Unity* magazine explained the benefits of attending:

What is the advantage in coming to the Summer School? You come into the atmosphere and influence of Unity School and those who devote their entire time to studying and demonstrating Truth. You have the advantage of attending lessons presented by teachers who are selected because of their ability to explain Truth simply and clearly. You have the opportunity to receive individual help in your particular problem.[44]

Since the Fillmores were now both over sixty-five and no longer assuming full responsibility for teaching the classes, Unity School sought to assure students of the qualifications of the faculty, observing: "These teachers are not only consecrated students of Truth but are also living examples of what Truth will demonstrate in its disciples. They are practical Christians, and in these lessons, they will give the rules of study, prayer, meditation and application by which they became what they are."[45]

The 1920 summer session was evidently a success, as additional two-week sessions of the "Intensive Training School," as it was then called, were scheduled for the fall of 1920—one in September and another in November.[46] The September session, which was called the Extension School because it followed within a few days an International New Thought Alliance Congress held in Kansas City, was attended by over two hundred people.[47] A Thanksgiving School was the fourth and final session of the intensive training for 1920.

The courses taught in the Easter School of 1921 were typical of those presented during the three-year period (1919–1922) the Intensive Training School was in operation. In addition to Charles's basic principles course, they included Spiritual Prosperity, Healing Principles, Practical Applications of Truth, The Cosmic Christ, Bible Interpretation, The Purpose and Practice of the Silence, and First Steps in Spiritual Growth.[48]

For reasons never explained in official Unity publications, there were no more sessions of the Intensive Training School after the summer of 1922. Lack of attendance does not appear to be the cause. Space was undoubtedly a problem, as the small Unity auditorium at Ninth and Tracy in Kansas City was not big enough to handle large gatherings of people. It is also probable that the teaching and administrative loads were too big for the staff to handle. Those who taught in the Intensive Training School were Unity's most highly skilled people, and all had full-time jobs in Unity School, either in editing and writing, field lecturing, or as heads of departments.

SUMMER CONFERENCES (1922–1930)

While the Intensive Training School itself no longer existed, the summer program, which had been an important part of the school, remained as an ongoing part of Unity School's effort to reach out to its students beyond Kansas City. The summer session for 1923, "A Mid-summer Conference with Healing Revival," was presented on schedule. In May 1923, *Unity* magazine announced the details of the conference: "Instead of the regular Midsummer Intensive Training School, a Unity Conference and Healing Revival will be held. Speakers and delegates from Unity centers all over the world will be invited to take part. Lecturers and teachers at Unity headquarters will also speak."[49]

Healing was to be the central theme of the conference, and Charles and Myrtle Fillmore, in contrast to the previous sessions of the Intensive

Training School, were the featured teachers. The rationale for the conference was articulated in the announcement: "The early Christian church did healing. Later, healing became largely lost to the church. It is our purpose at this time to prove that healing is a part of the Christian ministry. Here is an opportunity for all people not only to get an understanding of Unity principles, but also to be healed."[50]

The Fillmores were to be responsible for facilitating the six-day course "for healing the sick," which was to take place during the first week of the conference. The announcement indicated: "This six-day course of healing lessons had been used by the Silent Unity Society for thirty-five years, and thousands have testified to its efficiency."[51] It further stated, "[E]ach day will have its dynamic spiritual atmosphere as an invisible accompaniment."

From the post-conference report in *Unity* magazine, it appeared that the conference fulfilled all the high expectations set for it. "Hundreds" evidently attended, and the Unity auditorium "was filled all the day long."[52] The magazine reported:

That spiritual healings are performed on the earth today was very forcibly demonstrated during the two weeks of the conference. The Christ Spirit of healing rested lovingly upon many of those who were present at the conference. On one occasion a request was made that those in the audience who had experienced healing during the conference might rise. About nine-tenths of the audience stood up.[53]

During the next four years, from 1924 to 1929, conferences featuring lectures, workshops, and classes were held annually in the summertime at Unity headquarters. The meetings did not focus on particular themes, but covered the major subjects addressed in the Unity teaching: the nature of God and man, the role of Jesus, the Christ Consciousness, Bible interpretation, meditation and prayer, the power of thought, health and healing, and prosperity. In summary, the conferences focused on metaphysics and Practical Christianity. Sessions seemed to be aimed more at the beginning student than at the more advanced.

In the summer of 1927, Charles Fillmore encouraged all Unity students to come to Kansas City for the annual conference. In an article entitled "Forget Not the Gathering," he pointed out the many compelling reasons for attending and urged every Unity center around the world to send a representative. He explained:

Unity people should not neglect this gathering. It is through these gatherings that we form an intimate acquaintance with the evangelical side of the teaching. At these conventions we not only become acquainted with one another, but our resultant unification strengthens our capacity to teach Truth to others. Truth is contagious and can be imparted to others when those who are broadcasting it are resourceful and enthusiastic.[54]

Charles ended the invitation with an emotional appeal that reflected the depth of his belief in the importance of the work that was being done by Unity. He declared:

There is great need of these spiritual outpourings by men and women who are consecrated to the cause. The world must be saved from its ignorance, violence, and sensual insanity. Christianity is the great panacea, and Jesus Christ the only Savior of this age. Every Unity center should send a delegate to this convention to the end that all the people may make contact with the spiritual outpouring which will take place at this gathering.[55]

The 1928 convention, which met August 19–29, was the first to be held at Unity Farm, seventeen miles from downtown Kansas City. Advertised as "Ten Days of Spiritual Fellowship at Unity Farm," the attendees were told that it would be held in a "tent city," since no permanent conference buildings had been constructed. Rain, which came down heavily at times, evidently did not dampen spirits or cut down on attendance.

In the summer of 1930, Unity offered an expanded program that was similar in many respects—including its name—to the Intensive Training School that existed from 1919 to 1922. The "Summer School of Intensive Training" provided four weeks of "intensive training and study" for both "Truth students and teachers."[56] This work set the stage for a new development in Unity adult education.

THE UNITY TRAINING SCHOOL (1931–1965)

The success of the summer programs in the 1920s convinced Unity School of the need to create a new organization to manage its instructional program for adults. In the spring of 1931, the Unity Training School was established to develop and manage a training program that was to go beyond what had been attempted in the past. It featured a series of four sessions annually, each one lasting one month, beginning in late May and ending in early October. Students were encouraged to complete a four-year course, attending one month each year.[57] The 1931 program attracted

663 students from thirty-one states and six foreign countries. Attendance continued to increase throughout the 1930s.[58]

The program was made feasible by the existence at Unity Farm of a beautiful new building constructed in 1929 to house the Silent Unity Healing Department. When Silent Unity vacated the building after a year's residency and returned to its former quarters in downtown Kansas City, the building was available for use by the training school. Its location on the lovely grounds of Unity Farm, which had recreational facilities available for students, made the training school a much more inviting place for out-of-town students than Unity headquarters in crowded downtown Kansas City, which was hot in the summer.

One of training school's primary goals was "to provide a course of metaphysical instruction for those who earnestly seek a deeper understanding of Truth."[59] Aimed at adults, the program provided them, according to the prospectus provided by the school, with "an opportunity to receive instruction under outstanding metaphysicians."[60] Courses in Practical Christianity were offered each year during the thirty-five years of the training school's existence. These included classes on Bible interpretation, healing principles and practice, prayer and meditation, as well as seminars on the works of H. Emilie Cady (*Lessons in Truth* and *How I Used Truth*) and the works of Charles Fillmore (*Christian Healing, Talks on Truth, The Twelve Powers,* and *Jesus Christ Heals*).

In 1952 the Unity Training School began a teacher certification program aimed at providing skilled instructors for centers and churches. Unity students who had completed the correspondence course and forty-five credits in the training school over a period of at least two summers could become licensed as Unity teachers. In 1955 it was stipulated that the forty-five credits could be acquired at the Unity Training School in sixteen courses of four weeks each in which classes met four times each week. Not more than twenty-four credits could be earned in one year. Licensed teachers were described by Unity as "those teachers in a Unity center and conducting class work under the direction of the Field Department."[61] In 1962 the number of credits required for certification rose to fifty; in addition, students were required to maintain a grade point average of 90 or higher in each course of study.[62]

SCIENCE OF LIVING TRAINING PROGRAM
(1962–1965)

In 1962 Unity School established a special training program for adults called the "Science of Living Training Program." It was designed for men and women who wished to pursue "an orderly course of spiritual instruction," but who did not intend to become a Unity teacher or minister. Classes were offered in many of the same subjects as in the Unity Training School, including the Bible, metaphysical principles, prayer, and meditation. Unity selected the name "Science of Living" because it viewed the "knowledge of Truth principles" and an understanding of their functional application as "a scientific study."[63] Four full terms of study, each lasting a month, were required for graduation. In addition, students were required to complete two courses in the correspondence school to graduate. Unity indicated that those who completed the program would be better able to serve as Sunday school teachers, members of boards of directors of centers, and planning committee members at centers.[64]

THE GREAT VISION (1964–1965)

In June 1964, the board of trustees of Unity School announced a twenty-five year plan for educational expansion called "The Great Vision." It called for the establishment of an educational program in which a student could be exposed to Unity teachings from preschool through high school, college, and graduate-level education. It was indicated that by 1989, the one hundred year anniversary of the Unity movement, the entire program would be implemented according to the following schedule: preschool in 1966, graduate school in 1970, elementary school in 1976, college in 1980, and high school in 1985.[65]

The plan grew out of a meeting in October 1963 of three members of the Unity Ministerial Association and three members of Unity School board of trustees, including its executive vice president, Charles R. Fillmore. The members asked themselves how Unity could better serve humankind in the future. They agreed to form an education committee of Unity School staff to explore possibilities for "upgrading, strengthening, and making more flexible and better in every way" Unity's educational program.[66] The Great Vision, a twenty-five-year, $25 million program to build a major educational facility, grew out of the deliberations of this committee. The plan was ultimately approved by the Unity board.

The kickoff for The Great Vision was a groundbreaking ceremony, attended by 250 people at Unity School on June 7, 1964, for new preschool facilities. The first step in implementation of The Great Vision was the takeover of the Wee Wisdom School, a preschool that had been operated privately for several years at Unity Village.[67] It was determined at the outset that funding would be solicited from new sources and would not be derived from funds currently used to support and sustain Unity School. School officials hoped to interest national foundations, such as the Ford Foundation in New York City, as well as wealthy persons not currently acquainted with Unity.[68]

The educational facilities proposed in The Great Vision were never constructed at Unity Village. Construction was held back in part because of difficulties in raising money. James Dillet Freeman, who was appointed director of educational expansion and was responsible for implementing The Great Vision, indicated that the concept was "too ambitious," and "not achievable." The money for it, he reported, did not come in.[69]

Money apparently wasn't the only reason for the failure to implement The Great Vision. Questions arose within the school concerning the viability of the concept. William Underwood, who assumed a leadership position in Unity after successfully introducing a computerized system in Silent Unity, was opposed on the grounds that Unity did not have the resources, managerial and logistical as well as financial, to make the project successful. Underwood, who had been involved in the Oral Roberts organization and its attempts to found a university, recognized the difficulties involved and considered it unwise for Unity to attempt it. His voice apparently carried weight with the Unity board of trustees.[70]

The issue of parochialism was also raised by those in Unity who were opposed to implementing The Great Vision. Was it really in Unity's best interests to establish schools for the purpose of keeping its young people faithful to the teaching and to interest them in a ministerial career? Did Unity want to take on the responsibilities of a Principia, the Christian Science educational institution near St. Louis, which educated students from preschool through college? The Unity leadership, including Charles R. Fillmore, James Freeman, Dale Batesole, and David Williamson, visited Principia in 1964. As time passed, it became clear that this institutional model was not appropriate for Unity.[71]

Examination of track records of religious organizations that established schools for all levels of students raised further questions. Those that succeeded in attempts at establishing comprehensive educational programs tended to be the more rigid denominations, such as Christian Science, Bob Jones University, and Oral Roberts University, as well as fundamentalist groups. These organizations slanted their teaching more toward indoctrination than education. Unity, which views itself as nondoctrinaire, does not fit this profile.[72]

Williamson believed that The Great Vision had a positive impact on educational planning within Unity, even though the program itself wasn't implemented. He believed the Unity leadership became more open to new ways of reaching people with the Unity message, more willing to explore and experiment. Williamson indicated that Warren Kreml, director of the Omega Center, observed that Unity needed inspiration to move ahead with new educational approaches. By embracing The Great Vision, a far-reaching departure from past practices, the stage was set for experimentation.[73]

THE OMEGA CENTER (1969–1972)

In the fall of 1969, David Williamson, director of education, submitted a proposal to Charles R. Fillmore and the Unity board of trustees to conduct an experimental educational training program aimed at people both inside and outside Unity. The mixture of students required for "creative experimentation" included, according to Williamson, "Catholics, Methodists, psychologists, educators, social workers, osteopaths, housewives, and business men and women, young, old, blacks and whites."[74] Williamson viewed the Omega program as an attractive alternative to The Great Vision. In a note to the Unity leadership, he offered the following reasons to support his position:

Rather than trying to more or less duplicate the many struggling private colleges which already exist, it seems a better course to develop programs which utilized Unity's concept of man's inherent potential for growth and helpfulness. Instead of teaching undergraduate college students physical education, biology and ancient history, etc., it seems more creative of us to offer courses and programs for supplemental education for college students and continuing education for professionals as well as growth programs for the general public.[75]

An important inspiration for the creation of the Omega Center, according to Phil White, a Unity minister who had been a member of the Omega staff, came at a Unity summer conference in 1964 from a presentation on adult education by the respected Unity center leader and author

Eric Butterworth. Unity leadership's decision to go ahead with the Omega experiment was also influenced, according to White, by the work of the National Training Laboratory, headquartered in Bethel, Maine, which from 1967 to 1969 conducted its Midwest personal growth programs at Unity School.[76]

The Omega Center was approved by the Unity board and went into operation in early 1970. Williamson indicated that the decision to move in the direction of human development and adult education, rather than starting an elaborate system of schools, allowed Unity to offer what could really be called "higher education." As a result, Omega utilized many of the techniques and practices for personal growth employed by the growing human potential movement, and presented in the 1960s at the Esalen Institute in Big Sur, California.[77] These included Gestalt therapy, encounter exercises, sensory awareness games, transactional analysis, role playing, psychodrama, hatha yoga, and intensive journaling.

The program at Unity was initially called "The Center for the Development of Human Potential." Its name was changed in early 1970 to the "Omega Center," because it was felt that the original name was too long and that the term Omega aptly characterized the work. Warren Kreml, a Unity minister, holder of a doctorate in religion from the Chicago Theological Seminary, and director of the center, explained why the new name was chosen. He indicated:

Omega means the end point. It comes from the idea that God is the Alpha and the Omega, the beginning and the end point of all things. Omega stands for the fulfillment towards which man is moving. The term is used a great deal by Teilhard de Chardin who sees mankind moving toward a point of fulfillment of human potential in the Christ idea . . . The term is one of deep religious significance.[78]

Kreml was convinced that the Omega program embodied the modern-day expression of the teachings of Charles Fillmore. The philosophical ideas espoused by the center were, in Kreml's view, "in complete agreement with the ideas of Charles Fillmore . . . The Omega Center would be a logical expression of the ideas Charles Fillmore offered to the modern world in a way that is in tune with the times."[79] Kreml praised the breadth of the program, viewing it as "interdisciplinary, integrating the sciences of man, religion, arts and humanities, joining the intuitive spiritual insights of West and East, with the logic and precision of science and the visions of the artist."[80]

Unlike other Unity adult education programs that were directed primarily at people who had already been identified as Unity students, Omega was aimed at the general public, most of whom lived in the metropolitan Kansas City area. Unity indicated in its promotional material that the program was "open to the public," though it would be of special interest to "teachers, students, ministers, and counselors." Like Esalen and other growth centers in the United States and abroad in the 1960s, Omega sought to help participants get in touch with their feelings. A Unity news release indicated:

The goals of the workshops are: to know yourself and your feelings better, and to understand how your feelings affect behavior . . . to become more comfortable in expressing your own feelings openly and honestly . . . to develop a greater ability to listen, and to be empathic with other persons, and finally to try new behaviors in a interpersonal climate that encourages, rather than inhibits, change.[81]

During the two-plus years the program existed, some of the leading figures in the human potential movement presented their work at Unity, including Alan Watts, an English Episcopal priest who served as a popularizer of Eastern thought and tradition in the 1960s; Dr. Thomas Harris, a psychiatrist specializing in transactional analysis and author of *I'm Ok—You're Ok;* Dr. Ira Progoff, a depth psychologist and founder of Dialogue House in New York City and of the Intensive Journal Program; Elmer Green, a consciousness researcher from the Menninger Institute in Topeka, Kansas, and developer of biofeedback; Dr. Herbert Otto of the Human Potentialities Research Project at the University of Utah; Viktor Frankl, Holocaust survivor and developer of logo-therapy; psychiatrist John Sears of Menlo Park, California; and Laura Huxley, author and widow of Aldous Huxley, author, thinker, and consciousness explorer.

As the program progressed, opposition to it grew from within Unity School, particularly from Silent Unity. James Dillet Freeman, who became director of Silent Unity and who was also a member of the Unity School board of trustees, indicated that the content of the Omega program was "not Unity."[82] Several of the workshops used methods never before used in Unity, including those which employed highly confrontational encounter exercises. In forty-eight-hour "humanist-gestalt marathons," participants were sleep-deprived as a part of an effort to achieve "profound personal breakthroughs."[83] Criticism within Unity centered on the perception that the methods used for achieving transformation in the Omega program were not in conformity with basic Unity teaching, which stressed biblical interpretation, metaphysics, prayer, and spiritual healing.

In retrospect, John Anderson, who was on the staff of Omega and has just completed thirty years as a Unity minister, believes that the "old line" at Unity was totally unprepared for the type of experiential learning that Omega employed. The Omega staff saw the program as "a natural next step to implement the Unity teachings," while most on the Unity staff saw it "as disturbing the wonderful thing that had been developed."[84] It should be pointed out that the transformational methods of Omega were also controversial outside the Unity movement.

In January 1972, Charles R. Fillmore and the Unity board conducted a review of the Omega program, asking both Williamson and Kreml to present a report on the progress of the two-year-old Omega Center. Specifically, they wanted to know how Omega fit into Unity School and served its purposes. They asked how many people had been reached and the effect the trainings had upon them. In particular, they wanted statistics on how many people had become involved with the Unity teachings as a result of this work. The Board also asked for a summary of the financial return of the trainings to the school.[85] Answers to these questions were difficult to provide, because Williamson did not view Omega as a money-making operation. He believed that its primary purpose was to bring Unity into contact and conversation with, and service to, the "outside world," including younger people, rather than for the specific purpose of bringing people into the Unity movement.[86]

The board of trustees of Unity School, headed by its president, Charles R. Fillmore, concluded that the Omega Center was not benefiting the school and on April 25, 1972, decided to discontinue it. A memo to Unity staff signed by Charles R. Fillmore, Barney Rickets, and James Dillet Freeman indicated that Unity School was "not a proper vehicle" for this program. The board concluded:

While it is recognized that much of the experimental programming of Omega is worthwhile, experience has proved that Unity School is not a suitable sponsoring organization for such activities. Perhaps the greatest value of the "Omega" experiment was to reemphasize that Unity has a unique contribution to make toward teaching man to recognize his divine potential, and that we should focus our efforts toward assisting the spiritual unfoldment of the individual.[87]

Anderson believes that, while the Omega approach failed at Unity School, it had a positive impact on the Unity ministers who went through the program. Exposure to this new learning technology, Anderson observed, resulted in more effective ministries in the field. Anderson reported that experiential learning programs like Omega, which have been widely used in the human potential movement, have been extensively used in Unity churches for many years. He believes that many Unity students have benefited from them.[88] Williamson agrees with Anderson, observing that in the ensuing years, Unity's training in the churches "has gone in the direction I pushed." As a result, he considered the Omega program a success. Williamson stated, "The educational approaches in Unity today of more experiential education are similar to what we introduced in the '60s."[89]

CONTINUING EDUCATION PROGRAM (1967–2000)

In 1967 the Unity Institute for Continuing Education took over the adult education functions that had been previously performed under the auspices of the Unity Training School. The new program combined study at Unity School with work done by correspondence and extension classes in centers and churches. Unity School's part of the program was offered in four sessions, two weeks each during the summertime, from June to August. By 1977 the program at Unity Village had been extended from four sessions each year to six. Classes began in March and ended in November. The program was aimed at those who were working toward "greater personal unfoldment," as well as toward those interested in becoming Unity teachers.[90]

Courses were given in four basic areas of study: biblical, metaphysical, interpersonal, and historical. A wide variety of classes were offered, including study of the New and the Old Testaments, Biblical Interpretation, The Life of Prayer, Christian Healing, Prosperity, The Background of New Thought, and Myrtle Fillmore's Healing Letters. An additional feature was "Action Afternoons" at Unity School in which students participated in a course called "Service to Modern Man." After attending classes in the morning, students would go out into the Kansas City community and engage in social action service projects that were described as "experimental community action experiences."[91]

The institute sought to facilitate people in gaining a deeper understanding of the "ideas of Truth," helping them make progress in attaining the "inner directedness" needed to manifest "the Christ Consciousness."[92] Philip White, a Unity minister and director of the program, indicated that people attended these workshops for various reasons. He explained: "They come to clarify and better understand their own religious beliefs, or in some cases, discover what those beliefs are. The courses serve to spark and motivate. . . . This variety of courses helps people to integrate their emotional and intellectual nature, to impart information, and especially to learn to think and interpret."[93]

White believed that the institute's program offered people a time to step out of their routine and reflect on the meaning of their lives. During such time, people could seek and find positive solutions to problems they faced in everyday life. The program proved to be very popular: enrollment reached six hundred for the 1975 summer session and more than doubled by 1980, when approximately fifteen hundred attended.[94] White believed that the program succeeded in enabling those who participated in finding "more meaningful and satisfying ways of living." Many, he felt, ultimately developed into "serving person[s] for mankind."[95]

The program also helped train those who wanted to become licensed Unity teachers. Students who completed 150 credits of class work fulfilled one of the principal requirements for licensing by the Association of Unity Churches. At each of the six yearly sessions, a total of twenty-five credits could be obtained. In addition, designated extension courses presented in Unity churches could also be applied toward credit. It was possible for a student to accumulate the necessary credits to graduate in two years and apply for licensing.[96]

In 1980 the Unity School for Religious Studies was established for the purpose of managing and coordinating the education and retreat programs of Unity School. Its adult education programs were developed out of the foundation laid by the former Institute for Continuing Education. Now called the "Continuing Education Program," or CEP, this program, like its predecessor, was presented in six sessions, each two weeks long, beginning in March and ending in November. While classes were open to anyone who wanted to attend, the curriculum was designed primarily for those preparing for service in the Unity movement as licensed teachers or for those engaged in preministerial training.[97]

The titles of the courses were similar to those of the Institute for Continuing Education and included: Development of the Unity Movement, Comparative Religion, Principles of Communication, and Counseling Experience. The program emphasized the need "to inspire students to see themselves as unfolding spiritual beings and to encourage them to expand and deepen their own consciousness."[98] Those who sought eligibility to become licensed teachers needed to complete 150 credits of class work;

120 were required and 30 were electives. Some of the class work could be completed through extension study in churches. The diligent student could complete the course requirements in two years.[99]

In 1996 the Continuing Education Program was revised significantly by Unity School for Religious Studies. Two tracks were established for students participating in continuing education: the Personal Development Program for those desiring to study primarily for their own personal and spiritual growth, and a Leadership Development Program for those preparing for service as teachers in the Unity movement. Both programs seek to help people bring a consciousness of God into everyday life and to inspire them to express their God-given potential. Those who pursue the Personal Development Program engage in four major areas of study: biblical, metaphysical, prayer, and interpersonal. A new system for measuring credit hours has been introduced. For each hour spent in satisfactory class work, one credit is awarded. Approximately twenty-five courses are offered, each requiring ten hours of class work or credit hours to complete. A diploma of graduation and achievement is given to those who complete the 250 credit hours of work.[100]

Classes are offered in three different venues at Unity Village during weeklong CEP sessions held three times each year—spring, summer, and fall; in larger Unity churches that sponsor weeklong "CEP-in-the Field" sessions; and in extension study in most Unity churches. The ten hours of class work required to complete each course given in Unity churches must be spread over a five-week period. Included among the courses are: Jesus' Teachings, Interpreting the Bible, the Metaphysical Experience, How to Let God Help You, The Twelve Powers of Man, Discovering the Power Within You, Life of Prayer, and the Development of the Unity Movement.[101] Many students combine course work at Unity Village with classes taken in their own churches. The range of classes given in Unity centers and churches is now so extensive that students can complete all the course work for the Personal Development Program in their local communities.[102]

The Leadership Development Program requires significantly more work than before to qualify students for recognition as licensed Unity teachers. Students must first complete the 220 credit hours in the Personal Development Program before they can begin teacher training. Courses in the Leadership Development Program include Advanced Bible Study, Metaphysics and Prayer, Pastoral and Ministry Studies, and Communication and Counseling Theory. Classes in these subjects can be taken only at the Unity School for Religious Studies at Unity Village.[103] About nine weeklong sessions taken over a three-year period are needed to satisfy the requirements of the program. Those who complete the work will qualify for licensing as Unity teachers by the Association of Unity Churches. First, they must work for one year as volunteers in a Unity ministry, indicate the area of church work they want to pursue (adult or youth education, pastoral care or administration), receive a letter of recommendation from their local minister, and pass a general written examination.[104]

UNITY RETREAT PROGRAM

Retreats are one of Unity School of Religious Studies' major areas of service. Since 1951, retreats have been offered several times each year and have provided an opportunity for people to relax, get away from daily cares, and revitalize themselves, physically, psychologically, and spiritually. For many years the emphasis was more on relaxation and entertainment than on serious spiritual work. In 1960s and 1970s, Foster and Paula Mc-Clelland directed retreats and and were the "heart and soul" of the program. They came up with the idea of vacation retreats. Unity students were encouraged to come to Unity Village to spend part of their summer vacation. Recreational facilities were available, including golf, tennis, and swimming.[105]

In the 1990s, the program shifted under the direction of Christine Dustin, a Unity minister who holds a master of arts in religion. She has been in charge of the program since 1997. Rather than repeat the same content for each retreat, as was the practice in the 1980s, Dustin introduced themes to address particular aspects of the spiritual work. Themes included: Prayer and Possibilities, Creating Spiritual Community, Caring for Each Other, Honoring the Paths to God, Prosperous Living, and Living the Abundant Life.[106]

Retreats now reflect one of two approaches. They are categorized either as a "celebration" or as a "reflection."[107] The retreat brochure describes the differences between the two styles of retreat and how a person might choose between them, explaining: "As you may seek peace at differing times in your life you may want different things from a retreat. At one time you may want lots of stimulating new spiritual ideas, joyous music, and celebration. At other times you may need inner communion, with more time for reflection, renewal and quiet joy."[108]

Unity now offers approximately twelve retreats yearly, with from 40 to

180 people in attendance at each. Most are a week long, beginning on a Saturday and ending the following Friday. A few are held on weekends, beginning on Thursday evening and ending Sunday morning. About 60 percent of the content is experiential, with lectures occupying a significant portion of the remaining time. Unity describes the format of the retreats as follows: "You will find a gentle wake-up exercise, uplifting music, dynamic speakers and programs, fascinating workshops, spirit-filled prayer groups, quiet times, Village tours and sacred ceremonies."[109]

Dustin indicated that the people who come to retreats usually have something serious going on in their lives. It may be a personal problem, a job-related issue, an illness, or a major personal loss. Most who come are not Unity church members. Many come as a result of their reading of *Daily Word*. Unity points out that one of the benefits of a retreat is growth—both personal and spiritual.[110] Prospective participants are advised: "You will have a chance to relax, reflect, and enter into a creative prayer-based dynamic of change. Our retreat programs are designed to offer a structured flow of experience and thematic development that supports a shift in consciousness and creates an environment for spiritual and personal growth."[111]

Unity views the ultimate purpose of a retreat as affording the retreatant an opportunity for an experience of the self and God. "A retreat," Dustin explains, "is a time to be alone with God and reflect."[112] The retreat brochure indicates: "A retreat gives us a chance to step outside our busy day-to-day existence and seek clarity about who we are and what we should do. Our top priority is to create a safe space for all people to grow in spirit and discover their deepest connection with God."[113]

Unity also views retreats as a way to interest people in Unity teachings. Dustin reports, "Retreats serve as a springboard for people to come into Unity."[114] Fees for retreats are in the moderate range and vary depending upon length, whether for a weekend or for a full week.[115] The continued emphasis that Unity School is placing on retreats is indicated by the construction of a new $7 million retreat center at Unity Village, to be completed in 2002, which can handle as many as three hundred retreatants.

Unity Ministerial Training

A systematic program for training ministers and teachers was established by Unity School in 1931, over forty years after the initial presentation of the Unity spiritual teaching. The delay reflected the Fillmores' ambivalence regarding the establishment of Unity churches. From 1906 when the first Unity ministers were ordained until 1933 when classes of Unity students were ordained annually, no more than fifty people received Unity ordination. Those who were ordained prepared themselves by participating in adult education classes, by completing the correspondence course, by serving as Silent Unity workers, or by teaching classes in Practical Christianity at Unity School. Described below are the five programs for training ministers that evolved from 1931 to 2000. This is a story of experimentation that ultimately produced a remarkably successful program.

UNITY TRAINING SCHOOL (1931–1965)

The creation of a leadership training program for those who would serve in the growing number of centers and churches was a first priority in the founding of the Unity Training School in 1931. A "Call for Leaders," published in *Weekly Unity,* explained that the Unity Training School was "now giving special attention to the development of leaders."[1] The training school offered instruction in one-month classes throughout the summer at Unity Farm. A student could fulfill the class requirements for ordination to the Unity ministry by attending a minimum of one month per summer for a four-year period.[2] The first ordination of training school graduates was conducted on August 23, 1933, when eleven candidates who "had completed the requirements and necessary preparation for spiritual leadership were received into the Unity ministerial body."[3]

In 1952 the minimum requirements for ordination were expanded. Ministerial students now needed to complete the Unity correspondence course and accumulate at least forty-five credits of class work at the Unity Training School during at least two summer sessions. In addition, students were expected to serve at least one full year in a Unity center ministry.[4] The curriculum consisted of courses commonly associated with Practical Christianity, including: The Bible and Its Metaphysical Interpretation, The Practice of Scientific Prayer, Spiritual Principles, Center Ministry—Organization and Operation, Healing Practice, Spiritual Counseling, Public Speaking, and World Religions.[5]

Elizabeth Sand Turner, a Unity minister and author of *Let There Be Light, Your Hope of Glory,* and *Be Ye Transformed,* commented on what motivated Unity students to become ministers, and the requirements for success. She indicated:

Almost everyone who hears the call to train for the Unity ministry does so because he [or she] has been healed of some illness of body or affairs and wishes to share with others the knowledge of God that has proved to be of such benefit to himself . . . If he loses sight [of the goal] and succumbs to the desire to use the center as a means of livelihood, or yields to the subtle temptation to exploit himself, he but paves the way for disaster personally and for disaster to his center.[6]

The Unity Training School ministerial education program was nonresidential and required a minimum of preparation. A student could complete the academic requirements for ordination by attending summer school. This program was weak when compared to the ministerial training programs that followed, which required two years of formal training in residence at Unity Village and boasted a far more demanding curriculum.

SILENT UNITY MINISTERIAL TRAINING PROGRAM (1945–1969)

Unity's first residential ministerial training program was begun in 1945 under the leadership of a man who was to become one of the leading expositors of Unity teaching, James Dillet Freeman. The program combined work in the Silent Unity healing ministry with an academic program. The curriculum required two to three years to complete, and the school year was divided into two semesters, from September to May. The student was required to take a course load comparable to that of college undergraduates. The content of the courses was similar to that required of the students in Unity Training School's ongoing ministerial education program offered during summer school. In addition, ministerial candidates were expected to engage in fieldwork in Unity centers, teaching adult education classes or engaging in Sunday school work. A student completed the program when all work required under all three phases was finished. Before assuming the responsibilities of Unity center ministry, a student had to be deemed qualified by an examining committee of the Unity Ministerial Association.

Only men were allowed to matriculate in this program. The rationale for excluding women was based in part on the view that, before 1945, the Unity movement was based overwhelmingly on the involvement of women. It was assumed that gender balance was needed in Unity center ministries. The student was paid a salary for work in Silent Unity and was not required to pay tuition for ministerial training. Many men who matriculated were World War II veterans, who received benefits under the GI Bill. The program succeeded in its goal of attracting men to leadership positions, as several men were ordained each year from the inception of the program.[7]

In 1964, as a part of The Great Vision, Unity School began investigating the requirements for gaining accreditation of its ministerial training program with the American Association of Theological Schools. The association's director, Dr. Charles L. Taylor, visited the school, reviewed its program, and outlined the improvements needed to upgrade the program for accreditation by the association.[8] Specifically, the curriculum needed to be broadened, teachers with doctoral degrees added to the faculty, library holdings increased in the field of religion, and buildings constructed to house the program.

From 1965 to 1969, Unity set about improving its ministerial education program to meet these requirements. The Silent Unity Ministerial Training Program was discontinued and the School for Ministerial and Religious Studies was established in its place. During the four years of the school's existence, the teaching staff was increased and the course offerings significantly enhanced.[9] Courses were offered in four basic areas: metaphysical studies and skills, biblical studies and skills, historical studies and skills, and interpersonal studies and skills.[10] By 1969 the curriculum contained by far the largest number of course offerings for ministerial students at Unity School up to that time.

Unity School, as it sought to enhance its academic standing, increased the requirements for graduation. The program now required the equivalent of three years to complete instead of two. Only if a student matriculated in two summer sessions, each the equivalent of a fall or spring semester, could the work be finished in less than three years. Two primary tracks were offered: a graduate study program that would lead to a master of divinity degree when accreditation was granted, and a Ministerial Academy program, for which a diploma was awarded.[11] Entrance requirements for the two programs differed. The graduate study program required a bachelor's degree to qualify for entrance, while a high school diploma plus some college or evidence of a successful career was all that was needed to enter the Ministerial Academy.[12]

Both programs stressed academic achievement. In biblical studies, students were expected to integrate "the most recent scholarly historical understanding with metaphysical principles."[13] In historical studies, the student was expected to be able, through the study of world religions, ancient religions, philosophy, and church history, to place the Unity movement in historical perspective. The school emphasized the need for "intellectual attainment,"[14] which included the ability "to appreciate the relationship between understanding of ideas and the demonstration of ideas."[15] An integrative seminar offered on Wednesdays for two hours required the student "to integrate classroom theory and concern for what is really happening in the world." All students were offered the opportunity to serve in the Silent Unity Prayer Room and were expected upon graduation to be grounded in Silent Unity healing methods.[16]

In 1969 Unity School decided to postpone its efforts to achieve accreditation by the American Association of Theological Schools, close its School for Ministerial and Religious Studies, and transfer responsibility for ministerial training to the Association of Unity Churches. The decision was based in part on the high cost of meeting the standards of the American Association of Theological Schools in terms of faculty, buildings, and library holdings.[17] Another motivating factor was the belief that ministerial training could be more appropriately handled by the Association of Unity Churches.[18] Freed of the responsibility of training ministers as well as that of administering churches, Unity School could devote time, energy, and resources to its experiment with the Omega Center. The school could also now claim to be a nondenominational spiritual organization devoted to prayer, the publication of magazines and books, and adult education.

UNITY MINISTERIAL SCHOOL (1969–1983)

In 1969 the Association of Unity Churches, at the request of Unity School, assumed full responsibility for the training of Unity ministers. Unity School continued to cooperate by providing classroom facilities, opportunities for students to have practical experience, funds to support grant-in-aid awards, and supplemental faculty members and counselors. The association developed the curriculum, established the teaching philosophy, handled admissions, selected the faculty, established procedures for ordination, and funded the program.[19]

The curriculum covered the same basic areas as that of its predecessor organization, the School for Ministerial and Religious Studies. This included truth fundamentals, biblical history and interpretation, prayer and meditation, communication skills, and counseling practices.[20] The coverage, however, was in much less depth, and the school was less concerned with academic achievement than its predecessor. The number of course offerings was reduced as was the size of the faculty. In addition, the length of the program was reduced from three years to two.[21] The association showed no interest in pursuing accreditation by the American Association of Theological Schools.[22]

The qualifications for admission remained basically unchanged. Students needed to have acquired an associate of arts degree or equivalent work experience. In addition, the equivalent of one year's class work at the Unity Institute for Continuing Education was required, as well as one year's participation in the work of a Unity ministry. The ministerial school indicated that it sought "to help candidates deepen their knowledge of Truth and hone their skills to communicate that knowledge to others."[23] The school described the aims of the program as twofold: "First, to enable [students] to understand and develop their own potential through prayer, study and application of spiritual principles in their own lives, and second, to provide a high quality training program which prepares [students] for service [in the Unity ministry]."[24]

In 1981 Unity School decided to resume full responsibility for ministerial training. The conflict with the Association of Unity Churches over the proposal to establish Unity International had convinced school officials that the ministerial program, as managed by the association, was alienating ministers from the school.[25] Unity School officials also believed that the school was in a good financial position to create and sustain a quality ministerial education program. James Dillet Freeman recalled that he argued strongly for its return, believing that the Unity movement would be split if the association continued to maintain full control.[26] In June 1982, a proposal was made at the business meeting of the annual conference of the association to return ministerial training to Unity School. When the proposal was voted down by members of the association in attendance, officials announced that Unity School would establish its own ministerial training program.[27]

The conference then entertained and passed a motion to establish a committee of the association to negotiate with the school for the purpose of exploring joint management of the program.[28] An agreement was reached in September 1982 between the board of the school and the executive committee of the association that resulted in shared responsibility for ministerial training.[29] Administrative and financial responsibility was

transferred from the association to the school, as was responsibility for selection of the faculty. The association retained control of admissions policies and standards, licensing and ordination, and placement of ministers
and teachers. It also retained the right to appoint one member of the faculty.[30] A six-member ministerial education council was established to set
policy concerning the curriculum. Each organization has the right to select
three members of the council.[31]

UNITY SCHOOL FOR RELIGIOUS STUDIES
(1983–2000)

In the fall of 1983, Unity School of Christianity, through its School for
Religious Studies, again assumed responsibility for leading the program to
train Unity ministers. Phil White, dean of education, a Unity minister who
had received a master of divinity degree from St. Paul School of Theology,
and a Methodist, introduced a two-year program of academic studies for
annual classes of approximately thirty students. Organized around the
idea of a written credo that would be developed by each student through a
two-year study, the first year focused on five major areas: metaphysical
studies, biblical studies, historical studies, counseling theory and skills,
and communication theory and skills. The second year core units were devoted to ministry as healing, education, worship, and administration. In
contrast to previous methods of studying the Unity teachings by taking up
each individual Unity book, necessitating much repetition, the new school
introduced the method of pulling from the vast material the main themes
and ideas, and using the books as reference resources.[32]

The curriculum was organized to "maximize the student's experience
of the subject matter."[33] Large blocks of time were allocated so that students would be able "to study the subject fully," and by so doing meet the
standards of the licensing and ordination committee of the Association of
Unity Churches. Studying ministry this way, it was explained, was to
"structure the learning process to maximize the integration of theory and
practice." The objective of this academic approach, which informed the
school's educational philosophy throughout the 1980s, was to facilitate
the student "in thinking through the spiritual and metaphysical basis for
an effective ministry."[34]

By 1990 members of the faculty began expressing concerns about the
effectiveness of this approach to the study of ministry. The retention rate
of ministers continued to be low—almost half those graduating did not re-

main in ministerial service.[35] Robert R. Barth, who in 1988 became senior director of education for the Unity School for Religious Studies, concluded that the program was too intense and too demanding, leading to student burnout.[36] Gary Jones, who in 1990 was appointed dean of education, felt that the program was "too hard" on future ministers. Jones was alerted to this problem when in 1988, as a member of the licensing and ordination committee of the Association of Unity Churches, he interviewed a graduate of the ministerial program who, instead of seeking employment in a Unity ministry, took six months off to seek counseling and a time to heal. It was Jones's understanding that many new ministers took their unresolved personal issues and their anger into their first ministry.[37] School officials concluded that they had created a three-year program that they expected students to complete in two years.[38]

As a result, the ministerial education committee, comprised of representatives of the school and the Association of Unity Churches, began planning a ministerial program that would take three years to complete, reducing the stress and strain of the current program and providing time for students to serve summer internships in Unity churches around the country. While many ministers supported the idea, an influential minority were able to defeat the plan, arguing, "If I was required to go through a three-year program, I would never have been able to attend."[39]

With the failure of the effort to establish a three-year ministerial training program, in 1992 Unity School for Religious Studies devised a two-year program that reduced academic requirements, placed less emphasis on what students learned, and focused more on how students developed spiritually. As with the previous program of studies, begun in 1983, students continued to be told: "You will develop a clearly articulated personal belief system or credo . . . The goal of this study is to help you to systematically consider what you believe and organize that belief in a way that can be effectively communicated to others."[40] The school articulated the educational philosophy that underlies this approach, explaining:

The learning method has developed because it has become clear that students graduating from the ministerial program and assuming leadership positions in a Unity ministry do not take with them separate disciplines such as metaphysics, history, Bible, communication, counseling, and prayer. They take with them a developed or undeveloped, effective or ineffective consciousness (belief system) made up of their beliefs, relevant convictions, and experiences that will be externalized through them as ministers.[41]

The school alerted students to the fact that their belief systems would be challenged and that they were expected, by graduation, to have developed a fully integrated credo or set of beliefs. Students were advised:

The faculty recognizes that you enter school with your personal credo already functioning and then the disciplines of metaphysics, Bible, history, communications counseling and prayer are either effectively or ineffectively integrated into that belief system. Our conviction that ministerial education must not only present the basic disciplines, but must also include the process of the student's reflection upon his or her individual credo and encourage and support its unfoldment. For this reason the USRS ministerial program seeks to help you surface your individual credo and reflect upon it in an organized way.[42]

The school assured students that the ministerial education program would help them "begin the formal process of thinking through and clarifying what your system of belief really is and how you want to present it."[43]

The two-year curriculum that was developed to support this program was presented in eight themes or stages of growth. Students were advised that it was designed "to take you through the steps of your spiritual journey." Four themes are explored in the first year of the program and four in the second.[44] Theme one, "Spiritual Self-Awareness," asks the student to develop his or her life story, or "How I got to here." The goal is to experience the self—spirit, soul, body. Three questions are then addressed: "Who am I? What do I believe? How am I living my beliefs?" The learner explores, among other things, the concepts of the Christ within that are taught in Unity metaphysics.[45] The learner is also expected to become aware of his or her own core issues and to get involved in the healing process. Toni Boehm, dean of administration, explained how this process facilitates the student's spiritual development and prepares them for service in the Unity ministry. The process, she indicated:

Helps each person grow beyond the confines of his or her past history, through healing of the core "false" beliefs. This healing allows one to express and grow in a more authentic way and as a greater reflection of the Christ Consciousness that is inherent within. The assumption is that the more whole and healed a candidate is, the greater is the potential for healing and wholeness to be reflected in his or her ministry.[46]

Theme two deals with spiritual awakening. Three questions are asked: "What is it? How does it work? What do I do with it? Theme three, "The Wilderness Experience," is the key to the success of the ministerial program. The student's belief system and faith are tested and, according to Barth, "things often start falling apart. Students go through a kind of hell at this time."[47] During this part of the program students look at practical ways of practicing forgiveness.

Three themes explore the transition to Unity ministry, focusing on the nature of the ministry and its spiritual foundations. Two themes are devoted to exploring and serving the Unity community. In a recent interview, Barth indicated that the current ministerial program is more experiential than those in the past, with less time devoted to lectures and tests that require the regurgitation of information. The program is concerned as much with developing "the heart" as well as "the head."[48] As in the past, the student is encouraged to devote time to prayer and to experience the silence. The importance of prayer was indicated when the school stipulated "a consciousness of God through prayer is the foundation of ministerial education." The ministerial program continued to incorporate planned times for prayer such as the Silent Unity prayer service and the student chapel service as well as specific prayer instruction in class work.[49] In addition, every student goes on silent retreat, one day during the first year of study and two days during the second.

In 1999, the School for Religious Studies undertook its first comprehensive evaluation of the new curriculum based on an adult education model that had been in place for seven years. It examined the careers of 194 men and women who had graduated from the program since 1992. A total of 178 students, 81 percent of the graduates, were still serving in the field. The drop rate that historically had approached 50 percent of all ministerial school graduates was now at 19 percent. Both Robert Barth and James Rosemergy, executive vice president of Unity School, consider this strong evidence of the success of the current ministerial education program.[50]

Phil White, who as dean of education directed the ministerial education program in the 1980s, indicated that the high dropout rate of ministers in the eighties was in part due to the fallout from the controversy between the school and the association over the proposal for Unity International (see Chapter 11). White also indicated that the higher retention rate for ministers was also the result of a stricter admission policy for ministerial candidates, better opportunities for field placement, and a more effective licensing and ordination process.[51]

CHAPTER 11

The Development of Unity Centers and Churches

Introduction

Several years elapsed after the establishment in the 1890s of the first Unity church in Kansas City before efforts were made to develop Unity centers and churches throughout the United States. The Fillmores spent years in experimentation before they developed an organizational model that Unity students could replicate in their own communities. While the early organizations were structured like churches, the Fillmores referred to them as "Unity centers." This was because of a strong interest in preventing Unity from becoming another religious sect and a desire to locate these centers in Protestant and Catholic churches.

The Unity movement was thirty years old before Unity School gave significant attention to the work of these centers, and forty years before they developed a ministerial program to support them. Nevertheless, by the time of Charles Fillmore's death in 1948, the centers, or churches, as many of the centers were called by then, were located in major cities throughout the United States and had become a significant part of the Unity movement. Centers and churches were supported logistically for several decades by the field department and the Unity Ministers Association, both organizational components of the Unity School of Christianity.

In 1966 the Association of Unity Churches, an independent nonprofit group with no organizational connection to Unity School, took over the work of the field department and Unity Ministers Association. By 2000 there were over one thousand Unity ministries.

The First Unity Church: The Kansas City Unity Society
of Practical Christianity

The origins of the church organization that later became known as the Kansas City Unity Society of Practical Christianity can be traced to meetings the Fillmores held with fellow Christian Scientists in Kansas City during the summer of 1889. At the outset, the group went by a different name and was not considered a church. The group's original purpose was twofold: to support those who wanted to deepen their knowledge and understanding of metaphysics, particularly Christian Science; and second, to practice mental healing. The announcement that stated the group's purposes and the facilities available for meetings was published by Charles in *Modern Thought* in August 1889. Evidently the group, which Charles was part of from the beginning, had not yet named itself, for the news item in *Modern Thought* announcing its existence did not specify a name. The news item, most likely written by Charles, stated:

Pursuant to a call issued to those in Kansas City interested in the promulgation of metaphysical thought, a meeting was held July 13th, at Room 1, Journal Building, for the purpose of devising ways and means for the establishment of a free reading room, and Sunday meetings . . . As a result of that meeting quarters have been secured in the Deardorf building, corner of 11th and Main streets, in which a reading room has been established and in which regular meetings will be held.[1]

Modern Thought went on to indicate the times when the rooms would be available for use and contained an appeal to all interested in Christian Science to make use of the facilities and the available materials, stating:

The rooms will be open from 9 A.M. to 6 P.M. and the public is cordially invited to visit them during these hours. Those interested in Christian Science and kindred subjects are earnestly requested to make them their headquarters. They are not dedicated to any particular school of metaphysics, but open to all teachers and healers. The object is to spread the truth, and it is thought that can be done most effectively by a generous invitation to all workers. A circulating library has been established in connection with the free reading rooms, from which books can be taken at nominal price.[2]

Six months later, in February 1890, *Modern Thought* reported on the growing activity of "The Christian Science Association of Kansas City," the name that the group had chosen for itself. Weekly meetings were now being held on Sundays and Wednesdays, as the statement below indicates:

The rooms of the Christian Science Association of Kansas City, in the Deardorf building, are becoming the popular centre for those interested in progressive thought. Meetings are held Sunday and Wednesday afternoon at 3 o'clock, to which the public is cordially invited. The rooms are also open each day from 9 A.M. to 5 P.M., and there is generally someone in attendance to answer questions of strangers who desire information on the subject of mental or Christian Science.[3]

In September 1890, Charles published another announcement regarding the activities of the association in *Christian Science Thought*. In addition to regular Sunday meetings, a Sunday school was begun. The need for more space, prompted by the association's rapid growth, led the group to rent a larger facility. The announcement stated:

The Christian Science Association of Kansas City has grown so rapidly of late that more commodious quarters were found necessary, and in order to seat the increasing numbers that are attracted by the glorious gospel of freedom from any ills of humanity, a larger hall has been fitted up at 820 Walnut Street. A Sunday School commencing at 2 P.M. has also been inaugurated. The public is cordially invited to attend these meetings, viz, Wednesday at 3 P.M., and Sunday at 3 P.M. preceded by Sunday School at 2 P.M.[4]

In October *Christian Science Thought* indicated that meetings of people interested in Christian Science were now taking place in Kansas City in many different locations. "Kansas City is unusually blessed," it was noted, "in the apprehension by its people of the pure teachings of Jesus Christ. Regular meetings are being held in a number of places in town and classes constantly taught."[5] In November *Christian Science Thought* described in detail the order of business at the Wednesday and Sunday meetings. Though no preacher or minister had been officially designated, Sunday meetings were taking on the character of church services, with speakers, healing work, meditation, and music. The role of "speaker" was being shared by many members of the association, as the "No Name Lecture Series" described below indicated. The announcement in *Christian Science Thought* stated:

Regular meetings of Christian Scientists are held at 820 Walnut Street, Kansas City, as follows:

EVERY WEDNESDAY AT 3 P.M.

Open meetings for general exchange of views and experiences in the work. Largely given to the discussion of practical everyday questions and their relation to Divine Science. These conference gatherings are especially interesting to Scientists.

EVERY SUNDAY AT 3 P.M.

Open meetings to which strangers and those familiar with the teachings of Christian Science are attracted. For this reason the remarks are usually of a character to elucidate the subject from a primary standpoint.

EVERY SUNDAY AT 7:30 P.M.

"No Name Lecture Series." These lectures are delivered by the various teachers and students of Christian Science and cover in their variety the whole metaphysical field. The subject only of the lecture is announced one week in advance of its delivery. The speakers are changed every Sunday and their identity remains unknown to the public until the moment of going onto the platform.

At each of these meetings the uplifting and healing presence of the Holy Spirit is invoked, in both silence and song. Many people come to them suffering mentally and physically and go away well. We have no preacher or leader of any description—the one in the chair always appointing another to take his or her place at the next meeting.[6]

Charles was evidently one of the association's speakers for a long address entitled "Deception Removed," which was delivered before the association on November 29, 1891, and published the following month in *Unity* magazine.[7]

It appears that by 1892 the phrase "Christian Science" had been dropped from the group's name. In an announcement in which the articles of association adopted by the Kansas City society were published, the term "Divine Science" was used to characterize the work. It stated:

We, whose names are hereinafter appended, appreciating the importance of doing all things "decently and in order," with a profound love for unity and harmony, and with a joyful, serene and faithful devotion to Truth, purity and unselfish service, as taught and exemplified by Jesus Christ, hereby associate ourselves together for the purpose:

1. of maintaining Divine Science services at stated times.
2. of healing the sick, raising the fallen, and helping the misled child to return to the Father.
3. of teaching Divine Science and preaching the gospel to every creature, and of publishing and circulating Divine Science and other metaphysical literature.[8]

The duties and responsibilities of the officers of the association were spelled out as well as those of the executive board. It was stated that the executive board shall "make all provisions for meetings, lectures, classes, healings and order of exercise, and shall have charge of the hall, furniture and other property."[9] Membership was open to all who wanted to join, regardless of their religious convictions: "Every man, woman and child with a purpose in harmony with the preamble and purposes of this organization, herein set out, is invited to become a member of this association, and no test of opinion or belief shall ever be required as a qualification for membership."[10]

By 1894 the regular weekly meetings were being referred to as "Unity meetings." The venue had been changed to Rooms 510 and 511 Hall Building, and the weekly schedule contained several more gatherings. In December 1894 the Unity group met according to the following schedule:

Sunday—11:00 A.M. Bible Study
Tuesday—7:30 P.M. Silent Meeting
Wednesday—3:00 P.M. Association Meeting
Friday—7:30 P.M. Questions and Answers
Saturday—Daily High Noon 12:00 to 1:00 Silent Unity Treatment (a prayer for healing)

All meetings were open to the public and "everybody is cordially invited to be present."[11]

In 1896 the Sunday schedule shifted as a result of an effort by the various metaphysical groups in Kansas City to meet together instead of separately on Sunday morning. The kickoff meeting was to be led by the Reverend D. L. Sullivan, a Divine Science minister who, until his death in 1906, was one of Charles's most trusted friends and associates. The October 1895 issue of *Unity* carried the following statement:

The leading liberal scientists of Kansas City have decided to combine their efforts in the matter of Sunday meetings. Sunday, October 6th at 3 P.M., they will begin a regular service in Woodland Hall, 1016 Grand Avenue, to be led by different teachers and speakers . . . The Bible Class which has been held at Unity rooms on Sunday mornings will be discontinued. The other Unity meetings will be carried on as heretofore.[12]

The first meeting turned out to be a great success and Sullivan evidently inspired the Kansas City "liberal scientists" with his message. Charles wrote, "Kansas City was blessed with a very large attendance and the outpouring of the spirit through Brother Sullivan was beyond description."[13]

Sunday meetings continued at Woodland Hall for ten months, after which the site of the meeting was shifted to rooms adjacent to Unity head-quarters in the Pythian Building at Ninth and Walnut. An announcement in *Unity* magazine in August gave details of the transfer and indicated that a Rev. W. G. Todd would officiate during July and August. In this same August issue, the editors of *Unity* provided a detailed description of the "order of exercises" for Sunday meetings. While containing elements of many Christian services—silent prayer, scripture reading, congregational singing, and silent meditation—the sermon, which is a central feature of most services, was left out. In its place was a discussion of the Bible facilitated by the person chosen to lead the meeting. *Unity* magazine provided the following details:

While the congregation is gathering several songs are sung. The meeting is then formally opened with silent prayer, or silent meditation upon some statement or passage of Scripture given out by the leader. Next singing, followed by the Lord's Prayer repeated in concert aloud: then silently. We then distribute copies of *Unity* to each person and read the Bible Lesson text for the day—the leader reading the first verse, the congregation the second, and so on through. Then each verse is taken up and in general discussion, in which all present take part, the inner meaning is brought out and applied in the most practical ways consistent with the Science of Mind, based upon Man's relations to God.[14]

Experience of the group with this process indicated the greatest illumination took place when all participated. Implied was the notion that Scripture was best understood when the collective mind of the group was at work rather than the mind of a single individual. Accordingly: "We impress upon everybody the necessity of taking part in the discussion, and we find that those who are the most backward frequently bring out points that escape the leaders. It is understood of course that a leader has been by common consent selected, whose duty is to give general direction to the meetings."[15] The Sunday meeting ended with the usual formalities, a collection, announcements, and hymns. *Unity* reported:

After the lesson has been discussed, the allotted time usually about one hour, collection is taken up to meet expenses, during which the leader makes any announcements that may be sent in. Sometimes we have a solo or other voluntary performances during the collection. Then all arise and sing some familiar hymn, the benediction is pronounced either silently or audibly, as suits the leader, and the congregation disperses.[16]

In June 1897, *Unity* magazine identified the group as "The Unity Society of Practical Christianity" for the first time. The organization used this

name when it incorporated in 1903 and would continue to use it throughout the twentieth century.[17] Members of the society conducted services,
both on Sunday and during the week, and engaged in mental healing in a
large, four-bedroom house at 1315 McGee Street, Kansas City. The Sunday meetings of the Unity Society of Practical Christianity were held in
two large parlors at the front of the house. During the week Charles and
Myrtle Fillmore used the parlors for seeing clients for spiritual healing and
for their editorial duties. The two parlors could hold, when cleared of office furniture, a maximum of about one hundred people.[18]

The Sunday meetings, now called "religious services," were held in the
Unity parlors for three years. It was during this time that sermons by a
member of the society replaced the Bible discussions as the central feature
of the service.[19] Information on how these services were conducted was
contained in a news item describing the Easter service in 1901:

We wish every *Unity* subscriber could have been present at our Easter service in
Kansas City, Sunday April 7th. The solos by Mrs. Hazeltine and Mrs. Scott were
superb, and the lesson by Mrs. Croft and sermon by Mr. Fillmore were worthy of
equal praise. Mr. Prather directed the service with his usual grace, and a profusion
of flowers added to its pleasure. The only drawback was our overcrowded rooms.
We need a larger place.[20]

The need for more space for Sunday services was quickly addressed; in
May 1901, the site of the services of the Unity Society of Practical Christianity was moved to larger quarters at Arlington Hall at Tenth and Walnut Streets.[21] The work at Unity headquarters continued to grow in 1902.
In addition to Charles, who led the Sunday morning service, Myrtle directed a service at 2:30 on Wednesday afternoons, and Cassius Shafer,
who was soon to leave for Chicago to establish a Unity center there, directed a Sunday evening service. The society's first annual picnic was held
on July 4. Over two hundred people attended.[22]

The year 1902 marked the first time that Charles Fillmore was listed as
"speaker" for the Sunday morning service. This was a title he was to hold
until he retired from active church work in 1933. As speaker he performed
pastoral duties for the congregation and presided over the Sunday meeting.[23] A news item in *Unity* in April 1902, following the Easter service that
year, gave an indication of his ability as a speaker. The writer stated: "Mr.
Fillmore's address was in his usual happy vein, sparkling with wit and
studded with gems of Truth. He always rises to the occasion, and at this
time he outdid himself."[24] The writer also indicated how the society com-

pensated Charles for his services as speaker, stating: "At the close of the address a special Easter offer, mostly in gold, was presented to him through W. G. Haseltine, president of the Society. Mr. Fillmore responded, in a few well chosen words of thanks for this love-offering from the Society."[25]

In 1903 the Unity Society for Practical Christianity was incorporated "for scientific and educational purposes" under the laws of Missouri. Twelve people, headed by W. G. Haseltine of the Kansas City Board of Trade, were named to the board of the society.[26] It would be reasonable to assume that Charles and Myrtle also would have served as board members, since they were responsible for the society's creation and its continued existence. Such was not the case. Why they were left off remains a mystery, because their work was essential for the continued success of the society. It is possible that their involvement with the publishing work of Unity, which was not a part of the society's nonprofit mission, precluded them from participation in the work of the board.

The society decided to incorporate primarily because it wanted to purchase property and erect a building suitable for the needs of the expanding Unity work. Incorporation enabled the society "to hold any and all kinds of property."[27] Fund-raising began immediately, and by the summer of 1905 sufficient funds had been accumulated to purchase property at 913 Tracy Avenue. Excavation began in December for a building that was intended to be "a church, a school and a health dispensary."[28] Construction was completed the following summer, and the first Sunday meeting was held in the new Unity auditorium on July 29, 1906.[29]

The completion of the building was marked by special dedication exercises, which were held August 19–25, 1906. The program consisted of "speakers, musicians, teachers and healers" from around the country who came to participate in "lectures, lessons in healing, concentration classes, and healing through musical vibrations."[30] The program was entitled "Unity Building Dedication and Mid-Continent Convention of Practical Christians." As a part of the convention, the history of the Unity movement, its place in the spectrum of American religion, and its purposes were reviewed. The printed program stated:

The Unity Society of Practical Christianity is a revival of primitive Christianity. It seeks to put into everyday life the principles taught by Jesus Christ and practiced by early Christians, viz., "Preach the Gospel, heal the sick, cleanse the lepers, raise the dead, cast out devils. Freely ye have received, freely give." It is not connected with any of the orthodox religious organizations, but stands as an independent movement, with headquarters in Kansas City, Missouri. It had its inception some twenty years ago in what may be termed a Society of Modern or New Thought principles, which carried on meetings under various names and leaders. This Society gave the original name of the New Thought movement when it called its first monthly periodical, *Modern Thought*, the first number of this magazine being issued in April 1889. The Society is organized for religious, scientific and educational purposes, viz., the study and demonstration of Universal Law; (and) for matriculating, graduating and conferring the degrees through curriculum instruction and training in schools, colleges and universities. . . . The whole world is its field, and it is helping people everywhere to a fuller understanding of the One True God, and Man's relation thereto. Its aim is to make this the nucleus of a chain of similar institutions in many cities. . . . It will soon be sending forth representatives trained in the work, and through them will be planted everywhere the latest revelations of the Gospel of Jesus Christ, called Practical Christianity.[31]

In August 1906, the Unity Society of Practical Christianity, in order to fulfill its mission to "send forth representatives trained in the work," sought and was granted permission to revise its state charter to authorize the society to educate and train ministers. Unity students who were "ready and willing to give their lives and their ambitions to the service of God" were invited to come to Kansas City to study for the Unity ministry. The course of instruction would consist of "a thorough study of mind healing, Scripture interpretation and public speaking." One to two years would be required to complete the program and qualify for ordination, depending on the experience of the student.[32]

William G. Haseltine, president of the board of trustees of the society, explained the organization's intentions regarding ordination, indicating that the society was committed to aiding those who sought to establish Unity centers in their communities. Haseltine explained: "It is the intention of the Board to hold regular schools for the education of those who wish to take up this work, and having examinations of those who are desirous of becoming pupils, and in regular order submitting their work to an examination committee for the purpose of becoming ordained as teachers of Truth."[33]

For those Unity centers that could not send a student to Missouri for training, the Kansas City Society would send teachers who might help the center establish itself. Haseltine stated: "It is our desire to establish a lecture bureau so that our lecturers and teachers may be sent out to those centers who request them in the aiding of the building and growth of these centers, so that each center may, in time, become a power in itself, greater than is being manifested today."[34] Ordination of those who were considered sufficiently ready began immediately. Among the twelve people ordained in August 1906 were Charles and Myrtle and several members of the staff at Unity headquarters, including Jennie Croft, Cassius Shafer, and Charles Edgar Prather.[35]

A report in the March 1907 issue of *Unity* indicated that the Unity Society of Practical Christianity was "an independent movement established in 1889, with headquarters in Kansas City," and that it now enjoyed an attendance of "about 500" at its various meetings. The magazine further stated that the doctrine promulgated by the Society could be summed up in its name, "Practical Christianity."[36]

In August 1907 at the "First Annual Jubilee" of the dedication of the new Unity building, Charles reflected on the nature of the Unity teachings and their relationship to that of other religious denominations. He also indicated Unity's desire to reach out to all who were interested in the unification of all religions. He stated:

We are not a sect, we have merely a loosely woven organization that holds us together sufficiently to do a certain work, and that work is what our name represents, Unity in Christ—to bring together all the divergent thoughts of all the people on earth. For that reason we are not Methodists, Baptists, or Christian Scientists, but we select the good in them all and aim to practice it. . . . We are the mental and spiritual center of a great movement, greater than any of us can perceive, yet in its infancy, for the ultimate union of all religions.[37]

In February 1909 the Unity Society of Practical Christianity in Kansas City put out a strong appeal to Unity students worldwide to provide an endowment for the Unity teaching in Kansas City. The funds would go toward preparing teachers to carry forward the work. The announcement stated:

The work of the Society has been going forward long enough to prove its efficiency, and there is an urgent demand for enlargement and extension in every direction. A great awakening to the healing phase of Christianity is taking place both within and without the church and there is a call for us to teach the healing system of Jesus Christ and give to the work a rational, logical and scientific explanation of the Law which He used in performing the so-called miracles of the New Testament . . . There is a need for thoroughly equipped institutions with instructors who understand the science of mind as Jesus understood it. A generous number of the colleges of America have endowments over ten million dollars each, but a very much less amount will establish an institution here that will in a few years demonstrate an efficiency as an educator above anything ever attempted on earth. Our plans contemplate not only a college but a Rest Home also, where invalids will be received and educated into health.[38]

After the Unity School of Christianity was organized in 1914, the Kansas City Unity Society of Practical Christianity found it necessary periodically to distinguish its work from that of Unity School. In 1914 an article in *Weekly Unity* stated:

Our Society is an incorporated body, otherwise we would not be able to hold property under state law. We have no creed and place no obligations upon our members, except the unwritten creed of love of God and man. The bonds of love and understanding of Truth hold our people together. We do not have a "hired preacher," as our speakers give their ministry freely, and the congregation, in turn, makes them voluntary offers . . . We are not in any way allied with Christian Science. We are an entirely independent society, teaching and living the principles of Practical Christianity.[39]

It was made clear that concerning matters of belief, the society left that question entirely up to the individual. Although the society put forth specific teachings on a variety of subjects, membership did not require that persons subscribe to a particular doctrine or set of beliefs. The same article continued:

We do not observe the sacrament of the Lord as orthodox churches do, because we believe in the constant communion with the Spirit, which does not depend on outer symbols. The questions of dancing, card parties, theater-going and other matters of this sort, are left entirely to the discretion of our people. As we said before, we place no obligations on anyone, nor do we place restrictions, believing and teaching that the Spirit of Truth will, according to promise, "lead into all Truth." We know that each individual will be led to govern his life accordingly, and we do not interfere with personal matters.[40]

A decade later, in 1926, the society wanted it understood that it was not legally connected to Unity School, even though it was located in a building adjoining that of the school. Its work was similar to that of the other Unity centers that had come into existence around the world. *Weekly Unity* stated:

The Unity Society in Kansas City is known as the Unity Society of Practical Christianity and its property is held in trust by twelve directors who are elected by the members. This society is entirely separate from the Unity School of Christianity, just as all other Unity centers and Unity societies in different parts of the world are separate from the Unity School. It happens that the Unity Society of Practical Christianity in Kansas City occupies the building adjoining the buildings of the Unity School of Christianity and that some of the directors of the Society are members of the board of directors of Unity School, but the two are nevertheless entirely separate organizations.[41]

The same point was made five years later in 1931, when the lines of authority between Unity School and the Kansas City society again seemed blurred. A bulletin from the Field Department stated:

The Unity Society of Practical Christianity of Kansas City is the local organization and is a separate corporation from the Unity School of Christianity. The local Society owns the building adjoining the School's property, and its work is closely in harmony with the work of the School. The local Society's business is conducted by a board of twelve directors, who are elected for a term of three years. Its finances are entirely separate from those of Unity School.[42]

In 1940 the Kansas City Unity Society of Practical Christianity again found it necessary to distinguish its work from that of Unity School. The two groups shared a teaching function, and the society wanted to make it understood how its teaching fit in with the overall Unity work. *Weekly Unity* explained:

The Unity Society of Practical Christianity, though affiliated with Unity School of Christianity, is a separately incorporated organization. Unity School of Christianity publishes the Unity literature and includes the ministry of the Society of Silent Unity as well as the activities of the Unity Training School and of Unity Farm. The Unity Society of Practical Christianity is a necessary part of the Unity movement, and it is a work in which Charles Fillmore and all the workers at Unity School are interested. The Unity Society carries on the functions of Christian education and of Christian worship. Through its Selected Study Course and its Sunday school it gives instructions in the Unity teaching. Devotional services are held every Sunday and Wednesday . . . The Unity Society serves not only the people of Kansas City and the surrounding communities, but all Unity friends who visit Kansas City.[43]

The work of the Kansas City Unity Society of Practical Christianity and that of Unity School was not fully separated geographically until 1949, when the society moved into a new facility in the Country Club Plaza district of Kansas City and Unity School moved its headquarters to Unity Village, seventeen miles from downtown Kansas City. Only then did the two organizations function as fully independent units. The Kansas

City society flourished in its new facility. Called Unity Temple on the Plaza, it has become the home of one of Unity's largest congregations.

The Early Unity Center Leaders

By the turn of the century, the Kansas City Unity Society of Practical Christianity, through the effective leadership of Charles and Myrtle Fillmore, had become well established. Through daily meetings, including Sunday services, it carried out an active program of teaching and healing. The Fillmores and members of the board of the Kansas City society encouraged Unity students outside Kansas City to emulate the work of the local center and start Unity centers in their communities.

While exercising no control or jurisdiction over the new Unity groups, Unity headquarters provided center leaders with a variety of services that included helpful literature from Unity magazines, pamphlets, and books; opportunities for continuing education through classes in Practical Christianity in Kansas City and course work by correspondence from the Unity Correspondence School; counsel and advice from Unity field lecturers; and publicity which notified Unity students of towns and cities where Unity work was conducted. Aid to centers outside Kansas City, however, did not include financial support.

During the first two decades of the twentieth century, several teachers and healers who trained themselves by working for significant periods of time at Unity headquarters started centers in various cities around the country. Inspired by the teaching and healing work of Charles and Myrtle Fillmore, these Unity students set out to develop centers modeled after the Kansas City Unity Society of Practical Christianity. A review of the efforts of six of these leaders indicates the challenges they faced. Some succeeded; others failed. Nevertheless, these were the pioneers, the people that demonstrated that Unity work could be conducted successfully outside Kansas City. They set an example, provided inspiration for others, and enabled Unity School to learn from their experiences and to set up a support system within the school to facilitate the work of future leaders.

CASSIUS SHAFER AND THE CHICAGO UNITY SOCIETY OF PRACTICAL CHRISTIANITY

The first known center for conducting Unity work outside Kansas City was established by a Silent Unity healer, Cassius Shafer, in the summer of

1903 in Chicago. Shafer, who began working with the Fillmores at Unity headquarters in 1899, trained himself by taking part in a wide range of Unity activities in Kansas City. While he worked in Silent Unity as a letter writer, he mailed words to heal correspondents who requested prayer. In addition, he served as a practitioner of spiritual healing for Kansas City clients who came to Unity headquarters to work with him personally. He further prepared himself for conducting the ministerial work of a Unity center by teaching courses on the Bible and by lecturing on Sunday evenings before the Unity Society of Practical Christianity.[1]

In May 1903 Shafer left for Chicago, accompanied by his wife Recca, who had been employed in the Unity printing shop, to begin work as a "Christian teacher and healer."[2] In an article published in *Unity* in August 1903, "A Silent Unity Epistle," Shafer expressed his admiration for the work of Silent Unity and stated his intention to carry on that work in Chicago. He indicated:

Silently, but surely, the mighty current of thought, known as the Silent Unity current, is converting the world to the Truth as it is in Jesus Christ. From my four years' association with the work at Unity headquarters, Kansas City, I can testify of their fidelity and of the pure stream of powerful thought that pours forth from that center to heal the weak world that leans on Jesus Christ. But now I have taken up my residence in Chicago, and from there will speak forth my word in the only name that heals, the name of Jesus Christ.[3]

Unity magazine commented favorably in November 1903 on the quality of Shafer's work in Chicago and indicated that the basic and advanced courses he was teaching in Practical Christianity were patterned after those taught at Unity headquarters by the Fillmores. The magazine stated:

Mr. and Mrs. C. A. Shafer, formerly of Unity Headquarters, are now doing an excellent work in Chicago. They are nicely located at 243 LaSalle Ave. . . . where a good class is now being instructed. The primary course consists of two divisions: The foundation—God, whom Man can and must know; Christ, the divine idea as the universal man . . . the calling forth of all powers . . . the advanced course consists of exercises in concentration and drills, and is of such a nature that it cannot be conveniently outlined. Mr. and Mrs. Shafer teach the I AM doctrine of Spirit, and work on the free-will or love-offering plan, and many have already been blessed under their ministrations.[4]

Unity magazine in June 1904 continued to look with favor upon Shafer's teaching and healing work, and identified the center in which he worked as "Chicago Unity Society of Practical Christianity."[5] In July 1905 *Unity* published the full schedule of weekly services. These included a Sunday morning gathering at 11:00 A.M. Classes were offered during the week in "Concentration and Thought Control, Realization and Inner Development."[6] The Fillmores' satisfaction with Shafer's progress was indicated in a comment contained in the July 1905 issue of *Unity*. They commented, "The Center is becoming one of the strongholds of Truth teaching in Chicago, and good work is being done."[7]

While the center in Chicago received no financial backing from Unity in Kansas City, the Fillmores showed their personal support for Shafer by traveling to Chicago in October 1905 to teach a weeklong course. *Unity* magazine reported:

Great interest is aroused in Chicago in the work being done at the Unity Headquarters there. Mr. and Mrs. Fillmore are teaching a Basic Course and the hall is crowded to its utmost capacity every night. It is a most appreciative and enthusiastic class and among them are a number of prominent physicians, lawyers and ministers and business men. Good healing is being done and the people are thoroughly awake to the Good there is for them.[8]

Unity then noted the magnitude of the work Shafer was doing in Chicago, commenting: "Since going to Chicago Mr. Shafer has had to enlarge his quarters four times, and he is now in Hall 802, Masonic Temple. All classes and meetings are well attended."[9]

From October 1905 until August 1906 *Unity* carried no news of activities at the Chicago center. In August 1906 Shafer traveled to Kansas City to attend the dedication of the new Unity headquarters building and to take the examination for ordination to the Unity ministry.[10] Shafer expressed his strong personal commitment to the Unity movement in response to the question, "Have you dedicated yourselves?" Shafer replied: "I have dedicated myself many, many times as I always do whenever I think of it. I think everyone should do so whenever it comes to him. This body is God's body and I belong to him . . . So I have the pleasure of dedicating myself again, Spirit, Soul and body, to do the work of God in the name of Jesus Christ."[11]

Shafer, who was ordained on August 31, evidently did not return to Chicago after the ordination ceremony but apparently remained in Kansas City until June 1907. During this time there was no news on activity at the Chicago center. In June 1907 in an announcement by Shafer published in *Unity*, it was indicated that he had returned to Chicago, had resumed teaching and healing, and was joining with his wife in the operation of a metaphysical bookstore. Shafer indicated:

I desire to announce to the readers of *Unity* that, after having been in Kansas City cooperating with the Unity workers there since the dedication of the new Unity Building in August last, I have now returned to my home in Chicago and resumed the teaching of the fundamental principles of Practical Christianity, with head-quarters at 87 Washington St. . . . . We have also purchased the business known as the Liberal Book Concern, located in these rooms, which will be under the man-agement of Mrs. Shafer. It is said that we now have, and will continue to carry, the largest stock of metaphysical and occult literature in the world and we will furnish any book of that class of literature—or what is called New Thought—there is in print or procurable . . . I shall give my whole attention to the teaching of the fun-damental principles of Practical Christianity of the Truth which alone can heal man and make him free indeed.[12]

Shafer's work in Chicago was never again mentioned in the pages of *Unity*. There was no news on the whereabouts of either of the Shafers un-til 1917, when Shafer's wife Recca, who at the time had been living in New Baltimore, Michigan, returned to Unity headquarters in Kansas City to take over management of the Unity Inn. In reporting on her arrival, no mention was made of her husband's work in Chicago. Shafer himself was identified only as a former Silent Unity worker. *Daily Unity* reported: "Mrs. Shafer was the founder of the embryonic Unity Inn when the entire work of the Unity Tract Society was in a little frame house down on McGee Street. She lived in the house and cooked lunch for the workers. Mr. Shafer was the first worker in Silent Unity besides Mr. and Mrs. Fill-more, which then consisted of three people."[13]

What happened to Cassius Shafer after June 1907 remains a mystery. No evidence exists that indicates the Chicago Unity Society of Practical Christianity existed beyond October 1905. Shafer himself appears to have simply dropped out of sight. It can be presumed from the language of the 1917 statement in *Daily Unity* that Recca Shafer and her husband were no longer living together. Whether Shafer was alive at the time is un-known.

PROFESSOR LEROY MOORE AND
THE FIRST UNITY SOCIETY OF CHICAGO

Several years before he became actively involved in Unity work, LeRoy Moore enjoyed a career as a New Thought teacher and healer both inside and outside Kansas City. Moore's work was first mentioned in *Unity* in February 1904, when he served as speaker for the "New Thought Club" that held services every Sunday in Woodman Hall.[14] *Unity* continually referred to him as "Professor LeRoy Moore," though the academic credentials that entitled him to be addressed as "Professor" were never published. In November 1904 Moore participated with Charles Fillmore and Divine Science minister D. L. Sullivan in a Union New Thought service held at the Athenium Hall in Kansas City.[15] He also was a participant in the program of the Fourth Annual New Thought Convention held in St. Louis in October 1904, speaking at one of its sessions.[16]

Moore's first involvement with Unity appears to have occurred in 1906. His work as a spiritual healer evidently took him to Unity headquarters, where he remained for at least two years. By 1907 his workload was such that he needed larger quarters and moved to a space down the street. In November 1907 *Unity* published the following report on his work: "Professor LeRoy Moore has taken apartments in the building next to Unity headquarters, his success as a Christian Healer demanding more room. Call him over the Home Phone, Main 6096. He will also respond to calls outside the city for treatment or lectures or teaching."[17]

Moore was one of seventeen persons who applied for ordination to the Unity ministry and took the qualifying examination. He was one of five who failed to receive a passing score. He was allowed at a subsequent date to retake the examination. Though he passed, it is not clear whether he was ever ordained as a Unity minister.[18] Moore continued his work at Unity headquarters and by the summer of 1908 was conducting regular weekly meetings. On Easter Sunday he gave the lesson "Health and Harmony," and conducted the same service during the month of August.[19]

In October 1908 the Kansas City Society of Practical Christianity inaugurated its field lecturer program and LeRoy Moore was selected to be its first field lecturer. It is interesting to note that none of the twelve who were ordained in 1906 was selected for this assignment. An announcement in *Unity* described Moore's credentials and suggested that those who desired to establish centers for Unity work in their communities take advantage of Moore's services. The announcement indicated:

We are prepared to send out into the field a most successful teacher, lecturer and practitioner of Practical Christianity. Do you wish to awaken a greater interest in work already established in your midst? Do you desire to start a Truth Center? Send to us and we will send to you our Professor LeRoy Moore, a teacher and healer whom we recommend, and who has been a co-worker at Unity Headquarters for some years. In case you decide to make such a movement, it is well to arrange for classes beforehand, having place and people ready for work when the Professor comes. Write us for further information.[20]

In the following issue of *Unity* (November 1908), the magazine elaborated further on Moore's work, announcing: "Professor Moore will also cooperate with those who desire to establish Truth Centers, or to build up Centers already established. If you really want to do the Lord's work, form a class right in your own neighborhood and send for Professor Moore to come and give a course of lessons and healing demonstrations."[21]

By early 1909 Moore was on the road as a Unity field lecturer. In February he was in Champaign, Illinois, and conducted what *Unity* described as "a very successful class in Practical Christianity."[22] In April he was in Decatur, Illinois, "teaching a large class and meeting with success under the blessing of the Spirit."[23] In May the magazine announced that a new center, "The Unity Branch of Practical Christianity," had been established in Decatur. "This is the result," *Unity* commented, "of the work of Professor LeRoy Moore, who has been teaching and lecturing in that city and who organized the Center April 16th ... Much enthusiasm is reported and great good will follow." From Decatur, Moore went to Rogers, Arkansas, to lecture, teach, and heal.[24]

Moore spent the summer on vacation in Blossburg, Pennsylvania. *Unity* advised its "Eastern friends" to contact Moore and secure his services "while he is in that part of the country." In November Moore was in Chicago engaged in "Christian healing and teaching" at 2449 Indiana Avenue.[25] In January 1910 Moore was on the road again, teaching classes in Nashville, Tennessee, and Ashville, North Carolina.[26] In February he was teaching in Champaign, Illinois.

In March 1910 Moore returned to Chicago, but not in the capacity of a Unity field lecturer. He had decided to forgo the lecture circuit and to establish a Unity center there. *Unity* magazine announced that Moore had opened a "Unity Truth Center" in the LeMoyne Building at 40 Randolph Street, and that regular classes were held on Mondays, Tuesdays, Thursdays, and Fridays at 2:30 P.M., and a healing service every Wednesday at 2:30 P.M.[27]

In 1910 Moore again spent the summer in Blossburg, Pennsylvania, closing the Chicago center in his absence. He returned, however, in September. In November *Unity* stated that Moore was conducting a "Unity Society of Practical Christianity and doing excellent work teaching classes and healing."[28] Moore evidently combined this work with field lecturing, since in December he went to Detroit, where he taught a large class. According to *Unity* "great interest and enthusiasm are reported."[29] In January 1911 Moore returned to his Chicago center and apparently gave up field lecturing for good. In October 1911 the center changed its name to "The Unity Society of Chicago." At that time, a membership of thirty was reported.

After 1911 Moore's work was mentioned only on rare occasions. Brief notices appeared in 1914, 1917, and 1918. It appears that for the next several years the Chicago center operated on a full schedule of services, classes, and meetings. The November 1917 announcement stated: "First Unity Society of Chicago, order of services; Sunday morning in Silence at 10:30, lecture at 11 o'clock at Auditorium Lyceum Hall. Order of Classes, Monday and Thursday evening at 7:30. Healing Class Wednesday afternoon at 2:30. Only free will offerings received . . . Mr. and Mrs. LeRoy Moore in charge."[30]

CHARLES EDGAR PRATHER AND THE
SECOND DIVINE SCIENCE CHURCH OF DENVER

The son of a Methodist minister, Charles Edgar Prather was in his early thirties when he came to Unity in 1899. Like Cassius Shafer, he performed a wide range of duties during his eight-year stay at Unity headquarters. In addition to being the business manager of the Unity Tract Society, the organization that produced Unity books and magazines, Prather served as director of the Sunday services for the Unity Society of Practical Christianity, as assistant superintendent of the Sunday school, and as a member of the society's board of directors.[31]

Prather was Unity's most active participant in the work of the International New Thought Federation, playing a role in the planning and organizing of the federation's annual meetings in Chicago in 1903; in Nevada, Missouri, in 1904; in St. Louis in 1905; and in Denver in 1906. He presented a paper at the 1904 convention entitled "Man His Own Redeemer." *Unity* magazine applauded it and noted that Prather "delivered an able and forceful argument for toleration in all phases of thought and life and proved the power of men to redeem themselves from all inharmony." His articles in *Unity* magazine, particularly one entitled "What Is the

New Thought?" helped alert readers to the development of the movement. In 1904 the members of the federation honored him by electing him as one of its five officers.[32]

In August 1906 Prather served on the Kansas City Unity Society of Practical Christianity's examining committee for ordination to the Unity ministry. Charles and Myrtle Fillmore prepared the examination questions. Seventeen Unity students, including Prather, took the examination. Prather was one of twelve who passed. On August 31 he was ordained with the eleven others. In accepting ordination, he commented: "Ever since I came into the knowledge of Truth it has been a blessing. Never have I faltered in my intention to live the life . . . and I now dedicate myself to the Truth."[33]

Given his background and credentials, Prather would have been an ideal candidate to serve as a field lecturer or center leader. Instead, on April 23, 1907, less than one year after his ordination, Prather submitted his resignation from Unity. In a letter to Charles and Myrtle Fillmore, he indicated his intention "to enter into a broader service to humanity."[34] Prather closed his letter to the Fillmores stating, "I will leave you a loyal friend and trust that we may cooperate in the future for the upliftment of humanity."[35] The Fillmores responded by commenting favorably on his eight years of "faithful and most efficient service." Prather took with him, they said, "our blessings and our best wishes for his success and prosperity, and the love and respect of his co-workers."[36]

Prather left Unity in 1907 to join Divine Science teacher Nona Brooks in Denver and associated himself with the Denver Divine Science College. Not long after his arrival in Denver, Prather assumed the pastorate of the Second Divine Science Church of Denver, a post he held until his death in 1930.[37] In Denver Prather founded a New Thought magazine entitled *Power*, which he edited and published for over a decade. In 1910 he authored a book entitled *Spiritual Healing*. A review of the book in *Unity* magazine complimented Prather for presenting information concerning healing that was "necessary to a clear understanding of the principle involved." While in Denver, Prather also continued to involve himself deeply in the work of the International New Thought Federation. One of the few times he returned to Kansas City was in 1920, when Unity hosted the organization's annual convention.

Prather's leaving Kansas City was clearly a loss to the Unity movement. His eight-year association with the Fillmores at Unity headquarters equipped him to play an expanded role at a time when the leaders of the Unity Society of Practical Christianity had expressed their intention to establish libraries and centers outside Kansas City. Few others in Unity at the time possessed Prather's credentials for developing new centers outside Kansas City. We can only speculate why Prather left Unity. It is possible that, given his strong commitment to New Thought, he disagreed with the Fillmores' decision in 1907 to withdraw from the New Thought Federation. In Divine Science he may have found a metaphysical group committed to advancing the work of the federation. It is also possible that, after eight years at Unity headquarters, he needed a bigger challenge than Unity was able to provide. He may have concluded that the Unity structure did not give sufficient support to its workers who went into the field either as lecturers or as center leaders. Last, he may not have felt fully appreciated by the Fillmores. A comment made in passing in his letter of resignation indicates that, as a professional member of the Unity Tract Society staff, he did not feel that he was given the respect his position deserved. Prather stated, "My only suggestion is that a business manager should be considered as such and not merely a clerk."[38]

While Prather chose to work through the auspices of the College of Divine Science, it is likely that the favorable reviews of his writings that appeared in *Unity* magazine, as well as the occasional references to his work, came about because his metaphysical teaching continued to be aligned with that of Unity.

JUDGE HENRY H. BENSON AND THE UNITY CENTER OF PRACTICAL-SCIENTIFIC CHRISTIANITY, LOS ANGELES

Judge Henry H. Benson was identified with New Thought groups for several years before he became associated with Unity. His work was first brought to the attention of readers of *Unity* magazine in November 1904, when he was listed as speaker for the New Thought League of Kansas City.[39] In March 1905 Judge Benson (it was never stated where or when he served in the judiciary) was listed as the speaker at services held every Sunday at 8:00 P.M. for the New Thought Center.[40] Benson was also associated with the International New Thought Federation, speaking at its annual convention in Chicago in October 1906. In addition, at the federation's business meeting in Chicago in October, Benson was elected second vice president of the organization.[41]

In 1906 Benson began his work with Unity, an association that lasted until 1918. In February Benson began speaking regularly on Sunday evenings at 8:00 P.M. in Unity auditorium. It is not clear when he fully identified himself with the Kansas City Unity Society of Practical Christianity. He was not a candidate for ordination in August 1906, something he might have done if he had wished to fully identify himself at the time with Unity teaching. In 1908 he appeared to have aligned himself more closely with Unity, because his Sunday evening lectures were labeled "Unity Meetings."[42]

In January 1909 Judge Benson and his wife moved to Oklahoma City for the purpose of establishing a Unity center there. In May *Unity* reported that the Bensons had firmly established themselves and that the success they were having was due to their long experience in spiritual work. The magazine stated:

Judge Henry H. and Mrs. Benson have established a permanent center in Oklahoma City, Oklahoma. They are teaching classes in Truth with great success. This part of our country has long needed a work of this kind, and now that such experienced spiritual teachers and healers are located in one of the most flourishing cities in the new state, we may look for encouraging results.[43]

Unity carried no further reports on the work of the Bensons until June 1911, when the editor of the "Notes from the Field" column, after crediting the Bensons with "conducting a very successful work in Oklahoma City," noted that the couple was planning to spend the summer on the West Coast visiting several major cities.[44] The magazine further indicated that the Bensons were looking for speaking and teaching engagements. While the Bensons proposed speaking engagements that could have been described as "Unity field lectures," that terminology was never used to characterize their effort in the West. The following itinerary was listed along with Unity's description of the nature of their work: "On July 1st they go directly to Long Beach, California ... They expect to visit San Francisco, Portland and Seattle before returning to Oklahoma. Arrangements may be made with the Judge to deliver lectures or for courses of lessons and engagements to speak, teach or heal."[45]

Though it was never fully acknowledged in *Unity* magazine, the underlying purpose of the Bensons trip to the far West appears to have been to cut their ties in Oklahoma and to find a suitable place to establish a new center. They did not return to Oklahoma City, but announced their intention in November 1911 to open a center of Practical Christianity in Los Angeles.[46] *Unity* never indicated why the Bensons left Oklahoma City or whether another center leader was selected to serve the Unity community in Oklahoma City. The name of Benson's new center in Los Angeles was revealed in December, along with the schedule of services. The center was called "The Unity Center of Practical-Scientific Christianity," and Sunday services were being held in the Independent Church of Christ at Seventeenth and Figueroa Streets.[47]

No further mention was made of the Bensons' work in Los Angeles or of the Unity center they founded there. It was two years before their activities were covered again in *Unity*. In December 1913 it was reported that the couple had just completed "a successful tour" through northern California and Washington, and had returned to their apartment in Los Angeles.[48] Another two-year lapse in information on the Bensons occurred between 1913 and 1915. In May 1915 they were reported doing healing work in San Francisco.[49] After another three-year silence, *Unity* noted that the Bensons could be found in Long Beach, California. Evidently Judge Benson was still engaged in Unity work, because the article stated: "Treatments for health and teachings of the principles of Practical Christianity could be secured upon application."[50] *Unity* carried no further information on the work of the Bensons.

SOPHIA VAN MARTER AND THE UNITY SOCIETY OF PRACTICAL CHRISTIANITY OF NEW YORK CITY

Mrs. Sophia Van Marter became associated with Unity in Kansas City in 1907 and rose quickly to a position of leadership, first at Unity headquarters in Kansas City and then in the field. An Englishwoman, her talents as a speaker became evident almost immediately. In August 1908 she was assigned to give the lessons on "Health and Harmony," offered at Unity headquarters on Wednesday and Saturday afternoons from 3:30 to 4:00 P.M.[51] At the Unity Society Christmas service in 1908, she was listed as the "assistant" to the speaker, Charles Fillmore.[52] She taught a Bible class, worked in Silent Unity as a spiritual healer, and in May 1909 was elected to the board of directors of the Kansas City Unity Society of Practical Christianity.

In June 1909 Van Marter left Kansas City to work as a field lecturer on the West Coast, establishing headquarters in Seattle. In June 1909 *Unity* magazine publicized her intention to work with Unity centers in the West. A statement in the magazine indicated the high regard for Mrs. Van Marter at Unity headquarters. *Unity* stated:

Mrs. Sophia Van Marter, who has been associated with the Unity Society in Kansas City for the past two years, and who is a most capable and successful teacher and healer, is going to the Pacific Coast for the summer, and will be open to engagements anywhere in that locality. Mrs. Van Marter is one who embodies in her work the very substance of the Spirit and adds character to the teaching she gives, for she *lives* the Truth she proclaims. As an accomplished lecturer she endeared herself to the whole Unity household and goes out from us with the love and blessing of each one with whom she has been connected. Unity Society endorses and recommends Mrs. Van Marter, knowing that any society or community which may secure her services will receive great benefit.[53]

While in the West, Mrs. Van Marter taught two classes in Practical Christianity in Seattle before returning to Unity headquarters in the fall. She remained in Kansas City until the following summer, when she left for the East Coast. She planned to teach and heal there before returning to England on vacation. The high esteem Van Marter was held in by her coworkers was indicated by the sendoff she received at Unity headquarters. *Unity* reported:

Mrs. Van Marter's services have been highly appreciated by Unity people, and warm welcome awaits her whenever she shall return to us. Wherever she may minister her hearers, her students, her patients, all may be sure of the most faithful and careful attention and able exposition of the principles underlying the Science of Being and Christian Living. Unity Society gave her a rousing Testimonial service, morning, afternoon and evening of the last Sunday she was with us and sent her forth with a royal God-speed.[54]

After a vacation in her native England, Mrs. Van Marter returned to the United States but she did not proceed to Kansas City, choosing to remain in New York City, first to teach classes, then to found a Unity center in Manhattan.[55] By March 1911 it appeared that she had established herself. *Unity* reported: "nearly every mail brings letters from our New York friends, telling of some good that they have received from the work there." *Unity* also published a letter from Van Marter in which she reported on activities at the new center. She wrote: "God is mightily blessing our work here. The meetings are well attended and I am kept busy all day long—really from early morning until late at night. Ever and ever so many people are glad we have a Unity Center in New York, and I am sure it will grow into a pillar of light and life."[56]

In 1912 *Unity* reported twice on the activities at the center in New York. In 1913 *Unity* lauded the good work that was being done by Mrs.

Van Marter, noted the continued growth of the center, and appealed to Unity students in the city to support the work being carried on there. The magazine commented:

The Unity Society of Practical Christianity, 305 Madison Avenue, New York, has now a Sunday evening meeting. The other meetings and classes are continued as heretofore. Mrs. Van Marter and her co-workers are being blessed in their ministry in the great city. There is a steady increase in attendance at the classes and open meetings, and the people are more and more appreciating the pure truth taught there. Our New York friends should see to it that their faithful workers are sustained in all ways.[57]

The New York center evidently continued to grow, and Mrs. Van Marter reported in August 1915 that the society "is in a most flourishing condition" and that "a real new baptism of the Holy Ghost has come in and upon us."[58] By 1916 the New York center had expanded to the point that much larger quarters were necessary. A four-story brownstone house at 28 West 72nd Street was leased and converted into classrooms, offices, and an auditorium.[59] In June 1916 Mrs. Van Marter made a trip back to Kansas City, evidently her first return to Unity headquarters since leaving for New York in 1910. Her visit was properly noted, as was her Sunday talk before the Kansas City Unity Society of Practical Christianity.[60]

In May 1918 Mrs. Sophia Van Marter evidently resigned her position as center leader of New York Unity Society of Practical Christianity to return to her native England. *Unity* magazine expressed concern that the New York center might not continue under the leadership of a Unity-trained center leader, because William Weston, president of the Society of the Inner Life, would be in charge of the center. *Unity* reported: "Mr. Weston has not been directly associated with Unity work, and as we are not familiar with his teaching we cannot say how clearly his presentation of the Truth will correspond with that adopted by the Unity School of Practical Christianity. Our New York students will have to judge for themselves in this respect."[61]

A number of Unity students at the New York center evidently were not satisfied with Weston, because one year later, in June 1919, he was no longer its leader. Jennie Croft, who had worked at Unity headquarters in a variety of capacities for two decades, including as a field lecturer, went to New York to troubleshoot and take over the leadership of the center on a temporary basis. Her job was to present "the principles of Truth as taught by the Unity School" and to help form a nucleus of people that would ultimately "effect a permanent organization."[62] Croft returned to Kansas City in December, according to *Unity* magazine, having "completed a very successful ministry in New York."

RICHARD LYNCH AND THE NEW YORK UNITY SOCIETY OF PRACTICAL CHRISTIANITY

Richard Lynch was a Kansas City native who was involved with Unity work from a young age. He was employed by Unity while in his early twenties and spent several years working at Unity headquarters in a variety of capacities. In 1918 at age twenty-eight, he was sent out by Unity School to work as a Unity field lecturer. He conducted Sunday services in May at the Unity Society in St. Joseph, Missouri. He went on to Cleveland in September and during October and November lectured in Iowa, Illinois, Indiana, and Ohio. He returned to Kansas City in February 1919.[63] He was on the road again in the fall, this time to New York City. Lynch came to the New York Unity Society of Practical Christianity in October 1919, while Jennie Croft was still serving on a temporary basis. In January 1920, just after Croft returned to Kansas City, Lynch was invited to take charge of the New York center. Evidently Lynch did not make an immediate decision, although he remained in New York through the spring of 1920. According to a correspondent from the New York congregation, Lynch had done "wonderful work" and his teaching was in great demand. In July 1920, however, he was in Los Angeles working as field lecturer. Again, his ability to speak and hold a congregation was evident. A report from Los Angeles quoted in *Weekly Unity* indicated good results: "The result of Richard Lynch's meeting here, as a field lecturer, is most gratifying and inspiring to all who attended. Everyone is praising and giving thanks to the Father for this good work. Each message has found its way deeply into the hearts of many people. All keenly feel the Christ Spirit as given forth by Mr. Lynch. Every word is bearing a wealth of spiritual fruit."[64]

In late summer Lynch left Los Angeles and returned to New York. In October *Unity* reported that the New York congregation grew rapidly upon his return. It indicated: "The work of the New York Unity society has received a great impetus since the return of its speaker, Richard Lynch, the audience almost doubling in number and overflowing the ball room of the Astor Hotel. Many people testified to healing and uplift from his powerful message of spiritual Truth."[65]

One month later, in November, *Unity* magazine carried a report from the leaders of the New York congregation. It indicated that Lynch had accepted a permanent appointment, and that great things were expected of him. The report stated: "The Unity Society of New York City is glad to announce that Richard Lynch has accepted their call to remain with them as their permanent speaker. He has built up a large and growing center, and his powerful message is much needed in this city."[66]

Lynch remained in New York City for sixteen years, returning to Kansas City in 1936 to serve as a lecturer and teacher in Unity's ministerial training program. Lynch was a prolific writer and during his career was the author of thirteen books and many magazine articles. He was the first Unity center leader who was able to sustain a ministry on a long-term basis.

Unity Field Department (1919–1965)

INTRODUCTION

Many Unity students who completed the correspondence course, attended classes in Kansas City, and read Unity literature sought to establish centers of Unity work in their local communities. In 1919 Unity School decided to support these efforts by establishing a "Field Department" within Unity School. The Field Department saw its mission as "assisting in organizing study classes and centers among groups of students who are interested in applying the Jesus Christ principles in their lives and in their affairs."[1] The purpose of the work was "to encourage cooperation, harmony and constructive methods in the advancement of Truth."[2]

The Field Department provided operating guidelines for centers and churches; facilitated the development of "study classes" in local communities; published a newsletter, the *Field Department Bulletin*, that kept ministers and teachers informed on matters of mutual interest and gave helpful suggestions about work in the field; published a directory of centers and churches in *Unity* magazine; sent Unity-trained lecturers to local groups to provide advice and counsel; and organized an annual conference each summer at Unity Village.[3] In addition, the Field Department participated with the Unity Training School in the ordination of ministers and the licensing of Unity teachers. Since 1965 these functions have been performed by the Association of Unity Churches, an independent nonprofit organization not affiliated with Unity School of Christianity.

UNITY STUDY CLASSES

In 1917 *Unity* magazine began urging its readers in towns and cities to form study classes. A "study class" was a Unity center in miniature. The work, however, was less formal, requiring a minimum of organizational structure and leadership.[4] The rationale for study classes was presented in *Unity* magazine: "One is helped . . . by meeting with people whose desires, thoughts, realizations and manner of expression conform to his own. It is for this reason that Unity School encourages the organization of classes for cooperative study. We gladly assist in forming study classes in any city or town, and we have a special department which looks after this work."[5]

One of the advantages of a study class was that no leader was required. *Unity* magazine indicated:

In order to have effective Unity work in any community it is not at all necessary to have a leader. Cooperative study is often of more value than merely listening to some leader expound his realizations of Truth. For this reason the Unity study class is becoming more and more popular. It is estimated that Unity literature now is read by a million people every month, and nearly every community has enough interested Unity students to form a good study class. There is therefore no reason why every community should not have its own study class. . . . Remember that under our study class plan there is no particular need of having a leader. All that is necessary is a group of interested students who wish to study together. We can doubtless help you to get a group together.[6]

By the early 1920s, *Unity* was urging A STUDY CLASS IN EVERY COMMUNITY. Ease of organization and administration was a key advantage. The magazine commented: "About the only thing that is necessary, in the organizing of such a class, is for someone to make arrangements for a place to hold the opening meeting and to notify us a few weeks in advance. We will notify our readers of the meeting. In this way a class is easily brought together."[7]

In 1924 the study-class idea was catching on. During the year ending March 1, 1924, Unity School received 800 inquiries in relation to the organization of study classes, and 340 new study classes were reported to have been organized.[8] The emphasis on study classes and centers, as opposed to churches and ministries, supported the long-held position of Charles and Myrtle Fillmore that Unity—although it presented a spiritual teaching and its work was in the field of religion—was not a sect, nor was it a church. This position was presented most succinctly in a statement in *Weekly Unity* in April 1913: "The Unity Society is not a church, but a school for the training and discipline of all who would develop spiritually. It aims to prepare teachers for the work of spreading the Truth. In keeping, therefore, with our mission, every session should bear out the school ideas and each member of the various classes should enter heartily into his privileges as a student."[9]

As the Unity centers grew stronger and trained new leaders were available, the study-class program declined. No study classes were reported after 1930.

UNITY FIELD LECTURER PROGRAM

As the Fillmores committed themselves to supporting the development of Unity libraries and centers outside Kansas City, they realized that literature alone would not provide all the necessary knowledge and information. If centers for Unity teaching were to be established across America, Unity headquarters must send out men and women thoroughly grounded in Unity teachings to provide fledgling groups with counsel and advice. New centers often asked for help. "There are calls for teachers and lecturers," it was noted in *Unity* in May 1906, "from all parts of the country coming in constantly."[10] Unity pledged itself to provide lecturers who were sufficiently trained to give the needed aid. "This school," it was stated, "will meet the demand."[11]

The first field lecturer from Unity headquarters to travel to centers outside Kansas City was Professor LeRoy Moore. In 1908, two years before he became the leader of the Chicago Unity Center of Practical Christianity, Moore traveled from city to city, mainly in the Midwest and East, providing assistance to centers that requested help. During the thirteen years from the time the field lecturer program was established until 1919, when the Unity Field Lecture Department was established, only a few Unity teachers served as field lecturers. Most of those who did participate in the early years—like Judge Henry Benson, Sophia Van Marter, and Moore—accepted the invitation of a local group to found a center within a short time after they began touring on the lecture circuit.

It appears that despite a strong 1906 statement of intention to establish a field lecture program, no serious effort was made for over a decade to start this project. In February 1916, Unity began to offer a training program for workers at Unity headquarters who were interested in becoming field lecturers. A news release for Unity staff asked, "Do you want to be a teacher of Truth?"[12] It went on to explain:

Many workers at Unity have a more or less clearly defined ideal of themselves as public lecturers of the Truth. Many are afraid to make the start, to get up before a real audience and speak; others are willing, but feel that they need training and practice. For these people who feel the urge of Truth within calling for expression, we have decided to offer an opportunity for practice and training in lecturing.[13]

In 1916 Kate Nevill, an Australian woman in her late twenties who had worked at Unity headquarters for several years, began a four-year career as a field lecturer. She traveled outside Kansas City almost constantly, lecturing from New York to California and from Montana to Texas. Her ability as a speaker was revealed in an item in *Daily Unity* on September 25, 1911:

In a heart-stirring lecture yesterday morning, Miss Kate Nevill set a good many people to thinking about their conditions in life. Her language was simple enough to be understood by all, and her gestures sometimes verged on the dramatic. Her audience was not by any means asleep when she began her talk, but she certainly did wake them up. She created anew, in many people who just take this truth as a matter of course, the desire to really make demonstrations.[14]

Nevill drew sizable crowds wherever she went. During a lecture tour of Nebraska in the summer of 1916, *Daily Unity* reported that during the two months she was on the road, the average attendance at her lectures, even on the hottest days, was about two hundred.[15] Between 1916 and 1920 Nevill, who was ordained as a Unity minister in 1918, was by far the most traveled of the Unity field lecturers. In June 1918 *Unity* magazine listed the names of the Unity School field lecturers. In addition to Nevill, there were six others: Mary O'Neill, E. V. Ingraham, Ida Mingle, Richard Lynch, George Huston, and Jennie Croft. Of those listed, only Nevill had, up to that date, traveled extensively outside Kansas City.

In August 1919 *Unity* magazine announced that the demand for Unity lecturers had increased and that a Field Lecturer Department had been established within Unity School to deal with the increasing workload. The announcement in *Unity* stated:

From every corner of the globe the call for Unity lecturers and teachers is increasing. More and more are the people seeking to understand clearly the principles taught by this School. In an attempt to meet this demand, the Unity School is constantly seeking to evolve plans whereby the Truth may be more broadly and effectively presented. Their latest effort in this direction has been to establish a Field Lecture Department to look after this branch of work. As rapidly as possible, lecturers and teachers thoroughly familiar with Unity principles and ideas are being sent to communities calling for instructors. A plan has been evolved whereby centers and study groups in other cities may easily secure the services of one of the Unity lecturers, and particulars may be secured by communicating direct with the Field Lecturer Department.[16]

This announcement also indicated that three field lecturers were available for bookings: Nevill, Richard Lynch, and Viva January. By 1920 Nevill had given up the work, having married and settled down outside Kansas City. Lynch traveled extensively in 1919 before taking charge of the work at Unity Society of Practical Christianity in New York in January 1920. Viva January traveled for about one year before becoming the center leader of the Church of Life and Joy in Washington, D.C. Ida Mingle, a longtime Unity worker, began field lecturing in 1918; like many field lecturers before her, she accepted a center leadership position. Her choice was the First Unity Society of Chicago.[17] The experience of Lynch, January, and Mingle was similar to that of Moore, Benson, and Van Marter a decade earlier. After a short time traveling, field lecturers opted for the more settled life of a Unity center leader.

During the 1920s and the early 1930s, the Unity Field Department sent out several well-trained and committed lecturers to work with Unity centers requesting help. E. V. Ingraham, Francis J. Gable, H. B. Jeffery, Ralph Boileau, and Ernest Wilson, each an important staff member of Unity School, made periodic trips outside Kansas City. Wilson and Ingraham ultimately accepted the call to lead a center, but only after having spent several years in fieldwork. In 1929 Ingraham, who had worked at Unity headquarters in a variety of capacities for two decades, reported that he had talked with over thirty thousand people in three hundred lectures and had traveled over three thousand miles.[18]

Ralph Boileau, who headed the Field Department for several years, also traveled extensively. He developed a course called "The Absolute Science of Truth," which he gave in large cities in the United States. *Unity* gave the following description of the nature of Boileau's efforts to support the work of centers in the field. It reported:

The most valuable part of instruction lies not in lecture work alone, but in the phase of the work that embraces, on the part of the individual, definite study and application of the principles taught. The value of closed-class work has been emphasized, and out of this revelation has come the course known as the Absolute Science of Truth, now being given by Ralph E. Boileau in the larger cities in the United States. The course is now being given in the form of eight or ten open lectures followed by closed-class instruction in which each member of the class registers for enrollment and thereby agrees to follow through with the seven constructive lessons in the course. This class has been given recently in Jacksonville, Florida; Detroit, Michigan; and Cleveland, Ohio with very gratifying results.[19]

Unity viewed this approach to be highly successful and reported in October 1930 on the results of Boileau's work: "The closed classes following the R. E. Boileau lecture campaigns in Jacksonville and Detroit proved to be a marked success. In each instance there was a large enrollment and the general atmosphere was one of sincere interest and enthusiasm."[20]

Unity School's *Field Department Bulletin* occasionally provided news on the activities of its field lecturers. An announcement in the December 1931 issue of the *Bulletin* is indicative of the kind of reports published:

Francis J. Gable, upon his return from lecture engagements in Texas, reports encouraging growth and activity in the centers visited.

E. V. Ingraham's lectures through the state of Montana show increased attendance over the last year's work there, and an encouraging evidence of Spirit activity in the local class and center groups. Mr. Ingraham's lectures in Winnipeg, Canada, and in Minneapolis met with enthusiastic response.

H. B. Jeffery's lecture work through Ohio and cities in New York brought a hearty response from the leaders of the centers where he spoke, as well as from individual students.

Kate Nevill Orange, who is well known and loved by many students throughout the country as a Unity teacher and lecturer, but who had not been active in the work for some three or four years, filled a lecture engagement with Unity Temple in San Francisco this summer.[21]

One of the most extensive field lecture tours was conducted in 1937 by Charles Fillmore himself. Then eighty-three years old, he traveled for five months with his second wife, Cora, throughout the western United States. *Unity* reported:

During January and February 1937 Charles and Cora Fillmore gave fifty-eight talks in Unity center classes in Los Angeles, California and vicinity. During March Mr. and Mrs. Fillmore lectured in Oakland, San Francisco and Alameda. On Easter Sunday they opened their engagement in Portland, Oregon with thirteen hundred in attendance. After leaving Portland they were at the Seattle, Washington Unity center for two weeks. Subsequently they lectured in Yakima, Washington;

Bozeman, Butte, Livingston and Billings, Montana; Denver, Colorado Springs and Pueblo, Colorado; arriving in Kansas City the first week in May.[22]

Unity continued to send lecturers into the field during World War II even though travel was restricted. In August 1944 the Field Department reported on the upcoming work of Francis Gable and Richard Lynch. It stated: "This fall Francis J. Gable will visit centers in Illinois, Ohio and Indiana. In the new year it is planned that he will speak in California . . . Richard Lynch will be available to cover the East and such societies as Syracuse, Rochester, Buffalo, Detroit and Cincinnati."[23] After World War II the field lecture program accelerated. It was the goal of Unity School to have a field lecturer visit a Unity center at least once annually. The school saw it as a valuable service. In April 1948 a Field Department letter stated: "We try to send a field lecturer to each center once a year, as nearly as possible. The purpose of this is three-fold: first, to stimulate interest in the local center; second, to assist the leader in any way possible; and third, to establish a closer contact between the work in the field and Unity headquarters."[24]

Unity literature in the 1950s contains little or no information on the activities of field lecturers. The program was evidently discontinued. No explanation was given in the public record as to why it was dropped.

OPERATING GUIDELINES FOR CENTERS AND CHURCHES

While Unity headquarters expected Unity centers to confine their teaching to those of Unity, not all centers complied with these wishes. By 1916 the Fillmores recognized that this matter needed to be addressed, because complaints were being received at Unity headquarters from students who indicated that centers were presenting teachings that contradicted those of Unity. Charles, in a commentary in the "Publisher's Department" of the March 1916 issue of *Unity,* expressed exasperation with center leaders whose teachings were at odds with those of Unity. He pointed out:

Coming to us from various quarters are letters telling of Unity centers that are not teaching the Unity doctrine. These letters ask how we can endorse these centers which take our name when they depart so radically from what is set forth in our literature. We do not endorse them. We do not endorse anybody's teaching. It is all we can do to endorse our own, let alone hold up the standard set by many teachers now so profusely scattered throughout the country.[25]

While Charles made it clear that Unity School did not endorse centers' teaching diluted doctrine, Unity headquarters did not dictate to centers, even though incorrect teachings were presented. He observed:

Many of our readers take for granted that we have established the Unity centers that are carrying on propaganda work in our name. This is a wrong supposition. We are a school, but not a church, nor a society with branches. The Unity centers are independent movements and we have no jurisdiction or directive over them. We have no copyright on the name "Unity" and cannot prevent anyone from using it.[26]

Charles wanted it understood that Unity's basic mission was to provide literature that spelled out the Unity teachings. Those who used the true teachings, in Charles's view, got marvelous results. Unity, however, had no desire to force the teachings on anyone or to act as a policing agent. He explained:

Over a quarter of a century ago we began sending out literature advocating life based upon the plain teachings of Jesus. Our explanations of what Jesus taught were so simple and practical that people began applying them, and the results were just as promised in the New Testament. As the years go on, people are more and more accepting this simple doctrine, and we are finding our hands full in supplying the literature. Thus we do not have the time, even if we had the inclination, to censor the teaching of the various Unity centers. The only way to measure them is by that sure plumb-line given by Jesus: "By their fruits ye shall know them."[27]

These statements did not put the matter to rest and Charles felt compelled a year later, in May 1917, to respond to a Unity student who thought Unity headquarters should take more responsibility for what was being taught in the centers. Charles took the position that given Unity's teachings about the importance of consulting the indwelling presence to determine spiritual truth, it was impossible to require centers to adhere to specific doctrines, even though it was desirable that they do so. He commented: "The Spirit of Truth is the One Teacher and Guide, and each one who is called to the work of establishing meetings in any place where those interested in spiritual unfoldment may gather together for mutual benefit, must be led by his own indwelling Spirit of Truth, not by us nor by the Spirit through us."[28]

Charles believed that all students of truth were engaged in a continuing process of discovery, and what was believed true today might not be believed true tomorrow, hence the need for openness to new possibilities. He explained:

One must know the peculiar needs of the people to whom he is ministering to be able to decide just how to reach and aid them. Neither could we set forth any specific creed or dogma for others to follow, because we are all progressing, and will no doubt in a year from now be far ahead of that which we are giving out today. We are glad to help all we can by prayer or instruction in Truth but we would not dare to do anything that would tend to lessen the freedom of even our students to progress in their own way.[29]

Charles concluded that Unity headquarters should not take responsibility for the operation of Unity centers, because both Unity and the centers needed to be free to follow their own inner guidance. Charles, however, did not want to be associated with those centers that used the Unity name but diluted the teaching. He stated: "There may possibly be some so-called Unity Centers that we would not care to have associated with us ... since they would be our representatives, in a way, and would not be giving out a right idea at all, of the Truth we are seeking to promulgate. Therefore we feel that we must be free and allow all others the same liberty."[30]

Although Unity headquarters had encouraged Unity students to found centers since 1903 and to conduct study classes since 1917, guidelines had never been developed that might be used by leaders interested in either operating a center or facilitating a study class. In 1924 the field department of Unity School, which was described as "a field station for centers, classes and teachers," developed a six-part document entitled "Methods and Ideals for Conducting Centers and Study Classes." It dealt with organization, administration, teaching and healing work, and financing of both centers and study classes.[31]

The goal of the field department document was to aid leaders and centers and study classes to develop "the ways and means of building up a successful work." "Methods and Ideals" was the result of study over a period of several years of the activities of centers and classes. It attempted to answer questions most asked by center leaders and teachers and to provide a "general method of procedure" whereby individuals in a center could work most effectively together. The ultimate goal was to provide a road map for "those who feel the urge of Spirit to take up this work."

1. Teaching Truth Principles

"Methods and Ideals" stressed the fact that a center or study class, to be a true representative of Unity, must present the true teachings of Jesus.

This work consisted of "interpreting and explaining Practical Christianity and the workable nature of Divine Law." "Methods and Ideals" made this point explicit when it suggested: "The only permanent work that a Truth center or study class can accomplish is the thorough grounding of its students and workers in an understanding of the underlying Principle of Life, which we call God."[32] It went on to explain:

There can be but one reason for organizing a center or study class along Truth lines, and that is, for a fuller expression of Christian principles than is ordinarily permitted in the regular church organizations. The commands of Jesus, "Go ye into all the world, and preach the Gospel," "Heal the sick," "Raise the dead," "Cleanse the lepers," "Cast out demons," should be the ideals governing every center and study class.[33]

A primary objective of the teaching in a center or study class was to provide an atmosphere in which students would be able to connect with the indwelling Spirit and to find that place within where truth was revealed. "Methods and Ideals" indicated: "It would seem that the primary object of a center's ministry is to acquaint its individual students with the power and the presence of God within themselves, and to establish them in conscious relationships with the Spirit of truth within themselves."[34]

"Methods and Ideals" emphasized the fact students must learn to find truth for themselves and not rely on a teacher for obtaining it. It suggested:

The knowledge of greater importance to the seeker of Truth is not in what someone else is teaching, or in what someone else has taught or written, or in what any religious system is teaching; it is in what the Spirit of Truth within the individual reveals to him. The inspiration of Truth within each individual is the only source from which real understanding can come to that individual. No man really knows the things of God except the Spirit of God in him which will reveal them.[35]

Two books were recommended for study classes: *Lessons in Truth* by H. Emilie Cady and *Christian Healing* by Charles Fillmore.

2. Spiritual Healing

In addition to teaching truth principles, it was essential that each center or class incorporate spiritual healing into its regular activities. "Methods and Ideals" indicated:

One of the outstanding phases of the ministry of a Truth center is its healing work. To be a true exponent of practical Christianity, a center must not only recognize healing as a part of Christianity, but must make the healing work a practical part of the center's ministry . . . A Truth center should be strong in its healing ministry . . . The most successful centers and study classes are those that have established a strong healing ministry as a part of their work.[36]

Spiritual healing, the document indicated, grew out of the student's capacity to create union with the power and presence of God. "Methods and Ideals" noted: "Spiritual healing is the direct relation of the all-conquering power of God. A spiritual healer endeavors to expand his consciousness to comprehend more and more of the allness of God, to let the emanations be the voicing of divine impulses."[37] True spiritual healers, "Methods and Ideals" indicated, worked with words—powerful words—rather than by physical means of any kind, particularly bodily contact. The document continued:

Many methods of healing are now in vogue in the modern movement toward the re-establishment of spiritual healing in connection with religious organizations. Most of these methods produce problems which we feel can be avoided if the healing ministry is confined to the plan followed by Jesus in the case of the centurion's servant. The account of this healing shows that by speaking the healing word Jesus Christ restored the centurion's servant to health. One who has made study of metaphysics soon learns that words are a stronger medium than hands for transmitting the healing power. Too often, when one makes a practice of laying on hands, his own personality enters into the practice and he descends to the plain of magnetic healing.[38]

Meditation was a highly recommended spiritual practice for all Unity centers and study classes because it established a state of consciousness from which healing work could proceed. "Methods and Ideals" pointed out:

We should always remember that it is not the teacher or the teaching that is important. The important thing is to help each individual to a realization of Truth for himself. This readily leads us to the realization that with the teaching presented in a center there must be ample provision for meditation by the leader and by the student. Only in the stillness can each individual come to a realization of his own indwelling Lord . . . Ample provision should be made for silent meditation in all centers and classes.[39]

The document continued: "The great purpose of meditation is man's realization of the power and presence of God as an actual working principle within the life of the individual, and not only for his own enlightenment and physical exaltation, but for the radiation of Spirit for the uplift of his fellow man everywhere."[40]

While meditation facilitated the healing work of the center or study class, so did regular healing meetings. When people engaged in spiritual healing together as a group, that good work was accomplished and a strong community consciousness was developed in the center. "Methods and Ideals" noted:

It is well, particularly in centers, to establish regular healing meetings at which various members of the center take an active part in sending forth the realization of the healing power of Spirit. In such meetings is the real strength of a center, and when this phase of the ministry is developed to a great degree, the center will be a strong factor in lifting the consciousness of the community from a material to a spiritual level.[41]

Centers in which only one person did the healing work never seemed to flourish, because the group energy so important to the healing process was lacking. "Methods and Ideals" indicated:

Some centers have struggled along with a small following while the entire healing ministry was resting upon one individual, but have grown and flourished when the healing ministry was emphasized and other members of the center were drawn into the healing work. It would be well for any center or study class to hold regular weekly meetings wherein all persons interested in spiritual healing may join in the realization of spiritual health for themselves and for other members of the center.[42]

"Methods and Ideals" indicated that the most successful centers have been those in which the healing group met on a daily basis:

The centers that have found the healing ministry to be a vital help are those that have a meeting of the healing group every day. . . . The greater the number of persons who become actively engaged in the healing ministry in connection with the center, the greater the number of those who will be attracted to the center; in this way the center will become a more vital factor in the community and thereby a stronger and more stable work will be the final outcome.[43]

While spiritual healing was vitally essential to the success of a center, it was to be understood that if the healing work overshadowed that of spiritual teaching, the center would not flourish. "Methods and Ideals" indicated: "Healing should never be made the paramount issue in a center, but should be a vital factor in the center's ministry."[44]

3. Leadership

"Methods and Ideals" had many suggestions about how a center or study group should be led. It seemed apparent that one of the major problems a center faced concerned the quality of its leadership. It seems that some leaders had attempted "to make a one-man-affair" out of the center or study class, making "the entire spiritual and physical well-being of the community" rest upon one person alone. The leader rarely succeeded when "simply trying to carry on his own personal ministry."[45]

"Methods and Ideals" offered the following guidelines for leaders:

• When the vision or purpose of the work is always kept in the foreground, the teacher or leader is necessarily kept in the background. This eliminates personality, which as a rule is the greatest handicap in attempts to establish a Truth ministry.[46]

• The individual who conducts the work should ever strive for a greater realization of the knowledge and power of God working in and through him. Unless he has clear realization of this fact it will not be easy for him to impart it to another.[47]

• One of the purposes of a Truth center is to develop coworkers. Every center or study class should be considered as a formal training school for the purpose of developing coworkers, not only those who are capable of assisting with the teaching work of the center, but also those who are capable of taking a vital part in the healing ministry of a center. . . . When a teacher sets out actively to produce other teachers and healers, the weight of responsibility is considerably lightened.[48]

• The purpose of a center is not to promote the purpose of individuals who wish their own ideas carried out. The leader must learn to set aside his own personal ideas and in all instances, both in teaching and in practice, adhere to the principle which was paramount in the life of Jesus Christ. Only then are we practical Christians.[49]

• The leader of a Truth center or study class should always realize that the success of a work is not dependent upon numbers. Some of the most successful Truth organizations in the country started with only one or two members who stood by Truth until Truth became a conscious working principle in their daily lives . . . Instead of seeking to build up a larger class, the leader should work to increase the realization of the power and presence of Spirit in those who come.[50]

• The Truth teacher is not the promulgator of philosophies and "isms." He merely presents a fundamental principle by which an individual may find himself and his conscious unity with God.[51]

4. Finances

In regard to finances, "Methods and Ideals" indicated that it was "never consistent with the principles of Truth to make direct appeals to the people for money. A spiritual ministry should be conducted on a freewill offering basis." The document provided the following advice to leaders:

If the leader is constantly appealing to the student to give, it is clear that the leader believes the source of supply to be the student, rather than the real source.... Supply is in Spirit, and the wise and understanding leader is the one who relies solely upon Spirit. In case the supply of the leader is not commensurate with his desires or needs, it is necessary for him to understand two things: that his supply comes from God, and that he must be constantly at work, opening his consciousness to receive the supply which is his by virtue of his relationship to God.[52]

If finances were running low at a center, "Methods and Ideals" recommended that the services the center provided needed to be increased:

There is a secondary phase of supply which the leader should understand: His supply comes very largely in accordance with the fullness of service that he gives to the students that come to the class or center. When one feels that his supply is getting low, it is not necessary for him to consider ways and means by which he may stimulate or increase his supply. The thing for him to consider most is how he may give a more effective service to those who come to him. In other words, the surest way to get anything is to proceed at once to give its equivalent in service.[53]

5. Organization

As to the form of organization, the document had no specific recommendations, other than to keep it as simple as possible. "Methods and Ideals" indicated:

The question of organization is often brought up. We are asked whether it is advisable for a society to organize with a president, secretary, and other officers. This is a matter for each center to decide for itself. We believe that all the activities of a center or study class should be carried on in a businesslike manner. When organization is kept simple and is used as a means to better service, it is well, but when the organization becomes the predominating thought it hinders the work.[54]

6. Unification with Christian Churches

It was important that center leaders and workers recognized their ultimate goal was the incorporation of Unity teaching into local Protestant churches. Centers were not to compete, but to cooperate in every possible way so that the centers and study classes could contribute to the organized teaching of existing churches. "Methods and Ideals" explained:

> If a center is conducted along the lines here designated, no antagonism is likely to arise between the center and the churches. The ministry of the center is not to build up a new organization but to establish a center of vital spiritual service to the community. The work of the center or class is but supplementary to that of the churches. It will no doubt be only a short time until the churches recognize this fact, and admit the center or study class to the church. This is a condition to be desired; a condition toward which every sincere center or study class should direct its efforts.[55]

With the publication in 1924 of "Methods and Ideals," and its availability to Unity students as a correspondence course, Unity School, through its field department, involved itself more directly than before in the work of the centers. In an article published in *Weekly Unity* on July 11, 1925, RAISING THE STANDARD, Unity School urged center leaders to complete both the correspondence course and the "Methods and Ideals" course. Unity sought to make sure when it publicized the work of the centers in *Unity* and *Weekly Unity* magazines that center leaders were properly equipped to teach. It indicated:

> When notices concerning a class appear in *Weekly Unity* readers get the idea that we have virtually endorsed the work of that class or center. When our readers are led to attend, how can we be assured they will receive inspiration and help measuring up to Unity standards? It seems necessary and justifiable that a certain amount of preparation be required for those who would conduct a study class before we invite Unity readers through published notices to attend that class.[56]

A primary goal of the field department in 1926 was to make sure that Unity-affiliated organizations presented only the pure teaching, not the mixed bag apparently being offered in many centers. In a piece in *Weekly Unity* entitled THE MINISTRY OF UNITY SCHOOL, addressed primarily to center leaders, Unity School acknowledged that it "does not assume authority over any center." Nevertheless, it expected those who used the name "Unity" to maintain certain teaching standards. *Weekly Unity* stated: "When a center takes the name 'Unity' that name is a sign to Unity students everywhere that the center is teaching only Unity principles. When a center takes the name 'Unity' and teaches a mixed doctrine, that center is unfair to Unity students who come to it with the expectation of receiving Unity instructions."[57] *Weekly Unity* wanted it understood that it meant no criticism of other truth teaching—it was the labeling that was at issue. The magazine stated: "Unity School rejoices in every Truth movement, whether the teaching is strictly in accordance with the teaching of Unity or not, but it feels that any center whose teaching is not strictly in accordance with Unity principles should take some other name and not pretend to be a Unity center for the purpose of drawing Unity students."[58] The magazine made it clear that Unity School had no objection to its students' studying other teachings or participating in other spiritual practices. It was concerned, however, that the teachings presented in Unity centers were those of Unity and not a potpourri of metaphysical doctrines. *Weekly Unity* stated:

Unity School has no objection to its students going to other centers or to their taking up other teachings or to their studying Unity principles part of the time and some other teaching the rest of the time, but it does object to the mislabeling of centers. Whether a person studies a teaching of Unity or of some other school, he has the right to know the correct name of the doctrine which he is studying. It is unjust to students and to Unity School for a center to suggest by any means whatever that it is a Unity center when it is not a Unity center both in spirit and fact.[59]

It appears that by 1928 only a small minority of the Unity center leaders had become members of the Unity Annual Convention, because Unity School again found it necessary to inform its students that, just because a center used the Unity name, it did not necessarily mean that Unity principles alone were being taught. Unity students needed to be aware that they themselves had to be the final judges of whether a center bearing the Unity name was presenting the unadulterated teachings. In a piece entitled IN-FORMATION FOR STUDENTS, *Unity* magazine posed the following questions and answers:

Q. Has Unity School of Christianity any officially authorized or affiliated branches, centers or study classes?
A. No. Some centers bearing the name of Unity do give a true spiritual ministry, but we have no arbitrary rules by which we make them do so.
Q. When the name Unity is used in connection with a center or study class, should that be taken to imply endorsement by Unity headquarters?

A. No. The name Unity used in connection with a center or study class does not necessarily imply endorsement by Unity headquarters.

Q. How are readers and students of Unity literature to know where they may receive dependable teaching and instruction in centers bearing the name of Unity?

A. Since centers and societies in other cities have incorporated the name "Unity" into the name of their societies, yet are not under the management of Unity School of Christianity, Kansas City, we wish to make it clear that Unity School is not responsible for what they do or what they teach. Unity School puts out its teaching in its literature. When any center teaches things that do not conform to what is published in Unity literature, that center is to that extent not a Unity center. Each student must be his own judge as to whether or not a center is measuring up to the Unity standards . . . The fact that a center bears the name Unity and sells Unity literature does not necessarily make it a one-hundred-percent Unity center.[60]

Unity School remained concerned that truth students in towns and cities where no organized Unity groups were in existence would establish centers that presented an eclectic brand of teaching, only part of which was sanctioned by Unity School. An article entitled THE PURPOSE OF UNITY was published in the May 1931 issue of *Unity* as a part of an effort to inform potential center leaders about the nature of Unity fieldwork and to encourage them to consult with Unity School before founding a new center. *Unity* commented:

Unity centers provide a place of religious research for all people regardless of creed, and give helpful instruction in Christian living through devotional services, systematic study and individual instruction. Each center through its ministry demonstrates its own financial supply. No one should open a Unity center or study class without consulting the Unity Field Department. Contact with the department is necessary in order to conform with the standards of preparation required of Unity teachers and leaders, as well as to comply with the code of ethics and policies developed for Unity fieldwork.[61]

In May 1932 Unity School, through its field department, took more direct action to help Unity students outside Kansas City identify centers using the Unity name that presented the pure teachings. A "classified directory" was developed for publication in *Unity* that would "assist readers and the public to know how to contact a representative Unity ministry" and to "give recognition to leaders whose work is truly representative."[62] Those centers getting three stars (***) before their names were those "whose teaching and practice are in keeping with what Unity states." Two stars were for those centers "where organization and teaching ability had not yet been made to conform to Unity standards." One star was for centers where "the teaching program and visiting speakers do not permit us to include them under the classification of Unity work."[63]

The criteria the Field Department applied in developing the classifications included indices of a leader's preparation for teaching and standards of conduct maintained by the center. The criteria were based on resolutions taken by the Unity annual conference in 1926 for establishing cooperation between Unity headquarters and centers in the field.[64] The indices and standards required to attain a three-star rating were as follows:

1. Completed the Unity Correspondence Course.

2. Completed the Methods and Ideals Course, or at least completion of this study within the next two years.

3. An established ministry consistent with the Unity School standards and methods of presenting the teaching and center conduct.

4. Platform open only to Unity speakers, and independent speakers whose message is consistent with Unity teaching (Centers and leaders are required to confer with headquarters on this point).

5. Center program shall include regular course of study of fundamentals (Unity textbooks and Bible).

6. Quarterly reports sent regularly to the Unity School Field Department.

7. Satisfactory rating with the Sales Department.[65]

When the CLASSIFIED DIRECTORY OF UNITY CENTERS AND UNITY-LITERATURE DEALERS appeared in *Unity* magazine in January 1933, the language used to describe the classifications had been revised and made more palatable to those centers that received less than the highest rating. A new category was added for related truth teaching that was not under the auspices of Unity School. The revised categories are indicated below.

[***] indicates Permanent centers whose teaching and practice are uniformly in keeping with Unity School standards. [**] indicates Unity study classes and probationary center ministries. [*] literature dealers and independent Truth centers that carry Unity literature, but whose teaching and visiting speakers do not come strictly under the classification of Unity work.

[&] indicates: either Home of Truth, Divine Science, Christian Assembly, or Church of Truth center. These centers sponsor various presentations of Truth differing slightly from Unity, but all in harmony with the Christ message.

A total of 195 organizations were classified, with the ratings as indicated below:[66]

Three stars (***)	94
Two stars (**)	46
One star (*)	40
Other (&)	15
TOTAL	195

It is not surprising that fewer than half the centers received a three-star rating, given the relatively small membership of the Unity Annual Conference in the 1930s. Attendance of members at annual meetings at Unity Farm in the 1930s ranged between fifty and sixty. In 1933 a total of fifty "recognized Unity leaders" attended the conference. In 1934 there were fifty-six. The full list of members was published for the first time in 1935. It showed a total membership of eighty-six. Obviously, not all came to Unity Farm for the annual meetings held every summer.[67]

It is notable that Unity School listed far fewer centers or affiliated organizations in 1933 than in 1926. A section entitled "A Few Facts About Unity" in the program of the Fourth Annual Convention in October 1926 stated: "Unity has 1,700 centers or branch schools or study classes."[68] While Unity School provided no explanation for the drastic drop in numbers, it is probable that very few of the 1,700 organizations listed in 1926 would have met the criteria for a three-star rating.

At the 1933 meeting of the Unity Annual Conference (the name had been changed back from "Unity Annual Convention" to "Unity Annual Conference"), the fifty center leaders present discussed the Field Department's system for categorizing two- and three-star centers, asking for an interpretation of the code by which centers were identified.[69] Existing records do not provide the Field Department's response to this request. The star system again came up for discussion when the Unity annual conference met a year later, in August 1934. Some members "resented the idea" of classifying centers and indicated their belief that the system should be dropped. Frederick Andrews, center leader from Cincinnati and former president of the conference, defended the system, indicating that it was the logical outgrowth of the adoption in 1926 of a constitution and bylaws that pledged members to live up to certain standards in conducting Unity work at the centers. Andrews commented:

Back in 1926, in cooperation with the Field Department, the leaders that were here at the convention met together and agreed upon certain rules and regulations that we thought were right and just for the centers and the School. These were published by the School and sent out to the centers. They have been revised and added to or dropped as the need seemed to be, but they were the foundation upon which the star movement began. Time for action, and we have had since 1926 to conform to our own standard. In 1932 the star plan was inaugurated and two more years were given for conforming to the plan. The School has very leniently given three stars to many who did not measure up to the standard in preparation, but who, it was hoped would continue their study and do creditable work.[70]

The field department agreed with Andrews that the star system had helped improve teaching standards at Unity centers. In 1934 it came to the conclusion, however, that improved quality of the work in the field made the system unnecessary. Members of the department commented as follows:

We feel that the star listing has accomplished a good work, and that the leaders are now ready to adopt a more permanent program that will help us stand together in praise and rejoicing. It is encouraging to look back over the accomplishments of the past 3 or 4 years. While the star system has proved irksome to some, it is evident that a definite step toward higher standards has proved a blessing for us all, for there are more substantial centers in the field than we have ever had before.[71]

The star system was dropped in 1934. Listings in *Unity* magazine of work at Unity centers were shown under the title "Unity Annual Conference Members." In 1936 a total of ninety-one Unity centers in the United States and abroad were led by members of the Unity Annual Conference.[72] The magazine contained the following statement describing the work of these leaders and the activities at their centers: "Members of the Conference are recognized Unity leaders who are conducting a spiritual ministry in keeping with the Christ teaching as interpreted by Unity School. Centers are open daily for teaching, healing, devotional services, and the sale of Unity literature."[73]

ORDINATION OF UNITY MINISTERS/
LICENSING OF UNITY TEACHERS

In 1933 the officials of the Unity Training School and the Field Department and leaders of the Unity Annual Conference agreed to resume ordinations to the Unity ministry. Before the 1930s, ordination had occurred irregularly. No established policy existed in Unity School with regard to it. The first group of twelve was ordained in 1906. It was twelve years later (1918), however, before another eighteen were given the honor. Small numbers were ordained in 1923 and 1924, but no record of any more in the 1920s. It had been the practice of some center leaders to ordain within their centers. Unity School looked upon this with disfavor but had taken no formal action to prevent it. In 1934 the constitution of the Unity Annual Conference (Article 9) was amended for the purpose of disallowing these ordinations. The board of the conference decided, "[W]e should recognize but one headquarters, and we want to work wholly in cooperation with Unity School of Christianity. Centers therefore should not start separate colleges and schools, ordain students and send them into the field."[74]

In October 1933 the field department made an announcement that indicated the change in Unity School policy regarding ordination. The announcement read: "In considering whether ordination is necessary and how it may be helpful in promoting a spiritual ministry, the School has decided that those whose preparation and ministry fulfill the letter and spirit of Unity work will be invited from time to time to receive ordination."[75] The department then listed the requirements for ordination. These included satisfactorily completing the Unity correspondence course and the "Methods and Ideals" course, completing one term (one month) at the Unity Training School, and conducting a representative Unity ministry during a period of at least three years. Marie Handly, director of the field department, also listed additional expectations regarding teaching and healing:

It is expected that leaders upon whom the School confers this highest honor which it has to give shall have passed the experimental stage in all phases of Unity center work. Their teaching and healing program shall be established on the Jesus Christ foundation as presented by Unity School, and they are expected to present no visiting speakers except those whose message and ethics conform to the high ideals of this movement.[76]

In 1933 a group of eleven Unity teachers, having completed all of the school's requirements, were ordained at Unity Farm during the 1933 Annual Unity Conference.[77] Classes were ordained each year throughout the 1930s and 1940s. None of them was large. Most classes had fewer than ten students.

In 1936 the qualifications of a candidate for ordination were made a part of the bylaws of the Unity Annual Conference.[78] The requirement for conducting "a representative Unity ministry during a period of at least three years," which undoubtedly was considered to be stiff, was reduced to one year, while the course work at Unity Training School was increased from one month's attendance to two.[79] These were considered "minimum requirements," and completion of the course work and center residency requirements did not assure a candidate's ordination. The Field Department indicated, "there are many factors to consider in connection with the conferring of this highest honor, and the matter is left to the discretion of the Ordination Committee."[80]

The center service requirement may have been a major hurdle, even though it had been reduced to one year. Each ministerial candidate was required to complete one year's "independent center ministry that satisfies Unity School and the Unity Annual Conference Executive Board that the candidate's teaching and ethics are of the Christ standard." A candidate's ordination undoubtedly rested on how stringently that requirement was interpreted. This question was discussed at length at the business session of the Unity Annual Conference on July 1, 1936. Francis Gable, a long-time Unity field lecturer, expressed strong views on what constituted a year of successful ministry. His observations and conclusions were reported in the minutes: "Mr. Gable stated that from his experience in contacting the many centers in the field he felt a year of successful center ministry was a showing on the part of the leader to deal with the problems confronting a center—the ability to guard his platform against outside influences and stability in adherence to principle."[81]

The president of the conference, Mrs. Jessie Maloney, stressed the need for fiscal responsibility. Her comments were also included in the minutes: "The President expressed her opinion regarding a successful center ministry, stating it was necessary to have a balanced budget and that the leader be able to meet the law of need and supply, leaving personal self out of the question and following Jesus Christ."[82] Members of the conference agreed that serving as an assistant to someone who had an established or growing work would not satisfy the center service requirement. The prospective minister had to demonstrate that he or she could succeed on his own before ordination would be conferred.[83]

In 1942 the executive board of the conference placed another hurdle in the way of those who were working towards ordination. The board recommended that candidates for ordination should successfully pass an examination that demonstrated they were familiar with the constitution, by-laws, and code of ethics of the Unity Annual Conference, and that they had a clear understanding of how they were to conduct a ministry in accordance with these regulations.[84] Given these restrictions, it is not surprising that the ordination classes in the 1930s and 1940s were small. As noted below, it was not necessary at this time to be ordained to lead a center. Licensed Unity teachers were certified by the school and the conference to do the work, and the certification process was much less stringent.

In July 1935 the Field Department, in cooperation with the Unity Annual Conference, came up with a plan for providing credentials for those center leaders and teachers who had not yet completed the course requirements for ordination but who were doing effective Unity center work. The school and the conference decided to recognize those leaders with the title of "licensed Unity teacher." Leaders who applied for status as licensed teachers committed themselves to continued course work, both by correspondence and at the Unity Training School, until they fulfilled the requirements for ordination. In return, they got full cooperation from the Field Department in fostering the growth of their ministries and the right to use the word "Unity" in the name of their center. Article 11 was added to the conference bylaws of the Unity Annual Conference that set forth the ground rules for the licensing program. The article stated:

Authorized teachers not yet ordained who are actively engaged in fulfilling the required preparation for ordination and who have a good record in their present field work are eligible to become licensed teachers. Licensed teachers have the privilege of having their names listed in the Unity Annual Conference Yearbook in a separate group. The right to use the name "Unity" is also extended to them, as well as the cooperation that the Field Department extends to authorized teachers. From year to year the names of those who have discontinued their studies or their active cooperation with the Unity School shall be dropped from the list of licensed teachers.[85]

A total of twenty-one Unity teachers applied for and received recognition as "licensed Unity teachers" in July 1935 at the annual meeting at Unity Farm. The bylaws were subsequently revised to allow licensed teachers to lead recognized Unity centers. Article 6 was amended to read:

A recognized Unity Center shall have as its head an accredited member of this conference, or a teacher working under the dispensation of the Field Department, and shall teach the principles of practical Christianity, using the textbooks and literature published by the Unity School of Christianity, Kansas City, Missouri, and following the teaching prescribed by that School.[86]

In 1936 an additional twenty-four new applicants were voted on and accepted as licensed Unity teachers at the annual conference, and in 1937 another twenty-one were added.[87] Conference leaders pointed out that licensed teachers would be given an adequate period to complete their studies but, it was indicated, they should keep in mind "that it is a privilege conferred upon them by the Conference in consideration for their continued study and cooperation with the Field Department."[88] Names of those who discontinued study or active cooperation would be dropped from the list.

Nine licensed teachers lost their accreditation in 1938 because they "had not been consistent in their study during the past year."[89] Georgiana Tree West, president of the conference, suggested that the Field Department should point out in writing to these individuals that they had been voted in on the promise they would consistently continue their study and that the conference "anticipated welcoming them back next year." Those who lost their status as licensed teachers, however, were not required to give up leadership of their centers. Consensus at the business session in 1938 was "that suspended licensed teachers should be free to continue with center ministry, the only difference being that his or her name will not be listed in the Yearbook of the Conference or in the Unity directory."[90]

By 1938 a significant number of the centers were led by non-ordained teachers. Of the 144 centers listed in *Unity* magazine in March 1938, licensed Unity teachers headed fifty-eight of them. The conference executive board meeting on June 29, 1939, acknowledged that many licensed teachers were doing excellent work. "There are centers in the field," it was noted, "just as strong as those headed by Conference Members, which are under the direction of Licensed Teachers." In judging the quality of leadership, conference membership was not as important as "the good work that is being done."[91]

Non-ordained Unity leaders had the privilege of using the title "minister" if they chose to do so. The Unity Annual Conference considered this to be "wholly an individual matter." The conference did not feel that a leader had to be ordained to use the title. Conference members agreed: "Each leader should follow his own leading as to whether to call himself 'leader' or 'minister' . . . Each individual is free to use the title that seems best in his particular locality."[92]

In 1940 a decision was made by the Field Department and conference that confused many Unity leaders, students, and workers. "Licensed Unity teachers" were now to be called "licensed Unity ministers," even though they had never been ordained. The change in title was made because of legal barriers to teachers performing ministerial functions. The Unity Field

Department stated, "According to the laws of various States and communities, unless a person has the status of a minister it is difficult for him to
realize the privileges granted those who serve in religious work."[93] In addition, because of war conditions in Canada, it was necessary for a center
leader to be known as a minister, rather than as a teacher, in order to
properly identify his or her work.[94] The Field Department acknowledged
that the decision had caused confusion, particularly in centers where there
were several licensed teachers, only one of whom was the center leader.
The guidelines the Field Department and conference gave in 1941 to clarify the situation were as follows: "Licensed Teachers will be designated as
licensed teachers or as licensed ministers according to the kind of work
they are doing. The leader of a center should be designated as a licensed
minister and the teacher serving in connection with or conducting classwork as a licensed teacher."[95]

The Unity Annual Conference and the Unity Ministers Association (1925–1966)

In 1925 the Unity Field Department established an organization of
Unity center leaders called the "Unity Annual Conference." The organization operated under this name until 1946 when its name was changed to
the Unity Ministers Association. The director of the Unity Field Department, Ralph Boileau, brought together on October 13, 1925, the "recognized Unity leaders" who were in Kansas City attending the Third Annual
Conference. They met to create an organization of "ministers, healers and
teachers" within Unity School. Twenty-five leaders were present when
Boileau called the meeting to order and encouraged the group to form a
permanent organization. He asked that they draft a set of resolutions that
would serve as the organization's constitution and bylaws. The group responded by appointing a ten-person resolutions committee, chaired by
Frederick Andrews, center leader from Cincinnati, to meet for the purpose
of working on an appropriate document.

ORGANIZATION AND OPERATION

Within two days the committee drafted resolutions that set forth the
purposes of the new organization, established ground rules for conducting
business, spelled out relationships with Unity School, and committed
members to presenting only those teachings prescribed by Unity. The key

resolutions, which became the constitution and bylaws of the "Unity Annual Conference," are as follows:[3]

• This organization shall be known as the "Unity Annual Conference."[1]

• The purpose of this organization shall be to cooperate with the Unity School of Christianity, Kansas City, Missouri, in promoting the annual conference of ministers, leaders and teachers and those interested in the study and application of Practical Christianity, who meet in annual conference in Kansas City, Missouri, to exchange ideas for the uplift and advancement of the teaching.[2]

• Members of the Unity Annual Conference shall consist of all ministers, leaders, teachers and members of churches and centers who are working in cooperation with the Field Department of the Unity School of Christianity, Kansas City, Missouri.[3]

• A recognized Unity center shall be one that teaches the principles of Practical Christianity, using the textbooks and literature published by Unity School of Christianity, Kansas City, Missouri, and following the course of teaching prescribed by that School.[4]

• In order to be accepted as a recognized Unity center, that all text books and teaching which do not conform to the Christ standard, as recognized by Unity School of Christianity, Kansas City, Missouri, be eliminated. This does not exclude any books or lessons by other authors which conform to this standard.[5]

The remaining resolutions dealt with the election of officers, the composition of the executive board, the regularity of meetings, and the process by which the bylaws could be amended. The constitution itself was adopted at the second meeting of "recognized Unity leaders" in Kansas City on October 15, 1925.[6]

A notable omission from the document was a statement of intention regarding the integration of Unity work with that of the Christian churches. One of the key provisions in the Field Department's 1924 document, "Methods and Ideals for Conducting Centers," concerned the relationship of the centers with churches. The work of the centers was to be "supplementary to that of the churches," and if the work in the centers was conducted properly, it would be only a short time "until the churches recognize this fact and admit the center or study class to the church."[7] The omission of this objective from the constitution and bylaws of the Unity

Annual Conference may have been the result of a change in policy by Unity School. In subsequent meetings of the Unity Annual Conference and in discussions of amendments to its bylaws and the development of its code of ethics, the integration of Unity centers into the churches is never mentioned.

The files in the Unity archives on the activities of the Unity Annual Conference contain little information from 1927 to 1933. A meeting presumably took place in 1926, although no record exists. The minutes of the meetings of the Unity Annual Conference held in August 1927 indicate that a meeting took place in 1926.[8] In 1927 the board of directors established the qualifications a local Unity group needed to possess in order to become recognized as a "Unity center." The board also stipulated that Unity School was solely responsible for developing and presenting the teaching. On August 29, 1927, the convention body approved the resolutions of the board with the following statement:

A Unity Center is an independent association of Unity students formed to provide, maintain and conduct a Center and place of assembly where the principles of Practical Christianity, as set forth by Jesus Christ and interpreted in the light of present-day experiences by Unity School of Christianity of Kansas City, Missouri, shall be taught and practiced. A Unity center is a place of religious research for all people regardless of creed, and a place where helpful instruction in Christian living may be received. They are voluntary associations of Unity students who may desire to band themselves together for study, mutual help and service.[9]

While the Unity Annual Conference had operated since 1926 under the provisions of its constitution and bylaws, it had not adopted a code of ethics. Such a code would address the question of what standards center leaders should live up to both personally and professionally and the rules of conduct center leaders should observe in dealing with one another and with Unity School. Members of the 1934 Unity Annual Conference decided to tackle this issue. They saw themselves as committed to "maintaining a high and dignified standard for Unity centers," and decided to adopt "the standards that seemed right to them."[10]

H. B. Jeffery, a field lecturer who had been associated with the Unity movement for over a quarter century, believed that the absence of a code of ethics for the conference was a major omission. Jeffery, who had spent a great deal of time working with center leaders, was aware that erroneous teaching had been presented regularly in the name of Unity. He felt this might be prevented if center leaders adopted a code of conduct. Jeffery made an impassioned appeal to members of the Conference in 1934 to adopt a code. He argued:

To my mind Unity at the present time has reached a critical stage in the field work, and it is a question of whether you are going to unite and have a standard, principles, and a code of ethics whereby you are going to be known and read of by all men, or have no code of ethics at all. You cannot have a living organism unless you have standards. Societies cannot cooperate with each other without a plan . . . You must have an ideal around which all things revolve. If you can form a constitution or statement of principles and standard of conduct, and a code of ethics governing your relationships to one another and the public, then you can progress in an orderly way, and Unity can become a living, vital organism in the world. But you cannot go hit or miss as you have done; for Unity has been misrepresented by many so-called teachers. . . . We want ever to lift the consciousness of the Unity Training School and send out into the field duly qualified, devout teachers and students. The ideals here and in the centers must be those of the Christ, and it takes consecrated souls to carry on such a work. It will take the cooperation of all to hold and to sustain those ideals in a world that is constantly challenging them.[11]

The key provisions of the code of ethics adopted by the Unity Annual Conference in 1934 stipulated that only Unity teachings could be presented in centers and only those teachers approved by the Field Department could speak on Unity platforms. The code spelled out the role of the Field Department in monitoring work in the centers. The key provisions read as follows:

• Each member shall conduct his work, private and public, after the standards, and in accord with the teachings and ideals of Unity School of Christianity at Kansas City, Missouri.

• It is in the sense of this organization that we shall work in perfect harmony and accord with the Field Department of Unity School in our speaking and teaching program, and that we shall place no speaker or teacher on our platforms who is not acceptable to the Field Department, and that we shall consult with the Field Department whenever the teacher, lecturer or course of lessons is in doubt.

• We will not attempt to set up a Unity work in any city without first securing full approval of the Field Department for that work and receiving the cooperation of any already active and progressing Unity work in that vicinity.

• We recognize the advisability of the Field Department sanctioning the establishment of an additional Center in any city where statistics and information show that the field is not already adequately covered.[12]

Members of the conference had no objections to the code of ethics and adopted it unanimously on August 24, 1934. Center leader Georgiana Tree West, who within a few years was to become president of the conference, called the code of ethics "a statement of basic principles of right action for this particular type of body."[13]

The relationship of center leaders with spiritual leaders of other truth movements was a major topic of discussion at the 1935 conference. W. I. Hoschouer, center leader from Chicago and former teacher at Unity headquarters, asked the questions: "What is our attitude of fellowship as a center leader, with other movements, New Thought, Divine Science etc.? Shall center leaders belong to other organizations?"[14] After considerable discussion, it was the consensus that "it was not the best policy for center leaders to belong to other organizations." Most leaders felt that it was not wise to mix other truth teachings with Unity. Marie Handly of the Field Department reminded the leaders of their commitment to Unity teaching: "As ministers of the Unity movement we should stand for what Unity teaches, and also know what it teaches. We can have a spirit of fellowship with other movements of Truth work and still retain the integrity of our own teaching."[15]

Other leaders agreed with her, as the minutes of the July 1 meeting show. "Many leaders responded," it was indicated in the minutes, "with their ideas that each center will be stronger as the center leader is definite in the Unity teaching." As one leader put it, "If we are sold on our own teaching we will not have to carry a sideline."[16]

A related question had to do with inviting speakers from other New Thought groups to present their teachings from Unity platforms. Members in attendance at the 1935 conference agreed that outside speakers were a distraction and that Unity platforms should be for the presentation of the Unity teaching only. The *Unity Field Bulletin* of July 1935 reported the members' ideas on the question:

Various members made comments on the subject of the true stand of Unity with relation to outside speakers and fellowship with other movements. The general opinion was that every Unity leader should use discrimination in inviting an outside speaker to take a Unity platform, not because Unity claims to be the only movement presenting the Jesus Christ message, but because it does have a definite work to do. It is necessary to know our own teachings, our own methods and when we are busy learning these, we are occupied in our own work.[17]

At the 1935 Unity Annual Conference, Charles Fillmore added his support for the position taken by the center leaders regarding the sanctioning of other movements, reiterating his belief in the value of placing emphasis on Unity teaching. He noted: "We are teaching real Christianity and all I endorse is what Unity is teaching—the Jesus Christ message. Many of these other movements are going forth saying that Unity endorses them 100 percent, but that is not true. We want to adhere to Principle and reach the really spiritually minded people in the church and out of the church."[18]

A review of the contents of the bylaws of the Unity Annual Conference and the public statements of the ministers who led it indicates that the organization worked in close cooperation with the Unity Field Department and treated its staff members as superiors. In making decisions, the leaders of the conference often deferred to the Field Department, asking for guidance and advice. Meeting only once each year and with no staff of its own at Unity headquarters, the Unity Annual Conference was dependent on the Field Department for implementing its resolutions and directives. In a 1933 resolution of the general meeting of the Unity Annual Conference, the group referred to the head of the Field Department as "our immediate supervisor." The resolution indicated the respect its leaders had for the school: "Be it further resolved that we vote a whole-hearted fellowship and thanks to our immediate supervisor, the Head of the Field Department, Marie Handly, and a pledge of sincere cooperation with her and through her department, with every branch of our great School, its every department, every head, and every teacher in true Unity fellowship."[19]

A further indication of the close working relationship existing between the conference and the Field Department can be seen in the composition of the organization's executive board. In addition to the twelve members from the conference membership itself, there were two members from Unity School, director of the Field Department Marie Handly, and Unity School general manager Lowell Fillmore. On occasion, field lecturers E. V. Ingraham, H. B. Jeffery, and Francis Gable, and Unity School president Charles Fillmore, participated in the work of the executive board. Lowell Fillmore served for several years as the conference's secretary/treasurer.[20]

Some of the more independent-minded leaders thought the conference should be organized as a separate nonprofit organization. The question was looked into by center leader Paul M. Rigby of Seattle, Washington. He reported that the obstacles to separating seemed insurmountable. He reported: "We cannot incorporate as a church and to incorporate as a religious society would be too complicated. The lawyer advised against incorporation until such time as we own property. He indicated there would be little if any advantage in incorporating."[21] The issue of incorporation was never acted upon throughout the organization's forty-year history.[22]

On occasion board members criticized the school for dominating the conference. At an executive board meeting on June 28, 1938, Dr. Arthur Hall of Unity in Boston expressed the view that Unity School, "through the Field Department, is inclined to be too dictatorial."[23] Some center leaders felt that the conference should act more independently, suggesting that the Field Department act primarily in an advisory capacity. In 1939 the executive board rejected these recommendations, indicating they were satisfied with the existing relationship and commenting: "The Field Department is the executive arm of the Conference body and is acting in an executive way for the Conference. It was suggested that there should be greater cooperation with the Field Department, if anything, rather than wanting to act independently."[24]

As the quality of center leadership improved, a result of the work of the Unity Annual Conference and the Field Department, the leadership of Unity School became more confident in the reliability of the teaching in the centers. In the late 1930s the school began promoting the work of the centers in its magazines as it had never done before. The following statements, published in 1939, 1940, and 1947, are indicative of the efforts the school made to encourage Unity students to join in the work of the centers. The 1939 statement in *Weekly Unity* read:

For further enlightenment upon spiritual principles set forth in Unity literature we suggest that you attend your nearest Unity center. There you will find fellowship with other sincere students who are learning the practical application of these principles on human problems. The authorized Unity center leaders have been trained by Unity School and endeavor to provide a teaching and healing ministry of the same Christ standard as that of Unity School. You will find your center leader and local staff of consecrated workers glad to consult with you and pray with you that the "overcoming spirit" of Jesus Christ may bless you too. Classes helpful in spiritual instruction and healing are of inestimable value for the proper "living out" of the Truth that is taught in the Unity literature. Refer to the list of authorized local ministries in the back pages of *Unity* magazine, and write the Field Department at Unity School for the location of your nearest center.[25]

The 1940 announcement in *Weekly Unity* was equally enthusiastic in its support of the work being done in the centers. It suggested:

Perhaps there is a Unity center in your city or in a nearby city. If you do not already have a church affiliation there is much happiness and satisfaction awaiting you in a Unity center. Have you looked in your telephone directory or in the back of *Unity* magazine to find out if there is a Unity center in your community? Doubtless you have friends and acquaintances who are also interested in Truth and you should like to tell them of the nearest Unity center activity.[26]

In 1947, when the number of authorized Unity centers had risen to over two hundred, *Unity* magazine reported on the Unity field ministry. The magazine encouraged Unity students to take advantage of the services provided there. It reported:

More than two hundred Unity ministers conduct devotional and healing services and study classes in all parts of the United States. Constituting the Unity field ministry, these men and women serve all who come to them for prayer and instruction in the application of Truth. If there is a Unity center in your city, why not plan to enroll in one or more of the study classes that will be offered in the fall and winter months? You will be blessed by your fellowship with others who attend the classes, and you will be a blessing to them.[27]

Lowell Fillmore, who had served as general manager of Unity School since 1916 and was to become president with his father's passing in 1948, commented in March of that year how Unity School had come to view the centers as much a part of Unity School as its own departments. In answer to the question "What is Unity School's ethical relationship to Unity centers?" he responded:

It is our responsibility to consider the centers as a part of the Unity movement just as we do the various departments here at headquarters. In addition to giving spiritual support through faith and prayer we must be on the alert for new ways to help the centers build a substantial work. Besides mailing announcements and arranging lecture tours we are finding other ways to serve. *Daily Word,* in addition to the other publications, will occasionally give information as to how to find the address of Unity centers. Our radio program, "Unity Viewpoint," will also tell listeners how to find the addresses of local Unity centers and where they are located. We are publishing more and more material in the form of pamphlets, etc., designed to be helpful in Unity ministries. These things are being done because we feel that our ethical responsibility to the centers is to do everything possible to help them spread the Christ message.[28]

Several members of the Unity Annual Conference felt the name of the organization was unrepresentative and needed to be changed. Conference member Garnet January argued that the name failed to describe the work of the conference to the public. He suggested the group change its name to the "Unity Ministers' Conference." After a discussion of the pros and cons, a vote was taken. Of the forty-two members present, twenty-two voted for continuing to call themselves "Unity Annual Conference." Not until 1946 was the name changed to the Unity Ministers Association.[29]

Until its dissolution in 1966, the Unity Ministers Association continued to hold an annual meeting and address issues of common concern. The meetings were well attended and were the highlight of the year's activities. The association's bylaws were revised in 1953 in order to make the association even more responsive to the school. The association agreed "to conform to regulations and policies established by Unity School of Christianity for conduct and operation of authorized or accredited Unity centers." Centers were to conduct their work and ministry "in cooperation with Unity School of Christianity in order that the teachings of Jesus Christ may be furthered among mankind."[30] The bylaws also indicated that only members of the association could serve as heads of Unity centers or churches. The level of managerial control exercised by the Field Department was indicated by the fact that ministers and teachers worked "under the dispensation of the Field Department." Teachers were required to "teach the principles of Practical Christianity" and follow the guidelines of the school in choosing teaching materials. They were expected to use "the textbooks and literature published or approved by Unity School of Christianity . . . and follow the course of teaching prescribed by that School."[31] In 1963 the mission of the Unity Ministers Association was further expanded to include initiating, recommending, and coordinating the expansion of the program of the Unity field ministries and to assist in the establishment of Unity centers in new areas in North America and throughout the world. Not until 1964 did the association employ a full-time executive secretary. The group relied on the Unity Field Department for staff support and services.[32]

The Association of Unity Churches (1966–2000)

In December 1965, Unity School shifted its policy with regard to centers and churches. The directors of the school decided to allow the field ministries to operate independently, with no guidance or control from the school. It implemented this decision by abolishing its field department, the organization that for five decades had been responsible for guiding, directing, and supporting centers and churches. The school encouraged the Unity Ministers Association to incorporate and assume responsibility for church- and center-support functions. In *Unity School Bulletin #4*, dated December 14, 1965, Charles R. Fillmore, executive vice president of Unity School, outlined the school's new position regarding centers and churches, commenting on the strength and capability of the field ministries and the appropriateness of their being self-supporting. He stated:

Each year the Field Ministry has demonstrated its growing capacity to assume increased responsibility for the administration of its own affairs. The Unity Ministers' Association itself consistently has taken effective steps in this direction through the expansion of its Executive Board, the establishment of an Executive Secretary's office, and the assuming of a number of administrative functions. During the growth of the Field Ministry, the Unity School has, wholly or in part, performed many functions which by their very nature can be handled more efficiently by the Field itself. These functions include licensing ministers and teachers; ordaining ministers; placing ministers; obtaining and keeping personnel and center records; matters of Field discipline and ethics, administering the Sunday School and Y.O.U. activities and many others. The Field Ministry now has both the capacity and the need to take over these administrative functions.[1]

Fillmore indicated that Unity School, as a "non-sectarian-based spiritual educational institute," was not the appropriate institution for administering an organization of local churches.

The response of the ministers to the school's decision was mixed. Many viewed the abolishment of the Field Department as an opportunity for increased self-determination for the field ministries and considered the school's initiative the right course of action for the Unity movement. Sig Paulson, minister at the Unity Village Chapel, agreed that the Unity ministry "should be responsible for its own operation." He felt an association run solely by ministers from the churches would unite the movement. "We are going to be closer together," he commented, "because we will be responsible for our own areas of service."[2] Robert Sikking, the executive secretary of the Unity Ministers Association, was enthusiastic about the prospects of independence from the school. He declared: "This is a tremendous time to be a part of the Unity Movement, because what has happened during the past four or five weeks is that we have grown up, in a sense. We have taken steps that have created the greatest sense of unity that the Unity Movement has ever been able to express. We have taken a tremendous, wonderful step of growth and unfoldment and fulfillment in the movement."[3]

Other ministers were slow to see these possibilities, considering themselves to have been "kicked out" of the school. The decision communicated in *Bulletin #4* provoked feelings of abandonment and resentment.[4] Rev. Stan Hampson, who went on to have a long and successful career as a Unity minister and church leader, reported that when he read *Bulletin #4* as a young minister in his twenties, he burst into tears. Having grown up in Unity, he recalled that his whole identity up to that time was Unity School. He felt he had been "abandoned, disinherited, removed from the clan."[5]

Many Unity ministers were taken by surprise and were unsure how to respond. A sizable number of ministers believed they needed to band together. Ralph Rhea, a longtime Unity minister and former head of the Field Department, urged the ministers to organize. He declared: "I am sure we could not give serious thought to the possibility that we all can go our independent ways, not communicating with each other very well, and still accomplish the work that can be accomplished if we all work together . . . There must be commitment—commitment to a something that is bigger than ourselves as individuals, bigger than our local work."[6]

Other ministers saw no need for formal organization, feeling that the ministries should remain independent of each other and the school. The Reverend Joel W. Boehr of Tacoma, Washington, argued the case for complete freedom. He stated:

Most of the blessings that an "organization" would offer the individual leader could be handled in other ways or gotten along without. Let us be independent . . . This will put us on our own, which is basically the way most of us want to operate anyway. There will no longer be the "they" running things in the Field Department. What we teach will be up to us, and no one need fear "policy makers." Our ministries will be our responsibility.[7]

Some ministers questioned the school's motives, believing that financial concerns were the real issue and that the school was dumping the Field Department because it was no longer willing to pay the cost. Still others surmised that the school had decided to concentrate on its educational and healing mission and no longer wanted to be bothered with churches.[8] The school's decision created a great deal of controversy, some of it apparently meanspirited. Rev. David Williamson, head of Unity School's Institute for Continuing Education, was disturbed by negative comments from within Unity, reporting that he was "greatly shocked by the suspicion, character assassination, witch-hunts for heresy, and resistance to change that is being shown in Unity today."[9]

Whatever the motivation, the abolishment of the Field Department and the granting of autonomy to the churches signaled a major shift in direction for the school. No longer would it be able to exercise authority over the operation of the churches or control the content of their teaching. No longer would the school act, as one observer put it, "like the pampering parent," and no longer would the churches be able to behave as "immature children."[10]

In the summer of 1966 the Unity Ministers Association met at their annual conference in July and formulated a plan of action. Rather than seek incorporation as a nonprofit organization, which could take months to complete, the ministers decided to disband their association and join an already existing Unity nonprofit organization. In 1964 a group of Unity ministers, desiring to establish a tax-exempt organization for the purpose of investing funds to aid the expanding Unity field ministry, founded, in the state of Georgia, an organization called the Association of Unity Churches.[11] In July 1966, the board of that association agreed to expand its membership to include the leadership of the Unity Ministers Association and add to its bylaws the essential functions of both the Unity Ministers Association and the Unity Field Department.[12]

The Association of Unity Churches, with its new bylaws and expanded scope, became operational on July 22, 1966. It was empowered to formulate policy pertaining to Unity churches and the conduct of Unity ministers, ordain ministers and license teachers, hold an annual conference, and handle the business affairs of the group. The membership would consist of those Unity churches operating in accordance with the standards outlined in the bylaws of the association. All teaching in the centers would follow the principles of Practical Christianity as taught by the Unity School and the board of trustees of the association.[13] Almost all of Unity's 213 churches joined the Association of Unity Churches. Only eighteen refused, basing their decision on the assumption that the association, in order to survive financially, would tax on them which would be beyond their ability to pay.[14] Several of these churches eventually joined the association when it became clear that the organization would support itself through freewill offerings and grants rather than through levies upon the membership.

The establishment of the association met with the approval of the directors of Unity School, which offered the association office space for the organization at Unity headquarters in Unity Village. The school's satisfaction with the work of the association was demonstrated in 1968, when it turned over responsibility for the training of Unity ministers, offering free classroom space and paying the salaries of most of the faculty. The association remained at Unity Village for twenty-five years, moving in 1991 to an office building of its own in Lee's Summit, Missouri, a short distance from Unity Village.

The association has grown and developed in the three-plus decades of its existence. The number of ministries increased from 213 in 1966 to over 1,000 by December 1999. Just over 200 are outside the United States, Canada, and Puerto Rico. The number of congregants now totals 170,000.[15] The association's services to churches have also expanded and now include guidance for church administration, consultation for development and fund-raising, ministerial assistance, mentoring and spiritual renewal programs, training for key leaders, communication through a variety of publications, placement of ministers, conflict management, and assistance in the starting of new study groups and churches.[16]

Unity: A School for Spiritual Education or a Religious Denomination?

From its earliest beginnings in 1889, Unity has considered its mission to be spiritual education and prayer. Is Unity, at the same time, a religious denomination? This question has been long debated within Unity. Most of those who have written on the subject from within Unity have argued that Unity is not a religious denomination. Time after time until his death in 1948, Charles Fillmore argued that Unity was not a new church or a religious sect, but an educational institution. A part of his dream for Unity School was to have it work closely with Christian churches. In the April 1915 issue of *Unity* he explained:

The Unity School of Christianity should not be confounded with any of the modern religious movements that are setting up new standards and establishing new cults. We are not striving to add another sect to the world's surplus, nor set up another church on earth. This is a school in which is taught primitive Christianity. We are striving to set forth in its simplicity what Jesus taught, and as we do this we find that it opens up principles of truth that are acceptable to all men at all times and places.[1]

In the 1920s the ultimate goal of Unity work was to locate centers and study classes within the structure of the Christian churches. This objective was expressed most clearly in a piece entitled "Unity and the Churches" in *Weekly Unity* on March 26, 1921:

For many years the Unity School has looked forward to the time when it might do much of its work in the churches. Unity has never tried to establish another church or system of belief, but has endeavored to confine its teachings to the practical application of Christian Principles as demonstrated in the life of Jesus Christ, and to give this teaching to all the people, independent of their church affiliations. It has never been the desire to take people out of the churches, but rather to educate them in the spirit of their teaching and thus to restore the Christian spirit to the church.[2]

At the time this piece was written, Unity School had evidence that this goal was now within reach. *Weekly Unity* noted:

This long felt and cherished desire is more and more becoming realized . . . Unity study classes are now being conducted in Baptist, Methodist and Congregational and other denominational churches in various cities in this country. This is indeed encouraging and is but the herald of a great work, which every Truth student is about to realize, and in which he will have an opportunity to participate.[3]

In the January 1922 issue of *Unity,* Charles again stressed the fact that Unity School sought a cooperative relationship with the churches rather than a competitive one. Despite the fact that the teachings of Practical Christianity differed in many respects from those of traditional Christianity, Charles saw no reason why Unity students should abandon their churches to attend Unity services. He pointed out:

We do not object at all to having our members, patients or students remain in the churches. We seek to help men, women and children, in every walk of life, and we are always glad to cooperate with the churches. Our mission is to help people to become more spiritual; to help them to learn how to make Truth more practical in their everyday lives and affairs, and so to bring about the kingdom of heaven on this earth.[4]

In the October 1923 issue of *Unity,* Charles emphasized that Unity did not set itself apart from the churches and that its teachings were in addition to those of traditional Christianity. He declared: "Unity is not a sect, not a separation of people into an exclusive group of know-it-alls. Unity is the Truth that is taught in all religions, simplified and systematized so that anyone can understand and apply it."[5] Again, in the February 1924 issue of *Unity,* Charles restated his long-held contention that Unity was not in competition with Christian churches, having no creed Unity students must adopt in order to be in good standing with the school. He stated:

It is not our purpose to establish another sect. We are a school or a society, and our members are at liberty to belong to other religious organizations, or to remain in their churches. We have no creed to which our members must subscribe. We only require of those who study and worship with us a certain consecration to the things of Spirit and an earnest desire to come to an understanding of the fullness of the Christ Truth that alone makes one free. We are willing to cooperate with the churches and to help their members to make more practical in their lives the truths which Jesus Christ taught and demonstrated.[6]

In a speech before the Second Annual Unity Conference in 1924, Charles told Unity students that it was part of their task to bring life back into the traditional churches. The special emphasis on "primitive Christianity" that Unity could impart was needed by the churches. He explained: "Students of Unity do not find it necessary to sever their church affiliations. The church needs the vitalization which the renaissance of primitive Christianity gives it. Every member of the church needs a larger comprehension of the life-giving proclamations of Jesus. 'I came that they may have life, and may have it abundantly.'"[7]

In May 1924 Charles presented a proposal in *Unity* magazine for a "Unity Church Universal," which was a further attempt to achieve union with Christian churches. He stated:

The time is ripe for the expression in the world of the church of Christ, which has always been recognized as existing eternally in the heavens or realms of spiritual ideals. Unity people the world over are asking for a closer relation and a more definite fellowship with the foundation church. To meet this need it has been decided to form a Unity Church Universal for Unity people everywhere.[8]

Charles had concluded that the Protestant churches, despite sincere efforts, had been unable to find any common basis for unification. He noted: "The Protestant Christian churches are agitating for a church union, but they have so far been unable to agree as to the basis for the combination. The forms and ceremonies in which spiritual truths are taught and symbolized are barriers to a great church coalition." Charles believed Unity School could play a role in bringing the churches together, and it was for this reason that he proposed the Unity Church Universal. As a possible solution he suggested:

There is a need of a church organization that can interpret and demonstrate the spiritual realities back of the church symbols. All Christians could join such a church without breaking their present religious affiliations. Unity in Spirit and practice is the ideal Christian Church Universal, and it offers to people everywhere a spiritual church membership in which Christ will demonstrate His power to save His people here and now from the ills of mind, body, and affairs.[9]

Charles then went on to describe several of the principles of Practical Christianity that would be taught by Unity Church Universal. He concluded his proposal by stating that "membership in the Unity Church Universal will be based upon spiritual understanding." Charles's proposal evidently made little headway in Christian churches, because there are no further references to Unity Church Universal in the Unity literature.

Charles continued to state and restate the purposes of Unity School for the remainder of his life, embellishing upon it, emphasizing different aspects of it, but sticking to the basic proposition that the school was not a sect, not a church, and not in competition with other Christian churches. A primary goal was to find creative ways to work with the churches so that the Unity message could be delivered from inside rather than from outside traditional Christianity. In a statement made in June 1927, he emphasized the research aspect of the school. He explained:

Unity School is fundamentally a school of religious research. It is not a sect, it is not a church, neither is it in any way divorced from the prevailing teachings of Christianity. We should like it understood that we do not lay claim to any new revelations. The only thing that is revealed to Man at any stage of his development is Universal Truth. . . . One of the objects of the Unity School is to answer these questions scientifically, yet religiously . . . The Unity interpretation of Christianity may not harmonize in all ways with the popular teaching of the day, but it would be found to be the sound doctrine of the Scriptures.[10]

In November 1930 Myrtle restated the purposes of Unity School in a letter to Mrs. Dorff, one of her correspondents, indicating the importance of reaching people who were in Christian churches with the Unity message. Mrs. Dorff evidently was attempting to work within one of the Christian churches. She was finding it a difficult task to convince others of the correctness of Unity teaching. Myrtle suggested that Mrs. Dorff be patient, advising:

Our purpose is not to take members away from the churches, but to bring all Christians, and those of other faiths, into an understanding of the true character of God, and to teach them how to demonstrate spiritual laws. Through the study of

Unity teachings church members will come into a new and higher understanding of what the churches have been trying to teach . . . Those of you who are Unity students have the opportunity of so living Christ principles and practicing them in your daily living, that you will be an example for all the world to follow. The church members will see the proof that you have something vitally worth while, and they, too, will want to know how to demonstrate the Truth.[11]

In 1931 with the establishment of the Unity Training School, Unity began a training program for ministers. The first class was graduated and ordained in 1933. Ordinations took place each spring thereafter. Eric Butterworth, a Unity minister who knew Charles personally, believed that Charles came to have second thoughts about the advisability of ordaining ministers, because it weakened his argument that Unity was not a church. In a manuscript entitled "Unity Centers and Churches: A Historical Perspective," Butterworth reported his observations as well as those of May Rowland, director of Silent Unity and a close associate of Charles. Butterworth noted:

Charles Fillmore was never completely comfortable with the idea of Unity leaders being ordained. One summer he was particularly disturbed by the performance of ministers at the summer conference, acting for all the world like clergymen engaged in denominational hassles. There was a time when I was equally disturbed by a similar conference struggle. I was sharing my feelings with May Rowland . . . She said, "Eric, some years ago I was sitting in this very room with 'Poppa' Charlie, when he was expressing regret that he had agreed to ordain Unity ministers, since it seemed to encourage them to think and act like traditional ministers. He expressed the concern that it was a precedent that was moving the whole Unity Field operation into more formal and even ecclesiastical directions."[12]

Even though the Field Department's actions gave credence to the supposition that Unity was a denomination, Charles, in his public statements in the 1930s, adhered to his long-held position that Unity was not a church. In a radio interview in 1936, Charles was asked whether Unity had become a church, given the fact that a large number of Unity center leaders were now ordained ministers. Charles responded in the negative, as the following exchange indicates:

Q: Mr. Fillmore, I understand there are hundreds of "Unity Centers" in various parts of the world where doctrines of Unity are taught and the literature distributed. Is Unity a church?
A: No. Unity is not a church and we strive to keep its centers nondenominational. However, as students of the centers organize they tend to form what appear

to be church groups, but the majority of our students are regular members of orthodox churches.[13]

Marcus Bach, a University of Iowa professor and author of several books on Unity, interviewed Charles in the mid-1940s and asked him whether Unity had become a sect. Again the answer was no. Bach reported the conversation as follows: "I asked him frankly, 'Is Unity becoming a denomination?' And he said to me, 'Unity is a school of Christianity. As such it is an independent educational institution. All of our centers are places of religious research for all. We have no creed, but we are eager to serve the people of every creed.'"[14]

By 1945 a number of Unity center leaders had come to favor Unity's declaring itself a religious denomination or sect, so as to enable it to gain admission to the Federal Council of Churches. It comes as no surprise that Charles was strongly opposed to the idea. In presenting his position to Unity center leaders, he quoted at length from a letter sent to Lowell Fillmore by William H. Anderson, who was a member of both the Unity center in New York and of the Foundry Methodist Church in Washington, D. C. Anderson made a strong case against Unity's joining the Federal Council of Churches, stipulating in particular that such a move would alienate many Protestant ministers who heretofore were inclined to view Unity favorably. Anderson pointed out:

It would be exceedingly unwise from the Unity angle, with special reference to its rapidly widening influence, and particularly in view of unexpected new opportunities to carry the Truth teaching into new fields . . . to secure recognition from and admission to the Federal Council of Churches.

In my judgment (the organization of church constituencies as citizens under the leadership of their ministries having been my life work) this proposal to make a denomination of Unity will cut two ways, and both of them to Unity's disadvantage. In the first place, it will be utterly impossible for Unity, even if it should so desire and attempt, to carry over and deliver into any "denomination" its whole constituency. This is true because there are many Unity students, even members of centers, who are also members of churches, mainly Protestant churches.

Then I feel Unity would lose out from another angle . . . Untold thousands of perhaps somewhere near 150,000 Protestant ministers, a large proportion of whom today are hospitably inclined toward the Truth teaching, might feel, if not actually antagonized, that they must be cautious and reserved if Unity should set up as a "denomination" and thus on the face of it put itself in line to become a "competitor" of the now-established churches.[15]

In a letter to Georgiana Tree West, the leader of the Unity center in New York, Charles indicated the board of Unity School had unanimously endorsed the position suggested by Anderson. "We all agreed," stated Charles, "that the points Mr. Anderson makes against Unity's tendency toward sectarianism are well taken." Charles indicated that Unity School's firm stance against allowing itself to be considered a sect or a church should continue to be maintained. He stated, "We feel we should make it plain that we stand solidly for the continuance in the future, as in the past, of a non-sectarian policy." Charles went on to indicate that Unity's efforts to reach the Protestant churches through its literature were having an impact. He pointed out: "The fact is that a large number of orthodox churches are joining Unity in spirit and in due time will cut loose from their materialism and accept the living Christ. It would amaze their congregations if they knew how many of their ministers are readers of Unity literature."[16]

Charles ended the letter with a restatement of his belief that for the Christian churches to adhere completely to the message of Jesus Christ it would be necessary for them to incorporate Unity doctrines into their teaching. He declared: "Unity will be found to be the salvation of true Christianity, and it is essential that it continue as a school in which all sects may gain the truths that will save them from extinction."[17]

One month after rejecting the proposal of its ministers for Unity School to seek membership in the Federal Council of Churches, the school clarified further its position regarding its status as a church or sect. In a statement prepared by the Field Department for the Unity Annual Conference of ministers and center leaders, Unity School stated that while many Unity "churches" had come into existence, these organizations were independent of Unity School. The school itself was not a church or sect. The statement read as follows:

Unity School of Christianity, Kansas City, Missouri, is a religious-educational institution and is not a church. However, in disseminating the teachings of Unity, based upon the Bible and especially upon the teaching of Jesus Christ, teachers have formed organizations for study and worship and these organizations have evolved into groups called centers, societies, assemblies and churches. These groups are a part of the Unity fellowship and work closely with the Unity School of Christianity, but Unity is not a denomination or sect. Those who study Unity teachings and who attend a Unity center or a Unity church are free to keep their affiliation with any church they desire.[18]

This statement was incorporated into "The Purpose of Unity" and was carried in *Unity* magazine until after Charles's death.[19] It represents the final position that Charles took regarding the question of whether Unity School of Christianity functioned as a church or sect.

The issue of whether Unity had become a religious sect came up periodically in the proceedings of the Unity Annual Conference. At the business session of the conference on July 1, 1936, the question was asked whether centers should be called churches. The minutes contain a statement by Lowell Fillmore, general manager of Unity School, indicating that Unity was started as a school and should remain as such—that the Unity teaching should be distinct and separate from that of regular churches.[20] In a piece entitled, "Unity's Vision of the Field," appearing in a 1939 Field Department bulletin, the department, while acknowledging that the centers had taken on the characteristics of churches, asserted that Unity's principal mission was instruction in Christ principles and that the school was known primarily for its teaching. The editors commented:

The ideal upon which the Unity movement was founded is not to form a new sect or church but to give helpful service to people of every faith and creed, to give instruction in Christian living to men and women of every church, and to those who have no church affiliation, and to set forth the truths underlying all religions without being critical of any.

While it has been the Unity ideal through the years not to form churches, it has become necessary for leaders and centers to perform many of the functions of a church, and they are doing some of the things that the churches are doing. It is still our ideal, however, to be known as a school for interpreting the Jesus Christ teaching and presenting practical instruction for the development of the Christ nature in the soul of the individual.[21]

A long-term goal of Unity had been to influence the teaching that was presented in Christian churches. Maintaining its position as a school rather than as a church made Unity more creditable in the eyes of Protestant clergymen. The Field Department pointed out the influence of Unity literature in the churches and commented on its impact: "There are in the orthodox churches a large number of ministers who are Unity readers and who incorporate Truth in their services. At one time it was estimated from a check of the records that there were fifteen thousand ministers subscribing to Unity literature."[22]

Testimony of ministers who benefited from reading Unity literature was published periodically in *Unity* magazine. Appearing in October 1946 was a testimonial written by "a minister from a prominent, world-wide denomination," published under the headline MINISTER LIKES UNITY LITERATURE. The minister commented:

For many years I have had in my churches leading members who have read Unity literature. I have found them without fail to be the most poised and powerful Christians in my church. Only recently have I read any Unity literature myself. It seems very helpful. Because I wish to know what has helped my members and because I wish to find any additional help for victorious Christian living in my own life and home, I desire to subscribe to some of your publications. Please send me *Daily Unity* and *Weekly Unity* for one year.[23]

Charles Fillmore maintained throughout his lifetime that Unity was nondenominational. He never changed his mind, or came to view Unity as a religious sect or a church. In one of his last statements on the subject, published in the *Unity Field Bulletin* of September 1943, he reaffirmed the validity of the movement's original inspiration. He testified:

The Lord came to me in a dream and outlined the ideas for this work. I was told not to form a church, but a school that would teach all people regardless of their religions. I was given the name "Unity" and told plainly that Unity was not a sect, nor a church and that if we wanted to teach persons we must not allow it to become sectarian. These were the principles taught by Jesus Christ. We should therefore be careful not to draw ourselves apart into an exclusive group. If we call ourselves a denomination we immediately cut off the opportunity to serve other organizations. Ours is a spiritual church and our purpose is to establish the true church in the minds and hearts of men.[24]

The debate within Unity as to whether the movement was denominational continued after Charles's death. In the 1950s two of Unity's most articulate and successful ministers, Eric Butterworth and Ernest Wilson, took opposing sides on the question. Butterworth defended the position of Charles Fillmore, as the following statement indicates:

Unity as a religious movement has a distinct role to play. Since it is not an offshoot of any church organization or world order, it owes no allegiance to established doctrines, rituals or observances. Unlike the traditional church, which stresses the practice of sacred rites, Unity is concerned essentially with the therapeutic use of spiritual principles by every individual. Unity is not primarily a church in the usual sense of the word. It emphasizes practical spiritual instruction, prayer and healing, but it does not embody the old belief that the church is the mediator between God and man . . . Why should the Unity leader and the center that he conducts strain and strive for community recognition as a church? Actually, if we are successful in achieving that recognition, we restrict our more universal mission. Then we are branded with the inescapable stigma of seeking to undermine other churches to gain new converts to Unity. A Sunday morning service in Unity is not just a worship service, but an assembly of enthusiastic Truth students, who are engaging in collective study and the practice of powerful spiritual principles. Let us not slip into thoughts of competition, for the inevitable result will be to pattern our services more and more after the more "professional ritualists." A Unity service should be simple, dignified, prayerful and joyous. But it must always be a place of learning as well as of prayer.[25]

Ernest Wilson, who was groomed by Charles Fillmore to succeed him as speaker for the Kansas City Unity Society of Practical Christianity, took a view opposed to that of his mentor. Wilson argued that based on the religious practices of Unity in the field ministries, Unity School had all the characteristics of a religious denomination. Wilson believed the leadership should acknowledge what in fact existed. Wilson explained:

Unity centers have been established as persons have found a form of faith in which they have received more help than in the orthodox churches. Unity centers perform nearly all the functions of the average church. Unity centers or churches provide places of worship and instruction for thousands of persons who cannot accept the dogmas of other religious groups, but seek nevertheless, an acceptable form of worship and instruction. If we in Unity do not want to be called a church, I believe we should "give up the game." This expression means that we should just have classes of instruction, present "Sunday School" on a weekday, schedule classes at times that do not compete with denominational churches, stop ordaining ministers, and leave marriages, christenings and funerals to the denominations. If we do all the essential things that churches do, why balk at the name?[26]

Wilson's position was not accepted within Unity School, as indicated in statements of purpose appearing in Unity periodicals from the 1940s to the 1960s. *Unity* magazine constantly repeated the assertion that "the purpose of Unity School is not to found another sect." Rather, Unity's goal was to help churchgoers apply to their daily lives the principles taught by Jesus Christ, and thereby make "any church affiliation more practical."[27] Unity often stressed its educational mission, while disavowing its existence as an ecclesiastical body, as was indicated in *Weekly Unity* in July 1956. The magazine stated:

Unity School . . . is a nonsectarian religious educational institution. It is devoted to demonstrating that the Jesus Christ teaching is a practical seven-days-a-week way of life. Unity is not a church or sect and does not aim to found a new church or sect. Rather it is a school that is prepared through its activities to help anyone, irrespective of church affiliation, to find health, peace, joy, and plenty through his day-by-day practice of Christian principles.[28]

Like his grandfather Charles Fillmore and his uncle Lowell Fillmore, who had both headed Unity School before him, in 1966 Charles R. Fillmore continued to reject the idea that Unity was a denomination or sect. He viewed Unity as a spiritual organization that took "a broad non-sectarian approach to spiritual development which cut across denominational lines."[29] The teachings, he indicated, were spiritual, and "should never be obscured by submergence in organized religion."[30] Charles R. again made the case that Unity was an educational institute. He explained: "Unity is an open system for teaching and demonstrating the spiritual potential of man. It avoids strict creeds."[31] He further indicated that Unity's purpose was carried out through four activities: "Prayer and Healing, Education and Publication, Professional Preparation, Research and Study."[32]

Unity School's nondenominational stance was strengthened in 1966 when it disbanded its Field Department and turned over support responsibility for churches and centers to the Association of Unity Churches. Its nondenominational position was further enhanced when in 1969 the association assumed full responsibility for the training of Unity ministers. During the 1970s Unity School could, for the first time since it was incorporated in 1914, legitimately claim that its spiritual work in the areas of its primary focus—publications, prayer, healing, and education—was nondenominational.

While Unity School viewed itself as a nonsectarian spiritual organization, the Association of Unity Churches, which was founded in 1964, always considered itself a religious denomination.[33] A review of its activities indicates that it qualified as such. Over one thousand ministries belong to the association, most of them Unity churches. The association is directly involved in church management, including the licensing of ministers and teachers and inservice training. In addition, the association is committed to a specific spiritual teaching or doctrine—one of the primary criteria for determining whether an organization is denominational. Its bylaws prescribe the nature of the teaching, stating: "All teaching conducted in the center ministry shall follow the principles of practical Christianity as taught by the Unity School of Christianity at Lee's Summit, Missouri, and approved by the Board of Trustees of the Association of Unity Churches, Inc."[34]

While the association itself functions as a denomination, a number of

Unity ministers from churches belonging to the association still see Unity as nondenominational. Glenn Mosley, president and chief executive officer of the association, commented on this anomaly when he observed: "Most of us have colleagues with whom we have discussed the question: Unity is a denomination vs. Unity is not a denomination. Some believe it is not, and most of those who contend that it is, devoutly wish that it wasn't."[35]

Unity School moved toward denominational status again in the 1980s when it assumed responsibility for establishing and supporting Unity centers and churches in Europe, Africa, and parts of South America.[36] Its return to church work was furthered in 1983, when it again took on the task of educating Unity ministers.[37]

In the early years of Connie Fillmore Bazzy's tenure as Unity School's chief operating officer (she became executive vice president in 1983 and president and chief executive officer in 1987), she did not address the issue of Unity's denominational status. In a Unity School "Statement of Purpose" written in 1986, Unity's role as a denomination was not mentioned. The statement indicated that the school's mission was in the area of spiritual development. The school was "dedicated to teaching and demonstrating the spiritual truth of life as taught by Jesus Christ . . . All the activities of Unity School are designed to help people understand their own spiritual nature and to express spirituality in their lives in practical ways."[38]

A mission statement written in 1993 again omitted any mention of Unity as a denomination and stressed the school's commitment to spiritual education:

Unity School of Christianity is a center of spiritual light for the people of the world. We are dedicated to letting this light shine so brightly that people become aware of their spiritual nature and express it in their daily lives. We address physical, mental and emotional needs through affirmative prayer and spiritual education. We serve those who seek inspiration and prayer support as well as those who use Unity teachings as their primary path of spiritual growth.[39]

Bazzy addressed the issue of Unity's denominational status in early 2000, departing from positions taken by former presidents of Unity School. In an article in *Contact* magazine in April, "The Nature of the Unity Movement: Nondenominational and Denominational," Bazzy acknowledged that, given the existence of many Unity churches in the United States and other countries, "Unity currently fits the definition of a denomination."[40] She was quick to point out that it would be inaccurate to view Unity as nothing more than a denomination. She noted that Unity

encompasses many nondenominational components that are directly related to its mission. One of Unity's greatest strengths, she believes, is that it is
"both denominational and nondenominational."[41] With the position stated by Bazzy, the issue of Unity's denominational status appears to have
been resolved. Along with being a movement devoted to prayer, healing,
teaching, and publishing, Unity is also a religious denomination.

An Organizational Controversy within the Unity Movement

THE PROPOSAL FOR UNITY INTERNATIONAL

In October 1979 the president and board of directors of the Association of Unity Churches proposed a new organizational structure for the
Unity movement. In a communication to Unity School, the association's
board recommended that the activities of the school and the association
be brought together under the umbrella of an organization to be called
"Unity International." The new group would be governed by an eight-
member board, with four members each from the school and the association. A ninth member from outside the board would be elected chairman.
Unity International would be granted full financial responsibility and the
power to allocate resources. Both the school and the association would be
required to divest themselves of all funds and assets and place them under
the control of the new organization.[1]

The association's objective in making the proposal was to enable itself
to become an equal partner with Unity School in the Unity movement, and
by so doing gain an equal voice in the allocation of resources and the determination of policy.[2] Unity School income was in the $15 million range
and its assets over $27 million, while the association's income was some-
what less than $300,000. As a tenant of Unity School and without an en-
dowment, the association had relatively few assets.[3]

The sequence of events that led to the proposal appears to have been
initiated by a letter to the association dated September 26, 1979, from
Charles R. Fillmore, president of Unity School. Fillmore indicated that the
school wanted the association to pay "for the fair market value of office
space, storage space and related services."[4] The school also requested that
the association set up its accounting records to show the value of the
school's financial contribution to the association and publish this informa-

tion in the association's newsletter, *Contact*. The association was at the time occupying office and classroom space at Unity School; some of the space was free and some was not.[5]

On October 22 the association, in a letter signed by President Jack Boland, a Unity minister from Detroit, indicated that before the association could respond to the school's request, a full accounting was needed of all the school's income and expenses, including not only its major programs, such as publications and Silent Unity, but the Unity Country Club, the village chapel, and the Unity Inn as well. It asked for the disposition of what was presumed to be a $1.5 million profit from operations in 1978, as well as a statement of the "current shareholder's equity in the corporation." The association said it required this information "to fully analyze the financial position of the school and its tax-exempt status." The letter also called into question the qualifications of the school as a nonprofit organization under the IRS code. In addition, the association indicated that it was "concerned about the question of conflict of interest" on the part of the shareholders of the corporation, including James Dillet Freeman, director of Silent Unity, and Charles R. Fillmore.[6]

Both the proposal for Unity International and the above letter were delivered personally on October 22 by Jack Boland to William B. Dale, public relations director, at his office at Unity School. In a follow-up letter the next day to Dale, Boland threatened to do battle in the press if the school went public with the information contained in the two documents. Boland wrote: "It might perhaps be trite to point this out to you, but we must stress that if the AUC [Association of Unity Churches] was forced to respond to a public campaign with regard to the revelations in these documents, we would not hesitate to do so."[7]

The directors of Unity School (its president Charles R. Fillmore and its vice presidents James Freeman and Otto Arni), in a letter dated November 5 to Jack Boland, president of the association, rejected the proposal for Unity International. They stated:

We do not believe the plan is in keeping with the avowed purposes of the Unity School of Christianity as set forth by its founders, Charles and Myrtle Fillmore. Neither do we find it compatible with the School's traditional interdenominational emphasis nor workable for carrying on our successful present ministries. In short, we do not feel that the proposal is practical or in the best interests of the Unity movement.[8]

The school's directors indicated that the association's request for financial information went far beyond what was needed to respond to the school's letter of September 26. They expressed their distress at the presumption of wrongdoing contained in the association's letter, noting that it "is replete with numerous untrue inferences, insinuations, and innuendoes concerning the integrity and good faith of both the Unity School and its directors."[9] The directors continued: "We are astounded and deeply hurt by the contents of your letter of October 22, 1979, especially when we learn in your letter to Bill Dale that the contents and publication of your letter, so obviously injurious to the relationship of our two organizations, were unanimously approved by the present members of the AUC Board."[10]

Boland responded on November 16, indicating that the plan for Unity International "was worked out after much careful consideration." He urged the school to reconsider its decision, and noted that he did not believe that his October 22 letter would be "injurious to the relationship between our two organizations."[11] Boland and the association's board evidently believed that the rank-and-file ministerial leadership in the field would support the proposal for Unity International.[12] It soon became evident that many Unity ministers disagreed with the association board's action. In an effort to deal with the impasse and resolve the dispute, an influential group of Unity ministers brought together seventeen past presidents of the Unity Ministers Association and the Association of Unity Churches. The group of past presidents, which included some of the movement's most respected leaders, met with representatives of both the school and the association, considered the matter, and took the position that Boland and the association board had acted improperly.[13] The board was persuaded to withdraw its proposal for Unity International and apologize "for the pain and unrest" caused by the letter of October 22. A letter to that effect, which also indicated intent to establish a working relationship with the school based on mutual trust and respect, was signed by Jack Boland and sent to Unity School on January 14, 1980.[14]

When further actions by the association board led the school to doubt the sincerity of the board's publicly stated intentions, the school, by action of the board of trustees, in a letter dated February 14, 1980, and signed by William B. Dale, threatened to "dissolve the relationship existing between the AUC and the School," to establish a field department to service Unity ministries, and to "transfer the total operation of the Unity Ministerial School to Unity School."[15] In an effort to resolve the crisis, the leadership of the school then invited the seventeen past presidents to Unity Village during the week of March 10 to meet and help establish a better working relationship between the School and the field ministry.

The past presidents gathered at Unity School in mid-March; after four days of meetings, the group drafted a five-point agreement that was ultimately signed by the association board and Unity School. The association agreed to suspend its bylaws until its annual conference in 1982. The executive committee of the association was dissolved and an eight-member executive council of four past presidents and four members of the association board was put in its place. The council was given authority to ratify all decisions of the association board before they could be implemented.[16] In the agreement the association board acknowledged "the sanctity of the Unity School of Christianity as a corporate entity, distinct and separate from the AUC."[17] The association also recognized "it neither has, nor can claim entitlement in the government or assets of the Unity School," nor does it have the right "to demand an accounting from the Unity School of Christianity, financial or otherwise." Jack Boland was not forced to resign (his one-year presidential term ended in June). However, James Sherman, the association's vice president and a strong advocate of Unity International who was in line for the presidency, was not elevated to that position.[18]

In retrospect, it is surprising that the president and board of the Association of Unity Churches, before presenting their proposal for Unity International the previous October, did not ask themselves:

1. Why would Unity School agree to become part of an organization like Unity International, whose mission included the management of churches, when in December 1965 the school made it clear in *Bulletin #4* that it no longer viewed church activities as a part of its own mission and divested itself of church-related responsibilities?

2. In the face of charges of malfeasance and conflict of interest, what would motivate the school to join forces with the group making these charges? James Dillet Freeman, who was a member of the Unity board of trustees at the time, indicated that the board of the association totally alienated the leadership of Unity School with charges of conflict of interest and mismanagement.[19]

Had the leadership of the association been more cognizant of the history and tradition of Unity School, they would have understood that it was highly unlikely that the school would grant the association equal status. The leadership of Unity School, taking their cue from Charles Fillmore himself, did not view Unity as a religious denomination. Acceptance of the Unity International proposal would have required the abandonment of that position. Since the association's leaders were not newcomers to Unity, it would seem that they would have been aware of these longstanding points of view. It would also seem that the association's leaders would have recognized that the association's predecessor organizations, the Field Department and the Unity Ministers Association, were two of the school's smaller internal divisions, and both were phased out because they were no longer considered central to the school's purpose.

James Dillet Freeman believes that the leadership of the association, specifically Jack Boland and James Sherman, totally underestimated the commitment of Charles R. Fillmore to the Unity movement and to the vision of its founders. Fillmore was nearly sixty years old at the time, and nearing retirement age. Boland and Sherman, Freeman believes, felt that by presenting an organizational alternative that brought the divided leadership of the Unity movement under one organizational head, they were giving the school's president an opportunity to lay down the burdens of his office, retire honorably from the work he had engaged in for over thirty-five years, and pursue full time his interests in hunting, fishing, and the out-of-doors. Freeman concludes that the association leadership was unaware of Fillmore's deep interest in preserving Unity traditions and was therefore out of touch with reality.[20]

David Williamson, a Unity minister who was at the time a member of the association board and who until his death in the year 2000 was a minister at a Unity church in Hollywood, Florida, continued to believe that the organizational structures envisioned in the proposal for Unity International had a great deal of merit and, if implemented, would have benefited the Unity movement. He was convinced that a significant number of Unity ministers continue to share this view. Williamson acknowledged that the manner in which the proposal for Unity International was presented to Unity School precluded its being accepted. Inept leadership on the part of the association and an unwillingness on the part of the school to consider a viable alternative to the existing dual organizational system, he believed, were responsible for the ensuing conflict between the association and the school, a conflict that could have resulted in a split in the Unity movement.[21]

The conflict over the proposal for Unity International indicated both to the leadership of Unity School and the Association of Unity Churches that better communication between the two organizations was needed. In 1987, in an effort to promote better understanding between the two groups, coordinate their joint activities, and facilitate the progress and growth of the Unity movement, the Unity Movement Advisory Council was organized. Created at the instigation of Connie Fillmore Bazzy, president of Unity School, the council has met regularly to deal with issues of common concern. The presidents of both the school and the association are members, as are their top-level administrators. The council has served as an arena where issues of common concern are addressed. Glenn Mosley, president of the association, views the council as a place to work out problems that cause difficulty in the day-to-day business of both organizations. "Before the council was created," Mosley recalled, "we had a tendency to step on each other's toes without knowing it, or doing it intentionally."[22]

Jimmie Scott, a Unity minister who served as chairman of the association board in 1999, viewed the council as an effective vehicle for bringing the leadership of the two organizations together. In the year in which he attended meetings he recalled nothing "earthshaking" being decided.[23] This may be in part because the council does not consider itself to be a governing body or involved in making substantive decisions. Scott viewed the council as a place where each organization can exert "a gentle influence" on the other, rather than an arena where major policy decisions are made.

Joint projects have occasionally been undertaken. One was the creation and development of the "Quest" books, which have been popular with Unity students. Surveys of Unity readership and church members have also been carried out to discover what people in the movement are thinking and saying.[24] Mosley believes that one of the council's most important achievements has been to create a friendly atmosphere between the school and the association.[25] The work of the council has apparently made an important contribution toward dispelling the atmosphere of suspicion and distrust that followed in the wake of the controversy over the proposal for Unity International.

CHAPTER 12

The Role of Women in the Unity Movement

Women played major roles in the struggle for social and economic reform that swept the nation as Populism and Progressivism in the late nineteenth and early twentieth centuries. Acting out of religious and spiritual
motives, women joined in a variety of reform efforts that included temper-
ance; prison reform; improved care of the ill, insane, and handicapped;
Native American rights; and the abolition of child labor. Many became
professional social and settlement workers under the banner of "Christianity, Science and Philanthropy."[1]

Two major, female-led organizations came on the scene in the nineteenth century: Christian Science and the Shakers. Mary Baker Eddy not
only founded and led Christian Science but also brought many women
into the movement as practitioners. The Shakers were founded and led by
a woman, Mother Ann Lee, and developed a consistent system of empow-
erment for women.[2]

The Unity movement developed out of the context of women being active in spiritual organizations. Co-led by a woman, Myrtle Fillmore, from
the outset Unity encouraged the participation of women. In December
1889, in the eighth issue of the first volume of *Modern Thought* magazine,
Charles and Myrtle Fillmore published a piece that set the tone for Unity's
future position regarding the role of women. An article entitled "Woman's
Advancement and Social Purity" by Lucinda B. Chandler declared: "The
advancement of social purity and the spiritualization of humanity to a
greater degree, depend on a revolution in the theological, civil and industrial position of women."[3]

During Unity's one hundred-plus years, women have played major
roles, both as leaders of the movement and as participants who have

found in Unity their primary spiritual path. A recent survey indicated, "nearly nine out of ten Unity people are female."[4] From the movement's earliest beginnings, it appears that women have predominated. Many were attracted because they were inspired by the spiritual presence of Myrtle Fillmore. Her ability as a teacher and healer drew women to classes in Kansas City and to the healing work. Most of the practitioners of spiritual healing who worked with Myrtle over a period of four decades at the Kansas City Unity Society of Practical Christianity were women. Most of the letters Myrtle received, asking for prayer and healing during the last three years of her life (1928–1931), were from women.[5] It is safe to assume that most of the letters she received during her four decades in Unity, as well as those letters sent directly to Silent Unity, were also from women. In recent years most of the personal contact with Silent Unity has been by telephone rather than by letter. It has been estimated that women comprise 90 percent of the callers.[6]

When Unity began a ministerial training program in 1931, most of the students were women. Approximately 85 percent of the ministerial students who graduated (and were ordained) from the Unity Training School between 1933 and 1945 were women—eighty-three out of ninety-five candidates.[7] In 1945, in an effort to attract men to the Unity ministry, a special Silent Unity training program was initiated for men only. The move did not markedly shift the gender balance of those entering the Unity ministry. Of the 104 graduates between 1945 and 1953, 70 were women.[8] In almost all the graduating classes since then, women have been in the majority.[9]

Charles Fillmore was well aware that Unity was more attractive to women than to men. He saw women as inherently more spiritual. He commented: "Women are more receptive to Truth than men. Women have more spirituality and faith than men."[10] He believed this was due to women's ability to use intuition. He observed, "Women as a rule know more about pure mind on its own plane than men, because they trust that inner faculty of pure knowing called intuition."[11] Women have exerted strong leadership in the Unity movement. As co-founder of Unity, Myrtle Fillmore played a leading role for over forty years. While she never held the title of president of Unity School, anyone reading her lengthy correspondence realizes that, throughout her long career in Unity, she made her voice heard. Without a doubt, she involved herself in all major decisions affecting the development of the movement.

May Rowland was another towering female figure in Unity. Her official title was director of Silent Unity, but her impact went far beyond that of the head of a major department of Unity School, important though that was. May grew up in Unity. Her father was a member of the board of directors of the Kansas City Unity Society of Practical Christianity.[12] She came to work for the Silent Unity Healing Department in 1912, shortly after graduating from high school. Four years later she was appointed by the Fillmores to be director of the department, which at the time had thirty-five prayer workers. Myrtle Fillmore sensed that, though May Rowland was only in her early twenties, she was to make an important contribution to the movement. Myrtle told her, "You are going to be a great harmonizer in Unity."[13]

For the next fifty-five years, May provided strong leadership. Charles R. Fillmore, who worked closely with her for several years, described her as "the guiding spirit of the work, the power behind the scenes." He saw her as "living the teachings in every aspect of her life" and "having a strong influence over the direction of the movement."[14] According to Charles R., May was the one who got the ministerial training program off the ground in the 1930s, and it was her influence that resulted in the establishment in 1945 of the Silent Unity Ministerial Training Program for men. In addition, she had a major impact on the direction of the Unity Training School, which operated from 1931 to 1965. Though Rickert Fillmore was the chancellor, May, according to Charles R., was the key figure in getting the school's educational program "organized and going in the right direction."[15]

May Rowland was also a member of the Unity School board of trustees and a stockholder in the corporation.[16] Charles R. viewed her as a stabilizing influence on the board. "She could calm things down and keep things on track," he reported. "She saw the big picture."[17] When Lowell Fillmore, president of the school, had a difficult problem, Charles R. reported, Lowell went to May for advice. Lowell ran Unity, he recalled, "with a lot of help from May."[18] Charles's father, Rickert Fillmore, admired May and would turn to her, rather than to his brother Lowell, when he needed counseling and advice.

May, like Myrtle, served as an inspiration for many future leaders of the movement. Eric Butterworth, who has been one of the leading articulators of the teaching, found her to be an "amazing person . . . the soul of Unity School."[19] Ernest Wilson, who was Charles Fillmore's chosen successor in 1933 as speaker for the Kansas City Unity Society of Practical Christianity, viewed her as "a great lady, perhaps one of the greatest teachers and spiritual leaders of this present time."[20] He reported in 1973 after her retirement from Unity School: "Perhaps the greatest thing of all is what she is rather than what she does. She radiates a spirit of youthfulness and joy and inward peace and strength that has been a bulwark of strength and power, faithfulness and steadfastness to principle all throughout the many years she has served."[21]

Stan Hampson, who worked under May in Silent Unity before serving as a Unity minister for forty years, experienced her as a "deeply profound, spiritual person with a strong aura of saintliness about her." She loved to laugh and have fun, he recalled. Hampson said he "felt blessed to have been around her."[22] Phil White, a coworker at Unity School with her for over two decades, regarded her as "the second mother of Unity," a woman who "symbolized, in her way of conducting herself and in her demeanor, the basic Unity teaching."[23] Frank Gudici, who was chairman of biblical studies at Unity School, said she was "like an anchor, a firm anchor that you could really depend on." May, he observed, "symbolized strength."[24] Richard Billings, a Unity minister who knew her well, observed the same qualities. He reported: "After the Fillmores' transition, May became the constant we all looked to. She was the person you could depend on. She was what most of us considered to be the Spiritual Leader of Unity."[25]

James Freeman, who worked with her for several years and succeeded her as director of Silent Unity in 1971, viewed her as "the leader, a very wonderful person who never pushed her weight around."[26] He saw her contribution as equaling that of the co-founders, Charles and Myrtle Fillmore, stating: "I do not believe anyone has made a deeper impression on the Unity movement, and on us who were fortunate enough to work with her. May made her contribution not so much by what she did as by what she was."[27]

Dorothy Pierson, who began her long ministerial career as a Silent Unity worker in the 1930s, continues at this writing to view May as the guiding spirit in her life. She indicated: "May Rowland was my close friend and mentor, and the spiritual inspiration for my life. She had a beautiful presence and seemed to glow with an inner radiance that brought light to every situation. She was so supportive of me. I continue to feel at one with her in consciousness. My love for her is so deep that her spirit lives in me today."[28]

Several other women have played important roles at Unity School in leading various aspects of the work. Almost all of the departments within the school have been run, at one time another, by women. Martha Smock, after working in Silent Unity, became editor of *Daily Word* in the 1940s and served for thirty-five years. Under her leadership, subscriptions to the magazine mushroomed. In addition, she was the author of *Half Way Up the Mountain,* a book well regarded within Unity.[29] Elizabeth Sand Turner was director of the Unity Training School and taught classes on the Bible and biblical interpretation. Her two books on the Bible, *Let There Be Light* and *Your Hope of Glory,* written in the 1950s, are still widely used in Unity. She was a brilliant speaker and built a church in Florida where she was minister for several years.[30]

Celia Ayers, like many who came to work for Unity School, started in Silent Unity. She was given responsibility for directing the Unity Correspondence School and did so successfully for several decades.[31] Billie Freeman served Unity School for more than fifty years, was head of Silent Unity's special letter writers department, and edited *Daily Word* for ten years. She wrote articles for Unity publications and taught in the School for Continuing Education.[32] The Unity Field Department was, until the creation of the Association of Unity Churches in 1966, the organization within Unity School responsible for supporting Unity centers and churches. For several years Elsie Shaw, according to Charles R. Fillmore, did an outstanding job running the department.[33]

Several woman have contributed to the movement's growing body of literature. As indicated in Chapter 3, the works of H. Emilie Cady have had a great impact in Unity for over a century. Cady, a late nineteenth-century New York City homeopathic physician, laid out the basics of Unity metaphysics.[34] Jennie Croft, a Kansas City native, was one of the first professional women employed by Unity. During her thirty-year career, which began in the 1890s, she served as associate editor of *Unity Magazine,* represented the school at meetings of the International New Thought Alliance, traveled as a field lecturer, and authored a booklet on meditation titled *Methods of Meditation.* For many years this work was considered the standard authority within Unity on the subject.[35] Imelda Octavia Shanklin came to Unity in 1907 and wrote articles for *Wee Wisdom* magazine before becoming its editor in 1919 and chief editor of all Unity publications in the 1920s. Her book *What Are You?* continues to draw high praise from within Unity, because it presents a strong argument for the power of the mind to create human experience.[36]

Frances Foulkes, a New York City businesswoman who enrolled in the

Unity Intensive Training School in 1921 and became a "local healer" with Myrtle in Kansas City, was constantly encouraged by Myrtle to write for Unity publications. Her book, *Effectual Prayer*, written in the 1930s, provides a useful review of the Unity practice of prayer and meditation.[37] Mary Lou Kupferle, who came to Unity in 1935, became a prolific Unity author, contributing over the course of her career some 237 articles, poems, and pamphlets. Her book *God Never Fails* is still considered a basic Unity text.[38] Mary-Alice Jafolla and her husband Richard have provided a contemporary presentation of the Unity teachings in *The Quest*. This book was commissioned by Unity School and the Association of Unity Churches as part of an effort to present an overview of the Unity teaching in an appealing way to a modern audience.[39]

Catherine Ponder is a widely known author and lecturer whose background is in Unity. Her several books on the subject of healing and prosperity have had strong sales, both inside and outside the movement. They include: *The Healing Secret of the Ages*, *The Dynamic Laws of Prosperity*, and *The Prosperity Secret of the Ages*.[40] Although she is an ordained Unity minister, her teaching on prosperity departs in some respects from that of Unity. Charles R. Fillmore sees Ponder as having her own approach to prosperity that does not fit the Unity mold.[41] Connie Fillmore Bazzy's books dealing with the same topics, *The Unity Guide to Healing* and *The Unity Guide to Prosperous Living*, have found a much more receptive Unity audience.[42] In 1987 Unity School named Connie Fillmore Bazzy its first woman president. In 1983, four years before her elevation to that post, she became executive vice president and chief operating officer.

Several women ministers, too numerous to mention, have succeeded in building important ministries. Probably the most successful graduate of the Unity ministerial program has been Johnnie Colemon, an African American minister from Chicago. Her Universal Temple, which she founded in the late 1950s, has fifteen thousand members. About four thousand attend Sunday services. In addition, she has formed a telephone prayer ministry much like Silent Unity.[43]

CHAPTER 13

The Participation of Blacks in Unity Work

Over the course of Unity's one hundred-plus years, many African Americans have been attracted to the Unity teaching. Today they attend Unity churches, read Unity publications, and use the healing services of the Silent Unity ministry. A corps of Black ministers (over one hundred in all, many of whom are women) provide leadership in Unity centers and churches.[1]

It took several years before Blacks became involved in Unity work. The Fillmores began their teaching in 1889 in Missouri, a state in which Southern cultural and racial attitudes prevailed. Kansas City, where Unity was founded, had a sizable Black population. The races were segregated and Blacks and Whites attended separate churches. It comes as no surprise that Whites, rather than Blacks, were the first to be attracted to Unity teaching and its healing practices. Blacks were apparently never enrolled in the classes given by the Fillmores for the Kansas City Unity Society of Practical Christianity, nor is there any indication that any of the early Silent Unity healers were Black.

An illustration on the cover of *Wee Wisdom* magazine in March 1901 gave the first indication that Blacks were involved with Unity. Shown is a drawing of an angel looking down on a group of a dozen children, ages four to eight, both boys and girls. All are White, except for one Black child. Blacks apparently became aware of Unity teaching through reading Unity literature. In 1919 several "colored people's" study groups were listed in *Weekly Unity* magazine in cities as far-ranging as Jacksonville, Florida, and Columbus, Ohio. In 1920 the first center for Blacks, listed in Unity publications as "The Unity Society of Practical Christianity," was opened in New York City.[2]

By 1930 Blacks were in charge of several centers and study groups. In August 1928, there were a sufficient number of Blacks attending Unity's annual summer convention that they were invited to present one of the programs. Ralph Boileau, director of the Unity Field Department, introduced the first presenter, Mr. G. Page of the colored people's center in Kansas City, and commented on the contribution of Blacks to the Unity movement. Boileau noted that the "great natural faith" of "our colored brothers," seemed to work "greater miracles for them than it does for their white brothers."[3] Mr. Page then took the platform and explained why Blacks were drawn to Unity teaching and "why Truth takes such a hold" on them. Page indicated: "His [the Black man's] problem is one of tradition handed down from the days when the black men were slaves and were led to believe that they were not so well-born as other men. But Truth teaches men to break the limitations of old beliefs and to see themselves as they actually are; therefore it is especially fitted to helping the colored man."[4]

Page was specific about how Unity teaching helped Blacks achieve health and prosperity. Pointing to some fifty Black men and women in the audience, he exclaimed: "Behold then our demonstration. See what God hath wrought! There sit fifty men and women, healthy and happy. Some of them have been blind and otherwise afflicted. They have been healed through "the Truth."[5] Page evidently believed that equality for Blacks would ultimately be achieved as men and women practiced Unity principles. *Weekly Unity* reported: "As for the present differences that exist between the two races and the erasing of these differences, Mr. Page is not worried about them. He said that the practice of love itself will be sufficient to solve the problem; that we must let the problem work itself out gradually, and patience and love will accomplish this."[6]

Several Blacks took the platform to explain their attraction to Unity teaching. Dorothy Brownlow of the "Indianapolis Unity Study Class for Colored People" testified to the inner satisfaction she experienced when she started reading "Truth" literature. "It didn't seem like reading," she commented, "It was more like eating."[7] Madam E. M. Pratt of the study class in Dallas, Texas, saw liberation in the Unity message. "We are made in the image and likeness," she declared. "This is the Truth that will set us free."[8]

While Blacks were drawn to the Unity teaching, until the mid-1960s Unity School itself made it difficult for them to participate. Unity rhetoric supported equality. Charles Fillmore in a speech to the Unity summer conference in 1927 declared, "We see no separation in color, in race, in sect, in creed, in anything. We are all one in Spirit."[9] Unity practices did not live up to this rhetoric. The school followed the segregationist policies of the South in dealing with those who came to Kansas City to study. The Unity Training School allowed Blacks into classes and workshops, but refused them accommodations on the grounds of Unity Farm. Housing was available for Whites only. Announcements like the following one in the *Training School Bulletin* in 1934 were repeated year after year for twenty years. It stated: "Owing to limited living accommodations at Unity Farm, it will be necessary for all colored students who register for classwork to live in Kansas City."[10]

In an effort to dispel doubt that food service at the school would be denied them, training school bulletins indicated: "Meals will be served a la carte to Negro students in the Terrace Tea Room."[11]

Unity's segregation policy came under attack in 1934 from *The Call*, a Kansas City newspaper. Unity School had agreed to host a meeting of the National Conference of Social Work in May at Unity Farm. *The Call* reported that Negro delegates had been "Jim Crowed."[12] They were given meals at the Unity dining room, but refused rooms for the night. When White delegates offered to share their rooms with Blacks, Unity managers refused to allow it. As a result, Negro delegates, totaling about a half dozen, withdrew from the conference. *The Call* interviewed Lowell Fillmore and took him to task for Unity's policy of discriminating against Negroes. Lowell's response indicated the Southern bias that prevailed in the Unity leadership on the question of race in the 1930s. *The Call* indicated that "after hedging a bit,"[13] Lowell stated: "You do not quite understand. We are feeling our way along. This is Missouri and the Missouri people are not educated to the point, as yet, where they will accept Negroes on a basis of equality."[14]

Until 1934 the Unity Ministers Association had no Black members. At a meeting of the board of directors on August 25, 1934, the issue was raised. The minutes indicate that there was "much discussion as to whether we should accept colored members at this time."[15] It was finally decided to accept them as members "if they desired to join." Only one Black woman, Lily Saunders of Jacksonville, Florida, was viewed as eligible to join. The minutes stated, "Let her ask for membership."[16]

Until 1937 Unity maintained racial distinctions in the licensing of teachers. In that year the Great Lakes Conference voted to recommend to the Unity Field Department and Unity Annual Conference that qualified teachers be licensed "without distinction as to race."[17] On July 1, 1937, a motion to that effect was carried at a conference board meeting. No longer would a licensed Black teacher be listed in Unity publications as "Colored Teacher."[18]

Blacks had to rely on public transportation to get back and forth from Kansas City. Infrequent service of buses without air-conditioning made it difficult for students to attend scheduled classes and meetings during the hot summer months in Kansas City. At a business meeting of the 1938 Annual Conference, it was recommended by Whites in attendance that quarters be made available at Unity Farm for Blacks, as many were missing meetings because of the need to commute.[19] Unity School did not act on the recommendation.

Concern about how to handle matters of race at Unity was indicated in a 1946 office memo. May Rowland, head of Silent Unity, in submitting a testimonial for publication in a Unity magazine, asked the editors: "Would it be wise to print it since the woman mentioned that she was Negro?"[20] The response was in the affirmative, though the rationale was dubious. The memo continued: "Everyone agreed that it would be a good idea, as it might create a good feeling among the Negroes as regards our efforts to help them."[21]

Eric Butterworth, who was a ministerial student at Unity School in the 1940s, characterized Unity School as "a Southern product," and Rickert Fillmore, who was chancellor of the training school at the time, as "a dyed-in-the-wool Southerner." Butterworth recalled that when he was in youth work for Unity he "had to carefully instruct Blacks not to make waves. I told them, 'You can't go in the swimming pool, so don't try.' They had to sit and watch. I felt it was terribly wrong."[22]

An article in *Unity*, "Why Call It 'Race' Prejudice?" written in 1947 by the popular Unity minister Ernest Wilson, was based on the assumption that Blacks still had more catching up to do before they would be equal to Whites. Wilson indicated that before Blacks were accorded equality, they needed to demonstrate their worthiness. Wilson acknowledged that "the American Negro" had "progressed rapidly" in the past century, because "exposure to the contact with peoples of other origins has greatly hastened their development." Nevertheless, further opportunities for Blacks would depend on how well they lived up to their responsibilities. Laws guaranteeing their civil rights were not the answer. Wilson asked:

Does the colored man feel that a caste system is operating against him? Let him abolish it within his own people. Does he demand the recognition his rights and abilities deserve? Let him know others will be watching, perhaps with undue concern, to see how he adjusts himself to them as they come. Wisdom, patience and good judgment will [win] for him a place of dignity and respect that no enactment of law can do.[23]

For several decades only a few Blacks were employed at Unity School. A Unity staff photograph taken February 2, 1954, and published on the cover of *Unity News*, showed several hundred workers, only a handful of whom were Black.[24] Those Blacks who were employed apparently were well regarded, if we can assume that the testimony to the work of Mary Walker is representative. Mrs. Walker, a Black woman who supervised the cooking and arranged for Black student accommodations in Kansas City and transportation to and from the school, died in 1952 after forty-three years of service. *Unity News* reported, "thousands of Unity workers and visitors the last 43 years knew her and respected her for her gentle manner toward all with whom she came in contact."[25]

The first glimmer of hope for the Blacks that Unity would open up living accommodations at Unity School came in 1953. The Unity Training School prospectus stated, "We hope in time to have living accommodations on Unity Farm for our Negro students."[26] By 1955 nothing had been done. A letter to the Unity board of trustees from "A True Friend" expressed growing frustration with Unity's segregation policies. Written June 28, 1955, the writer made the following request: "I am asking that you please pray with me for and about the following: The fact that Negroes are not allowed to stay in our cottages when our government rules there is to be no segregation. Are they children of God too?"[27]

The issue came to a head in 1955. A Black female ministerial student, Johnnie Colemon of Chicago, whom Dorothy Pierson, a training school teacher at the time, characterized as "an excellent student and true leader,"[28] threatened to quit the ministerial program if the school continued to refuse her housing on campus. In an article in the winter 2000 issue of *New Thought* magazine, Colemon recalled her experience: "Everyday we read out of the *Daily Word* about love and how much we loved each other. But before the sun would go down every day, I had to be on my way to Kansas City. That was fifteen miles one way. Thirty miles going and coming because of the color of my skin."[29]

Colemon reached a crisis point during her last summer at Unity

School, shortly before she was to graduate and qualify for ordination. She reported: "One morning I drove through pouring rain and by the time I got there I'd had it . . . I walked into the restaurant and said: 'This is it! I can't take anymore. I'm finished. I won't be back.' . . . They [her fellow students] said to me; 'You're not going to leave. You've given too much. We love you. We will sign a petition and you will live here.'"[30]

A group of ministerial students led by David Williamson developed a petition requesting that Colemon be housed at Unity Village and they submitted it to the school administration.[31] The school responded favorably, as Colemon reported: "I received a letter that I could live in the cottage at the end of the farm where the workers live. It was not a nice cottage. They expected me to say 'no.' I said, 'Fine. Take me to it.' . . . That was the beginning of Black students living at Unity Farm."[32]

Colemon's action officially ended segregated housing at Unity School. Bulletins issued by the Unity Training School, beginning in 1956, no longer indicated that Black students who attended classes at the school had to find living accommodations in Kansas City.[33]

Colemon herself went on to be one of the most successful ministers to graduate from Unity School. She became the founding minister of Christ Universal Temple in Chicago, which now [in 2000] has fifteen thousand members. About four thousand attend Sunday services, which Colemon continues to conduct. There are thirteen hundred adult students in weekly classes and seven hundred young people in a broad range of programs.[34]

Unlike student housing, recreational facilities at Unity School, particularly the tennis courts and the golf course, were apparently available to Black students and employees of the school. Unity publications announced each year, "all Unity workers are automatically eligible for membership in the Unity Country Club."[35] The same nondiscriminatory policy was not applied with regard to the use of the Unity swimming pool. The pool was off-limits for Blacks until the summer of 1963.[36] Rev. David Williamson, who was on the staff of the Unity Ministers Association at the time, described how the pool was integrated. He recalled:

In the summer of 1963 the Y.O.U. (Youth of Unity) was holding a conference at Unity Village. A number of black youths were in attendance. On a hot summer afternoon everyone, black and white, went down to the pool. Only the whites went in for a swim. Blacks stood on the deck watching. Ralph Rhea, the veteran Unity minister who at the time was co-director of the Unity Field Department, happened by the pool. Finding the situation intolerable he hollered, "Everyone swims." The blacks jumped in and from then on the pool was integrated.[37]

Who was responsible for Unity's continued policy of racial segregation in its public accommodations? Dorothy Pierson, the longtime Unity minister who was at Unity School in the 1940s and 1950s, stated that the difficulty lay in the general acceptance of segregation in the Kansas City area.[38] It is generally conceded, she noted, that the leadership of Unity School conformed to the policy of segregation at that time.[39] Dorothy indicated that Unity School's attitude toward Blacks changed when in 1962 Rickert's son, Charles R. Fillmore, became executive vice president and chief operating officer. He did not share the racial views of the local community, she noted, having been exposed to more enlightened attitudes during his service in the Navy in World War II.[40] In an interview with this writer, Charles R. Fillmore downplayed his role in integrating Unity School. He acknowledged that Unity was not in the forefront of the national effort to bring segregation to an end, and took no credit personally for Unity's changed policy. "We evolved with the rest of society," he explained. "We were not pioneers."[41]

It should be noted that, in the period prior to the Civil Rights movement, Unity's record on integration was no better or worse than that of other Christian churches in the South, Protestant or Catholic. Churches with White congregations that welcomed Blacks were few and far between before the walls of segregation came down nationally in the 1960s. Charles R. Fillmore acknowledged that Unity benefited greatly from integration. Increasing numbers of Blacks came to the training school and to the retreats when facilities were open to them.[42]

Despite the fact that Unity School did not take the lead in the Civil Rights movement, Blacks continued to be drawn to Unity's message. The Reverend John Anderson, the first Black Unity minister to teach at Unity School, indicated that Blacks in particular resonated with Unity's teaching regarding the healing of mind and body. Blacks, according to Anderson, easily identify with the Unity belief that God is the source and heals all things. Anderson noted that the example of Myrtle Fillmore in overcoming tuberculosis had an impact on Blacks. "It was testimony," Anderson indicated, "to the way God works in the world."[43]

While Blacks attend Unity churches, Anderson believes that Unity's biggest impact on the Black community is upon those who have no connection with a Unity congregation. He sees the Unity teaching having the greatest effect on those who have remained faithful to their Black churches, most of which are Baptist. In his thirty years in Unity, Anderson has encountered countless Blacks who read *Daily Word* and other Unity literature, use Unity tapes, and call Silent Unity for healing work. "Unity is alive in the black churches," noted Anderson, "but they don't call it Unity."[44]

David Williamson, a White Unity minister who for eighteen years led a Detroit congregation that was 95 percent Black, concurs with Anderson. According to Williamson, the parts of the Unity teaching that attract Blacks are: "That every person is divine, a child of God, and therefore has great dignity and self-worth; that men and women are not by nature sinful; and that prosperity and good health are the natural state for all humankind."[45]

Williamson, like Anderson, observed that most Blacks who identify with Unity do not attend Unity churches. He based this conclusion on a survey he did in Detroit in the late 1970s. At that time Unity School provided the Association of Unity Churches with a printout by ZIP code of all Unity contacts through subscriptions to Unity periodicals or calls to Silent Unity throughout the United States, including the Detroit metropolitan area. In checking ZIP codes in the center of the city, which is all Black, there were several thousand contacts, a total of one in ten households, far more than belonged to Unity churches there. Williamson concluded that while his Black congregation in central Detroit was large (about 1,000), its numbers were small compared to those who read Unity literature or contacted Silent Unity. Williamson's observations were confirmed in a conversation he had with a Black minister from a United Church of Christ in Detroit, who told him begrudgingly, "A lot of my people read your literature and ask for prayers and get involved with Unity."[46]

CHAPTER 14

Unity and New Thought

Introduction

"New Thought" was the term used to describe the nineteenth century
metaphysical movement in which mental healing was the key feature.
New Thought had its origins in the teachings of Emanuel Swedenborg,
Franz Anton Mesmer, Ralph Waldo Emerson, Warren Felt Evans, P. P.
Quimby, and Emma Curtis Hopkins.[1] Those who came to consider themselves as "New Thoughters," as they were sometimes called, might have at
one time identified themselves with liberal Christianity, Swedenborgianism, Transcendentalism, Theosophy, Spiritualism, Christian Science, or the
religions and philosophies of the East. They might also have used such
terms as "Mental Science," "Mind Cure," "Practical Metaphysics," or
"Divine Science" to describe their work.[2] New Thoughters were united in
the belief that the inner, or real self of men and women, is divine.[3] They
dissented from the common Christian view that men and women, though
created in the image and likeness of God, did not share God's divine nature.[4] The writings of the Fillmores, H. Emilie Cady, and Unity are considered by many in the New Thought movement to fall within the scope of
New Thought teaching.

Unity and the Organization of the New Thought Federation

Those who accepted New Thought ideas in the 1890s were a disparate
group, and no one organization on the regional or national scene met their
needs. An organization called the International Metaphysical League,
which attempted to serve as a clearinghouse, held conventions in various

large cities in the 1890s, but it disappeared from the scene before the turn of the century. An attempt to organize at the national level did not begin in earnest until 1903. A Chicago group that called itself the "Union New Thought Committee" served as a catalyst. This committee, comprised of representatives from several New Thought centers in Chicago, decided to bring together representatives from all New Thought organizations worldwide for the purpose of establishing a federation of like-minded groups.[5] Invitations went out to all individuals and organizations which engaged in mental healing, including Unity.

In addition to bringing groups together to discuss common goals and to receive inspiration from each other, one of the principal objectives of the meeting was to form an organization that served the needs of the member groups on an ongoing basis. Charles and Myrtle Fillmore, along with two members of their staff, Charles Edgar Prather and Jennie Croft, traveled to Chicago to attend the International New Thought Convention, which was held November 17–20, 1903. Both Fillmores were on the program and presented papers. In response to the question "What is New Thought?" the convention adopted a statement that, except for references to the role of Jesus, reflected the Fillmores' thinking on the nature of God and man. The statement read as follows:

God—Universal Spirit, Mind, Principle, is omnipresent, omniscient, and omnipotent.

Man is the individual expression of God, possessing inherently and capable of manifesting, all the aspects of God.

Man unfolds to a constantly expanding consciousness and manifestation of these aspects through right thinking and right living.

The consciousness of harmony is Heaven, here and now, in the realization of which abide peace of mind and health of body.[6]

A committee was formed to discuss organizational issues and to draft a resolution for the formation of a New Thought Federation. The resolution was presented for approval at the 1904 convention, held in St. Louis October 25–28. The Fillmores were pleased with the results of the Chicago convention and believed that a federation of New Thought organizations was a positive step. *Unity* magazine commented:

Through experience it was found that the method of one would not, and could not, fulfill the ideals of another, yet permeating all were the same basic principles of universal law. Instead, then, of an organization with a creed or doctrine of its own, to which many could not fully subscribe, it was found that co-operation or federation, regardless of method or creed, was the one thing necessary for the proper advancement of the movement as a whole.[7]

The Fillmores returned to Kansas City believing that their work and that of the other soon-to-be members of the New Thought Federation had been very productive. *Unity* magazine reported: "Unity staff, consisting of Charles Fillmore, Myrtle Fillmore, Jennie H. Croft, and Charles E. Prather, returned to their several posts of duty filled with enthusiasm over the good accomplished by this gathering together of the exponents of so many different phases of the New Thought."[8]

The major work of the 1904 convention in St. Louis was the adoption of the constitution of the New Thought Federation and the appointment of a board of directors and officers. Article II spelled out the purpose of the federation. It indicated:

The purposes of the Federation are: To promote the better and wider knowledge and appreciation of the unity of all life, and to assist in the manifestation of this unity by means of cooperation, to stimulate faith in, and study of, the higher nature of man in its relation and application to health, happiness and character; to foster the New Thought movement in general; to publish such literature as may be found advisable.[9]

Membership in the organization did not require individuals or groups either to alter or give up their teaching. It was further explained: "In accomplishing these purposes, the Federation in nowise shall interfere with, infringe upon or be responsible for the teachings and interpretations of affiliating individuals or organizations."[10] Charles's approval of the goals, purposes and operating procedures of the federation was further indicated when he accepted appointment as a member of the board of directors of the new federation.

Unity's participation in the activities of the New Thought Federation appears to have resulted in an increased involvement with New Thought groups in Kansas City. In November 1904 *Unity* magazine reported that a "Union New Thought Service" was held at the Athenaeum Hall. Those who participated included, in addition to Charles, Henry Harrison Brown, president of the New Thought Federation, who was visiting from San Francisco, and Dr. D. L. Sullivan, vice president of the federation and a resident of Kansas City. *Unity* further reported, "much interest is being taken in higher thought," and that all New Thought centers in Kansas City are "working together in love and harmony."[11]

In March 1905 *Unity* magazine reported on the opening of the New Thought Center in Cleveland, stating, "Unity extends congratulations and blessings to this new society and affirms unbounded success of the work." *Unity* further reported that "[T]he New Thought Movement is gaining strength and power and new centers are being organized on all sides."[12]

Unity played a significant part in the 1905 convention of the newly formed New Thought Federation, as it helped organize the meeting that was held from September 26 to 29 in the small town of Nevada, Missouri, not far from Kansas City. As the convention drew to a close, *Unity* magazine's associate editor, Jennie Croft, reported on the benefits many people derived from attending. She observed: "Thus closed the most successful convention in the history of the Federation, successful from every standpoint. The spirit of unity, harmony and love was most noticeable, and the enthusiasm awakened among the members to go home to work for the cause was marked."[13]

Withdrawal from the Federation

As 1905 drew to a close, Charles Fillmore began to harbor reservations about the desirability of Unity's continued participation in the New Thought Federation. In a long article in *Unity* magazine Charles expressed his misgivings. He was primarily concerned about the contradictions he saw in the teachings, all of which were classified as "New Thought." He commented:

New Thought is the common denominator of a complex and often contradictory mass of metaphysical doctrines which have sprung up in the past few years. . . . What may be termed the Mental Science School holds that God is not a being of Love and Wisdom, but a force of attraction. They repudiate the Loving father proclaimed by Jesus Christ and hold that man is the highest form of self-consciousness in the universe.[14]

A basic problem, Charles indicated, was that many people who branded themselves as New Thoughters lacked discrimination in spiritual matters, as evidenced by the leaders they followed. Charles reported: "A large number of New Thoughters are not using spiritual discrimination nor spiritual independence, but are following the way pointed out by some enthusiastic half-truth discoverer. Thus there are sharp divisions based upon different understandings of the expositions of the Divine Law in New Thought circles."[15]

Charles found that disagreement existed even among New Thought people with a Christian orientation. He expressed disappointment that common ground had not been reached, stating:

There is another class of New Thought people who accept Christianity in its true sense and try to live up to the teachings of Jesus Christ . . . There are a number of schools, passing under the general name of New Thought, that adhere to this Christian interpretation, yet even among them there are minor differences. Each teacher tinges with his mental bias the philosophy he promulgates. Not one seems yet to have attained that place where the revelation from the Spirit of Truth, promised by Jesus to his followers, is wholly transparent. For this reason disciples are never safe in accepting the teachings of any school as final.[16]

Charles believed that people who were being introduced to New Thought teachings for the first time should be warned that much effort would be required to discover "the unadulterated truth." He explained: "It will be seen that the New Thought student has a broad field to select from, also that he should have his eyes open in order that he may know to choose the truth from the great mass of matter labeled as 'New Thought.'"[17]

Charles admitted that he had concluded that in many respects Unity teaching differed from that of other New Thought leaders and schools. As a result, he found it difficult to be an active participant in the work of the New Thought Federation. He indicated: "So far as the Society of Practical Christianity (the local Unity society in Kansas City) is concerned we must candidly say that its teachings differ widely from those of the majority of New Thought doctrines, and we do not feel at home in the average gathering under that name, although we try to harmonize with all truth seekers."[18] Possibly as a result of his growing disenchantment with the group, Charles left the board of the federation. His name no longer appeared in 1906 on the roster of its board members.[19]

While Charles expressed reservations about the desirability of Unity's continued participation in the federation, no decision was made to pull back in 1905. When it came time for the annual 1906 New Thought convention, to be held in Chicago, October 23–26, Unity students were encouraged to participate. *Unity* magazine suggested: "All who can, should attend and let their friends know. These are all speakers who are too well known to need any introduction, and you are sure of a treat."[20]

Charles and Myrtle attended the Chicago convention, along with other Unity staff. Charles's continuing reservations about the work of the federation were reflected in comments made in *Unity* magazine after the adjournment of the convention. His principal complaint concerned the content of the teaching being presented under the "New Thought" label. A large percent of the subject matter, he reported, "was far from New Thought as I understand it."[21] He himself took issue with many of the teachings that were presented, and could not defend them to Unity students. He explained: "Quite a number of people who had taken our lessons last year asked me if I endorsed certain doctrines set forth by some of the speakers. I had to admit that I did not, yet they were accepted by the officials of the Convention without protest or explanation, and those unfamiliar with absolute Truth would naturally take for granted that they were New Thought teachings."[22]

The proceedings at the 1906 Chicago convention convinced Charles that he could no longer proceed under the 'New Thought' label. The teachings were too far removed from "the Truth" as he saw it. He observed: "It dawned upon me that the name 'New Thought' has been appropriated by so many cults that had new theories to promulgate, that it has ceased to express what I conceived to be Absolute Truth."[23]

It is not surprising, given Charles's disillusionment, that Unity withdrew from the New Thought Federation. Charles defended the decision in the following announcement:

The New Thought Federation is attempting to carry this load of thought diversity, and I can see no success in it. There are too many lines of thought to harmonize. When I hear what, to me, is rank error set forth by New Thought speakers, I protest and say, "If this is New Thought, then I must find a new name for my philosophy." In the face of these facts I have decided that I am no longer a New Thoughter. I have a standard of faith, which is true and logical, and I must conform to it in my teaching without compromise. We call it Practical Christianity, and under this name we shall henceforth do our work.[24]

In January 1907, Charles elaborated further on the weaknesses he perceived in the people who had enrolled as members of the federation. The principal difficulty was that many failed to accept "statements of truth" because they had not yet reached a high enough level of spiritual consciousness. He observed:

What I saw as a hopeless task was the attempt to unify so many lines of individual thought, the basis of which was not in the absolute, but the relative, and must therefore always be disintegrating. There is but one foundation upon which we can have a permanent federation, and that is the One Absolute Mind. From that

Mind, statements of truth can be formulated that will be accepted by all who are functioning in the top brain, where the superconsciousness has its seat of action. Those in whom the tide of life flows no higher than intellectual perception will not rise to this consciousness of the Absolute, hence we cannot expect them to accept its basis of the origin of things.[25]

Charles then restated a long-held belief that only those who commit their lives to the regeneration of the body can achieve advanced levels of spiritual consciousness. He was confident that more and more people would commit themselves to this ideal, and that over time a sizable number would reach this advanced state. He wrote: "Only those who think purely and act virtuously in all ways, conserving the vitalities of mind and body, can rise and stay in the top brain, hence we may not get together a very large convention in the beginning, but it will come, and be a permanent federation of men who are truly seeking unselfishly to do the will of God."[26]

For several years after 1907, the pages of *Unity* magazine contained no information on the activities of the New Thought Federation or its annual conventions. In April 1913 *Weekly Unity* broke the silence with the following announcement: "We are requested to announce that the New Thought Convention, to be held at Detroit, has changed the date of opening to June 16th. We make this announcement for the information of our readers and not as a matter in which we are directly interested."[27] *Weekly Unity* then restated the position Unity had taken regarding its involvement in the activities of the New Thought Federation, again indicating that contradictions in New Thought teaching had caused Unity to refrain from further participation:

A number of years ago we decided that the holding of the New Thought conventions was unprofitable, and our views have not changed. Our work has grown much faster since we decided to stay at home and attend to it, and we are satisfied that the energy put into conventions would bring far greater returns to the cause, and the individuals concerned, if we expended it in local fields. Besides, the mass of contradictory statements presented at such gatherings is confusing the public as to the true character of the doctrines for which we stand.[28]

In April 1916 *Unity* magazine, in an editorial note presumably written by Charles, expressed misgivings about the current direction of the New Thought movement. Reference was also made to an earlier and happier time in the history of the movement, when there was more general agreement on the content of the teaching. The item reported:

There was a time in the history of what is called New Thought when it had a standard of principles that were universally accepted by its teachers. These principles were the expression of mind that had been illuminated by the inspiration of the untrammeled I Am. But there was neither head nor organization to New Thought, and of later years it has become a Babylon of voices crying in the wilderness. The name has been adopted by every kind of new doctrine, and has almost wholly lost the spiritual significance for which its early students regarded it. So do not take for granted that the name "New Thought" represents any defined spiritual doctrine.[29]

Unity and the International New Thought Alliance

Three years later in November 1919, with no prior indication that Unity's position had shifted regarding New Thought, it was announced that Unity had rejoined the International New Thought Alliance (the name the New Thought Federation had adopted in the interim) and that I.N.T.A.'s Congress in 1919 would be held in Kansas City under Unity sponsorship.[30] In a brief note entitled "Unity and the International New Thought Alliance," presumably written by Charles but not identified as such, the background of Unity's involvement in the organization was briefly traced: "Early in the organization of I.N.T.A., Unity was active in its movements and represented on its program. However, as time went on, certain ideas were introduced into the Alliance which, from our point of view, were not in keeping with the Christ message, and we therefore withdrew from the organization."[31]

The item further indicated that officials of I.N.T.A. had been striving to make the organization acceptable to Unity: "During the last few years there have been those in the Alliance who sought untiringly to eliminate from their programs and practices those things which had, in a sense, placed a stigma upon the name New Thought."[32]

The result of these efforts was an acknowledgment that Christ was the head of the New Thought movement, and its "invisible inspiration and guide." This was made official in 1919 by the action of I.N.T.A. in its Cincinnati congress by the adoption of "Bulletin 17," which stated:

The universe is spiritual and we are spiritual beings. This is the Christ message to the twentieth century, and it is a message not so much of words but of works. To attain this, however, we must be clean, honest and trustworthy, and uphold the Christ standard in all things. Let us build our house upon this rock, and nothing can prevail against it. This is the vision and mission of the Alliance.[33]

Based on I.N.T.A.'s action in adopting "the Jesus Christ Standard," Unity agreed to rejoin the alliance. In so doing, however, it was acknowledged that Unity was still not in agreement with a number of the teachings that were classified as "New Thought." The Fillmores noted:

The entrance of Unity into the New Thought Alliance does not mean that Unity endorses everything which has been and is now being taught under the name of New Thought. There are yet teachers who are giving forth ideas which are entirely inconsistent with the principles of Truth. Our action in this connection does indicate, however, that Unity believes in the spirit activating the International New Thought Alliance at this time, and that we propose to support this spirit in every way possible.[34]

The I.N.T.A. conference held in Kansas City, September 19–23, 1920, came off exceedingly well from Unity's point of view. *Unity* magazine used words of high praise to characterize the proceedings and the impact of Unity's participation, observing:

It is impossible for us to convey in words of exultation of spirit, the democratic camaraderie, the lovely accord which characterized all the proceedings of the Seventh International New Thought Alliance Congress. And why not this beautiful harmony? The spirit of the living Christ, active in all the business deliberations, the lectures, and the speeches, proved as ever, when invoked, a great, loving, brooding, harmonizing presence. . . . It is not too much to assume that the Unity spirit, which we have been cultivating at this center for years, came to perfect fruition at this Congress.[35]

The key to the success of the event from the Unity perspective was the emphasis placed on the role of Jesus Christ in the work of I.N.T.A. *Unity* magazine reported: "The dominant note sounded by all the speakers was 'conformity with the Christ standard.' As the week went on and the sessions continued, one could in one's mind's eye see that gleaming banner, far-flung to the nations, inviting the weary, the disconsolate, the wretched, into the pure white light of the Christ self."[36]

Unity magazine considered it remarkable that such a widely diverse group could join in acknowledgment of "the Jesus Christ Standard." *Unity* noted:

It must be remembered that most of the different cults of the New Thought movement were represented at the Congress. Yet Jew, Gentile, Divine Scientist, Mental Scientist, Episcopal minister in the Immanuel movement, a pastor of the Universalist Church, even those who have been taught to heal by suggestion—these all proclaimed themselves as followers of the Jesus Christ standard as set by Unity over thirty years ago! Glory to His holy name.[37]

The relationship between Unity and I.N.T.A. continued on a high note in 1921. The I.N.T.A. congress held in Denver, July 17–24, 1921, was equally as successful as that held under Unity sponsorship in Kansas City in 1920. After the convention Charles, in remarks made at Unity headquarters to the Unity school staff, gave his personal assessment of the progress that had been made as a result of Unity's involvement with I.N.T.A. He explained:

Many of you know that two years ago the Unity School here at Kansas City, through its President, decided to join the Alliance, and last year the congress met at Kansas City . . . Many of our people thought we were getting along very well, and that it would be better not to go into any by-paths or make alliances with other movements so long as we were growing so rapidly. But we have always been classed with what is broadly termed the New Thought movement, and our sympathies have been with them in the advanced religious ideas which they are advocating. Consequently, when at the Cincinnati convention they adopted what is called the Jesus Christ Standard, we felt that we could no longer refuse to cooperate with them. As some of you doubtless know, in this move we have had to meet situations that were not altogether harmonious, but on the whole, we are pleased to report that our work with them has been satisfactory, and that the fundamental doctrine for which we all stand are being furthered and more freely accepted by people everywhere as a result of our cooperation.[38]

Charles was particularly impressed by the spirit of cooperation that existed at the congress and the good will that existed between all the participants. He noted:

The peace, harmony, and love of the Christ Spirit were so apparent at the various meetings that many of the speakers commented on it. Lecturers and teachers representing every branch of New Thought were present, but the doctrines they set forth did not conflict in the least, and it was universally conceded that there had never been such perfect harmony at any convention before. This was proof that the Christ Spirit was present, and that we were working according to Divine Principle.[39]

Charles felt that the convention in Denver was particularly successful because of the stress that had been placed on spiritual healing. He was particularly pleased with the way convention presenters had addressed the subject, stating:

Unusual attention was given at this congress to the practical application of public healing. Every meeting closed with healing demonstrations ... No attempt was made in these meetings to stimulate the emotional nature, and thereby get temporary results, as is the rule in most faith healing gatherings. Appeal was made directly to the understanding and realization of the truth that health is man's normal condition, and by having faith in the one omnipresent Life, Love, Substance Power, and Intelligence, man can come into such close relations with the source of health that he may be instantly restored. This feature of the Alliance is to be more fully brought out in future congresses.[40]

Charles also expressed pleasure with changes that had been made in the constitution of the alliance, and expressed his belief that I.N.T.A. would be even stronger if the word "Christian" were added to its name. He indicated:

Quite a few changes were made in the constitution of the Alliance, and an open acknowledgment of Jesus Christ as the head of the movement, and the New Testament as its textbook was incorporated. The matter of adding the word "Christian" to the official name of the Alliance was brought up in the Plans Committee meeting, but it was decided to postpone the question until next year. Of course the Unity people thought that the word "Christian" added to the name of the Alliance would be notice to the world that it was a Christian organization.[41]

Withdrawal from the International New Thought Alliance

With no advance warning, and just five months after Charles's statement indicating that the Unity-I.N.T.A. relationship was flourishing, on March 22, 1922, Unity withdrew from the International New Thought Alliance. The announcement that appeared in *Unity* magazine under the headline UNITY WITHDRAWS FROM I.N.T.A. was short and gave few details as to the reasons for the action. The announcement read as follows:

On March 7, 1922, a special meeting was called to consider the relationship of the Unity School of Practical Christianity with the International New Thought Alliance. Our directors, department heads and teachers were in attendance. It was unanimously voted, that, on account of the many protests received from our students against our membership in the I.N.T.A., and owing to the fact that the present methods of the Alliance make it virtually another metaphysical school rather than an association of schools, thereby rendering it impracticable for the Unity School to give time and support to it, the Unity School of Christianity resigned from the Alliance, the resignation to take effect at once.[42]

The brief announcement did not satisfy Unity students, and many wrote to the school asking for more information. Charles, in responding, acknowledged that the school had hoped to avoid a full disclosure, stating, "[I]t had not been our intention to give publicly all the causes of the withdrawal from I.N.T.A."[43] The desire for more details on the part of *Unity* readers convinced him that it was necessary to provide a fuller explanation. Charles listed as a primary reason I.N.T.A.'s refusal to add the word "Christian" to its name. He commented:

The Unity School has from the beginning stood for certain religious ideals which the New Thought people have not adopted. We have proclaimed Jesus Christ as the head of our work, and have so notified the world by putting the word "Christian" into the name of our organization. This the I.N.T.A. has refused to do, although it claims to carry out Christian principles. When we advocated a change of name to include the word "Christian" the proposal was quickly hushed up in the executive board meeting. The argument was that, although I.N.T.A was a Christian movement, it should not put anything in its name to antagonize non-Christians who might otherwise be induced to join.[44]

Secondly, Charles listed I.N.T.A.'s refusal to adopt Unity teachings regarding the regeneration of the body. As a result, Charles felt Unity was hampered in presenting to the world the correct view of physical death and the afterlife. Charles indicated:

Unity teaches that the eternal life taught and demonstrated by Jesus is not gained by dying, but by refining the body until it becomes the undying habitation of the soul. This refinement of the body requires the renunciation of certain sense habits and appetites, such as the lust for meat, tobacco, stimulants, sex, coarse dances, and all pleasures that exalt sense above soul. Unity teaches that to gain the spiritual life man must sacrifice the animal life. "He that loseth his life for my sake shall find it." New Thought people do not advocate the renunciation of sense life in order to gain eternal life. They teach that man goes on to higher fields of action by dying. We hold that Christianity, rightly understood, teaches a science by which life can be attained here and now, and that dying is a loss instead of a gain.[45]

Charles concluded that only by being free from the New Thought connection could Unity properly put forth these teachings. He observed:

Unity has certain ideals to carry forward, and it must have the greatest freedom in presenting them because they are revolutionary, and some of them, like eternal life here and now in the body, apparently visionary and beyond attainment. But these ideas are capable of attainment, and admitted by progressive philosophers in various fields of physical science. Unity people are aiming to demonstrate these ideals, although the ideas may appear to be beyond present human achievement . . . The Unity School found that it was hampered in the expression of its ideals through its intimate association with New Thought.[46]

Charles also felt that, rather than being truly committed to it, I.N.T.A. gave only lip service to "the Jesus Christ Standard." They never fully accepted it as part of their teaching. He explained:

We cooperated with the I.N.T.A. when that organization agreed to the Jesus Christ Standard, but we found that their concept of that standard was not ours, and they insisted that we should cooperate on the interpretation which they give to the ideas which we are working out. This hampered us instead of helped us. We must all in the end be set free, and Unity has declared its freedom from all organizations that advocate anything less than the highest idealism of Jesus.[47]

Charles noted that confusion and consternation were experienced at Unity centers in the field when I.N.T.A. members were granted a forum at these centers and then presented teachings that contradicted those of Unity School. Charles elaborated:

New Thought requested the open platform at all Unity centers for its field lectures, because Unity was a member of the I.N.T.A. When this was granted and the lecturers opposed, as they nearly always did, the plain teachings of Jesus on these points, the congregations were confused and often dismayed at the apparent change of doctrine at the Unity center. It then required continued explanation and much effort on the part of Unity teachers to clear up points in which the two schools differed.[48]

Charles was particularly dismayed because, after Unity joined I.N.T.A., the organization shifted its focus from being a federation of like-minded organizations to becoming a school espousing a doctrine that on many points contradicted Unity teachings. As a result, a cooperative relationship devolved into a competitive one. Charles explained:

The I.N.T.A. directors are doubtless not aware of it, but they are making the Alliance another school of New Thought people, instead of a federation of schools that already exists. We were continually urged by the I.N.T.A. to cooperate in building up their school, which was working along lines parallel with Unity, yet so different in many respects that we did not harmonize with them. We see that the demand for a New Thought School has so crystallized around the I.N.T.A. that it will continue in spirit to be a school instead of an alliance of schools . . . We have no objection whatever to the institution, but we do object to its trying at the same time to be a federation of institutions . . . This and similar methods were pulling right away from the idea of a federation of schools for mutual benefit, causing many of our centers to complain of I.N.T.A. competition, instead of cooperation which we had expected.[49]

Unity's withdrawal from the I.N.T.A. in 1922 apparently ended official contact with the organization. In the two decades preceding World War II, Unity publications carried little information on I.N.T.A activities. In October 1923 in a piece in *Unity* magazine, Charles emphasized the distancing from other New Thought groups when he declared: "We were also classed as New Thought people, Mental Scientists, and Theosophists, and so on, but none of these sufficiently emphasized the higher attributes of man, and we avoided any close affiliation with them."[50]

While most of the statements in the public record concerning Unity's relationship with New Thought groups were made by Charles, Myrtle evidently held views similar to his. Her thinking on the subject of New Thought was revealed in a letter to a Mrs. Kramer, written in 1928. Myrtle advised the woman, who apparently had involved herself with New Thought teachings, to let go of her attachment to ineffective teachings and devote herself to the teachings of Jesus. In her characteristically direct and forthright manner, Myrtle suggested:

Instead of thinking and saying "New Thought" would it not be better for you to think and speak of "God Thought"? It is not "New Thought," it is thought which is founded in the unchanging spiritual reality. "New Thought" lets one in for all sorts of conjectures and experiments and isms. To identify one's self with "New Thought" is to open the mind to the winds and waves of the race thought which is being built up. While to identify one's self with the Jesus Christ Standard of thinking which is made known in the individual's mind and heart through the action of the Holy Spirit, keeps one poised and freed and filled with Light.[51]

In the late 1930s, Charles, at a board meeting of Unity ministers, again restated the principal reasons for Unity's final departure from the I.N.T.A. The meetings recorder paraphrased Charles's remarks, stating:

Mr. Fillmore mentioned that in 1920 the Unity ministry in Kansas City joined the I.N.T.A. and soon after that they were invited to Kansas City for their meeting, but it was discovered that members of the organization were teaching ideas entirely opposite from what Unity teaches . . . Also, certain (I.N.T.A.) members felt they should be allowed to present their teachings from Unity platforms. For this reason the Unity work in Kansas City immediately withdrew its membership from I.N.T.A.[52]

The recorder then appears to have quoted Charles directly, who summed up his views by saying: "Since we have chosen the Unity way, it is our duty to stay true to the Jesus Christ teachings. . . . We should become so strong in our definite presentation of the Jesus Christ message that eventually all those leaders who are associated with I.N.T.A. will see this clearly."[53] This last remark clearly reflects Charles's long-held hope that New Thought would ultimately incorporate into its teachings the Unity interpretation of the Jesus Christ message.

Unity Remains Outside the I.N.T.A.

In the late 1940s the Unity School board of directors again took up the question of the school's relationship with I.N.T.A. Lowell Fillmore observed that Unity had withdrawn from the I.N.T.A. when it discovered that "members of the organization were teaching ideas entirely opposite from what Unity teaches." Lowell took the position, "Since we have chosen the Unity way, it is our duty to stay true to the Jesus Christ teaching." He expressed the view that Unity work in centers and churches could not have been conducted properly if Unity teachings had been mixed with that of other New Thought groups.[54]

Unity School has continued to maintain its position of nonaffiliation and non-involvement. Connie Fillmore Bazzy, president of Unity School, indicated that the school's position is based on the view that I.N.T.A. represents a spectrum of teaching, some of which is not consistent with that of Unity School. While I.N.T.A. proclaims the divinity of humanity, it does not officially establish Jesus as the standard and authority. While the school sees no benefit in joining forces with I.N.T.A., it has no objection to Unity ministers who see value in participating. Unity School has maintained the same position regarding the Association for Global New Thought, a group that was organized in 1955 by members of the I.N.T.A. who were dissatisfied with the leadership and direction of the organization.[55]

CHAPTER 15

Unity and the New Age

Introduction

The New Age is an international social, religious, and spiritual movement begun in the late 1960s. It is aimed at promoting personal and spiritual growth and provides individuals with an opportunity to experience a wide variety of spiritual principles, practices, and disciplines. It has no single leader, no central organization, no agreed-upon agenda, and no official spokesperson.[1] The movement has been particularly attractive to people who have experienced apathy or disillusionment in their spiritual life.[2] The New Age is comprised of a variety of teaching and healing modalities, including:

• Mind/body practices such as Yoga (in its various forms), Tai Chi, aikido, massage, Rolfing, biofeedback, Feldenkrais and reflexology.

• Psychological therapies such as Gestalt, psychosynthesis, encounter, hypnosis, rebirthing, Progoff journaling, and past-life therapy.

• Holistic healing methods including acupuncture and acupressure, homeopathy, therapeutic touch, A Course in Miracles, prayer, and affirmations.

• Meditation in several forms including Eastern practices such as Zen and Vipassana, Transcendental Meditation, and a variety of centering techniques.

• Metaphysical practices including the Kabbalah, channeling, crystals, and dream interpretation.

• Psychic readings, including ESP (Extra Sensory Perception), clairvoyance and clairaudience.

• Divination, including astrology, the tarot, palmistry, numerology, the I Ching and shamanic practice.

• Dietary regimens including vegetarianism and macrobiotics.[3]

The above methods have been presented by a wide variety of practitioners in local settings as well as at retreat centers such as Esalen in Big Sur, California; the Omega Institute at Rhinebeck, New York; and the Kripalu Center for Yoga and Health in Boulder, Colorado. In addition, these techniques have been presented in personal growth seminars such as EST (now called the Forum), Mind Dynamics (renamed Lifespring), PSI Seminars, Life Dynamics, Hoffman Quadrinity Process, Actualizations, Dimensional Mind Approach, Pathwork, and others.

The "New Age" is somewhat of a misnomer, because many of the techniques and practices associated with it are not new, having been available for generations prior to the 1960s in a wide variety of venues. New Age antecedents can be found in Swedenborgianism, mesmerism, Transcendentalism, Spiritualism, Christian Science, New Thought, Theosophy, parapsychology, and Eastern spirituality and philosophy. The term " New Age" has been used pejoratively by those outside the movement because many who identify themselves with it appear, according to many observers of the movement, to be self-preoccupied, undisciplined, shallow, tending to flit from one fad to another.[4]

Commonalities in Unity and New Age Practices

The basic Unity spiritual practices (mental self-discipline, affirmations, visualizations, prayer, meditation, accessing intuition, dream work, and focusing on the here and now) are presented in one form or another in many New Age modalities. Consequently, it is not surprising that many ministers in Unity churches, as they seek to deepen their own spiritual experience and that of their congregations, have incorporated modalities identified with the New Age into the work of the churches. Unity churches have served as hosts for "A Course in Miracles" groups as well as for holistic healers, mind/body practitioners, meditation teachers, and personal growth workshop leaders.

While many Unity churches have presented work of practitioners associated with the New Age, the Unity School of Christianity has preferred to confine itself to the presentation of the pure Unity teaching. For the most

part, it has resisted attempts to influence the contents or method of presentation of its teaching from individuals or groups outside the Unity
movement. For two years during the late 1960s, New Age teachings were
presented by Unity through its Omega Center. The center was disestab-
lished when leaders of Unity decided its programs compromised the work
of the school. Since the 1960s Unity School and the Association of Unity
Churches have separated themselves from teachings and practices branded
as New Age. Leaders have made it clear that Unity teachings do not include the use of tarot cards or the practice of astrology, numerology, channeling, Kirlian photography, or healing through crystals.[5] Unity's perception of the New Age was expressed by Connie Fillmore Bazzy in the following statement:

What then is the New Age and what is Unity's attitude toward it? The New Age is
a potpourri of many different ideas, philosophies, doctrines and practices. It has
attracted such a variety of people under its banner that it is difficult to define exactly what it is and what it is not. The New Age that Unity seeks to teach is an inner, spiritual journey which is available to us all and which can be undertaken at
any time.[6]

Unity's Impact on the New Age

Since Unity principles and practices are used by New Age practitioners, it is likely that, given Unity's century-long history, some of these practitioners consulted Unity teachings during the course of their own spiritual
search. The work of Alexander Everett, a Unity student in his formative
years, provides one concrete example of how Unity teachings found their
way into the personal growth workshops associated with the New Age.

Born in England in 1921 and raised in the Church of England, Everett
encountered Unity work early in life. His mother subscribed to *Daily
Word* and, according to Everett, used the affirmations presented there to
heal him as a child from asthma. Everett indicates that during the Great
Depression, after his family lost all its money, his mother relied on Unity
teaching and prosperity affirmations to get the family through major financial difficulties. As a teenager in an English boarding school, Everett
subscribed to both *Unity* and *Weekly Unity* magazines. Charles Fillmore's
ideas on the oneness of all religion had a major impact on him. "That
woke me up," Everett recalled. By the time he finished school, his spiritual
ideas were more in alignment with Unity than with Anglicanism. "Inspira-

tional articles in Unity magazine," he commented, "bolstered my vision and led me to believe that someday I would be a spiritual teacher."[7]

As an adult Everett continued to read Unity literature. He did not attend Unity church services, because no Unity center was available in his locality. At the age of twenty-nine, while serving as headmaster of an English preparatory school in Sussex, Everett had a major health crisis. He contracted polio and was told by medical authorities that he would never walk again. He healed himself, he reported, through using the affirmations contained in Unity's "Prayer of Faith," written by Hannah More Kohaus.[8] The prayer reads:

> God is my help in every need;
> God does my every hunger feed;
> God walks beside me, guides my way
> Through every moment of the day.
>
> I now am wise, I now am true,
> Patient, kind, and loving, too.
> All things I am, can do, and be,
> Through Christ, the Truth that is in me.
>
> God is my health, I can't be sick,
> God is my strength, unfailing, quick;
> God is my all; I know no fear,
> Since God and love and Truth are here.[9]

He repeated this prayer several times during the day for one month, at which time, he reported, he regained the use of his legs. "The doctors could not believe it," he indicated. They considered his recovery to be a medical miracle. As he regained his health, Everett's interest in Unity grew. After founding and becoming headmaster of Shiplake College in his thirties, he decided in 1962 at the age of forty to give up his work, come to the United States, and pursue a career as a spiritual teacher.

Everett enrolled in the ministerial training program at Unity School with the idea of becoming a Unity center leader. At Unity Village, in addition to pursuing ministerial studies, he served as a prayer worker and letter writer in Silent Unity. During his stay at Unity School, he was profoundly affected by the spiritual presence of Lowell Fillmore, then president of the school, who spent considerable time with him. He developed a high regard for May Rowland, director of Silent Unity, who took a personal interest in him and was eager for him to succeed. He continued in the ministerial program for only one year, deciding that he was not cut out for pastoral work. Unity School officials agreed that Everett should seek a different venue for his spiritual work.[10]

In 1964 Everett went to Fort Worth, Texas, at the request of a friend who asked him to help found the Fort Worth Country Day School, an institution whose academic program was to be based on the English curriculum. On weekday evenings he taught a meditation course in which he facilitated people in going into the silence. His sessions were so well attended that in 1968 he increased his efforts, conducting workshops that required attendance over the course of two weekends. Included in these sessions, in addition to meditation, were guided imagery, closed-eye processes, and the use of affirmations directed toward basic human needs—health, prosperity, and success. He named this experiential teaching "Mind Dynamics."

In 1970 Everett relocated to San Francisco, believing that Californians were more ready for Mind Dynamics than were Texans. Through lectures at a metaphysical bookstore and by making contact with doctors at a hospital for children, he enrolled sixty people in his first weekend workshop, which was given at a downtown hotel. By the end of the year he had conducted several Mind Dynamics training sessions, with increasing numbers of people. He taught people "how to use the mind in a positive manner . . . how to think right, feel right, and act right." Mind Dynamics promoted itself by using the slogan "Change the world, one mind at a time." Everett earned over $100,000 during its first year of operation.[11]

The work quickly became too large for one facilitator, so Everett began teaching others to present the workshop. By 1974 Mind Dynamics had expanded to the point where workshops were being given several times each year in San Francisco and in many major cities in the United States as well as in Switzerland and Australia. In 1974 Everett concluded that Mind Dynamics was placing too much stress on the development of mind power alone, and that he himself was on the wrong track. He decided to leave the organization and create a workshop that helped people enter "the spiritual state of human consciousness." He named this new spiritual development seminar "Inward Bound."[12]

Mind Dynamics was taken over by two of Everett's assistants, John Hanley and Robert White, and continued under a new name, "Lifespring." Several Mind Dynamics workshop leaders proceeded in the 1970s to establish their own personal growth organizations. These included: Werner Erhard, who founded EST (Erhard Seminar Trainings); Stewart Emery, who created Actualizations; Randy Revell, who developed Context; James Quinn, who organized Lifestream; and Thomas Willhite, who founded PSI Seminars. At this writing most of these organizations (or their successors) continue to exist.[13]

By 2000 Everett had taught Inward Bound for twenty-five years, presenting it annually in several locations in the United States, Europe, and the Far East. The seminar incorporated many of the same spiritual principles he had learned through his lifelong interest in Unity teaching. Several thousand people have attended the workshop. At this writing, although approaching eighty years of age, Everett continues to teach both in the United States and abroad.[14]

Nine personal growth organizations have grown out of Mind Dynamics. These include EST (now called "The Forum"), Lifespring, Lifestream, Context Training, PSI Seminars, Personal Dynamics of Switzerland, Life Dynamics of Japan and Hong Kong, Alpha seminars in Australia, and Actualizations. While each added experiential exercises that included confrontational encounter work and role-playing, all retained some of the original program created by Everett.[15] This included Unity practices such as going into the silence, affirmations, focusing the mind on the positive rather than the negative, and listening for the intuitive inner voice.[16]

Over the course of the past three decades (1970–2000), over one million people have enrolled in the personal growth trainings spawned by Mind Dynamics. Everett, in looking back over the course of his career as a spiritual teacher, acknowledged that Unity principles and practices played an important role in his own work, as well as in that of Mind Dynamics and its successors.[17] He considers Unity, both Unity School and Unity churches, as reflecting spiritually "the energy of this age." "Unity," he asserted, "is absolutely in tune with the spiritual needs of today." He believes that the Unity movement will continue to grow and prosper.[18]

The similarity in content between the Unity teaching and the personal growth seminars spawned by Mind Dynamics was brought to my attention in the mid-1980s. After participating in a Lifespring workshop, I was told by a fellow participant that if I wanted to explore the Lifespring teachings in greater depth, I should attend a Unity church. Similarities in the content of the teaching was apparent to me as I explored Unity at church services in Washington, D.C., and attended, in addition to Lifespring, other Mind Dynamics-related trainings (EST, Actualizations, and PSI Seminars).

Are there others, in addition to Alexander Everett, who nurtured themselves spiritually through Unity and then injected Unity teachings into New Age modalities? The answer is probably yes, though at the time of this writing, my research has not uncovered additional examples. One of Charles Fillmore's principal goals was to insert Unity teaching into the spiritual framework of Christian denominations. He would probably be pleased to know that Unity teachings have found their way into the structure of New Age spirituality.

Perspectives on Unity: Commentaries from Other Spiritual and Religious Vantage Points

Unity has provoked wide-ranging responses from those representing other spiritual and religious vantage points. Presented below are commentaries from representatives of mainstream Christian denominations, scholars in the field of American religion, and non-Unity teachers of New Thought principles.

Representatives of Mainstream Christianity

Many Roman Catholics and mainstream Protestants, including Episcopalians, Lutherans, and Presbyterians, view Unity as out of alignment with traditional Christian beliefs. The Christian Right has been most vocal in labeling Unity as "heretical" and "anti-Christian." Unity is viewed as taking non-Christian positions on such issues as the nature of God and man, the role of Jesus, sin and salvation, hell and the nature of the afterlife, and the role of Satan or the Devil. Constant Jacquet Jr. of the National Council of Churches summarized the view of many traditional Christians when he observed, "Unity does not fit in with mainstream Christianity."[1]

MISINTERPRETATION OF THE BIBLE

Critics of Unity indicate that errors in Unity teaching are derived from its metaphysical interpretation of sacred Scripture, which they view as undermining the biblical message. William J. Whalen, a Roman Catholic, author of *Separated Brethren,* views the Unity teaching as robbing the Bible of its true meaning, noting: "Unity students interpret the Bible allegorically and strip Christianity of its essential doctrines."[2] Writing in *The Sunday School Times,* the Reverend George A. Brown was blunt in his criticism, stating: "Unity in its metaphysical interpretation of the Bible, falsifies its true meaning."[3] Rev. Louis T. Talbot, who served as the chancellor of the Bible Institute of Los Angeles, was particularly caustic in his condemnation of Unity's approach to biblical interpretation. He indicated that Unity's teaching was "thoroughly saturated with some of the most soul-destroying and Scripture-denying doctrines ever foisted upon the world."[4] He continued:

You do not find any outright denials that the Bible is the Word of God in Unity. You find something far more subtle and deadly. The "metaphysical interpretation" can make any verse mean whatever the teacher desires without reference to semantics whatsoever. What utter arrogance to take the plain words of Scripture and thus "interpret" them. Unity distorts the Word of God, destroys its meaning and leads its followers into [an] intellectual spiritual maze.[5]

Dr. Gordon Lewis, professor of theology at the Conservative Baptist Theological Seminary in Denver, Colorado, agreed, saying, "Unity subverts the Bible's message." Lewis observed: "Unity students select the Bible' s statement only when they displace its original meaning with a spiritualized meaning . . . The Unity interpretation of Scripture is made to the measure of the Fillmores' preconceived ideals and interests."[6]

Dr. James Teener, who wrote a Ph.D. dissertation in American religious history on Unity in 1939, revisited Unity work in 1952 in an article entitled "The Challenge of Unity," published by *Crossroads,* a publication of the Board of Christian Education of the Presbyterian Church of the United States. Teener viewed Unity from his position as general presbyter for the Kansas City Presbytery, rather than from his role as a scholar and academic. He criticized Unity for its method of biblical interpretation, stating: "The Bible is not to be interpreted by recognized historical methods, but by intuition . . . Because it is wholly dependent on individual whim, lacking any intellectual controls, it has enabled Unity to interpret the simplest Biblical statements in terms of mystical systems of Hinduism and its dependents, Theosophy and New Thought."[7]

In *The Kingdom of the Cults,* Walter R. Martin accused Unity of subterfuge in presenting its interpretation of the Bible, indicating that Unity, through chicanery, misleads people. He noted: "The Unity School adopts Biblical language to portray its essentially anti-Christian theological propositions. But when its theological teachings are projected against the backdrop of Biblical revelation, and stripped of their protective terminology camouflage, the entire system is revealed to be a . . . clear counterfeit of the genuine Gospel of Jesus Christ."[8]

FALSE VIEW OF THE NATURE OF GOD AND MAN

Unity's teachings on the nature of God have drawn sharp criticism from a variety of Christian sources. Unity has been attacked for rejecting the belief that God is a person, and for viewing God as impersonal "principle."

The Reverend A. Jase Jones, a high-ranking Southern Baptist, indicated that Unity's concept of God as principle was inaccurate. He declared: "God is more than impersonal principle. He is person, self-knowing, distinct from man, able to infill but maintain separate identity, with characteristics and powers beyond man's ability to possess."[9]

Rev. Louis T. Talbot chided Unity for its failure to accord "personality" to God. He asserted: "It is clear that Unity does not believe . . . that God is a Person, with intelligence, will, emotion and ability to think and act which denotes personality."[10]

In an article entitled "The Unity Cult," Walter Martin pointed out the same inadequacy in the Unity approach, observing: "The Father objectively loved the world, hence He is a Person who is capable of love, not love itself, as Unity would have us believe."[11]

Several Christian authorities considered Unity's conception of the nature of God to be pantheistic, more in alignment with Hinduism than Christianity. Rev. Louis Talbot noted that Unity viewed God as existing in nature "in inanimate things, in animals, in you—all in different degrees but all a part of His substance." Talbot declared, "This is Hinduism; this is pure pantheism; this is heathenism of the most degraded type."[12] In *Christianity Today*, J. K. van Baalen viewed Unity in the same negative light, observing, "The basic error of Unity . . . is its pantheism. Unity literature is full of pantheism. We must "find Christ in us . . . God is all . . . God is principle." Unity reduces God to a Do-gooder, not one to be served and glorified, but a principle to serve and obey the human will."[13]

Unity was also criticized for failing to acknowledge the doctrine of the Trinity. In *Christianity and the Cults*, Dr. Harold Lindsell asserted: "Unity does not believe in the Trinity as it is taught in our great creeds and confessions. Unity is pantheistic, teaching that God is all in all, and each person is a part of the divine essence."[14]

Unity misconstrued the doctrine of the Trinity, according to James Teener, by substituting "mind, idea and expression" for the Christian Trinity of "Father, Son, and Holy Spirit."[15]

Unity critics indicate that in addition to putting forth a false conception of the nature of God, Unity also holds an incorrect view of human nature. Unity's error lies in its belief that humankind possesses divine attributes. Talbot asserted: "Unity members believe the lie of Satan that they may be gods by recognizing their own inner divinity, thus making themselves equal with God."[16] Gordon B. Lewis, in *Confronting the Cults*, maintained that Unity falsely teaches that "men by creative thoughts can achieve perfection for themselves and their world."[17] Teener commented that in Unity teaching, God is always accessible, that God is "your highest self." Teener observed: "This is the weakness of Unity, for in experience we discover that our 'highest self' is still far short of the glory of the God and Father of our Lord Jesus Christ."[18]

H. A. Ironside, Litt.D., writing in *Heresies Exposed,* condemned as heretical Unity's belief that God was an indwelling Spirit in humankind. He declared:

This is the very antithesis to the Scriptural teaching which insists that there can be no unity between a holy God and sinful men till regeneration and justification by grace. And even then the saved man does not become part of God, but is a partaker of the divine nature imparted only when he believes the gospel, so that he becomes a child of God by a second birth and a son of God by faith in Jesus Christ . . . This is a complete denial of the gospel of the grace of God. It is salvation by enlightenment and by human merit.[19]

Several Christian commentators considered Unity to be a revival of Christian Gnosticism, a heresy that flourished in the first century and was stamped out by the early Church. Human spirits, the Gnostics believed, are sparks of human light.[20] Walter Martin viewed Unity as the largest "Gnostic cult in Christendom," and its teaching as a "Gnostic masquerade."[21] The Reverend Gerald L. Claudius, an Anglican minister, saw Unity as nothing more than a "revival of this ancient heresy."[22] William Whalen indicated that if one dug deeply into Unity, "they would find a school not of practical, but of Gnostic Christianity."[23]

Talbot saw the work of the Devil in Unity's teaching that men and women had divine attributes. He reported: "Unity members believe the lie of Satan that they may be gods by recognizing their own inner divinity, thus making themselves equals with God . . . Unity believes through the perfection of the body they will become equals of God Himself . . . This blasphemous teaching that man can attain deity is the result of the Unity conception of man."[24]

Critics indicate that Unity's incorrect view of human nature is in part due to its rejection of the doctrine of original sin. Dr. Harold Lindsell put it bluntly when he pointed out, "Unity does not believe in original sin."[25] Dan Olinger indicated that Unity's error lies in its interpretation of Luke 17:21, which states, "The Kingdom of God is within you."[26] Olinger asserted:

The verse does not say that all men, even the Pharisees to whom Christ was speaking, have some sort of divine spark in them. The word "within" means "in the midst of," and Christ is saying that He, as the King, is standing in the midst of His hearers. Unity's interpretation of the verse flies in the face of the rest of Scripture which tells us that there is nothing good in unregenerate man.[27]

Traditional Christianity sees human nature as depraved and in need of God's redeeming grace. Walter Martin, in *The Kingdom of the Cults*, chastised Unity for its naiveté and blindness regarding humankind's true condition. He noted: "The Unity philosophy has one 'filling the mind with happy thoughts and kind ideas,' thereby banishing forever the awful concept that man is essentially an unregenerate rebel against the laws of the Holy God, and desperately in need of personal redemption."[28]

Unity's blindness to the true nature of the human condition was in part due to its failure to take into consideration the work of the Devil. "Those who follow Unity," Dr. Harold Lindsell reported, "have been blinded by the prince of this world."[29] Rev. George Brown also considered Unity blind to the machinations of the Devil. He observed: "Unity denies the personality of the Devil. Again Charles Fillmore tells us that 'there is no personal devil' . . . Certainly nothing can please the Devil more than for men to believe that he does not exist."[30]

Unity's most severe critics indicate that the Unity teaching itself is the work of the Devil. J. K. van Baalen asserted: "In view of the vehemently anti-Christian doctrine of Unity, we should not forget that St. Paul ascribes to Satan the power of doing 'lying wonders' through his human agents. Satan is never more dangerous than when he walks in velvet slippers."[31]

FAILURE TO ACKNOWLEDGE JESUS' ROLE AS LORD AND SAVIOR

Critics charge that Unity has a mistaken view of Jesus, failing to accord him his true nature, to acknowledge his divine origins, and to consider him an equal participant in the godhead. Critics chastise Unity for downgrading Jesus by suggesting that only through spiritual work over the course of several lifetimes did he reach the level of the Christ-self. Walter R. Martin viewed Jesus as infinitely superior by nature to any human being and criticized Unity for failing to accept the prevailing Christian view.[32] He observed: "Unity reduces the Lord Jesus Christ to the level of a mere man who had within him 'the perfect Christ idea.' Thus it is taught by Unity that all men are miniature Christs, sharing in His nature and power. . . . The Word of God in its entirety stands arrayed against such outright perversions of the true gospel."[33]

A. Jase Jones stated traditional Christianity's objection to Unity's teaching on the Christ Consciousness, explaining: "On His human side Jesus and man are alike, but on His divine side He has characteristics which are forever superior to human characteristics. Man can have the spirit of Christ . . . but not the Christ-spirit, if one means by that a spirit of the same quality and power that Jesus had. Man can never be Christ."[34]

Jerry Cooper, pastor of the Faith Bible Church of Rocky Mount, North Carolina, and author of an article on "the cults" included in a book entitled *The Best from All Religions,* challenged Unity's belief that Jesus was born human like all other men and women, and developed within himself the Christ-self or the Christ Consciousness. Cooper commented:

Unity teaches that the Christ dwells within every man. Each person must bring "the Christ" forth . . . Unity students believe that Jesus of Nazareth was a mere man, separate and distinct from the Christ. They say He was successful in bringing forth the Christ so that "the flesh of his body was lifted up, purified, spiritualized and redeemed . . . In other words, Unity teaches that Jesus needed purification and redemption. Heresy again![35]

Unity's rejection of traditional Christian teaching regarding Jesus' role as Savior and redeemer of humankind from sin has provoked strong criticism. A. Jase Jones declared:

Jesus was more than a "way-shower." His mission and his supreme accomplishment on earth was to serve as a sacrifice for man's sin, and by his death and resurrection to break the power of sin and death. His mission was of such character and magnitude that only Deity could accomplish it . . . It was a unique sacrifice and atonement for sin, and the basis for man's justification in God . . . Man's only hope lies in Jesus' death and resurrection.[36]

Rev. Louis T. Talbot criticized Unity for failing to acknowledge Jesus as the Savior of humankind. He observed: "Jesus Christ is never represented as the one who gave his life to save us from our sins. Unity does not acknowledge that man needs a savior or that he is seeking salvation. The cross of Christ, the substitutionary death of Christ, is made of no effect by Unity . . . Man is not a sinner; therefore there is no need of a savior."[37]

Harold J. Berry, author of *What They Believe*, chastised Unity for its failure to acknowledge humankind's need for a personal savior. Berry declared: "They have ignored or have reinterpreted God's clear revelation in His Word concerning the fall of man and His clear plan of redemption through the sacrifice of His only Son . . . Until the followers of Unity recognize the reality of sin and their need for a personal savior, no amount of wisdom and mental enlightenment will be able to save them."[38]

Rev. A. Jase Jones also believed that Unity was not entitled to call itself "Christian," because its beliefs had little resemblance to traditional Christian teachings. He observed: "The Unity approach to Jesus Christ is a source of controversy because it differs markedly with most Christian denominations. Some critics refuse to recognize Unity as 'Christian' because of this."[39]

ACCEPTANCE OF THE EASTERN DOCTRINE OF REINCARNATION

The Unity co-founders, Charles and Myrtle Fillmore, believed that life was continuous, and that each person had continuing opportunities, through reincarnation, to realize the divine self. Since there was no such place as hell, eternal damnation played no part in the Unity teaching. Harold Berry asserted that nothing in the Scriptures supports reincarnation, that men and women receive either an eternal reward or eternal punishment. He observed:

In the teachings of Unity, reincarnation takes the place of salvation in Christ and eternity in heaven for the redeemed. Nowhere in the Bible do we find the doctrine of reincarnation. The Scriptures state emphatically that each person experiences physical death only once. And after we die, our chances for salvation are gone. Instead of reincarnation, the word of God teaches the resurrection of the body.

When Christ returns, those who have accepted Him as Savior will receive their bodies back from the grave as incorruptible, glorified bodies. They will spend eternity with the Lord . . . Those who have rejected Jesus Christ as their savior will receive their bodies back at a later resurrection to stand before the Great White Throne of Judgment. They will then be cast into the lake of fire.[40]

Dan Olinger argued that the doctrine of reincarnation has no place in the biblical literature and that Unity, by embracing reincarnation, fails to adhere to the teaching of Jesus. Olinger explained: "The Unity doctrine of salvation is its belief in reincarnation, 'until man's life force gains divine protection and lives eternally.' This belief in reincarnation not only finds no support whatsoever in Scripture, but the universalism that results from it would make Christ a liar."[41]

Rev. Jerry Cooper asserted that the Bible flatly rejected reincarnation, quoting Hebrews 9:27, which states, according to Cooper, "man is destined to die once, and after that to face judgment." William Whalen, writing from the perspective of a Roman Catholic, indicated that a Hindu would be more attracted to Unity than a Christian because of Unity's teaching on reincarnation.[42] Whalen explained: "A Hindu would find little to upset his religious sensibilities in Unity literature. In fact the Hindu might feel more at home with Unity books than the Christian since the sect teaches that the soul passes through various incarnations, 'till we all come to Unity.'"[43]

Rev. Talbot asserted that Unity followers, through their belief in reincarnation, forfeit their claim to bodily resurrection upon the return of Jesus on Judgment Day. Talbot declared: "Many persons are shocked to learn that Unity unequivocally teaches the doctrine of Reincarnation. Resurrection of the body at the coming of Christ, as taught in the Scriptures, when spirit and body will be reunited, is not the hope of the Unity followers; it is rather the heathen belief that the soul of the dead successively returns to earth in new forms or bodies."[44]

Unity teaching on reincarnation was also attacked on the basis that it negated traditional Christian teachings on existence of heaven and hell. James Teener indicated that Unity was not concerned with heavenly rewards after death. "Unity is not interested in some future heaven where saints immortal reign," Teener observed. "Unity teaches body salvation, here and now."[45] Rev. Talbot took issue with Unity's ideas on the nature of hell. He asserted that for Unity, "hell is a figure of speech which represents a corrective state of mind. This is wholly false. The Lord Jesus spoke of hell as a literal place of torture."[46] J. K. van Baalen viewed Unity as blind to the penalty for sin. He commented: "Unity denies the guilt of sin . . . There is no sentence of death as the 'wages of sin' . . . Unity resents the biblical teaching that sickness and death may be a punishment inflicted by a just and holy God."[47]

FAULTY METHODS OF SPIRITUAL HEALING

Unity was also criticized for the emphasis it placed on spiritual healing. In 1960 the thirty million-member United Presbyterian Church distributed a thirty-seven thousand-word document to its delegates in which it made a case for helping the ill through the responsible use of Christian healing. The document warned, however, against the rise of cults and the use of false healing practices. Both Christian Science and Unity were singled out as presenting healing work that did not meet the Christian standard.[48] Other traditional Christians expressed reservations that bodily healing should be a part of spiritual practice. The Reverend William Smith of the Gospel Ministry Union in Kansas City lamented: "People are so much more interested in a sound body than in a saved soul that they are selling their souls in damnable heresies like [Unity] in order to get healing. What a caricature of prayer is here! Mere talking to the parts of one's body."[49]

Unity's healing practice, which focuses on the use of affirmations, was seen as creating false hopes in people and served as a form of deception. H. A. Ironside observed:

The devotees are taught to repeat over and over certain formulas such as I am that I am. I am Spirit. I am Life. I am the Christ. I know no evil. I deny all sin and sickness. I have all power. I am God manifest in the flesh . . . The constant reiteration of the blasphemies until they become an obsession gives a sense of superiority to the ordinary ills that flesh is heir to, which makes for cheerfulness and peace of mind—albeit a false peace.[50]

Unity's method of prayer was considered in the same negative light, viewed as ineffective and not in accordance with Christian practice. Rev. Talbot observed: "It is not surprising that their kind of prayer would be contrary to the teaching of the Word of God. Their conception of God as 'inexorable Principle' and of Christ as one like themselves does not lead one into a spirit of humble, believing prayer."[51]

The prayer work of Silent Unity was also seen as being of no help. Talbot declared: "The hundreds who write into Silent Unity for prayer have no idea of the anti-Christ nature of Unity's teaching . . . Certainly they will have no help from the throne of God through Unity, Silent or otherwise. God pity those who are ensnarled and bewitched by the Christian appearance of heresy."[52]

IMPROPER DECORUM AT UNITY CHURCH SERVICES

Some Christians find the Unity church services disturbing. Stephen Miller, an editor and writer for the Church of the Nazarene who explored Unity in depth by attending church services, reading Unity literature, and interviewing ministers, was upset by the lack of decorum on the part of the congregants at a Sunday service at Unity Village. He reported:

I broke out into a clammy sweat during the first Unity worship service I attended. It's because I'm not a toucher. I don't even put my arm around my wife when I settle in to listen to the sermon in my home church. But the morning I stepped into the 1,000-seat auditorium of Unity Village chapel at Unity headquarters near Kansas City, I realized I had been engulfed by a swarm of huggers, kissers and hand-holders.

I didn't start sweating until the end of the service. Since no one knew me, I thought I'd be able to escape with nothing more intimate than a handshake. I was wrong. Most Unity churches, this one included, close each service by having everyone stand, hold hands and sing "The Peace Song." (Let there be peace on earth. And let it begin with me . . .)

As I stood there in the aisle, fumbled through the unfamiliar song from the '50s, and held the hands of two women I didn't know, my pores began to pump out a chilling sweat. Then everybody started to sway, left and right to the rhythm of the music.

With the last phrase of the song, everyone raised their hands up high over their heads. Mine got lifted too, and with the last one came the hand squeezes. I got one for each hand. I can't remember if I gave any back by reflex. I was so unnerved by all this, I nearly decided to leave and skip the second service, which featured a different speaker. But I convinced myself to stay.

Unity lives on the fringe of Christianity. Some critics say beyond the fringe, over the edge, off the wall.[53]

Miller might have had the same negative response had he attended a worship service in a liberal Protestant church. The hand holding and hugging in a Unity Sunday service are similar in many respects to the personal intimacies encouraged in services in liberal Christian settings, Protestant or Roman Catholic.

Scholars in the Field of American Religion

Unity began drawing the attention of scholars of American religion in the 1940s. The movement was a half century old and had grown to the extent that it was making an impact on the American religious scene. Silent Unity was doing extensive prayer work, handling thousands of prayer requests each week. Unity periodicals reached over five hundred thousand subscribers; centers and churches were growing around the country; and Unity Village was in the process of being built.

Marcus Bach, a professor in the School of Religion at the State University of Iowa and author of *The Unity Way of Life,* was one of the first to examine Unity's work and report on it. Bach concluded that Unity appealed across the spectrum of American religion because of its spiritual practices. He observed: "The secret has to do with a mystical attitude. Unity students believe and have proved that power is generated in united prayer; that success is a result of basic spiritual laws; that wealth is based on stewardship according to plan; that health and happiness and freedom from worry are the natural consequences of seeking first the kingdom of God."[1]

Bach, who was also an ordained minister in the United Church of Christ, saw Unity putting into action the practices traditional churches had theorized about. Bach reported: "I am convinced that there is nothing in Unity which the established churches do not have. But Unity has pinpointed and practiced these things through well-defined techniques."[2]

Bach believed that Unity set an example for the churches, stating: "We in the traditional churches are coming more and more to realize that we must provide ways of doing as well as ways of knowing. We have been strong in our knowing. Unity is strong in its doing and know-how."[3]

From the vantage point of the 1950s, Bach considered Unity to have made a major contribution to religion in America. He indicated:

No modern religious movement has made more of an impact upon American faith than the Unity School of Christianity. No emerging group has been so widely accepted by a large number of Protestants and Roman Catholics. No new group has so impressively got its literature into Christian homes. No new group has appealed to the unchurched as strongly as Unity has in its fifty years of history.[4]

J. Stillson Judah, a faculty member at the Pacific School of Religion, Berkeley, California, and author of *Metaphysical Movements in America,* observed in the mid-1950s the same wide-ranging impact of Unity teaching on both ministers and members of traditional Christian churches. He reported: "Of all the branches of the Metaphysical movement Unity must be regarded as being the most influential upon organized churches of the Judeo-Christian tradition. . . . A number of ministers in the United States are preaching the Unity doctrines in their churches, although only a few will admit it openly."[5]

Judah attributed Unity's influence to the wide circulation of its literature, which reached far beyond Unity students. Judah indicated: "While Protestant denominational literature is read largely by those in the particular denomination, most of Unity's periodicals are being read by people who are not classified in religious statistics as Unity students, but as Catholics, Protestants or Jews."[6]

Judah acknowledged that even though a wide gap existed between Unity spiritual teaching and that of traditional Christianity, the Unity message had a strong appeal. He explained: "Even though there are still great differences between traditional Christianity and Unity School of Christianity, many members of denominational churches have found reassurance in Unity's optimism, its spirit of devotion, and its affirmative thought."[7]

One of the longest and most in-depth discussions of the growth and development of the Unity movement was provided by Charles Braden, a professor of the history of religion at Northwestern University. In his book *Spirits in Rebellion,* published in 1963, Braden told the story of how Unity grew from prayer meetings in the Kansas City homes of the Fillmores in the 1880s to a worldwide spiritual movement by the 1950s. He gave particular attention to Unity's connection with teachings associated with New Thought. He observed: "Its practice of affirmation and denial as major techniques, its concern about healing by the Christ method is central. It affirms the availability of substance, prosperity and well-being. All these are earmarks of New Thought, even if slightly more orthodox in terminology than the more intellectual formulations of New Thought."[8]

Braden found only minor distinctions between the Unity approach and New Thought, noting: "If Unity differs from New Thought it is mainly in the degree of emphasis upon what Charles Fillmore called the Jesus Christ teaching."[9]

It might be assumed that given the interest in Unity received in the 1950s and 1960s on the part of Bach, Braden, and Judah, all professors in the field of American religion at major universities, Unity would continue to be reported on by academics in this field. A review of the scholarly literature published from 1960 to 2000 indicates that Unity has for the most part gone unnoticed by specialists in American religion. Most of those who currently exhibit the greatest familiarity with Unity are located in the Kansas City area, the site of Unity headquarters.

Joseph P. Schultz, who served for many years as professor of Judaic studies and director of the Center for Religious Studies at the University of Missouri-Kansas City, provided a critique of Unity from the point of view of a scholar steeped in the literature of Judaism. He saw strong connections between aspects of the Jewish tradition and that of Unity. He observed:

From a Jewish perspective, there are many positive elements in Unity. In fact, the very name "Unity" evokes echoes of the Shema, "Hear O Israel, the Lord is our God, The Lord is One (Deuteronomy 6:4–9), the central affirmation of Judaism ... The metaphysical interpretation of Scripture, so central in Unity teaching, has its roots in midrash, the exegetical method of the Rabbis and, in the writings of Philo, the Alexandrian Jewish philosopher and exegete of the first century C.E. The emphasis in Unity on meditation and healing has strong affinities to the Jewish kabbalistic tradition where these practices remained pivotal for centuries and are being revived and renewed throughout the Jewish world today.[10]

Schultz stressed the fact that while Unity was an American contribution to religion, its teaching cut across several spiritual traditions.

The Unity School of Christianity is a uniquely American Midwestern religious movement. Though related to the New Thought and spiritualist traditions of American Christianity, the theology and structure of the movement, founded by Charles and Myrtle Fillmore of Kansas City, are highly eclectic and pragmatic, drawing from many sources East and West. In its Christology, the Unity Movement, like Unitarianism, emphasizes the human qualities of Jesus and His missions to serve as a teacher and role model for humanity, a conception very acceptable to liberal Jewish religious denominations.[11]

Al Truesdale is a recently retired professor of philosophy of religion and Christian ethics at the Nazarene Theological Seminary in Kansas City and author of *If God Is God, Then Why?—Letters from Oklahoma City* (Kansas City: Beacon Hill Press, 1997). Truesdale expressed his admiration for Unity, as well as reservations about the content of its teaching. He observed:

I deeply respect the commitment to beauty and wholeness of life that Unity embraces. Unity has a strong aesthetic as well as religious commitment. My major reservations have to do with what I perceive to be a failure by Unity to practice intellectual and existential rigor with reference to evil. I realize that I say this as a person committed to classical Christianity. For me the problem that evil presents to religious faith cannot be adequately resolved as Unity proposes. I respect an intellectual rigor that lives with hard unresolved problems more than I do a solution that, as I see it, does not treat the problem with sufficient seriousness.[12]

Vern Barnet, minister in residence of the Center for Religious Experience and Study in Kansas City, provides one of the most balanced and in-depth critiques of Unity. Barnet, who holds a doctorate of ministry from the University of Chicago Theological Seminary and is religion editor for the *Kansas City Star,* indicated that Unity attracts men and women who are disaffected from traditional teachings. He noted: "Many find the acceptance Unity offers, and its emphasis on continuing growth, to be a healing change from a competitive judgmental religious environment. This attitude makes it possible for people to learn from many sources and weakens authoritarian ecclesiastical structures. The very name 'Unity' suggests values or kinships that underlie all faiths."[13]

Barnet also sees important values in the Unity message itself and in its spiritual practices. He observed:"The skillful, positive presentation of the Unity message uplifts those of almost any faith, and contributes to society important reminders that the focus of religion can be appreciation and love. The techniques Unity has employed, such as the use of affirmations and visualizations, may not be magic, but in some situations, including illness, can be useful."[14]

Barnet's reservations about Unity teaching have to do with the way Unity students interpret it. He commented: "Unity's emphasis on prosperity, and indeed on God as Law, at times has been interpreted as a doctrine that says that if we hold the right thought, all will be well for us. This reduces morality to merely self-interested, prudential behavior."[15]

Barnet has observed the same difficulty as Truesdale concerning the problem of evil. "The reality of evil is sometimes denied," he observed. "A few in the movement even explain the horrors of the Nazis as the result of the karma of those who suffered." Barnet also believes that some Unity students use affirmations in inappropriate ways. "In dealing with personal issues," he noted, "the overlay of affirmations over a truly troublesome situation can lead to behavior that fails to correct the problem."[16]

The only recent American scholar outside Kansas City who has demonstrated a familiarity with Unity's work is J. Gordon Melton, director of the Institute for the Study of American Religion at the University of California, Santa Barbara. As editor of the *Encyclopedia of American Religions,* published by Gale Research, Melton acknowledged the growth of Unity churches, the impact of *Daily Word,* and the prayer work of Silent Unity.[17] While he acknowledged Unity for its spiritual contribution, he nevertheless did not see Unity as playing a major role in American religion. "Unity," he commented, "is still on the fringe of the American religious scene."[18]

Melton's acknowledgment of Unity and other New Thought organizations is sparked in part by his own interest in the emerging New Age and consciousness movements. Melton's *New Age Encyclopedia,* published by Gale Research in 1990, is "a guide to the beliefs, concepts, terms, people and organizations that make up the new global movement toward spiritual development, health and healing, higher consciousness and related subjects."[19] The encyclopedia contains several references to the work of Unity.

One general encyclopedic work, the *Encyclopedia Britannica,* gives a brief description of the history of the Unity movement, the work of Silent Unity, and the Unity publishing program.[20] Another, more prestigious one in the field of religion, *The Encyclopedia of Religion,* edited by Mircea Eliade and published by Macmillan (1987), has nothing to say about Unity.

Dictionaries on world religion, while containing information on many obscure religious groups, make no mention of Unity. These include: *The Perennial Dictionary of World Religions,* published by Harper and Row, San Francisco, and *The Dictionary of Religion and Philosophy,* published by Paragon House in New York.

A few specialists in the field of American religion give brief attention to Unity, indicating only a superficial knowledge of the movement. Martin Marty, a foremost authority on religion in America, Fairfax M. Cone distinguished service professor of history and modern Christianity at the University of Chicago, and author of over thirty books, characterized Unity as having expertise "at the spiritual healing of mind-cure." Marty viewed Unity as "a mail-order movement for self help."[21] When requested to comment specifically on Unity's contribution to American religion, he indicated that he had "an interest" in Unity, but did not give more details.[22] Winthrop Hudson, who taught history of religion at the University of Chicago and the University of Rochester, viewed Unity in his *Religion in America* as "emphasizing the power of positive thinking to guarantee prosperity as well as physical health."[23] He described Unity as "a less amorphous expression of mind-cure ideas."[24] Paul J. Williams, a faculty member in the department of religion at Mount Holyoke, in his *What Americans Believe and How They Worship*, viewed Unity "as emphasizing Education" and making "a systematic use of Silence."[25] Thomas Tweed, a professor of religion at the University of North Carolina, in *Retelling U.S. Religious History*, viewed Unity as emerging from "the forging of mesmerist and healing traditions."[26] Clifton Olmstead, a professor of religion at George Washington University and author of the *History of Religion in the United States*, described Unity as "more orthodox in their doctrine of Jesus Christ than other New Thought groups."[27] James Ward Smith, author of *The Shaping of American Religion*, published by Princeton University Press in 1961, considered Unity, Christian Science, and Mormonism as cults, "unassimilable deviants, entitled to all respect yet not to be confused with traditional Christianity."[28]

Two authors treat New Thought without mentioning Unity. These include: Benson Y. Landis, author of *Religion in the United States*, and Edwin Scott Gaustad, author of *A Religious History of America*. R. Laurence Moore, professor of history and former chairman of the department of history at Cornell University, is the author of a book that by its title seemed to address the work of Unity. Moore's book, *Religious Outsiders and the Making of America*, focuses on the Mormons and on Christian Science, but makes no mention of Unity or New Thought.[29]

An indication that both New Thought and Unity have not made a major impact on the American religious scene is evidenced by the fact that many scholars in the field of American religion make no mention of either in their work. These include: Robert Wuthnow, Gerhard R. Andlinger professor of social sciences and director of the Center for the Study of American Religion at Princeton University and author of *The Restructuring of American Religion: Society and Faith Since World War II* (Princeton University Press, 1988); Huston Smith, former professor of religion at Massachusetts Institute of Technology and Syracuse University and author of *Religions of Man*; Catherine L. Albanese, professor of religious studies at the University of California, Santa Barbara, and author of *America: Religions and Religion* (Belmont, Calif.: Wadsworth, 1992); Harold Bloom, Sterling professor of humanities at Yale University and author of *The American Religion: The Emergence of the Post-Christian Nation* (New York: Simon & Schuster, 1992); Jacob Needleman, former professor of philosophy at San Francisco State University and author of *The*

New Religions (New York: E. P. Dutton, 1977); Mark Noll, professor of church history at Wheaton College and author of *A History of Christianity in the United States and Canada* (Grand Rapids: Eerdmans, 1992); Jack O. Neusner, distinguished professor of religious studies at the University of South Florida and editor of *World Religions in America;* Leo Rosten, a former faculty member at Yale, Columbia University, and the University of California, Berkeley, and editor of *Religions in America* (Simon & Schuster, 1963); F. E. Mayer, former professor of systematic theology at Concordia Seminary, St. Louis, Missouri, and author of *The Religious Bodies of America* (Concordia Publishing House, 1961); W. Seward Salisbury, former professor of sociology and chairman of the social science department at the State University of New York at Oswego and author of *Religions in American Culture: A Sociological Interpretation* (Homewood: Dorsey Press, 1964); George C. Bedell, a faculty member at Florida State University and author of *Religion in America* (New York: Macmillan, 1982); David Lotz, formerly Washburn professor of church history at Union Theological Seminary, New York, and editor of *Altered Landscapes: Christianity in America 1935-1985* (Eerdmans, 1985).

The relative neglect of Unity by a significant segment of religious scholars in the United States can be attributed in part to the relatively small size of the Unity movement. Unity church membership is slight in comparison to that of the larger Protestant denominations and the Roman Catholic Church. The membership in traditional churches is in the millions, while the Association of Unity Churches claims only 170,000 members.

Size might not have mattered if Unity made a bigger impact on the American intellectual establishment. Unitarian Universalist churches claim no greater membership than Unity and, like Unity, live outside the American religious mainstream. Yet Unitarianism is treated in depth in many scholarly works on American religion. Vern Barnet indicated that Unitarianism has gained the limelight because of the social, economic, and intellectual attainments of its membership. In addition, more so than Unity, liberal mainline Christian churches see Unitarianism as a resource for their own development. Barnet indicated that Unity was discounted because it did not project a distinct religious image. Unity churches are inconsistent in their teaching, and Unity School has adopted a nondenominational stance for years. Barnet observed: "Unity is difficult to write about with precision, not only because its churches vary considerably from one to another and have no creed, but because the Unity School of Christianity focuses on traditional 'nondenominational' prayer rather than promoting a denominational identity."[30]

Non-Unity New Thought Teachers

New Thought shares with Unity many of the same guiding principles. These include the centrality of mind, the focus upon the immanence of God and the divine within, the clear distinction between Jesus of history and the Christ, and the practice of metaphysical healing.[1] As a result, many teachers whose works are based on New Thought themes and principles and who identify themselves as part of the New Thought movement hold Unity in high regard and acknowledge Unity for the contribution it has made to spirituality in the twentieth century. Among the most influential was Emmet Fox, English author of the best-selling *Sermon on the Mount* (New York: Harper & Row, 1938) and a Divine Science minister. In the 1930s, 1940s, and 1950s, Fox attracted thousands to his services in New York City's Church of the Healing Christ. Fox's influence on the spread of New Thought ideas was in part due to the popularity of his writings. *Sermon on the Mount* alone sold several hundred thousand copies. He also had an impact on traditional Christianity, because his works were widely read by ministers of all denominations and passed along by them to their congregations.[2] Fox had strong Unity connections. He was a frequent visitor to Unity School, and was highly appreciative of Unity's teachings. At talks given at Unity School in 1944 and 1946, he declared: "Coming to Unity is like coming home. I am spiritually a Unity man, though not technically in the outer. I have been reading Unity literature for about forty years ... I look upon Charles Fillmore as being among the prophets. He has given us something that the great prophets have given us."[3]

Fox also commented in 1946 on the impact of the Unity movement worldwide, observing: "I doubt whether Unity people in Kansas City realize how very far spreading the influence of Unity is. Unity in fifty years or more, perhaps sixty years now, has done a work in the world far beyond anything which appears in the outer, not only in teaching the Truth, but infusing a certain spirit into the churches and the general public."[4]

Norman Vincent Peale, like Fox, was not officially associated with

Unity, though he maintained a close personal connection with the school. Peale, whose *Power of Positive Thinking* (New York: Prentice Hall, 1952) sold millions of copies, was also a New York City minister, serving for many years as pastor of the city's Marble Collegiate Church.[5] Peale felt spiritually at home not only at Unity Village, but with the Unity teaching. In a talk at Unity Village in 1972, he acknowledged his spiritual debt to Unity, stating: "I have been spiritually fed by this place for many years. I am personally glad to acknowledge the debt of gratitude that I owe to Unity for many spiritual insights and growth, and for the help that it has given me in my ministry over the years."[6]

Peale also commented on the importance of connecting the mind with the life of the spirit, and Unity's part in facilitating that connection. He observed: "I know that Unity is a good movement because it produces good people and has brought the Divine into the consciousness of untold thousands of people. You have related mind to the spiritual life and you have taught people to think."[7]

Charles Braden, author of *Spirits in Rebellion,* considered Peale one of New Thought's major advocates. Braden observed:

The man through whose ministry essentially New Thought ideas and techniques have been made known most widely in America is Norman Vincent Peale . . . He is reaching more people than any other single minister in America and perhaps the world, and is using consistently ideas and methods which have been the peculiar earmarks of New Thought since at least the turn of the century.[8]

Ministers of other New Thought religions, particularly Religious Science, also have a high respect for Unity. Rev. Dr. Michael Beckwith, founder and senior minister of the Agape International Spiritual Center in Culver City, California, indicated that the spiritual contribution of Unity has had an important impact on Religious Science. He observed:

As a Religious Science minister, I take the liberty of speaking for our movement in expressing the profound respect and appreciation Religious Science has for the influence of Unity upon the New Thought-Ancient Wisdom teachings. In our classes and in the Holmes Institute for Consciousness Studies for the ministry, Charles and Myrtle Fillmore are recognized as two of the spiritual giants upon whose metaphysical shoulders we stand. The spiritual contribution of the Fillmores is as vibrantly alive and operable today through Unity's prayer practitioners, its churches and Unity School of Christianity as it was when they lived and taught the timeless Truth principles of the Master Teacher's prediction that "greater works than these shall ye do." Indeed, their compassionately powerful work radiates a beacon of light, inviting a world hungry for unconditional love to "come unto me all ye who labor and I will give you rest."[9]

Rev. Noel McInnis, a contributor to New Thought periodicals who has served in Religious Science churches in Washington, D.C., and in the San Francisco Bay area, also expressed appreciation for Unity teaching. He commented:

I was for the first thirty-five years of my life a Methodist. I eventually concluded that Jesus' teachings were obscured by Christian orthodoxy, and for several years was without a church until I discovered Unity. It was immediately apparent to me that while Christianity is all about Jesus, Unity is more akin to what Jesus Himself was about. My entire family was active in Unity for several years. Then one day I picked up a *Science of Mind* magazine in a Unity church bookstore, and within a year decided to become a Religious Science minister. In retrospect, I see that Unity served as my "entry point" to New Thought metaphysics, which is more true to my understanding of Jesus' message and role than is traditional Christianity.[10]

CHAPTER 17

Unity in the Twenty-First Century: Challenges to Be Met

The Unity movement faces a variety of challenges at it proceeds into the twenty-first century. Its continued success depends upon how well its leadership meets the challenges and resolves the issues. Specifically, can Unity School of Christianity:

1. Make a successful transition from the long term, dedicated, and effective leadership provided by the Fillmore family to high quality leadership provided by skilled managers well grounded in Unity principles?

2. Continue to create the funds needed to maintain the large facility and grounds at Unity Village and provide sufficient compensation to attract and maintain a staff of high quality professionals?

3. Provide a work environment that fosters high employee morale?

4. Efficiently organize and administer its internal operation to gain maximum benefit from its financial resources?

5. Continue to provide the prayer work and spiritual healing through Silent Unity that benefits a wide range of constituents, both inside and outside Unity?

6. Operate a publications program, both books and magazines, that serves to inform and inspire Unity students, attract new people to the Unity teachings, and sustain itself financially?

7. Provide ministerial training through its School of Religious Studies that enables large numbers of its graduates to succeed in Unity ministries?

8. Offer a continuing education program for Unity students that enables them to deepen their knowledge and understanding of Unity principles, develop their capacity for spiritual healing, and qualify them to teach classes in Unity churches?

9. Expand its retreat program to benefit larger numbers of people and more effectively utilize the assets of the 1,400-acre facility at Unity Village?

Can the Association of Unity Churches:

1. Continue as an effective vehicle for administering the affairs of Unity churches and ministries?

2. Secure the funding required to provide high quality educational services and administrative assistance to support the churches and the field ministries?

3. Assist Unity ministries in sharing with people everywhere the spiritual principles presented in the works of the founding teachers and Unity School?

4. Develop and expand the overseas ministries?

5. Through the Unity Movement Advisory Council, continue to work together in cooperative ways with Unity School to maintain open communication, find agreement on matters of policy that affect both organizations, and avoid the misunderstandings that led to the proposal to establish Unity International?

Can the field ministries:

1. Present Unity teaching in the classroom and from the pulpit in a way that provides spiritual sustenance to an expanding number of people?

2. Provide a church environment that provides for the spiritual needs of congregants?

Can the Unity movement at large:

1. Present its goals, purposes, and teachings in such a way that traditional Christianity will view Unity as falling within the broad spectrum of its teachings rather than as a cult or heretical sect?

2. Gain wider acknowledgment for its contribution to American religion from the media, traditional Christianity, and the academic community?

The growth and development of the Unity movement will depend upon how well the leadership of the school, the association, and the churches meet these challenges.

NOTES

Introduction

1. Bruce F. Campbell, *Ancient Wisdom Revived: A History of the Theosophical Movement* (Berkeley: University of California Press, 1980), 16. A sizable portion of the original source materials cited in this manuscript can be found in the archives of Unity School of Christianity. These include: Myrtle Fillmore Collection, Charles Fillmore Collection, Mary G. Fillmore Collection, Lowell Fillmore Collection, W. Rickert Fillmore Collection, Royal Fillmore Collection, Charles R. Fillmore Collection, Rosemary Fillmore Rhea Collection, H. Emilie Cady Collection, May Rowland Collection, James Dillet Freeman Collection, Charles Edgar Prather Collection, Ernest Wilson Collection, and Eric Butterworth Collection. Also included in the collection in the Unity archives are unpublished materials relating to the organization, development, and management of Unity School of Christianity.

2. Ibid., 8–9.

3. Paul Starr, *The Social Transformation of American Medicine* (New York: Basic Books, 1982), 54–55.

4. Ibid., 60.

5. Ibid., 30–31.

6. Ibid., 104–105.

7. Ibid., 55–56.

8. Ibid., 72.

9. Ibid., 105.

Part I: The Unity Teachings: Yesterday and Today

1. Charles Fillmore, *Atom Smashing Power of Mind* (Unity Village, Mo.: Unity School of Christianity, 1949), 13.

2. Charles Fillmore, *Christian Healing* (Kansas City, Mo.: Unity School of Christianity, 1909), 74.

3. H. Emilie Cady, *God a Present Help* (New York: R. F. Fenno & Co., 1912), 114–15.

4. Ibid.

Chapter 1: Myrtle Fillmore: Spiritual Visionary

1. Myrtle Fillmore, *How to Let God Help You,* ed. Warren Meyer (Unity Village, Mo.: Unity School of Christianity, 1957), 178–186.

2. Ibid.

3. Myrtle Fillmore to Grace Norton, 9 August 1928, Myrtle Fillmore Collection, Unity Archives. All letters cited in Chapter 1 are from Myrtle Fillmore to her correspondents; unless otherwise noted, they are found in the Myrtle Fillmore Collection.

4. "Report of Midweek Services," *Unity,* July 1899, 28.

5. Myrtle Fillmore, "How I Found Health," *Unity,* August 1899, 68.

6. M. Fillmore to Jean, 31 July 1931.

7. M. Fillmore, *How to Let God Help You,* 178–186.

8. Myrtle Fillmore, "Health in the Home," *Unity,* October 1911.

9. M. Fillmore to Jennie Koerner, 3 December 1929.

10. M. Fillmore to Lillian Gibbon, 28 June 1929.

11. M. Fillmore, "How I Found Health," 68.

12. Ibid.

13. M. Fillmore to Momsey (Mrs. Mary G. Fillmore), 27 December 1890, Mary G. Fillmore Collection, Unity Archives.

14. *Weekly Unity,* August 18, 1923.

15. M. Fillmore to Herbert Fry, 22 January 1931.

16. M. Fillmore to Paula Verdu, 15 March 1929.

17. M. Fillmore to Mrs. Tracy, 1 August 1928.

18. M. Fillmore to Mrs. Elgin and Mrs. Miles, 2 March 1928.

19. M. Fillmore to Marion Irons, 4 February 1931.

20. M. Fillmore to Marie Bell Irwin, 4 May 1928.

21. M. Fillmore to Marion Crichton, 16 March 1929.

22. M. Fillmore to Bee Phillips, 28 July 1928. Myrtle used first names only in letters to personal friends or longtime correspondents.

23. M. Fillmore to Mr. Anderson, 9 April 1929.

24. M. Fillmore to Gertrude DeFrates, 11 February 1931.

25. M. Fillmore to Mrs. Dowling, 6 April 1928.

26. M. Fillmore to Petrenella Gunteman, 29 April 1929.

27. M. Fillmore to Telleta R. Clutton, 15 March 1928.

28. M. Fillmore to Ella Randolph, 19 March 1929.

29. M. Fillmore to Jennie Koerner, 3 December 1929.

30. M. Fillmore to Martha Rieck, 3 December 1928.

31. M. Fillmore to Mr. Weir, 26 March 1929.

32. M. Fillmore to Eleanor Weaver, 31 July 1931.

33. M. Fillmore to Mrs. Weir, 26 March 1929.

34. M. Fillmore to Martha Rieck, 7 September 1928.

35. M. Fillmore to Bess Smith, 10 November 1928.

36. M. Fillmore to Mrs. Brown, 17 July 1928.

37. M. Fillmore to Ella Richards, 26 May 1928.

38. M. Fillmore to Stella Paulus, 6 October 1930.

39. M. Fillmore to Nina Free, 7 June 1929.

40. M. Fillmore to Mary Kahout, 9 June 1928.

41. M. Fillmore to Mrs. Hornbeck, May 1929.

42. M. Fillmore to Jennie C. Koerner, 3 December 1929.

43. M. Fillmore to Laura Carlson, 30 June 1928.

44. M. Fillmore to Lady Norma, 17 June 1928.

45. M. Fillmore to Elizabeth Berlinghoff, 26 June 1928.

46. M. Fillmore to Helen Mack, 29 June 1928.

47. M. Fillmore to Mrs. Kramer, 12 June 1928.

48. M. Fillmore to Mrs. Rubert, 6 June 1928.

49. M. Fillmore to Ella Richards, 20 February 1931.

50. M. Fillmore to Hattie Johnson, 12 February 1930.

51. M. Fillmore to Marion Crichton, 16 March 1929.

52. M. Fillmore to Jannie Wingate, 9 December 1930.

53. M. Fillmore to Elizabeth Berlinghoff, 1 September 1931.

54. M. Fillmore to William Green, 23 February 1928.

55. M. Fillmore to Helen Glass, 19 July 1928.

56. Ibid.

57. M. Fillmore to Flora Reeder, 9 August 1928. In contrast to Charles Fillmore in his treatment of the twelve powers, Myrtle did not identify each of the twelve disciples with one of the respective powers. Moreover, she, for the most part, ignored four of the powers

—strength, order, elimination, and renunciation. Because she addressed the faculties in response to questions, her treatment of the twelve powers is not systematized. Her approach might have been more in depth had she chosen to present her ideas in an article or a book.

58. M. Fillmore to Jennie Koerner, 3 December 1929.
59. M. Fillmore to Mrs. Knickerbocker, 27 July 1928.
60. M. Fillmore to Madie, 11 June 1930.
61. M. Fillmore to Mary Elizabeth, 2 December 1929.
62. M. Fillmore to St. Lawrence, 5 May 1930.
63. M. Fillmore to Elizabeth Griffiths, 28 August 1931.
64. M. Fillmore to Elsie Cade, 15 April 1929.
65. M. Fillmore to Aunt Ella, 13 February 1930.
66. M. Fillmore to John Fuhring, 25 November 1930.
67. M. Fillmore to Marian Richardson, 6 August 1928.
68. M. Fillmore to Valerie Padelford, 31 August 1928.
69. M. Fillmore to Mrs. Whittlemore, 13 December 1930.
70. M. Fillmore to Mrs. Hollis, 26 June 1929.
71. M. Fillmore to Mamie Horne, 31 August 1928.
72. M. Fillmore to Mrs. Zimmer, 4 February 1930.
73. M. Fillmore to Helen Mack, 29 August 1930.
74. M. Fillmore to the Berlinghoffs, 2 March 1929.
75. M. Fillmore to Jean May, 4 May 1931.
76. M. Fillmore to Eleanor Weaver, 31 July 1931.
77. M. Fillmore to Evelyn Day, 6 November 1928.
78. M. Fillmore to Mrs. Hazelhurst, 21 March 1930.
79. Myrtle Fillmore, ed., "The Family—Harmony in the Home," *Unity*, September 1910, 231.
80. Ibid.
81. "Motherhood Department," *Unity*, May 1921, 452.
82. M. Fillmore to Ida Lathrop, 11 August 1928.
83. M. Fillmore to Miss Ware, 30 April 1928.
84. M. Fillmore to Alice, 23 January 1929.
85. M. Fillmore to Mrs. Griffiths. 21 October 1930.
86. M. Fillmore to Bertha Haney, 24 June 1929.
87. M. Fillmore to Mrs. King, 5 December 1929.
88. M. Fillmore to Madge Bartlett, 6 December 1928.
89. Ibid.
90. M. Fillmore to Harold, 19 March 1930.
91. M. Fillmore to Emily Peckham, 6 August 1930.
92. M. Fillmore to Eva Stafford, 21 August 1929.
93. M. Fillmore to Mrs. Clarke, 24 December 1929.
94. M. Fillmore to Elodia Gonzalez, 3 January 1931.
95. Ibid.
96. M. Fillmore to Mrs. Smallwood, 7 July 1931.
97. M. Fillmore to Lucy Kellerhouse, 17 March 1930.
98. M. Fillmore to Elodia Gonzalez, 3 January 1930.
99. Ibid.
100. Ibid.
101. M. Fillmore to Mrs. Ainsworth, 5 June 1930.
102. M. Fillmore to Marion Irons, 15 July 1930.
103. M. Fillmore to Ida Lathrop, 13 July 1929.
104. M. Fillmore to Ewing Duval, 1 August 1928.

105. M. Fillmore to Mrs. Brown, 17 July 1928.

106. M. Fillmore to Clara Joseph, 8 November 1929.

107. M. Fillmore to Fannie Wingate, 22 May 1928.

108. M. Fillmore to Mrs. Ungerer, 13 June 1928.

109. M. Fillmore to Mrs. Kramer, 12 June 1928.

110. M. Fillmore to Mary Eaglehoff, 9 April 1929.

111. M. Fillmore to Morris, 26 May 1928.

112. M. Fillmore to Mary Bronner, 30 June 1930.

113. Ibid.

114. M. Fillmore to Josie Ford, 9 October 1929.

115. M. Fillmore to Anna Nicolay, 20 March 1930.

116. M. Fillmore to Alida d'Isay, 20 July 1931.

117. M. Fillmore to Mrs. Balleau, 12 April 1929.

118. M. Fillmore to Harold, 30 September 1929.

119. M. Fillmore to Louise Wardell, 10 December 1930; M. Fillmore to Mrs. Smith, 8 November 1928.

120. M. Fillmore to Mary Kohout, 9 June 1928.

121. Ibid.

122. M. Fillmore to Ben and Ellen, 21 September 1928.

123. M. Fillmore to Mrs. Luce, 16 November 1928.

124. M. Fillmore to Mrs. Ken, 22 September 1928.

125. M. Fillmore to Mrs. Brown, 13 June 1929.

126. M. Fillmore to Mary Eaglehoff, 17 June 1929.

127. M. Fillmore to Mrs. Livingston, 1 June 1931.

128. M. Fillmore to Ruth Dalrymple, 17 June 1929.

129. M. Fillmore to Maria Caldwell, 6 February 1929.

130. M. Fillmore to Earl, 24 September 1928.

131. M. Fillmore to Mrs. Tracy, 1 August 1928.

132. M. Fillmore to Lennel Clark, 7 January 1930; M. Fillmore to Mrs. Flint, 3 February 1931.

133. M. Fillmore to Maude Armstrong, 30 January 1931.

134. M. Fillmore to Blanche, 25 April 1929.

135. M. Fillmore to Lady Norma, 27 March 1931.

136. M. Fillmore to Mrs. Davis, 26 December 1928.

137. M. Fillmore to Juliet Heer, 31 October 1929.

138. M. Fillmore to Mrs. d'Isay, 23 July 1928.

139. M. Fillmore to May Eaglehoff, 25 May 1928.

140. M. Fillmore to May Bailey, 26 October 1928; M. Fillmore to Peter Wistran, 3 February 1931.

141. M. Fillmore to Fannie Wingate, 9 December 1930.

142. M. Fillmore to Edith Hennessey, 12 June 1931.

143. M. Fillmore to Flora B. Plumstead, 6 March 1928.

144. M. Fillmore to Elizabeth Patterson, 22 March 1928.

145. M. Fillmore to Fannie Wingate, 9 December 1930.

146. M. Fillmore to Mrs. d'Isay, 23 July 1928.

147. M. Fillmore to Marion Irons, 7 August 1930.

148. M. Fillmore to Laura Bolles, 1 November 1928.

149. M. Fillmore to Rowena Benadom, 31 July 1928.

150. M. Fillmore to Ester Berlette, 23 February 1928.

151. Ibid.

152. M. Fillmore to Earl, 24 September 1928.

153. Ibid.

154. M. Fillmore to G. N. Hansen, 24 August 1931.

155. M. Fillmore to Mrs. Chaplin, 3 November 1930.

156. M. Fillmore to Mrs. DeFrates, 25 November 1930.

157. M. Fillmore to Gene Eller, 26 September 1928.

158. M. Fillmore to Gertrude DeFrates, 11 February 1931.

159. M. Fillmore to Mrs. Goodyear, 22 January 1929.

160. M. Fillmore to Maude Armstrong, 30 January 1931.

161. M. Fillmore to the Lathrops, 5 March 1931.

162. M. Fillmore to Ella Randolph, 19 March 1929.

163. M. Fillmore to Mrs. Shutts, 14 November 1930.

164. M. Fillmore to Stella Paulus, 19 June 1930.

165. M. Fillmore to Mrs. Piatt, 15 August 1930.

166. M. Fillmore to Ida Peters, 8 March 1929.

167. M. Fillmore to Elizabeth Griffiths, 13 March 1931.

Chapter 2: Charles Fillmore: Spiritual Teacher and Leader

1. U.S. Bureau of the Census, "Inhabitants in Sauk Rapids District in the County of Benton (Minnesota)," *Census of the United States,* 1850.

2. U.S. Bureau of the Census, "County of Stearns (Minnesota)," *Census of the United States,* 1860; and "3rd Ward of the City of St. Cloud (Minnesota)," *Census of the United States,* 1870.

3. "Unity Founder Tells What It Means," Unidentified New York City newspaper article (copy), 1934, Charles Fillmore Collection, Unity Archives.

4. Dana Gatlin, *The Story of Unity's Fifty Golden Years* (Kansas City, Mo.: Unity School of Christianity, 1939), x–xiii.

5. M. Fillmore to Mrs. Murphy, 21 January 1931, Myrtle Fillmore Collection, Unity Archives.

6. *Unity,* September 1896, 262. Gatlin, *Fifty Golden Years,* x–xiii.

7. Charles Fillmore, radio interview, 1936, as reported in "Master Way Shower," Unity School pamphlet, September 1974, Charles Fillmore Collection, Unity Archives.

8. Gatlin, *Fifty Golden Years,* x–xiii.

9. "Unity Founder Tells What It Means."

10. Gatlin, *Fifty Golden Years,* x–xiii.

11. Ibid.

12. "Rest for Unity Founder," *Kansas City Times,* 29 November 1933.

13. *Weekly Unity,* September 10, 1924.

14. "Unity Founder Tells What It Means," *Thought,* February 1894, 447. (Charles and Myrtle Fillmore began publishing spiritual magazines in April 1889 with the inaugural issue of *Modern Thought.* Within a year they changed the magazine's name to *Christian Science Thought.* In 1891 the name was changed again to *Thought.* In 1891 *Unity* magazine was first published. In 1895 *Thought* was incorporated into *Unity.* Renamed *Unity Magazine* in 1994, the periodical continues to be published by Unity School of Christianity. *Weekly Unity* was begun in 1909 and continued in publication until 1972.

15. Ibid.   16. Gatlin, *Fifty Golden Years,* x–xiii.

17. Ibid.   18. *Weekly Unity,* May 9, 1954, 5.

19. *Unity,* February, 1894, 6–7.   20. Ibid.

21. Ibid.   22. Ibid.

23. Ibid.   24. Ibid.

25. Editor, "The Silence of God," *Unity,* June 1891, illegible page number.

26. James Dillet Freeman, *The Story of Unity* (Unity Village, Mo.: Unity School of Christianity, 1949), 167–168.

27. Ibid.

28. Editor, "Developing Psychic Powers," *Modern Thought*, April 1889, 12.

29. *Unity*, May 1921, 408–409.

30. *Unity*, September 1920, 212.

31. *Unity*, February 1920, 168.

32. *Unity*, April 1902, 198.

33. *Unity*, July 1907, 11–12.

34. *Thought*, December 1892, 362–64.

35. *Unity*, January 1905, 9.

36. *Unity*, February 1901, 88.

37. *Unity*, November 1, 1895, 9.

38. *Unity*, April 1, 1898, 260.

39. *Unity*, March 1895, 531.

40. *Thought*, June 1889, 9.

41. *Christian Science Thought*, January 1891, 11.

42. *Thought*, June 1892, 405.

43. *Unity*, July 1907, 8.

44. *Unity*, November 15, 1896, 493.

45. *Unity*, October 1913, 271–272.

46. *Thought*, June 1890, 10.

47. *Unity*, May 1905, 261.

48. *Unity*, February 1902, 69.

49. *Unity*, May 1903, 260.

50. *Unity*, May 1903, 261–263.

51. *Unity*, April 15, 1898, 309.

52. *Unity*, January 1905, 9.

53. *Unity*, February 1905, 68.

54. Charles Fillmore, *Prosperity* (Kansas City, Mo.: Unity School of Christianity, 1936), 161.

55. *Unity*, December 1907, 354.

56. *Thought*, October 1894, 283.

57. Charles Fillmore, *Christian Healing* (Kansas City, Mo.: Unity School of Christianity, 1909), 26.

58. *Modern Thought*, June 1889, 9.

59. Charles Fillmore, *Jesus Christ Heals* (Kansas City, Mo.: Unity School of Christianity, 1939), 130.

60. *Unity*, July 1894, 11.

61. *Unity*, August 1894; *Unity*, August 15, 1897, 143.

62. Charles Fillmore, *Prosperity*, 161.

63. Charles Fillmore, *Christian Healing*, 112.

64. *Unity*, January 102, 25.

65. *Thought*, July 1894, 156.

66. *Christian Science Thought*, September 1891, 242.

67. *Modern Thought*, January 1890, 5.

68. *Unity*, December 1920, 506.

69. *Unity*, July 1, 1896, 93–94.

70. *Unity*, April 1908, 198.

71. *Unity*, August 1920, 111; *Unity*, October 1908, 203.

72. *Unity*, November 1891, 224.

73. *Thought*, September 1895, 9.

74. *Unity*, November 1898, 224.

75. *Unity*, August 1895, 206.

76. *Thought*, June 1892, 99.

77. Charles Fillmore, *The Twelve Powers of Man* (Kansas City, Mo.: Unity School of Christianity, 1930), 155.

78. Charles Fillmore, *Christian Healing*, 41.

79. Charles Fillmore, *Twelve Powers*, 27.

80. Ibid., 107, 167.

81. Charles Fillmore, *Jesus Christ Heals*, 59.

82. Ibid.

83. *Christian Science Thought*, December 1891, 7.

84. *Thought*, January 1895, 444–45.

85. *Unity*, October 1894, 12.

86. *Unity*, July 1929, 1.

87. *Thought*, June 1895, 114.

88. *Unity*, June 15, 1897, 52.

89. Charles Fillmore, *Twelve Powers*, 155.

90. Ibid., 16.

91. *Unity*, March 1907, 187.

92. *Unity*, May 1908, 284.

93. *Unity*, September 1920, 212.

94. *Unity*, June 1904, 336.

95. *Unity*, June 1920, 507.

96. *Unity*, March 1900, 388.

97. *Unity*, February 1902, 75.

98. Charles Fillmore, *Christian Healing*, 91.

99. *Thought*, January 1894, 349–50.

100. *Unity*, December 1908, 376. Quoted from Henry Drummond, *The Greatest Thing in the World* (London: Collins, 1930), 47–64. Drummond analyzes love and portrays its various manifestations found in Paul's love poem included in 1 Corinthians 13.

101. *Modern Thought*, May 1889, 10.

102. Charles Fillmore, *Talks on Truth* (Kansas City, Mo.: Unity School of Christianity, 1926), 153.

103. *Unity*, October 1903, 209.

104. *Unity*, December 1903, 321–23.

105. *Unity*, August 1908, 65; Charles Fillmore, *Christian Healing*, 96.

106. *Unity*, February 2, 1902, 75.

107. *Unity*, August 1920, 103.

108. *Unity*, July 15, 1897, 51–52; *Thought*, December 1894, 376.

109. *Unity*, January 1902, 25.

110. *Unity*, March 1930, 13.

111. *Unity*, April 1908, 244.

112. *Unity*, January 1896, 10.

113. *Unity*, June 1920, 504.

114. *Unity*, February 1, 1896, 3.

115. *Unity*, June 1920, 505.

116. *Unity*, July 15, 1897, 53.

117. *Unity*, March 1920, 204.

118. *Unity*, February 1920, 104.

119. *Unity*, June 1929, 4–6.

120. *Unity*, September 1908, 139.

121. *Unity*, April 1930, 2–5.

122. Charles Fillmore, *Twelve Powers*, 162–163; *Thought*, June 1895, 114.

123. *Unity*, April 15, 1897, 333.

124. *Thought*, January 1895, 447–48.

125. *Unity*, September 1903, 147.

126. *Thought*, October 1894, 286.

127. *Unity*, March 1902, 151.

128. Charles Fillmore, *Christian Healing*, 43.

129. *Unity*, December 19, 1891, 2.

130. *Thought*, October 1894, 188.

131. *Unity*, September 1, 1896, 287.

132. *Unity*, March 1907, 189.

133. *Unity*, January 1908, 50.

134. *Unity*, September 1920, 213.

135. *Unity*, February 1904, 83.

136. *Unity*, April 1, 1898, 260.

137. *Unity*, December 1891, 7.

138. *Unity*, February 1907, 91.

139. *Unity*, September 1898, 132.

140. *Unity*, November 1903, 272.

141. *Unity*, November 1903, 273.

142. *Unity*, March 1907, 187.

143. *Unity*, January 15, 1897, 15.

144. *Unity*, February 1892, 1.

145. *Unity*, October 1, 1896, 376.

146. *Unity*, April 1920, 307.

147. *Unity*, April 1894, 6.

148. *Modern Thought*, April 1889, 9–10.

149. Charles Fillmore, radio interview, 1936.

150. Gatlin, *Fifty Golden Years*, x–xiii.

151. Charles Fillmore, radio interview, 1936.

152. Ibid.

153. *Unity*, August 1902, 69; Charles Brodie Patterson, "Charles Fillmore: A Biographical Sketch," reprinted from *Mind* magazine.

154. Ibid.

155. *Unity*, May 1903, 301.

156. M. Fillmore to William Ray, 31 October 1928.

157. M. Fillmore to Mary Eaglehoff, 9 November 1928.

158. *Unity*, August 1929, 5–7.

159. Freeman, *Story of Unity*, 167–68.

160. James W. Teener, "Unity School of Christianity" (Ph.D. diss., University of Chicago, 1939).

161. Marcus Bach, *The Unity Way of Life* (New York: Prentice Hall, 1962), 4–5.

162. Hugh D'Andrade, *Charles Fillmore: The Life of the Founder of the Unity School of Christianity* (New York: Harper & Row, 1976), 125.

163. Charles Fillmore, *Atom Smashing Power of Mind* (Unity Village, Mo.: Unity School of Christianity, 1949), 132–33.

164. *Unity*, September 1948, 10.

165. D'Andrade, *Life of the Founder*, 130.

166. Charles Fillmore, *Atom Smashing Power*, 132–33.

167. D'Andrade, *Life of the Founder*, 130.   168. Ibid.

169. Freeman, *Story of Unity*, 212.   170. *Unity*, January 1907, 58.

171. *Unity*, May 15, 1897, 421.   172. *Unity*, August 1891, 7.

173. Ibid.

174. Charles Fillmore, *Twelve Powers*, 174.

175. *Unity*, May 15, 1897, 421.

176. *Unity*, January 1, 1897, 3.

177. Charles S. Braden, *Spirits in Rebellion: The Rise and Development of New Thought* (Dallas: Southern Methodist University Press, 1963), 260.

178. Ibid.   179. *Unity*, May 1903, 282.

180. *Unity*, June 1901, 258.   181. *Unity*, January 1903, 35.

182. *Unity*, December 1902, 329.   183. Ibid.

184. Ibid.   185. Ibid.

186. Ibid.   187. *Thought*, September 1894, 233.

188. Charles Fillmore, *Atom Smashing Power*, 168.

189. *Unity*, January 1907, 6–8.   190. *Unity*, August 15, 1897, 138.

191. Ibid.   192. *Unity*, June 1901, 263.

193. *Unity*, February 1902, 75.

194. Charles Fillmore, *Atom Smashing Power*, 13.

195. *Thought*, February 1895, 479.

196. Charles Fillmore, *Christian Healing*, 74.

197. *Unity*, May 1905, 275.

198. Ibid.

199. Ibid.

200. *Unity*, August 1894, 213; *Unity*, August 15, 1897, 143.

201. Charles Fillmore, *Atom Smashing Power*, 22.

202. *Unity*, June 1, 1897, 445.

203. *Unity*, January 1907, 6–8.

Chapter 3: H. Emilie Cady: Articulator of the Unity Teaching

1. *Weekly Unity*, February 1917, 7.

2. *Weekly Unity*, July 1920, 7.

3. M. Fillmore to H. Emilie Cady, 7 January 1929, Myrtle Fillmore Collection, Unity Archives.

4. *Unity*, September 1945, 75.

5. *Weekly Unity*, February 19, 1938.

6. *Weekly Unity*, June 12, 1937.

7. Martha Smock, "Ideas We Live By," *Daily Word*, September 1959, 7.

8. Ibid.

9. *Foundations of Unity* 2 (Unity Village, Mo.: Unity School of Christianity, 1974), vols. 1–3.

10. Michael Maday, interview by author, 17 November 1998.

11. Russell A. Kemp, "H. Emilie Cady: Physician and Metaphysician," *Unity*, August/September 1975.

12. Ella Pomeroy, "From Medicine to Metaphysics: The Story of Dr. H. Emilie Cady," *New Thought Bulletin*, winter/spring 1946, Unity Archives.

13. Ibid.

14. H. Emilie Cady, *Lessons in Truth* (Kansas City, Mo.: Unity Tract Society, 1901), 71.

15. H. Emilie Cady to Lowell Fillmore, 11 November 1937.

16. Ibid.

17. Pomeroy, "Medicine to Metaphysics."

18. Cady, *Lessons in Truth*, 19.

19. H. Emilie Cady, *Miscellaneous Writings* (Kansas City, Mo.: Unity School of Christianity, 1917), 59.

20. Cady, *Lessons in Truth*, 20.

21. H. Emilie Cady, *God a Present Help* (Kansas City, Mo.: Unity School of Christianity, 1940), 54–55.

22. Ibid.

23. Cady, *Lessons in Truth*, 22; Cady, *Miscellaneous Writings*, 76.

24. Cady, *Lessons in Truth*, 100.

25. Ibid., 53.

26. Ibid., 34.

27. Ibid.

28. Ibid., 17–18.

29. Cady, *God a Present Help*, 53.

30. Cady, *Lessons in Truth*, 41.

31. Ibid., 75.

32. Ibid., 119, 129.

33. Cady, *God a Present Help*, 56.

34. Cady, *Lessons in Truth*, 6.

35. Cady, *God a Present Help*, 56.

36. Cady, *Miscellaneous Writings*, 14.

37. Cady, *Lessons in Truth*, 29–30.

38. Ibid., 12, 70.

39. Ibid., 72.

40. Cady, *Miscellaneous Writings*, 13.

41. Cady, *Lessons in Truth*, 84.

42. Ibid., 31.

43. Cady, *God a Present Help*, 83.

44. Ibid.

45. Ibid., 84.

46. Cady, *Lessons in Truth*, 34–35.

47. Cady, *God a Present Help*, 83.

48. Cady, *Lessons in Truth*, 31.

49. Ibid., 47.

50. Ibid., 30.

51. Ibid.

52. Cady, *Miscellaneous Writings*, 37.

53. Cady, *God a Present Help*, 83.

54. Cady, *Lessons in Truth*, 89.

55. Ibid., 31.

56. Ibid., 73.

57. Cady, *Miscellaneous Writings*, 77–78.

58. Ibid., 110–11.

59. Cady, *Lessons in Truth*, 14.

60. Ibid., 88.

61. Ibid., 84.

62. Cady, *Miscellaneous Writings*, 13.

63. Cady, *Lessons in Truth*, 69.

64. Ibid., 63.

65. Cady, *Miscellaneous Writings*, 120.

66. Ibid.

67. Ibid., 121.

68. Cady, *Lessons in Truth*, 36.

69. Ibid., 10.

70. Ibid., 33.

71. Ibid., 31.

72. Ibid., 33.

73. Ibid., 63.

74. Ibid., 90.

75. Ibid., 28–29.

76. Ibid.

77. Ibid., 85.

78. Ibid., 87.

79. Ibid., 77.

80. Ibid., 78.

81. Ibid., 28.

82. Ibid., 26.

83. Ibid.

84. Ibid., 95.

85. Ibid., 94.

86. Ibid., 79.

87. Ibid., 13.

88. Ibid., 289–95.

89. Ibid., 12.

90. Ibid., 11.

91. Ibid., 108–109.

92. Ibid., 109.

93. Ibid., 102.

94. Ibid.

95. Ibid., 103.

96. Cady, *Miscellaneous Writings,* 113.

97. Cady, *Lessons in Truth,* 40.

98. Cady, *Miscellaneous Writings,* 100.

99. Cady, *Lessons in Truth,* 56.

100. Ibid., 50.

101. Cady, *Miscellaneous Writings,* 99.

102. Cady, *Lessons in Truth,* 57.

103. Cady, *Miscellaneous Writings,* 37.

104. Cady, *Lessons in Truth,* 16.

105. Cady, *God a Present Help,* 44.

106. Cady, *Lessons in Truth,* 74–75.

107. Ibid., 37.

108. Ibid.

109. Ibid., 41.

110. Ibid., 42.

111. Ibid.

112. Cady, *Miscellaneous Writings,* 79.

113. Cady, *Lessons in Truth,* 56.

114. Ibid., 55.

115. Cady, *God a Present Help,* 72.

116. Ibid., 66.

117. Cady, *Miscellaneous Writings,* 71.

118. Cady, *God a Present Help,* 41–42.

119. Ibid.

120. Cady, *Miscellaneous Writings,* 71.

121. Ibid., 29.

122. Ibid.

123. Ibid., 10.

124. H. Emilie Cady, "Finding the Christ in Ourselves," *Thought,* October 1891, 3.

125. Cady, *God a Present Help,* 60–61.

126. Cady, *Miscellaneous Writings,* 12.

127. Ibid., 17.

128. H. Emilie Cady, *God a Present Help* (New York: R. F. Fenno & Co., 1912), 116.

129. Ibid.

130. Ibid., 105.

131. Ibid., 118.

132. Ibid., 109.

133. Ibid., 116.

134. Ibid., 106.

135. Ibid.

136. Ibid., 114–15.

Chapter 4: Lowell Fillmore: Clarifier and Popularizer

1. Lowell Fillmore, unpublished 7-page autobiographical sketch, n. d., probably early 1950s, Lowell Fillmore Collection, Unity Archives 2.

2. Ibid., 5.

3. Unidentified Unity School staff member, "Remember to Smile," unpublished 46-page profile of Lowell Fillmore; n. d., probably 1963 or 1964, Lowell Fillmore Collection, Unity Archives, 4.

4. Ibid., 9.

5. Ibid., 10.

6. Ibid., 15.

7. Ibid., 26.

8. Ibid., 28.

9. Ibid., 17.

10. M. Fillmore to Ellen Dorrah Clackley, 23 August 1928, Myrtle Fillmore Collection, Unity Archives.

11. Charles Fillmore to Lowell Filmore, 4 January, 1931, Charles Fillmore Collection, Unity Archives.

12. *Unity News,* May 1, 1928, 11.

13. *Unity News,* January 18, 1933.

14. "Remember to Smile," 38.

15. Ibid.

16. Francis Fillmore Lakin interview by author, 11 October 1995.

17. "Remember to Smile," 13.

18. Ibid., 13–14.

19. Ibid., 39.

20. Ibid.

21. Ibid., 42–43.

22. "Editorial," *Youth,* November 1928, 13.

23. "Remember to Smile," 27.

24. Ibid., 28.

25. Rosemary Fillmore Rhea interview by author, 17 October 1994.

26. Charles R. Fillmore interview by author, 1 November 1995.

27. Marcus Bach, *The Unity Way of Life* (New York: Prentice Hall, 1962), 34.

28. Ibid., 56.

29. Charles R. Fillmore interview.

30. Bach, *Unity Way of Life,* 53.

31. "Remember to Smile," 18–19.

32. Bach, *Unity Way of Life,* 70–71.

33. *Weekly Unity,* September 4, 1936.

34. *Weekly Unity,* March 19, 1954.

35. *Weekly Unity,* March 12, 1932.

36. *Weekly Unity,* December 9, 1944.

37. *Weekly Unity,* February 27, 1959.

38. *Weekly Unity,* October 24, 1954.

39. *Weekly Unity,* September 28, 1929.

40. *Weekly Unity,* September 4, 1925.

41. *Weekly Unity,* November 3, 1928.

42. *Weekly Unity,* September 4, 1925.

43. *Weekly Unity,* August 23, 1941.

44. *Weekly Unity,* May 23, 1936.

45. Ibid.

46. *Weekly Unity,* April 13, 1940.

47. *Weekly Unity,* January 18, 1953.

48. *Weekly Unity,* May 23, 1936.

49. *Weekly Unity,* August 24, 1940.

50. *Weekly Unity,* February 10, 1946.

51. *Weekly Unity,* September 14, 1947; *Weekly Unity,* December 30, 1939.

52. *Weekly Unity,* May 21, 1932.

53. *Weekly Unity,* February 21, 1954.

54. Ibid.

55. *Weekly Unity,* September 9, 1939.

56. *Weekly Unity,* December 30, 1939.

57. *Weekly Unity,* September 27, 1927.

58. *Weekly Unity,* January 4, 1948.

59. *Weekly Unity,* April 19, 1949.

60. *Weekly Unity,* June 7, 1941.

61. *Weekly Unity,* September 10, 1927.

62. *Weekly Unity,* December 10, 1932.

63. *Weekly Unity,* August 1, 1942.

64. *Weekly Unity,* February 21, 1942.

65. *Weekly Unity,* May 21, 1932.

66. *Weekly Unity,* February 14, 1942.

67. *Weekly Unity,* March 30, 1925.

68. *Weekly Unity,* February 16, 1947; *Weekly Unity,* November 20, 1937.

69. *Weekly Unity,* January 6, 1952.

70. *Weekly Unity,* November 20, 1937.

71. *Weekly Unity,* November 4, 1956.

72. Lowell also equated divine law with "Principle" and "Truth." He explained, "Divine law or principles, sets men, who obey it, free from the bondage of selfishness, fear, greed, worry, jealousy, and unhappiness. A man is truly free only when he is an obedient servant to the laws of God . . . God's laws are eternal spiritual principles, which sustain all things in heaven and in earth. These principles are true and unchanging and they benefit all who cooperate with them in Spirit . . . Many Truth students have a very clear intellectual conception of how the laws of Truth work, and when they make affirmations they perceive clearly that the law is perfect and that God is all-powerful." *Weekly Unity,* June 2, 1957; *Weekly Unity,* March 8, 1953; *Weekly Unity,* February 12, 1938.

73. *Weekly Unity,* June 9, 1928.

74. *Weekly Unity,* December 21, 1921.

75. *Weekly Unity,* February 17, 1940.

76. *Weekly Unity,* September 11, 1955.

77. Ibid.

78. *Weekly Unity,* October 7, 1945.

79. *Weekly Unity,* August 12, 1939.

80. *Weekly Unity,* January 7, 1928.

81. *Weekly Unity,* September 9, 1939.

82. *Weekly Unity,* May 28, 1932.

83. *Weekly Unity,* June 9, 1928.

84. *Weekly Unity,* April 21, 1928.

85. *Weekly Unity,* February 1, 1930.

86. *Weekly Unity,* August 16, 1941.

87. *Weekly Unity,* September 12, 1942.

88. *Weekly Unity,* March 12, 1927.

89. *Weekly Unity,* September 7, 1940.

90. *Weekly Unity,* September 6, 1941.

91. *Weekly Unity,* March 23, 1940.
92. *Weekly Unity,* June 13, 1931.
93. *Weekly Unity,* September 7, 1940.
94. *Weekly Unity,* August 21, 1926.
95. Ibid.
96. *Weekly Unity,* March 23, 1940.
97. *Weekly Unity,* October 26, 1935.
98. Ibid.
99. *Weekly Unity,* August 5, 1944.
100. *Weekly Unity,* November 11, 1945.
101. *Weekly Unity,* August 22, 1945.
102. *Weekly Unity,* November 11, 1945.
103. *Weekly Unity,* November 25, 1939.
104. Ibid.
105. Ibid.
106. *Weekly Unity,* November 13, 1943.
107. *Weekly Unity,* November 22, 1941.
108. *Weekly Unity,* Ibid.
109. *Weekly Unity,* July 27, 1940.
110. *Weekly Unity,* March 21, 1948.
111. *Weekly Unity,* November 17, 1945.
112. *Weekly Unity,* March 21, 1948.
113. Ibid.
114. *Weekly Unity,* October 21, 1939.
115. *Weekly Unity,* June 3, 1957.
116. *Weekly Unity,* March 21, 1948.
117. *Weekly Unity,* April 29, 1944.
118. *Weekly Unity,* January 16, 1937.
119. *Weekly Unity,* June 5, 1944; *Weekly Unity,* October 5, 1944.
120. *Weekly Unity,* June 9, 1949.
121. *Weekly Unity,* September 3, 1961.
122. *Weekly Unity,* November 10, 1928.
123. *Weekly Unity,* June 8, 1929.
124. Ibid.
125. *Weekly Unity,* November 6, 1960.
126. *Weekly Unity,* June 9, 1949.
127. *Weekly Unity,* March 10, 1945.
128. *Weekly Unity,* September 22, 1928.
129. Ibid.
130. *Weekly Unity,* June 6, 1931.
131. *Weekly Unity,* September 16, 1957.
132. *Weekly Unity,* August 23, 1930.
133. *Weekly Unity,* October 10, 1935.
134. *Weekly Unity,* December 28, 1935.
135. *Weekly Unity,* February 9, 1947.
136. *Weekly Unity,* September 9, 1939.
137. *Weekly Unity,* March 8, 1953.
138. *Weekly Unity,* February 21, 1954.
139. *Weekly Unity,* January 4, 1953.
140. *Weekly Unity,* October 22, 1927.
141. *Weekly Unity,* April 20, 1935.
142. *Weekly Unity,* October 28, 1939.
143. *Weekly Unity,* April 21, 1946.
144. *Weekly Unity,* June 7, 1941.

Chapter 5: Unity's Spiritual and Intellectual Antecedents

1. *Unity,* August 1895, 9; *Unity,* October 1923, 203.

EMANUEL SWEDENBORG: SEER AND MYSTIC

1. J. Gordon Melton, "New Thought's Hidden History: Emma Curtis Hopkins, Forgotten Founder," 198, paper, Unity Archives.

2. George F. Dole, ed., *Emanuel Swedenborg: The Universal Human and Soul-Body Interaction* (New York: Paulist Press, 1984), back cover.

3. Ibid.

4. Harry W. Barnitz, *Existentialism and the New Christianity: A Comparative Study of Existentialism and Swedenborgianism* (New York: Philosophical Library, 1969), 198.

5. Ibid., 201.

6. *Modern Thought,* November 1889, 11.

FRANZ ANTON MESMER:
THE HEALING POWER OF THE MIND

1. Roy Udolf, *Hypnosis for Professionals* (New York: Van Nostrand Reinhold Co., 1981), 2.

2. Stephen Zweig, *Mental Healers: Franz Anton Mesmer, Mary Baker Eddy, Sigmund Freud,* (New York: Frederick Unger Publishing Co., 1932), 18.

3. Ibid., 19.
4. Ibid., 27.

5. Udolf, *Hypnosis*, 2. 6. Ibid., 3.

7. Zweig, *Mental Healers*, 96. 8. Ibid.

9. Charles Fillmore, *Jesus Christ Heals* (Kansas City, Mo.: Unity School of Christianity, 1939), 46.

RALPH WALDO EMERSON:
THE TRANSCENDENTALIST CONNECTION

1. *Modern Thought*, April 1889, 8.

2. Information on the life and teachings of Ralph Waldo Emerson is from Robert D. Richardson, Jr., *Emerson: The Mind on Fire* (Berkeley: University of California Press, 1995). Richardson, a faculty member at Wesleyan University, has written a superb biography of Emerson; it is the product of eight years of research and writing. Richardson consulted the vast written works of Emerson, including his essays, letters, lectures, addresses, sermons, and journals. The result is a work that gives highly useful information on Emerson's life and in-depth coverage on his philosophical and spiritual ideas and teaching.

3. Ibid., 254.

WARREN FELT EVANS:
THE RECORDING ANGEL OF METAPHYSICS

1. Gail T. Parker, *Mind Cure in New England: From the Civil War to World War I* (Hanover, N.H.: University Press of New England, 1973), 50.

2. Horatio W. Dresser, *A History of New Thought* (New York: Thomas Y. Crowell Co., 1919), 75.

3. Charles S. Braden, *Spirits in Rebellion: The Rise and Development of New Thought* (Dallas: Southern Methodist University Press, 1963), 126.

4. H. Emilie Cady to Lowell Fillmore, 11 November 1937, Lowell Fillmore Collection, Unity Archives.

5. *Unity*, May 1908, 283.

6. Braden, *Spirits in Rebellion*, 90.

7. Warren Felt Evans, *Mental Medicine* (Boston: H. H. Carter, 1872), 210; *Esoteric Christianity and Mental Therapeutics* (Boston: H. H. Carter & Karrick, 1886), 134; *The Primitive Mind-Cure: or Elementary Lessons in Christian Philosophy and Transcendental Medicine* (Boston: H. H. Carter & Karrick, 1884), 50; *Soul and Body: The Spiritual Science of Health and Disease* (Boston: Colby & Rich, 1876), 32.

PHINEAS P. QUIMBY: MENTAL HEALER

1. J. Stillson Judah, *The History and Philosophy of Metaphysical Movements in America* (Philadelphia: Westminister Press, n.d., est. 1960), 25.

2. Braden, *Spirits in Rebellion*, 84.

3. Annetta Dresser, *The Philosophy of P. Quimby* (Boston: Geo. H. Ellis, 1899), 38.

4. Ibid., 40.

5. Erwin Seale, ed., *Phineas Quimby, The Complete Writings* (Marina Del Rey, Calif.: DeVorss and Company, 1988), 137. From the late nineteenth century onward, the material in the *Complete Writings* has been referred to by historians as well as by students of New Thought as the "Quimby Manuscripts." They are referenced in this way below.

6. Dresser, *P. Quimby*, 40.

7. Seale, "Quimby Manuscripts," 40.

8. Several scholars credit Phineas Quimby with founding the New Thought movement. Included among these are: C. Alan Anderson, "Quimby as Founder of New Thought," *Journal of the Society for the Study of Metaphysical Religion* (spring 1997):5–22; Deborah G. Whitehouse, "Process New Thought: Uniting Science and Religion on An Updated Philo-

sophical Foundation," *Journal of the Society for the Study of Metaphysical Religion* (fall 1999):153–63; and Dell de Chant, "Taproots of the New: New Thought and the New Age," *The Quest* (winter 1991):68–77.

J. Gordon Melton disagrees with their assessment, noting that, except for Julius and Annetta Dresser, none of the leaders of the New Thought movement had met Quimby, read any of his material, or made reference to his teachings during the movement's first four decades. Melton credits Emma Curtis Hopkins with founding the New Thought movement. (See "The Case of Edward J. Arens and the Distortion of the History of New Thought," *Journal of the Society for the Study of Metaphysical Religion* (spring 1996):13–29; and "New Thought's Hidden History: Emma Curtis Hopkins, Forgotten Founder," *Journal of the Society for the Study of Metaphysical Religion* (spring 1995):5–39.

Charles and Myrtle Fillmore, their son Lowell, and H. Emilie Cady fall within the category of metaphysical spiritual teachers whose work has been identified with New Thought but who give no indication in their writings of acquaintance with Quimby's spiritual ideas or healing techniques. It also should be noted that the Fillmores, although they acknowledged their intellectual debt to Warren Felt Evans, ultimately distanced themselves from New Thought. While embracing the New Thought movement at the turn of the century, they soon saw their work as differing in several important respects with that of most of the teachers and healers who were members of the New Thought Federation and its successor organization, the International New Thought Alliance.

MARY BAKER EDDY AND CHRISTIAN SCIENCE

1. Gillian Gill, *Mary Baker Eddy* (Reading, Mass.: Perseus Books, 1998), 137. This fine biography, written by a woman with solid academic credentials from outside Christian Science, is a comprehensive, balanced, and insightful work. Gill, who writes from a feminist perspective, views Eddy's work as the result of a resilient and determined woman's attempt to insert unconventional spiritual ideas into a culture dominated by paternalism and traditional Christianity. Though attracted to her subject, Gill is not blind to Eddy's many foibles.

2. Robert Peel, *Mary Baker Eddy: The Years of Trial, 1876–1891* (New York: Holt, Rinehart & Winston, 1971), vol. 2, 63.

3. *Thought,* September 1894, 273–74.

EMMA CURTIS HOPKINS: TEACHER OF TEACHERS

1. *Modern Thought,* January 1890, 8. Emma Curtis Hopkins, *High Mysticism* (Marina del Rey, Calif: DeVorss & Co., Publishers, n.d.), 281; first printing Cornbridge, Conn.: High Watch Fellowship, 1907. Emma Curtis Hopkins, *Scientific Christian Mental Practice* (Marina del Rey, Calif.: DeVorss & Co., Publishers, n.d.), 64.

2. *Christian Science Thought,* April 1890, 13.

3. *Thought,* September 1894, 273–74.

4. J. Gordon Melton, "New Thought's Hidden History: Emma Curtis Hopkins, Forgotten Founder" (paper presented at the 1987 annual meeting of the American Academy of Religion, Boston, December 5–8, 1987).

5. Information for this biographical sketch is from: Gail Harley, "Emma Curtis Hopkins: 'Forgotten Founder' of New Thought" (Ph.D. diss., Florida State University, 1991), 3–74.

6. Ibid.

7. Ibid.

8. Ibid.

9. Ibid.

10. Ibid.

11. Ibid.

12. Ibid.

MADAME HELENA PETROVNA BLAVATSKY
AND THE THEOSOPHISTS

1. *Modern Thought,* April 1889, 9–16.

2. *Thought,* December 1892.

3. Bruce F. Campbell, *Ancient Wisdom Revived: A History of the Theosophical Movement* (Berkeley: University of California Press, 1980), 2, 6.

4. Ibid., 2–6.   5. Ibid., 22.

6. Ibid., 20–22.   7. Ibid., 26.

8. Ibid., 27–28.   9. Ibid., 29.

10. Ibid.   11. Ibid.

12. Helena Petrovna Blavatsky, *The Key to Theosophy* (Pasadena, Calif.: Theosophical University Press, 1972), 39; first printing 1875.

13. Ibid., 28.

14. Mircea Eliade, ed., *The Encyclopedia of Religion* (New York: Simon & Schuster, 1995), 465.

15. Ibid.

16. Jonathan Z. Smith, ed., *The HarperCollins Dictionary of Religions* (San Francisco: HarperSanFrancisco, 1995), 1071.

17. Campbell, *Ancient Wisdom,* 35.   18. Ibid., 40.

19. Ibid., 48.   20. Ibid.

21. Ibid., 53–55.   22. Blavatsky, *Key to Theosophy,* 290.

23. Ibid., 280.   24. Campbell, *Ancient Wisdom,* 61.

25. Ibid., 33, 56–61.

26. John Hinnells, ed., *Who's Who in World Religions* (New York: Simon & Schuster, 1992), 57.

27. Campbell, *Ancient Wisdom,* 53.   28. Ibid., 86.

29. Ibid., 104.   30. Ibid., 176.

Part II: *The Growth and Development of the Unity Movement*
Chapter 6: Organizing and Financing Unity School

1. Ralph Waldo Emerson, Warren Felt Evans, Phineas Quimby, H. Emilie Cady, and Emma Curtis Hopkins might be included within this group.

2. *Unity,* July 1909, 29.   3. *Weekly Unity,* July 3, 1909, 1.

4. *Weekly Unity,* October 30, 1909.   5. *Unity,* March 1910, 273.

6. *Weekly Unity,* November 24, 1910, 1.   7. *Weekly Unity,* April 13, 1913, 5.

8. *Unity,* June 1913, 530.   9. *Unity,* September 1914, 254.

10. *Unity,* June 1914, 529.

11. U.S. Board of Tax Appeals, "Findings of Fact About Unity School of Christianity," *Appeal of Unity School of Christianity,* docket no. 1799, submitted February 4, 1926, decided April 23, 1926, before Sternhagen, Lansdon, and Arundell, Corporate Documents, Unity Archives.

12. *Unity,* February 1915, 1.

13. Ibid.

14. *Unity,* August 1918, 178; *Unity,* July 1927.

15. "Findings of Fact About Unity School of Christianity."

16. Ibid.

17. Convention program, Fourth Annual Convention, October 3–7, 1926, 8, Unity Archives.

18. Ibid.

19. Amendment to Articles of Incorporation, August 26, 1951, signed by Walter Tester-man, Secretary of State, State of Missouri, September 30, 1951, Unity School of Christianity Corporate Documents, Unity Archives.

20. Ibid.; and "Findings of Fact About Unity School of Christianity."

21. Charles R. Fillmore interview by author, 22 June 2000; Connie Fillmore Bazzy interview by author, 22 June 2000.

22. Connie Fillmore Bazzy, "President's Message to Coworkers," March 13, 2001, Unity School of Christianity administrative files; Connie Fillmore Bazzy, "Memorandum to All Unity Ministers," March 14, 2001, Unity School of Christianity administrative files.

23. Ibid.

24. Ibid.

25. *Weekly Unity,* May 5, 1910, 5. All information from unpublished sources cited in this section can be found in the Unity Archives, Unity School of Christianity, Unity Village, Mo.

26. *Unity News,* February 2, 1924.

27. *Weekly Unity,* May 5, 1910, 1.

28. Ibid.

29. *Weekly Unity,* May 12, 1910.

30. Ibid.

31. *Unity News,* February 2, 1924, 2.

32. *Weekly Unity,* April 1911, 373.

33. *Unity,* April 1911, 373.

34. Ibid.

35. *Weekly Unity,* May 1911, 462.

36. *Unity,* August 1911, 180.

37. *Unity,* September 1911, 270.

38. *Weekly Unity,* July 5, 1911, 4.

39. *Unity,* December 1911.

40. Ibid.

41. *Unity,* January 1912, two-page ad on the two back pages. Although Charles Fillmore continued to served as the editor of *Unity* magazine, it is likely that the copy for the Prosperity Bank advertisements was written by other copywriters on the staff. It is unlikely that any claims made for the effectiveness of the banks would have been published without his prior approval.

42. *Unity,* January 1912.

43. Ibid.

44. *Weekly Unity,* May 25, 1940.

45. *Daily Unity,* September 4, 1916.

46. *Unity,* April 1913.

47. Ibid.

48. *Unity,* August 1913.

49. *Unity,* April 1914.

50. *Unity,* May 1915.

51. *Unity,* July 1915.

52. Ibid.

53. Ibid.

54. *Unity,* February 1925, 170.

55. *Weekly Unity,* February 26, 1910.

56. *Weekly Unity,* December 18, 1912.

57. *Unity,* February 1915, 179.

58. *Unity,* February 1916, 79.

59. Ibid.

60. *Unity,* July 1920, 86.

61. Ibid.

62. Ibid.

63. *Unity,* August 8, 1920, 178.

64. *Unity,* January 1921, 80.

65. Ibid.

66. *Unity,* June 1921, 579.

67. *Unity,* May 1922.

68. Ibid.

69. *Unity,* August 1922, 177.

70. Ibid.

71. *Unity,* June 1923, 489.

72. *Unity News,* November 10, 1923, 2.

73. *Unity News,* June 10, 1922.

74. *Unity News,* February 2, 1924.

75. *Unity News,* August 4, 1923, 1.

76. Ibid.

77. *Unity,* June 1925, 482.

78. *Unity News,* February 7, 1925.

79. *Unity,* January 1924, 182.

80. *Unity,* August 1924, 182–83.

81. *Weekly Unity,* September 17, 1927, 8.

82. *Unity,* July 1927, 96.

83. *Unity,* December 1929.

84. *Weekly Unity,* December 18, 1912, 15.

85. *Daily Unity,* September 4, 1916; *Unity News,* May 1919; *Unity,* April 1922, 304; *Unity,* January 1924, 78; *Weekly Unity,* February 9, 1924; *Weekly Unity,* August 20, 1927, 8; *Weekly Unity,* February 23, 1939; James W. Teener, "Unity School of Christianity," 109, 139.

86. *Weekly Unity,* November 1926.   87. *Unity,* December 1901, 375.

88. *Daily Unity,* September 4, 1916.   89. *Weekly Unity,* May 14, 1913.

90. *Unity,* April 1922, 376; *Unity,* June 1924.

91. *Unity,* September 1924.

92. *Wee Wisdom,* July 1922, back cover.

93. *Daily Unity,* September 4, 1916; *Unity,* April 1922, 376.

94. *Unity,* February 15, 1896.   95. Ibid.

96. *Unity,* September 1902, 169.   97. *Unity,* April 1924, 383.

98. *Unity,* May 1924, 481.   99. Ibid.

100. Unity School subscription manager to Lowell Fillmore, 2 September 1927, Lowell Fillmore Collection, Unity Archives.

101. *Unity,* October 1926, 386.   102. *Unity,* February 1928, 187.

103. *Unity,* November 1926, 487.   104. *Unity,* December 1926, 598.

105. Teener, "Unity School of Christianity," 109.

106. *Unity,* July 1922, 77.

107. *Weekly Unity,* January 6, 1923.   108. *Unity,* June 1924, 580.

109. Inez Russell, "He Deals in Ideas: A Close-up of Lowell Fillmore," *Progress* (August 1934), 10–15.

110. "What Is a Prosperity Bank?" *Unity Catalog of Books, 1931,* Unity Archives.

111. John A. Garraty, *The American Nation: A History of the United States Since 1865,* 3d ed. (New York: Harper & Row, 1975), vol. 2, 713–725.

112. *Weekly Unity,* February 23, 1929, 2.

113. *Weekly Unity,* February 23, 1939; Teener, "Unity School of Christianity," 109.

114. *Weekly Unity,* February 9, 1925, 7; *Unity,* September 1924, 281; Teener, "Unity School of Christianity," 109.

115. *Weekly Unity,* November 20, 1926, 7.

116. *Weekly Unity,* March 10, 1934.

117. *Unity Catalog, 1934,* Unity School of Christianity, Unity Archives.

118. Ibid.   119. *Weekly Unity,* April 27, 1935, 15.

120. Ibid.   121. Ibid.

122. *Weekly Unity,* May 28, 1938, 8.   123. Ibid.

124. *Unity,* May 1932, 93.   125. *Unity News,* January 18, 1933.

126. Lowell Fillmore to H. Emilie Cady, 6 January 1935, Lowell Fillmore Collection, Unity Archives.

127. Gatlin, *Fifty Golden Years,* 82.

128. *Weekly Unity,* February 23, 1929; Teener, "Unity School of Christianity," 109.

129. Charles Fillmore, *Prosperity,* 171, 47.   130. Ibid., 16.

131. Ibid., 83.   132. Ibid., 67.

133. Charles Lelly, interview by author, 10 July 2000.

134. Much of the information provided in this section was obtained during telephone interviews with Charles Lelly, July 10–11, 2000. Additional information is available in Charles Lelly, "The Unity School Years, 1964–1972," *Memories Notebook, July 1999,* Lelly's personal papers, Louisville, Ky.

135. Phil White, interview by author, 25 September 2000. *New* magazine was a continuation of a magazine entitled *Good Business,* which Unity School published for several years beginning in the 1920s. According to Phil White, *New* magazine went out of existence in the late 1960s.

136. Regular Unity supporters include people who subscribe to *Unity* magazine and *Dai-*

ly Word, have contacted Silent Unity for prayer, have attended adult education classes at Unity School, or have attended a retreat.

137. Charles R. Fillmore, interview by author, 22 June 2000; Jim Sproul (retired Unity School staff member), interview by author, 20 June 2000; see also Allen Noel to Connie Fillmore Bazzy, memo, June 19, 2000, Unity School of Christianity. Unity officials agree that the Premium Booklet promotion program, currently used by Unity School, is based on the program designed by Charles Lelly. They recognize, as Lelly did, that the program required the close collaboration of several people. It was not possible to credit any one person for the success of the program. Charles Fillmore indicated that Unity officials Rod Friend, May Rowland, and Martha Smock also contributed.

138. Chris Jackson (executive vice president, Unity School of Christianity), interview by author, 2 May 2000; Allen Noel (senior director, promotion department, Unity School of Christianity), interview by author, 3 May 2000. See also promotion packet, "Take a closer walk with God through prayer" (spring 2000), Unity School of Christianity.

139. Ibid.

Chapter 7: W. Rickert Fillmore and the Development of Unity Village

1. James Dillet Freeman, *The Story of Unity,* rev. ed. (Unity Village, Mo.: Unity Books, 1978), 145.

2. Thomas E. Witherspoon, *Mother of Unity* (Unity Village, Mo.: Unity Books, 1977), 124–25.

3. Proposal on company letterhead to decorate Hillcrest Country Club, Kansas City, April 3, 1916, Rickert Fillmore Collection, Unity Archives.

4. Witherspoon, *Mother of Unity,* 150.

5. Dorothy McLaren, "God's Service Station," *New Magazine,* June 1967, 21, Rickert Fillmore Collection, Unity Archives.

6. *Unity News,* December 30, 1922, 1; Rickert Fillmore Collection.

7. Witherspoon, *Mother of Unity,* 151.

8. Dorothy Pierson, interview by author, 19 October 1995, Unity Christ Church, Sacramento, Calif. Her name during her years at Unity Village in the 1940s and 1950s was Dorothy O'Connor. She was then married to a Unity minister, Donald O'Connor.

9. Ibid.

10. Rotary Club of Kansas City, *Newsletter,* October 14, 1965, Rickert Fillmore Collection, Unity Archives.

11. *Kansas City Times,* 9 October 1965, Rickert Fillmore Collection, Unity Archives.

12. Rotary Club, *Newsletter.*

13. *Kansas City Times,* 9 October 1965.

14. Ibid.

15. McLaren, "God's Service Station," 22; Capital Press Bureau, Inc., "W. Rickert Fillmore, Kansas City, Missouri" news release, Rickert Fillmore Collection, Unity Archives; Charles R. Fillmore, interview by author, 1 November 1995.

16. Pierson interview.

17. McLaren, "God's Service Station," 21.

18. Ibid., 22.

19. Pierson interview.

20. Ibid.

21. Ibid.

22. Ibid.

23. Ibid.

24. Rosemary Fillmore Rhea, interviews by author, 18 October 1994, and 25 October 1995.

25. Ibid.

26. Pierson interview.

27. McLaren, "God's Service Station." 28. Rhea interview, 25 October 1995.

29. Pierson interview.

30. Ibid.

31. Ibid.; *Unity News,* March 28, 1925, 1.

32. Marcus Bach, *The Unity Way of Life* (Unity Village, Mo.: Unity Books, 1972), 61.

33. Rhea interview.

34. McLaren, "God's Service Station," 22.

Chapter 8: *The Fillmore Family and the*
Operation of Unity School

1. *Unity News,* June 6, 1925, 4.

2. Charles R. Fillmore, interview by author, 1 November 1995.

3. Charles R. Fillmore, interview by author, 17 October 1994; and "Charles R. Fillmore," biographical information file, Unity Archives.

4. Charles R. Fillmore, interview by author, 1 November 1995.

5. Ibid.

6. Ibid.

7. William B. Dale, interview by author, 4 May 2000.

8. Charles R. Fillmore, interview by author, 26 April 2000.

9. Dale interview; Harry Jones, "Unity School Led by Ardent Believer," *Kansas City Star,* 30 June 1979.

10. Charles R. Fillmore, interview by author, 26 April 2000.

11. Reinhard Bendix, *Max Weber: An Intellectual Portrait* (Berkeley: University of California Press, 1977), 299–328.

12. Charles R. Fillmore, interviews by author, 8 December 1998, and 26 April 2000.

13. Charles R. Fillmore, *The Adventure Called Unity* (Unity Village, Mo.: Unity School of Christianity, n. d.), pamphlet, probably mid–1960s, 1–11.

14. Ibid.

15. "Unity Meeting Is Under Way," *Kansas City Star,"* 25 June 1970.

16. Ibid.

17. James Dillet Freeman, interview by author, 28 April 2000.

18. Dale interview.

19. "Charles R. Fillmore," biographical information file, Unity Archives.

20. *Kansas City Times,* 16 September 1907; *Lee's Summit Journal,* 24 June 1971, 7 June 1978.

21. Charles R. Fillmore interview, 1 November 1995.

22. *Lee's Summit Journal,* 12 December 1968.

23. "Charles R. Fillmore," biographical information file, Unity Archives; Charles R. Fillmore interview, 22 June 2000.

24. "Connie Fillmore Bazzy," biographical information file, Unity Archives.

25. *Lee's Summit Journal,* 9 December 1983, 9; *Lee's Summit Journal,* 4 September 1985, 22A; *Lee's Summit Journal,* 16 January 1987; *Blue Springs Examiner,* 31 January 1987, 6.

26. Connie Fillmore Bazzy, interview by author, 22 June 2000.

27. Ibid.

28. Ibid.

29. *Lee's Summit Journal, Blue Springs Examiner.*

30. Ibid. 31. Bazzy interview.

32. Ibid. 33. Ibid.

34. Ibid. 35. Ibid.

36. Ibid.   37. Ibid.

38. Connie Fillmore Bazzy, *Unity Today* (Unity Village, Mo.: Unity School of Christianity, n.d., presumably 1990s), pamphlet, Unity Archives.

39. Ibid.

40. Charles Burke, "Unity Readies for Centennial," *The Blue Springs Examiner,* 31 January 1987, 6.

41. Bazzy interview.   42. Ibid.

43. Dale interview.   44. Bazzy interview.

45. Ibid.   46. Ibid.

47. Ibid.   48. Ibid.

49. Connie Fillmore Bazzy, "President's Message to Coworkers," March 13, 2001, administrative files, Unity School of Christianity.

50. Connie Fillmore Bazzy, "Interoffice Memo to All Unity School Employees," July 18, 2001, administrative files, Unity School of Christianity.

51. Charles R. Fillmore, interview by author, 17 October 1994.

52. Thomas E. Witherspoon, "The Royal Fillmore," *Unity,* June 1979, 10.

53. *Unity News,* November 10, 1923.   54. *Unity,* February 1905.

55. Witherspoon, "The Royal Fillmore."   56. Ibid.

57. Ibid.   58. *Wee Wisdom,* April 1917, 16.

59. Thomas E. Witherspoon, "Essence of Unity," audiotape transcription, Unity Archives, n.d., probably 1970s.

60. *Weekly Unity,* December 25, 1919.

61. *Weekly Unity,* January 1912, 7.

62. *Kansas City Daily Sun,* 14 February 1916.

63. *Unity,* August 1914, 252.

64. *Unity,* May 1913; *Daily Unity,* October 5, 1916.

65. Birthday note, Myrtle Fillmore Collection.

66. M. Fillmore to her sister, 27 November 1923, Myrtle Fillmore Collection.

67. Thomas E. Witherspoon, *Mother of Unity* (Unity Village, Mo.: Unity Books, 1977), 154; *Unity News,* July 28, 1923.

68. Witherspoon, *Mother of Unity,* 155–56.

69. *Unity News,* November 10, 1923, 4; M. Fillmore to her sister, 23 September 1923.

70. Unity staff member to Mr. and Mrs. Sleater, 10 September 1923, Royal Fillmore Collection, Unity Archives.

71. Certificate of Death, State of Michigan, Department of State, Division of Vital Statistics, September 9, 1923, Royal Fillmore Collection, Unity Archives.

72. M. Fillmore to her sister, 23 September 1923.

73. Joan Baker, "Rosemary Fillmore Rhea, Beloved Ambassador" (term paper, Unity School for Religious Studies, 1983), Unity Archives.

74. "Rosemary Fillmore Rhea," March 26, 1976, biographical information file, Unity Archives.

75. *Kansas City Star,* 29 June 1958.

76. Rosemary Fillmore Rhea, interview by author, 12 April 2000.

77. "Rosemary Fillmore Rhea"; *Kansas City Star,* 30 August 1963; *The Independence and Jackson County Examiner,* 9 November 1963.

78. "Rosemary Fillmore Rhea."

79. Rhea interview.

80. "Rosemary Fillmore Rhea."

81. "Petition for Accounting," *Rosemary Fillmore Rhea v. Unity School of Christianity and Charles R. Fillmore, James Dillet Freeman, and Otto J. Arni,* Circuit Court of Jackson County, Missouri, administrative file, Unity Archives.

82. Rhea interview.

83. *Rhea v. Unity School of Christianity.*

84. In January 1980, Rosemary Fillmore Rhea also filed a complaint with the Equal Opportunity Commission alleging that Unity School was discriminatory in removing her as head of the radio and TV department. She withdrew this complaint for the same reasons she withdrew the suit before the Circuit Court of Jackson County.

85. Rhea interview.

86. Ibid.

Chapter 9: *Silent Unity and the Practice of Spiritual Healing*

PRACTITIONER WORK IN KANSAS CITY

1. This sign hung outside the offices of Charles and Myrtle Fillmore in the 1890s. The sign is in the Charles Fillmore Collection, Unity Archives. All of the unpublished material cited in the references below may be found in the Unity Archives, Unity School of Christianity, Unity Village, Mo.

2. *Unity,* February 1908, 114.

3. *Unity,* March 1910, 206.

4. Neal Vahle, *Torchbearer to Light the Way: The Life of Myrtle Fillmore* (Mill Valley, Calif.: Open View Press, 1997), 15–29.

5. Dana Gatlin, *The Story of Unity's Fifty Golden Years* (Kansas City, Mo.: Unity School of Christianity, 1939), 8.

6. *Unity,* March 15, 1896, 13.

7. Vahle, *Torchbearer,* 15–29.

8. *Unity,* February 1908, 114.

9. *Weekly Unity,* November 20, 1909, 1.

10. *Unity,* October 1911, 336.

11. M. Fillmore to Millie Lee Goodbred, 28 September 1928, Myrtle Fillmore Collection, Unity Archives.

12. M. Fillmore to Alice Carpenter, 11 March 1931.

13. M. Fillmore to Mrs. Davis, 16 December 1930.

14. M. Fillmore to Mrs. Smith, 28 November 1928.

15. M. Fillmore to Elizabeth Money, 25 March 1929.

16. *Weekly Unity,* August 9, 1924.

17. M. Fillmore to Mrs. Syderstricker, 2 June 1930.

18. Ila White to an unnamed correspondent, n.d. but circa 1929–1930, Myrtle Fillmore Collection, Unity Archives.

19. Ibid.

20. M. Fillmore to Jane Morgan, 15 August 1930.

21. *Unity,* February 1908, 114.

THE SOCIETY OF SILENT UNITY:
A COMMUNITY FOR MENTAL HEALING

1. *Unity,* June 1891.

2. The Fillmores published three other magazines in the early 1890s. These magazines differed from *Unity* in that they were addressed to a broader reading audience. *Unity* magazine, in the period 1891 to 1895, was published solely to present truth principles to members of the Society of Silent Unity. The other three magazines *(Modern Thought, Christian Science Thought,* and *Thought),* published from 1889 to 1895, served as a platform for the Fillmores to present their developing spiritual ideas. When *Thought* was merged with *Unity* in 1895,

Unity became the flagship magazine of the Unity movement, the primary publication for presenting the Unity teachings to a worldwide audience.

3. *Unity,* June 1891; *Unity,* January 1894, 4.

4. *Thought,* July 1892, 386.

5. *Unity,* May 1902, 295.

6. *Christian Science Thought,* April 1890.

7. *Christian Science Thought,* November 1890, 8.

8. *Unity,* June 1894, 14.

9. Ibid.

10. *Unity,* June 1891, 2.

11. *Christian Science Thought,* April 1890, 9; *Unity,* June 1891, 1.

12. *Unity,* June 1891, 1.

13. *Unity,* August 1894, 216.

14. *Christian Science Thought,* February 1891, 11.

15. *Unity,* October 1, 1896, 375–76.   16. *Unity,* February 1902.

17. *Unity,* October 1, 1896, 375–76.   18. *Unity,* August 1905, 104.

19. Ibid.

20. *Christian Science Thought,* July/August 1890, 12.

21. *Christian Science Thought,* October 1890, 12.

22. *Unity,* November 1894, 349.

23. Ibid.

24. Ibid. and *Christian Science Thought,* September 1891, 239–40.

25. Ibid.

26. Ibid.

27. *Unity,* December 1892, 386–87.

28. *Unity,* October 1896, 375; *Unity,* August 1896; *Unity,* January 1907, 52; *Unity,* September 1909, 148.

29. *Unity,* May 1893, 11.   30. *Unity,* September 15, 1896, 330.

31. *Thought,* November 1892, 352.   32. *Unity,* April 1894, 6–7.

33. *Unity,* May 1894, 76.   34. *Thought,* January 1895, 409.

35. *Unity,* August 1894, 216.   36. *Unity,* February 1905, 95.

37. *Unity,* September 1907, 176–77.   38. Ibid.

39. *Unity,* October 1905.   40. *Unity,* January 1906.

41. *Unity,* February 1906.   42. *Unity,* April 1906, 255.

43. Ibid.   44. *Unity,* January 1908, 58–59.

45. *Unity,* January 1906, 32–34.   46. Ibid., 106.

47. *Unity,* February 1906, 131.   48. Ibid., 106.

49. *Unity,* September 1906.   50. *Unity,* April 1906, 239.

51. Ibid.   52. Ibid.

53. Ibid.   54. Ibid., 254.

55. Ibid.   56. *Unity,* May 1906, 335.

57. Ibid.   58. *Unity,* September 1906, 126.

59. Ibid.   60. Ibid.

61. Ibid.   62. Ibid., 126.

63. *Unity,* December 1906, 385.   64. *Unity,* February 1907, 125.

65. Ibid., 126–127.   66. *Unity,* January 1908, 58.

67. *Unity,* May 1915, 399.

SILENT UNITY

1. *Weekly Unity,* February 1910, 1.

2. *Unity,* January 1912, 56.

3. *Thought,* July 1892.

4. *Unity,* July 1893, 10. Mental or spiritual healing can take either one of two forms. It can take place in a setting where the practitioner gives personal treatments to a physically present client. The Fillmores called this kind of practitioner work "local healing." Mental or spiritual healing can also take place in a setting where the practitioner and client are physically removed from each other by hundreds, even thousands, of miles. "Absent healing" is the term used to describe the work of a spiritual healer when the client and healer are not physically present in the same room with each other at the time the healer does the work. This was the form practiced by the Silent Unity Healing Department.

5. *Unity,* September 1912, 257.

6. *Unity,* September 1891, 240.

7. *Unity,* September 1906, 217.

8. *Unity,* July 1911, 261.

9. *Unity,* January 1902, 37.

10. *Unity,* December 15, 1897, 517; *Unity,* December 1, 1897, 463–64; *Unity,* January 1895.

11. *Unity,* December 1, 1897, 463–64.

12. *Unity,* January 1902, 37.

13. *Unity,* February 1902, 71.

14. *Unity,* April 1907, 261.

15. *Unity,* January 1902, 37.

16. *Unity,* December 15, 1897, 517.

17. *Unity,* January 1901, 27.

18. Ibid., 28–29.

19. *Unity,* May 1905.

20. *Unity,* March 1906, 166.

21. *Unity,* October 1906, 311.

22. Ibid.

23. Ibid.

24. *Unity,* January 1907, 54.

25. Ibid.

26. Ibid., 55.

27. *Unity,* August 1908, 172.

28. *Weekly Unity,* February 19, 1910, 11.

29. Ibid.

30. *Unity,* October 1911, 332.

31. Ibid., 336.

32. Ibid., 334–35.

33. Ibid., 335.

34. Ibid., 336.

35. *Unity,* March 1915, 225–27.

36. Ibid.

37. Harry L. Reed, "At the Feet of the Master," n.d., circa 1920–1930, Charles Fillmore Collection, Unity Archives.

38. Ibid.

39. Ibid.

40. *Weekly Unity,* March 12, 1927, 7.

41. *Weekly Unity,* June 1919, 6.

42. M. Fillmore to Mary Grater, 16 June 1930, Myrtle Fillmore Collection, Unity Archives.

43. M. Fillmore to Mrs. Allen, 16 January 1931.

44. M. Fillmore to Marion Irons, 7 August 1930.

45. M. Fillmore to Ella Tabor, 5 February 1930.

46. May Rowland, "Reminiscing About Charles Fillmore," 2, May Rowland Collection, Unity Archives.

47. Ibid.

48. *Daily Word,* September 1960, 2.

49. Ibid., 4.

50. Ibid., 2.

51. Ibid.

52. Ibid., 4.

53. *Daily Word,* September 1960, 11.

54. *Weekly Unity,* May 27, 1922, 1.

55. Ibid.

56. Ibid.; *Daily Word,* September 1960, 9.

57. Ibid., 1–2.

58. *Weekly Unity,* September 1922, 2.

59. May Rowland, *Daily Word,* September 1960, 11.

60. *Weekly Unity,* May 27, 1922, 3.

61. Ibid.

62. *Unity,* January 1940, 45; *Unity,* February 1939, 13.

63. "The Work of Silent Unity," *Weekly Unity,* April 23, 1938, 13.

64. *Weekly Unity,* May 4, 1940, 4.   65. Ibid.

66. *Unity,* October 1940, 10.   67. Ibid., 13–14.

68. Ibid., 14.   69. Ibid.

70. Ibid., 14–15.   71. Ibid., 13.

72. Ibid.   73. *Daily Word,* May 1953, 2.

74. Ibid.   75. *True Confessions,* March 1958, 5.

76. Ibid.   77. Ibid.

78. Ibid.

79. On February 21, 1919, *Unity News* reported that in January, Silent Unity answered 12,100 letters. On June 6, 1919, *Unity News* reported that 12,386 letters were answered in May of that year.

80. *Unity,* March 1915, 225; *Kansas City Star,* 1 April 1972.

81. Phil White, interview by author, 21 January 1997.

82. Rosemary Fillmore Rhea, interview by author, 11 September 1997.

83. James Dillet Freeman, interview by author, 19 September 1994.

84. *Seattle Times,* 14 January 1975, A5.

85. Ibid.

86. *Seattle Post Intelligencer,* 14 March 1975; *Seattle Times,* 14 January, 1975, A5.

87. *Hemet-News-Hemet* (Calif.), 19 July 1977, 5.

88. *Seattle Times,* 14 January 1975.

89. *Hemet-News-Hemet,* 19 July 1977, 5.

90. George R. Plagenze, *The Citizen Journal,* 19 February 1997.

91. *Hemet-News-Hemet,* 19 July 1977.

92. *The Houston Chronicle,* 27 January 1979.

93. Unity School "Vision," September 1989, 4.

94. *Independence/Blue Springs Weekend Examiner* (Mo.), 28/29 August 1993; *Seattle Times,* 4 January 1975 (statement by James Freeman), *Unity School Field Update* 1, October 1992.

95. *Kansas City Star,* 15 May 1989.

96. Ibid.

97. *Unity School Field Update,* March 1993, 1.

98. *Independence/Blue Springs Weekend Examiner,* n.d. or p.

99. *Unity School Field Update,* October 1992, 1.

100. Lynne Brown, Debbie Bryant, and Peggy Pifer (Silent Unity staff members), interview by author, 27 April 2000; and Unity School, *Silent Unity: The Light that Shines for You,* n.d., probably late 1990s, booklet.

101. Ibid.

102. Ibid.

103. Ibid.

104. Ibid.

DAILY WORD

1. *Unity,* March 1924, 383; *Unity,* April 1924, 481.

2. *Auburn Journal* (Calif.), 15 July 1974, D4; *Daily Word and You,* 8-page Unity pamphlet, n.d.

3. Association of Unity Churches, *Contact,* July/August 1974, 22.

4. *Kansas City Times,* 28 June 1974, 16; *Kansas City Times,* 20 August 1974, E 11.

5. *Independence/Blue Springs Examiner,* July, n.d., 1994.

6. *Blue Springs Sentinel* (Mo.), July 1974, n.d. or p.
7. *Auburn Journal*, 15 July 1974.
8. *Lee's Summit Journal* (Mo.), 11 July 1974.
9. *Grandview Tribune Progress*, January 1978, 6B.
10. *Kansas City Star*, 20 July 1974, 3.
11. Public Relations Department, Unity School of Christianity "Report," July 1983.
12. *Auburn Journal*, 15 July 1974.
13. *Progress Tribune* (Tempe, Ariz.), 16 July 1994.
14. *Dallas Morning News*, 10 May 1997.
15. Ibid.
16. *Auburn Journal*.
17. *Progress Tribune*.

Chapter 10: *Training Unity Students*

CONTINUING EDUCATION PROGRAMS FOR ADULTS

1. *Unity,* August 1, 1896, 207. All of the unpublished material cited in this section can be found in the Unity Archives, Unity School of Christianity, Unity Village, Mo.

2. *Unity,* March 1, 1897, 216.
3. *Unity,* January 1, 1899, 325.
4. Ibid.
5. *Unity,* May 1899, 524–26.
6. *Unity,* December 1902, 371–72.
7. Ibid.
8. *Unity,* December 1902, 371.
9. *Unity,* June 1903, 375.
10. *Unity,* September 1903.
11. *Unity,* June 1903, 375.
12. *Unity,* December 1920, 582.
13. *Unity,* April 1909, 263.
14. Ibid.
15. Ibid.
16. *Weekly Unity,* June 5, 1909.
17. *Unity,* November 1910, 366.
18. *Unity,* March 1910, 277.
19. *Unity,* November 1910, 366.
20. Ibid., 367.
21. *Unity,* December 1910, 544–45.

22. Dana Gatlin, *The Story of Unity's Fifty Golden Years* (Kansas City, Mo.: Unity School of Christianity, 1939), 73.

23. *Unity,* August 1912, 164.
24. *Unity,* September 1912, 258.
25. *Unity,* March 1913, 224.
26. *Unity,* December 1917.
27. *Unity,* December 1913, 533; *Unity Catalog, 1926.*
28. *Weekly Unity,* December 11, 1912, 6.
29. *Unity,* December 1920, 582.
30. *Unity,* September 1912, 259.
31. *Unity,* March 1913, 223.
32. *Unity,* September 1914, 56.
33. *Unity,* May 1919, 263.
34. *Unity,* December 1920, 582.
35. *Unity,* October 1923, 283.
36. *Unity,* March 1933, 85.
37. *Unity,* November 1933, 86.
38. *Weekly Unity,* October 21, 1944, 7; *Unity,* January 1947.
39. *Weekly Unity,* September 4, 1960.

40. Janet Hankins, "Development of the Unity Movement: The Unity Society Correspondence School," March 3, 1982, Correspondence School Collection, Unity Archives.

41. Unity School for Religious Studies, *Continuing Education Program, 1984,* 15.
42. *Unity,* May 1919, 486.
43. *Unity,* September 1919, 5–6.
44. *Unity,* May 1920, 476.
45. *Unity,* June 1920, 573.
46. *Weekly Unity,* October 1920, 7.
47. Ibid.
48. *Unity,* January 1921, 75; *Unity,* May 1921, 480.
49. *Unity,* May 1923, 481.
50. Ibid.
51. *Unity,* July 1923, 78.
52. *Unity,* September 1923, 281.
53. Ibid.
54. *Unity,* July 1927, 85.

55. Ibid.

56. *Unity,* August 1930, 86.

57. *Weekly Unity,* June 27, 1936, 7.

58. Ibid.

59. *Unity,* February 1933, 86.

60. *Weekly Unity,* April 8, 1939.

61. Unity Training School, *1952 Prospectus;* Unity Training School, *1955 Prospectus;* Unity Training School, *1959 Prospectus.*

62. Unity Training School, *1962 Prospectus.*

63. Unity Training School, *Science of Living Program,* 13, Unity Archives, n.d.

64. Ibid.

65. Charles R. Fillmore, "1964–Year of Decision: Unity's Educational Expansion Plan" (speech presented at meeting of Unity Workers, July 14, 1964), Unity Archives.

66. *The Great Vision: 1964 Year of Decision, Education—A New Emphasis,* n.d., brochure, Unity Archives.

67. *Kansas City Times,* 8 June 1964. The Wee Wisdom School was the only educational program of "The Great Vision" to be implemented by Unity School. Wee Wisdom School continued in operation for over a decade.

68. Charles R. Fillmore, "1964–Year of Decision."

69. James Dillet Freeman, interview by author, 28 April 2000.

70. David Williamson, "Add to Report on Accreditation," n.d., probably early 1970s, handwritten note, David Williamson Papers, Unity of Hollywood, Hollywood, Fla.

71. David Williamson, typed notes, n.d., David Williamson Papers. A commentary on *The Great Vision.*

72. Ibid.

73. Ibid.

74. David Williamson, "The Place of Outreach and Omega in Strengthening Unity," n.d, probably between 1970 and 1972, typed paper, David Williamson Papers.

75. Ibid.

76. Unity Institute for Continuing Education, "Omega Program," April–July 1970, and Winter/Fall 1971. Phil White, interview by author, 19 January 2000.

77. Walter Truett Anderson, *The Upstart Spring: Esalen and the American Awakening* (Reading, Mass.: Addison-Wesley Publishing Company, 1983), 207–29.

78. Charles R. Fillmore, "Memo to Unity School Staff," February 9, 1970.

79. Ibid.

80. *Community Observer* (Independence, Mo.), 30 March 1970.

81. Unity School of Christianity, "News Release," January 17, 1970.

82. Freeman interview, April 28, 2000.

83. "Omega Program," April–July 1970.

84. John Anderson, interview by author, 25 January 2000.

85. Unity School of Christianity, "Meeting of the Unity Trustees with David Williamson and Warren Kreml," January 18, 1972, David Williamson Papers.

86. David Williamson, handwritten notes, n.d., probably early 1970s, David Williamson Papers; and David Williamson, interview by author, 30 May 2000.

87. Unity School Board of Trustees to All Department Heads, "Evaluation Results, April 25, 1972," interoffice memo, Unity Archives.

88. Anderson interview.

89. David Williamson to Neal Vahle, 12 April 2000, Neal Vahle Papers, Mill Valley, Calif.

90. Education Department of Unity School of Christianity, "Programs for Personal Growth, Licensed Teacher Preparation, Vacations with a Purpose," 1977, Unity Archives.

91. "Action Afternoons," *Unity Village News,* August 1, 1970, 1.

92. Unity Institute for Continuing Education, *Prayer•Service•Study: 1971 Bulletin,* 2, Unity Achives.

93. *Lee's Summit Journal,* 25 June 1980.

94. Unity Institute for Continuing Education, *Education Newsletter* (fall 1975), 1; *Independence/Blue Springs Examiner,* 24 February 1978, 4D; *Lee's Summit Journal,* 25 June 1980, Unity Archives.

95. Unity Institute for Continuing Education, *Education Newsletter,* 1971, 2, Unity Archives.

96. Education Department of Unity School of Christianity, "Programs for Personal Growth."

97. Unity School for Religious Studies, "1984 Continuing Education Program," Unity Archives.

98. Unity School for Religious Studies, "1989 Brochure for the Continuing Education Program"; Unity School for Religious Studies, "Continuing Education Program," *1992 Catalog,* Unity Archives.

99. Ibid.

100. Unity School for Religious Studies, "Continuing Education Program," *2000 Catalog,* Unity Archives.

101. Ibid.

102. Robert R. Barth (senior director, education, Unity School for Religious Studies), inteview by author, 26 April 2000.

103. Ibid.

104. Unity School for Religious Studies, *2000 Catalog.*

105. Barth interview; Christine Dustin (director, Unity retreat program), interview by author, 3 May 2000; James Rosemergy (executive vice president, Unity School of Christianity) interview by author, 25 April 2000; Phil White, interview by author, 13 October 2000.

106. "Creating Tomorrow Today: Transforming for the New Millennium," January 2000, Unity retreat brochure.

107. Dustin interview.

108. "Creating Tomorrow Today."

109. Ibid.

110. Dustin interview.

111. "Creating Tomorrow Today."

112. Dustin interview.

113. "Creating Tomorrow Today."

114. Dustin interview.

115. "Creating Tomorrow Today."

UNITY MINISTERIAL TRAINING

1. *Weekly Unity,* June 29, 1933, 7.

2. *Weekly Unity,* May 16, 1936, 7.

3. *Unity,* November 1933.

4. Unity Training School, *1952 Prospectus;* Unity Training School, *1955 Prospectus;* Unity Training School, *1959 Prospectus;* Unity Training School, *1962 Prospectus.*

5. Ibid.

6. Elizabeth Sand Turner, "Unity in the Field," *Unity Field Bulletin* (conference issue, 1946).

7. Information on the Silent Unity ministerial training program is contained in the following pamphlets: "Special Training Program for Unity," 1954; *Unity Training School Bulletin,* 1964; "Silent Unity Ministerial Training Program," 1964, all Unity Archives, Unity School of Christianity.

8. "News of Education," *Unity Spirit* (winter 1964–65), 9; *The Examiner, Independence and Jackson County, Missouri,* 1 March 1966.

9. *Unity Journal of Education* (catalog edition 1968–1969).

10. Ibid.

11. Ibid.

12. Ibid.

13. Ibid.

14. Ibid.

15. Ibid.

16. Ibid.

17. David Williamson, notes, n.d., probably early 1970s. Williamson was chairman of Unity School's educational administrative cabinet in 1969.

18. Glenn Mosley (president and CEO, Association of Unity Churches), interview by author, 4 May 2000.

19. "A Report from the Association of Unity Churches," *Contact* (March 1969), 1; *Contact* (November 1969).

20. Association of Unity Churches, Unity Ministerial School, "Information Brochure, 1981–82 School Year."

21. Ibid.

22. Mosley interview.

23. Unity Ministerial School, "Information Brochure, 1981–82."

24. Ibid.

25. Mosley interview.

26. James Dillet Freeman, interview by author, 28 April 2000.

27. Mosley interview.

28. Ibid.

29. Unity School for Religious Studies, *Spring Newsletter* (1983), 1.

30. Unity Ministerial School. The number of faculty chosen and paid for by the Association of Unity Churches was reduced from two to one.

31. Unity School for Religious Studies, *Spring Newsletter.*

32. Phil White, interview by author, 22 June 2000; Unity School for Religious Studies, "Ministerial Education Program," *Catalog, 1984–85*, 47–49.

33. "USRS Ministerial Education, A Unique Appproach," *USRS Newsletter* (fall 1983), 1.

34. Ibid.

35. Toni Boehm to Bob Barth, "New Curriculum—7 Years Later," memo, April 24, 2000, Unity School for Religious Studies.

36. Bob Barth, interview by author, 26 April 2000.

37. Gary Jones, "Evaluation of the M. E. Program," memo, April 18, 2000, Unity School for Religious Studies.

38. White interview.

39. Ibid.

40. Unity School for Religious Studies, "Ministerial Education Program," *Catalog, 1992*, 35–37. Previous catalogs carry much of the same information

41. Ibid.

42. Ibid.

43. Ibid.

44. Unity School for Religious Studies, "Ministerial Education Program," *1996 Catalog.* Previous catalogs carry much of the same information.

45. Ibid.

46. Boehm memo.

47. Barth interview.

48. Ibid.

49. Unity School of Religious Studies, "Ministerial Education Program," *1994 Catalog.* Previous catalogs carry much the same information.

50. Boehm memorandum; Rosemergy interview.

51. White interview.

Chapter 11: The Development of Unity Centers and Churches

THE FIRST UNITY CHURCH: THE KANSAS CITY UNITY SOCIETY OF PRACTICAL CHRISTIANITY

1. *Modern Thought,* August 1899, 9. All information from unpublished sources cited in this section can be found in the Unity Archives, Unity School of Christianity, Unity Village, Mo.

2. Ibid.

3. *Modern Thought,* February 1890, 10.

4. *Christian Science Thought,* September 1890, 8.

5. *Christian Science Thought,* October 1890, 8.

6. *Christian Science Thought,* November 1890, 13: *Christian Science Thought,* December 1890, 11.

7. *Unity,* December 1891, 1.

8. *Thought,* June 1892, 143.

9. Ibid.

10. Ibid.

11. *Thought,* December 1894, 414.

12. *Unity,* October 1895, 16.

13. Ibid.

14. *Unity,* August 1, 1896, 200.

15. Ibid.

16. Ibid.

17. *Unity,* June 1, 1897, 1.

18. *Unity,* June 1, 1898, 113; *Unity,* June 15, 1898, 416, 427.

19. *Unity,* June, 1899, 553; *Unity,* March 1900, 423.

20. "Publisher's Department," *Unity,* April 1901.

21. Ibid.

22. *Unity,* January 1902, 54; *Unity,* July 1902, 52.

23. *Unity,* May 1902, 199.

24. *Unity,* April 1902, 249.

25. Ibid.

26. *Unity,* August 1903, 120.

27. Ibid.

28. *Unity,* September 1906, 202.

29. *Unity Building Dedication and Mid-continent Convention of Practical Christianity, August 19-25, 1906, Unity Building, 913-915 Tracy Ave., Kansas City, Missouri,* convention program, conferences and conventions file, Unity Archives.

30. *Unity,* July 1906, 29.

31. *Unity Building Dedication,* convention program.

32. *Unity,* May 1906, 341.

33. *Unity,* October 1906, 243-48.

34. Ibid.

35. "Ordination Guidelines and Questions for Theological Students," August 1906, box 89, Charles Fillmore Collection, Unity Archives.

36. *Unity,* March 1907.

37. *Unity,* August 1907, 182.

38. *Unity,* February 1909, 140-141.

39. *Weekly Unity,* June 12, 1914, 5.

40. Ibid.

41. *Weekly Unity,* December 11, 1926, 1.

42. *Field Department Bulletin,* December 1931, 1, Unity Field Department Bulletins 1931-1939, Unity Archives.

43. *Weekly Unity,* October 26, 1940, 3.

THE EARLY UNITY CENTER LEADERS

1. *Unity,* July 1902, 52.

2. *Unity,* August 1903, 122; *Unity,* May 1903, 370.

3. *Unity,* August 1903, 94.

4. *Unity,* November 1903, 311.

5. *Unity,* June 1904, 37.

6. *Unity,* July 1905, 46.

7. *Unity,* July 1905, 50.

8. "A Note from Chicago," *Unity*, October 1905.

9. Ibid.

10. "Ordination Guidelines and Questions for Theological Students," August 1906, manuscript, Charles Fillmore Collection.

11. Ibid.

12. *Unity*, June 1907, 408.

13. *Daily Unity*, February 24, 1917.

14. *Unity*, February 1904; January 1905, 52.

15. *Unity*, November 1904, 307.

16. Ibid.

17. *Unity*, November 1907, 309.

18. "Ordination Guidelines."

19. Sunday School of the Unity Society of Practical Christianity, "Easter Program," *Unity*, April 1908, 2; *Unity*, August 1908, 108.

20. *Unity*, October 1908, 262.

21. *Unity*, November 1908, 345.

22. *Unity*, February 1909, 139.

23. *Unity*, April 1909, 238.

24. *Unity*, May 1909, 319.

25. *Unity*, November 1909, 359.

26. *Unity*, January 1910, 86.

27. *Unity*, March 1910, 267.

28. *Unity*, November 1910, 465.

29. *Unity*, December 1910, 539.

30. *Unity*, November 1917, 3.

31. *Unity*, April 1901; *Unity*, July 1902, 52; *Unity*, August 1903, 121; *Unity*, January 1904, 55.

32. *Unity*, March 1904, 138.

33. "Ordination Guidelines," 6–7.

34. Charles Edgar Prather to Charles and Myrtle Fillmore, 23 April 1907, Charles Edgar Prather Collection, Unity Archives.

35. Ibid.

36. *Unity*, May 1907.

37. A new name for the church was adopted in 1919 when Prather returned from chaplain service in the U.S. Army. The church was renamed "The Church of the Indwelling Spirit," *Unity*, May 1919, 487.

38. Charles Edgar Prather to Charles and Myrtle Fillmore, 23 April 1907.

39. *Unity*, November 1904, 307.

40. *Unity*, March 1905.

41. *Unity*, January 1906, 47.

42. *Unity*, August 1908, 127.

43. *Unity*, May 1909, 318.

44. *Unity*, June 1911, 558.

45. Ibid.

46. *Unity*, November 1911, 453.

47. *Unity*, December 1911, 540.

48. *Unity*, May 1915, 425.

49. Ibid.

50. *Unity*, January 1918, 5.

51. *Unity*, August 1908, 127.

52. "Christmas Greeting from Unity," 1908, 4, Unity Archives.

53. *Unity*, June 1909, 385.

54. *Unity*, July 1910, 68.

55. *Unity*, November 1910, 454.

56. *Unity*, March 1911, 268.

57. *Unity*, January 1, 1913, 72.

58. *Unity*, August 1915, 176.

59. *Weekly Unity*, January 1, 1916, 5.

60. *Weekly Unity*, June 10, 1916, 5.

61. *Weekly Unity*, May 11, 1918, 5.

62. *Weekly Unity*, September 1919, 7.

63. *Unity*, May 1918, 479; *Unity*, June 1918, 575; *Unity*, August 1918, 176; *Unity*, September 1918, 281.

64. *Unity*, July 3, 1920, 7.

65. *Weekly Unity*, October 30, 1920, 7.

66. *Weekly Unity*, November 27, 1920, 7.

UNITY FIELD DEPARTMENT (1919–1965)

1. *Unity News,* February 21, 1965.   2. Ibid.

3. Ibid.   4. *Weekly Unity,* March 1917.

5. *Unity,* March 1923, 281.   6. *Unity,* September 1923, 181.

7. *Unity,* August 1924, 181.   8. *Weekly Unity,* May 10, 1924.

9. *Weekly Unity,* April 9, 1913, 5.   10. *Unity,* May 1906, 319, 341.

11. Ibid.

12. *Kansas City Daily Sun,* 2 February 1916.

13. Ibid.   14. *Daily Unity,* September 25, 1916, 4.

15. Ibid.   16. *Unity,* August 1919, 181.

17. *Weekly Unity,* May 3, 1919, 6; *Weekly Unity,* May 31, 1919, 7; *Weekly Unity,* July 5, 1919; *Unity,* January 1920, 25.

18. Ernest Wilson to Lowell Fillmore, 24 April 1929, Ernest Wilson Collection, Unity Archives.

19. *Unity,* September 1930, 85.

20. *Unity,* October 1930.

21. Unity Field Department, *Field Department Bulletin,* December 1931, Unity Archives.

22. *Field Department Bulletin,* May 1937, 2.

23. "Unity Field Department Letter," August 31, 1944.

24. "Unity Field Department Letter," April 8, 1948.

25. "Publisher's Department," *Unity,* March 1916, 259.

26. Ibid.   27. Ibid.

28. *Unity,* May 1917, 424–25.   29. Ibid.

30. Ibid.

31. Field Department, "Methods and Ideals for Conducting Centers and Study Classes," 1924, Unity School of Christianity, Field Department files, Unity Archives.

32. Ibid.   33. Ibid.

34. Ibid.   35. Ibid.

36. Ibid.   37. Ibid.

38. Ibid.   39. Ibid.

40. Ibid.   41. Ibid.

42. Ibid.   43. Ibid.

44. Ibid.   45. Ibid.

46. Ibid.   47. Ibid.

48. Ibid.   49. Ibid.

50. Ibid.   51. Ibid.

52. Ibid.   53. Ibid.

54. Ibid.   55. Ibid.

56. *Weekly Unity,* July 11, 1925, 8.

57. *Weekly Unity,* December 11, 1926, 1–2.

58. Ibid.   59. Ibid.

60. *Unity,* October 1928, 327.   61. *Unity,* May 1931, 87.

62. *Field Department Bulletin,* May 1932, 1.

63. Ibid.

64. The operative resolutions were as follows:

• That a recognized Center shall be one that teaches the principles of Practical Christianity, uses the textbooks and literature published by Unity School of Christianity and follows the course of teaching prescribed by that school.

• That all leaders of Unity centers be requested to complete the Correspondence Course and Methods and Ideals Course before the next annual convention.

• That all centers shall make regular reports to the Field Department and that a copy of all printed matter mailed out from centers be mailed to the Field Department.

65. *Field Department Bulletin,* May 1932, 1.

66. *Unity,* January 1933.

67. Unity Annual Conference, August 19–26, 1934; Minutes, general business meeting, Unity Annual Conference, July 1, 1933; conferences and conventions files 1906–1939, Unity Archives.

68. "Fourth Annual Convention Program," October 3–7, 1926, back cover, conferences and conventions file 1906–1939, Unity Archives.

69. Minutes, General Meeting, Unity Annual Conference, August 22, 1933, conferences and conventions file 1906–1933, Unity Archives.

70. "Highlights in discussions at Business Meetings and Luncheons, 1934 Conference," *Field Department Bulletin,* October 1934, 3.

71. Ibid.

72. *Unity,* February 1936, 88–91.

73. Ibid.

74. *Field Department Bulletin,* October 1934, 4.

75. *Field Department Bulletin,* October 1933, 1.

76. Ibid., 2.

77. *Weekly Unity,* October 7, 1933.

78. *Field Department Bulletin,* August 1936, 2.

79. Ibid.

80. Ibid.

81. Minutes, Business Session, Unity Annual Conference, Kansas City, Mo., July 2, 1936.

82. Ibid.

83. Business Session, Unity Annual Conference, Kansas City, Mo., July 1, 1936.

84. *Field Department Bulletin,* September 1942.

85. *Field Department Bulletin,* July 1935, 1.

86. Minutes, Executive Board Meeting, Unity Annual Conference, Kansas City, Mo., June 26, 1939.

87. *Field Department Bulletin,* August 1936, 4.

88. Ibid.

89. Executive Board Meeting, Unity Annual Conference, Kansas City, Mo., June 1, 1938.

90. Business Session, Unity Annual Convention, Kansas City, Mo., July 1, 1928.

91. *Unity,* March 1938, 87; Executive Board Meeting, Unity Annual Conference, Kansas City, Mo., June 29, 1939.

92. *Field Department Bulletin,* August 1936, 2.

93. *Field Department Bulletin,* August 1940, 4.

94. *Field Department Bulletin,* September 1941.

95. Ibid.

THE UNITY ANNUAL CONFERENCE AND THE UNITY MINISTERS ASSOCIATION (1925–1966)

1. "Minutes of the Meeting of Recognized Unity Leaders," October 25, 1925, Third Annual Conference, October 4–17, 1925, conferences and conventions file 1906–1939, Unity Archives.

2. Ibid.   3. Ibid.

4. Ibid.   5. Ibid.

6. "Minutes of the Second Meeting of Recognized Unity Leaders with the Unity Field Department," October 15, 1929, conferences and conventions 1906–1939, Unity Archives.

7. Field Department, "Methods and Ideals for Conducting Centers and Study Classes," 1924, Unity School of Christianity, Field Department files, Unity Archives.

8. General Meeting of the Unity Convention Body, August 22, 1927, conferences and conventions 1906–1939, Unity Archives.

9. Ibid.

10. Ibid.

11. *Field Department Bulletin,* October 1934, 1.

12. Ibid., 4.

13. "Code of Ethics of the Unity Annual Conference," adopted at Kansas City, Mo., August 24, 1934, Unity Annual Conference, 1934, conferences and conventions 1906–1939, Unity Archives.

14. Business Session, Unity Annual Conference, July 1, 1936, conferences and conventions 1906–1939, Unity Archives.

15. Board Meeting, Unity Annual Conference, Kansas City, Mo., July 1, 1937.

16. Ibid.

17. Ibid.

18. *Field Department Bulletin,* July 1935, 1.

19. *Field Department Bulletin,* August 1936, 2.

20. *Field Department Bulletin,* October 1933, 2.

21. Executive Board Meeting, Unity Annual Conference, Kansas City, Mo., June 30, 1936.

22. Business Session, Unity Annual Conference, Kansas City, Mo., June 29, 1936.

23. Ibid.

24. Executive Board Meeting, Unity Annual Conference, Kansas City, Mo., June 28, 1938.

25. Executive Board Meeting, Unity Annual Conference, Kansas City, Mo., June 29, 1939.

26. *Weekly Unity,* July 8, 1938, 8.

27. *Weekly Unity,* June 1, 1940.

28. *Unity,* September 1947.

29. "Unity Field Department Letter," 29 March 1948, Unity Archives.

30. Unity Annual Conference, Kansas City, Mo., June 30–July 5, 1935.

31. Fannie Baldwin (president, Unity Ministers' Association) to members, August 21, 1953, with copy of association bylaws attached, Unity Archives.

32. Ibid.; and Unity Ministers Association, "A presentation for Board Members, Trustees and staff members of Unity centers," 1963, Unity Archives.

THE ASSOCIATION OF UNITY CHURCHES (1966–2000)

1. Charles R. Fillmore, "Planning Toward Self-government in the Unity Field Ministry," Unity School Bulletin #4, December 14, 1965, Unity Archives.

2. Executive Board and Committee Meeting, Council of the Unity Ministers Association, January 18, 1966, Unity Archives.

3. "Message from the new Executive Director in a Talk to Unity School Employees on January 25, 1966," *Unity News,* February 1, 1966.

4. Glenn Mosley (president and CEO, Association of Unity Churches), interview by author, 17 January 2000.

5. Rev. Stan Hampson, interview by author, 31 March 2000.

6. Ralph R. Rhea, "In Unity There Is Strength," notes from the Unity Ministers Association, June 1966, Unity Archives.

7. Ibid.

8. Mosley interview.

9. "In Unity There Is Strength."

10. "The Unity Ministers Association Becomes the Association of Unity Churches: An Explanation," Unity Archives.

11. Ibid.; and William Helmbold (chairman, Unity Ministers Association) to UMA members, March 1966, Unity Archives; "'History of the Association of Unity Churches' to be included in *Wings Across Time*," report, January 2000, Association of Unity Churches.

12. Unity Ministers Association, Annual Conference, July 1966, Unity Archives.

13. Association of Unity Churches, bylaws, Unity Archives.

14. Mosley interview.

15. "History of the Association of Unity Churches."

16. "Yearbook," Association of Unity Churches, January 1998.

UNITY: A SCHOOL FOR SPIRITUAL EDUCATION OR A RELIGIOUS DENOMINATION?

1. *Unity,* April 1915, 339.

2. *Weekly Unity,* March 26, 1921.

3. Ibid.

4. *Unity,* January 1922, 58.

5. *Unity,* October 1923, 306.

6. *Unity,* February 1924, 267.

7. Second Annual Unity Conference, June 16–28, 1924; "Unity Conference Daily Program," June 24, 1924, Unity Headquarters, Kansas City, Mo.

8. *Unity,* May 1924, 438.

9. Ibid.

10. *Weekly Unity,* June 25, 1927, 1.

11. M. Fillmore to Mrs. Dorff, 8 November 1930, Myrtle Fillmore Collection.

12. Eric Butterworth, "Unity Centers and Churches: A Historical Perspective," January 1980, Eric Butterworth Collection, miscellaneous file, Unity Archives.

13. Radio interview, 1936, published in "Modern Way Shower," Unity pamphlet, September 1974, Unity Archives.

14. Marcus Bach, *The Unity Way of Life* (Unity Village, Mo.: Unity Books, 1972), 124.

15. William Anderson to Lowell Fillmore, 15 May 1945, Lowell Fillmore Collection.

16. Charles Fillmore to Georgiana Tree West, 8 June 1945, Charles Fillmore Collection.

17. Ibid.

18. "Field Department Letter," July 18, 1945, Field Department file, Unity Archives.

19. *Unity,* April 1947, 861.

20. Business Session, Unity Annual Conference, July 1, 1936.

21. "Unity's Vision for the Field," *Field Department Bulletin,* April 1939.

22. Ibid.

23. *Unity,* October 1946, 92.

24. *Field Department Bulletin,* September 1944.

25. *Unity Ministers' Association Journal* (Annual Conference, 1958), 27–28.

26. Ibid., 29.

27. *Weekly Unity,* March 17, 1945.

28. *Weekly Unity,* July 22, 1956.

29. Charles R. Fillmore, *Unity School of Christianity Bulletin #3,* December 14, 1965, Unity Archives.

30. Charles R. Fillmore, "Purposes of the Unity Movement," *Unity School of Christianity Bulletin #3* and *Bulletin #10,* January 14, 1966, Unity Archives.

31. Ibid.

32. Ibid.

33. Glenn R. Mosley, "Unity, a Denomination and So Much More," *Contact,* April/ May 2000.

34. Association of Unity Churches, Inc., Bylaws, Article IV, Section 4.01 (b), Unity Archives.

35. Mosley, "Unity, a Denomination."

36. Ron Tyson (director, international services, Unity School of Christianity), interview by author, 2 May 2000.

37. "USRS Ministerial Education, A Unique Approach," *USRS Newsletter* (fall 1983), 1.

38. Connie Fillmore Bazzy, "Mission Statement," November 7, 1986, Unity Archives.

39. Unity School of Christianity, "Mission Statement," March 1, 1994, Unity Archives.

40. Connie Fillmore Bazzy, "The Nature of the Unity Movement: Non-denominational and Denominational," *Contact,* April 2000. A denomination can be defined as consisting of churches which are affiliated with each other and are independent of other religious churches and teachings.

41. Ibid.

AN ORGANIZATIONAL CONTROVERSY WITHIN
THE UNITY MOVEMENT

1. "Unity International (proposed structure)," Association of Unity Churches, Unity Archives.

2. Mosley interview, 4 May 2000.

3. Charles R. Fillmore to the Association of Unity Churches, 26 September 1979; Hampson interview, 31 March 2000; Mosley interview, 17 January 2000.

4. Charles R. Fillmore to the Association of Unity Churches; Glenn Mosley believes that the proposal for Unity International was apparently considered by the association board at its meeting in June 1979. David Williamson, who was a member of the board, does not recall whether it was discussed at that meeting. James Sherman, an officer of the association at the time, and at this writing a Unity minister in Toronto, Canada, could not be reached for comment. Whether or not the proposal was considered by the association board for a significant period of time does not obviate the fact that the Unity School board presumed that the proposal for Unity International was prepared quickly in response to Charles R. Fillmore's letter of September 26.

5. Phil White (editor, *Unity Magazine*), 25 March 2000.

6. Jack Boland to Charles R. Fillmore, 22 October 1979, Unity Archives.

7. Jack Boland to Bill Dale, 23 October 1979, Unity Archives.

8. Charles R. Fillmore to Jack Boland, 5 November 1979, Unity Archives.

9. Ibid.

10. Ibid.

11. Jack Boland to Charles R. Fillmore, 16 November 1979, Unity Archives.

12. Mosley interview, 7 January 2000.

13. *Kansas City Star,* 2 March 1980, Unity Archives; Mosley interview, 4 May 2000.

14. "President's Letter," *Contact,* March 1980, 2; William B. Dale to Rev. Jack Boland, 14 February 1980, William B. Dale papers, Unity School of Christianity.

15. Ibid.

16. *Kansas City Star,* 16 March 1980, Unity Archives.

17. *Lee's Summit Journal,* 19 March 1980, including comments from Bill Dale, director of public relations, Unity School, Unity Archives.

18. Mosley interview, 4 May 2000.

19. Freeman interview, 28 April 2000.

20. Ibid.

21. David Williamson, interview by author, 30 May 2000.

22. "Connie Fillmore Bazzy," biographical information file, Unity Archives; Mosley interview, 4 May 2000.

23. Jimmie Scott, interview by author, 1 May 2000.

24. Mosley interview, 4 May 2000.

25. Ibid.

Chapter 12: The Role of Women in the Unity Movement

1. Rosemary R. Reuther and Rosemary S. Keller, *Women and Religion in America*, vol. 1, *The Nineteen Century* (San Francisco: Harper & Row, 1981), 295–303.

2. Ibid., 50–51.

3. Ibid., viii, xii.

4. Lucinda B. Chandler, "Woman's Advancement and Social Purity," *Modern Thought*, December 1889; Chris Jackson, *Unity School Update*, September 23, 1991, 2.

5. After reading more than two thousand letters by Myrtle Fillmore, written from 1928 to 1931, it was evident to me that a substantial majority of her correspondents were women.

6. *Kansas City Star*, 30 June 1979, 1.

7. This information was obtained May 3, 2000, from the pictures of each class of ministerial students who were ordained from 1933 to 1953. The pictures are currently on the wall of a corridor in the Education Building, Unity School of Christianity, Unity Village, Mo.

8. Ibid.

9. Glenn Mosley, interview by author, 4 May 2000.

10. Charles Fillmore, *Atom Smashing Power of Mind* (Unity Village, Mo.: Unity School of Christianity, 1949), 88.

11. Ibid., 145.

12. Ernest Wilson, "Reminiscing About Charles Fillmore: Remarks by May Rowland," Unity on the Plaza, January 21, 1974, Unity Archives.

13. Ibid.

14. Charles R. Fillmore, interview by author, 1 November 1995.

15. Ibid.

16. According to Rosemary Fillmore Rhea, May Rowland held one-third of the fifty shares of Unity School stock during most of the period she served on the board of trustees of Unity School; Rosemary Fillmore Rhea, interview by author, 12 April 2000.

17. Charles R. Fillmore interview.

18. Ibid.

19. Eric Butterworth, interview by author, 30 October 1995.

20. Wilson, "Reminiscing About Charles Fillmore."

21. Ibid.

22. Stan Hampson, interview by author, 5 April 2000.

23. Phil White, interview by author, 19 January, 2000.

24. Patricia Young, "Influence of the Light Touch" (research paper, March 20, 1988), 9, Unity Archives.

25. Ibid., 10.

26. James Dillet Freeman, interview by author, 26 October 1995.

27. *Unity*, April 1989, 34–35.

28. Dorothy Pierson, interview by author, 10 August 2000.

29. *Kansas City Times*, 28 January 1974; 7 July 1984; Charles R. Fillmore, interview by author, 26 April 2000.

30. Charles R. Fillmore interview; James Freeman, "Life Is a Wonder," *Unity*, May 1987, 32.

31. *Unity News*, February 1, 1928.

32. "Billie Freeman," biographical file, Unity Archives.

33. Charles R. Fillmore interview.

34. See Part I of this work for a bibliographical sketch of H. Emilie Cady.

35. Ernest Wilson, "Great Woman of Unity," *Unity,* December 1979, 19.

36. "Imelda Octavia Shanklin," biographical file, Unity Archives; Ernest Wilson, "Valiant Lady," *Unity,* September 1979, 5–8.

37. "Who's Who in Unity," n.d., newspaper clipping file, Unity Archives.

38. "Mary Louise Kupferle," biographical data file, Unity Archives.

39. *Lee's Summit Journal,* 11 October 1989; Mosley interview, 4 May 2000.

40. Eastern Editor, "Pictorial News," *Independence* (Lee's Summit), 2 January 1969.

41. Charles R. Fillmore interview, 26 April 2000.

42. Neal Vahle, "Survey of Books That Most Effectively Present the Unity Teaching," January 2000, Personal Papers of Neal Vahle, Corte Madera, Calif.

43. "A Woman Called Johnnie: The Minister and Her Message," *New Thought* (winter 2000), 39.

Chapter 13: The Participation of Blacks in Unity Work

1. Jimmie Scott, interview by author, 1 May 2000.

2. *Weekly Unity,* July 1919, 7; *Unity,* November 1920.

3. *Weekly Unity,* September 29, 1928.

4. Ibid.   5. Ibid.

6. Ibid.   7. Ibid.

8. Ibid.

9. Charles Fillmore, "Speech to Unity Conference–1927," Charles Fillmore Collection, Unity Archives.

10. *Unity Training School Bulletin, 1934,* 13, Unity Archives.

11. *Unity Training School Prospectus, 1944,* Unity Archives.

12. *The Call* was a Kansas City newspaper published in the 1930s. The copy in the Unity Archives is a reproduction and does not contain a date. The article was probably published on or about Monday, May 21, 1934.

13. Ibid.

14. Ibid.

15. Board of Directors Meeting, Unity Annual Conference, August 25, 1934, Unity Ministers Association Files, Unity Archives.

16. Ibid.

17. *Field Bulletin,* May 1937, Unity Archives.

18. Minutes of the Board Meeting, Unity Annual Conference, July 1, 1937, Unity Archives.

19. Business Session, Unity Annual Conference, June 30, 1938, Unity Archives.

20. Office memo, July 18, 1946, Unity School of Christianity administrative files, Unity Archives.

21. Ibid.

22. Eric Butterworth, interview by author, 30 October 1995.

23. *Unity,* April 1947, 9.

24. Ibid.

25. *Unity News,* March 11, 1954; *Unity News,* n.d. but probably spring or summer, 1952, 5.

26. *Unity Training School Prospectus, 1953,* Unity Archives.

27. "True Friend" to the Board of Trustees, Unity School of Christianity, 28 June 1955, Lowell Fillmore Collection, Unity Archives.

28. Dorothy Pierson, interview by author, 10 August 2000.

29. *Chicago Sun Times,* 31 October 1968; "A Woman Called Johnnie: The Minister and Her Message," *New Thought* (winter 2000), 39.

30. Ibid., 6.

31. David Williamson, interview by author, 11 April 2000.

32. "A Woman Called Johnnie," 39.

33. *Unity Training School Prospectus, 1956,* Unity Archives.

34. "A Woman Called Johnnie," 6, 39.

35. *Unity Office Bulletin,* April 1952, Unity Administrative Files, Unity Archives.

36. Pierson interview, 19 October 1995.

37. Williamson interview, 11 April 2000.

38. Pierson interview, 19 October 1995.

39. Ibid.

40. Ibid.

41. Charles R. Fillmore interview, 1 November 1995.

42. Ibid.

43. John Anderson, interview by author, 25 January 2000.

44. Ibid.

45. Williamson interview, 30 May 2000.

46. Ibid.

Chapter 14: Unity and New Thought

1. J. Stillson Judah, *The History and Philosophy of Metaphysical Movements in America* (Philadelphia: Westminster Press, n.d.), 172; Catherine L. Albanese, *America: Religion and Religions* (San Francisco: Wadsworth Publishing, 1981), 181.

2. Charles S. Braden, *Spirits in Rebellion: The Rise and Development of New Thought* (Dallas: Southern Methodist University Press, 1963), 140; J. Gordon Melton, "New Thought's Hidden History: Emma Curtis Hopkins, Forgotten Founder," paper presented at the 1987 annual meeting of the American Academy of Religion, Boston, December 5–8, 1987; Gail M. Harley, "Emma Curtis Hopkins: 'Forgotten Founder' of New Thought" (Ph.D. diss., Florida State University, 1991), 5–10.

3. Harley, "Emma Curtis Hopkins," 11–15.

4. Ibid.

5. The Baha'is, Chicago Truth Center, The Circle of Light, College of Freedom, Englewood Spiritual Union, Esoteric Extension, The Higher Thought, Illinois Metaphysical College, The Mental Advocate, Mental Science Institute, Prentice Mulford Club, Sara Wilder Pratt Rooms, Stockholm Publishing Company, Suggestions Publishing, Universal Truth Club. See *Unity,* December 1903, 126–127.

6. *Unity,* December 1903, 326–27.

7. Ibid., 327.

8. Ibid., 333.

9. *Unity,* November 1904, 275.

10. Ibid.

11. Ibid., 307.

12. *Unity,* March 1905.

13. *Unity,* October 1905, 238.

14. Charles Fillmore, "New Thought: A Second Explanatory Lesson," *Unity,* October 1905, 195.

15. Ibid.

16. Ibid.

17. Ibid.

18. Ibid.

19. *Unity,* January 1906, 47.

20. Ibid.

21. Charles Fillmore, "About the New Thought Convention in Chicago," *Unity,* December 1906, 384.

22. Ibid.   23. Ibid.

24. Ibid.

25. Charles Fillmore, "Editorial Note," *Unity,* January 1907, 63.

26. Ibid.   27. *Weekly Unity,* April 30, 1913.

28. Ibid.   29. *Unity,* April 1916, 292.

30. *Unity,* November 1919, 471.   31. Ibid., 471–73.

32. Ibid.   33. Ibid.

34. Ibid.

35. *Unity,* November 1920, 473; *Weekly Unity,* October 9, 1920, 3.

36. Ibid.

37. Ibid.

38. Charles Fillmore, "About the International New Thought Convention," *Unity,* October 1921, 375.

39. Ibid.   40. Ibid.

41. Ibid.   42. *Unity,* May 1922, 49.

43. *Unity,* July 1922, 49–52.   44. Ibid.

45. Ibid.   46. Ibid.

47. Ibid.   48. Ibid.

49. Ibid.   50. *Unity,* October 1923, 305.

51. M. Fillmore to Mrs. Kramer, 15 May 1928, Myrtle Fillmore Collection.

52. Board of Directors meeting, Unity School of Christianity, Lowell Fillmore, Secretary, n.d., presumably late 1930s, Lowell Fillmore Collection, Unity Archives.

53. Ibid.

54. Board of Directors meeting, Unity School of Christianity, Lowell Fillmore, Secretary, n.d., presumably late 1940s, Lowell Fillmore Collection, Unity Archives.

55. Connie Fillmore Bazzy, interview by author, 18 August 2000.

Chapter 15: Unity and the New Age

1. J. Gordon Melton, *New Age Encyclopedia* (Detroit: Gale Research, Inc., 1990), xiii–xxxiii.

2. Steven S. Sadleir, *The Spiritual Seeker's Guide* (Costa Mesa, Calif.: Allwon Publishing, 1992), 148.

3. Melton, *New Age Encyclopedia.*

4. Rev. Vern Barnet, interview by author, 17 September 2000.

5. *Unity View of New Age and New Thought,* a pamphlet published by the Unity Movement Advisory Council, a joint committee of the Association of Unity Churches and Unity School of Christianity, n.d., probably late 1990s, 9.

6. Ibid., 11.

7. Alexander Everett, interview by author, 13 August 2000, and 9 September 2000; Alexander Everett, *Inward Bound: Living Life from the Inside Out* (Wilsonville, Ore.: Book Partners, 1998), 10. This book is now available by mail order only from Box 456, Veneta, OR 97487.

8. Ibid.

9. Thomas E. Witherspoon, *Mother of Unity* (Unity Village, Mo.: Unity Books, 1977), 121.

10. Everett interview, 13 August 2000; Phil White, interview by author, 24 September 2000.

11. Ibid.

12. Everett, *Inward Bound,* 5, 71; Everett interview, 5 September 2000.

13. Everett, *Inward Bound,* 72.

14. Everett interview, 13 August 2000.   15. Ibid.

16. Everett, *Inward Bound*, 4–5.   17. Everett interview, 13 August 2000.

18. Everett, *Inward Bound*, 42. Everett interview, 9 September 2000.

Chapter 16: Perspectives on Unity: Commentaries from Other Spiritual and Religious Vantage Points

REPRESENTATIVES OF MAINSTREAM CHRISTIANITY

1. "Unity School Predates Groups Espousing Positive Attitudes," *Kansas City Times,* 12 June 1989, A5.

2. William J. Whalen, *Separated Brethren: A Survey of Non-Catholic Christian Denominations in the United States* (Milwaukee: The Bruce Publishing Co., 1958), 154.

3. George Lewis, "The Unity School of Christianity," *The Sunday School Times,* March 31, 1956, 255.

4. Louis T. Talbot, "Cults of Our Day, Unity," *The King's Business,* official publication of the Bible Institute of Los Angeles, October 1955, 12.

5. Ibid.

6. Gordon R. Lewis, *Confronting the Cults* (Denver: Presbyterian and Reformed Publishing Co., 1966), 135.

7. James W. Teener, "The Challenge of Unity," *Crossroads: A Study and Program Magazine for Adults,* the publication of the Board of Christian Education of the Presbyterian Church in the USA, July–September 1952, 10.

8. Walter R. Martin, *The Kingdom of the Cults* (Grand Rapids: Zondervan Publishing House, 1965), 275.

9. A. Jase Jones, "The Unity School of Christianity," *Home Missions,* a publication of the Home Mission Board, Southern Baptist Convention, March 1975, 31; *Kansas City Star,* 29 July 1979, 10A.

10. Talbot, "Cults of Our Day," 17.

11. Walter R. Martin, "The Unity Cult," *Eternity: Magazine of Christian Truth,* February 1955, 8.

12. Talbot, "Cults of Our Day," 18.

13. J. K. van Baalen, "Unity," *Christianity Today,* December 19, 1960, 10.

14. Harold Lindsell, *Christianity and the Cults* (Glendale: Gospel Light Publications, 1963), 26.

15. Teener, "The Challenge of Unity," 10.

16. Talbot, "Cults of Our Day, 16.

17. Lewis, *Confronting the Cults,* 141.

18. Teener, "The Challenge of Unity," 11.

19. H. A. Ironside, *Heresies Exposed* (Loizeaux Brothers, 1955), 199–201. The reproduction of the book in the Unity Archives tells nothing about the author, city or country where the book was published.

20. Jan Knappert, *Middle Eastern Mythology and Religions* (Rockport, Mass.: Element, 1993), 132.

21. Martin, *The Kingdom of the Cults,* 275.

22. Rev. Gerald L. Claudius, "Heretical Cults," *Kansas City Times,* 20 June 1989.

23. Whalen, *Separated Brethren,* 154.

24. Talbot, "Cults of Our Day," 16–17.

25. Lindsell, *Christianity and the Cults,* 26.

26. Dan Olinger, "The Word on Unity," *Faith,* November 1982, 1.

27. Ibid.

28. Martin, *The Kingdom of the Cults,* 275.

29. Lindsell, *Christianity and the Cults*, 26.

30. Lewis, "The Unity School of Christianity," 255.

31. Van Baalen, "Unity," 10.

32. Martin, "The Unity Cult," 44.

33. Ibid.

34. Jones, "The Unity School of Christianity," 31.

35. Jerry Cooper, "Unity Doctrine May Look and Sound Christian, but It Is Not," *The Best from All Religions*. The information in the Unity Archives does not give the author, the publisher, or the date published. There are no page numbers, but this is a 2-page article. Apparently the article is the sixth in a series on the cults by Jerry Cooper, pastor of the Faith Bible Church of Rocky Mount, North Carolina.

36. Jones, "The Unity School of Christianity," 31.

37. Talbot, "Cults of Our Day," 17.

38. Harold J. Berry, *What They Believe*, 298. The Unity Archives has only a reproduction of the cover of the book plus a chapter on Unity, but no information on the publisher or the date published.

39. *Kansas City Star*, 29 July 1979, 10A.

40. Berry, *What They Believe*, 298.

41. Olinger, "The Word on Unity," 14.

42. Cooper, "Unity Doctrine," 1.

43. Whalen, *Separated Brethren*, 154.

44. Talbot, "Cults of Our Day," 18.

45. Teener, "The Challenge of Unity," 10.

46. Talbot, "Cults of Our Day," 18.

47. Van Baalen, "Unity," 10.

48. George Dugan, "Faith Healing Assembly Topic," *Kansas City Times*, 24 May 1960, from *The New York Times* news service.

49. William M. Smith, "The So-called Unity Movement," published by the Gospel Missionary Union, 1841 East 7th St., Kansas City. No more information was available in the Unity Archives on the book from which the piece was taken.

50. Ironside, *Heresies Exposed*, 199–201.

51. Talbot, "Cults of Our Day," 18.

52. Ibid.

53. Stephen Miller, ed., *Misguiding Lights*, 63. No publishing information is available on this book. A reproduction of the front cover is all that is available in the Unity Archives. Miller is listed as an editor and writer for the Church of the Nazarene Headquarters in Kansas City.

SCHOLARS IN THE FIELD OF AMERICAN RELIGION

1. Marcus Bach, "Unity School of Christianity," Adult Fellowship Series, lesson 5, November 1956, 45, Unity Achives.

2. Ibid.

3. Ibid.

4. Ibid.

5. J. Stillson Judah, *The History and Philosophy of Metaphysical Movements in America* (Philadelphia: Westminster Press, n.d., c. 1960), 229.

6. Ibid., 230.   7. Ibid., 255.

8. Charles S. Braden, *Spirits in Rebellion: The Rise and Development of New Thought* (Dallas: Southern Methodist University Press, 1963), 261.

9. Ibid.

10. Joseph Schultz to Neal Vahle, 1 August 2000, Neal Vahle Papers, Corte Madera, Calif.

11. Ibid.

12. Al Truesdale to Neal Vahle, 20 August 2000, Neal Vahle Papers, Corte Madera, Calif.

13. Vern Barnet to Neal Vahle, 9 September 2000.

14. Ibid.

15. Ibid.

16. Ibid.

17. J. Gordon Melton, *Encyclopedia of American Religions,* 6th ed. (Detroit: Gale Research, 1999), 141.

18. J. Gordon Melton, *Kansas City Times,* 12 June 1989, A5.

19. J. Gordon Melton, *New Age Encyclopedia* (Detroit: Gale Research, 1990), iii.

20. *Encyclopedia Britannica,* volume 12 (1998), 162.

21. Martin Marty, *Pilgrims in Their Own Land: 500 Years of Religion in America* (Boston: Little Brown & Co. 1984), 331.

22. Martin Marty to Joseph Schultz, 24 August 2000, Joseph Schultz Papers, Golden. Colorado, Neal Vahle Papers, Corte Madera, Calif.

23. Winthrop S. Hudson, *Religion in America: An Historical Account of the Development of American Religious Life* (New York: Charles Scribners Sons, 1981), 270–271.

24. Ibid., 291.

25. Paul J. Williams, *What Americans Believe and How They Worship* (New York: Harper & Row Publishers, 1952), 428.

26. Thomas A. Tweed, ed., *Retelling U.S. Religious History* (Berkeley: University of California Press, 1997), 77.

27. Clifton Olmstead, *History of Religion in the United States* (Englewood Cliffs, N.J.: Prentice Hall, 1960), 520–21.

28. James Ward Smith, *The Shaping of American Religion* (Princeton: Princeton University Press, 1961), 216–19.

29. R. Laurence Moore, *Religious Outsiders and the Making of Americans* (New York: Oxford University Press, 1986), 25–48, 105–128.

30. Vern Barnet to Neal Vahle, 9 September 2000.

NON-UNITY NEW THOUGHT TEACHERS

1. Charles S. Braden, *Spirits in Rebellion: The Rise and Development of New Thought* (Dallas: Southern Methodist University Press, 1963), 285.

2. Ibid., 352.

3. *Unity,* December 1946, 7; *Weekly Unity,* September 30, 1944, 8.

4. Ibid.

5. Braden, *Spirits in Rebellion,* 386.

6. *Kansas City Star,* 1 April 1972, 2B.

7. *Lee's Summit Journal,* 16 June 1989; *Raytown Post,* 21 June 1989, 15.

8. Braden, *Spirits in Rebellion,* 386.

9. Rev. Dr. Michael Beckwith to Neal Vahle, 22 August 2000, Neal Vahle Papers, Corte Madera, Calif.

10. Noel McInnis to Neal Vahle, 22 August 2000, Neal Vahle Papers, Corte Madera, Calif.

BIBLIOGRAPHY

Albanese, Catherine L. *America: Religion and Religions.* San Francisco: Wadsworth Publishing, 1981.

———, ed. *The Spirituality of the American Transcendentalists.* Macon, Ga.: Mercer University Press, 1988.

Anderson, Walter Truett. *The Upstart Spring: Esalen and the American Awakening.* Reading, Mass.: Addison-Wesley Publishing Co., 1983.

Bach, Marcus. *The Unity Way of Life.* New York: Prentice Hall, 1962.

Barnitz, Harry W. *Existentialism and the New Christianity: A Comparative Study of Existentialism and Swedenborgianism.* New York: Philosophical Library, 1969.

Bendix, Reinhard. *Max Weber: An Intellectual Portrait.* Berkeley: University of California Press, 1977.

Berry, Harold J. *What They Believe.* The Unity Archives has only a reproduction of the cover of the book, plus a chapter on Unity. No information is available on the publisher or the date published.

Blavatsky, Helena Petrovna. *The Key to Theosophy.* Pasadena: Theosophical University Press, [1875] 1972.

Braden, Charles S. *Spirits in Rebellion: The Rise and Development of New Thought.* Dallas: Southern Methodist University Press, 1963.

Butterworth, Eric. *Discover the Power Within You.* New York: Harper & Row, 1968.

Campbell, Bruce F. *Ancient Wisdom Revived: A History of the Theosophical Movement.* Berkeley: University of California Press, 1980.

Channing, William Ellery. *The Collected Works of William Ellery Channing.* Rev. ed. Boston: American Unitarian Association, 1886.

D'Andrade, Hugh. *Charles Fillmore: The Life of the Founder of the Unity School of Christianity.* New York: Harper & Row, 1976.

Dole, George F., ed. *Emanuel Swedenborg: The Universal Human and Soul-Body Interaction.* New York: Paulist Press, 1984.

Dresser, Annetta. *The Philosophy of P. P. Quimby.* Boston: Geo. H. Ellis, 1899.

Dresser, Horatio W. *A History of New Thought.* New York: Thomas Y. Crowell Co., 1919.

Drummond, Henry. *The Greatest Thing in the World.* London: Collins, 1930. Quoted in *Unity,* December 1908, 376.

Eddy, Mary Baker. *Miscellaneous Writings.* Boston: First Church of Christ, Scientist, 1924.

———. *Science and Health with Key to the Scriptures.* Boston: First Church of Christ, Scientist, [1875] 1994.

Eliade, Mircea, ed. *The Encyclopedia of Religion.* New York: Simon & Schuster, 1995.

Evans, Warren Felt. *Esoteric Christianity and Mental Therapeutics.* Boston: H. H. Carter & Karrick, 1886.

———. *The Mental-Cure: Illustrating the Influence of the Mind on the Body Both in Health and Disease.* Boston: William White & Co., 1869.

———. *Mental Medicine.* Boston: H. H. Carter, 1872.

———. *The Primitive Mind-Cure: Or Elementary Lessons in Christian Philosophy and Transcendental Medicine.* Boston: H. H. Carter & Karrick, 1884.

————. *Soul and Body: The Spiritual Science of Health and Disease.* Boston: Colby & Rich Publishers, 1876.

Everett, Alexander. *Inward Bound: Living Life from the Inside Out.* Wilsonville, Ore.: Book Partners, 1998.

Fox, Emmet. *Sermon on the Mount.* New York: Harper & Row, 1934.

————. *The Ten Commandments, The Master Key to Life.* New York: Harper & Row, 1953.

Fuller, Robert C. *American National Biography.* New York: Oxford University Press, 1999.

————. *Mesmerism and the Cure of Souls.* Philadelphia: University of Pennsylvania Press, 1982.

Gill, Gillian. *Mary Baker Eddy.* Reading, Mass.: Perseus Books, 1998.

Harley, Gail. "Emma Curtis Hopkins: 'Forgotten Founder' of New Thought." Ph.D. diss., Florida State University, 1991.

Haskins, David Green. *Ralph Waldo Emerson: His Maternal Ancestors.* Boston: Cripples, Upham & Co., 1887.

Hinnells, John, ed. *Who's Who in World Religions.* New York: Simon & Schuster, 1992.

Hopkins, Emma Curtis. *High Mysticism.* Marina del Rey, Calif.: DeVorss & Co., n.d. Originally published in 1907 by the High Watch Fellowship, Cornwall Bridge, Conn.

————. *Scientific Christian Mental Practice.* Marina del Rey, Calif.: DeVorss & Co., n.d. Originally published by the High Watch Fellowship, Cornwall Bridge, Conn.

Hudson, Winthrop S. *Religion in America: An Historical Account of the Development of American Religious Life.* New York: Charles Scribners Sons, 1981.

Ironside, H. A. *Heresies Exposed.* Loizeaux Brothers, 1955. The reproduction of the book in the Unity Archives tells nothing about the author, city, or country where the book was published.

Jonsson, Inge. *Emanuel Swedenborg.* New York: Twayne Publishers, 1971.

Judah, J. Stillson. *The History and Philosophy of Metaphysical Movements in America.* Philadelphia: Westminster Press, n.d., c. 1960.

Keller, Helen. *My Religion.* New York: Swedenborg Foundation, 1945.

Knappert, Jan. *Middle Eastern Mythology and Religions.* Rockport, Mass.: Element, 1993.

Lewis, Gordon R. *Confronting the Cults.* Denver: Presbyterian and Reformed Publishing Co., 1966.

Martin, Walter R. *The Kingdom of the Cults.* Grand Rapids: Zondervan, 1965.

Marty, Martin. *Pilgrims in Their Own Land: 500 Years of Religion in America.* Boston: Little Brown & Co., 1984.

Melton, J. Gordon. *The Encyclopedia of American Religions.* 6th ed. Detroit: Gale Research, 1999.

————. *New Age Encyclopedia.* Detroit: Gale Research, 1990.

Moore, R. Laurence. *Religious Outsiders and the Making of Americans.* New York: Oxford University Press, 1986.

Olmstead, Clifton. *History of Religion in the United States.* Englewood Cliffs, N.J.: Prentice Hall, 1960.

Parker, Gail T. *Mind Cure in New England: From the Civil War to World War I.* Hanover, N.H.: University Press of New England, 1973.

Pavri, P. *Theosophy Explained.* Adyar, Madras, India: Theosophical Publishing House, 1930.

Peel, Robert. *Mary Baker Eddy: The Years of Discovery, 1821–1875.* Vol. 1. New York: Holt, Rinehart & Winston, 1966.

————. *Mary Baker Eddy: The Years of Trial, 1876–1891.* Vol. 2. New York: Holt, Rinehart & Winston, 1971.

————. *Mary Baker Eddy: The Years of Authority, 1892–1910.* Vol. 3. New York: Holt, Rinehart & Winston, 1977.

Reuther, Rosemary R., and Rosemary S. Keller. *Women and Religion in America*. Vol. 1, *The Nineteenth Century*. San Francisco: Harper & Row, 1981.

Richardson Jr., Robert D. *Emerson: The Mind on Fire*. Berkeley: University of California Press, 1995.

Sadleir, Steven S. *The Spiritual Seeker's Guide*. Costa Mesa, Calif.: Allwon Publishing, 1992.

Seale, Erwin, ed. *Phineas P. Quimby: The Complete Writings*. Marina Del Rey, Calif.: DeVorss and Co., 1988. Referred to as the "Quimby Manuscripts."

Sigstedt, Cyriel O. *The Swedenborg Epic: The Life and Works of Emanuel Swedenborg*. New York: Bookman Associates, 1952.

Smith, James Ward. *The Shaping of American Religion*. Princeton: Princeton University Press, 1961.

Smith, Jonathan Z., ed. *The HarperCollins Dictionary of Religions*. San Francisco: HarperSanFrancisco, 1995.

Starr, Paul. *The Social Transformation of American Medicine*. New York: Basic Books, 1982.

Swedenborg, Emanuel. *Angelic Wisdom Concerning Divine Providence*. New York: Houghton Mifflin, [Amsterdam, 1764] 1907.

Talbot, Louis T. "Cults of Our Day, Unity." *The King's Business*. Bible Institute of Los Angeles, October 1955.

Teener, James W. "Unity School of Christianity." Ph.D. diss. University of Chicago, 1939.

Trowbridge, George. *Swedenborg: Life and Teaching*. New York: Swedenborg Foundation, 1955.

Tweed, Thomas A., ed. *Retelling U.S. Religious History*. Berkeley: University of California Press, 1997.

Udolf, Roy. *Hypnosis for Professionals*. New York: Van Nostrand Reinhold Co., 1981.

Vahle, Neal. *Torchbearer to Light the Way: The Life of Myrtle Fillmore*. Mill Valley, Calif.: Open View Press, 1997.

Whalen, William J. *Separated Brethren: A Survey of Non-Catholic Christian Denominations in the United States*. Milwaukee: The Bruce Publishing Co., 1958.

Williams, Paul J. *What Americans Believe and How They Worship*. New York: Harper & Row, 1952.

Zweig, Stephen. *Mental Healers: Franz Anton Mesmer, Mary Baker Eddy, Sigmund Freud*. New York: Frederick Unger Publishing Co., 1932.

Publications of the Unity School of Christianity

Bach, Marcus. *The Unity Way of Life*. Unity Village, Mo.: Unity Books, 1972.

Bazzy, Connie Fillmore, ed. *The Unity Guide to Healing*. Unity Village, Mo.: Unity School of Christianity, 1974.

———, ed. *The Unity Guide to Prosperous Living*. Unity Village, Mo.: Unity School of Christianity, 1973.

Brumet, Robert. *Finding Your Life in Transition: Using Life's Changes for Spiritual Awakening*. Unity Village, Mo.: Unity Books, 1995.

Butterworth, Eric. *Spiritual Economics*. Unity Village, Mo.: Unity School of Christianity, 1983.

Cady, H. Emilie. *God a Present Help*. Kansas City, Mo.: Unity School of Christianity, 1940.

———. *Lessons in Truth*. Kansas City, Mo.: Unity Tract Society, 1901.

———. *Miscellaneous Writings*. Kansas City, Mo.: Unity School of Christianity, 1917.

Fillmore, Charles. *Atom Smashing Power of Mind*. Unity Village, Mo.: Unity School of Christianity, 1949.

———. *Christian Healing*. Kansas City, Mo.: Unity School of Christianity, 1909.

————. *Jesus Christ Heals*. Kansas City, Mo.: Unity School of Christianity, 1939.

————. *Prosperity*. Kansas City, Mo.: Unity School of Christianity, 1936.

————. *Talks on Truth*. Kansas City, Mo.: Unity School of Christianity, 1926.

————. *The Twelve Powers of Man*. Kansas City, Mo.: Unity School of Christianity, 1930.

Fillmore, Lowell. *New Ways to Solve Old Problems*. Unity Village, Mo.: Unity School of Christianity, 1958.

————. *Remember*. Kansas City, Mo.: Unity School of Christianity, 1929.

————. *Things to Be Remembered*. Unity Village, Mo.: Unity School of Christianity, 1952.

Fillmore, Myrtle. *How to Let God Help You*. Selected and arranged by Warren Meyer. Unity Village, Mo.: Unity School of Christianity, 1957.

Fischer, William L. *Alternatives: New Approaches to Traditional Christian Beliefs*. Unity Village, Mo.: Unity Books, 1980.

Foulkes, Frances Warder. *Effectual Prayer*. Kansas City, Mo.: Unity School of Christianity, 1945.

Freeman, James Dillet. *The Story of Unity*. Unity Village, Mo.: Unity School of Christianity, 1949; rev. ed. 1978.

Gaither, James. *The Essential Charles Fillmore: Collected Writings of a Missouri Mystic*. Unity Village, Mo.: Unity Books, 1999.

Gatlin, Dana. *The Story of Unity's Fifty Golden Years*. Kansas City, Mo.: Unity School of Christianity, 1939.

Hausmann, Winifred W. *Your God-given Potential*. Unity Village, Mo.: Unity Books, 1978.

Ingraham, E. V. *Meditations in the Silence*. Lee's Summit, Mo.: Unity School of Christianity, 1969.

Jafolla, Richard and Mary-Alice. *The Quest: A Journey of Spiritual Rediscovery*. Unity Village, Mo.: Unity Movement Advisory Council, 1993.

Kupferle, Mary L. *God Never Fails*. Lee's Summit, Mo.: Unity School of Christianity, 1959.

Roth, Charles. *The Master Power*. Unity Village, Mo.: Unity Books, 1974.

Rowland, May. *Dare to Believe*. Lee's Summit, Mo.: Unity School of Christianity, 1961.

Shanklin, Imelda Octavia. *Who Are You?* Kansas City, Mo.: Unity School of Christianity, 1924.

Smock, Martha. *Half Way Up the Mountain*. Unity Village, Mo.: Unity Books, 1971.

Tait, Vera Dawson. *Take Command*. Unity Village, Mo.: Unity School of Christianity, 1984.

Turner, Elizabeth Sand. *Be Ye Transformed*. Lee's Summit, Mo.: Unity School of Christianity, 1969.

————. *Let There Be Light*. Lee's Summit, Mo.: Unity School of Christianity, 1954.

West, Georgian Tree. *Prosperity's Ten Commandments*. Lee's Summit, Mo.: Unity School of Christianity, 1944.

Wilson, Ernest C. *The Emerging Self*. Unity Village, Mo.: Unity Books, 1970.

————. *The Great Physician*. Lee's Summit, Mo.: Unity School of Christianity, 1959.

Witherspoon, Thomas E. *Mother of Unity*. Unity Village, Mo.: Unity Books, 1977.

INDEX

(The following abbreviations are used: CF for Charles Fillmore; CRF for Charles Rickert Fillmore; MF for Myrtle Fillmore.)